Market Power, Competition, and Antitrust Policy

Irwin Publications in Economics
Advisory Editor   Martin S. Feldstein   *Harvard University*

Market Power, Competition, and Antitrust Policy

William L. Baldwin

1987

Homewood, Illinois 60430

© RICHARD D. IRWIN, INC., 1987

All rights reserved. No part of this publication may be
reproduced, stored in a retrieval system, or transmitted,
in any form or by any means, electronic, mechanical,
photocopying, recording, or otherwise, without the prior
written permission of the publisher.

ISBN 0-256-02806-0

Library of Congress Catalog Card No. 86-081648

Printed in the United States of America

1 2 3 4 5 6 7 8 9 0 DO 4 3 2 1 0 9 8 7

PREFACE

This book focuses on market power—the ability of business firms to exercise monopolistic control over the prices of their products and to restrict entry into their markets. It examines sources of such power, various forms in which it is exercised, and the consequences for economic welfare. Two basic restraints on the rise and use of market power are emphasized: first, competition from other firms and, second, public policies (embodied in antitrust law) that evolved to maintain or restore competition. Hence, the title, *Market Power, Competition, and Antitrust Policy*.

The book is intended primarily as a basic text for an intermediate or upper-level undergraduate course in the economics of industrial organization or as a general reference book for a graduate course in that field. In addition, the book may be interesting and useful to those who, apart from formal classroom study, wish to delve into a challenging and crucially important subject. Although some knowledge of microeconomic theory will be helpful to the reader, models and diagrams are explained thoroughly enough to make their assumptions and results, if not the underlying analysis, accessible to those without such background.

The bulk of the book deals with the topics that comprise the mainstream of industrial organization and that are the standard components of a solid course in the field. Rather than being proselytized concerning controversial aspects of these topics, the reader is exposed to leading divergent views. Although this is the principal obligation of a textbook writer, I have also indulged a few of my idiosyncracies.

Early in my career at Dartmouth College, Martin L. Lindahl and William A. Carter gave me the insight that, since the overwhelming preponderance of market power in the United States today is held by firms organized in the corporate form, an understanding of the modern corporation is necessary to fully appreciate the current nature of such power and how it is exercised. Thus, there are unusually detailed treatments of corporate attributes and decision-making processes throughout the book, including a complete chapter on the rise of the modern corporation (Chapter Three).

Chapters Thirteen and Fourteen are devoted to paradigms other than the conventional one of structure, conduct, and performance. All these paradigms are treated as essentially complementary rather than contending approaches to industrial organization.

An instructor may want to cover some topics in different order. For example, the full model of static resource allocation under competition and monopoly is not presented until Chapter Eleven, which reflects my experience that, while early introduction of the topic provides students with a useful analytical background, the motivation for detailed study of such an abstract model is lacking. Chapter Two and Chapter Four should contain sufficient exposure to the implications of market power for consumer welfare to carry the reader through until an appropriate foundation has been laid for discussing static resource allocation in the context of the structure-conduct-performance paradigm. But if the instructor prefers a more conventional organization, Chapter Eleven could be assigned earlier, perhaps immediately after Chapter Two.

Another innovation is the early discussion, in Chapter Five, of the basic antitrust response to the problem of market power, although antitrust matters are not taken up again until Chapters Fifteen through Twenty. I made a trade-off between logic and motivation, presuming that reader interest is best served by including a general survey of antitrust in the initial overview of industrial organization, while more detailed discussion of the law and policies must draw on the economic principles and paradigms developed in the intervening chapters. Should the instructor weigh the trade-off differently, however, Chapter Five need not be assigned until just before Chapter Fifteen.

Chapter Two, introducing the reader to the Schumpeterian methodological approach employed throughout the book, contains a rather long appendix on quantitative analysis. This section is not intended to impart econometric skills but rather to give the reader a sense of both the power and the limitations of modern econometrics. The appendix may be omitted, but if so, the instructor should explain those terms characterizing the accuracy, reliability, and significance of some of the empirical findings described in other parts of the book.

Chapter Eleven includes a section on competition and optimal rates of depletion of nonreproducible resources. While the topic is increasingly significant for public policy, it is not customarily included in industrial organization texts, and the section can be omitted without any loss of continuity.

I am grateful to a number of current and former colleagues in Dartmouth's Economics Department who have read all or portions of the manuscript for this book at various stages and have made thoughtful and constructive comments. These include Meredith O. Clement, William R. Dougan, Alan L. Gustman, Lawrence G. Hines, Daphne A. Kenyon, Meir G. Kohn, Michael C. Munger, Robert D. Plotnick, and David C. Stapleton. I am particularly indebted to John T. Scott, both for his reading of various drafts and for innumerable hours of discussion from the inception of this project several years ago.

William P. Albrecht of the University of Iowa, John Rapoport of Mount Holyoke College, and Anthony A. Romeo of the University of Connecticut reviewed the manuscript for publication. The final version owes much to all three for their careful readings, perceptive observations, and constructive suggestions.

Sony Lipton has provided incisive and extensive editorial advice on both early and revised versions and has also prepared the index. Marcia H. Baldwin is responsible for many improvements in presentation. Deborah Hodges typed the manuscript with care and unfailing good judgment

Despite my appreciation for all the help that I have received from these people, I accept the author's usual burden of full responsibility for any remaining errors or inadequacies, in part at least because I have not accepted all of the suggestions they have made.

Finally, I wish to acknowledge my indebtedness to Jesse W. Markham, who does not have the slightest responsibility for this particular text, since he has not seen any of it. I hope and expect, though, that he will recognize the profound and pervasive influence he has had on my thinking about industrial organization, in part through his writings but, more important, in both formal and informal ways as my graduate school instructor, dissertation adviser, and long-time friend.

William L. Baldwin

CONTENTS

PART FOUR Epilogue

PART ONE

Introduction and Overview

CHAPTER ONE

The Business Firm and Economic Activity in the United States

Economists refer to the study of the activities of private business firms in various market settings as *industrial organization*. This term may be misleading to those hearing it for the first time, since it refers more to the organization of entire industries and markets than to the internal organization of individual firms. The German term for the field, *Marktform* (form of market), is more accurate.

Activities of private business firms in the United States range across a broad economic spectrum and take place in diverse market settings. Over 15 million firms of widely varying sizes and organizational forms filed U.S. tax returns in 1981. The ultimate interest of industrial organization economists is in understanding the determinants of the economic *performance* of these firms and how effectively they contribute to the well-being of the nation's people.

MARKET POWER

One of the most important determinants of economic performance is market power, or the abilities of firms to influence the prices of their products either through independent actions or through actions coordinated with others. The long-run effectiveness of raising price above costs depends, in turn, on the ability to exclude others from the market. In defining monopoly as "the power to control prices or exclude competition,"[1] courts in the United States have recognized these two basic attributes of market power. Much of this book, therefore, deals with private economic power and the appropriate public policy responses to the existence and uses of that power—that is, the antitrust policies of the United States.

Economic activity in the United States is largely carried out by private business firms, and the bulk of this activity is shaped and motivated by market transactions. At the outset, it is useful to put the study of industrial organization into the perspective of the modern U.S. economy through an overview of the composition of this activity and of the population of business firms engaged in it.

Table 1–1 breaks down the gross domestic product (GDP) (defined as the total value of final goods produced within the country) by institutional sector of origin for the year 1983. As indicated, private business firms accounted for nearly 86 percent of the total final goods and services produced in the United States. Government's share, just under 11 percent, may seem surprisingly small, since total federal, state, and local government expenditures amounted to $1,167.5 billion, or 35.9 percent of GDP, in 1983. The explanation is, in part, that a substantial portion of government expenditures is transfer payments (such as social security and unemployment compensation), which do not contribute to the value of GDP since they do not involve production of final goods and services. Further, a substantial portion of government spending involves purchases from, and therefore economic activity originating in, private firms. Total government purchases of goods and services for 1983 amounted to $685.5 billion, or 21.1 percent of GDP.[2] The $349.2 billion shown in Table 1–1 for total GDP origi-

TABLE 1–1 U.S. Gross Domestic Product by Institutional Sector of Origin, 1983

Sector	Amount ($ billions)		Percentage of Total
Business			
Nonfarm	$2,728.9		83.8%
Farm	61.5		1.9
Total business		$2,790.4	85.7%
Households and nonbusiness institutions		116.5	3.6
Government			
Federal	107.8		3.3
State and local	241.4		7.4
Total government		349.2	10.7
Statistical discrepancy		0.5	
Total gross domestic product		$3,256.5	100.0%

SOURCE: U.S. Council of Economic Advisers, *Economic Report of the President and Annual Report of the Council of Economic Advisers, 1985* (Washington, D.C.: U.S. Government Printing Office, 1985), p. 242.

nating in government represents direct purchases of labor. Virtually all of the remainder of the $685.5 billion, with the minor exception of government enterprises such as the postal service and naval shipyards, consists of the activities of private firms in constructing roads and schools, manufacturing tanks and missiles, and otherwise dealing with the government as a customer.

A second way of breaking down GDP to shed light on its composition is by industrial sector of origin, as shown in Table 1–2.

TABLE 1–2 U.S. Gross Domestic Product by Industrial Sector of Origin, 1983

Industry		Amount ($ billions)		Percentage of Total
Agriculture, forestry, and fisheries		$ 72.7		2.2%
Mining		112.4		3.5
Construction		130.7		4.0
Manufacturing				
Durable goods	$389.7		12.0%	
Nondurable goods	295.5		9.1	
Total manufacturing		685.2		21.0
Transportation and public utilities		306.8		9.4
Wholesale and retail trade		536.2		16.5
Finance, insurance, and real estate		542.5		16.7
Services		477.5		14.7
Government and government enterprises		392.1		12.0
Statistical discrepancy		0.5		
Total gross domestic product		$3,256.5		100.0%

SOURCE: U.S. Council of Economic Advisers, *Economic Report of the President and Annual Report of the Council of Economic Advisers, 1985* (Washington, D.C.: U.S. Government Printing Office, 1985), p. 244.

Governmental Restraints on Market Freedom

The essential characteristics of a free market include the freedom of firms to choose the goods and services they wish to produce and the methods used in that production, to set their own prices (or to elect to sell or not sell at the current market-determined price), to determine their own rates of production and amounts offered for sale, to sell or refuse to sell to specific customers, and to enter or leave the market without any restraints imposed by public authorities. Under this set of criteria, there are limitations on market freedom throughout the U.S. economy. Typically, regulatory commissions prescribe rates or prices to be charged and the services to be offered by public utilities. These commissions also have the power to approve or deny requests for new firms to enter the market or for existing ones to abandon, expand, or modify their current services. This pervasive regulation is based on the notions that public utilities such as gas, electricity, and water companies are by definition natural monopolies serving markets in which competition is not feasible and that they provide essential goods or services in which the exercise of private monopoly power would be intolerable. Most forms of public transportation and communication have been subject to similar regulation by commission; but in recent years, a marked trend towards deregulation in these industries has surfaced. Finance and insurance are subject to substantial federal and state regulation of rates and services as well as control of entry into new markets either by new firms or by expansion of existing ones. Real estate agents are subject to state certification.

Even in the private sectors usually described as unregulated— agriculture, forestry, fisheries, mining, construction, manufacturing, wholesale trade, retail trade, and services—accounting in total for 62 percent of GDP by origin, there are substantial governmental restraints on market freedoms. The freedom to produce whatever one wishes by whatever methods of production one wishes to use is limited by product safety, controlled-substance, pure food and drug, environmental, and occupational safety laws and regulations. For a number of agricultural products, output is limited and prices are supported under federal programs. Output and prices of petroleum and natural gas have been regulated. Entry to diverse economic activities such as liquor wholesaling and retailing, medicine, law, and barbering is controlled by license, franchise, and certification requirements.[3]

Nevertheless, throughout these "unregulated" sectors, the primary determinants of the product mix, prices, rates of output, and investment levels are private profit-seeking firms' decisions made in the face of existing and expected market conditions.

Competition as a Limiting Force

As indicated in both Tables 1–1 and 1–2, private business accounts for the overwhelming majority of economic activity in the United States. Most of the markets in which private-sector goods and services are exchanged are free enough from public control so that business firms may exercise whatever market power they possess. The primary economic force limiting this power is the actual and potential competition of other private business firms; antitrust laws are predicated on the belief that government has a role in maintaining and restoring such competition.

CHANGES IN COMPOSITION OF ECONOMIC ACTIVITY

Economic development and technological advances change the composition of economic activity over time. In 1859, on the eve of the Civil War, agriculture accounted for 30.8 percent of total private income earned from production in the United States; manufacturing accounted for 12.5 percent. Seventy years later, on the eve of the Great Depression, the positions were reversed: agriculture had fallen to 14.8 percent, and manufacturing had risen to 30.7 percent. The "services" sector (trade, finance, service, and other miscellaneous activities) rose slightly in relative importance over the period, from 34.4 percent to 39.1 percent.[4]

As reflected in Tables 1–1 and 1–2, agriculture has continued to decline to well under 3 percent of GDP in the 1980s. This falling share does not, however, reflect a weakened agricultural sector; to the contrary, it results from a spectacular increase in agricultural productivity. A host of improvements—including mechanization, irrigation, rural electrification, new techniques of soil conservation such as contour plowing, technical advance in and more widespread use of chemical fertilizers, new and more effective pesticides, improved seed varieties, introduction of new crops, new techniques for raising livestock and preventing animal diseases, agricultural extension services, better education of farmers, and the development of an infrastructure including such things as road and rail networks, refrigerated storage and shipping facilities, and efficient channels of trade—have been responsible for building up an agricultural sector with an output that more than meets the nation's needs for food (net agricultural exports amounted to 31.1 percent of total agricultural production in 1980 and to 26.8 percent in the more depressed year of 1983),[5] while absorbing only a small fraction of its productive resources.

Table 1–2 indicates that by 1983, manufacturing output had fallen to 21 percent of GDP, in current prices. Some observers conclude from this decline that the United States has made the transition from an industrial to a "postindustrial" economy, or they view with concern the "deindustrialization" of the nation.[6] Yet the smaller relative contribution of manufacturing to GDP, like that of agriculture, results primarily from the disproportionate growth of productivity in that sector. In a 1984 study, Robert Z. Lawrence noted that if one corrected for the fall in the prices of manufactured goods relative to other prices (attributable to greater increases in productivity and thus lower real resource costs of production in the manufacturing sector), there had been virtually no change in the ratio of output of manufactured goods to gross national product from 1950 to 1980.[7]

This increased productivity of agriculture and manufacturing has allowed the United States to become an increasingly service-oriented economy. A summation of the relevant figures in Table 1–2 indicates that the shares of wholesale and retail trade, finance, insurance, real estate, and services rose to 47.9 percent of GDP by 1983. And when government services are added to that total, the share of the service-oriented sectors amounts to around 60 percent. Thus, antitrust must be concerned not only with the effects of market power in manufacturing industries but also with the impact on economic performance of such developments as the growth of chain stores and large nationwide distributors in both wholesaling and retailing, interstate bank mergers and the formation of diversified bank holding companies offering varied financial services, and restraints on competition imposed by the rules and practices of professional societies including those of medical doctors, lawyers, and engineers.

MARKET POWER IN THE MODERN CORPORATION

In a leading textbook published in 1945, Harry L. Purdy, Martin L. Lindahl, and William A. Carter emphasized the role of the modern corporation in attaining and wielding economic power.[8] "To the early nineteenth-century economist," they noted, "the business unit was a small personal venture most commonly organized and directed by an individual or set of partners. Today, the corporation has become the typical business form, and in many industries we must recognize the fifty-million-dollar corporation as a small organization."[9] Modern economic power, Purdy et al. insisted, cannot be assessed and explained without first understanding the role of the corporation in the economy. This book follows in the same tradition by devoting a chapter to a discussion of the attributes of the modern corporation that have led to the predominance of that particular form of business and by linking these attributes to the exercise of economic power in the U.S. economy today.

Table 1–3 indicates the dominant position of the relatively small number of corporations among private business firms in the United States. While corporations make up about 16 percent of the nation's business population, they account for around 89 percent of net business receipts.

Table 1–4 breaks down the information from Table 1–3 by sector of the economy. In every sector, corporations comprise a minority of the number of business firms. Yet in every sector except agriculture, forestry, and fisheries, corporations account for a substantial majority

TABLE 1–3   Number of U.S. Firms Filing Tax Returns and Net Receipts from Sales and Services, by Form of Business, 1981

Form of Business	Number of Returns (000)	Net Receipts* ($ billions)
Proprietorships	12,185	$ 523
Partnerships	1,461	272
Corporations	2,812	7,076

*Receipts from sales and services less allowances, rebates, and returns.
SOURCE: U.S. Department of Commerce, Bureau of the Census, *Statistical Abstract of the United States, 1985* (Washington, D.C.: U.S. Government Printing Office, 1984), p. 516.

of the economic activity. The situation is most marked in manufacturing, where corporations account for nearly 99 percent of net receipts.

Concentration within the corporate sector is illustrated in Tables 1–5 and 1–6. The four smallest size classes in Table 1–5 comprise a total of 99.29 percent of the nation's corporations, but these corporations as a group own only 13.73 percent of total corporate assets. The four largest size categories, representing 0.71 percent of the corporate population, account for 86.26 percent of corporate assets. Table 1–6 shows that concentration among the giants of U.S. business—the

TABLE 1–4   Number of U.S. Firms Filing Tax Returns and Net Receipts from Sales and Services, by Industry and Form of Business, 1980

Industry	Number of Returns (000)			Net Receipts* ($ billions)		
	Proprietor-ships	Partner-ships	Corporations	Proprietor-ships	Partner-ships†	Corporations†
Agriculture, forestry, and fisheries	3,279	126	81	$101.1	$21.6	$ 48.9
Mining	120	35	26	8.6	13.2	167.4
Construction	1,073	67	272	47.8	18.4	260.4
Manufacturing	296	30	243	14.8	15.3	2,301.1
Transportation and public utilities	439	20	111	20.0	5.9	507.4
Wholesale and retail trade	2,527	200	800	202.3	65.8	1,919.3
Finance, insurance, and real estate	1,049	637	493	21.5	87.1	697.5
Services	3,843	263	671	88.0	58.6	266.1

*Receipts from sales and services less allowances, rebates, and returns.
†Includes total receipts from finance, insurance, and real estate industry, whether business receipts or otherwise. Total for all industries therefore exceeds total in Table 1–3.
SOURCE: U.S. Department of Commerce, Bureau of the Census *Statistical Abstract of the United States, 1984,* (Washington, D.C.: U.S. Government Printing Office, 1983), p. 533.

TABLE 1–5 Number and Assets of Active U.S. Corporations, by Asset Size, 1981

Asset Size ($000)	Number of Returns (000)	Total Assets ($ billions)	Percentages of Total Returns	Percentages of Total Assets
Under $100	1,570.0	$ 50	55.82%	0.59%
100–1,000	1,004.0	322	35.70	3.77
1,000–10,000	201.1	526	7.15	6.15
10,000–25,000	17.5	275	.62	3.22
25,000–50,000	8.4	296	.30	3.46
50,000–100,000	5.2	372	.18	4.35
100,000–250,000	3.4	540	.12	6.32
Over 250,000	3.1	6,165	.11	72.13

SOURCE: U.S. Department of Commerce, Bureau of the Census, *Statistical Abstract of the United States, 1985* (Washington, D.C.: U.S. Government Printing Office, 1984), p. 523.

large corporations comprising the "big business" sector of the economy—is high, whether measured by sales, assets, or number of employees.

CONCLUSION

The principal characters in this book are (1) the nation's consuming households (the individuals and families whose material welfare is the ultimate standard by which the performance of the economy must be judged); (2) the private business firms producing nearly all of the goods and services that provide this welfare, dominated by a form of business—the modern corporation—that has shown itself particularly well suited to the acquisition and exercise of economic power; and (3) the government, viewed here in its role as a public agent responsible for establishing market conditions and rules of business conduct designed

TABLE 1–6 Sales, Assets, and Number of Employees of the 500 Largest U.S. Industrial Corporations,* by Group Rank, 1983

Rank by Sales Group	Sales Dollars (billions)	Sales Percent of Group Total	Assets Dollars (billions)	Assets Percent of Group Total	Employees Number (000)	Employees Percent of Group Total
First 100	$1,161.1	68.8%	$913.6	67.5%	8,313	59.2%
Second 100	262.9	15.6	227.0	16.8	2,767	19.7
Third 100	132.9	7.9	109.9	8.1	1,397	9.9
Fourth 100	78.6	4.7	65.6	4.8	967	6.9
Fifth 100	51.2	3.0	37.8	2.8	608	4.3

*Firms deriving more than 50 percent of revenues from manufacturing or mining.
SOURCE: U.S. Department of Commerce, Bureau of the Census, *Statistical Abstract of the United States, 1985* (Washington, D.C.: U.S. Government Printing Office, 1984), p. 530.

to promote optimal economic performance. The setting is the world's largest, most diverse, and to date most productive national economy. And the plot—an ongoing story line without resolution or conclusion— consists of the responses and interactions of the main characters as they seek to cope with the opportunities, challenges, and problems posed by a relatively free market economy.

ENDNOTES

[1]United States v. E. I. du Pont de Nemours & Company, 351 U.S. 377, 391 (1956). See also United States v. Grinnell Corporation, 384 U.S. 563, 571 (1966).

[2]U.S. Council of Economic Advisers, *Economic Report of the President and Annual Report of the Council of Economic Advisers, 1985* (Washington, D.C.: U.S. Government Printing Office, 1985), p. 233.

[3]For a survey of the scope of government regulation and a critical analysis of its costs and effects, see Murray L. Weidenbaum, *Business, Government, and the Public,* 2d ed. (Englewood Cliffs, N.J.: Prentice-Hall, 1981). See also Ronald J. Penoyer, *Directory of Federal Regulatory Agencies,* 3d ed. (St. Louis, Mo.: Washington University, Center for the Study of American Business, 1981).

[4]U.S. Department of Commerce, Bureau of the Census, *Historical Statistics of the United States, 1789–1945* (Washington, D.C.: Government Printing Office, 1952), p. 14.

[5]U.S. Council, *Economic Report and Annual Report,* pp. 244, 342.

[6]See, for example, Robert L. Heilbroner, *Business Civilization in Decline* (New York: W. W. Norton, 1976); Lester C. Thurow, *The Zero-Sum Society* (New York: Basic Books, 1980); Barry Bluestone and Bennett Harrison, *The Deindustrialization of America* (New York: Basic Books, 1982).

[7]Robert Z. Lawrence, *Can America Compete?* (Washington, D.C.: Brookings Institution, 1984).

[8]Harry L. Purdy, Martin L. Lindahl, and William A. Carter, *Corporate Concentration and Public Policy* (New York: Prentice-Hall, 1945).

[9]Ibid., p. 34.

The Basic Tools of Analysis: History, Theory, and Quantitative Methods

Joseph A. Schumpeter, one of the great economists of the 20th century, wrote in *History of Economic Analysis*, "What distinguishes the 'scientific' economist from all other people who think, talk, and write about economic topics is a command of techniques that we class under three heads: history, statistics, and 'theory.' These three together make up what we shall call Economic Analysis."[1] All three of Schumpeter's analytical tools are essential to understand industrial organization and appropriate public policy toward business in the United States today. But, as Schumpeter noted in a footnote to the passage just quoted, command of a technique "sufficient to constitute scientific level" need "not require any elaborate methods that the layman could not understand."[2] The remainder of this chapter is devoted to such a "layman's" understanding—presuming, however, that most students who use this text have already taken a course in introductory microeconomic theory.

ECONOMIC HISTORY

In introducing his discussion of economic history, Schumpeter stated:

> Of these fundamental fields, economic history—which issues into and includes present-day facts—is by far the most important. I wish to state right now that if, starting my work in economics afresh, I were told that I could study only one of the three but could have my choice, it would be economic history that I should choose. And this on three grounds. First, the subject matter of economics is essentially a unique process in historic time. Nobody can hope to understand the economic phenomena of any, including the present, epoch who has not an adequate command of historical *facts* and an adequate amount of historical *sense* or of what may be described as *historical experience*. Second, the historical report cannot

be purely economic but must inevitably reflect also "institutional" facts that are not purely economic: therefore it affords the best method for understanding how economic and non-economic facts *are* related to one another and how the various social sciences *should* be related to one another. Third, it is, I believe, the fact that most of the fundamental errors currently committed in economic analysis are due to lack of historical experience more often than to any other shortcoming of the economist's equipment.[3]

A sense of past experiences and present-day realities in any area of applied economics is immensely valuable in, if not crucial to, the construction of relevant and applicable theoretical models and to the formulation of meaningful hypotheses for statistical testing. Contrary to popular stereotype, the great economic theorists have not worked in an "ivory tower," nor have they been indifferent to the course of economic events. Rather, those who made the most important contributions to economics were motivated by the problems and crises of real economies and by the actual struggles of people to utilize their resources efficiently. As Alexander Gray noted in *The Development of Economic Doctrine,* "It is no accident that Malthus wrote on population at a time when the population was rapidly increasing, or that Ricardo explored the intricacies of currency problems when the currency system was disorganized."[4] The most prominent 20th-century economist, John Maynard Keynes, wrote his best-known book, *The General Theory of Employment, Interest, and Money,*[5] in reaction to his shock and dismay at capitalism's failures during the Depression of the 1930s and his concern that capitalism might not survive the crisis.

The need for history as a guide to policymaking is captured in George Santayana's oft-quoted remark, "Those who do not remember the past are condemned to repeat it."[6] We can learn from both the successes and the mistakes of our predecessors. Those who formulate economic legislation and regulations, as well as those who apply the laws and rules, ought to be aware of both the achievements and the failures of past policies, particularly their unanticipated problems and side effects. "Progress," Santayana wrote, "far from consisting in change, depends on retentiveness. When change is absolute . . . no direction is set for possible improvement: and when experience is not retained, as among savages, infancy is perpetual."[7]

In an area of frequent controversy and advocacy such as economics, those who do not remember the past may be unduly influenced by those who do—or who claim to. Only those with their own knowledge of history can evaluate the pertinence and accuracy of inferences that others draw from the past—or from the incomplete and distorted historical record we have today.

There is yet another need for historical perspective in the study of economics. In 1931, Schumpeter described a form of "infantilism" that permeated discussions of economic issues, noting that "the subjects we deal with are so much bound up with practical interests and the struggle of social classes that most people find it difficult to look upon a scientific result dispassionately, and not to *love* it or hate it according as it seems to fit their predilections or not."[8] Where values, ideologies, and self-interest are involved, people tend to indulge in wishful thinking or rationalizations. Catching the essence of such self-delusion, Mark Twain reportedly remarked that we know much less about the past than we do about the future.[9] A sound knowledge of history is essential to throw off preconceptions and "look upon a scientific result dispassionately."

This book draws heavily on the historical record for an adequate comprehension of corporate concentration and antitrust policy in the United States. The significance of the corporate form of business is developed by tracing the rise of the modern corporation and noting how its specific attributes emerged over time in response to changing conditions and needs of the business community. Similarly, current attitudes toward big business and private market power are traced from their origins to assess their current strength and relevance. Present-day interpretations of antitrust law by the courts and enforcement agencies are explained through review of earlier questions and problems that led to these interpretations. A rationale for the view that preservation of competition is essential to the survival of the free-enterprise system is derived from perceived historical imperatives.

ECONOMIC THEORY

In essence, all theory is *abstraction*—literally, a drawing away or pulling out. If an underlying reality is too complicated or cumbersome to analyze and understand completely, we must concentrate on only a few important features. An economy such as that of the United States is highly complex, involving millions of diverse business firms producing millions of products—both intermediate products purchased by other businesses and final products sold to consumers. A population of over 200 million is organized into household consuming units of varying ages, numbers, incomes, and tastes. The number of market transactions is immense. Markets themselves, or the conditions under which goods are bought and sold, are diverse in organization and scope. A basic need of microeconomic theory, therefore, is to abstract.

Theoretical Models

The primary purpose of theory is to identify and, if possible, explain cause-and-effect relationships to describe how the real world behaves and to predict the effects of certain phenomena—including, in the social sciences, the effects of proposed public policies. This general objective of describing and predicting in terms of cause and effect guides the process of abstraction: the theorist's job is to identify and concentrate on the most important causal factors in explaining significant effects. In many instances in the physical sciences, and in a much smaller number of cases in the social sciences, the hypothesized causal relationships can be tested in controlled experiments. But some physical phenomena and nearly all social phenomena cannot be replicated in a laboratory, so models—or artificial constructs based on hypothesized causal relations—must substitute for controlled experiments.

Theory, therefore, seeks to simplify the real world. Good theory is linked indissolubly to reality. A theoretical model that abstracts away from the important causal factors or that fails to consider the most interesting and significant effects is a poor one, no matter how elegant and internally consistent it may be.

The use of abstract modeling in depicting a fundamental cause-and-effect relationship may be illustrated by the most basic model of economics, that of supply and demand in a competitive market. In Figure 2–1, the demand curve D plots the quantities of a particular product (a consumer good in this instance) that would be purchased at various prices, if available, *holding everything else constant.* In other words, the quantity that households wish to purchase is treated as a function of the product's own price. We know that many other factors influence the purchase decision, such as prices of other goods, introduction of new products, incomes of consumers, and changes in taste, style, and habit. But under the *ceteris paribus* (everything else constant) assumption, we assume that the mix and prices of other goods, consumers' incomes and tastes, and anything that could affect the amounts demanded other than the product's own price are all unchanged. This simplifying assumption, or abstraction, is made because we want to concentrate on the role of price. The functional relationship can then be expressed as

$$Q_d = d(P)$$

where Q_d stands for quantity demanded and P is the price of the product.

Similarly, the supply curve S shows the quantities that firms would offer for sale at various prices, *ceteris paribus.* Technology, costs of factors of production, and all influences on the firm's willingness to sell except the price it receives are assumed away by invoking the phrase *ceteris paribus.* We thus have in the model a supply function,

$$Q_s = s(P)$$

where Q_s represents the quantity supplied.

The model incorporates fundamental cause-and-effect relation-

FIGURE 2–1 Supply and Demand Curves in a Competitive Market

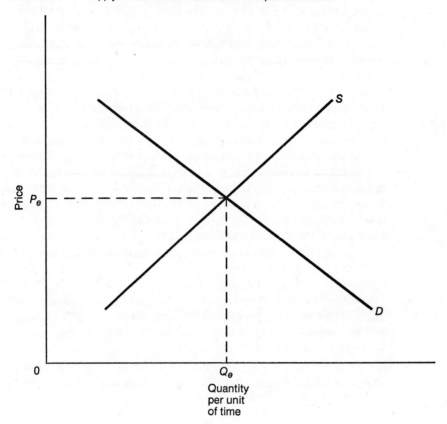

ships based on the assumed behavior of competing sellers and buyers. If the quantity that households wish to buy is less than the quantity firms are offering for sale, as would be the case at any price above P_e in Figure 2–1, the theory predicts that those who are left holding goods that they would like to have sold at the going price will offer these goods at lower prices. As the price falls, the quantity demanded will rise, as shown on the demand curve, eliminating the unsold "glut." Similarly, at any price below P_e, there will be some unsatisfied buyers, and they will bid the price up. The price will be at equilibrium, or under no pressure to either rise or fall, only when

$$Q_d = Q_s$$

or the amount buyers wish to purchase is just equal to the amount suppliers wish to sell.

We have a set of three simultaneous equations and, assuming that the functions $d(P)$ and $s(P)$ are independent of each other, these equations can be solved for the three variables Q_d, Q_s, and P.

This simple supply-and-demand model of a market-clearing price is a highly abstract one. If we could depict real-world supply and demand curves, they would be in continual motion, constantly changing both slope and position as other prices, incomes, tastes, and technology change throughout the economy. The equilibrium point would have to be replaced by a tendency of actual prices and outputs to gravitate toward an ever-shifting equilibrium target. It is not too difficult to construct more complex models, introducing the prices of complementary and substitute goods, for example, as variables causing the demand curve to shift. Such models can be expressed as a set of simultaneous equations and solved if the number of unknowns is equal to the number of independently determined equations. Nevertheless, the simple model—yielding a fundamental insight into the role of price as the equilibrating mechanism in a free-market economy, and reducible to a two-dimensional graph—has been one of the most important tools of economic analysis.

Economics as a Behavioral Science

In applying and interpreting economic theory, keep in mind that economics is a *behavioral* science. Rather than testing cause-and-effect relationships among natural phenomena, the behavioral sciences seek to develop the consequences of human motives and behavior. Stable equilibrium in the supply-and-demand model, for example, is assured by a downward-sloping demand curve and an upward-sloping supply curve. The negative slope of the demand curve derives from the psychological principle of diminishing marginal utility of consumption and the assumption that all consumers distribute their purchases to maximize total utility obtainable from a limited budget. The principles of diminishing marginal utility and utility maximization, taken together, form the basis for a general theory of consumer behavior. Similarly, the behavioral assumption that businesses are run to maximize the profits of their owners permits us to develop a general theory of the firm. The upward-sloping short-run supply curve is derived from the behavioral assumption of profit maximization coupled with the technical or engineering law of diminishing returns.

In actuality, consumers cannot possibly be perfect utility maximizers, and plausible business objectives other than profit maximization have been identified. Nevertheless, some abstraction is essential to form manageable general models, and utility and profit maximization are elemental features of actual economic behavior.

From time to time, we must modify these behavioral assumptions to analyze a particular issue. One example is the rise of the large corporation, in which the managers who make the operating decisions may have goals of their own, distinct from and conflicting with maximization of profit for the owners.

Positive and Normative Economics

Finally, economic theory can be either positive or normative. *Positive economics* is value free: it describes and predicts economic phenomena but does not evaluate them. *Normative economics* seeks to establish standards or norms by which we can rate the performance of the economy as good or bad. Both positive and normative theory must be applied in a field such as industrial organization, which involves the prescription of appropriate public policies towards business. Like the theory in other social sciences but unlike most theory in the physical sciences, then, economic theory derives from subjective preferences as well as objective relationships. A theoretical model, no matter how well it describes and predicts the real world, can rarely be used to "prove" that one public policy is superior to another, unless those to be convinced share the theorist's relevant social goals.

Microeconomic theory remains an indispensable tool in the study of industrial and market organization in a large modern economy. But like any good tool, a theory can be used properly and effectively only by those who understand what it is designed to do and how to pick the right one for the job.

QUANTITATIVE ANALYSIS

Modern scientific inquiry involves a process of *hypothesis, verification,* and *rehypothesis*. First, a hypothesis is formulated to explain a certain natural or social phenomenon. The hypothesis is then tested by experiment, observation, collection of data, or some combination, followed by analysis to interpret the empirical findings. Such testing might verify, discredit, or suggest modifications in the original hypothesis. No hypothesis, regardless of how thoroughly tested and verified, is immune from challenge by new experimental or statistical methods or from retesting in the light of additional data. Indeed, a hypothesis not capable of being disproved is not a strictly "scientific" one.

In the social sciences, verification is usually achieved by observation of human behavior in uncontrolled environments rather than through controlled experiment. In economics, the observed variables of interest are frequently quantitative (prices, costs, profits, rates of output and sales, inventory levels, numbers of firms and their sizes, market shares, advertising expenditures, and spending on research and development, for example). The ability of economists to analyze quantitative data to test and verify hypotheses is therefore crucial for a scientific approach to the discipline. To meet this need, *econometrics* has evolved as a specialized form of economic statistics.[10]

Econometric techniques, properly used, provide far more powerful and reliable tools for testing hypothesized causal effects than do tables, graphs, or straightforward unanalyzed averages and percentages. There are econometric standards, for example, for evaluating the adequacy of the sample. There are tests to determine the likelihood that the observed relationship could have resulted from chance rather than cause and effect. And investigators can "control" for extraneous influences by including variables representing features to be held constant under the *ceteris paribus* assumption. But these techniques can be grossly misused by those who do not understand the underlying economic relationships involved. Equally true, econometric analysis poses pitfalls for the researcher who, no matter how knowledgeable of empirical matters and skilled in theory, does not understand the relevant statistical principles.

Econometric testing is no substitute for historically based empirical knowledge and the sound application of economic theory. To the contrary, sensible application of econometric techniques requires empirical and theoretical sophistication. To ask which of Schumpeter's three techniques of economic analysis is the most important is rather like asking which of the three legs of a tripod contributes most to its stability.

The Appendix to this chapter introduces the reader with no prior background to the rudiments of econometrics.

APPENDIX: ECONOMETRIC TECHNIQUES

Regression Analysis

The most widely applied econometric technique is known as *regression analysis.* A simple regression is a mathematical technique for fitting an equation of the general form $Y = f(X)$.[11] Suppose, for example, we wish to ascertain whether there are economies of scale in the production of a particular commodity—call it a goofus—and we have data for the month of April on 10 goofus factories, all of which operated for eight hours a day, five days a week, throughout the month (see Table 2–1). The data suggest that there may be a relationship: The greater the number of goofuses produced per month, the lower the average cost of production. Or, Y (average cost) appears to be a decreasing function of X (rate of output). The statistical relationship could also be displayed on a *scatter diagram,* as shown in Figure 2–2.

TABLE 2–1 Goofus Production Data, by Factory, for April

Factory	(X) Number of Goofuses Produced (000)	(Y) Average Cost of Goofus Production
1	252	85 cents
2	278	74
3	310	87
4	335	77
5	401	72
6	456	74
7	523	69
8	588	71
9	647	67
10	720	68

A simple linear regression fits a straight-line equation of the form $Y = a + bX$ to the data, with values calculated for a (the intercept) and b (the slope) that minimize the sum of the squares of the differences between the actual values of Y and those predicted by the equation. The least squares regression equation for the goofus data is:

$$Y = 89.476 - .034X \qquad (2.1)$$

FIGURE 2–2 Average Production Cost (Y) and Rate of Output (X) of 10 Goofus Factories, and Y as a Straight-Line Function of X

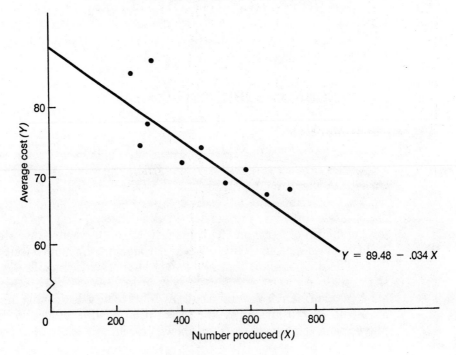

Graphed onto the scatter diagram, Equation (2.1) appears as the downward-sloping line in Figure 2–2.

According to the estimating equation, if production were cut back, toward a limit of zero, average cost of production would rise toward 89.476 cents. For each additional 1,000 units produced per month, average cost would fall by .034 cents. The difference between predicted and actually observed values of Y can be illustrated by inserting an observed value for X in the equation and solving for Y. For example, when a factory produces 523,000 units per month, the equation becomes $Y = 89.476 - (.034)(523)$, and $Y = 71.694$ cents. This estimated cost can be compared with the observed cost of 68 cents per unit.

The regression equation could also be used to *project*, or estimate costs outside of the range of observations. Thus, if we wanted to estimate average production costs when the rate of output was 150,000 goofuses per month, we could set $Y = 89.476 - (.034)(150)$, and calculate an average cost of 84.376 cents. Similarly, the equation predicts average costs of 62.276 cents at a production rate of 800,000 per month. Econometric models are used in this fashion to predict, as well as to test, hypotheses. Note that even within the range of observations, costs calculated from the estimating equation may provide more accurate predictions than the costs actually observed; due to some atypical experiences in April, actual costs may be far from the average.

The equation fitted need not be a straight-line one. If the underlying hypothesis suggests an exponential relationship, the equation $Y = aX^b$ can be used and transformed to the linear equation $\log Y = \log a + b \log X$. Or a quadratic function can be used to fit a U- or inverted U-shaped curve to the data. A straight-line equation is clearly not designed to project costs at all possible rates of goofus output. According to Equation (2.1), unit costs of production would fall to zero at an output rate of 2,631,647 goofuses per month and would be negative at still higher rates of production! Further, the principle of factor indivisibility strongly suggests that average costs would rise exponentially if production were cut back to very low levels. In logarithmic form, which is probably more appropriate than a straight-line estimate for a cost function, our estimating equation becomes:

$$\log Y = 2.399 - .201 \log X \qquad (2.2)$$

Graphically, Equation (2.2) yields the line shown in Figure 2–3.

At some high rate of output, economies of scale presumably would be exhausted (so that the line plotting the estimating equation would become horizontal) or possibly diseconomies of scale would set in (so that the regression line would turn up). If we had more data, particularly for higher levels of output, some functional form other than the two (linear and logarithmic) already estimated might suggest itself.

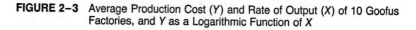

FIGURE 2–3 Average Production Cost (*Y*) and Rate of Output (*X*) of 10 Goofus Factories, and *Y* as a Logarithmic Function of *X*

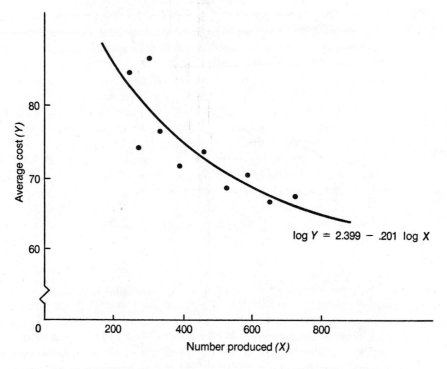

$$\log Y = 2.399 - .201 \log X$$

But unless there is some economic reason to believe that the hypothesized form is plausible, or unless the hypothesis is simply that there is some causal relationship of unknown form, it is impermissible to fit a complex exponential or kinked function to the data simply to get a closer fit.

Statistical Inference

Econometric analysis, concerned with testing of causal hypotheses, is grounded on principles of *statistical inference,* a branch of statistical theory derived from principles of probability. Most of the data sets used in economic analysis are in the form of a *sample,* or a limited number of observations made from the *universe* or *population* of all possible observations of the phenomenon.

One problem of statistical inference is how representative the sample is or how reliable the inferences are that can be drawn from analysis of that sample. There may, for example, have been several hundred goofus factories producing during the month in which we obtained our 10 "typical" observations from a small random sample. From month to month, such things as down time on machinery, employee absenteeism, and delays in receipt of raw materials will cause production to vary. Some of our firms would have had random good luck in April but bad luck in other months, with the luck of the draw bearing no plausible relationship to size.

Statistical inference theory, drawing on principles of probability that will not be discussed here, is used to determine the confidence that can be placed in the various inferences drawn from econometric analysis. At the most basic level, we want to design a test with a low probability of either rejecting a true hypothesis (called a type I error) or accepting a false one (type II error).

Coefficient of Determination. One measure of the statistical relationship between the dependent and independent variables in a regression equation is the *coefficient of determination,* or the square of the *correlation coefficient.* The correlation coefficient, customarily designated as *r* is formulated in such a way that an absolute value of one indicates no differences between observed and estimated values, so that all actual data points lie squarely on the regression line. A value of zero indicates no difference between dispersion around the mean and dispersion around the regression line, or a random scattering of points with no statistical linear relationship between the dependent and independent variables. A positive value for the correlation coefficient indicates a direct relationship between the variables (an upward-sloping line on a graph relating Y to corresponding values of X), while a negative value indicates an inverse relationship (a downward-sloping line). The closer r is to an absolute value of one, either positive or negative, the better the fit of the regression line to the data. Examples are shown in Figure 2–4.

The square of the correlation coefficient is reported more often than the coefficient itself, since the equation for calculating r is constructed so that r^2 (always positive) is equal to the percentage of total deviations from the mean that are incorporated into or are statistically "accounted for" by the regression equation.

The *statistical significance* of the coefficient on an independent variable, or its *confidence level,* measures the reliability of the estimate. There are standard methods for calculating the level of statistical significance from the correlation coefficient and the number of observations. Roughly, to say that a variable is significant at the 5 percent confidence or significance level is to say that if the true value of the coefficient for the universe is zero (or in general, if the *null hypothesis* of no relationship between the variables is true), the chances are only 5 out of 100 that the investigator would have found a coefficient as large as that calculated from the sample.

In our goofus example, $r = -.799$ and $r^2 = .638$ for the linear

FIGURE 2–4 Some Illustrative Scatter Diagrams and Correlation Coefficients

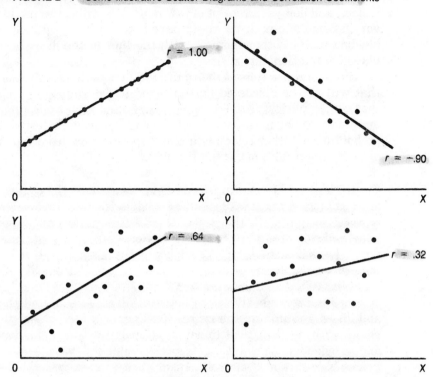

regression, while for the logarithmic form of the estimating equation, $r = -.832$ and $r^2 = .693$. The coefficient on X, the size variable, is statistically significant at the 1 percent confidence level in both equations.

Perhaps the single most important warning in both use and interpretation of regression results is that high correlation and level of statistical significance do not demonstrate causation. Consider the following examples:

- There may be no causal relationship at all between the variables. One might find, for example, that from 1960 through 1980, the average height of students admitted to college rose, while the average scholastic aptitude test scores of those admitted fell. One would not, presumably, infer from this that short people are more scholastically apt than tall ones.
- Both variables may move in the same direction because they are effects of the same cause. If in a particular community the numbers attending church and the number of violent crimes were positively correlated, certainly it would be more plausible to as-

sume that both were the results of an increasing population than to conclude that church members are particularly prone to violence.

- Even if there is a causal relationship between the variables, correlation does not identify the direction in which the causation runs. A positive correlation between sales of umbrellas and average rainfall would lead no sane person to believe that one could cause more rain to fall by increasing the sales of umbrellas.

Thus, a high correlation cannot by itself verify a causal hypothesis. It can only provide evidence to support a reasoned or intuitively plausible hypothesis.

Multiple Regression. Our simple straight-line regression yielded an estimating equation of the form $Y = a + bX$. An equation completely describing the data would have the form $Y = a + bX + u$, where u is the *error*, or *disturbance*, term accounting for movements in Y that are not "explained" in the equation by movements in X. If these error terms are not randomly distributed, the inclusion of additional independent variables may often be called for to improve either the fit or the reliability of the estimate.

Suppose, in our goofus example, that the error terms were larger for low values of X than for high values. This would indicate that the low rates of output did not appear to predict average costs as well as high ones. Perhaps some factories operated at closer to full capacity in April than did others, and the higher the rate of output, the greater the probability that a firm was fully utilizing its capacity. Thus, the effect of rate of output on average costs would be shown more accurately if we *controlled* for the extent that capacity was utilized by adding a variable such as percentage of optimum or rated capacity in operation during April. Since operating at less than full capacity presumably raises average costs, the effect of adding this variable should be to flatten the slope of the regression line while improving its fit and lessening the statistical significance of the rate of output. Or, suppose we found that the mean value of the error term was negative in repeated observations for particular values of X and positive for other values. It might be that the 10 factories for which we have data are of different ages and that the newer ones tend to be more efficient regardless of size or rate of output. This would indicate the advisability of adding a new independent variable, age of factory.[12]

Thus in many (perhaps most) econometric studies, it is advisable to regress the dependent variable on more than one independent variable, or to estimate the parameters for equations of the general functional form $Y = f(X_1, X_2, X_3 \ldots X_n)$. A technique known as *multiple regression* can be used for this purpose. Properly used, multiple regression compares to a controlled laboratory experiment in the sense that adding independent variables is akin to controlling for influences other than the one being tested. For example, we would be trying to *isolate* and thus identify the effect of the goofus production rate on average production cost by adding variables for capacity utilization and age of factory.

There are tests of significance for multiple regressions similar to those for simple regressions. A *multiple* correlation coefficient and its square can be calculated and used to measure goodness of fit. (It is customary to use R to designate the correlation between a dependent variable and a set of two or more independent ones, while r is the standard symbol for a simple correlation coefficient.) Levels of statistical significance, or confidence levels, can also be calculated for each of the independent variables and for the equation as a whole.

As a simple illustration, suppose that investigation indicated that all 10 goofus factories operated at nearly the same capacity in April but turned out to be of substantially different ages (see Table 2–2).

TABLE 2–2 Goofus Production Data, Introducing Age of Factory

Factory	(X₁) Number of Goofuses Produced (000)	(X₂) Age of Factory	(Y) Average Cost of Production of a Goofus
1	252	9 years	85 cents
2	278	3	74
3	310	10	87
4	335	8	77
5	401	4	72
6	456	9	74
7	523	1	69
8	588	8	71
9	647	2	67
10	720	6	68

A multiple regression of Y on both X_1 and X_2 yields

$$Y = 77.99 - .0262X_1 + 1.039X_2 \qquad (2.3)$$

For Equation (2.3), $R = .925$ and $R^2 = .855$. Thus, a greater percentage of the total variance in cost is "explained" by including the data on factory age. However, the coefficient on X_1 (the rate of output) remains statistically significant at the 1 percent level of confidence, providing further verification for our original hypothesis. The coefficient on X_2 is significant at the 5 percent level but not at the 1 percent level, identifying factory age as another significant factor in explaining differences in cost.

. The results of this econometric test would be difficult to interpret unless both rate of output and factory age exerted independent influences on cost. If, for example, the new factories also tended to be the larger ones, we would be faced with the problem of *multicollinearity,* or an inability to distinguish the causal effect of either independent variable. The mathematical effect of multicollinearity is to reduce the level of statistical significance of each of the mutually correlated variables. In the goofus case, the statistical evidence for the hypothesized effects of both variables is strong. That the correlation between the independent variables X_1 and X_2 is quite low ($r = -.339$ and $r^2 = .115$) and not statistically significant further indicates that multicollinearity is not a problem in this example.

The objective of multiple regression is most definitely not to obtain the highest possible R^2. We could probably improve the fit of our goofus equation greatly by adding rate of profit as an independent variable because, presumably, the lower the average cost, the higher the profitability, *ceteris paribus;* but this would not strengthen the test of the hypothesis in any way.

Simultaneity describes the situation that arises when variables are mutually determinative. Suppose we want to test the hypothesis that advertising is one of several determinants of profitability, but we also recognize that there may be a reverse causal flow in our model, with advertising being a function of profit as well as profit being a function of advertising. We would then have, rather than a single equation, a system of simultaneous equations to estimate. We could no longer speak strictly of dependent and independent variables. We should, instead, refer to Y and X_1 as *endogenous* variables determined within the system and X_2 through X_n as *exogenous* variables.

The coefficients of a single equation with one variable identified as independent are estimated through a process known as ordinary least squares (OLS) regression. If we have a simultaneous-equation system, we must resort to a more complicated process. One such estimator commonly used in such situations is known as two-stage least square (TSLS) regression.

ENDNOTES

[1]Joseph A. Schumpeter, *History of Economic Analysis* (New York: Oxford University Press, 1954), p. 12.

[2]Ibid.

[3]Ibid., pp. 12–13 (italics original).

[4]Alexander Gray, *The Development of Economic Doctrine* (London: Longmans, Green, 1931), p. 12.

[5]John Maynard Keynes, *The General Theory of Employment, Interest, and Money* (London: Macmillan, 1936).

[6]George Santayana, *The Life of Reason,* vol. 1: *Reason in Common Sense* (New York: Charles Scribner's Sons, 1906), p. 284.

[7]Ibid.

[8]Quoted in "The Crisis in Economics—Fifty Years Ago," *Journal of Economic Literature* 20, no. 3 (September 1982), p. 1051 (italics original).

[9]I am indebted to Professor Leo Grebler for the attribution.

[10]A number of excellent treatments of econometric techniques introduce the unfamiliar reader to the subject. The material in this chapter draws heavily on the following: Alan A. Walters, *An Introduction to Econometrics* (New York: W. W. Norton, 1968); Christopher A. Achen, *Interpreting and Using Regression* (Beverly Hills, Calif.: Sage Publications, 1982); William J. Baumol, *Economic Theory and Operations Analysis,* 4th ed. (Englewood Cliffs, N.J.: Prentice-Hall, 1977), especially Ch. 10, "On Empirical Determination of Demand Relationships," pp. 227–66; Franklin M. Fisher, "Multiple Regression in Legal Proceedings," *Columbia Law Review* 80, no. 4 (May 1980), pp. 702–36; Peter Kennedy, *A Guide to Econometrics* (Cambridge, Mass.: MIT Press, 1979); David L. Sjoquist, Larry D. Schroeder, and Paula E. Stephan, *Interpreting Linear Regression Analysis: A Heuristic Approach* (Morristown, N.J.: General Learning Press, 1974).

[11]Read as: Y (the dependent variable) is a function of X (the independent variable).

[12]As we add independent variables, however, we tend to reduce the statistical significance of our regression, since each additional independent variable causes us to lose one *degree of freedom*. Probabilistic tests of significance are based on degrees of freedom rather than on number of observations. In general, the degrees of freedom equal the number of observations minus the number of coefficients on the right side of the equation, including the intercept.

CHAPTER THREE

The Rise of the Modern Corporation

In this chapter, we take a closer look at a curious artifact of commercial and industrial civilization, the business corporation.

Exxon, the largest industrial firm in the United States, had 1982 sales slightly greater than the gross domestic product (GDP) of all but 19 of the 118 nations listed in the World Bank's 1984 *World Development Report*. General Motors, the nation's largest industrial employer, had 748,000 employees in 1984, a year when the total military personnel of the U.S. Army numbered 780,000.[1]

However, business gigantism is hardly a new phenomenon. Indeed, relative to the markets and nation-states they operated in, some preindustrial business enterprises make Exxon and General Motors look like small-scale operators. Consider, for example, the following description of England's great 16th- and 17th-century trading companies, taken from Miriam Beard's *History of Business*.

> From the first, the Navy was a merchants' affair. They had most of the ships originally, for which the Tudors had to bargain; the English State conducted its warfare on a contractual basis with them.... Like feudal lords, they [the merchants] undertook the defense of their sovereign in expectation of titles, loot, grants and vast rewards.
>
> And they were rewarded like feudal lords, by grants to enormous domains, greater in extent than those of landed dukes at home, but which lay overseas, in Asia and the Americas, where they could not be supervised.... They could make treaties with heathen potentates, declare and wage war on their own account, enjoy rights of ruling and taxing their heathen subjects.... A supreme example of this mercantile feudalism is provided by the East India Company.... The merchants of this Company

received the entire rights over all of India that they could bring under their sway. Their enemies complained that they "have half the known world in their charter, and that's too much for any company."[2]

Beard's study abounds with similar instances, mostly drawn from the centuries when a rising mercantile class successfully challenged the feudal orders of Europe. In 13th-century Genoa, she writes, "the Bank of St. George was, in fact, the State."[3] In 1340, a consortium of Florentine bankers successfully demanded, as security for a loan to Edward III of England, "the whole reverend person of the Archbishop of Canterbury."[4] For over 100 years, in the 17th and early 18th centuries, a small group of Amsterdam merchant families ruled Holland under what Beard called "the business concept of empire."[5]

In sum, large and wealthy business enterprises, enjoying enormous economic and political strength, are not unique to modern industrialized economies. What is new, however, and what sharply distinguishes today's private-enterprise economies, is the pervasiveness, permanence, and impersonal character of the modern large corporation.

ATTRIBUTES OF THE BUSINESS CORPORATION[6]

A corporation is an *association* of natural persons, formed to achieve some *common purpose* of the group. This fundamental feature holds for religious societies, municipal governments, charities, and educational institutions, as well as for business enterprises. The corporation is different from other associations, such as a business partnership or an unincorporated social club, because it is recognized in law as an entity separate and distinct from its flesh-and-blood members. Ancient Roman, medieval English, and modern U.S. law alike based such recognition on the presumption that the corporation performs some social function that will promote the public welfare. Yet the private corporation is a *voluntary* association, designed to promote the interests of its members. "The almost insuperable difficulty in the use of the corporate form," according to the author of one of the leading studies of its origins and development, "has been to reconcile the private motive and public purpose of the activity exercised within it."[7]

Characteristics of Unincorporated Businesses

To understand the distinctive features of the business corporation, it is useful first to consider some fundamental attributes of unincorporated businesses as they have evolved over centuries out of English and U.S. common law. In a *single proprietorship* the owner is free to transfer funds in and out of the business (e.g., to take money out of the cash register for an evening's entertainment, or to put money back in to build up the change fund) without the permission of any other person or governmental body. All assets may be mingled (a basement workshop or an automobile may be used for both business and personal purposes). In turn, there is no legal distinction between business and personal assets or between business and personal debts. A single proprietor's personal assets may be attached to pay business debts and vice versa.

In an *unincorporated general partnership,* serious conflicts may arise unless partners have a clear understanding as to who can draw on the assets of the business for personal purposes and under what circumstances. The partners are likely to insist that the contributions and withdrawals of each be accounted for separately, to determine how earnings should be distributed, and, in the event that the firm is dissolved, how each partner's share should be ascertained. But as far as the government is concerned, these are private matters, to be resolved by the partners.

Principles of Partnership

Three general principles of partnership evolved in British common law and became part of the common law of the United States following the American Revolution. The first of these is *mutual agency,* a concept under which any and all partners may be held responsible and liable for the business acts of every other partner, whether authorized by the group or not.

Second is the familiar principle of *unlimited liability.* Since the law recognizes no separation of business assets of the partnership from the personal assets of each partner, neither does it recognize any limit on the rights of business creditors to sue for and collect amounts owed from the personal assets of the partners. While the courts will "marshall" the assets, or assure that business assets are exhausted before unsatisfied creditors of the business turn to partners' personal assets, such creditors are then free to sue any partner they wish—presumably the one most able to pay—regardless of degree of involvement in incurring the debt.

Mutual agency and unlimited liability make a potent and dangerous combination. One partner may be sued and have personal assets taken—even be driven into bankruptcy—as the result of some ill-advised action of another partner, regardless of any understanding (even a written contract) between them specifying that the latter would not engage in such activities on behalf of the partnership.

The third principle, that of *delectus personae* (choice of a person) ameliorates the harshness and possible unfairness of this situation. Under this principle, no one may be admitted to a partnership without the approval of all of the existing partners. No one, therefore, can be forced into an unwilling exposure to the two-barreled threat of mutual agency and unlimited liability. No one may inherit a share in any ordinary partnership or buy it from a retiring partner. In such an event, the existing partnership is dissolved and, with full consent of all involved, may be reconstituted as a new firm with new membership.

These three principles—mutual agency, unlimited liability, and *delectus personae*—are hard to fault in terms of general equity or fairness both in relations between a partnership and outsiders dealing with it and in internal relations among the partners. But as equitable as these three general principles may be, they are not particularly suitable for the efficient operation of a large-scale enterprise over a protracted period.

Characteristics of the Modern Corporation

The modern U.S. corporation is a result of entrepreneurs' and investors' centuries-long efforts to escape the limitations of the partnership form of business. The legal concept of the corporation, "that brilliant intellectual achievement of the Roman lawyers, the juristic person, a subject of rights and liabilities, as is a natural person,"[8] was first applied in England to noncommercial associations such as convents and monasteries, municipal governments, and universities. But leading economic historians who have studied the evolution of the modern business corporation generally agree that its functional (as opposed to legal) ancestry can be traced to the joint-stock company, especially the great trading companies of Elizabethan and Stuart times. Among the most important were the East India Company, the Hudson's Bay Company, the Africa Company, and the South Sea Company. The first two joint-stock companies, the Russian Company and the African Adventurers, were established under royal charters issued by Queen Elizabeth I in 1553.

A royal charter customarily granted the company a monopoly on trading in a particular region of the world. In return, the Crown (later Parliament) expected the company to perform some political services— exploration or pacification of an area, suppression of piracy (sometimes defined to include trade by other Europeans or nonchartered English merchants), or liaison between governments in the style of an embassy. The East India Company governed colonial India for nearly two centuries, from 1687 to 1858.[9]

The term *joint stock* does not refer to share capital but rather to the company's real assets, or stock in trade. Initially, the joint-stock trading companies solicited investors to contribute to the joint ownership of a stock of goods to be traded overseas, with any proceeds divided among the investors at the end of each voyage. At that time, the joint stock was dissolved and a new one solicited for the next voyage.

As trade grew and the companies sought to meet their responsibilities to the government, creating and then disbursing a succession of separate joint stocks became increasingly difficult. The companies needed warehouses and trading stations (known as factories), wharves, shipyards, and fortifications abroad with resident representatives and garrisons at these posts. Trading became a continuous function, with incoming ships unloading a new supply of English goods at the factory and reloading with items acquired by the resident trader, or factor.

Under these conditions, the companies needed a group of permanent investors. Yet investors were unwilling to commit their funds to a company with no obligation to return the principal for any reason other than dissolution, unless they were free to sell their shares to others or transfer them to heirs. And, if there were a risk of being held personally responsible for the acts of fellow investors under the principle of *delectus personae,* no one would invest in a company that had issued freely transferable shares without control over who purchased them. In any event, investors could not manage the company directly, and a great deal of authority had to be delegated to distant agents—ships' captains, supercargoes, factors, garrison commanders, and, in some instances, governors of foreign enclaves.

The solutions to such problems lay in the attributes of the corporation:

1. Legal recognition as an entity.
2. The right to issue transferable shares.
3. Delegation of authority and responsibility.
4. Uninterrupted life.[10]
5. Limited liability.

1. Legal Recognition as an Entity. The most fundamental attribute of the corporation, legal recognition, is inherent in charters issued by governments since Roman times. A name or title distinguishes the corporation from its human members. Under its own name, the corporation can sue or be sued, take title to property, and enter into agreements and contracts. It has its own "signature" in the form of a corporate seal.

2. The Right to Issue Transferable Shares. Efforts to win this right have led to the most protracted struggle and, along with limited liability, to the greatest controversies in the development of the modern corporation. The issuance of fractional shares, along with the owners' freedom to sell these shares to whomever they please at whatever price they can get and the buyers' freedom to obtain shares without the approval of anyone but the seller, distinguishes the business corporation from its ecclesiastical, municipal, educational, and charitable counterparts.

As a result of the widespread issuance of such shares by English joint-stock companies, both incorporated and unincorporated, organized securities trading evolved (initially in London's Exchange Alley). Speculation has always been an integral part of this trading. A spectacular stock market boom and collapse in 1719–20, the so-called South Sea Bubble, led to England's passage of the Bubble Act—more accurately, "An Act to Restrain the Extravagant and Unwarrantable Practice of Raising Money by Voluntary Subscriptions for Carrying on Projects Dangerous to the Trade and Subjects of this Kingdom." According to this act, "presuming to act as a corporate Body or Bodies, pretending to transfer or assign any Share or Shares in such Stock or Stocks without legal authority either by Act of Parliament or by any Charter from the Crown to warrant such acting as a Body Corporate . . . shall forever be deemed to be illegal and void."[11]

Despite repeal of the Bubble Act in 1825 (in large part because of savage medieval penalties coupled with incomprehensible prohibitions), it is now settled law in both Great Britain and the United States that only duly chartered corporations may issue transferable shares and thus escape the constraints of *delectus personae* imposed on partners.

3. Delegation of Authority and Responsibility. If a large number of investors, whose membership is continually changing as transferable shares are traded, are to establish and maintain an efficiently operating business enterprise for any length of time, they must delegate management authority and responsibility to a smaller group. Not only would the full body of stockholders be too large to act promptly and efficiently but, in a company with transferable shares, at least some owners would be poorly informed as to the firm's affairs or less than competent participants in intelligent decision making. Further, most stockholders do not care to devote more than a small fraction of their time to matters affecting their companies. In any event, no rational investor would give up the right of *delectus personae*, no matter how attractive the investment in transferable shares might be, unless the common-law authority of every partner to obligate the business could also somehow be abrogated.

Typically, corporate shareholders elect a board of directors, who in turn appoint and dismiss managers responsible for day-to-day business operations. The board of directors is also responsible for major decisions such as declaration of dividends, issuance of new shares, and formulation of broad company policies. Stockholders and directors have no authority to act individually on behalf of the corporation. They exercise their powers only collectively at duly called meetings.

4. Uninterrupted Life. From legal entity status, the right to issue transferable shares, and delegation of authority, it follows that the life of a corporation can be completely independent of the life of any of its owners. This attribute of the corporation, often referred to as unlimited life or perpetual succession, implies a sort of corporate immortality. These phrases can be misleading; any corporation can be terminated and its net assets distributed to shareholders, either voluntarily by vote of the shareholders or through bankruptcy or insolvency proceedings. Early charters normally specified a date on which the corporate grant terminated, requiring periodic renewal by the granting authority. Today, in the United States, corporate charters issued by the various states routinely provide for indefinite continuance, with no terminal date set but with the charter-issuing state retaining the right of revocation for cause.

5. Limited Liability. Under this concept, the creditors of a corporation have a claim against the assets of the firm but not against the personal assets of individual shareholders. Thus, the shareholder's maximum loss can be no more than the cost of his or her investment in the firm (or the amount of stock subscribed for, if not fully paid and issued).

From the 16th through the first three quarters of the 18th century, a period during which joint-stock companies were clamoring for other corporate characteristics, there was little concern over limited liability. It was not a typical feature of the early English business corporations. Its earliest known mention as a motive for incorporation was in 1768, when counsel for the Warmley Company argued, "In case of common partnership every man's private fortune is liable in toto for ye misconduct of any one in ye partnership transactions. What we pray is that they may not be liable beyond what they have subscribed."[12] Nor was limited liability of much concern to colonial companies in the United States.[13]

Most scholars agree that limited liability is not an inherent corporate attribute. However, 19th-century legislation and litigation in both Great Britain and the United States that followed bitter and protracted controversies made limited liability an integral feature of the corporations of both countries, routinely prescribed in the charter but virtually impossible to obtain without registration (in Great Britain) or issuance of a corporate charter (in the United States).[14]

Leading legal and economic students of the corporation generally agree that the advantages of limited liability are often exaggerated by the business community. For example, a great deal of exposure to business risk can be eliminated by insurance and bonding of employees. Lenders, well aware of limited liability, often require personal guarantees for loans to corporations of dubious financial standing. Wage and tax liabilities, along with routine trade credit, are the major sources of uninsurable and normally unsecured claims.[15]

The Business Community's Push toward Incorporation

Throughout the 18th century and well into the 19th, corporate charters were granted sparingly and only by special act of the king or Parliament in England or by a state legislature in the United States. There was widespread acceptance of Adam Smith's view that "the only trades which it seems possible for a joint stock company to carry on successfully, without an exclusive privilege [i.e., grant of monopoly], are those, of which all the operations are capable of being reduced to what is called a routine, or to such a uniformity of method as admits of little or no variation."[16] Smith added that only banking, insurance, canal construction and maintenance, and municipal water supply appeared to meet these criteria.

Despite the reluctance of governments to issue corporate charters, unincorporated firms organized as joint-stock companies were flourishing by the beginning of the 19th century, claiming all of the attributes of corporations: issuing shares described on the face as transferable, electing courts of directors and appointing managers, transacting business in the company name, and asserting both perpetual succession and limited liability in their articles of association. The Bubble Act was not enforced and was generally ignored by English businessmen. As DuBois notes, "The significance of the seventeenth century for the history of the business company organization lies in the perfection of the framework. The contribution of the eighteenth century is in the settlement of certain details of internal organization."[17]

What remained for the 19th century was to make this form of organization readily available, while denying corporate attributes to unincorporated enterprises. Great Britain accomplished this by a series of Parliamentary acts, from 1844 to 1862, providing for incorporation by the mere act of registration and (after protracted debate) for limited liability of all registered corporations. In the United States, a series of general incorporation acts were passed by the various states (beginning with Connecticut in 1837).[18] These general incorporation acts set standard requirements for a corporate charter; and a state official, usually the secretary of state, was required to issue a charter to every qualified applicant who filed articles of incorporation meeting these requirements and who paid the prescribed fee.

In the late 19th and early 20th centuries, competition grew among the states for chartering revenues. In 1891, on the advice of a New York corporate lawyer, New Jersey enacted legislation allowing corporations to own the shares of other corporations, thus legalizing the holding company and greatly facilitating the process of combining independent firms in the merger movement of that period.

Figure 3–1 illustrates, in a highly simplified example, the basic principle behind the holding company device for consolidation and control of a large assemblage of assets through a small investment. Companies A, B, C, and D are operating companies, each consisting of $2,000 of productive assets financed by equal amounts of stockholders' equity in the form of voting common stock and debt. It is assumed that ownership of exactly one half of each firm's common stock confers control; thus, ownership of $500 worth of the common stock of Company A, B, C, or D is needed to control that company. (Creditors holding the bonds or other forms of debt of a corporation are not owners and do not share in its control, except on a contingency basis in times of default or bankruptcy.) Company E, formed to control Companies A, B, C, and D, has sole assets of $500 worth of the common stock of each of the four operating companies, totaling $2,000. These paper assets are financed by Company E through $1,000 of common-stock equity and $1,000 of debt. An investment of $500 in the common stock of holding Company E yields control of that firm and, thus, of the $8,000 productive real assets of the four operating companies. One more tier in the pyramid of control, shown as Company F in Figure 3–1, would permit indirect control of Companies A, B, C, and D by an individual owning $125 of the common stock of Company F.

The magnification of control made possible by the holding company device could be even greater than that illustrated in Figure 3–1. Working control of a corporation can frequently be obtained through

FIGURE 3–1 An Illustration of Pyramided Asset Control through the Holding Company Device

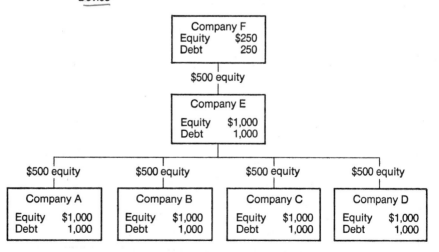

ownership of far less than half of the voting stock, and the proportion of debt in the capitalization can exceed 50 percent. The holding company, particularly through multiple tiers, could also be used to conceal the identity of the individuals or firms in ultimate control of an operating corporation.

In 1896, New Jersey further relaxed incorporation requirements pertaining to capitalization, stockholders' meetings, and disclosures made to owners, creditors, and potential investors. In 1899, Delaware followed, and even outstripped, New Jersey in the privileges offered to incorporators. Further, Delaware undercut New Jersey's fees for initial issuance of a corporate charter. The results for state revenues were impressive. Revenues from corporate chartering fees and franchise taxes allowed New Jersey to abolish property taxes in 1902 and to eliminate the state debt. By 1929, such fees and franchise taxes accounted for 42 percent of the total revenue of the state of Delaware. Other states, faced with the principle of interstate comity under which corporations chartered in one state may do business in all of the others, concluded that they had no choice but to join the competition.[19] This situation has led reformers such as Ralph Nader and his associates to advocate federal chartering of all large corporations engaged in interstate commerce.[20]

The Corporation as a State Grant of Privilege

Legally, corporate attributes are granted by a sovereign state through issuance of a charter, and corporations cannot exist in the absence of such a grant. Thus, entity status, issuance of transferable shares, and the rest are reviewed by the courts as privileges. Yet there is little historical basis for this legal presumption.

The Bubble Act attempted in vain to curb the routine practice by unincorporated joint-stock companies of writing into their articles of association provisions for delegation of authority, issuance of transferable shares, and independent life. Before the passage of the Joint Stock Companies Registration and Regulation Act of 1844, unincorporated British associations frequently had clauses in their articles limiting the liabilities of members to the amounts of their stock subscriptions. When the courts held such clauses invalid against claims by outsiders, firms resorted to a contract provision limiting recovery to the assets of the firm. Livermore's survey of early land companies in the United States showed that "business associations at the end of the eighteenth century were not modified partnerships, but had become corporations in all but the technical legal sense."[21] He concluded that by the time the movement for acts of general incorporation spread among the various states, "the undercurrent of economic evolution was in the direction of free incorporation as a *right* of business bodies, not as a privilege to be granted or withheld."[22]

Until recently, the issue seemed unimportant outside legal circles and academia since obtaining a corporate charter had become so routine. But in a 1979 book, Robert Hessen noted a revival of the debate, with what he viewed as significant implications for public policy:

> When critics demand, for example, that Congress compel corporations to adopt a new system of internal decision making, the obvious question is why do the critics believe that government has any right to regulate the internal affairs or dictate the internal structure of private business. The reason they offer is that corporations, unlike other organizations or associations, are "creatures of the state" because they require governmental permission to exist. From this basic premise, they conclude that in return for this permission, corporations must submit to whatever constraints or demands government may choose to impose upon them.[23]

Hessen contended, to the contrary, that conferring corporate attributes by grant of a charter is merely a convenience. Under basic principles of freedom of association and freedom of contract, any business firm could obtain these "privileges" for itself. He listed three special features that distinguish the corporation: entity status, perpetual life, and limited liability. The equivalent of entity status, he noted, can be obtained by any group of people who designate a trustee to represent them in court and hold property for their benefit. Agreements assuring that a partnership will be reorganized rather than liquidated on the withdrawal of one partner offer de facto continuity. Limited liability can be written into contracts. And after arguing that the law of torts (which holds individual owners of unincorporated enterprises liable for acts committed by employees or agents) is unjust and illogical, he concluded that modern forms of insurance make the issue largely irrelevant.

Hessen did not explicitly discuss transferable shares and delegation of authority, although he commented on the partnership principles of mutual agency and *delectus personae,* noting that the latter is a safeguard made necessary by the former. He merely observed, without elaboration, that these "automatic features" of a partnership can be modified by agreements among the partners and by "notification to outsiders."[24]

THE SEPARATION OF OWNERSHIP AND CONTROL

In the 20th century, control of corporations largely passed from individual investors to managers. Writers at the turn of the century noted the increasing numbers of stockholders and growing use of voting by proxy. But the first thorough and systematic treatment of the matter was contained in Berle and Means' influential 1932 study *The Modern Corporation and Private Property.*

Stockholders have ultimate control of the corporation. They can, if mobilized into a majority, elect any board of directors they wish; and the board, in turn, can set corporate policy as well as dismiss and appoint managerial personnel. But the day-to-day control of the real properties and operations of the corporation is vested in its management. To get at the essence of the concept, Berle and Means define control of the corporation in a special way: "Since direction over the activities of a corporation is exercised through the board of directors, we may say for practical purposes that *control lies in the hands of the individual or group who have the power to select the board of directors (or its majority),* either by mobilizing the legal right to choose them . . . or by exerting pressure which influences their choice."[25]

What Happened to Stockholder Control?

Why then is it that for practical purposes, control may no longer lie with the stockholders? They still have the right to elect the directors, with voting strength proportional to the size of their stock holdings. The general answer, according to Berle and Means, is that the stockholder "has, in fact, exchanged control for liquidity."[26]

Late 19th- and early 20th-century industrial corporations, even the giants of the day, were typically controlled by individuals (e.g., James B. Duke of the American Tobacco Company and John D. Rockefeller of the Standard Oil Company of New Jersey) or by families such as the Du Ponts. As owners of majority or substantial minority stock holdings, the firms' founders or members of their families took active roles in day-to-day management.

By the end of the 19th century, concern was being expressed for the rights of the scattered minority stockholders. Controlling stockholders, with access to inside information, might be in a position to profit from buying or selling the company's stock before good or bad news became public, to the detriment of other stockholders. Large stockholders might try to manipulate the price quoted on a stock exchange. Those in control might let contracts to or make purchases from other companies in which they had an interest, on excessively generous terms. The controlling stockholders might appoint themselves or members of their families to managerial positions, irrespective of competence, and pay themselves excessive salaries.

By the 1930s, however, a more significant issue was the growing abdication of direction and control by *all* stockholders. Dominant holdings were being eroded by the diffusion of ownership made possible by transferable shares (the liquidity to which Berle and Means alluded) among large numbers of middle-class small investors, the scattering of founders' shares among descendants (and charitable foundations), the impact of inheritance taxes on individual wealth, and the growing difficulties of accumulating new fortunes under 20th-century income tax and antitrust laws. (The original Standard Oil, American Tobacco, and Du Pont companies were all dissolved into several successor firms by antitrust action in 1911). Berle and Means noted, for example, that the number of AT&T shareholders had risen from 10,000 in 1901 to 642,180 in 1931, while the Pennsylvania Railroad's stockholders had increased eightfold over the same period.[27] The process has continued apace. At the end of 1983, AT&T had 2,960,471 holders of its common stock.[28] And other *Fortune* 500 industrials have seen comparable increases.

Today, typical individual stockholders are passive investors; they invest discretionary income, savings, or inheritance to supplement income earned from some primary activity or to provide retirement income. Such stockholders probably own portfolios of several common stocks. Alternatively, individual stockholders who speculate buy and sell frequently. Neither type of stockholder has the time or inclination to become actively involved in corporate affairs. A dissatisfied stockholder is far more likely to sell and reinvest elsewhere than try to change a corporation's policies or unseat its directors and managers. Further, the individual stockholder probably prefers having the company controlled by professional managers rather than by a myriad of small and usually uninformed fellow investors.

Proxies: Mechanism for Control and Change. Management may obtain control of the corporation by proxy solicitation. Along with notices of the annual stockholders' meeting, management routinely sends out proxy forms. If signed by the stockholder, a proxy authorizes the secretary of the corporation or some other member of management to cast the absentee stockholder's votes. In most cases, management has to solicit proxies to assure a quorum for the meeting (although in some publicly held corporations managers' holdings alone may comprise a quorum). As a result, usually only a minuscule fraction of stockholders attend the meeting and vote in person—a far cry from the voting strength represented by management holdings of proxies.

A dissatisfied stockholder wishing to change either corporate policies or management has three options. First, he or she might buy enough outstanding stock to obtain control of the corporation or at least to seek representation on the board of directors. Such a tactic is far beyond the means of most individual stockholders.

Second, he or she might solicit proxies in competition with management. Such a solicitation is time consuming and costly. Legally, a corporation must provide a current list of its stockholders to any stockholder who requests it. Nevertheless, in a proxy fight, management usually refuses in order to force the dissident(s) to obtain a court order. Then the dissidents must assume the costs of assembling and mailing their proxy material, including a statement of their reasons for challenging the incumbent management. Management, on the other hand, has access to corporate funds for its own proxy solicitation as well as for the costs of any further communications with stockholders (additional mailings, public advertisements, press conferences, or speeches, for example) to defend itself against the assault.[29]

The third option for the individual is to attend the annual meeting and try to obtain the support of other shareholders through the force of arguments from the floor. In addition to the time and expense involved in traveling to and attending such meetings, the stockholder will face the full force of the proxies accumulated by management.

Given these options, it is hardly surprising that most dissatisfied stockholders simply sell their shares.

The Securities Exchange Act of 1934, which authorizes the Securities and Exchange Commission (SEC) to issue rules and regulations governing proxy solicitations, restrains use of the proxy machinery by management and dissidents. All corporations with shares traded on national securities exchanges or with at least 500 shareholders of at least one class of stock are covered by these regulations. The SEC requires full disclosure of all matters on which proxies are solicited, including the backgrounds of nominees for the board of directors. It also prohibits dissemination of fraudulent or deceptive materials and requires that management include stockholders' proposals in its own mailings, provided these proposals meet certain standards of brevity, relevance to the business affairs of the firm, and legality.

The Rise of Managerial Control

Managerial control has grown in importance over the century. Berle and Means, after warning the reader that reliable information was not always available and that "certain arbitrary judgments had to be made," concluded that by 1930, management exercised direct or indirect control of 88½ of the nation's 200 largest nonfinancial corporations in that there was no identifiable stockholder group owning more than 20 percent of the outstanding common stock and no published reports or "street knowledge" of any smaller controlling minority ownership. Of the 200, 41 others were controlled by a legal device such as a voting trust, nonvoting stock, or a special class of stock with greater than proportional voting power. Only 22 were found to be controlled by private or majority ownership. Minority control existed in 46½ of the group, and the remaining 2 were in receivership.[30]

In a 1970 study, Robert J. Larner updated Berle and Means' findings, concluding that by 1963, 167 of the 200 then largest nonfinancial corporations were controlled (in Berle and Means' sense) by management and 9 by a legal device. Larner, using a 10 percent cutoff criterion for minority control rather than the 20 percent used by Berle and Means, identified 18 companies in this class. He found only 6 of the 200 under majority ownership control and none subject to private control.[31]

A number of other investigations, employing less stringent criteria for identification of control (in the neighborhood of a 5 percent holding of outstanding common stock), have reached less dramatic conclusions regarding the rate of growth of managerial control.[32] Philip Burch, for example, regarded 4 to 5 percent stock ownership, coupled with evidence of active participation in management or representation on the board of directors, as evidence of control. He found that for 1965, 43 percent of the top 200 publicly owned industrial concerns (as listed by *Fortune*) were probably management controlled, 39.5 percent were probably under the control of an owning family, and the remaining 17.5 percent were possibly family controlled. Burch concluded that management control was far less widespread among large firms than Larner had contended and was growing less rapidly than either Berle and Means or Larner had believed. Still, Burch found that management control was increasing but that the phenomenon would not work itself out fully until "sometime well after the turn of the century."[33]

Perhaps the most sophisticated study of modern corporate control is Edward S. Herman's 1981 work *Corporate Control, Corporate Power*.[34] Herman notes conceptual shortcomings in the identification of control by simple numerical measures such as the percentage of voting stock owned or representation on the board of directors. He argues that stock holdings of 5 or 6 percent in and of themselves yield no power to control. The important issues are who owns the stock and who possesses a "strategic position" in the corporation. "In cases where companies are closely held or subject to majority ownership control," he observes, "the dominant owners occupy the top offices themselves, or they select (and can readily displace) those who do—with the result that strategic position, in the form of high office, is not a significant source of independent power."[35]

Herman states that he was unable to find any instance in which the purchase of 1 to 5 percent of the voting stock gave an outsider control of a large corporation; but holdings of less than 1 percent by founders or their families were sources of continuing authority. "Ownership has been and remains an important basis for obtaining strategic position; it has a solidity as a power base beyond that available to the promoter and banker, assuming retention of a large proportionate interest."[36] When "occupancy of the top positions becomes an independent source of power that can be built up by deliberate strategies and passed on to successors," the corporation should be regarded as managerially controlled.[37]

Although formal control of the corporation lies in the hands of the board of directors, Herman continues, "inside" directors nominated by and often members of management tend to have far more influence on the board's decisions than do "outsiders." Outsiders tend to defer to insiders' superior knowledge of the firm and its affairs, and they often hesitate to disturb the existing situation (particularly to displace managers) as long as crises are not imminent, for fear of doing unanticipated harm out of ignorance. "Outside director power is, in consequence, typically latent at best," he concludes, "activated mainly in response to serious economic or political setbacks to the company, which demonstrate serious management ineptitude or malfeasance that leave management in great disarray and threaten corporate financial integrity and survival."[38]

Financial institutions may exercise substantial influence and latent control over the affairs of a corporation. This power, Herman notes, may be based on a firm's anticipated needs for future capital—determined by its plans for growth, the requirements of its technologies, and its marketing costs—as well as on its past use of outside financing and its current capital position. The power of capital suppliers is frequently "negative in character," stemming "in part from management's unwillingness to proceed on programs looked upon with disfavor by institutions whose goodwill is important."[39]

Herman's attributions of control of the 200 largest publicly owned nonfinancial corporations and the 100 largest industrial corporations at the end of 1974, based on the considerations discussed above, are shown in Table 3–1.

Herman's concept of control—the possession of strategic position or the ability to designate holders of high office—is somewhat different from that formulated by Berle and Means and used by Larner—the ability to select a majority of the board of directors. But for all of these writers, the locus of control involves the current ability to set corporate policies and conduct the affairs of the firm. Control, in this broad sense, may be entrenched and almost impossible to wrench from its present holders, or it may be held tenuously. Managerial control, for example, does not mean that managers have freedom to flout the interests of stockholders in such matters as excessive managerial compensation and perquisites, growth of the firm beyond its most profitable size in the interests of managers' prestige, or perpetuation of an unprofitable enterprise in order to protect managers' jobs. Nor need it be true that a management-controlled firm can persistently disregard

TABLE 3–1 Ultimate Control* of Largest Publicly Owned Nonfinancial Corporations and Largest Industrial Corporations in the United States, December 31, 1974

	Number of Corporations	
Type of Control	200 Largest Nonfinancials	100 Largest Industrials
A. Inside management		
1. Significant ownership interest†	26	13
2. Financial representation or constraint	20	8
3. Regulatory constraint	58	6
4. Unconstrained	47	41
Net total‡	131	64
B. Inside management and outside board		
1. Significant ownership interest	15	8
2. Financial representation or constraint	18	7
3. Regulatory constraint	16	2
4. Unconstrained	3	3
Net total	34	14
Total management	165	78
C. Majority ownership	3	1
D. Minority ownership		
1. On board and significant committees	3	3
2. Active in management	18	12
3. Present on board	6	5
4. Small stock interest (5 to 10 percent) with more than residual power	2	0
Total	29	20
E. Government§	1	1
F. Financial	1	0
G. Receivership	1	0
Grand total	200	100

*Designates control form of minority ownership controlling company.
†One percent or more.
‡Some companies are classified in more than one subdivision.
§Standard Oil Company of Ohio was 25 percent owned by British Petroleum Company, which in turn was under majority control by the government of Great Britain.

SOURCE: Edward S. Herman, *Corporate Control, Corporate Power* (London: Cambridge University Press, 1981), pp. 58–61, 65. © by Cambridge University Press. Reprinted by permission of Cambridge University Press.

the concerns of present or potential suppliers of capital. Stockholders still possess the final power to elect the board of directors and, thus, through the board, place the people they wish in strategic positions. Further, those who exercise voting power are not necessarily individual investors. They may be financial institutions. It is, therefore, necessary to consider the growing role of institutional investors to round out a description of the modern business corporation.

THE EMERGENCE OF THE PARAPROPRIETAL SOCIETY

The Institutionalization of Stockholdings: Who Owns the Company?

In 1970 testimony before a subcommittee of the Joint Economic Committee, Roy A. Schotland, former chief counsel for the SEC's Institutional Investor Study, stated:

> Forty years ago, Berle and Means and others taught that there was a great difference between who managed a corporation and who owned it. . . . That was the first phase of the managerial revolution. We are now in the second phase, in which stockholders no longer manage even their own stockholdings. Stockholdings are being "institutionalized"—the reduction of direct stock investment by individuals and the rise of indirect investment through mutual funds, bank trust departments, investment advisers, variable annuities, and pension funds. In 1957, institutions held 23 percent of all outstanding stock, and they now hold between 35 and 40 percent.[40]

The dollar volume of this growth and the principal types of financial institutions involved, as estimated by the SEC, are shown in Table 3–2.

TABLE 3–2 Market Value of Stocks Held by Financial Institutions ($ billions)

Type of Institution	Stock Value		Average Annual Percentage Increase
	1968	1955	
Personal trusts	$80.1	$28.5	8%
Private pensions	59.6	6.1	19
Mutual funds	50.9	7.2	16
Insurance companies	27.5	9.0	9
Foundations	15.8	6.0	8
College endowments	9.0	2.6	10

SOURCE: U.S. Congress, Joint Economic Committee, Subcommittee on Fiscal Policy, *Hearings: Investment Policies of Pension Funds* (Washington, D.C.: U.S. Government Printing Office, 1970), p. 224.

What Does Ownership Mean? In 1959, Berle noted that while "the ultimate product of the stock is to be divided literally among tens of millions of beneficiaries or policyholders," the control of the largest industrial firms might well pass to a "few hundred large pension trust and mutual fund managers," if the trend continued.[41] By delegation of authority, noted Berle, the stockholder has given up control of and even access to the corporation's physical property, which is acquired, operated, and disposed of by management. But the stock certificate still contains several important attributes of ownership of the firm itself, if not of its trucks, machines, and buildings. Stockholders receive dividends, share in the proceeds if the corporation is liquidated or distributes a portion of its assets, and have the right to vote at annual stockholders' meetings. But the individual who invests in a fund managed by a financial institution gives up even these rights. The shareholders of a mutual fund receive payments based on the portfolio's performance, as do most beneficiaries of personal trusts; but pensioners and insurance claimants have contractual claims against the financial institution that are independent of the portfolio's earnings and thus cannot be viewed as risk takers. In any case, income paid to the individual recipient no longer depends on the earnings and other distributions of a single company. And the financial institution, which retains the title to the stock and its voting rights, is not the "owner" of the stock; it is merely a fiduciary manager of monies provided by others and held in trust for the benefit of others. The provider of the funds and the beneficiary may be the same person; or, as with a testamentary trust or employer contribution to an employee pension fund, they may be different people. Neither can be considered the owner of shares of particular corporations held in the portfolio of the institution. Berle concludes that in such a situation there is simply no answer to the question of who owns the trucks, machines, and buildings of a corporation or even who owns its shares. In his view, the concept of private property is no longer relevant.

A Society Beyond Property. Harbrecht, wrestling with the same issues in his 1959 study of pension funds and their investment policies, coined the phrase "paraproprietal society" (beyond property) to describe what he viewed as this new relationship between man and things.[42] In his words, "the concept of ownership is meaningless since the 'ownership' resides in the legal fiction, the financial corporation." The corporation, itself owned by others, holds a "bare title" to its real property; and with the growth of the financial institutions, "the concept of ownership of the corporation has reached a dead end and no longer has any functional meaning." In sum, "a bare title held by a legal fiction is an inert concept."[43]

"Pension Fund Socialism": Employee Ownership. Peter F. Drucker referred to the phenomenon as "pension fund socialism."[44] Concentrating on pension funds alone, Drucker noted that from 1959 (when Berle and Harbrecht dealt with the issue) to 1975, the assets of these funds had increased more than tenfold, and their shareholdings had gone from less than 3 percent to more than 30 percent of the nation's outstanding equity capital. By 1995, according to Drucker's projection, the pension fund holdings should exceed two thirds of the equity capital and roughly 40 percent of the debt capital of American industry. Apparently ignoring Berle's and Harbrecht's earlier observations on the shift of economic power toward the managers of the financial institutions, Drucker noted:

> In terms of Socialist theory, the employees of America are the only true "owners" of the means of production. Through their pension funds they are the only true "capitalists" around, owning, controlling, and directing the country's "capital fund." The "means of production," that is, the American economy—again with agriculture the only important exception—is being run for the benefit of the country's employees.[45]

Drucker does not suggest a mechanism through which employees might be able to exercise this control nor how they might wrest it from financial managers.

Current Trends

Recent government studies have confirmed this continued trend. In a 1973 document, a subcommittee of the Senate Committee on Government Operations reported that the 30 largest stockholders owned an average of 38.5 percent of the outstanding common stock of 89 large corporations (queries went to 324 of the nation's largest corporations, but only 89 replied in full). The trust departments of large New York banks, involved mainly in the management of personal trusts and pension funds, held an average of 11.3 percent of the outstanding stocks of these firms.[46] A 1980 Senate Governmental Affairs Committee staff study estimated that the average holding of institutional investors in 93 major publicly owned corporations was in the neighborhood of 40 percent. This study included only institutional investors reporting to the SEC—thus excluding those without investment discretion, those with discretionary accounts of less than $100 million, and a number of large financial institutions that simply failed to file with the SEC although required to do so by 1975 legislation. The reported figure therefore substantially understated the true extent of institutional holdings.[47] By comparison, a 1984 *Business Week* article cited the estimate of a large private bank that financial managers control (i.e., have authority to buy and sell) some 60 percent of the equity shares outstanding in the United States.[48]

CONCLUSION

As Harbrecht noted presciently in 1959, the paraproprietal society represents the latest step in the evolution of the modern corporation. In his words:

> The present concentration of financial power is not so much the result of a drive for power as it is of (1) social demands which require the aggregation of great wealth to provide security, and (2) the fortunate presence of the financial institutions as apt media for administering this wealth. The alignment of forces now taking shape is of an institutional and permanent character that will be part of our economic and social structure for some time to come.[49]

ENDNOTES

[1]Data obtained from U.S. Department of Commerce, Bureau of the Census, *Statistical Abstract of the United States 1985* (Washington, D.C.: U.S. Government Printing Office, 1984); World Bank, *World Development Report 1984* (New York: Oxford University Press, 1984); "The *Fortune* Directory of the 500 Largest U.S. Industrial Corporations," *Fortune,* May 2, 1983.

[2]Miriam Beard, *History of Business,* vol. 1, *From Babylon to the Monopolists* (Ann Arbor: University of Michigan Press, 1938), pp. 429–30. © by the University of Michigan. Used by permission of the University of Michigan Press.

[3]Ibid., p. 146.

[4]Ibid., p. 118.

[5]Ibid., p. 284.

[6]This section draws heavily on the following studies: Adolf A. Berle, Jr., and Gardiner C. Means, "Corporation" in *Encyclopaedia of the Social Sciences,* vol. 4, ed. E. R. A. Seligman (New York: Macmillan, 1930); Adolf A. Berle, Jr., and Gardiner C. Means, *The Modern Corporation and Private Property* (New York: Macmillan, 1932); John P. Davis, *Corporations: Their Origin and Development,* 2 vols. (New York: G. P. Putnam's Sons, 1905); Joseph S. Davis, *Essays in the Earlier History of American Corporations,* vol. 1 (Cambridge, Mass.: Harvard University Press, 1917); Arthur S. Dewing, *The Financial Policy of Corporations,* 5th ed., vol. 1 (New York: Ronald Press, 1953); Armand B. DuBois, *The English Business Company after the Bubble Act* (New York: Commonwealth Fund, 1938); L. C. B. Gower, *Gower's Principles of Modern Company Law,* 4th ed. (London: Stevens, 1979); Robert W. Hamilton, *The Law of Corporations* (St. Paul, Minn.: West Publishing, 1980); Bishop C. Hunt, *The Development of the Business Corporation in England 1800–1867* (Cambridge, Mass.: Harvard University Press, 1936); Shaw Livermore, *Early American Land Companies: Their Influence on Corporate Development* (New York: Commonwealth Fund, 1939); William R. Scott, *Joint Stock Companies to 1720* (Cambridge, Eng.: Cambridge University Press, 1912).

[7]J. P. Davis, *Corporations,* vol. 1, p. 29.

[8]Hunt, *Development of the Business Corporation,* p. 3.

[9]See, for example, Ramkrishna Mukherjee, *The Rise and Fall of the East India Company* (New York: Monthly Review Press, 1974).

[10]The phrase is taken from Livermore, *Early American Land Companies,* p. 237, who notes that it is more accurate than the more commonly used but misleading phrase "unlimited life."

[11]The most important portions of the Bubble Act are reprinted in DuBois, *The English Business Company*, pp. 41–42.

[12]Ibid., p. 95.

[13]Livermore, *Early American Land Companies*, p. 236.

[14]It is possible in the United States to establish a "limited partnership": one or more "general partners" have unlimited liability; but others, known as "limited partners," have no personal liability beyond their investment for obligations of the firm. Limited partners are severely restricted in the managerial authority they can exercise. A limited partnership can be created only by filing with a state a certificate naming the limited partners and stating that they have assumed limited liability.

[15]See Hamilton, *The Law of Corporations*, p. 22. After a brief but excellent discussion, Hamilton concludes, "On balance, it is fair to say that limited liability is a distinct plus for the corporate form of business from the investors' standpoint but is usually not the determinative factor in deciding whether to incorporate a small business."

[16]Adam Smith, *The Wealth of Nations*, ed. Edwin Cannan (New York: Modern Library, 1937), p. 713.

[17]DuBois, *The English Business Company*, p. 307.

[18]See Berle and Means, *The Modern Corporation*, p. 136.

[19]This paragraph draws heavily on Harry L. Purdy, Martin L. Lindahl, and William A. Carter, *Corporate Concentration and Public Policy* (New York: Prentice-Hall, 1945), pp. 46–49; and Ralph Nader, Mark Green, and Joel Seligman, *Taming the Giant Corporation* (New York: W. W. Norton, 1976), pp. 43–55.

[20]Nader et al., *Taming the Giant Corporation*, p. 240.

[21]Livermore, *Early American Land Companies*, p. 75.

[22]Ibid., p. 295.

[23]Robert Hessen, *In Defense of the Corporation* (Stanford, Calif.: Hoover Institution Press, 1979), p. xiv. Reprinted with permission of Hoover Institution Press. © 1979 by the Board of Trustees of the Leland Stanford Jr. University.

[24]Ibid., p. 38.

[25]Berle and Means, *The Modern Corporation*, p. 69. (Italics added.)

[26]Ibid., p. 286.

[27]Ibid., p. 53.

[28]*Moody's Public Utility Manual 1984* (New York: Moody's Investors Service, 1984).

[29]The initial steps and legal actions taken by both sides and the early measures and countermeasures in a proxy fight have become routine, almost stylized. For an excellent and entertaining account, including some victories by dissidents, see David Karr, *Fight for Control* (New York: Ballantine Books, 1956).

[30]Berle and Means, *The Modern Corporation*, chap. V, especially pp. 90–118. The fractional numbers reported for the management and minority control categories result from problems of classification where managers were also large stockholders. Several corporations were classified as doubtful because Berle and Means could not determine whether such stockholders exercised control independently from their managerial positions.

[31]Robert J. Larner, *Management Control and the Large Corporation* (New York: Dunellen, 1970), p. 12.

[32]See Philip H. Burch, Jr., *The Managerial Revolution Reassessed: Family Control in America's Large Corporations* (Lexington, Mass.: D. C. Heath, 1972); Jean-Marie Chevalier, "The Problem of Control in Large American Corporations," *Antitrust Bulletin* 14, no. 1 (Spring 1969), pp. 163–80; Raymond W. Goldsmith and Rexford C. Parmelee, *The Distribution of Ownership in the 200 Largest Nonfinancial Corporations*, U.S. Temporary National Economic Committee, Monograph no. 29 (Washington, D.C.: U.S. Government Printing Office, 1940); Lawrence Pedersen and William K. Tabb, "Ownership and Control of Large Corporations Revisited," *Antitrust Bulletin* 21, no. 1 (Spring 1976),

pp. 53–66; Don Villarejo, "Stock Ownership and the Control of Corporations," *New University Thought* II (Autumn 1961 and Winter 1962), pp. 33–77, 47–65. Villarejo's findings are summarized in Earl F. Cheit, ed., *The Business Establishment* (New York: John Wiley & Sons, 1964), pp. 172–73.

[33]Burch, *The Managerial Revolution Reassessed,* p. 105.

[34]Edward S. Herman, *Corporate Control, Corporate Power* (London: Cambridge University Press, 1981).

[35]Ibid., p. 26.

[36]Ibid., p. 27.

[37]Ibid., p. 26.

[38]Ibid., p. 48.

[39]Ibid., p. 22.

[40]U.S. Congress, Joint Economic Committee, Subcommittee on Fiscal Policy, *Hearings: Investment Policies of Pension Funds* (Washington, D.C.: U.S. Government Printing Office, 1970), pp. 129–30.

[41]Adolf A. Berle, Jr., *Power without Property* (New York: Harcourt Brace, 1959), pp. 53–54.

[42]Paul P. Harbrecht, *Pension Funds and Economic Power* (New York: Twentieth Century Fund, 1959), p. 287. See also Paul P. Harbrecht, *Toward the Paraproprietal Society* (New York: Twentieth Century Fund, 1960).

[43]Harbrecht, *Pension Funds,* p. 4.

[44]Peter F. Drucker, *The Unseen Revolution: How Pension Fund Socialism Came to America* (New York: Harper & Row, 1976).

[45]Ibid., pp. 2–3.

[46]U.S. Senate, Committee on Government Operations, Subcommittees on Intergovernmental Relations and on Budgeting, Management, and Expenditures, *Disclosure of Corporate Ownership* (Washington, D.C.: U.S. Government Printing Office, 1973). See also review by Peter C. Dooley, *Antitrust Bulletin* 21, no. 2 (Summer 1976), pp. 427–30.

[47]U.S. Senate, Committee on Governmental Affairs, *Structure of Corporate Concentration: A Staff Study,* 2 vols. (Washington, D.C.: U.S. Government Printing Office, 1980).

[48]"Will Money Managers Wreck the Economy?" *Business Week,* August 13, 1984, pp. 86–93, at p. 88.

[49]Harbrecht, *Pension Funds,* pp. 249–50.

CHAPTER FOUR

Economic, Political, and Social Criticisms of Business Power

As we have seen in Chapter Three, the modern business corporation is designed to accumulate large amounts of permanently committed capital from numerous small-scale investors and to operate efficiently over a sustained period of time. This form of organization was widely adopted during the 19th century, to utilize the large-scale, complex, interdependent, and hence highly coordinated techniques of production, communication, and distribution that spread through the industrializing nations.

Economic advances accomplished through the modern business corporation have made even greater contributions to human welfare in the 20th century. Labor productivity has increased many times over, standards of living have risen, work hours have fallen while work conditions have improved, life expectancy has increased, and human horizons have been broadened by new methods of transportation and communication. No one perceived these achievements of the modern capitalistic industrial order more clearly or described them more vividly, even when the outlines were barely emerging, than Karl Marx.

> The bourgeoisie during its rule of scarce one hundred years has created more massive and more colossal productive forces than have all preceding generations together. Subjection of nature's forces to man, machinery, application of chemistry to industry and agriculture, steam navigation, railways, electric telegraphs, clearing of whole continents for cultivation, canalization of rivers, whole populations conjured up out of the ground— what earlier century had even a presentiment that such productive forces slumbered in the lap of social labor?[1]

Marxists concede that capitalism was a necessary stage, required to eliminate the older feudal order, in the process of economic evolution. But they insist that at a certain further stage of development, the capitalist business properties should have been expropriated and a new socialist order introduced—by revolutionary force if necessary. Had governments assumed this function promptly enough, according to the Marxist and non-Marxist socialist theorists, the inequities and suffering that accompanied industrialization could have been avoided.

Those who advocate a private-enterprise system over socialism but see a major corrective role for government note that government intervention or labor unions were necessary to eliminate child labor, reduce work hours, and compel business firms to accept responsibility for on-the-job safety and compensation for those injured and unable to work. Some, including both socialists and nonsocialists, contend that the modern corporate capitalistic system is viable only because it is ameliorated by such governmental correctives as unemployment compensation, social security, public health and education programs, public housing and urban renewal programs, environmental and safety regulations, and redistribution of income through a progressive tax system and welfare programs, to say nothing of macroeconomic policies of full employment and price stability. In many developing countries today, planners and political leaders are trying to learn from, and thereby avoid, some of the worst aspects of the transition to industrialization experienced by the developed nations—most notably the misery and degradation suffered by workers and their families in the slums of industrializing cities.

Even some who regard the free enterprise system as vastly superior, in terms of both economic efficiency and personal freedom, have voiced concern over the emergence of private business power. A number of corporations may have grown larger than necessary to take full advantage of modern technology; in the process, they have—perhaps inadvertently—attained power. Such power, exercised in the self-interest of the corporation's owners or managers, may well have undesirable economic, political, and social consequences, even if it is the result of nothing more sinister than pursuit of economies of scale.

ECONOMIC POWER

The most fundamental aspect of economic power is power over price. At one extreme, the model of pure and perfect competition posits a large enough number of firms selling an identical product so that no one firm has the power to influence price. Such a firm would lose all its sales to others if it asked a price higher than that set by impersonal market forces of supply and demand; and it would have no incentive to quote a price lower than the current market price, since it can sell as much of its product as it wishes at the going price. At the other extreme, a pure monopolist—by definition the only seller of a particular product—must set a price for its product, recognizing that as the price rises, the quantity that customers will buy falls, and vice versa. Between these extremes, firms have varying latitude in setting price or influencing it by varying the quantities offered for sale.

Monopoly and Power

Economists no longer confine the word *monopoly* to a single seller. Instead, monopoly is viewed as a matter of the degree to which a firm is able to exercise control over the price of its products. Thus, we speak of a pure monopolist as the single seller of a particular product but recognize the existence of partial monopoly, or monopoly power, in many other markets.

A firm's power over price is enhanced or limited by its ability to influence rivals' prices. A purely competitive market is characterized by a complete absence of such power; in general, as the number of competing firms declines, the possibility increases that such influence will be exerted. Because of a dominant position in the industry (based on a substantially higher market share than that of any other firm), a firm may become a price leader, confident that the others in the market will follow its increases and decreases. Others may recognize a price leader out of fear of its power to retaliate against nonfollowers or because of its stature and reputation for mutually beneficial pricing practices that take into consideration the interests of the entire industry. In the absence of a dominant firm or recognized price leader, various firms' abilities to influence one another's pricing decisions may stem from collusive agreements or, alternatively, from each one's awareness that aggressive pricing practices may trigger equally aggressive and mutually harmful responses.

Whether the power over price is independent and derived solely from market share, or whether it stems from the ability to influence rivals' prices, the immediate determinant of such power is the elasticity of the demand curve facing the firm. Figure 4–1 illustrates an elementary microeconomic model that highlights the significance of demand elasticity, comparing pricing under conditions of pure or partial monopoly with pricing in the absence of any monopoly power, or under conditions of pure competition. In both diagrams, a firm's profit is maximized—the difference between its total revenue and total cost is greatest—when marginal revenue (*MR*) is equal to marginal cost (*MC*), regardless of the degree of competition it faces or monopoly power it enjoys.[2]

FIGURE 4-1 Equilibrium Price and Output of Firms with and without Market Power

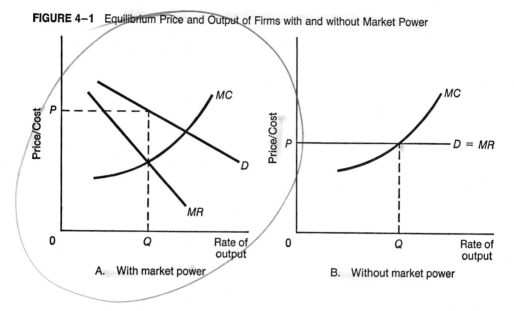

A. With market power

B. Without market power

The essential difference between the firm with market power in Figure 4–1A and the one without such power in Figure 4–1B is that the former faces a downward-sloping demand curve (D), reflecting the inverse relationship between the price received and the quantity offered for sale. MR lies below and to the left of a downward-sloping demand curve. But MR is identical with the horizontal or infinitely elastic demand curve faced by the firm in pure competition. Thus, while $MR = MC$ for both firms, the price (P) is higher than MC for the monopolistic firm, but $P = MC$ for the competitive firm.[3]

One of the most widely used indexes of monopoly power, the Lerner index, is based on this contrast. The Lerner index is

$$\frac{P - MC}{P}$$

The difference between P and MC represents the monopolist's ability to raise price and is standardized for different levels of price and cost by expressing it as a percentage of P. The Lerner index for a profit-maximizing firm is equal to $\frac{1}{\eta}$, where η represents the absolute value of the elasticity of demand.[4] Thus, the lower the elasticity, the greater the degree of monopoly power.

The relationship between the profit-maximizing price and demand elasticity may also be expressed as

$$P = MC \left(\frac{\eta}{\eta - 1} \right)^5$$

Thus, if $\eta = 2$ at the profit-maximizing price, that price would be set twice as high as marginal cost. If $\eta = 3$, then P is 1.5 times MC. Note that a firm with monopoly power will always operate on the elastic portion of its demand curve, where $MR > 0$, as long as MC is positive. If $\eta = \infty$, as is the case for the firm in a purely competitive market, $P = MC$. Therefore, unless the monopolist's costs are substantially lower than those of competitive firms, its price will be higher.

Resource Misallocation. The higher price charged by the monopolist implies that for any given market demand curve for a product, less will be produced and offered for sale than if the same product were produced by a competitive industry. The resource misallocation attributed to varying degrees of market power is, therefore, that too few resources are devoted to the production of monopolized goods. Under full employment, the corollary is that there is too great a use of some resources in competitive sectors.

Income Redistribution. A second effect of the use of market power that many would consider an evil of monopoly is income redistribution. The monopolist raises price to increase profits, thus gaining wealth at the expense of its customers. This wealth transfer is frequently viewed both as a form of unjust exploitation of customers by the monopolist and as leading to an inequitable distribution of real income or purchasing power. However, there are no rigorous and generally accepted criteria in economic theory for preferring any one income distribution over others; hence, the perceived injustice is treated by economists as a reflection of individual or societal values rather than as a failure in economic performance.

Resource misallocation, by contrast, is regarded as an unambiguous failure in economic performance by standards of welfare economics—that is, the allocation of existing resources is considered fully efficient only when the economic welfare of households is maximized, holding technology constant and taking the distribution of income as given. The use of pure and perfect competition as a *norm*, or standard, for efficient resource allocation is discussed at length in Chapter Eleven.

Economic power can be exerted against others, besides customers, having dealings with a firm. The sole or largest employer in a labor market may exert downward pressure on wages. Similarly, some firms may be in a position to demand and receive preferential price reductions or credit terms from suppliers. Firms large and wealthy enough to afford protracted and expensive legal actions may make more effective use of patents, franchises, leases, and other intangible claims.

The Influence of the Paraproprietal Society on the Profit Motive

The prospect of profit and its concomitant, the avoidance of loss, are the motivating forces driving business in a private-enterprise economy. The economic model determining a firm's price and output by equating *MR* and *MC* assumes that the firm is maximizing its profits. There is no difference in the motivation attributed to the competitive firm and the monopolist; rather, the extent to which profit-maximizing behavior contributes to or detracts from optimal resource allocation results from differences in the nature of the markets in which the firms operate. In a consumer-sovereign economic system, relative intensities of various consumer wants are signaled through market demand to the business sector as accurately and as promptly as possible, and firms have the maximum incentive to respond to these signals. The role of profit is to provide that incentive. In the long run, profit also induces entrepreneurs to undertake risky and uncertain business ventures and to engage in research and development aimed at both new products and new production processes.

The separation of ownership and control in the modern corporation and the subsequent emergence of a paraproprietal society have, therefore, been received with mixed reactions. A concern expressed by Adam Smith—that hired managers would not exercise the same degree of care and diligence in the affairs of a business as would owners if they managed the firm themselves—has its modern counterpart in Harvey Leibenstein's theory of "X-efficiency."[6] Inadequate managerial motivation, Leibenstein noted, may lead to slackness in managers' own work effort, failure to obtain acceptable levels of performance from subordinate employees, and excessive waste of material resources. The distinctive characteristic of X-inefficiency is that it results in sheer waste and loss of the output obtainable from the resources used rather than in a transfer of income.

In addition to lack of managerial motivation, several reasons have been given for why the management-controlled firm might not seek to maximize its own profits. Some lead to X-inefficiency and some to a transfer of wealth from owners to managers or others. Managers might want to maximize their own incomes through some combination of salaries, benefits, and perquisites of office. They might seek the stature and prestige of running the largest possible enterprise rather than the most profitable. To protect their own jobs, managers might be reluctant to terminate unprofitable enterprises. Also, it has been contended, the separation of ownership and control has given rise to a set of managerial ethics calling for recognition of managers' responsibilities to customers, employees, suppliers, creditors, and communities as well as to stockholders.

Some commentators feel managerialism ameliorates the exploitation of consumers and misallocation of resources that accompany profit maximization by monopolistic firms. Others condemn it as dampening the incentives for efficiency and full responsiveness to consumer demand. Still others argue that managerial control, whatever its implications for profit distribution between owners and managers, should have little effect on firms' market behavior because the highest possible profit provides the funds for the highest possible managerial compensation. Profit may also be needed to provide either the funds or the credit standing for expansion.

As the paraproprietal society evolves and managerial control shifts from the managers of individual industrial and commercial corporations to the managers of financial institutions, the force of the profit motive should be strengthened, at least in the nonfinancial sectors. Whatever a fund manager's personal motives or conflicts might be, it is in the joint interests of fund managers and beneficiaries that the portfolio's firms be as profitable as possible. Thus the paraproprietal society can be expected, for better or worse, to enhance the primacy of the profit motive.

Of far more fundamental concern, however, is the concentration of economic power that would accompany the growth in the proportion of voting shares held by a small number of financial institutions. If an institutional investor obtains influential positions in a number of corporations, particularly multiproduct concerns, it may—perhaps inadvertently—acquire the power to coordinate pricing and output policies and hence limit competition among some of them. Of equal concern is the possibility of coordinated action, perhaps fostered by interlocking directorates, among the large institutional investors themselves.

THE MARXIST VISION AND THREAT

Despite his profound appreciation for capitalism's productive efficiency, Karl Marx was not, of course, a proponent of the system.

> Modern bourgeois society with its relations of production, of exchange and of property, a society that has conjured up such gigantic means of production and of exchange, is like the sorcerer who is no longer able to control the powers of the nether world whom he has called up by his spells. For many a decade past the history of industry and commerce is but the history of the revolt of modern productive forces against modern conditions of production, against the property relations that are the conditions for the existence of the bourgeoisie and of its rule.[7]

The Self-Destruction of Capitalism

Marx's view of the process by which capitalism would inevitably destroy itself is best captured in a later and more mature passage from *Das Kapital*, a long paragraph described by Joseph Schumpeter as "the crowning finale not only of that volume [the first volume of *Das Kapital*] but of Marx's whole work."[8]

> As soon as this process of transformation has sufficiently decomposed the old society from top to bottom, as soon as the labourers are turned into proletarians, their means of labour into capital, as soon as the capitalist mode of production stands on its own feet, then the further socialisation of labour and further transformation of the land and other means of production into socially exploited and, therefore, common means of production, as well as the further expropriation of private proprietors, takes a new form. That which is now to be expropriated is no longer the labourer working for himself, but the capitalist exploiting many labourers. This expropriation is accomplished by the action of the immanent laws of capitalist production itself, by the centralisation of capital. One capitalist always kills many. Hand in hand with this centralisation, or this expropriation of many capitalists by few, develop, on an ever extending scale, the co-operative form of the labour-process, the conscious technical application of science, the methodical cultivation of the soil, the transformation of the instruments of labour into instruments of labour only usable in common, the economising of all means of production by their use as the means of production of combined, socialised labour, the entanglement of all peoples in the net of the world-market, and this, the international character of the capitalist regime. Along with the constantly diminishing number of the magnates of capital, who usurp and monopolise all advantages of this process of transformation, grows the mass of misery, oppression, slavery, degradation, exploitation; but with this too grows the revolt of the working-class, a class always increasing in numbers, and disciplined, united, organised by the very mechanism of the process of capitalist production itself. The monopoly of capital becomes a fetter upon the mode of production, which has sprung up and flourished along with, and under it. Centralisation of the means of production and socialisation of labour at last reach a point where they become incompatible with their capitalist integument. This integument is burst asunder. The knell of capitalist private property sounds. The expropriators are expropriated.[9]

This passage contains two of Marx's best known and most controversial projections regarding the future development of the capitalist order. ("Projection" of existing trends is a more accurate description of Marx's intention and contribution than is "prediction." Paul M. Sweezy notes that both proponents and critics of Marx often fail to understand this distinction. Sweezy quotes Marx himself as warning in "perfectly clear language" that his laws may be "modified . . . by many circumstances," and adds that such a law "constitutes in no sense a concrete prediction about the future.")[10] First, Marx noted a tendency for the concentration of business or "centralisation of capital" to grow: "One capitalist always kills many." Second, he held that the process of capital accumulation based on the surplus product exploited from labor assured a long-run fall in real wages, or the growing immiserization of the proletariat: "Along with the constantly diminishing number of the magnates of capital, who usurp and monopolise all advantages of this process of transformation, grows the mass of misery, oppression, slavery, degradation, exploitation."

The Inherent Contradiction of Capitalism

Marx used "contradiction" in a Hegelian sense. The early 19th-century philosopher Georg W. F. Hegel had posited a basic structure of social change in which an initial condition, or thesis, gives rise to opposition, or an antithesis. The conflict of thesis and antithesis produces a synthesis. The synthesis, in turn, becomes a thesis challenged by a new antithesis. The term *contradiction* was used to describe the features within a thesis that caused the antithesis to develop. In reading Marx, therefore, one must not interpret a contradiction as showing the logical impossibility of two contradictory conditions coexisting or the falsity of some hypothesized condition or statement contradictory to a true one.

The basic contradiction of capitalism, in Marx's analysis, is the private ownership of the means of production side by side with socialization of the processes of production. Large amounts of privately owned capital are accumulated and converted into the machines and factories of modern industries. Those working in these factories are supplied by the capitalist owners with the tools and materials needed for production. The workers become proletarians, dispossessed of their productive capital (such as the shop and tools owned by a craftsman) and supplying only their own labor. Simultaneously, the processes of production become ever more complex and interdependent, requiring large numbers of people working together, cooperating on tasks, coordinating their efforts, and accepting the discipline of organized factory labor. In Marx's words:

> Modern industry has converted the little workshop of the partriarchal master into the great factory of the industrial capitalist. Masses of labourers, crowded into the factory, are organized like soldiers. As privates of the industrial army they are placed under the command of a perfect hierarchy of officers and sergeants. Not only are they slaves of the bourgeois class and of the bourgeois State; they are daily and hourly enslaved by the machine, by the overseer and, above all, by the individual bourgeois manufacturer himself.[11]

The contradiction works itself out as the number of capitalists decreases and the ranks of the proletariat grow, ironically being augmented by former small capitalists displaced by the process of concentration. Thus, fewer people have a propertied stake in the survival of the capitalist system, and fewer benefit from it. At the same time, the number exploited by this system, and thus disaffected, grows. And the very nature of capitalist development assures that the exploited and immiserized class, the proletariat—rescued from what Marx referred to as "the idiocy of rural life"[12]—becomes more capable of revolutionary action, "a class always increasing in numbers, and disciplined, united, organised by the very mechanism of capitalist production itself."

Marx's Projections: Immiserization/Alienation

Concentration of business, in the form of the large modern corporation, came to pass much as Marx foresaw. But the second of his projections—the increasing immiserization of the proletariat—has proved an embarrassment for modern Marxists. In the early 20th century, the orthodox Marxist position was that the rise of imperialism and the development of overseas colonial markets had alleviated, if not temporarily eliminated, the forces of immiserization. A group of "revisionists" noted that Marx had failed to anticipate the development of government social services and effective trade unionism in capitalist nations. Still others have argued that Marx meant only *relative* immiserization—a growing disparity between incomes of capitalists and proletarians that does not preclude the possibility of rising absolute standards of living for all. But modern Marxists most commonly respond to the great increase in the proletariat's material welfare in advanced capitalist countries by maintaining that alienation of the proletariat, rather than its immiserization, generates the internal contradiction that must eventually destroy capitalism.

Marx expressed his views on alienation most fully in writings antedating *The Communist Manifesto*—that were virtually ignored until the 1930s.[13] But Marxist scholar Bertell Ollman places the concept of alienation at the very core of Marxist theory. "The theory of alienation," he contends, "is the intellectual construct in which Marx displays the devastating effect of capitalist production on human beings, on their physical and mental states and on the social processes of which they are a part."[14] As Ollman interprets Marx,

> Man is spoken of as being separated from his work (he plays no part in deciding what to do or how to do it)— a break between the individual and his life activity. Man is said to be separated from his own products (he has no control over what he makes or what becomes of it afterwards)—

a break between the individual and the material world. He is also said to be separated from his fellow man (competition and class hostility has rendered most forms of cooperation impossible)—a break between man and man.[15]

In much of the discussion of alienation by modern Marxists and interpreters of Marxism, the role of increasing concentration of capital is neglected, although for Marx himself it was crucial to the inherent contradiction of capitalist development. Recent empirical work, however, has led researchers to the conclusion that there is a significant correlation between size of establishment (concentration of capital) and alienation from work in the United States. Job satisfaction appears to decline steadily and significantly with the size of the establishment in which workers are employed. Recognition of this phenomenon by employers and efforts to overcome it are reflected in an equally clear pattern of higher wages in industries with larger average plant size.[16]

Is There a Cure for Marx's Capitalist Contradictions?

Marxists and others hostile to capitalism view Marx's depiction of capitalism's contradictions and its ultimate collapse as a promising vision. Among those who support the capitalist order, many regard his projected outcome as a serious—perhaps even imminent—threat. The question for this group is what, in light of the diagnosis, is the cure? Typically, limitations on increases in the size of business firms and levels of market concentration (such as the U.S. antitrust laws promote) are regarded as essential to preserve a private-enterprise system. For example, J. G. Van Cise, a prominent antitrust lawyer and former chairman of the Section on Antitrust Law of both the American and the New York State Bar Associations, writes:

> The dogma of Karl Marx that the competition of capitalism will necessarily lead to jungle warfare, in which competitor will eat competitor until only monopoly remains, has been refuted by our antitrust laws . . . . The objective of the antitrust laws has not been the "radical" desire to destroy, but rather the "reactionary" endeavor to defend, private enterprise, through harnessing it to produce a free, democratic, ethical economy. Not without reason, accordingly, do the principles underlying these laws today enjoy the support of such diverse groups as the Democratic and Republican parties, the AFL–CIO, the National Association of Manufacturers, and the United States Chamber of Commerce.[17]

THE IDEAL OF JEFFERSONIAN DEMOCRACY

Discussions of public policies promoting and protecting small business, even at the sacrifice of economic efficiency if necessary, often invoke the concept of "Jeffersonian democracy."

Christopher Lasch identifies three varieties of Jeffersonian democracy espoused even before Jefferson's death in 1826: "a pure agrarian version, which later became identified with the defense of states' rights; a mercantile version, somewhat more kindly disposed to the positive uses of central power; and a popular version associated with the rights and interests of the common man." He notes that "states' rights conservatives, liberals, and even socialists have all claimed descent from Jefferson," whose writings have been used to support diverse and mutually contradictory positions.[18] In the years before the Civil War, both Abraham Lincoln and South Carolina's John C. Calhoun (a brilliant spokesman for states' rights, nullification, and slavery) evoked Jeffersonian doctrines in support of their political principles.[19]

Harold Laski captured the essence of Jefferson's unwavering central concern in commenting, "His democratic ideas are those of a man who suspects all exercise of power and seeks above all the fullest means of its control."[20] Thus, whether or not he ever made the precise comment, Jefferson held throughout his life that "that government is best which governs least."[21] At the same time, he abhorred the idea of a hereditary or otherwise self-perpetuating aristocracy, whether based on birth or wealth, and he maintained that a democratic government needed the power to prevent the rise of such a class.

In Jefferson's view, for democracy to function and not degenerate into anarchy, a "natural" aristocracy of "talent and virtue" had to emerge to replace the older ones of entrenched wealth and privilege. In diametric opposition to socialist and Marxist thought, he believed that secure ownership of property was essential to provide the members of this natural aristocracy with the independence to express and act freely on their convictions. Yet he feared the rise of an oligarchy based on the accumulation of property, and he regarded extremes of inequality in income and living standards as incompatible with a stable democratic order. He thus advocated laws against primogeniture and favored a progressive property tax with rates high enough to prevent undue accumulations by individuals and families.

Jefferson had a strong sentimental attachment to an agrarian order, yet as president he recognized that development of the nation required encouragement of both industry and agriculture. Richard E. Ellis assesses Jefferson's efforts to reconcile agrarian and commercial viewpoints in the political sphere as both successful and of utmost importance to the development of the nation:

> Recognizing the vast richness and potential in the American economy, Jefferson moved to develop it in such a way that everyone could participate in the market revolution that was to transform American life in the nineteenth century. What the Jeffersonian economic system did was to democratize business enterprise and substitute for the fear and pessimism

prevalent in so much post-revolutionary thought that spirit of infectious optimism in America's future.[22]

The small business owner has been regarded as the current heir to the independent landowning farmer in providing the backbone of Jeffersonian democracy. With the transformation of the U.S. economy from basically agrarian to predominantly industrial, commercial, and service oriented, Jefferson's "natural aristocracy of talent and virtue" must draw more and more of its recruits from business rather than agriculture, according to this line of argument. Small-business owners—rising to and maintaining positions of respect and influence through their own efforts, freed from subservience by ownership of their own firms, and with a personal stake in the affairs of their communities—are regarded as the type of citizens needed to make representative democracy work. The fear is that the large, impersonal corporation, owned by scattered passive stockholders and managed by a hierarchy of hired executives, provides neither the independence nor the encouragement of individual initiative and excellence needed to foster a modern-day aristocracy of talent and virtue.

The Fate of Small Business in a Democracy

From a Jeffersonian perspective, two basic sociopolitical problems are posed for a democratic society by the rise of the modern corporation. The first is the possible threat of the displacement of small business by giant firms, and the second is the power that might be attained by these giants. Despite oft-repeated fears of Marxists and Jeffersonians alike, small business in the United States has not been swallowed up by big business. In 1977, small manufacturing establishments (defined as those with less than 500 employees) comprised 98.3 percent of all manufacturing establishments in the United States and accounted for 51.0 percent of the nation's value added by manufacture. Thirty years earlier, comparable figures had been 98.1 percent of establishments and 53.5 percent of value added by manufacture.[23]

Perhaps the best analysis of recent changes in the relative position of small business in the U.S. economy is found in a 1982 study by Lawrence J. White.[24] After noting problems of definition and measurement, and examining a number of reported size distributions based on both employment and sales, White concludes that "small business is still alive and well in the American economy. On an economy-wide basis, the relative importance of small business has declined modestly over the past two decades."[25] The slight overall decline, however, disguises more severe losses of share in the individual sectors of the

TABLE 4–1 Percentage of Employment in Companies with Fewer than 500 Employees, Including Owner, by Sector of the U.S. Economy

Year	All Industries	Mineral	Manu-facturing	Wholesale Trade	Retail Trade	Selected Services
1958	59.4%	63.0%	38.1%	94.7%	77.4%	88.1%
1963	57.1	70.1	35.5	94.3	74.4	86.2
1967	57.6	63.4	31.3	92.6	72.6	85.7
1972	58.1	50.6	29.8	92.4	69.3	84.3

SOURCE: Lawrence J. White, *Measuring the Importance of Small Business in the American Economy* (New York: New York University Graduate School of Business Administration, 1982), p. 37.

economy. As White explains, "this severe effect has been moderated by the changing emphasis of the overall economy—away from sectors like manufacturing, in which small business has not been prevalent, and toward sectors like retailing, wholesaling, and services, in which small business has been prevalent."[26] The phenomenon is shown in Tables 4–1 and 4–2. The decline of 1.3 percent for the small-business share of employment in all industries shown in Table 4–1 is consistent with declines of 8.3 percent in manufacturing and 8.1 percent in retailing, for example, because of the declining share of employment shown for manufacturing and the increasing share shown for retailing in Table 4–2.

White sees no cause for alarm over the future of small business, since he expects the shift to continue towards the sectors with higher shares accounted for by small firms. Further, he notes that the absolute number of new U.S. businesses, most of them small, increased at a 3.1 percent annual rate between 1947 and 1975.[27]

It is impossible to say to what extent small business has survived and flourished as a result of competitive efficiency or as a result of

TABLE 4–2 Employment Percentages, by Sector of the U.S. Economy

Sector	1962	1977
Agricultural services, forests, fisheries	0.3%	0.4%
Mining	1.5	1.3
Construction	5.6	5.5
Manufacturing	37.7	30.2
Transportation, public utilities	6.9	6.2
Wholesale trade	7.4	7.0
Retail trade	18.5	20.6
Finance, insurance, real estate	6.3	7.0
Services	15.2	21.6
Unclassified	0.7	0.1

SOURCE: Lawrence J. White, *Measuring the Importance of Small Business in the American Economy* (New York: New York University Graduate School of Business Administration, 1982), p. 11.

deliberate neo-Jeffersonian public policies to protect and promote it. Numerous federal, state, and local government programs, of varying degrees of effectiveness, are designed to assist small business in areas including procurement, finance, management, and technical advice. The 1984 edition of the federal government's *Catalog of Federal Domestic Assistance* lists small-business assistance programs, primarily loan or loan guarantee, of the Small Business Administration, General Services Administration, Department of Agriculture, Department of Commerce, Department of Housing and Urban Development, Internal Revenue Service, and Federal Trade Commission.[28]

As discussed in Chapter Five and in later chapters dealing with specific provisions of the antitrust laws, protection and promotion of small business has been a major source of controversy in the development of the nation's antitrust policy.

Corporate Wealth and Political Power

The obverse of admiration and support for small business is distrust of and hostility toward big business. Jefferson's belief that representative democracy was threatened by the existence of an aristocracy of inherited wealth and position has been translated into today's fear of the giant, self-perpetuating, and impersonal corporation. The wealth of huge corporations may be used to obtain undue political influence through access to the media, use of lobbyists, political contributions, and outright corruption of public officials. This political influence, in turn, may be used to enhance profits through such public measures as tariff protection, subsidies, favorable tax treatment (depletion allowances, for example), award of government contracts, and regulatory relief (both *from* burdensome regulations such as pollution abatement and *through* protective regulations such as the exclusive right to serve certain markets). Further, the wealth of the large corporations may give them privileged access to the legal system through the ability to retain the best lawyers and to pursue expensive litigation.

Modern Jeffersonians notwithstanding, it is not obvious that big business should have greater political power and influence than small business or any other special-interest groups. Two features do favor concentrated industries—those in which most of the activity is accounted for by a small number of firms. First, market power may be necessary to provide the profits used to attain and maintain political power. Second, the smaller the number of firms constituting an interest group, the easier it should be for them to form a coalition with coordinated tactics and common goals. As a corollary, the smaller the number of firms, the less serious will be the "free-rider" problem—the refusal of some individual firms to contribute to the industry's efforts knowing that they cannot be excluded from any benefits won for the entire group.[29]

Offsetting these considerations, however, is the vastly larger number of small businesses. Dollars cannot be translated directly into votes. The political power of the nation's 13,900,000 small-business owners and 3,370,000 farmers is based on the number of votes they and their families are prepared to cast for prosmall-business and pro-farm legislators rather than on their individual wealth and economic power.

Empirical Studies of Market Power: Results and Problems

If the industry is a large one and the benefits bestowed upon it represent losses to others (customers, workers, or suppliers), the size of the industry itself (regardless of the number or the size of its individual firms) may be a political liability. Presumably, there is a threshold below which individual consumers and voters do not perceive a cost to them (say, of a tariff), or do not let a small perceived cost influence their votes. But if perceived costs rise above the threshold, either because of the size of the tariff or the importance of the product, consumers might retaliate by voting against politicians who support the measure. On the other hand, industry size may be a positive factor, especially if the benefits of political favors are shared with large numbers of voters, including both the work force and customers, and if labor union support can be enlisted.

Empirical studies have yielded no clear results on the relationships between size or market power and political power.[30] Richard E. Caves sought to explain the level of tariff protection obtained by various Canadian industries in terms of industry characteristics, including labor intensity, seller concentration (percentage of sales accounted for by the four largest firms), buyer concentration, and economies of scale. Caves found that labor intensity was not a statistically significant determinant of tariff protection. Seller concentration had a negative coefficient, indicating that public disapproval of firms with market power was a political liability that more than overcame any superior abilities to finance political activities and solve the free-rider problem. Buyer concentration, designed to measure the intensity of opposition to a particular tariff, was statistically insignificant. Economies of scale, however, were positively correlated with the degree of protection.

Two other studies found that the size of the typical firm in a U.S. industry is positively correlated with the "tax avoidance rate"—the ability of the industry to obtain special tax concessions—but both size of industry and level of market concentration are negatively correlated with this measure of political influence. Lester M. Salamon and John

J. Siegfried found the relationship between size of firm and successful tax avoidance to be statistically significant; but Cathleen Coolidge and Gordon Tullock found the relationship to be insignificant after removing from Salamon and Siegfried's sample some industries they regarded as atypical or misleading. In both studies, the negative coefficient on the concentration variable was statistically significant, but that on the industry size variable was not.

Esty and Caves obtained information on the political goals considered most important in 35 industries between 1976 and 1980, on bills introduced during these years that affected these industries, and on the extent to which the industries' stated objectives were achieved. By use of weighted averages of activity (number of bills filed weighted by the extent to which they favored the industry) and of success (both passage of favorable and defeat of unfavorable legislation), Esty and Caves sought to overcome the problems of focusing on a single objective such as tariff protection or tax relief, which are at best only partial indications and do not take into account that achieving one objective may make success in others more difficult or impossible. They found that higher seller concentration increased both activity and success but that industry size and firm size were not significant. Further, political spending was more closely correlated with all three of these industry characteristics than with the degree of success. Spending did, however, exert some influence on political activity affecting an industry, regardless of such characteristics as seller concentration, industry size, and firm size.

Critics, including the authors of these studies, have noted severe problems with empirical studies. Most fundamental, the political power held by an industry or firm is difficult to measure statistically. Further, the basic theory of influence seeking by business organizations is weak and provides no adequate guidance as to hypotheses to be tested. Presumably, no profit-maximizing firm wishes to maximize political influence in and of itself but rather weighs the economic benefits of additional political favors against the costs of obtaining them. But there is no good theory on the optimal level of spending on political influence. In particular, no one has yet posited a generally accepted set of relationships between industry characteristics such as market concentration and average firm size on the one hand and the net benefit of political influence on the other.

There are technical problems with the statistical tests reported above. It is not always clear whether causation runs from industry characteristics to political influence or vice versa. Coolidge and Tullock, for example, argued that extractive industries should be removed from Salamon and Siegfried's sample because it is more plausible to assume that generous depletion allowances encourage growth than it is to assume that large firms are able to obtain generous depletion allowances. Caves, in commenting on Coolidge and Tullock's study, noted that multicollinearity is a pervasive problem in studies of political influence, since there are sound theoretical reasons for attributing independent influences to such closely related variables as firm size, market size, and concentration. He pointed out such a problem in his own study: When the seller concentration variable was omitted, the coefficient of the variable measuring labor intensity became negative and statistically significant, although when the concentration variable was included, labor intensity had no significant explanatory value. The problem grew out of the strong negative correlation between concentration and labor intensity.[31]

The Jeffersonian Vision Revisited

Modern commentators who invoke Jefferson's philosophy would be hard put to say how Jefferson himself would weigh the trade-off between limitations on private and public power in determining appropriate public policies toward the modern giant corporation. The modern corporation's effects on the democratic polity are not yet well understood. Nevertheless, the Jeffersonian vision of small government, small owner-operated enterprises, and an economically independent and self-reliant citizenry remains attractive and has had a pervasive influence on these policies.

SOME SPECIFIC CONCERNS

As the U.S. economy evolves and grows, new social and political problems arise. Recent and current issues include the role of the business Establishment, the influence of the military-industrial complex, the impersonal character of the modern corporation and the concomitant emergence of the organization man and woman, the use of business power to promote discrimination, and the financial support of political candidates and parties by business firms.[32]

The Establishment

The term *Establishment* (almost always capitalized) has become common in describing the relationship between top business and political leaders—a group labeled "the power elite" by sociologist C. Wright Mills.[33] Richard J. Barber depicted the relationship as one in which "new alliances are emerging and old concepts are losing their relevance. Government, once accepted as the regulator of business, is now its willing partner. Indeed, privately owned corporations are becoming so deeply immersed in functions which historically have been regarded as 'public' that the old demarcation of 'public' and 'private' no longer has meaning."[34] Until recently, the business Establishment was thought to comprise the senior executives of the nation's largest industrial and financial corporations. In Barber's words, "Today the executives of large enterprises are not only welcome at the White House but are deeply involved on a continuing though usually informal basis in the highest decision-making levels of the Executive Branch."[35]

The Establishment was epitomized by the Business Roundtable, a group organized in 1972, with a 1981 membership of 196 chairmen of major corporations. The Business Roundtable seeks to maintain close and free communication between its members and high government officers, providing information and advice as well as receiving briefings from cabinet-level officials.[36] Its predecessor, the Business Council, was described by Barber as "a cozy club, bringing together the top policy makers of government and business in an elitist environment that may be foreign to our traditional ways of making public policy but that is now coming to be an accepted way of life for the new partnership."[37]

The rise of the Establishment is, of course, anathema to modern Jeffersonians, who regard the limitation of business power as an essential function of the state. But some writers, including Barber and John Kenneth Galbraith, urge an even closer partnership. Barber argues that the public interest in corporate decisions on such matters as pricing, new-product development, merger, new investment, and product safety is so great that routine discussion, cooperation, and coordination between leading corporate executives and high public officials is needed.

In *The New Industrial State,* Galbraith argues that planning in the large industrial corporations and governmental economic planning are mutually interdependent. It is irrelevant whether cooperative business-government planning is welcomed or deplored, he notes, since such planning is inevitable. Galbraith, like Barber, sees the line between public and large corporate private activities fading.

> So comprehensive a relationship cannot be denied or ignored indefinitely. Increasingly it will be recognized that the mature corporation, as it develops, becomes part of the larger administrative complex associated with the state. In time the line between the two will disappear. Men will look back in amusement at the pretense that once caused people to refer to General Dynamics and North American Aviation and AT&T as *private* business.
>
> Though this recognition will not be universally welcomed, it will be healthy. . . . If the mature corporation is recognized to be a part of the penumbra of the state, it will be more strongly in the service of social goals.[38]

The issue itself may be irrelevant because the relationship is dissolving. Sydney Blumenthal described the political influence of the Business Roundtable, corporate managers, and New York financial circles as declining during the Reagan administration. The business Establishment may have identified itself too closely with an activist philosophy of government to retain its influence during a period in which reduction of the federal government's role appears to have broad political appeal. Independent business operators—"Sun Belt entrepreneurs" and "the small-business community"—are growing in political influence and power, Blumenthal noted, and are more interested in winning greater freedom from government interference.[39] In a 1985 *Fortune* article, Thomas Moore noted the growing influence among younger business leaders of libertarian views, or a "Jeffersonian" ideology that is "neither liberal nor conservative" but advocates "maximizing personal liberties and minimizing government controls."[40] These libertarian executives according to Moore, tend to avoid involvement in politics except to vote.

The Military-Industrial Complex

Another special relationship between big business and government was viewed with alarm by President Dwight D. Eisenhower: "In the councils of Government, we must guard against the acquisition of unwarranted influence, whether sought or unsought, by the military-industrial complex. The potential for the disastrous rise of misplaced power exists and will persist."[41]

The existence of a military-industrial complex seems unavoidable as long as world tensions continue and expenditures on national defense remain high. Most large defense contractors depend on the Department of Defense (DOD) for their continued survival; indeed, DOD may be their principal or even sole customer. Likewise, DOD depends on the contractors for scientific and technical knowledge and experience. Many procurement programs, particularly for high-technology weapon systems, involve close long-term relations between contractors and procuring agencies. There is also an easy flow of people between contractors and DOD: Contractors' technical personnel and executives often take temporary jobs with defense agencies; and retired DOD officials, both civilian and military, are frequently hired by contractors.

Most defense procurement expenditures are made with a small number of companies, some of them among the nation's largest. Concentration of defense procurement has been quite stable over the cold-war period. In the 1957 fiscal year, 68.4 percent of military prime contract awards were made to the 100 largest contractors: in fiscal 1983 the corresponding figure was 66.9 percent.[42]

The fundamental problem raised by concentration in the defense market is, as President Eisenhower noted, "unwarranted influence" on the nation's defense and foreign policies. It is not primarily one of private market power or even of excessive profits, since the government is the sole buyer in the defense market and thus normally bargains on at least an equal footing with its suppliers. In the long run, rates of return on investment in defense contracting may well be too low and uncertain to attract an appropriate level of private capital, despite high profits during occasional build-up periods.[43] Criticisms of the military-industrial complex have focused on waste, inefficiencies, false and excessive billings, cost overruns, delays in production, overdesigned ("gold-plated") products, and a large private-interest group pressing for high levels of defense spending.[44]

"The Organization Man"

In a 1956 book, William H. Whyte, Jr., gave the nation a new phrase, "the organization man."[45] The large corporation, in Whyte's analysis, had created an entirely new work ambience and set of values in its managers. "Once people liked to think, at least, that they were in control of their destinies," Whyte wrote, "but few of the younger organizational people cherish such notions. Most see themselves as objects more acted upon than acting—and their future, therefore, determined as much by the system as by themselves." The corporate system, Whyte continued, is seductive—essentially beneficial, if not paternalistic—and places an overwhelming premium on cooperation. He recognized the dangers in selfish individualism but feared an even greater danger in "a climate which inhibits individual initiative and imagination, and the courage to exercise it against group opinion."[46] The result, for Whyte, is a subtle tyranny. "No one wants to see the old authoritarian return, but at least it could be said of him that what he wanted primarily was your sweat. The new man wants your soul."[47]

Corporate Impact on the Community

Absentee top management and ownership may lead to corporate ignorance of or indifference to the impact of top-level decisions on local communities. Decisions on transferring operations or plant closings are likely to be impersonal. Plant managers without roots in a community may not play as informed, effective, and influential a role in political, cultural, and charitable community affairs as local independent owner-operators. Such managers, under performance pressure from distant central offices, may show less concern for a factory's effect on the local environment, traffic congestion, or housing problems.

Race and Sex Discrimination

These are particularly sensitive issues at both national and community levels. The underlying economic theory is ambiguous. Because competitive firms must minimize production costs, if the going wages of minority workers or women are lower than those of equally productive white males, competition should force firms to hire those discriminated against until the wage differentials are eliminated. But if local customs and standards of discrimination lead to lower productivity among white male workers or to costly troubles in the community unless existing discriminatory practices are followed, no competitive firm (regardless of the social views of its owners and managers) can afford to take the lead in eliminating discrimination. In general, competitive firms will be forced to pay wage differences equal to differences in the marginal productivities of workers in separable groups, whether the productivity differences result from different personal traits (education, physical strength, or job attitudes) or whether they are the indirect results of changes in the productivity of others.

According to this line of reasoning, competitive firms can adapt to but not change existing patterns of discrimination. Firms with the market power or size to be indifferent to community attitudes can, to some extent, indulge the social preferences of their owners or managers. Depending on these preferences, such firms may practice more or less discrimination than those in more highly competitive industries.[48] Empirical studies indicate that discrimination against blacks and women throughout the 1960s, both in wages and in types of jobs held, was a positive function of both size and market concentration, when other explanatory variables such as plant location and nature of product were held constant. During the 1970s, however, the differences vanished or at least shrunk to statistical insignificance, presumably as a result of antidiscriminatory legislation and regulations.[49]

The Corporation and Political Influence: PACs

Electoral reforms made in the Federal Election Campaign Act (FECA) of 1971 and its subsequent amendments have intensified interest in campaign contributions by both corporations and labor unions. Most dramatically, these reforms have led to an explosive growth of corporate financial support to congressional campaigns through political action committees (PACs).[50]

The period of rapid PAC growth appears to be ending. In late 1983, the *National Journal* reported a sharp decline in the rate of growth, from over 40 percent per year from 1974 to 1976, down to 20 percent per year between 1976 and 1982, and to approximately 10 percent per year since.[51]

Opinions vary on the impact of business PACs. Edwin M. Epstein, has observed that "it is not an exaggeration to say that the Federal Election Campaign Act . . . has legitimized the role of corporations and business-related groups in federal elections, greatly improving their position vis-à-vis labor and other social interests."[52] Gary J. Andres, on the other hand, points out that there has been more change in form than in substance, noting that "prior to the 1970s, business executives contributed to politicians in an unsystematic, ad hoc manner. Traditionally, corporate executives got together and bankrolled candidates of their choice with little pressure or need to disclose the recipients of their largess." The basic change, according to Andres, is that "the emergence of corporate political action committees represents an institutionalization of business involvement in campaign finance. Business campaign giving is now a much more systematic and strategic operation."[53]

Epstein noted a clear relationship between firm size and the propensity of corporations to form their own PACs, as shown in Table 4–3.

TABLE 4–3 PACs Established by *Fortune*'s Top 1,000 Industrial Firms Grouped by Relative Size, September 1978

Industrial Firms Ranked by Size	PACs Formed	
	Number	Percent
1–50	35	70%
51–100	34	68
101–150	30	60
151–200	25	50
201–250	17	34
251–500	52	21
501–750	24	10
751–1,000	7	3

SOURCE: Edwin M. Epstein, "The Business PAC Phenomenon: An Irony of Electoral Reform," *Regulation*, May–June 1979, pp. 35–41, at p. 39.

Andres looked at the same phenomenon from a different perspective, pointing out that by 1980 only 262 of the *Fortune* 500 had formed PACs. The percentage, he noted, differed greatly from industry to industry. PACs had been formed by 75 percent or more of the *Fortune* firms in the pharmaceuticals, rubber and plastic products, mining and crude oil production, motor vehicles, petroleum refining, and aerospace industries. At the other end of the spectrum, 25 percent or less of the firms from the top 500 in the jewelry, soap and cosmetic, publishing and printing, and apparel industries had formed PACs.[54] Andres hypothesized that the differences might be explained by size of firm, level of industry concentration, and degree of government regulation of the firm. In a regression analysis, he found that PAC formation did rise with all three of these variables but that only size and regulation were statistically significant at the 1 percent confidence level. Concentration was significant only at the 10 percent level.

CONCLUSION

Big business and the exercise of market power have raised a broad range of issues, with economic, political, and social concerns expressed by numerous critics of widely varying persuasions and ideologies. These concerns have been acknowledged repeatedly in the development of the nation's public policies toward business. Antitrust policy, to which we turn in the next chapter, cannot be understood and evaluated without being aware of the pervasive criticisms and sense of unease generated by the rise of the modern corporation.

But it is a long—and frequently wrong—way from concerned criticism to condemnation, with mixed evidence on the actual scope and effects of the evils attributed to big business. The research required to assess these effects must be continual, since the issue is current performance rather than past offenses. Further, a theme that runs through the economics of industrial organization, and hence through this book, is the frequent need to recognize trade-offs among desirable social objectives. The minimum scale of production required for technical efficiency relative to demand for the product, for example, may require a large firm with an otherwise objectionable degree of market power. It has also been contended, and is treated at length in Chapter Twelve, that only large firms with market power are capable of performing the research and development needed for an optimal rate of technological progress.

As the natures of both business firms and the society in which they operate evolve over time, so will concerns and criticisms raised. And in a pluralistic society with varied social and political values, we may not all agree on even the nature of the problem.

ENDNOTES

[1]Karl Marx and Friedrich Engels, *The Communist Manifesto* (1848), trans. Samuel Moore (1888), in *Birth of the Communist Manifesto*, ed. Dirk J. Struik, (New York: International Publishers, 1971), p. 94.

[2]For readers not familiar with diagrams such as those in Figure 4–1, marginal revenue (cost) is defined as the change in total revenue (cost) resulting from the sale (production) of one more unit, or the first derivative of total revenue (cost) with respect to quantity sold (produced). The typical shapes of the cost and revenue functions are such that at levels of output and sales below the profit-maximizing point, $MR > MC$.

As long as the firm can add more to total revenue *(TR)* by selling an additional unit than it adds to total cost *(TC)* by producing that unit, it should continue to expand output and sales. Or, from simple differential calculus, $TR - TC$ (i.e., profit) is maximized when its first derivative, $MR - MC$, equals zero.

[3]Under a very stringent set of assumptions, it can be shown that the total economic welfare of a society will be maximized for a given set of productive resources when all firms, in all industries, produce at the rate of output at which $P = MC$. Intuitively, *MC* represents the cost of the resources devoted to producing the last unit, while *P* reflects the value put on that unit by consumers. As long as the added cost is lower than the value of the product, welfare will be increased by producing more. Increased demand for resources will raise their costs to producers. If all resources were devoted to the production of various goods and services in such a way that $P = MC$ throughout the economy, it would be impossible to improve total economic welfare by any reallocation, taking the distribution of income among members of the society as given.

[4]To demonstrate this, consider a small change in the price charged for its product by a firm facing a downward-sloping demand curve. The change in total revenue is expressed as

$$\Delta TR = P \cdot \Delta Q + \Delta P \cdot Q \tag{4.1F}$$

That is, *TR* will rise (fall) by the increased (decreased) quantity sold multiplied by the price at which the product is now sold, but will decrease (increase) by the amount that the price is reduced (raised) multiplied by the quantity previously sold at the slightly higher (lower) price.

If we multiply $\Delta P \cdot Q$ on the right side of Equation (4.1F) by $\Delta Q \cdot P / \Delta Q \cdot P$ and rearrange, we obtain

$$\frac{\Delta TR}{\Delta Q} = P\left(1 - \frac{1}{\eta}\right) \tag{4.2F}$$

where $\eta = |\Delta Q / \Delta P \cdot P/Q|$.

Since by definition $\Delta TR / \Delta Q = MR$, Equation (4.2F) can be written

$$MR = P\left(1 - \frac{1}{\eta}\right) \tag{4.3F}$$

To maximize profit, the firm will set $MR = MC$. Substituting *MC* for *MR* and rearranging again, we obtain

$$\frac{P - MC}{P} = \frac{1}{\eta} \tag{4.4F}$$

[5]Obtained by rearrangement of Equation (4.4F) of Footnote 4.

[6]Harvey Leibenstein, "Allocative Efficiency versus 'X–Efficiency,' " *American Economic Review* 56, no. 3 (June 1966), pp. 392–415.

[7]Marx and Engels, *Communist Manifesto,* p. 95.

[8]Joseph A. Schumpeter, *Ten Great Economists* (New York: Oxford University Press, 1951), p. 46.

[9]Karl Marx, *Das Kapital* (1867), from the first American edition (1906), ed. Ernest Untermann, in *Capital* (New York: Modern Library, 1932), pp. 836–37.

[10]Paul M. Sweezy, *The Theory of Capitalist Development* (New York: Monthly Review Press, 1942), p. 19.

[11]Marx and Engels, *Communist Manifesto,* pp. 96–97.

[12]Ibid., p. 94.

[13]For a brief discussion of these early writings and their rediscovery in the 1930s, see Ignace Feuerlicht, *Alienation from the Past to the Future* (Westport, Conn.: Greenwood Press, 1978), pp. 31, 130–39.

[14]Bertell Ollman, *Alienation: Marx's Conception of Man in Capitalist Society*, 2d ed. (London: Cambridge University Press, 1976), p. 131.

[15]Ibid., pp. 133–34.

[16]For recent discussions, see Frederic M. Scherer, "Industrial Structure, Scale Economies, and Worker Alienation" in *Essays on Industrial Organization in Honor of Joe S. Bain*, ed. Robert T. Masson and P. David Qualls (Cambridge, Mass.: Ballinger, 1976), pp. 105–21; "Firm Size, Market Structure, and Worker Satisfaction," *The Economics of Firm Size, Market Structure, and Social Performance: Proceedings of a Conference Sponsored by the Bureau of Economics, Federal Trade Commission*, ed. John J. Siegfried (Washington, D.C.: U.S. Government Printing Office, July 1980), pp. 325–88.

[17]J. G. Van Cise, *The Federal Antitrust Laws*, 4th ed. (Washington, D.C.: American Enterprise Institute for Public Policy Research, 1982), pp. 68–69.

[18]Christopher Lasch, "The Jeffersonian Legacy" in *Thomas Jefferson: The Man . . . His World . . . His Influence*, ed. Lally Weymouth (New York: G. P. Putnam's Sons, 1973), pp. 229–45, at p. 229.

[19]Charles M. Wiltse, *The Jeffersonian Tradition in American Democracy* (Chapel Hill: University of North Carolina Press, 1935), pp. 222–36; and Lasch, *Jeffersonian Legacy*, pp. 238–40.

[20]Harold Laski, "Democracy," *Encyclopaedia of the Social Sciences*, vol. 5 (New York: Macmillan, 1932), pp. 76–85, at p. 80.

[21]Henry David Thoreau, in *Civil Disobedience* (1849), attributed this remark to Jefferson, but it has never been located in the latter's writings. Berger Evans, *Dictionary of Quotations* (New York: Delacorte Press, 1968), pp. 285–86.

[22]Richard E. Ellis, "The Political Economy of Thomas Jefferson" in *Thomas Jefferson*, ed. Weymouth, pp. 81–95, at p. 93.

[23]U.S. Department of Commerce, Bureau of the Census, *1947 Census of Manufactures* and *1977 Census of Manufactures* (Washington, D.C.: U.S. Government Printing Office, 1949, 1981).

[24]Lawrence J. White, *Measuring the Importance of Small Business in the American Economy*, (New York: New York University Graduate School of Business Administration, 1982).

[25]Ibid., p. 30.

[26]Ibid., p. 2.

[27]Ibid., p. 8.

[28]U.S. Office of Management and Budget, *Catalog of Federal Domestic Assistance* (Washington, D.C.: U.S. Government Printing Office, 1984).

[29]For a leading and excellent discussion of this free-rider effect, see Mancur Olson, *The Logic of Collective Action* (Cambridge, Mass.: Harvard University Press, 1965).

[30]For recent analyses by economists, see Richard E. Caves, "Economic Models of Political Choice: Canada's Tariff Structure," *Canadian Journal of Economics* 9, no. 2 (May 1976), pp. 278–300; Lester M. Salamon and John J. Siegfried, "Economic Power and Political Influence: The Impact of Industry Structure on Public Policy," *American Political Science Review* 71, no. 3 (September 1977), pp. 1026–43; Cathleen Coolidge and Gordon Tullock, "Firm Size and Political Power," in *Economics of Firm Size*, ed. Siegfried, pp. 43–71; Daniel C. Esty and Richard E. Caves, "Market Structure and Political Influence: New Data on Political Expenditures, Activity, and Success, " *Economic Inquiry* 21, no. 1 (January 1983), pp. 24–38. For a comprehensive review of the literature, see Edwin M. Epstein, "Firm Size and Structure, Market Power and Business Political Influence: A Review of the Literature" in *Economics of Firm Size*, ed. Siegfried, pp. 240–81.

[31]Richard E. Caves, "Commentary" in *Economics of Firm Size*, ed., Siegfried, pp. 314–18, at p. 317.

[32]The issues discussed are those of sociopolitical problems associated with the ac-

tivities of large firms and those possessing market power. The broader issues of the sociopolitical role of business in general in modern society are not discussed. The reader interested in the larger issues should refer to Charles E. Lindblom, *Politics and Markets* (New York: Basic Books, 1977).

[33]C. Wright Mills, *The Power Elite* (New York: Oxford University Press, 1956).

[34]Richard J. Barber, *The American Corporation: Its Power, Its Money, Its Politics* (New York: E. P. Dutton, 1970), p. 4.

[35]Ibid., p. 186.

[36]Sydney Blumenthal, "Whose Side Is Business on, Anyway?" *New York Times Magazine,* October 25, 1981, pp. 29–31, 92–98.

[37]Barber, *The American Corporation*, p. 200.

[38]John Kenneth Galbraith, *The New Industrial State* (Boston: Houghton Mifflin, 1967), pp. 393–94 (italics original). © by John Kenneth Galbraith. Reprinted by permission of Houghton Mifflin Company.

[39]Blumenthal, "Whose Side . . .?" p. 94.

[40]Thomas Moore, "The New Libertarians Make Waves," *Fortune,* August 5, 1985, pp. 74–78, at p. 74.

[41]"Liberty Is at Stake: Farewell Address by Dwight D. Eisenhower, President of the United States," *Vital Speeches of the Day,* February 1, 1961, p. 229.

[42]U.S. Department of Defense, Office of the Secretary of Defense, *100 Companies and Their Subsidiaries Listed According to Net Value of Military Prime Contract Awards,* FY 1957 and FY 1983.

[43]James K. Brown and George Stothoff, *The Defense Industry: Some Perspectives from the Financial Community* (New York: The Conference Board, 1976); John Nielson, "The Party's Over for Arms Makers," *Fortune,* August 5, 1985, pp. 89–92.

[44]For more detailed discussion and analysis, see Merton J. Peck and Frederic M. Scherer, *The Weapons Acquisition Process: An Economic Analysis* (Boston: Harvard University Graduate School of Business Administration, 1962); Frederic M. Scherer, *The Weapons Acquisition Process: Economic Incentives* (Boston: Harvard University Graduate School of Business Administration, 1964); William L. Baldwin, *The Structure of the Defense Market, 1955–1964* (Durham, N.C.: Duke University Press, 1967); Bernard Udis, ed., *The Economic Consequences of Reduced Military Spending* (Lexington, Mass.: Lexington Books, 1973); J. Ronald Fox, *Arming America: How the U.S. Buys Weapons* (Boston: Harvard University Graduate School of Business Administration, 1974); A. M. Agapos, *Government-Industry and Defense: Economics and Administration* (University: University of Alabama Press, 1975); Jacques S. Gansler, *The Defense Industry* (Cambridge, Mass.: MIT Press, 1980); U.S. Congress, Joint Economic Committee, *Economic Impact of Federal Procurement* (Washington, D.C.: U.S. Government Printing Office, 1966 through 1969).

[45]William H. Whyte, Jr., *The Organization Man* (New York: Simon & Schuster, 1956).

[46]Ibid., p. 395.

[47]Ibid., p. 397.

[48]The leading theoretical work is Gary S. Becker, *The Economics of Discrimination* (Chicago: University of Chicago Press, 1957).

[49]See especially William G. Shepherd, "Market Power and Racial Discrimination in White Collar Employment," *Antitrust Bulletin* 14, no. 1 (Spring 1969), pp. 141–61; William G. Shepherd and Sharon G. Levin, "Managerial Discrimination in Large Firms," *Review of Economics and Statistics* 55, no. 4 (November 1973), pp. 412–22; William S. Comanor, "Racial Discrimination in American Industry," *Economica* (new series) 40, no. 160 (November 1973), pp. 363–78; Sharon M. Oster, "Industry Differences in the Level of Discrimination against Women," *Quarterly Journal of Economics* 89, no. 2 (May 1975), pp. 215–29; William R. Johnson, "Racial Discrimination and Industrial Struc-

ture," *Bell Journal of Economics* 9, no. 1 (Spring 1978), pp. 70–81; Douglas F. Greer, *Industrial Organization and Public Policy* (New York: Macmillan, 1980), pp. 475–78; William A. Luksetich, "Market Power and Discrimination in White-Collar Employment, 1969–1975," *Review of Social Economy* 39, no. 2 (October 1981), pp. 145–64.

[50]For analysis of this growth, see Larry J. Sabato, *PAC Power: Inside the World of Political Action Committees* (New York: W. W. Norton, 1984); and Michael J. Malbin, ed., *Money and Politics in the United States: Financing Elections in the 1980s* (Chatham, N.J.: Chatham House, 1984).

[51]"PACs Still Growing, But More Slowly," *National Journal* 15, no. 34–35 (August 20, 1983), p. 1754.

[52]Edwin M. Epstein, "The Business PAC Phenomenon: An Irony of Electoral Reform," *Regulation*, May/June 1979, pp. 35–41, at p. 35.

[53]Gary J. Andres, "Business Involvement in Campaign Finance: Factors Influencing the Decision to Form a Corporate PAC," *PS* 18, no. 2 (Spring 1985), pp. 213–20, at pp. 214–15.

[54]Ibid.

CHAPTER FIVE

The Antitrust Response to Corporate Size and Power

Antitrust is one of the most fundamental public policy responses to the modern corporation and to the economic, political, and social problems attributed to its predominance. The basic presumption behind antitrust policy is that desired business performance will be fostered by competition.

Other major public policy responses to corporate size and power include direct regulation of rates and services in public utilities regarded as natural monopolies, and government controls over issuance and subsequent trading in corporate securities. Since this book focuses on the role of competition in restraining market power, these alternative and often complementary policies are not discussed.

Also omitted are public policies designed to deal with the general impact of business activities on society but not primarily and plausibly linked to size and market power. Thus, this book does not cover policies affecting all firms alike, such as control of industrial pollution of the environment, promotion of occupational health and safety, and protection of consumers from hazardous and unhealthy products.

THE SHERMAN ANTITRUST ACT OF 1890

In the spring of 1890, nearly two years after Ohio Senator John A. Sherman first introduced his antitrust bill, Congress passed the Sherman Antitrust Act.[1] By that time, several states had antitrust laws; but interstate comity made these laws difficult or impossible to enforce against corporations chartered in other states.

The Sherman Act contained only two substantive provisions,[2] short enough to be reproduced in full here:

> Sec. 1. Every contract, combination in the form of trust or otherwise, or conspiracy, in restraint of trade or commerce among the several States, or with foreign nations, is hereby declared to be illegal. Every person who shall make any such contract or engage in any such combination or conspiracy, shall be deemed guilty of a misdemeanor, and, on conviction thereof, shall be punished by fine not exceeding five thousand dollars, or by imprisonment not exceeding one year, or by both said punishments, in the discretion of the court.
>
> Sec. 2. Every person who shall monopolize, or attempt to monopolize, or combine or conspire with any other person or persons, to monopolize any part of the trade or commerce among the several States, or with foreign nations, shall be deemed guilty of a misdemeanor, and, on conviction thereof, shall be punished by fine not exceeding five thousand dollars, or by imprisonment not exceeding one year, or by both said punishments, in the discretion of the court.

During debate on the bill, Senator Sherman emphasized that the legislation was designed to eliminate only the types of business combinations that were already unlawful under common law. But, as then interpreted by the federal courts, the common law was ineffective in controlling trusts, since it was applied only in private suits alleging breach of contract or seeking to void all or parts of a contract, and only to ascertain whether certain restrictive provisions were legal and hence enforceable. Only parties to the contract could sue; and other than a ruling that the contract could not be enforced, there were no sanctions for having entered into an illegally restrictive agreement. Thus, the only new feature of Sections 1 and 2 of the Sherman Act, at least according to its original supporters, was the provision of criminal penalties for violation.

In addition, Section 4 provided that:

> The several circuit courts of the United States are hereby invested with jurisdiction to prevent and restrain violations of this act; and it shall be the duty of the several district attorneys of the United States, in their respective districts, under the direction of the Attorney General, to institute proceedings in equity to prevent and restrain such violations.

Further, Section 7 allowed individuals or business firms injured by any actions declared to be illegal in the Sherman Act to sue and, on proof of both a violation of the law and a financial injury, to recover three times the damages suffered.

The virtually unanimous approval given to this first piece of federal antitrust legislation did not, however, reflect a strong and unambiguous condemnation of business combinations. Congress's unease was reflected in the House of Representatives vote (85 members abstained; the measure passed by 242 to 0). Both Congress and informed commentators had trouble reconciling the perceived popular mandate to curb the trusts' increasing economic power with their alleged economic benefits.

Virtually all of the few economists of the time opposed the Sherman Act. Most agreed that technological developments resulting in lower-cost methods of production could be implemented only by very large business units. Even monopoly, it was asserted, could lower costs by eliminating the wastes of competitive selling. Some, on shaky economic reasoning, argued that by control of production, the trusts could eliminate overproduction and hence bring an end to periodic business crises.

The Issue of Laissez-Faire

Throughout the 1880s, the principal issue dividing economists was an attack on the doctrine of laissez-faire launched by an influential group of younger economists.[3] The advocates of laissez-faire contended that the rise of the trusts was a natural, evolutionary development stimulated by industrialization and that government intervention in such a natural phenomenon could lead only to harm. They further asserted that private monopoly could not survive without special privileges granted by government (such as patents, exclusive franchises, or tariff protection) unless justified by economies of scale and that the only appropriate public policy, therefore, would be the elimination of such privileges. In their view, any other government actions against the trusts, could only hurt the public by denying consumers the benefits of greater economic efficiency and lower costs.

Some laissez-faire economists, anticipating John Kenneth Galbraith's concept of countervailing power by over half a century, argued that the 20th century was inevitably going to be a time of combination rather than competition and that the answer to the trust movement was voluntary formation of offsetting combinations of workers, farmers, small-business owners, and consumers. Others argued that publicity alone could curb the abuses of the trusts, while retaining their benefits.

Those rejecting the doctrine of laissez-faire did not believe that unregulated competition, even in the absence of market power, necessarily promoted the public good. They noted, for example, that competition drove firms to the use of child labor.

These younger economists tended to favor interventionism and control of the trusts through positive regulation of their pricing and conduct rather than attempts to limit their formation or to dissolve them. Thus, neither the adherents to laissez-faire doctrine nor its critics gave any support to the antitrust approach.

The Intent of Congress

Today, it is difficult to ascertain the objectives Congress sought in passing the Sherman Act. In part, Congress was simply responding to strong but somewhat inchoate public pressure. William Letwin describes the public attitude "simply as a familiar feeling raised to a high pitch, intense because the speed with which the new trusts were being hatched made it seem that they would overrun everything unless some remedy were found soon."[4] Although there has been some disagreement among economic historians, most now accept the long-held idea that widespread and intense public hostility toward the trusts[5] led politicians to realize that something had to be done, at least to still the clamor. Both the Democratic and the Republican Party platforms in 1888 contained planks attacking the trusts and calling for legislation. After the presidential election of that year, it was virtually incumbent on Congress to enact some sort of antitrust law.

Public aversion to the trusts, as vehement as it evidently was, was not based on any consensus as to the nature of the problem. Granger and Populist criticisms leveled at the railroads shortly after the Civil War soon broadened into an attack on the entire combination movement for depressing farm prices while enhancing the prices of both manufactured goods used in agriculture and consumer goods. Labor held the trusts responsible for depressing wages and repressing unionization. Others feared that the wealth and ostentatious spending of the rising industrialists not only reflected new inequities in income distribution but were leading to social instability. Still others attacked the trusts on ethical grounds, claiming that they were ruthless in the methods used to destroy competitors and criminally immoral in use of their money to corrupt the political process. Jeffersonian concerns were expressed over the elimination of small business. Trusts were charged with overcapitalization and fraud against investors. And special-interest groups joined the assault: The Traveling Men's Anti-Trust League, for example, was obviously motivated by the salesmen's fear of discharge following mergers of previously competing firms. In all, it was unclear just what were the "monstrous evils"[6] that Congress was expected to correct.

Donald Dewey has observed that "generations of lawyers, judges, and economists have puzzled over what Congress 'really' intended to accomplish by the Sherman Act. One cynical school of investigators has concluded that the lawmakers of 1890 were merely denouncing corporate sin in order to placate their more rustic constituents." But

Dewey, noting that "the young reader is cautioned against the naiveté of cynicism," concluded that it is pointless to try to ascertain congressional intent from either the language of the Sherman Act or the record of the debate.[7] Letwin made a similar point, commenting that "the deceptive simplicity of the Sherman Act has led many historians to believe that the intention of Congress was equally simple. Although they have not agreed on what the intention was, these historians have shared the view that the motives of Congress were simple and unmixed and have differed chiefly over whether Congress was sincere."[8] Letwin contended, to the contrary, that congressional motives are inevitably mixed and complex, involving subjective assessments of public opinion, predicted reactions of constituents, individual ideologies, pride in professional legal craftsmanship, party loyalties, and the focused influence of interest groups and those most directly affected by the proposed legislation.

Hans B. Thorelli argued that while Congress felt consumers would be the ultimate beneficiaries of the legislation, small business proprietors were the immediate intended beneficiaries. "Perhaps," he continued, "we are even justified in saying that the Sherman Act is not to be viewed exclusively as an expression of economic policy. In safeguarding the rights of the 'common man' in business 'equal' to those of the evolving more 'ruthless' and impersonal forms of enterprise the Sherman Act embodies what is to be characterized as an eminently 'social' purpose."[9]

In sum, the Sherman Act made the common-law offenses of restraint of trade, monopolization, and attempts to monopolize statutory, providing both criminal sanctions and civil remedies. But federal authorities were left with broad discretion as to the number and types of cases to bring. The burden of interpreting the common-law language of the statute and reducing its generalities to specific application in deciding individual cases was put squarely on the courts.

EARLY INTERPRETATION OF THE SHERMAN ACT: PER SE VIOLATIONS AND THE RULE OF REASON

In early Sherman Act cases, the judges took on the burden of interpreting the language of Sections 1 and 2—language described by some as of "constitutional scope"[10] and by others (not inconsistently) as vague. From the start, they perceived the problem to be interpreting the common-law meaning of "restraint of trade" and "monopolization." The three leading contributors to this crucial process were Justice Rufus W. Peckham, Justice Edward D. White, and Circuit Judge William Howard Taft (later president of the United States and chief justice of the Supreme Court).

Early Judicial Debate: Landmark Cases

The main features of the early judicial debate and its resolution are found in the opinions in three landmark cases: the *Trans-Missouri Freight Association* case, decided by the Supreme Court in 1897 with an opinion by Peckham and a dissent by White; the circuit court of appeals decision written the following year by Taft in the *Addyston Pipe and Steel Company* case; and the opinion of White, by then chief justice of the Supreme Court, in the 1911 *Standard Oil Company* case.[11]

The *Trans-Missouri Freight Association* Case. The *Trans-Missouri Freight* case came to the Supreme Court with the basic issue laid out clearly in the lower courts' opinions. The case involved the legality of an association formed by 15 railroads to carry out an agreement that all freight rates and shipping regulations, except those dealing with freight shipments in competition with nonmembers, were to be subject to approval by the association. The district court had held that the common-law issue was whether this agreement was "prejudicial to the public interest."[12] The circuit court of appeals rejected this view without discussion. The three judges of the appeals court could agree on little else, however, coming to a split decision. The majority opinion stated that by the time of passage of the Sherman Act, it was well established in both British and U.S. jurisprudence "that the validity of contracts restricting competition was to be determined by the reasonableness of the restriction. If the main purpose or natural and inevitable effect of a contract was to suppress competition or create a monopoly, it was illegal." But if the contract had been made for a "lawful purpose" and was not "unreasonably injurious to the public welfare," it would be upheld, even if there was a "tendency to some extent to check competition."[13] The dissenting judge, however, expressed concern over the virtually impossible burden that would be imposed on a plaintiff "compelled to establish by competent evidence that the rate complained of was unreasonable," adding—in the best economic tradition—"the reasonable rates which the community is entitled to enjoy are those which result from free and unrestrained competition."[14]

The Supreme Court reversed. Justice Peckham, writing for a bare majority, rejected the notion that the courts could assume Congress intended only to codify the common law in Sections 1 and 2 of the Sherman Act. Addressing himself to the argument that proponents of the act had so stated repeatedly in debate, Peckham noted that many members of Congress who had voted for the act had been silent throughout the floor discussion, and their intentions were unknown. "All that can be determined from the debates and reports," he wrote, "is that various members had various views, and we are left to determine the meaning of this act, as we determine the meaning of other acts, from the language used therein."[15]

Peckham then proceeded to argue that the word *every*, which began both Sections 1 and 2, could only be read as broadening the scope of the prohibitions beyond those of the common law:

> A contract may be in restraint of trade and still be valid at common law. When, therefore, the body of an act pronounces as illegal every contract or combination in restraint of trade or commerce among the several States, etc., the plain and ordinary meaning of such language is not limited to that kind of contract alone which is in unreasonable restraint of trade, but all contracts are included in such language, and no exception or limitation can be added without placing in the act that which has been omitted by Congress.[16]

Peckham did not explain how a contract or agreement "in restraint of trade" was to be distinguished from other contracts, leaving himself vulnerable to the criticism that his interpretation was tantamount to treating all contracts that restrained the market behavior of at least one party as illegal. But he did go on to discuss the formidable problems that the courts would impose on themselves by adopting the appeals court's test of reasonableness. "If only that kind of contract which is in unreasonable restraint of trade be within the meaning of the statute, and declared to be therein illegal, it is at once apparent that the subject of what is a reasonable rate is attended with great uncertainty. What is a proper standard by which to judge the fact of reasonable rates?"[17] Peckham answered his own rhetorical question by asserting that he did not know of any such standard.

Peckham found further grounds for rejecting a standard of reasonable prices by arguing that the Sherman Act was not intended solely to protect consumers from unreasonable prices. In the tradition of Jeffersonian democracy, he noted that the trusts might lead to other social evils.

> In business or trading combinations they may even temporarily, or perhaps permanently, reduce the price of the article traded in or manufactured, by reducing the expense inseparable from the running of many different companies for the same purpose. Trade or commerce under those circumstances may nevertheless be badly and unfortunately restrained by driving out of business the small dealers and worthy men whose lives have been spent therein, and who might be unable to readjust themselves to their altered surroundings. Mere reduction in the price of the commodity dealt in might be dearly paid for by the ruin of such a class, and the absorption of control over one commodity by an all-powerful combination of capital.[18]

In elaborating on this matter, Peckham also made the point, fundamental to antitrust today, that it is the power to restrain trade—

whether or not it is exercised—that is of concern in the antitrust laws. He added that an inevitable concomitant of technical change and progress is the displacement of those engaged in obsolete lines or methods of business. But this natural process should be distinguished from elimination of independent businesses by combination.

Justice White, writing for the minority and supporting the court of appeals, contended that the title of the Sherman Act, "An Act to Protect Trade and Commerce Against Unlawful Restraints and Monopolies," reflected the intent of Congress. Only "unlawful" restraints and monopolies—those already condemned by the common law—were to be covered. Proceeding from this premise, he held that a review of the common law would "demonstrate that the words 'restraint of trade' embrace only contracts which unreasonably restrain trade, and, therefore, that reasonable contracts, although they, in some measure, 'restrain trade,' are not within the meaning of the words."[19]

White emphasized the basic vulnerability of the majority's position. "To define, then, the words 'in restraint of trade' as embracing every contract which in any degree produced that effect would be violative of reason, because it would include all those contracts which are the very essence of trade, and would be equivalent to saying that there should be no trade, and therefore nothing to restrain."[20]

Almost inadvertently, White introduced the phrase "rule of reason" into the jargon of antitrust, asking rhetorically "If the rule of reason no longer determines the right of the individual to contract or secures the validity of contracts upon which trade depends and results, what becomes of the liberty of the citizen or of the freedom of trade?"[21] White did not clarify whether his rule of reason referred to the common-law principle that only unreasonable restraints of trade were illegal or to the courts' duty not to interpret a statute in such a way as to be violative of reason.

The divided *Trans-Missouri* decisions, at both the appeals and Supreme Court levels, appeared to pose a fundamental dilemma. The dissenting circuit court judge and the majority of the Supreme Court now appear—with the benefit of hindsight—to have been absolutely correct and to have performed an extraordinarily important service in warning the judiciary against assuming the burden of trying to ascertain the inherent reasonableness or unreasonableness of particular prices or other economic effects of restrictive agreements. This is a responsibility for which courts and the legal process are particularly unsuited. On the other hand, some standard had to be devised to distinguish legitimate and illegitimate restraints, since literal interpretation of the word *every* would have made the Sherman Act either devastatingly destructive of economic activity or, more likely, unenforceable.

The *Addyston Pipe and Steel Company* Case. The dilemma was largely resolved by Judge Taft's decision the following year in the court of appeals decision in the *Addyston Pipe and Steel* case—a decision that Robert H. Bork has said "must rank as one of the greatest, if not the greatest, antitrust opinions in the history of the law."[22]

The *Addyston* defendants, six corporations manufacturing cast-iron pipe, had formed an organization known as the Associated Pipe Works. Through this association, the defendants divided markets in 36 states and territories among themselves and, among other schemes, agreed to allow each member firm to submit the low bids in its reserved area.

Taft circumvented Peckham's question of whether the Sherman Act made any acts illegal that had been legal under the common law. He stated that, without doubt, anything void at common law was illegal under the Sherman Act. Following a review of earlier common-law cases involving restraints of trade, he concluded "that no conventional restraint of trade can be enforced unless the covenant embodying it is merely ancillary to the main purpose of a lawful contract, and necessary to protect the covenantee in the enjoyment of the legitimate fruits of the contract, or to protect him from the danger of an unjust use of those fruits by the other party."[23]

Taft continued by observing that in a valid contract, "there is a main purpose, to which the covenant in restraint of trade is merely ancillary." But not all such contracts would be valid under the common law. If there was an ancillary restraint, "The main purpose of the contract suggests the measure of protection needed, and furnishes a sufficiently uniform standard by which the validity of such restraints may be judicially determined." If, on the other hand, the restraint is not ancillary, but is itself the purpose of the agreement, such an agreement would not be upheld under the common law. "But where the sole object of both parties in making the contract as expressed therein is merely to restrain competition, and enhance or maintain prices, it would seem that there was nothing to justify or excuse the restraint, that it would necessarily have a tendency to monopoly, and therefore would be void."[24]

Defendants had argued not only that the prices charged by the association were reasonable but that "the law now recognizes that competition can be so ruinous as to injure the public, and, therefore, that contracts made with a view to check such ruinous competition and regulate prices, though in restraint of trade, and having no other purpose, will be upheld." Taft, however, disagreed, writing, "We think this conclusion is unwarranted by the authorities when all of them are considered."[25] He then discussed a number of common-law cases and concluded:

Upon this review of the law and the authorities, we can have no doubt that the association of the defendants, however reasonable the prices they fixed, however great the competition they had to encounter, and however great the necessity for curbing themselves by joint agreement from committing financial suicide by ill-advised competition, was void at common law, because in restraint of trade, and tending to a monopoly.[26]

Finally, Taft repeated Peckham's point that the ability to raise prices, whether exercised or not, was the evil at which the Sherman Act was aimed, stating, "We do not think that at common law there is any question of reasonableness open to the courts with reference to such a contract. Its tendency was certainly to give defendants the power to charge unreasonable prices, had they chosen to do so."[27] The following year, in the first unanimous Sherman Act decision rendered by the Supreme Court, Taft's decision was upheld. The opinion was written by Peckham.[28]

The essence of the concept of per se (in and of itself) illegality under the Sherman Act, as formulated in Taft's opinion, has been reaffirmed on several occasions since and remains a fundamental feature of modern antitrust law. The basic question is whether a restraint is ancillary to a legitimate business purpose or the objective of the agreement. If the restraint is of the latter type—sometimes known as a "naked" restraint—it is illegal per se. Under the per se concept, agreements to fix price, restrict output, or share markets have been condemned solely on evidence that they existed. Pleas that the prices fixed were reasonable or that the restrictions were intended only to avoid "ruinous" competition are irrelevant and will not be admitted by the courts. Taft thus dealt with the troublesome word *every* by holding that ancillary restraints need not be in restraint of trade as that phrase is understood at law; and by redirecting the question to one of whether the agreement is ancillary, he met the concern over a court's inability to determine reasonable prices.

The *Standard Oil Company* Case. As basic as Taft's contribution was, it solved only part of the dilemma. It was clear that even if a restraint was ancillary, it might still run afoul of the law. It remained for White, by then chief justice, to grapple further with this issue in the 1911 *Standard Oil* case.

In 1906, when the case was filed, the Standard Oil Company of New Jersey was perhaps the best known and most infamous of the trusts, its notoriety heightened by Ida M. Tarbell's vivid 1904 exposé *The History of the Standard Oil Company*.[29] The word *trust* had come into popular usage as a result of the use of the trust form in 1882 to consolidate control of 40 firms engaged in "purchasing, transporting, refining, shipping and selling oil and the products thereof,"[30] including

John D. Rockefeller's Standard Oil of Ohio. In this trust, devised by Rockefeller's lawyer, S. C. T. Dodd, the voting rights to the common stocks of all of the firms included in the trust were assigned to a single trustee. In 1899, shortly after liberalization of New Jersey's incorporation law, the Standard Oil Trust was dissolved and succeeded by the Standard Oil Company of New Jersey, a holding company that acquired the trust's stockholdings. The indictment alleged that Standard Oil, in its various forms, had obtained and maintained control of 90 percent of the nation's petroleum refining and marketing through flagrantly abusive business methods, including solicitation of rebates from railroads, collusion with competitors, predatory pricing, espionage, operation of bogus independent companies, and division of markets.

The *Standard Oil* case, and the *American Tobacco* case decided on the same day,[31] both of which dealt with "close-knit" combinations (the absorption of a number of formerly independent firms into one corporation), posed a set of issues quite different from those raised by "loose-knit" combinations of firms retaining their organizational independence, such as the Trans-Missouri Freight Association or the Associated Pipe Works. In the case of the formation of a trust or close-knit combination, alleged practices—however they might restrain trade or monopolize a market—might arguably be ancillary to the establishment of a more efficient as well as larger business organization.

White, as those before him, reviewed the common law at length. And, like both the court of appeals majority in *Trans-Missouri Freight* and Taft in *Addyston Pipe and Steel,* he found ample precedent in the common law for treating the intent or purpose of the parties to the restraint as central to the matter. He wrote "that as to necessaries of life the freedom of the individual to deal was restricted where the nature and character of the dealing was such as to engender the presumption of *intent* to bring about at least one of the injuries which it was deemed would result from monopoly, that is an undue enhancement of price."[32] In a sentence that perhaps deserves to be noted for its length as much as for its crucial importance in the development of antitrust law, White wrote:

> Without going into detail and but very briefly surveying the whole field, it may be with accuracy said that the dread of enhancement of prices and of other wrongs which it was thought would flow from the undue limitation on competitive conditions caused by contracts or other acts of individuals or corporations, led, as a matter of public policy, to the prohibition or treating as illegal all contracts or acts which were unreasonably restrictive of competitive conditions, either from the nature or character of the contract or act or where the surrounding circumstances were such as to justify the conclusion that they had not been entered into or performed

with the legitimate *purpose* of reasonably forwarding personal interest and developing trade, but on the contrary were of such a character as to give rise to the inference or presumption that they had been entered into or done with the *intent* to do wrong to the general public and to limit the right of individuals, thus restraining the free flow of commerce and tending to bring about the evils, such as enhancement of prices, which were considered to be against public policy.[33]

Congress, in White's view, by declining to expressly define the contracts and acts covered, must have intended that "the standard of reason which had been applied at the common law"[34] be the measure for determining whether the Sherman Act had been violated. Subsequently, White referred to the "rule of reason" as the guide under "the construction which we have given the statute" and noted that "in every case where it is claimed that an act or acts are in violation of the statute the rule of reason, in the light of the principles of law and the public policy which the act embodies, must be applied."[35]

Taft's Interpretation of the Rule of Reason

In a 1914 book, Taft (who by then was a professor of law at Yale University) sought to describe the rule of reason in clearer and simpler language than that in White's opinion.[36] In fact, the rule of reason, as applied since the *Standard Oil* decision, owes as much to Taft's explication as to White's original construction. In outline, the court must first determine the "nature or character of the contract or act." If the court decides that the restraint is naked rather than ancillary, it is per se illegal. There is no test of intent or of reasonableness of the prices or profits either sought or realized. If, however, a restraint is determined to be ancillary to a legitimate business purpose, the court must then ascertain the primary intent of the defendant or defendants. The law is violated only when that primary intent is to reduce or eliminate competition.

One relatively minor issue appears to have divided White and Taft. White would have required the court to examine the inherent effect of a restraint as well as the intent of the parties. If the restraint would have had severe anticompetitive effects, relative to the main purpose of the act or agreement, it should be prohibited under the White version of the rule of reason, whether or not it could be shown that the effects were intended. In Taft's version, however, the only issue is whether the main purpose was to restrain trade or to forward a legitimate business objective. Scholars have since held that White's version of the common-law rule of reason was probably sounder than Taft's,[37] but the Taft version has become the more widely accepted of the two. In effect, the distinction is not significant. Discussing the question of intent, Taft referred to "necessary effect,"[38] by which he presumably meant the effect anticipated at the time a business arrangement was made. It is a standard principle of law that if individuals can be shown to have known the consequences of their behavior, they can be presumed to have intended those consequences.

ANTITRUST LEGISLATION, 1914

In the presidential election campaign of 1912, as in that of 1888, public control of the trusts was a leading issue. President Taft, running for reelection as the Republican candidate, endorsed the Supreme Court's enunciation of the rule of reason and saw no need for major new legislation, though he had for some time advocated federal incorporation of firms operating in interstate commerce. The Republican platform, however, did endorse an amendment to the Sherman Act specifying certain acts as criminal offenses. Theodore Roosevelt, running as the candidate of the newly formed Progressive, or "Bull Moose," party, and Woodrow Wilson, the Democratic party nominee, both made the trust issue the principal one in their campaigns.

Criticisms of the Sherman Act

Several criticisms were leveled at the Sherman Act and its enforcement, both during the election campaign and in the subsequent debate over the 1914 legislation.

The Rule of Reason. First, the rule of reason was widely criticized, mainly because it was widely misunderstood. Both politicians and the public shared a common but flagrantly incorrect belief that the Supreme Court had assumed responsibility for distinguishing inherently "reasonable" restraints of trade and acts of monopolization from "unreasonable" ones and would condemn only those that a majority of the justices thought were "bad" or unreasonable. A 1913 report of the Senate Committee on Interstate Commerce stated:

> The committee has full confidence in the integrity, intelligence, and patriotism of the Supreme Court of the United States, but it is unwilling to repose in that court, or any other court, the vast and undefined power which it must exercise in the administration of the statute under the rule which it has promulgated. It substitutes the court in the place of Congress, for whenever the rule is invoked, the court does not administer the law, but makes the law.[39]

Quite to the contrary, as Letwin noted, Chief Justice White "had taken infinite trouble when discussing the proper role of judicial discretion, to make certain nobody could think he was arguing that judges ought to have a wider scope for intruding their personal views of public policy."[40] Taft, in his 1914 book, wrote harshly:

> Politicians have seized on phrases that would attract the public eye, the meaning of which in the law they have not themselves understood, and have proposed amendments to accomplish purposes of a most indefinite character, without knowing or caring how they were to operate, if only the passing of the amendment gave them a ground for appeal for votes and a claim to the gratitude of their constituents.[41]

He added, "I have said little to my purpose if I have not made clear that the only reasonableness in the application of the statute which the court assumes to consider and decide is that of the restraint of trade, ancillary to a main contract with a different purpose and which the common law has for years furnished practical and definite legal rules for determining."[42]

Anticompetitive Practices.   There were other more valid concerns regarding the rule of reason. The *Standard Oil* and *American Tobacco* cases brought to light a number of practices used against independent firms in the process of consolidating an industry. Predatory pricing, or cutting price below the costs of rivals while holding it high in areas without competition, was alleged in both cases. Selling tactics included tying arrangements (the sale of one product only on the condition that the customer buy some other product or a full line of products) and exclusive dealing requirements (an insistence that a distributor not carry the products of any competitor). Independent companies had been bought out through purchase of controlling blocks of stock, sometimes surreptitiously and through secret agents. In some instances in both industries, the control was not revealed, creating bogus independents.

The Need for Preventive Legislation. As a result of these revelations and the thorough restructuring of the oil and tobacco industries that resulted (Standard Oil was broken up into 34 successor companies and American Tobacco into 14), some argued for preventive legislation, as opposed to remedial, to check the formation of trusts and monopolies in their incipiency rather than relying on a drastic, after-the-fact remedy under the Sherman Act. Among the foremost proponents of this argument was Wilson, who stated repeatedly in his election campaign that the proper policy was not to regulate monopolies—a policy he claimed Roosevelt supported—but rather to regulate competition by forbidding types of conduct that favored businesses with the greatest economic power rather than those that were most efficient.

The Need for a New Antitrust Agency. Wilson's charge that Roosevelt advocated regulation of the trusts was based on the latter's campaign proposal that a new agency be established "having the same power over industrial concerns that the Inter-State Commerce Commission has over railroads, so that whenever there is in the future a decision rendered in such important matters as the recent suits against the Standard Oil [and] Tobacco Trust—we will have a commission that will see that the decree of the court is really made effective; that it is not made a merely nominal decree."[43] In addition to regulatory powers, such an agency was expected to bring business, accounting, and economic expertise (presumably not possessed by most of the nation's judges) to bear on the trust problem. Roosevelt and his supporters hoped that an independent enforcement agency could implement a sustained and consistent, as well as informed, antitrust program. They contended that it was impossible for successive attorneys general, who were political appointees directly responsible to the president and subject to the president's views, to conduct such a program. Roosevelt proposed naming his commission the Federal Trade Commission.

Language of the Sherman Act. Finally, both supporters and opponents of antitrust complained that the language of the Sherman Act was too vague and general. They contended that the law would be both more effective and more equitable if the prohibitions were made more specific and more easily understandable.

All these concerns, with the arguable exception of the last, were addressed in the two laws passed in 1914, the Clayton Antitrust Act and the Federal Trade Commission Act.

The Clayton Antitrust Act

The Clayton Act[44] contains four substantive sections. These sections deal with price discrimination, tying arrangements, exclusive dealing agreements, acquisition of the stock of competitors, and interlocking directorates.

Section 2 forbids "any person engaged in commerce . . . to discriminate in price between different purchasers of commodities . . . where the effect of such discrimination may be to substantially lessen competition or tend to create a monopoly in any line of commerce." The Clayton Act does not make price discrimination illegal per se; but neither does it limit the prohibition to predatory price discrimination. Rather, price discrimination is illegal in any situation in which it may have substantial harmful effects on competition.

Section 3 forbids any lease, sale, or contract that provides that the lessee or purchaser shall refrain from using or dealing in commodities supplied by a competitor of the lessor or seller—a tying arrangement or exclusive dealing arrangement. Again, such transactions are illegal "where the effect of such lease, sale, or contract for sale . . . may be to substantially lessen competition or tend to create a monopoly in any line of commerce."

The first paragraph of Section 7 states:

> No corporation engaged in commerce shall acquire, directly or indirectly, the whole or any part of the stock or other share capital of another corporation engaged also in commerce where the effect of such acquisition may be to substantially lessen competition between the corporation whose stock is so acquired and the corporation making the acquisition or to restrain such commerce in any section or community or tend to create a monopoly of any line of commerce.

The following paragraph of the section forbids a corporation from acquiring the whole or part of the share capital of two or more corporations "where the effect of such acquisition or the use of such stock by the voting or granting of proxies or otherwise may be to substantially lessen competition between such corporations . . . or tend to create a monopoly of any line of commerce." Thus, Section 7 covers both direct acquisition of the stock of a competitor and the merger of two or more competitors through a formation of a holding company.

Section 8 deals with the problem of interlocking directorates. Its principal provision is that "no person shall at the same time be a director in any two or more corporations" capitalized at over $1 million, "if such corporations are or shall have been theretofore, by virtue of their business and location of operation, competitors, so that the elimination of competition by agreement between them would constitute a violation of any of the provisions of any of the antitrust laws."

There are no per se prohibitions in the Clayton Act; neither is there any rule of reason based on intent. Instead, specific forms of conduct are forbidden only in instances in which they may lead to certain anticompetitive effects. Not only is effect substituted for intent, but the test of illegality is prospective rather than retrospective in that the act requires the enforcement agencies and the courts to estimate probable future effects.

A final distinction between the Sherman and the Clayton Acts is that only civil remedies can be imposed for violations of Sections 2, 3, 7, and 8 of the Clayton Act—orders to cease and desist or otherwise correct the offending practices rather than fines or jail terms. Violations of these orders, however, constitute contempt of court and therefore are criminal offenses punishable by fine and imprisonment. Further, Section 4 extends the treble-damages provision of the Sherman

Act to cover injuries resulting from violations of any of the antitrust laws. Section 5 states that any decision against a defendant on either criminal or civil charges may be used as prima facie evidence of guilt in a subsequent treble-damage suit, leaving proof of injury and the monetary value of the damage as the major burden of a plaintiff. There is an escape clause, though, in that Section 5 is made inapplicable in the cases of consent judgments or decrees agreed to by the prosecuting agency or plaintiff and the defendant before testimony has been taken. The result is to put pressure on firms to settle with the enforcement agencies out of court.

The Federal Trade Commission Act

The Federal Trade Commission Act[45] established the Federal Trade Commission (FTC) as an independent commission with five commissioners, appointed for seven-year terms, no more than three of whom could be members of the same political party. The FTC was given authority to enforce the Clayton Act but not the Sherman Act.

The Federal Trade Commission Act contains only one substantive provision. The first paragraph of Section 5 reads, in full, "that unfair methods of competition in commerce are hereby declared unlawful." In drafting this section of the act, the 1914 Congress reverted to the tactic of its 1890 predecessors: the phrase "unfair methods of competition" was one long recognized in the common law. By 1914, it clearly covered practices such as industrial espionage, false disparagement of a competitor's products, bribery of competitors' employees, and misrepresentation of one's own products in such a way as to suggest that they were those of a competitor. In using common-law language, the proponents of the act stated they were giving the FTC authority to use its expertise to identify, define, and take action against new forms of unfair competition as business conditions and practices changed.

In enforcing the substantive provisions of both the Clayton and the Federal Trade Commission Acts, the FTC is empowered to investigate suspected violations, serve complaints, hold hearings, and issue cease-and-desist or affirmative orders. An order of the commission may be appealed to the courts, but the "findings of the commission as to the facts, if supported by testimony, shall be conclusive."[46]

An investigation by the FTC may lead to an informal settlement under which company officials and members of the FTC staff agree to a stipulation ending òr modifying the challenged behavior. If such an informal settlement cannot be reached or if the FTC attorney in charge of the investigation doubts the good faith of a firm in abiding by a stipulation, a formal complaint is issued. The complaint is heard by an administrative law judge, whose decision may be appealed to the full commission by either the cited firm or the FTC staff. Only after the commission has reached a decision and handed down an order may a firm appeal to the courts.

Conclusion

With passage of the 1914 legislation, the main features of the nation's antitrust policy were established. As Bork notes, "The rest of antitrust history is merely elaboration."[47]

In summary, under the Sherman, Clayton, and Federal Trade Commission Acts, there are four basic types of antitrust offense. First, some business activities, such as collusive price-fixing and market-sharing, are per se illegal. Second, other types of conduct that appear to be ancillary to legitimate business objectives but nevertheless restrain or monopolize trade will be judged by the rule of reason, under which the legal issue is the primary intent or purpose of the perpetrators. Third, still other practices—such as price discrimination, exclusive dealing, and acquisition of the share capital of another corporation— are judged by their probable effects, regardless of motive. Fourth, certain forms of conduct held to be unfair methods of competition, under changing standards of fairness, are proscribed.

The antitrust laws deal with business conduct. There is no provision forbidding monopoly itself. But conduct that is aimed at obtaining or maintaining monopolistic power is forbidden, whether or not the power is exercised.

Enforcement of the Sherman Act is the responsibility of the Antitrust Division of the Department of Justice. The Clayton Act is enforced by both the Antitrust Division and the FTC. Section 5 of the Federal Trade Commission Act is enforced solely by the FTC.

PRINCIPAL AMENDMENTS TO THE BASIC ANTITRUST LAWS

Of a number of amendments to the antitrust laws since 1914, three are particularly important: the Robinson-Patman Act, the Wheeler-Lea Act, and the Celler-Kefauver Act.

The Robinson-Patman Act

In 1936, Congress passed the Robinson-Patman Act,[48] amending Section 2 of the Clayton Act. The Robinson-Patman Act was introduced for the avowed purpose of protecting small independent retailers and wholesalers from the growing inroads of chain stores. Indeed, its supporters described it as an "anti-chain store" bill. The bill, initially introduced in the House of Representatives and incorporated into the act as passed, was drafted by the counsel for the United States Wholesale Grocers Association.[49]

One of the most basic changes made by the Robinson-Patman Act, in Section 2(a), broadened the test of illegality in Section 2 of the Clayton Act, so that it now reads "where the effect of such discrimination may be substantially to lessen competition or tend to create a monopoly in any line of commerce, *or to injure, destroy, or prevent competition with any person who either grants or knowingly receives the benefit of such discrimination, or with customers of either of them.*" The addition, indicated by italics, has been interpreted as a deliberate effort to protect individual competitors rather than to promote the process of competition. Other provisions of the Robinson-Patman Act are discussed in Chapter 18.

The Wheeler-Lea Act

In 1938, the Wheeler-Lea Act[50] amended Section 5 of the Federal Trade Commission Act by adding "unfair or deceptive practices in commerce" to the prohibition of unfair methods of competition. This amendment responded to a court decision that held that the FTC was not authorized to take action against a firm charged with false and misleading— indeed, medically dangerous—advertising of a thyroid obesity remedy when no effect on competition could be shown, but only deception of customers.[51] The Wheeler-Lea Act also strengthened the administrative power of the FTC by providing that an order of the commission becomes final unless appealed to the courts within 60 days.

The Celler-Kefauver Act

The Celler-Kefauver Act of 1950[52] amended Section 7 of the Clayton Act, converting it from a prohibition against acquisition of part or all of the outstanding stock of a competitor into a general antimerger statute. The act made two major changes. First, the prohibition against merger was made general by including asset acquisitions as well as those of share capital. Second, the test of illegality was broadened from a lessening of competition solely between the acquired and acquiring companies to a lessening of competition "in any line of commerce in any section of the country."

Other Antitrust Amendments

In a 1980 amendment, the scope of Section 7 was broadened again in response to a 1975 Supreme Court decision holding that the Celler-

Kefauver Act dealt only with mergers in interstate competition and not with those merely affecting such commerce.[53]   In the 1980 amendment, the word *person* was substituted for *corporation,* and the phrase "or in any activity affecting commerce" was inserted throughout, so that the section now reads:

> No person engaged in commerce or in any activity affecting commerce shall acquire, directly or indirectly, the whole or any part of the stock or other share capital and no person subject to the jurisdiction of the Federal Trade Commission shall acquire the whole or any part of the assets of another person engaged also in commerce or in any activity affecting commerce, where in any line of commerce or in any activity affecting commerce in any section of the country, the effect of such acquisition may be substantially to lessen competition, or to tend to create a monopoly.

Among other changes in the antitrust laws, criminal penalties under the Sherman Act have been raised several times.   Violations have been raised from misdemeanor to felony status.   Since 1974, individuals can be sentenced to a maximum of three years in prison and be fined a maximum of $100,000 for each criminal offense, and corporations can be fined up to $1 million per violation.   In 1984, the exposure to fines was increased by legislation providing that both corporations and individuals found guilty of felony violations of federal law may be fined (1) the amount specified in the statute violated, (2) twice the gross amount gained from the violation or lost by victims, or (3) $250,000 for individuals and $500,000 for firms, whichever is the largest of the three.

THE PURPOSES OF ANTITRUST: ECONOMIC EFFICIENCY AND SOCIOPOLITICAL REFORM

What *Are* the Objectives of Antitrust?

The generally accepted view of the intent of Congress in passing the Sherman Act is summed up in Thorelli's previously cited observation that "the Sherman Act embodies what is to be characterized as an eminently 'social' purpose."   The courts have reflected this view in several decisions, beginning with Peckham's observation that even permanently lowered prices set by the trusts could not justify driving out of business the "small dealers and worthy men whose lives have been spent therein."   One of the most widely cited of such passages is that of Judge Learned Hand in the *Alcoa* decision of 1945.

> [Congress] did not condone "good trusts" and condemn "bad" ones; it forbade all.   Moreover, in so doing it was not necessarily actuated by economic motives alone.   It is possible, because of its indirect social or

moral effect, to prefer a system of small producers, each dependent for his success upon his own skill and character, to one in which the great mass of those engaged must accept the direction of a few. These considerations, which we have suggested only as possible purposes of the Act, we think the decisions prove to have been in fact its purposes.[54]

In 1963, the Supreme Court, rejecting an argument that under the Clayton Act the anticompetitive effects of a merger in one market could be offset by procompetitive effects in others, stated, "Congress determined to preserve our traditionally competitive economy. It therefore proscribed anticompetitive mergers, the benign and the malignant alike, fully aware, we must assume, that some price might have to be paid."[55]

Maximization of Consumer Welfare. In a 1966 article, however, Bork contended that the intent of Congress in passing the Sherman Act was to maximize consumer welfare—the identical test of static economic efficiency as that applied in modern microeconomic theory. In Bork's words, "Congress intended the courts to implement (that is, to take into account in the decision of cases) *only* that value we would today call consumer welfare."[56]

Senator Sherman and his colleagues fortunately did not need help from the economists of 1890, with all of their antipathy to antitrust, to understand that the effect of market power exerted by a profit-maximizing firm would be to raise price through restriction of output. Bork correctly points out that in the Senate debate on the Sherman bill, the bill's most vocal supporters identified price enhancement as the fundamental evil wrought by the trusts. Nevertheless, other evils—sociopolitical in modern terms—were also identified. On the matter of protection of small business, for example, Sherman stated:

> I am not opposed to combinations in and of themselves; I do not care how much men combine for proper objects; but when they combine with a purpose to prevent competition, so that if a humble man starts a business in opposition to them, solitary and alone, in Ohio or anywhere else, they will crowd him down and they will sell their product at a loss or give it away in order to prevent competition, and when that is established by evidence that can not be questioned, then it is the duty of the courts to intervene and prevent it by injunction and by the ordinary remedial rights afforded by the courts.[57]

Senator Sherman, in expressing concern for the "humble man," did not face the fundamental issue posed by Bork: What if the humble man is forced out of business by a more efficient trust with a lower profit-maximizing price rather than one selling at a loss?

Sherman also warned his colleagues of the threat of political instability:

Sir, now the people of the United States as well as of other countries are feeling the power and grasp of these combinations, and are demanding of every Legislature and of Congress a remedy for this evil, only grown into huge proportions in recent times. . . . You must heed their appeal or be ready for the socialist, the communist, and the nihilist. Society is now disturbed by forces never felt before.[58]

Bork's study does not purport to show that consumer welfare was the only goal of congressmen who voted for the Sherman Act. Rather, he argues that consumer welfare was the "predominant" goal and that "other values are superfluous to the decision of cases since none of them would in any way alter the result that would be reached by considering consumer welfare alone." Bork concludes that "since the legislative history of the Sherman Act shows consumer welfare to be the decisive value it should be treated by the court as the only value."[59]

Multiple Objectives.   Not all legal scholars share Bork's view. For example, in the 1982 edition of his book *The Federal Antitrust Laws,* J. G. Van Cise maintains that the courts have "studied carefully the hearings, reports, and debates of our federal legislatures. In the course of this judicial research the courts have determined that Congress has sought to achieve—through prohibiting restraints threatening a competitive economy—the three-fold blessings of material prosperity, political democracy, and an ethical society."[60]

We are probably forced back to the insights of Dewey and Letwin, that the motives of Congress were mixed and complex and that it is fruitless to try to reconstruct congressional intent from the written record.

What *Ought* to Be the Objectives of Antitrust?

The more fundamental issue remains—what *ought* to be the proper objectives of antitrust policy. More specifically, should the efficiency with which the economy promotes consumer welfare be the sole standard, or should the impact of economic activity on social and political conditions also be considered? Arguments over the intent of the 1890 Congress probably cloud rather than clarify this question. The issue is in part a normative one: What values does society wish to foster? It is also, in part, one of administrative efficacy.

Even agreeing that there is need for public policies to deal with the sociopolitical problems raised by corporate concentration, it is still not at all clear that such policies are best implemented through antitrust laws. Political corruption, for example, might better be dealt with by the Federal Bureau of Investigation and state law enforcement agencies. Possible abuses against investors are now primarily the responsibility of the Securities and Exchange Commission. Redistribution of income poses far broader issues and is addressed in a comprehensive way through the nation's tax and welfare systems.

This book's approach is that the appropriate goals of antitrust are still open to question. The *economics* of industrial organization focuses on formulating a standard of consumer welfare, evaluating how well or poorly that standard is met in various markets (the basic test of economic efficiency), and appraising policy options in terms of how effectively they improve consumer welfare. But economists concerned with public policy must also be sensitive to conflicts between economic efficiency and social, political, and ethical goals (as well as areas of mutual reinforcement). To deny that such conflicts exist or are important is wishful thinking.

ENDNOTES

[1] Public Law No. 190, approved July 2, 1890 (1st sess. 51st Cong., U.S. Stat. L., vol. 26, p. 209). The vote was unanimous in the House of Representatives, and there was only one dissenting vote in the Senate.

[2] A *substantive* provision in law declares certain acts illegal, prescribes rights and obligations of individuals, or states the conditions under which a cause of action exists. *Procedural* provisions provide for implementation of the law—dates of effectiveness, enforcement authority and procedures, penalties, and special defenses. Essentially, the substantive provisions declare what is made illegal by a law, and the procedural provisions describe how the law is to be enforced.

[3] "Laissez-faire" has been given many meanings and been used to support widely differing ideologies and policies. Sidney Fine, *Laissez-Faire and the General Welfare State* (Ann Arbor: University of Michigan Press, 1956), p. vii, defines the basic meaning of the term: "to embrace the arguments of those who accepted government as a necessity but nevertheless wished to see its functions reduced to the narrowest possible limits." G. D. H. Cole, "Laissez Faire" in *Encyclopaedia of the Social Sciences*, ed. E. R. A. Seligman (New York: Macmillan, 1933), vol. 9, pp. 15–20, notes that U.S. economists in the 1880s, under the emerging influence of the marginal analysis school, held laissez-faire to imply that freely expressed consumer demand should determine supply without any interference with the conditions of supply. Under this concept of laissez-faire, control of supply by a private monopolist was to be just as much condemned as governmental interference. But the laissez-faire economists did not believe that private monopoly, in the absence of special governmental privilege such as patents, exclusive franchises, or tariffs, could survive unless it was justified by economies of scale.

[4] William Letwin, *Law and Economic Policy in America: The Evolution of the Sherman Antitrust Act* (New York: Random House, 1965), p. 70.

[5] In 1913, Oswald W. Knauth noted a "host of articles" that "flooded" the magazines during the late 1880s. He observed that "they were almost unanimously of a character to arouse popular fear of the new form of industrial organization" coming to prominence with the trust movement. See Knauth, "The Policy of the United States towards Industrial Monopoly," *Studies in History, Economics and Public Law*, no. 138 (New York: Columbia University Press, 1913), pp. 175–404, at p. 188. John D. Clark, in *The Federal Trust Policy* (Baltimore, Md.: Johns Hopkins Press, 1931), pp. 31, 53, subsequently criticized Knauth, arguing that he had merely "gathered a handful of eye-catching titles" and that a lack of strong public interest in the trust problem is evidenced by the hasty, almost casual manner in which Congress passed the Sherman Act. More recent writers,

notably Letwin and Thorelli (whose studies are discussed in this chapter), have concluded that Knauth's view was by far the more accurate of the two. The position of Knauth, Letwin, and Thorelli is bolstered by a passage in Senator Sherman's autobiography, in which he discussed the passage of his antitrust bill and commented, "I know of no object of greater importance to the people." See John Sherman, *Recollections of Forty Years in the House, Senate, and Cabinet: An Autobiography*, vol. 2 (New York: Werner, 1895), p. 1076.

[6]The phrase is taken from the 1888 presidential campaign platform of the Democratic Party. Quoted by Hans B. Thorelli, *The Federal Antitrust Policy: Origination of an American Tradition* (Winchester, Mass.: Allen & Unwin, 1954), p. 151.

[7]Donald Dewey, *Monopoly in Economics and Law* (Skokie, Ill.: Rand McNally, 1959), pp. 142–43, 157.

[8]Letwin, *Law and Economic Policy*, p. 53.

[9]Thorelli, *Federal Antitrust Policy*, p. 227.

[10]See, for example, Appalachian Coals, Inc. v. United States, 288 U.S. 344, 359–60 (1933), and United States v. E. I. du Pont de Nemours & Co., 351 U.S. 377, 386 (1956).

[11]United States v. Trans-Missouri Freight Ass'n., 166 U.S. 290; United States v. Addyston Pipe and Steel Co., et al., 85 Fed. 271; Standard Oil Co. v. United States, 221 U.S. 1. For interesting and perceptive studies of these and related cases and of the early interpretations of the Sherman Act, see Robert H. Bork, *The Antitrust Paradox: A Policy at War with Itself* (New York: Basic Books, 1978), and John R. Carter, "From Peckham to White: Economic Welfare and the Rule of Reason," *Antitrust Bulletin* 25, no. 2 (Summer 1980), pp. 275–95.

[12]53 Fed. 440, 449.

[13]58 Fed. 58, 72–73.

[14]91.

[15]166 U.S. 290, 318.

[16]328.

[17]331.

[18]323.

[19]346.

[20]351.

[21]355.

[22]Bork, *The Antitrust Paradox*, p. 26.

[23]85 Fed. 271, 282.

[24]282–83.

[25]283.

[26]291.

[27]293.

[28]175 U.S. 211 (1899).

[29]Ida M. Tarbell, *The History of the Standard Oil Company*, 2 vols. (New York: McClure Phillips, 1904).

[30]221 U.S. 1, 34.

[31]United States v. American Tobacco Co., 221 U.S. 106.

[32]221 U.S. 1, 54. (Italics added.)

[33]58. (Italics added.)

[34]60.

[35]66.

[36]W. H. Taft, *The Anti-Trust Act and the Supreme Court* (New York: Harper & Row, 1914).

[37]Letwin, *Law and Economic Policy,* pp. 266–67. See also Alan D. Neale and D. G. Goyder, *The Antitrust Laws of the United States,* 3d ed. (London: Cambridge University Press, 1980), pp. 23–30, esp. p. 29.

[38]Taft, *The Anti-Trust Act,* p. 96.

[39]Quoted in Henderson, *Federal Trade Commission,* p. 16.

[40]Letwin, *Law and Economic Policy,* p. 265.

[41]Taft, *The Anti-Trust Act,* pp. 5–6.

[42]Ibid., pp. 113–14.

[43]Excerpt from an address given in Milwaukee, Wisconsin, on October 14, 1912. Quoted in William Griffith, ed., *Roosevelt: His Life, Meaning, and Messages,* (New York: Current Literature Publishing, 1919), vol. 3, *New Roosevelt Messages,* p. 757.

[44]Public Law No. 212, approved October 15, 1914 (2d sess. 63d Cong., U.S. Stat. L., vol. 38, p. 730).

[45]Public Law No. 203, approved September 26, 1914 (2d sess. 63d Cong., U.S. Stat. L., vol. 38, p. 717).

[46]Section 5.

[47]Bork, *The Antitrust Paradox,* p. 47.

[48]Public Law No. 692, approved June 19, 1936 (2d sess. 74th Cong., U.S. Stat. L., vol. 49, p. 1526).

[49]United States Department of Justice, *Report on the Robinson-Patman Act* (Washington D.C.: U.S. Government Printing Office, 1977), p. 114.

[50]Public Law No. 447, approved March 21, 1938 (3d sess. 75th Cong., U.S. Stat. L., vol. 52, p. 111).

[51]Federal Trade Commission v. Raladam Co., 283 U.S. 643 (1931).

[52]Public Law No. 890, approved December 29, 1950 (2d sess. 81st Cong., U.S. Stat. L., vol. 64, p. 1125).

[53]United States v. American Building Maintenance Industries, 422 U.S. 271.

[54]United States v. Aluminum Company of America, 148 F. 2d 416, 427.

[55]United States v. Philadelphia National Bank, 374 U.S. 321, 371.

[56]Robert H. Bork, "Legislative Intent and the Policy of the Sherman Act," *Journal of Law and Economics* 9 (October 1966), pp. 7–48, at p. 7 (italics added).

[57]*Congressional Record* 21 (1890), p. 2569.

[58]Ibid., p. 2460.

[59]Bork, "Legislative Intent," p. 11.

[60]J. G. Van Cise, *The Federal Antitrust Laws,* 4th ed. (Washington, D.C.: American Enterprise Institute, 1982), p. 20.

PART TWO

Structure, Conduct, and Performance: The Analytical Framework

CHAPTER SIX

The Structure-Conduct-Performance Paradigm

WHAT IS A PARADIGM, AND WHY?

In the social sciences and other studies of human behavior, the word *paradigm* refers to a pattern, model, or example used as the underlying conceptual framework within which a set of social interactions can be studied. The Hegelian dialectic of thesis, antithesis, and synthesis is, for example, the paradigm, or pattern, used by Karl Marx in his theoretical and empirical analyses of capitalism. The lives of great religious figures are frequently cited as paradigms, since precepts of ethical, moral, and ritualistic behavior may be based as much on these models as on the actual teachings of a religion's founder.

To be relevant to the real world, a theory (which abstracts from reality in order to simplify complex real-world systems) must be premised on a meaningful and sensible paradigm. Such a paradigm provides a framework in which to ascertain elements of reality that should be abstracted (singled out) to identify the crucial cause-and-effect relationships and thus explain and predict actual phenomena. In the social sciences, which deal with man-made institutions and systems, the careful formulation of an appropriate paradigm is particularly important to successful analysis and is sometimes the most difficult stage of the process. Social organizations are the purposeful constructs of human beings, created to achieve particular goals and solve particular problems, although leading at times to unintended outcomes.

Most students of industrial organization are primarily interested in assessing how well the economy functions and finding ways to improve its performance. Thus, standards, or norms, are needed that will permit us to evaluate the economic performance of a particular industry or the market system and rate it as "good" or "bad." We also want to identify the most important determinants of such performance and the effects of various public policies.

FROM STRUCTURE TO CONDUCT TO PERFORMANCE: THE LINKS IN THE FUNDAMENTAL CHAIN

The most widely accepted paradigm of industrial organization stems from various concepts of the interactions among industry or market structure, business conduct, and the social and economic performance of an industry.

Structure as the Firm's External Environment.

Edward S. Mason, who first proposed and cogently argued the merits of the structure-conduct-performance approach, defined market structure in such a way that it followed from the definition itself that structure exerts a major influence on business conduct. "The structure of a seller's market, then," he wrote, "includes all those considerations which he takes into account in determining his business policies and practices. His market includes all buyers and sellers, of whatever product, whose action he considers to influence his volume of sales."[1] Mason went on to describe the structural conditions that would be likely to have the greatest impact on conduct. These included:

- The product's economic characteristics, such as whether it is a consumer or producer good, durable or nondurable, and differentiated or standardized.
- The firm's cost and production conditions, including ratios of fixed to variable costs at various levels of output.
- The numbers and relative sizes of buyers and sellers whose actions the firm had to take into account and the ease of entry for new firms.
- Demand conditions—including sales trends, seasonal or cyclical fluctuations around these trends, and buyers' knowledge of the product's characteristics.
- The nature of the distribution channels.

This list is a pioneering effort. Since Mason's initial formulation of the paradigm in 1939, others have identified additional structural features including extent of diversification, minimum efficient scale of operation, ease of exit, and advances in scientific and engineering knowledge. A more comprehensive and up-to-date list is presented and discussed in Chapter Seven. But Mason's basic insight is fundamental to the paradigm. As he stated, "Under similar market conditions may not firms be expected to pursue similar policies and practices? A careful study of the empirically determinable differences in market structure may go far in explaining observable differences in policy and practice."[2]

From Structure to Conduct

Industrial organization economists, particularly those concerned with antitrust policy and enforcement of the antitrust laws, are interested not only in price levels and rates of output under differing structural conditions but also why forms of conduct such as collusive price fixing, predatory pricing, price discrimination, tying arrangements, price leadership, pricing to limit or exclude entry, resale price maintenance, and agreements to divide markets or restrict output are found in some industries but not in others.

Since Mason's pioneering work, the concept of business conduct has been expanded to include areas other than determination of price and output. Industry structure has been studied to explain the forces either stimulating or retarding research and development (R&D) efforts, advertising, merger and acquisition activities, and product diversification.

The fundamental causal relationship between structure and conduct is inherent in the framework of microeconomic theory, as illustrated by the following propositions:

1. Firms will be able to set price (a form of conduct) only if their products are sold in the structural setting of a less than purely competitive market. Otherwise, all they can do is decide how much they wish to sell at the price determined by the impersonal market forces of supply and demand.
2. Successful collusion depends on structural characteristics; the two most important are the number of possible conspirators and the ease with which newcomers can enter the market.
3. Price discrimination requires at least two sets of customers with different demand elasticities, so that the profit-maximizing prices charged to each set will differ. Also, there must be some barrier to prevent those paying the lower price from reselling to customers charged the higher price.
4. The nature of the product and its users will determine whether false or misleading advertising is likely to be a profitable form of conduct.

5. The higher the target firm's fixed costs relative to its variable costs, the more effective a tactic predatory pricing is.
6. The degree of competition in and the ease of entry into the market for a potential new product are important considerations in a firm's R&D planning.

Recognition of the structure-conduct link as pervasive permits objective study of individual industries. A market characterized by price discrimination, overt collusion, predatory pricing, or false advertising is not necessarily or even probably populated by business men and women who are more venal, unethical, and less scrupulous than those operating in markets where prices and production are determined independently, advertising is truthful and tasteful, and all customers are treated equally. Indeed, the structure-conduct approach encourages us to understand business behavior without moral judgment of its practitioners.

From Conduct to Performance

While it is both possible and advisable to engage in value-free analysis of business conduct, normative judgments are necessary in dealing with industry performance. But economists, as social scientists, measure performance against societal rather than private criteria of what is "good" and "bad." In Mason's words, we want to know "the consequences ... for the functioning of the economy."[3] Further, we want to be able to evaluate performance to ascertain whether governmental interference in private markets is justified and, if so, what the probable effects of various policy actions will be.

The Criteria of Performance. Performance is a multidimensional concept. In his initial discussion, Mason identified two aspects: the allocation of resources among different users and the stability of production at full-employment levels. Shortly thereafter, Joseph Schumpeter argued that technical progress and the economic growth it engendered are far more important than static efficiency in resource use. "A system—any system," Schumpeter wrote, "economic or other—that at *every* given point of time fully utilizes its possibilities to the best advantage may yet in the long run be inferior to a system that does so at *no* given point of time, because the latter's failure to do so may be a condition for the level or speed of long-run performance."[4] Today, many economists would add equitable distribution of income to the list of performance criteria. While a precise and value-free standard of equity in income distribution cannot be formulated, most would agree that monopolistic profit represents unearned income to the monopolist and exploitation of the consumer.[5] The dollar value of the transfer may be much higher than the cost to society as a whole of the misallocation of resources.

The Complexity of Establishing Standards.   Granted that efficient resource allocation, macroeconomic stability with full employment, rapid rates of innovation and growth, and equitable income distribution (however defined) are all desirable economic goals, we still face problems of choice if all of our performance objectives cannot be pursued simultaneously and consistently.   People would disagree as to whether performance had improved or worsened if, to draw on Schumpeter's argument, the rate of innovation increased but, at the same time, resources became less efficiently allocated as an unavoidable side effect.   As the result of such a change in the economy's overall performance, we would be worse off today but would expect society to be better off at some time in the future.   Our judgment on performance and hence on public policy towards business would depend on the relative strengths of our desires for present and future income or even on how much importance we attach to the welfare of the next generation.

Further, standards of performance may vary among nations in different economic circumstances and with different economic problems.   Some nations, particularly developing countries, might regard a favorable balance of payments in international trade as crucial to growth and therefore consider the most important dimension of an industry's performance to be its contribution to an export surplus. Some people or societies may value goals that are anathema to others. For example, in "garrison states" consumer welfare is a subordinate consideration and economic activity is judged primarily on its contribution to the nation's military might.   Military might may be desired for purely defensive reasons, entirely aggressive ones, or to gratify some combination of national objectives.

Well-meaning people with no personal stake in the outcome may disagree on performance norms for many valid reasons.   The most that can be expected of the structure-conduct-performance paradigm, or any other systematic approach to the study of industrial organization, is that it identify the major determinants of performance and be able to describe and predict the effects of various public policy alternatives on these determinants and thus on performance.   Policymakers can sensibly indulge their preferences, or those they believe their constituents to hold, only to the extent that they are adequately informed as to the likely effects of their actions on the performance of the economy.   But although the weighing of performance norms is a subjective matter, it is a crucial feature of the quality of a society.   (Consider again the garrison-state example.)

In sum, the structure-conduct-performance approach posits a fundamental causal change running from market structure to business conduct to industry performance, as illustrated:

$$Structure \rightarrow Conduct \rightarrow Performance$$

The Structural Setting of Conduct: A Necessary Qualification

One important feature of the conduct-performance link cannot be captured easily in a simple sketch of the causal flow. We must recognize that in different structural settings, the same type of conduct may lead to different types of performance. For example, in two antitrust decisions, the Supreme Court sought to identify the economic effects of agreements among competing firms to exchange price information. In both of these cases, the majority opinions were against the defendants.[6] Yet the Court recognized that "the exchange of price data and other information among competitors does not invariably have anti-competitive effects; indeed, such practices can in certain circumstances increase economic efficiency and render markets more rather than less competitive."[7] In markets with many small firms, knowledge of other firms' current prices should facilitate flexible competitive price responses.

The majority opinions in both cases, however, took note that the structures of the defendants' industries differed in significant respects from the structural conditions associated with effective competition. These opinions held that where (1) each of a few sellers tries to take account of the effects of its pricing changes on the prices charged by the others, (2) demand is inelastic, and (3) customers typically shop around while making frequent small purchases for their immediate needs, the industrywide practice of providing competitors with information on individual sales to specific customers serves mainly to stabilize prices and to retard their downward movements. Since in both cases the defendants knew that the effect of the practice in their particular industrial structures was to restrain competition, they were presumed to have intended this effect and thus to be guilty of violating Section 1 of the Sherman Act under the rule of reason.

In later chapters, we will see that market structure may, similarly, be a basic determinant of the performance associated with other types of conduct, such as price discrimination, tying arrangements, territorial restraints on resale, and even collusive price-fixing. It does not follow from firm (albeit subjective) conclusions as to what constitutes good and bad economic performance, that certain forms of economic conduct are invariably good or bad. Rather, it is necessary to look at the market structure within which the conduct is occurring to assess its effect on performance.

THE STRUCTURALISTS AND THEIR CRITICS

The structure-conduct-performance approach lends itself to a simple interpretation if we ignore the complex features of goal determination and decision making within the modern large corporation. Micro-economic theory owes much of its power and precision to the assumption that the privately owned business firm's sole objective is the maximization of the present risk-adjusted value of future expected profit. Theorists recognize that this is an abstraction from a host of considerations motivating real-life business owners and managers, but the assumption does make it possible to construct a set of theoretical models with specified cause-and-effect relationships and determinate equilibrium levels of price and output. Further, it can be argued that the abstraction is not far from a realistic description of business goals and that theories using this abstraction are therefore not only manageable but also yield good approximations to reality.

If the assumption that profit maximization is the single goal of the firm is applied to the structure-conduct-performance paradigm, it is possible to drop conduct as an independent factor in the causal chain, leading to the proposition that structure determines performance:

$$\text{Structure} \rightarrow \text{Performance}$$

If structure includes all elements of the environment influencing business decision making and if all business owners and managers are strict profit maximizers, only one set of price and output decisions—the profit-maximizing combination—can result from a given market structure. The theorist need not be concerned with the forms of conduct and the specific tactics actually used by the various firms to impose their prices or dispose of their output. The prices and levels of production, within the structural context, in turn determine the industry's performance.

Defense of the Structuralist Approach

Economists who have accepted and used this variant of the paradigm have been labeled "structuralists." The structuralists do not believe the actual world of business is as utterly mechanistic as their model implies. Rather they contend that it is necessary to simplify and ignore qualifications (i.e., to abstract) to get to the essence of how business performance is determined and, more importantly, to be able to make statements relevant to large numbers of diverse firms and markets or to a nation's industrial sector in general.

Further pragmatic justification for the structuralist approach was cogently argued by Joe S. Bain in his book *Industrial Organization.*[8] Business conduct can take numerous, very different forms, within which various tactics are possible. Particular levels of industry price and output might, for example, be established by any one of several forms of overt collusion. Such collusion might involve either the price level or the rate of production. It could include various tactics such as conspiratorial meetings, agreed-upon signals, regular exchange of statistical data, or communication through an intermediary such as a trade association or interlocking memberships on boards of directors. If one type of collusion were suppressed, the firms might find it easy to adopt another. Further, in many if not most structural situations, different forms of conduct might lead to almost exactly the same results for price and output. Even if all possible collusive tactics could be eliminated, perhaps much the same outcome could be obtained through price leadership, actual or threatened predatory pricing, or merger of troublesome independent small firms with larger ones. Only the collective ingenuity of the nation's business people limits the nature and types of business conduct. Many different types of conduct will yield virtually identical levels of price and output and, therefore, economic performance as long as the structural setting remains unchanged.

The investigator may find it impossible to identify the conduct actually practiced in an industry. Firms engaged in illegal or unethical conduct will try to hide it. Also, honest and ethical firms may have legitimate competitive reasons for not wanting rivals to know their tactics. Both diversity and obscurity of conduct, Bain argued, lead to a situation in which "we find that actual patterns of market conduct cannot be fully enough measured to permit us to establish empirically a meaningful association either between market conduct and performance, or between structure and market conduct." Accordingly, he continued, "It thus becomes expedient to test directly for net associations of market structure to market performance, leaving the detailed character of the implied linkage of conduct substantially unascertained."[9]

Structuralism's Implications for Public Policy

Although most structuralists would, like Bain, plead expediency, they also contend that the direct structure-performance link is significant enough in the real world to have major implications for public policy. The most important of these implications has been that conduct-oriented proscriptions in the antitrust laws and remedies in individual civil antitrust cases forbidding or requiring certain forms of conduct are likely to be ineffective, as are fines for illegal conduct in criminal cases. If the law or a court decree forbids a certain type of conduct, the reasoning goes, firms will often find other ways to achieve the same ends, as long as the structural conditions in their industries remain unchanged. If they cannot find effective alternatives, structural pressures to persist in the original illegal conduct will be so great that enforcement of the law or decree will be difficult, time consuming, expensive, and often frustrated.

It is not an attractive prospect to have the government involved in a persistent round of investigations, trials, fines, imprisonments, and court decrees in protracted combat with the ever-changing business population of a particular industry. Nor, structuralists contend, do we want to be in a situation where effective antitrust enforcement involves the burdensome task of constant policing and may also require taking actions of dubious fairness against new and hitherto not illegal business tactics and practices. For the structuralists, the only generally effective remedies for industries that persistently perform badly are such forms of restructuring as dissolution, divestiture, or elimination of barriers to entry.

Legal scholars, judges, antitrust officials, politicians, and others who advocate more drastic restructuring of the economy under the antitrust laws are frequently labeled structuralists; and in some writings, the term has been synonymous with the older and more graphic term *trustbuster*. But throughout this book, the word *structuralist* will be confined to those economists who advocate an analytical approach premised on a direct causal link from structure to performance, regardless of whether they think that there are few or many U.S. industries today that are performing badly.

Alternatives to Structuralism

One of the earliest and most influential alternatives to the structuralist position was offered in a 1954 book by Joel B. Dirlam and Alfred E. Kahn.[10] The crux of their position is that, as an empirical matter, the market structure of the U.S. economy is conducive to rigorous competition throughout the private sector. Indeed, market forces put severe pressures to compete on firms in most industries that are not subject to direct regulation. "A broad sampling of opinion among economists," they wrote, "of a wide variety of general attitudes toward big business and the antitrust laws, discloses a surprising concurrence in the view that pure, noncollusive oligopoly is not the problem that has been popularly depicted."[11] The antitrust laws, in their opinion, were based on a similar view: "The theory underlying the antitrust laws is that except in certain unusual kinds of industries (the public utilities) monopoly will not become a serious problem so long as businessmen are prevented from engaging in collusive or exclusive tactics that suppress or subvert the competitive process."[12]

The primary role of antitrust policy, according to Dirlam and Kahn, should be to control the behavior of firms that are under the intense pressure of competitive market structures. (Firms' responses to a competitive environment might include seeking to eliminate or alleviate the pressures to compete through mutual agreement, predatory attacks on vigorous competitors, exclusionary practices, or attempts to monopolize through merger and acquisition.) If only "fair" methods of competition are permitted, performance will be good in most industries. Dirlam and Kahn, acknowledging the difficulty of defining fair competitive behavior, argued that the development of the rule of reason by the courts in interpreting the Sherman Antitrust Act, with the judiciary's emphasis on ascertaining the intent or purpose behind business behavior, provides an adequate standard of fairness.

This line of criticism is not inconsistent with the basic structure-conduct-performance framework. Rather, it provides an alternative to the structuralist approach through its emphasis on the independent role of conduct and the importance of the conduct-performance link. Dirlam and Kahn stated explicitly that "the market structure concept of monopoly still has an important role to play in antitrust policy." Knowledge of an industry's structure is necessary to determine appropriate legal remedies "by suggesting (for removal) the market elements that fostered illicit conduct."[13] The argument that they rejected was the deterministic one: that only variants of conduct yielding the same performance were consistent with a particular industry structure.

A causal diagram of the structure-conduct-performance paradigm, taking into account both the structuralist position and that taken by Dirlam and Kahn, must reinsert conduct into the linkage and recognize that the arrow showing the effect of conduct on performance designates more than mere transmission of structural effects, at the same time showing that structure may have an important direct influence on performance. The diagram thus appears as follows:

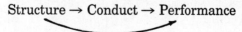

Structure → Conduct → Performance

FEEDBACK EFFECTS

The structure of an industry, like that of any social organization, is the result of human activities. Indeed, to a significant extent, the current structure of any industry is the result of the past conduct of the firms that have made up that industry since its inception.

From Conduct to Structure

Some aspects of industry structure that are largely determined by phenomena outside the industry's control or influence can be altered to some extent by the activities of the industry's firms. Optimal production techniques, and hence economies of scale, will be largely determined by the physical and chemical principles underlying processes of production and by current engineering knowledge, as well as by prices set by suppliers of inputs. But process R&D done within an industry changes at least some of the technological restraints on optimal techniques. The size of the market, and hence the number of optimally sized firms that the industry can support under any given set of production techniques, depends primarily on the level and elasticity of customer demand. But these demand characteristics are amenable to manipulation by advertising and by R&D aimed at the development of new and improved products.

Other changes in an industry's structure will be intentionally brought about by the behavior of its firms. The most obvious example is found in merger and acquisition activity. Another form of conduct with a deliberate feedback effect on structure is predatory pricing, which (although of dubious wisdom in most instances) will eliminate or reduce the market share of some firms and increase that of others when it does succeed. Barriers to entry of new firms, among the most important structural determinants of conduct, may be "natural," or unintended, such as scarcity of an essential resource or large technical economies of scale relative to the size of the market. But they may also be the "artificial" results of conduct, such as strong customer preferences for existing brands induced by heavy and persistent advertising, or acquisitions of patents that may or may not be used by the holder.

From Performance to Structure

There may also be feedback from performance to structure. The primary if not sole reason for using monopoly power to set prices above the competitive level and to restrict output below that level, and thus to misallocate resources, is to increase profits. Other things being equal, those firms in which performance, either good or bad, yields the highest rates of profit will have the greatest opportunities for growth

in existing markets and expansion into new ones, through both retained earnings and a greater facility in marketing new securities at
lower cost if they seek additional outside capital. The effect on structure may be direct (as in new investment in plant and equipment or
acquisition of rivals) or indirect, through conduct (if the reinvested
profits are used to finance higher levels of R&D, advertising, or even
predation).

Thus, our diagram of the complete paradigm should show these
feedback effects. Reflecting all of the considerations, the diagram now
appears as follows:

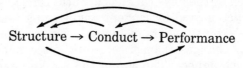

$$\text{Structure} \rightarrow \text{Conduct} \rightarrow \text{Performance}$$

A SUMMARY EVALUATION OF THE PARADIGM

It is unacceptably simplistic to treat industry or market structure as
the sole determinant of business conduct. Such a mechanistic link
requires two strong assumptions: First, we must assume that all business owners and managers in an industry (or the theorists putting
themselves in the role of the decision makers) have complete knowledge
of all relevant structural factors that will affect the outcomes of their
decisions. As a corollary, each owner or manager must know or assume that all other decision makers are similarly well informed. Second, we must assume that all of the firms are run by single-minded
maximizers of long-run profit.

The assumption of perfectly complete and accurate information on
structure is strained. Although the purpose of abstraction is to reduce
reality to a comprehensible set of interactions, abstractions must retain
the essential features of the real-world system being modeled. Remember that structure in its broadest conception is defined to include
all elements of the external environment impinging on business decisions. The flesh-and-blood business owner or manager, with human
limits on the capacity to absorb and use information (as well as the
economist analyzing the business system), must concentrate on an
analytically manageable number of important structural features. But
even among dedicated profit maximizers, this realistic limitation does
allow latitude for choice of behavior, based on differences in perception
of the operative structural influences.

Large firms in concentrated markets need not be long-run profit
maximizers. In less than highly competitive market structures, analogous to those found in the real world of modern large corporations,
many firms will earn above-normal returns, enabling them to continue

operation, even to thrive and grow, without constantly seeking to maximize their profits. As Sir John Hicks, 1972 winner of the Nobel Prize in economics, once noted, "The best of all monopoly profits is a quiet life."[14]

Thus the paradigmatic link between structure and conduct is perhaps best phrased as a proposition: *The structure of an industry or market is by far the most important, though not the sole, determinant of business conduct; and therefore, the economic analyst cannot adequately describe or fully understand the conduct of a business firm without putting it into the context of the industry's structure.*

Turning to the link between conduct and performance, we have already noted that the same forms of conduct may lead to very different kinds of performance in industries with different structures. Thus: *An industry's economic performance is determined by the conduct of its business firms within an underlying structural setting; therefore, one cannot identify the source of good or bad performance without making a study of both structure and conduct.*

Finally, we must never take the structure of an industry as given, or as the exogenously determined starting point of our analysis. Industry structure changes as time passes, often as a result of business firms' deliberate efforts to provide a more hospitable environment. In studying the problems of a particular industry and in evaluating public policy options toward it, understanding how the present structure evolved and identifying the existing forces contributing to its stability or change is often at least as important as depicting that structure as it now exists.

ENDNOTES

[1]Edward S. Mason, "Price and Production Policies of Large-Scale Enterprise," *American Economic Review* 29, no. 1 (March 1939), Part 2, pp. 61–74, at p. 69.

[2]Ibid., pp. 66–67.

[3]Ibid., p. 73.

[4]Joseph Schumpeter, *Capitalism, Socialism, and Democracy* (New York: Harper & Row, 1942), p. 83 (italics original).

[5]But, see John Rawls, *A Theory of Justice* (Cambridge, Mass.: Harvard University Press, 1971), for a leading attempt to formulate principles of a just income distribution derived from basic propositions of moral theory. For an alternative philosophic approach to the issue, see Robert Nozick, *Anarchy, State, and Utopia* (New York: Basic Books, 1974).

[6]United States v. Container Corporation, 393 U.S. 333 (1969); United States v. United States Gypsum Company, 438 U.S. 422 (1978).

[7]438 U.S. 422, 441.

[8]Joe S. Bain, *Industrial Organization*, 2d ed. (New York: John Wiley & Sons, 1968).

[9]Ibid., p. 329.

[10]Joel B. Dirlam and Alfred E. Kahn, *Fair Competition: The Law and Economics of Antitrust Policy* (Ithaca, N.Y.: Cornell University Press, 1954).

[11]Ibid., p. 33.

[12]Ibid., p. 141.

[13]Ibid., p. 34.

[14]John R. Hicks, "Annual Survey of Economic Theory: The Theory of Monopoly," *Econometrica* 3, no. 1 (January 1935), pp. 1–20, at p. 8.

CHAPTER SEVEN

The Elements of Industrial Structure

Having reviewed the fundamental structure-conduct-performance paradigm, we now turn to a closer examination of each of its three links. This chapter and the next discuss structure. Two chapters on forms of business conduct found in various structural settings follow, and then two on economic performance.

As defined by Edward S. Mason, *industry structure* comprises all aspects of the external business environment that a member of the industry "takes into account in determining his business policies and practices."[1] With such a sweeping definition, the most significant elements of this environment must be identified if the paradigm is to be of practical use. Initially, we might ask what general features of the business world—neglecting special characteristics of particular industries—would likely be of most concern to business men and women. Information relevant to most businesses would include answers to the following questions:

- Who are my competitors? How many are there, and how big are they, especially in comparison with me?
- In what market areas do I meet each of these competitors?
- What specific products do these competitors produce, and how closely do they resemble mine? Can I shelter myself from competition and increase customer loyalty by improving my products or making them more distinct from those of others?
- In what ways are market demand, cost conditions, or rivals' strategies likely to change, and how easily can I adjust to such changes? How rapidly and effectively can my competitors react to changes I might make in my price and output strategies? And how will my customers react to such changes?
- Under what conditions are new firms likely to enter one or more

of my markets or are existing firms likely to leave? How difficult would it be for me to enter new markets or withdraw from some of those I am now in?

- How dependent am I on a few suppliers for essential materials? Do I have adequate alternative sources of supply?

Such questions suggest an outline of the most commonly encountered elements of structure. Other elements are crucial in some industries but not all. In some, for example, current scientific and technological knowledge is an important part of the environment, while in others it has no significant effect. Also, the extent and effects of external economies and diseconomies vary widely from industry to industry.

MAJOR ELEMENTS OF INDUSTRIAL STRUCTURE

Elements of structure that the industrial organization literature suggests are central to application of the structure-conduct-performance paradigm are outlined below. Each of these elements is described in this chapter, and in a preliminary way, their primary links to conduct and performance are noted and discussed.

A. Size distribution of firms.
   1. At any one time.
   2. Over time.
      a. Entry to and exit from the industry.
      b. Stability of share and rank.
B. Nature of selling (customer) markets.
   1. Geographical boundaries.
      a. Local.
      b. Regional.
      c. National.
      d. International.
   2. Product boundaries.
   3. Problems in defining the market.
   4. Monopsonistic power of customers.
C. Nature of buying (supplier) markets.
   1. Monopsonistic and monopolistic power.
   2. Reliability of sources of supply.
   3. Vertical integration as an alternative to market exchange.
D. Nature of products.
   1. Consumer or producer goods.
   2. Homogeneous or differentiable products.
   3. Perishable or durable goods.
   4. Capital goods: the accelerator principle.

 E. Product diversification within firms.
  1. Corporate size and economic power.
  2. Advantages of product diversity.
   a. Tie-ins and reciprocal dealing.
   b. Mutual forbearance.
   c. Multimarket concept.
 F. Barriers to entry, mobility, and exit.
  1. Natural barriers to entry.
   a. Economies of scale relative to market size.
   b. Nonduplicable resources.
  2. Artificial barriers to entry.
   a. Public.
   b. Private.
    (1) Foreclosure.
    (2) Product differentiation.
    (3) Capital cost and access.
    (4) Imposition of higher cost.
  3. Barriers to mobility.
  4. Barriers to exit.
 G. Nature of costs.
  1. Absolute levels.
  2. Economies of scale and scope: real and pecuniary.
  3. Ratios of fixed to variable costs.
 H. Nature of demand.
  1. Elasticity.
   a. For the product.
   b. Facing the individual seller.
  2. Stability.
  3. Underlying rate of growth or decline.
 I. The technological base.
 J. Externalities.

This outline contains considerable overlap and duplication. As examples, the extent to which a product is durable or perishable is a major determinant of the stability of demand for it, and absolute cost advantages may represent a significant barrier to entry. But each of the items merits discussion in its own right.

SIZE DISTRIBUTION OF FIRMS

Perhaps the most immediately obvious elements of structure are the number of firms in an industry and their relative sizes. The standard market categories of microeconomic theory emphasize these elements, ranging from pure monopoly (a single seller) through various subcategories of oligopoly and imperfect or monopolistic competition (a few to a substantial number of price-setting firms that may be of similar or varying sizes) to pure competition (a large number of firms with each one so small that it cannot exert a perceptible influence on the price of the product.

Both the number of firms and differences in their sizes are regarded as determinants of market conduct. The larger the number of rivals each price-setting firm faces, the more difficult it becomes for any one of them to predict others' responses to a change in its price or other selling strategy. Further, the larger the number of competitors, the more likely it is that at least one will adopt a vigorously competitive strategy. The greater the variations in size, for any number, the greater the likelihood that optimal strategies and responses will vary.

If the market shares of various firms remain stable over a substantial period of time, a plausible inference is that competition among them has been restrained. If, on the other hand, an industry remains highly concentrated but the population of firms turns over rapidly, highly competitive conditions probably exist. Even without turnover, evidence of competition may be found in fluctuating market shares, regardless of the level of concentration at any given time.

NATURE OF SELLING (CUSTOMER) MARKETS

Geographical Boundaries

To a producer of ready-mixed concrete in Buffalo, New York, it is not particularly informative to know that there are about 4,500 ready-mixed concrete firms in the United States and that the largest four account for approximately 5 percent of the value of shipments. That producer is not worried about losing sales to a price-cutting competitor in Santa Fe, New Mexico. Markets for products with low unit costs of production and high unit costs of transportation are geographically limited.

Large numbers and low concentration ratios at the national level may disguise market power enjoyed by firms in local or regional market industries. Indeed, most pure monopolies in the United States are local-market ones; "everybody has seen towns with one bank, one hotel, one electric repair shop, one dry cleaner."[2] But nationwide firms may take advantage of multiplant economies of scale, and at the same time reduce shipping and other costs of serving regional markets, by operating plants in various locations around the country. In such cases, the figures for national and regional concentration may be similar.

At the other end of the market spectrum, national figures on size distribution may suggest an erroneously high degree of market power in industries whose products are sold worldwide. In industries such as automobiles, primary steel products, machine tools, and commercial aircraft, national boundaries no longer define markets, and domestic monopoly is a contradiction in terms unless bolstered by tariffs or import quotas.

Product Boundaries

To describe markets fully, we must identify product as well as geographic boundaries. Suppose, for example, a firm produces chocolate candy. Do its competitors include manufacturers of hard fruit candies, lollipops, or licorice who make sales in the same area? Or those selling cookies? What about other sweets such as ice cream? Or other snack foods such as potato chips and salted nuts? To add to the complexity, "competitors" may be in distinctly different industries: a local movie theater, for instance, might find that its strongest competitor is a nearby bowling alley.

Joan Robinson defined an industry as "any group of firms producing a single commodity" and went on to observe that "in some cases, where a commodity in the real world is bounded on all sides by a marked gap between itself and its closest substitutes, the real-world firms producing this real-world commodity will conform to the definition of an industry sufficiently closely to make the discussion of industries in this technical sense of some interest."[3] A "marked gap" in the chain of substitutes involves substitution in production as well as consumption. Some firms make products that are in no way substitutes in use—such as wooden bedsteads and bookshelves—but that are produced in similar factories by similar processes, so that production can easily shift from one to the other in response to changes in relative prices. These may appropriately be grouped in a single industry, such as wooden furniture and fixtures.

Problems in Defining the Market

In both antitrust cases and industry studies, defining the geographic or product markets is sometimes difficult, requiring informed judgment and common sense. Optimally, the definition needs to be clear, note the extent of intermarket penetration, identify the leading substitutes, and evaluate the effects of external influences.[4]

The Department of Justice has developed an approach to market definition to ascertain whether a particular merger will be challenged as anticompetitive. The department's 1984 "Merger Guidelines" offers the following definition:

> [F] or each product of each merging firm, the Department seeks to define a market in which firms could effectively exercise market power if they were able to coordinate their actions. Formally, a market is defined as a product or group of products and a geographic area in which it is sold such that a hypothetical, profit-maximizing firm, not subject to price regulation, that was the only present and future seller of those products in that area would impose a "small but significant and nontransitory" increase in price above prevailing or likely future levels. The group of products and geographic area that comprise a market will be referred to respectively as the "product market" and the "geographic market."[5]

A "small but significant and nontransitory" price increase is "in most contexts . . . a price increase of five percent lasting one year,"[6] but the Department of Justice modifies this general criterion to fit individual market circumstances.

The 1984 "Merger Guidelines" notes that the power to raise prices is constrained by both demand and supply responses. Four such responses are identified: "(1) consumers switching to other products; (2) consumers switching to the same product produced by firms in other areas; (3) producers of other products switching existing facilities to the production of the product; or (4) producers entering into the production of the product by substantially modifying existing facilities or by constructing new facilities."[7]

Monopsonistic Power of Customers

A final important structural feature of selling (customer) markets is the market position of customers, or the extent of monopsonistic power faced by sellers. In the case of bilateral monopoly—a single seller facing a single buyer—the equilibrium levels of price and output are indeterminate in the static profit-maximizing model. John Kenneth Galbraith has called attention to the phenomenon of "countervailing power," or the extent to which customers with market power can offset the similar power of their suppliers. "The first," he contends, "begets the second."[8] Countervailing power, however, will benefit consumers only if the monopsonistic customers resell in competitive markets or are themselves final consumers (e.g., a consumer cooperative).

NATURE OF BUYING (SUPPLIER) MARKETS

A firm's business environment includes the markets in which it buys its inputs—labor, materials, and capital goods—as well as those in which it sells its products. Typically, the number of factor markets in which a firm is a buyer is larger than the number of product markets in which it is a seller. The firm may thus face very different degrees of market power in dealing with its various suppliers.

Monopsonistic and Monopolistic Power

Firms may exert differing degrees of monopsonistic power on their suppliers. The largest firm, for example, may be able to extract from suppliers concessions that are unavailable to its smaller rivals, thus lowering its cost of production relative to theirs.

Steven R. Lustgarten has noted that collusion is generally more feasible among sellers than buyers: First, firms buy in many markets, making collusion in any one less important and an overall collusive purchasing strategy more complex. Second, suppliers commonly sell to firms in a number of industries, and collusion is difficult to organize among firms producing different products. But Lustgarten's study did not support the idea that buyers who cannot collude effectively necessarily lack market power. To the contrary, he found that buyer concentration is positively and significantly correlated with seller concentration, lending support to Galbraith's countervailing-power hypothesis.[9]

A firm's costs may be raised only slightly by even a large increase in the price of a single input. This feature may significantly lower the elasticity of demand and hence raise the market power of a monopolistic supplier selling a product without close substitutes. One basic feature of the demand for any factor of production is that it is a *derived* demand, stemming from demand for the product in which it is used. Steel, for example, accounts for roughly 10 percent of the cost of producing an automobile. Thus, a 10 percent increase in the cost of steel leads to approximately a 1 percent increase in the cost of an automobile. As a result, the quantity of steel demanded by the automobile industry is more responsive to changes in the quantity of automobiles demanded and produced (causing the demand curve for steel to shift) than it is to a change in the price of steel (leading to a movement along the demand curve for steel).

A similar phenomenon exists in the market for tin metal, since the cost of the tin incorporated in a "tin" can (actually a can made of tinplated steel) is usually less than 5 percent of the price of the canned product, and since solder (the second greatest industrial use of pure tin) is a similarly small component of the products in which it is used. For these reasons, the author of a pioneering econometric analysis of the world demand for tin treated the quantity demanded as a function of general economic conditions in the countries in which it was used and did not even include the price of tin metal as an explanatory variable in his regression equations.[10]

Suppliers may benefit from this aspect of derived demand (the importance of being unimportant); they may be able to set price levels far above their costs of production and experience only small reductions in quantities sold. But this power will persist over the long run only if its exercise does not attract lower-priced substitutes, such as tin-free steel, aluminum cans, and lead-based solder.

Reliability of Sources of Supply

If a particular factor of production is essential to the continued operation of firms in the purchasing industry, supply reliability will usually be far more important than price. Whenever possible, most firms avoid relying on a single supplier, from fear of losing that source as much as from aversion to monopolistic pricing.

Vertical Integration as an Alternative to Market Exchange

Another method of protection, often more feasible or effective than the development of alternative external sources, is upstream vertical integration into production of the needed material or component. The motives for upstream, or "backward," vertical integration may be mixed, and the effects—whether intended or not—may involve more than merely a greater assurance of stable supply. Shortly after its formation, the Pittsburgh Reduction Company and its 1907 successor, Aluminum Company of America (Alcoa), began a prolonged campaign to acquire bauxite mines and reserves. The company contended that it needed these assured sources of supply as insurance for its massive investments in expanded production capacity. But critics noted that lack of access to commercially workable bauxite sites made the entry of competitors impossible even after Alcoa's patents on the electrolytic reduction process expired in 1909.[11] Large firms, recognized by suppliers as having the financial and organizational capacity to make a product rather than buy it, have used this capability to bargain for concessions on price or other terms of sale.

Forward, or downstream, integration may have analogous motives (such as assuring outlets for production) and similar effects (such as denying outlets to competitors).

NATURE OF PRODUCTS

The inherent nature of a firm's product or products, as well as the market conditions it faces, will limit or enhance its market power and influence its strategic decisions.

Consumer or Producer Goods

Whether the product is sold to consumers or producers is often important. Usually, final consumers are numerous, are not organized to exert monopsonistic power, and spend only a small fraction of their total income on any one commodity. Buyers for a household are likely to be poorly informed about the quality and characteristics of many products purchased (e.g., durability, nutritional value, or safety), or about the availability of new or substitute products. Since numerous goods and services are available and most are of only minor importance to the household's overall utility, consumers lack the time and rational motivation to obtain detailed information on the great majority of products offered to them. There are obvious exceptions to these generalities: purchase of a house, automobile, or college education for a child makes deep inroads into a household's budget, and there are no substitutes for certain medical products.

In contrast to consumer products, those sold to producers are likely to be sold to a few well-informed customers. Not only is monopsony power more prevalent in producer goods markets, but industrial and commercial buyers tend to be knowledgeable. Purchasing agents are concerned with only a few products and are often technically trained or experienced in their use. Such buyers are expected to keep well informed as to technical characteristics of inputs, their firms' needs, available alternatives, and relative prices.

Advertising

Most consumer products companies must compete with numerous substitutes, promote brand names and quality, indicate where and at what prices their products can be bought, and either take advantage of or strive to overcome consumer habits or current fads. Thus, advertising and other forms of sales promotion are important features of conduct in many consumer goods markets.

In producer goods markets, sales promotion is likely to take forms other than brand-name advertising. More important are unique quality or performance characteristics, a reputation for superior service (e.g., ready availability, prompt delivery, and component repair), and a technically qualified rather than merely persuasive sales force.

Advertising, by shifting out the demand curve for a product, may raise both the price and the quantity sold; it may also be a vehicle for entry and greater price competition. A study by Lee Benham found that in states that prohibited optometrists from advertising the retail prices of eyeglasses, the average price was 25 to over 100 percent higher—primarily because in nonrestrictive states retailers could enter and thrive if they made their low prices known to the public.[12] A follow-up Federal Trade Commission (FTC) staff study found that the average quality of eye examinations and eyeglasses did not vary significantly between restrictive and nonrestrictive cities. In cities with no restrictions on advertising, however, the optometrists who did not advertise and charged higher prices for eyeglasses gave more thorough examinations.[13]

Homogeneous or Differentiable Products

The degrees to which products can be differentiated vary; thus, so does the extent to which they are amenable to advertising and other forms of nonprice promotion. Wheat, iron ore, ground beef, and cabbages are examples of basically homogeneous goods in the sense that the buyer does not usually distinguish the product of one firm from that of another. Aircraft, office machinery, cigarettes, and aspirin are examples of products successfully differentiated by their manufacturers, so that buyers perceive differences (real or imagined) in the products of various firms. Homogeneity can be a matter of degree (e.g., a grain elevator may establish a reputation for more carefully graded wheat with greater precautions taken against rodent and insect contamination). The more homogeneous the product, the more important price competition will be relative to other forms—and price differences will be less sustainable among various producers. Pure competition, of course, requires a homogeneous product.

Durable or Perishable Goods

Analysts have long been aware that the demands for durable goods, both consumer and producer, fluctuate more over the business cycle than do the demands for perishable products. In times of financial stringency, both households and business firms can postpone the purchase of durables (make the old refrigerator or the old lathe last another year). Demand instability, as we shall see below, can have important consequences for market behavior.

Frederic M. Scherer has observed another way in which durability of a product—or more strictly, its costs of storage—determines a firm's market behavior.[14] Inventories, he points out, serve as a buffer between production and sales. A firm in a less than perfectly competitive market must either set a price and estimate the rate of sales that will result or set a rate of output and estimate the price at which that output will be absorbed by the market. In oligopolistic industries, collusive or not, firms find it exceedingly difficult to formulate an appropriate strategy in terms of both price and sales volume. "Characteristically, therefore," Scherer notes, "the coordination process in oligopoly focuses primarily on price."[15] But if, because of perishability or inordinately high storage costs, all that is produced must be sold immediately, any errors in estimating market demand will make the predetermined price unsustainable. Price maintenance at the desired level, in the absence of perfect prediction of demand, requires fluctuations in the level of inventory holdings (or back orders).

Capital Goods: The Accelerator Principle

Producer goods may be *capital goods,* usually defined as relatively long-lived machines, tools, or structures used in the production of other goods.[16] The *accelerator principle* describes how fluctuations in final demand lead to far greater fluctuations in the derived demand for capital goods. Suppose a factory is producing and selling 10,000 rocking chairs per year and requires 10 woodworking lathes for this level of production (i.e., each lathe turns out components for 1,000 chairs over a year). Suppose further that the useful life of a lathe is five years. On the average, as long as it continues to produce 10,000 chairs per year, the furniture factory will replace two lathes each year.

Now suppose the demand for rocking chairs rises and the furniture company increases its production to 12,000 per year. In the first year of increased production, it will order four new lathes—a 20 percent increase in demand for the final product has led to a doubling of demand for the capital good. But the furniture factory's demand for lathes will remain stable at the new rate of four per year only if the demand for rocking chairs continues to grow by 2,000 per year. If rocking chair demand remains at 12,000 per year, the number of lathes sold will fall back to two per year and then rise to three as replacement demand becomes effective.

The point of this simple example is that manufacturers of capital goods produce for inherently unstable markets.

PRODUCT DIVERSIFICATION WITHIN FIRMS

An overwhelming majority of large modern corporations are multiproduct, or conglomerate, firms. One of the first economists to call attention to the economic significance of size and multiproduct operation (distinct from the issue of concentration in specific product markets) was Corwin D. Edwards.

Corporate Size and Economic Power

In a 1949 book and in subsequent writings,[17] Edwards warned of several possible manifestations of economic power growing out of size alone. Sheer purchasing power, he wrote, gives the large firm the ability to "buy scarce materials and attractive sites, inventions, and facilities; pre-empt the services of the most expensive technicians and executives; and acquire reserves of materials for the future."[18] The large firm could afford a law office of its own as well as the services of the nation's best outside lawyers. It could afford expensive litigation. Such a firm, in Edwards's view, could obtain favorable discriminatory treatment from suppliers or customers through threats of refusal to deal or of vertical integration into the activities of either sellers or buyers. He observed, further, that the large firm could exploit advantages over its smaller rivals in political influence, public relations, and privileged access to financial institutions—advantages others have since questioned.[19]

Advantages of Product Diversity

Edwards also noted advantages of multiproduct operation, as distinct from sheer size (except to the extent that manufacture of additional products requires greater overall size).

Tie-ins and Reciprocal Dealing. Production of more than one product permits a firm to engage in tie-in sales (conditioning the sale of one product on the buyer's purchase of another) and reciprocal dealing (one firm agrees to buy a product from another in exchange for the seller's agreement to buy some product of the first firm).

Mutual Forbearance. Perhaps more significantly, as large firms diversify, they come into contact with each other in a greater number of markets. The result, Edwards hypothesized, would be greater pressures and incentives for mutual forbearance than would be generated by each of the firms' various market shares alone. The prospect of a successful punitive response to a competitive challenge in any one market is heightened by multimarket contacts, since a diversified firm could mobilize resources from its other lines of activity to meet such a challenge or could retaliate in another line of business in which it enjoys advantages over the challenger. Escalation and the spread of challenges, responses, and countermoves through several markets could magnify losses for all concerned. "Hence," Edwards concluded, "there is an incentive to live and let live, to cultivate a cooperative spirit, and to recognize priorities of interest in the hope of reciprocal recognition."[20]

Arnold A. Heggestad and Stephen A. Rhoades tested this mutual-forbearance hypothesis in an investigation of 187 banking markets. They found that the greater the number of markets throughout a state in which that state's three largest banks met one another, the more stable the market shares of these banks. The relationship was statistically significant, generally at the 5 percent confidence level, after controlling for the degree of concentration, rate of deposit growth, and extent of state regulation in each market. Interpreting market share stability as an indicator of a reduction in the vigor of competition, they concluded "that multi-market meetings between dominant banks do affect the degree of rivalry within markets."[21]

Market Contact. John T. Scott has examined both real economies of multiproduct operation and the heightened awareness of mutual dependence that might result from multimarket contact.[22] Looking at 437 of the 1,000 largest U.S. manufacturing firms, Scott found evidence of economies of both company-financed R&D and advertising. But, he argued, such economies could not explain higher profits in markets where multimarket contacts were greater: "The firms in these markets may be technically efficient, but if resources move freely their profits, *ceteris paribus,* should be no higher than those of other firms. My hypothesis is firms in markets where both seller concentration and multimarket contact are high will recognize their interdependence and not compete away their own profits."[23] Higher profits, he noted, could be explained only if the multiproduct firms refrained from taking full advantage of the ease of internal reallocation of capital to more profitable lines of business, and if there were impediments to entry by others.

Scott used a unique measure of multimarket contact: the extent of such contact over and above what would have occurred by pure chance as large firms diversified. In other words, he sought to examine the effects of purposive diversification with increased multimarket contact as one of the apparent objectives. His findings confirmed his hypothesis. "Profits," he reported, "were, *ceteris paribus,* about 3.0% higher in 1974 for lines of business where seller concentration and multimarket contact were both higher than their median values than for those where only multimarket contact was high." Further, "High multimarket contact alone is associated overall with *lower* profits," supporting the argument that capital mobility within multiproduct firms enhances competition, in the absence of heightened recognition of mutual dependence.[24]

BARRIERS TO ENTRY, MOBILITY, AND EXIT

Barriers to entry, or some impediment to the free flow of capital, are essential to any theoretical explanation of long-run monopolistic or monopsonistic profits. Virtually all industrial organization economists accept the proposition that in the real world, such barriers are essential for the persistence of profits substantially above a risk-adjusted competitive rate of return; but there is disagreement on how common such barriers and thus such profits are. Barriers to entry are customarily divided into two major classes—*natural* and *artificial*.

Natural Barriers to Entry

Economies of Scale Relative to Market Size. The most important natural barrier to entry is raised by economies of scale relative to size of the market. The qualifying phrase, "relative to size of the market," is crucial. Economies of scale alone, in the absence of imperfections in the capital market, do not constitute a barrier to entry. But the number of efficiently sized firms that the market can support clearly limits the number that can enter and survive. Figure 7–1 illustrates the point.

Suppose, for simplicity, that the demand curve for a product is the straight line *AB* in Figure 7–1, intersecting the horizontal axis at a sales rate of 300 units per day. Suppose also that the long-run average cost curve of a firm, either now producing the product or contemplating entry, is the curve *LAC*. (The assumption behind *LAC* is that existing firms have no cost advantage over entrants for an given rate of output.) A firm obtains all available economies of scale at a rate of output of *OE* units per day. The output *OE* is often referred to as the *MES* (minimum efficient scale) for a firm. A purely monopolistic firm could operate at a normal or higher profit anywhere in the range between a daily output of *OF* and of *OG*. If a second firm entered and the two share the market equally, the demand curve facing each would be *AC*, intersecting the horizontal axis at 150 units per day and with twice the slope of *AB* throughout. Each firm could still earn profits by producing between *OH* and *OI*, even though (as drawn in Figure 7–1) neither would be producing at the rate *OE*, which realized all available economies of scale. However, if under the same assumptions a third firm entered the market, the demand curve facing each would fall to *AD*—one third of the market demand curve—and there would be no rates of production and sales at which any of the firms could operate without loss. Under such circumstances, it can be said that the market will support one firm of efficient size and two firms at profitable levels of output but that entry of a third is barred.

There are three possible sources of erosion of this barrier over time. First, either technological advance or declines in resource costs may cause the entire *LAC* curve to fall. Second, technological change may shift *LAC* to the left, reducing the *MES*, or may cause the sloping

FIGURE 7–1 Economies of Scale as a Barrier to Entry

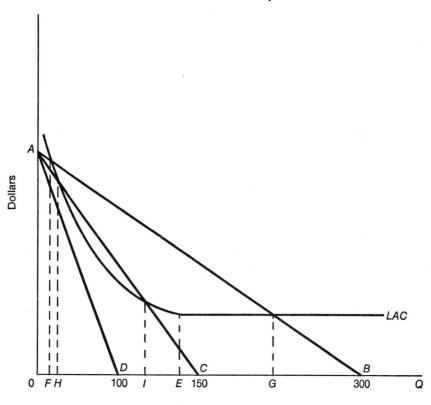

portion of LAC to become less steep, reducing the competitive disadvantage of less than optimally sized firms. Third, and often a key feature in the history of an industry, the market demand curve may shift out—perhaps as improvements in transportation convert local markets into regional or national ones.

Nonduplicable Resources. The second major source of natural barriers to entry is lack of accessibility to nonduplicable resources without good substitutes, such as naturally scarce raw materials, the unique features of an artist's talents, or advantages of location.

Artificial Barriers to Entry, Public and Private

Artificial barriers to entry may be of two general types. First, they may be *public,* or erected by the government. Such barriers include tariffs, patents, copyrights, exclusive franchises, and licenses. Second, barriers may be erected by the actions of *private* firms, either intentionally or as the unintended consequences of other actions. As discussed previously, firms may integrate upstream (and foreclose needed materials from potential competitors) or downstream (to preempt markets). They may acquire numerous patents, either through their own R&D or through purchase from others—in some cases, not to make use of the patented processes or products but to preclude others from doing so.

Product Differentiation.   Joe S. Bain, in an empirical study of barriers to entry in 20 U.S. industries, concluded that it is very likely that the most important source of artificial barriers is product differentiation—"at least of the same general order of importance as an impediment to entry as are economies of large-scale production and distribution."[25]   Product differentiation, Bain observed, could lead to buyers' preference for established brands.   A newcomer's promotional expenditures would then be raised by the need to overcome existing brand loyalties as well as inform potential customers of the new brand's availability and characteristics.

Subsequent writers have noted that early entrants may have to incur heavy advertising outlays to persuade consumers to try a new product, and that these outlays may pave the way for later entrants. A priori, it is not obvious whether promotional expenditures are likely to be heavier for the first firms to introduce a new product or for later entrants offering competing brands.

Both Thomas T. Nagle and Richard Schmalensee have argued that brand loyalty is not so much a function of advertising as it is a natural barrier, stemming from consumers' reluctance to search for alternative brands once they have found a brand that is of high enough quality. Such buying behavior, Nagle observed, is economically rational if the consumer believes that the value of the additional satisfaction from finding a better brand multiplied by the probability of success in doing so is lower than the anticipated costs of the search.   Advertising, for Nagle, does not raise barriers to entry so much as it breaks down brand-loyalty barriers: "Without advertising, consumers would sample until they found an exceptional brand and then simply purchase it repeatedly. . . .   But through advertising, and other promotional efforts, consumers may be induced to sample other brands, particularly those they perceive as most likely to be exceptional given their preferences."[26]

Schmalensee noted that Bain was well aware that advertising is not the main source of product differentiation.   Bain's basic argument, he contended, is strengthened by demonstrating the advantage of a first entrant in the absence of advertising.   This advantage stems from consumers' discovery that an existing brand performs satisfactorily. "[T]hat brand," Schmalensee observed, "becomes the standard against which subsequent entrants are rationally judged. It thus becomes harder for later entrants to persuade consumers to invest in learning about their quality than it was for the first brand."[27] Whereas Nagle emphasized the effect of advertising in breaking down barriers to entry; Schmalensee argued that if product-quality advertising is not completely credible to potential consumers, a later entrant's advertising is less effective than the pioneer's.

Bain also pointed out that competitive advertising outlays increase the nonproduction costs of a firm, and these outlays may be at the most efficient level (in terms of equating profits earned from making additional sales with the promotional costs of generating these sales) at rates of output in excess of those needed to obtain full economies of production and distribution, thus raising scale-economy barriers to entry. Further, some forms of sales promotion involve close and continuing relations between manufacturers and dealers and may thus raise problems of *preemption,* or "locking up" of existing dealers, making it difficult for entering manufacturers to find outlets for their products or, alternatively, for entering dealers to find satisfactory sources of supply.

Capital Cost and Access. Another barrier to entry, which may impose significantly higher absolute costs on entrants, is capital cost and access. Small and new firms seeking external financing almost invariably face steeper interest charges, more stringent credit rationing, higher investment bankers' fees, or lower subscription prices for newly issued stock than larger established firms.

The unresolved question is the extent to which such higher costs represent socially optimal allocation of capital (e.g., compensation to potential investors for extensive and costly investigations of new ventures, or a premium to induce investors to contribute capital to risky enterprises),[28] or instead reflect imperfections in the capital market. One such imperfection is frequent high concentration in local banking markets (to which smaller firms have access) in contrast to highly competitive conditions in the national financial markets serving large corporate borrowers. Another is the inherent conservatism attributed to bankers. Still a third stems from interlocking directorates among the nation's largest banks and industrial corporations, inevitably leading to suspicions of undue influence and favoritism.[29] (Capital cost barriers of this type are presumably negligible for one important class of potential entrants—large multiproduct corporations considering diversification into profitable new lines of business.)

Scott has identified a second kind of capital cost barrier to entry that exists even if potential entrants and incumbents have identical access to capital markets. Entry, Scott noted, may raise the cost of capital for all firms in the industry, incumbents and entrants alike. In a regression analysis of the data from a large sample of Canadian firms, Scott found an inverse relationship between seller concentration and cost of capital, after controlling for risk, diversification, size of firm, and financial leverage.[30] He explained that increased concentration reduces the probability that any one firm will be forced out of the market, *ceteris paribus*. "The reduction in that probability," he observed, "reduces capital cost by lowering expected bankruptcy costs and by offering downside return protection (i.e., skewness in returns)."[31] Entry, therefore, raises the cost of capital by reducing concentration. Scott referred to this effect, which abstracts from any capital market imperfections giving some firms capital cost advantages over others, as the "pure capital-cost barrier to entry."

Imposition of Higher Cost. Both limited access to needed resources and the capital cost barrier to entry represent *absolute cost* advantages for established firms. Existing firms may obtain an absolute cost advantage, and hence erect an artificial barrier to entry, by intentionally imposing higher costs on smaller rivals or potential entrants. As real-world examples of this strategy, Steven C. Salop has cited preemption of low-cost raw materials, the manufacture of a low-priced mainframe computer that was plug-incompatible with peripheral equipment produced by newer and smaller nonintegrated rivals, use of patents to deny best technology to entrants, and a union contract in which large firms using a capital-intensive technology agreed to pay higher wages, provided the union imposed the same wage scale on smaller, more labor-intensive rivals.[32]

John C. Hilke and Philip B. Nelson have observed that increased advertising may be used to counter a threat of entry by forcing higher advertising costs on the entrant.[33] Abnormally heavy advertising by the incumbent firm may also serve this purpose if it overloads consumers with more information than they can assimilate or remember. An entrant is particularly vulnerable to such a strategy, Hilke and Nelson maintain, since dealers often base reorder decisions on initial customer acceptance of a product and consumers overwhelmed or confused by a plethora of advertising messages are likely to stick with a familiar product. The overload strategy need only be temporary because consumers are most amenable to experimentation at the time of a new product's introduction.

In a 1962 article, John A. Menge observed that style competition in the automobile industry imposed higher unit costs on small manufacturers (both existing firms and potential entrants) than on their larger rivals, even without any predatory or exclusionary intent, because virtually every body style change in an automobile requires a new set of costly tools and dies.[34]   As an example, Menge discussed a special die stamping rear decklids and costing $40 million. At General Motors, such a die might be used on 2 million cars per year. If replaced and scrapped after two years, it would have turned out 4 million decklids at an amortized cost of $10 per unit. American Motors might have a similar die but be producing only 300,000 cars per year. If American Motors tried to meet General Motors' style competition by changing its decklid every two years, the die would have to be scrapped after stamping 600,000 decklids of a particular style, for an amortized cost of $67 per unit. Alternatively, if American Motors used the die until it had turned out 4 million decklids, it would be 13 years before the style could be changed.

In a review of the history of the U.S. automobile industry, Menge noted that Ford had initially won the largest share of the market by a 1910 decision to stress economy and standardization but was supplanted by General Motors after the latter's 1920s decision to emphasize style change. "This change in direction," Menge noted, "was not an attempt on the part of any one firm deliberately to select a market strategy which would impose disproportionate 'penalties' on its rivals and drive them from the field as a result." But whether intended or not, "smaller firms such as Hudson, Packard, Studebaker, Willys, Kaiser, Graham-Paige, et al., could not have been expected to stand and fight it out successfully with GM, Ford, and Chrysler. Slowly and inexorably a code of behavior based on rapid periodic style change tends to drive the small producers from the industry."[35]

Barriers to Mobility

Richard E. Caves and Michael E. Porter have formulated an important generalization of Bain's initial concepts of barriers to entry. They note that the theory of entry barriers "becomes much richer—yet remains determinate—when set forth as a general theory of the mobility of firms among segments of an industry, thus encompassing exit and intergroup shifts as well as entry."[36] Structural features, Caves and Porter observe, may segment an industry into groups of different sizes, degrees of product differentiation, and levels of integration and diversification. There may also be barriers, both natural and artificial, to intergroup mobility, the ability of firms to shift from one group in the industry to another. "All the standard sources of entry barriers," they state, "translate into mobility barriers in this obvious way."[37]

Potential entrants to a group include existing firms in other industries considering diversification, firms in the same industry contemplating a shift to another group, and completely new firms. Entry to a group thus depends on the height and nature of barriers both to entry into the industry and to intergroup mobility within the industry.

Barriers to Exit

Finally, an industry's economic performance may be as much influenced by barriers to exit, or immobility of capital, as by barriers to entry. An industry may be capital intensive, and the capital required may be long-lived, specialized, and not readily convertible into cash. If capital cannot easily be transferred out of an industry with declining demand, the result may be severe financial losses and concomitantly increased incentives to both price warfare and overt collusion. In 1940, J. M. Clark noted the case of a hypothetical industry with all of the characteristics of perfect competition but one. "Take away the saving grace of perfect two-way mobility," he wrote, "and leave the other conditions; let the demand decline, and competition becomes too strong: you have a 'sick industry' on your hands."[38]

NATURE OF COSTS

Absolute Levels

Cost levels may vary among firms within the same industry. A firm with unit costs lower than its rivals at all rates of output is said to enjoy an *absolute cost* advantage. Sources of absolute cost advantages already discussed include limited availability of scarce or nonreproducible resources and differences in costs of capital. Lower-cost methods of production and distribution, most often based on patents, secret know-how, and superior management, may also provide a firm with such an advantage. In addition to raising entry barriers, absolute cost advantages may allow firms to dominate collusive arrangements. Bain found absolute cost advantages to be slight, and temporary for entrants, in 16 of 20 industries he studied. In the other four, significant advantages stemmed from superior access to resources, patents, and secret know-how.[39]

Economies of Scale and Scope:[40] Real and Pecuniary

Economies of scale and scope are among the most important features of industrial structure, playing a major role in determining the size distribution of firms and the severity of barriers to entry in an industry. The significance of cost advantages for economic performance depends largely on whether the economies are real or pecuniary.

A real economy of scale or scope is one that lowers real social cost by reducing the resources used per unit of product or, alternatively, allowing for an improved product with the same mix of resources per unit. A pecuniary economy, on the other hand, represents a transfer of income in the sense that the cost saving to one firm is offset by a shift of the burden to another—typically a supplier or customer.

Consider, for example, economies of large-scale purchasing. It may be that the costs of processing a purchase—approving the request of a requisitioning department, searching for the best buy, placing the order, checking on delivery, validating the invoice, and arranging for payment—are roughly the same for small and large purchases or at least do not rise proportionately with the amount purchased. Also, unit shipping costs may be substantially less for truckload or carload lots. These represent real economies of large-scale purchasing, freeing resources for other economic activities. But discounts obtained by a large buyer through threats of shifting its business elsewhere or of vertical integration into the purchased item are pecuniary economies, involving no resource saving but merely a transfer of dollars from the seller to the powerful buyer.

The performance implications of pecuniary economies are often neutral, but one important exception arises in the case of counter-vailing power. If competitive market conditions in the industries ben-efiting from pecuniary economies force the firms to pass these benefits along to consumers, there is an unambiguous gain in economic welfare.

Ratios of Fixed to Variable Costs

The ratio of fixed to variable costs exerts a powerful influence on a firm's short-run behavior. And where capital is long lived and highly specialized, the "short run" may be quite lengthy. One of the basic principles of the theory of the firm is that in the short run, a producer will not shut down so long as its revenues cover variable costs of pro-duction and make some contribution, no matter how slight, to its fixed costs. Another elementary principle is that average fixed cost (AFC) falls as output increases and rises as output decreases, since total fixed cost (TFC), by definition, does not change with changes in output. Therefore, average variable cost (AVC) reaches a minimum at a lesser output than does average total cost (ATC).

These features of short-run cost curves are illustrated in Figure 7–2. AFC is a rectangular hyperbola, asymptotically approaching both axes, since the product of every cost and quantity determined by a point on ATC must equal the constant value of TFC. Since $ATC = AFC + AVC$, the vertical distance between AVC and ATC must equal the height of AFC, and thus AVC and ATC asymptotically approach each other as output increases and AFC decreases. Since AFC is falling throughout, it continues to reduce ATC even at rates of output beyond which AVC has started to rise. Indeed, ATC must reach a minimum at the rate of output at which the upward slope of AVC is

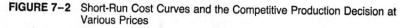

FIGURE 7-2 Short-Run Cost Curves and the Competitive Production Decision at Various Prices

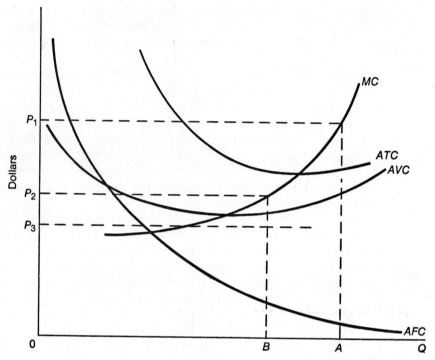

just equal to the downward slope of *AFC*. The marginal cost curve (*MC*) passes through the minimum of both *AVC* and *ATC*. At a price of P_1, a competitive firm will produce a rate of output of *OA*, earning a profit per unit equal to the difference between P_1 and *ATC* at that output.[41] If the price falls to P_2, the firm will cut production to *OB* sustaining a loss per unit equal to *ATC* − P_2. But notice that the firm will continue to produce rather than close down, since the loss per unit is less than *AFC*. Recall that *AFC* = *ATC* − *AVC*. Or, the rate of total loss while continuing to produce—average loss multiplied by *OB*—is less than the total cost that would be incurred after shut-down—*AFC* multiplied by *OB*. If, however, the price fell to P_3, or to any level below minimum *AVC*, the firm would be better off to close.

The essential point is that a firm with low fixed costs relative to its variable costs will cease operations when price falls slightly below *ATC* and either wait for market conditions to improve or start disposing of some of its plant and equipment. As a number of plants shut down and market supply is thereby curtailed, the price fall is checked. In such an industry, output responds flexibly to shifts in demand. But if fixed costs are high, price can fall well below ATC and firms can suffer heavy losses before any withdraw from production. For this reason, fluctuations in demand are particularly devastating to firms with high fixed costs relative to variable costs.

A heavy fixed cost burden has other consequences for business behavior. Since "spreading the overhead," or reducing AFC by increasing output, provides an incentive to keep production levels up, optimal scale and attendant barriers to entry are increased, *ceteris paribus,* as fixed costs rise relative to variable. Pressures to engage in price discrimination may become intense. Any one sale that earns enough revenue to cover its own variable costs, plus provide even a minute surplus to defray some small part of the overhead, is worth making, considered by itself. But, to make all sales on this basis would be ruinous; if the firm is to remain in business, the total revenue from sales must be sufficient to cover total fixed cost as well as variable cost. The obvious answer, where feasible and legal, is to discriminate in price, charging "whatever the traffic will bear," provided only that the lowest price accepted is barely above variable, or out-of-pocket, costs.

NATURE OF DEMAND

Elasticity

Both the elasticity of demand for a product and that facing the individual seller are extremely important determinants of the industry's performance.

For the Product. If the demand for a product is highly inelastic, there is, *ceteris paribus,* a stronger incentive for collusion than if a product has more elastic demand. Firms learn from experience that price-cutting throughout an industry tends to be mutually destructive if the quantity sold rises very little in response. Conversely, a marketwide increase in price will benefit all if only a few sales are lost. If collusion is difficult or impossible, firms in such an industry may turn to the government—witness the popularity of agricultural price support programs.

Facing the Individual Seller. The elasticity of demand facing an individual seller may be extremely difficult for an outsider to estimate. If the industry is a highly concentrated one, oligopolistic pricing may prevail, each seller's demand curve subjectively determined by the responses it anticipates from rivals as well as purchasers. Nevertheless, this elasticity is of basic significance to the exercise of market

power through pricing. Recall from Chapter Four that the firm ascertains its profit-maximizing price by setting $P = MC \, \eta/_{\eta-1}$. Or, the
greater the elasticity of demand facing it, the less the divergence of
price from marginal cost.

Stability

Fluctuations in demand, particularly those that are unpredictable, also
have important implications for business conduct. In particular, unstable and uncertain demand conditions in an oligopolistic setting make
tacit collusion more problematic. A firm experiencing a loss of sales
at the going price may find it impossible to ascertain, before it has to
decide on a response, whether the cause is a decline in demand or price-
cutting by a rival. Further, demand fluctuations make it harder for
a firm to know its actual market share at any one time; thus, live-
and-let-live policies based on mutual respect for traditional market
shares are less likely. Particularly severe problems are raised by
unstable demand coupled with high fixed costs or inflexible rates of
production. The overall effect of demand instability may be either to
enhance independence in price and output policies (to the detriment
of profits throughout the industry) or to encourage more structured
forms of overt collusion.

Underlying Rate of Growth or Decline. Demand may fluctuate
around long-run trends of growth or decline. Bain and others have
hypothesized that long-run growth in demand should ease barriers to
entry and improve the opportunities for small firms to expand their
output without retaliation by larger rivals—therefore reducing concentration.[42] Econometric tests have generally supported this hypothesis, but not strongly.[43]

THE TECHNOLOGICAL BASE

According to Joseph A. Schumpeter, "the kind of competition which
counts" is not price competition, but rather "the competition from the
new commodity, the new technology, the new source of supply, the new
type of organization (the largest-scale unit of control, for instance)—
competition which commands a decisive cost or quality advantage and
which strikes not at the margins of the profits and the outputs of the
existing firms but at their foundations and their very lives."[44] We
cannot evaluate these dynamic aspects of economic performance without considering an industry's underlying technological environment,
or the opportunities for technical progress. It makes no sense, for
example, to claim that the technological performance of the electronics

industry has been superior to that of the dairy products industry merely because the former has experienced greater technological advance. A more reasonable test would be to compare the relative technological performance of the U.S. and Japanese electronics industries.

EXTERNALITIES

In 1971, in a biting comment on the welfare implications of free-market competition, Robinson wrote:

> The distinction that Pigou made between private costs and social costs was presented by him as an exception to the benevolent rule of *laisser-faire*. A moment's thought shows that the exception is the rule and the rule is the exception. In what industry, in what line of business, are the true social costs of the activity registered in its accounts? Where is the pricing system that offers the consumer a fair choice between air to breathe and motor cars to drive about in? The economists were the last to realize what was going on and when they did recognize it they managed to hush it up again. *Laisser-faire* and consumer's sovereignty were still absolute except for a few minor points discussed under the heading of "externalities" that could easily be put right.[45]

Despite some hyperbole, Robinson's point is a telling one. No economist today can take seriously a model of economic welfare that fails to address problems of environmental pollution, urban congestion, and waste disposal. An externality is a cost or benefit imposed on society by the action of a producer or consumer but not borne or enjoyed exclusively by the one imposing it. Externalities will be ignored by the profit-maximizing firm or utility-maximizing household, but they cannot be ignored by anyone interested in assessing economic performance.

CONCLUSION

This chapter serves two purposes. First, it introduces many of the most generally important elements of industry structure—those aspects of the business environment that industrial organization economists' research indicates are the most pervasive and compelling determinants of business conduct and economic performance. Second, discussion of these elements provides insight into their sometimes complex causal relationships with conduct and performance. Subsequent consideration of specific forms of conduct and standards of performance should deepen such insight.

Before focusing our attention on conduct and performance, however, it is useful to take a closer look at a particular aspect of structure—the size distribution of firms, or market concentration. Since concentration is the most readily apparent and easily quantifiable element of structure, it has been the most often measured and studied and provides the most commonly used indices of concentration in statistical analyses. The next chapter discusses how concentration has been measured, its trends, and its causes.

ENDNOTES

[1]Edward S. Mason, "Price and Production Policies of Large-Scale Enterprise," *American Economic Review* 29, no. 1 (March 1939), part 2, pp. 61–74, at p. 69.

[2]Lloyd G. Reynolds, *Microeconomics: Analysis and Policy,* rev. ed. (Homewood, Ill.: Richard D. Irwin, 1976), p. 176.

[3]Joan Robinson, *The Economics of Imperfect Competition* (London: Macmillan, 1933), p. 17.

[4]For significant discussions of the problem, see Kenneth G. Elzinga and Thomas F. Hogarty, "The Problem of Geographic Market Delineation in Antimerger Suits," *Antitrust Bulletin* 18, no. 1 (Spring 1973), pp. 45–81; Ira Horowitz, "Market Definition in Antitrust Analysis: A Regression-Based Approach," *Southern Economic Journal* 48, no. 1 (July 1981), pp. 1–16; Gregory J. Werden, "Market Delineation and the Justice Department's Merger Guidelines," *Duke Law Journal* (June 1983), pp. 514–79; Kenneth D. Boyer, "Is There a Principle for Defining Industries?" *Southern Economic Journal* 50, no. 3 (January 1984), pp. 761–70.

[5]U.S. Department of Justice, "Merger Guidelines" (Washington, D.C.: June 14, 1984, mimeographed), p. 4. Reprinted in Commerce Clearing House, *Trade Regulation Reports,* no. 665 (June 18, 1984), part 2.

[6]Ibid., p. 7.

[7]Ibid., pp. 4–5.

[8]John Kenneth Galbraith, *American Capitalism: The Concept of Countervailing Power* (Boston: Houghton Mifflin, 1952), p. 118.

[9]Steven R. Lustgarten, "The Impact of Buyer Concentration in Manufacturing Industries," *Review of Economics and Statistics* 57, no. 2 (May 1975), pp. 125–32, at p. 130.

[10]Meghnad Desai, "An Econometric Model of the World Tin Economy, 1948–1961," *Econometrica* 34, no. 1 (January 1966), pp. 105–34.

[11]Donald H. Wallace, *Market Control in the Aluminum Industry* (Cambridge, Mass.: Harvard University Press, 1937).

[12]Lee Benham, "The Effect of Advertising on the Price of Eyeglasses," *Journal of Law and Economics* 15, no. 2 (October 1972), pp. 337–52.

[13]Ronald S. Bond, John E. Kwoka, Jr., John J. Phelan, and Ira Taylor Whitten, for the Bureau of Economics, Federal Trade Commission, *Staff Report on Effects of Restrictions on Advertising and Commercial Practice in the Professions: The Case of Optometry* (Washington, D.C.: U.S. Government Printing Office, 1980).

[14]Frederic M. Scherer, *Industrial Structure and Economic Performance,* 2d ed. (Skokie, Ill.: Rand McNally, 1980), pp. 193–97.

[15]Ibid., p. 193.

[16]Real capital includes all produced means of production—all goods and services made not for consumption but to aid in the production of other goods. Capital goods fall in the category of fixed capital.

[17]Corwin D. Edwards, *Maintaining Competition* (New York: McGraw Hill, 1949);

Corwin D. Edwards, "Conglomerate Bigness as a Source of Power," in *Business Concentration and Price Policy,* National Bureau of Economic Research (Princeton, N.J.: Princeton University Press, 1955), pp. 331–59; Corwin D. Edwards, *Big Business and the Policy of Competition* (Cleveland: Press of Western Reserve University, 1956).

[18]Edwards, "Conglomerate Bigness," p. 334.

[19]See the discussion of political influence in Chapter Four and comments on privileged access to financial institutions in this chapter.

[20]Edwards, "Conglomerate Bigness," p. 335.

[21]Arnold A. Heggstad and Stephen A. Rhoades, "Multimarket Interdependence and Local Market Concentration in Banking," *Review of Economics and Statistics* 60, no. 4 (November 1978), pp. 523–32.

[22]John T. Scott, "Multimarket Contact and Economic Performance," *Review of Economics and Statistics* 64, no. 3 (August 1982), pp. 368–75.

[23]Ibid., p. 372.

[24]Ibid., p. 374 (italics original).

[25]Joe S. Bain, *Barriers to New Competition* (Cambridge, Mass.: Harvard University Press, 1956), p. 142.

[26]Thomas T. Nagle, "Do Advertising-Profitability Studies Really Show that Advertising Creates a Barrier to Entry?" *Journal of Law and Economics* 24, no. 2 (October 1981), pp. 333–49, at p. 347.

[27]Richard Schmalensee, "Product Differentiation Advantages of Pioneering Brands," *American Economic Review* 72, no. 3 (June 1982), pp. 349–65, at p. 360.

[28]For statements challenging the view that limited access to capital poses an economically inefficient barrier to entry, see George J. Stigler, "Imperfections in the Capital Market," *Journal of Political Economy* 75, no. 3 (June 1967), pp. 287–92; and Robert H. Bork, *The Antitrust Paradox: A Policy at War With Itself* (New York: Basic Books, 1978), especially pp. 320–24.

[29]See U.S. Senate, Committee on Governmental Affairs, *Interlocking Directorates among the Major U.S. Corporations* (Washington, D.C.: U.S. Government Printing Office, 1978).

[30]This result is reported in "Corporate Finance and Market Structure," in *Competition in the Open Economy: A Model Applied to Canada,* Richard E. Caves, Michael E. Porter, and A. Michael Spence, with John T. Scott (Cambridge, Mass.: Harvard University Press, 1980), chap. 13.

[31]John T. Scott, "The Pure Capital-Cost Barrier to Entry," *Review of Economics and Statistics* 63, no. 3 (August 1981), pp. 444–46, at pp. 444–45.

[32]Steven C. Salop, "Introduction," in *Strategy, Predation, and Antitrust Analysis,* ed. Steven C. Salop (Washington, D.C.: U.S. Federal Trade Commission, 1981), pp. 1–42; Steven C. Salop and David T. Scheffman, "Raising Rivals' Costs," *American Economic Review* 73, no. 2 (May 1983), pp. 267–71. Studies drawn on by Salop include Oliver E. Williamson, "Wage Rates as a Barrier to Entry: The Pennington Case in Perspective," *Quarterly Journal of Economics* 82, no. 1 (February 1968), pp. 85–116; Janusz A. Ordover and Robert D. Willig, "An Economic Definition of Predatory Product Innovation," *Strategy, Predation, and Antitrust Analysis,* pp. 301–96.

[33]John C. Hilke and Philip B. Nelson, "Noisy Advertising and the Predation Rule in Antitrust Analysis," *American Economic Review* 74, no. 2 (May 1984), pp. 367–71.

[34]John A. Menge, "Style Change as a Market Weapon," *Quarterly Journal of Economics* 76, no. 4 (November 1962), pp. 632–47.

[35]Ibid., pp. 634, 635.

[36]Richard E. Caves and Michael E. Porter, "From Entry Barriers to Mobility Barriers," *Quarterly Journal of Economics* 91, no. 2 (May 1977), pp. 241–61, at p. 241.

[37]Ibid., p. 254.

[38]J. M. Clark, "Toward a Concept of Workable Competition," *American Economic Review* 30, no. 2 (June 1940), part 1, pp. 241–56, at p. 242.

[39]Bain, *Barriers to New Competition,* p. 155.

[40]An economy of scope is an organizational efficiency not related to economies of scale in production or distribution of any one commodity, such as centralized finance in a multiproduct firm.

[41]For simplicity, only the case of pure competition is diagrammed and discussed. The analysis can easily be extended to cover the downward-sloping demand curve of a monopolist.

[42]See, among others, Joe S. Bain, *Industrial Organization* (New York: John Wiley & Sons, 1959), pp. 180–82; Douglas Needham, *The Economics of Industrial Structure Conduct and Performance* (New York: St. Martin's Press, 1978), p. 174; Edith T. Penrose, *The Theory of the Growth of the Firm* (New York: John Wiley & Sons, 1959), especially chaps. 10 and 11.

[43]See especially James A. Dalton and Stephen A. Rhoades, "Growth and Product Differentiability as Factors Influencing Changes in Concentration," *Journal of Industrial Economics* 22, no. 3 (March 1974), pp. 235–40; William P. Hall, "The Learning Curve, Demand Growth, and Market Concentration," Economic Policy Office discussion paper (Washington, D.C.: U.S. Department of Justice, Antitrust Division, February 11, 1983, mimeographed).

[44]Joseph A. Schumpeter, *Capitalism, Socialism, and Democracy,* 2d ed. (New York: Harper & Row, 1950), p. 84.

[45]Joan Robinson, "The Second Crisis of Economic Theory," *American Economic Review* 62, no. 2 (May 1972) pp. 1–10, at p. 7.

CHAPTER EIGHT

Measures of, Trends in, and Determinants of Market Concentration

The size distribution of firms (concentration) is only one of the several elements of market structure reviewed in Chapter Seven. But it is the most frequently cited evidence of market power—both in numerical series showing how concentration has increased or decreased, by industry or for the economy in the aggregate, and in industry rankings to identify those in which the "monopoly problem" is presumably the most severe. The student of industrial organization needs to understand, therefore, the various measures of concentration, how patterns of concentration have evolved over time in the United States, and the principal forces explaining the levels of concentration found in various markets.

MEASURES OF CONCENTRATION

We need a unit of measurement for size of firm and market. Four have been used frequently in past studies: assets, employment, sales (or value of shipments), and value added by manufacture. None is perfect.

Units of Measurement

Assets. The reported dollar value of assets owned by a firm follows accounting conventions. One such convention, designed to promote conservative reporting and eliminate a possible source of deception, is "no recognition of revenue without a transaction." Under this convention, assets are listed on a firm's balance sheet at acquisition cost, and their dollar values are not increased unless they are sold or the company is merged, regardless of changes in replacement cost. Depreciation of long-lived assets such as buildings and machinery is not based on declines in market value but rather on the accounting principle of amortization, or spreading the initial acquisition cost over the estimated useful life of the asset (which often means the shortest life allowed by the Internal Revenue Service). Inventories with large numbers of identical goods and rapid turnover require arbitrary valuation assumptions—such as, the most recent unit bought is the first to be sold, known as last-in, first-out (LIFO). LIFO gives a reasonably accurate estimate of the real opportunity cost of the goods sold by a firm, since these are valued at the most recent purchase costs, but results in the inventory being valued as an asset on the balance sheet at the oldest and most out-of-date purchase costs.

Even if the analyst could obtain information on current market or replacement value of assets, another problem arises in multiproduct firms. Specific assets would have to be identified with the production and distribution of particular products, and the size of the market would have to be shown as the aggregation of such assets. Firms rarely report assets on this basis; even if they did, allocating "overhead" assets (e.g., central office buildings) among products would be arbitrary and economically meaningless. For such reasons, assets are now used only rarely in studies of concentration.

Employment. Employment, as a measure of size, avoids the problems of valuation based on assets' historical cost but raises similar problems of allocation (e.g., how much of the president's time is assigned to each product?). Further, employment may vary throughout the year. Typically, larger firms in an industry have higher ratios of capital to labor than smaller ones; so measures based on employment usually show substantially less concentration than measures based on assets.

Value of Shipments. Today, the most commonly used measure of firm and market size is value of shipments, a figure closely related to but not identical with sales revenue. (Actual shipping dates may be different from dates when sales are recorded, and value of shipments includes interplant transfers within the same company.)

Net value of shipments provides the best measure of market share, but it does not measure relative firm size accurately. The problem stems from the degree of vertical integration not involving interplant transfers. Two firms, for example, may have identical values of television set shipments but one may assemble components purchased from others, while the other manufactures all its own components and assembles them in a single plant. The two firms would be quite different in size if measured by assets or employment.

Value Added by Manufacture. Value added by manufacture (value of shipments minus costs of purchases from others or, alternatively, the sum of a firm's wages, interest, rents, and profit) does distinguish among degrees of vertical integration. It is therefore used to measure *aggregate* concentration, or the percentage of the nation's total manufacturing activity accounted for by the 50, 100, 150, or 200 largest manufacturing firms. It is not used to measure concentration in individual product markets, both because firms' accounting records often make it impossible to report value added for a specific product and because its relevance is questionable. It makes little difference to short-run market power, for example, whether a seller of televisions manufactures its own components.

The Standard Industrial Classification (SIC) System

The U.S. Bureau of the Census uses a standard industrial classification system (SIC) in which the nation's manufacturing industries are classified into 20 two-digit SIC major groups (numbered 20 through 39), subdivided into 144 three-digit SIC groups (201 to 399) and 452 four-digit industries (2011 to 3999). For example, Major Group 28 comprises Chemicals and Allied Products, Group 281 is Industrial Organic Chemicals, and Industry 2812 is Alkalies and Chlorine. Industry concentration in the United States is almost always measured within SIC three-digit groups or four-digit industries. The Census Bureau is sensitive to problems of product definition, and the varied needs of different users of its data. For this reason, the SIC system is revised periodically by an intergovernmental technical committee.[1]

Concentration Ratios

Once units of measurement are determined and industries defined, an index of concentration must be constructed. The concentration ratio, or the proportion of total value of shipments of a product accounted for by the 4, 8, 20, and 50 largest manufacturers (referred to as CR4, CR8, CR20, and CR50), is reported periodically in the *Census of Manufactures* for three-digit groups and four-digit industries. To assure confidentiality, CR4 is the finest breakdown published in the United States, although a number of other countries report CR3.

Most economists use CR4 or CR8, presumably on the assumption that 4 or possibly even 8 firms might constitute an oligopolistic group exercising collective market power, while current theory suggests that the share of the market held by the 20 or 50 largest is of little relevance to the state of competition in a market. But John E. Kwoka, Jr., using privately collected data on individual-company market shares, has concluded that the percentage of shipments by the two largest firms (CR2) accounts for differences in industry price-cost margins, and therefore presumably for market power, better than any other concentration ratio from CR1 to CR10.[2]

An obvious problem with the concentration ratio is that it measures concentration at only one point on the size distribution. Suppose that in Industry A, CR4 = 55 percent and CR8 = 72 percent. In Industry B, suppose CR4 = 49 percent and CR8 = 77 percent. There is no clear answer as to whether Industry A or Industry B is more "highly concentrated." Or suppose industries A and B are the same industry in, say, 1963 and 1977. Has the industry become more or less concentrated? Several measures of concentration have been devised to yield a single index number for the entire population of a size distribution; the most widely used are the Gini coefficient and the Herfindahl index.[3]

The Gini Coefficient. Figure 8–1 illustrates the Gini coefficient. The vertical axis shows the cumulative percentage value of shipments (or of whatever measure of firm and market size is used), and the horizontal axis shows the cumulative percentage of firms in the industry, ranked from smallest to largest. Thus the curved line, known as the Lorenz curve, indicates that the first 20 percent of firms, comprising the industry's smallest ones, collectively accounted for 5 percent of value of shipments and that the first 50 percent, so ranked, accounted for 25 percent. Clearly, 100 percent of the firms must account for 100 percent of the shipments.

If all firms made equal shipments, the Lorenz curve would be a straight line with a 45-degree slope, or the dashed line in Figure 8–1. The greater the degree of inequality among the firms in the values of their shipments, the greater the bowing out of the Lorenz curve. Or, as inequality increases, Area A increases and Area B decreases. The Gini coefficient is simply

$$G = \frac{A}{A + B}$$

ranging from a value of 0 for perfect equality towards 1 as inequality becomes greater.

FIGURE 8-1   The Lorenz Curve and Areas Used in Calculating the Gini Coefficient

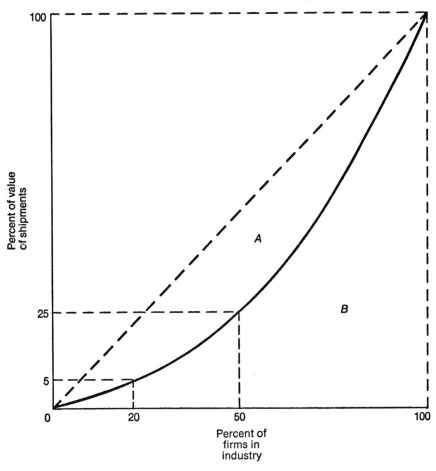

The Herfindahl Index.   Strictly speaking, the Gini coefficient measures inequality rather than concentration. Two, 5, or 50 firms with equal shipment values would all yield the same coefficient, $G = 0$. The Herfindahl index, designed to overcome this problem, takes into account the absolute number of firms in a market as well as their relative sizes. This index is simply the sum of the squares of the market share percentages of all firms in the industry. Or, if there are n firms in the industry,

$$H = \sum_{i=1}^{n} S_i^2$$

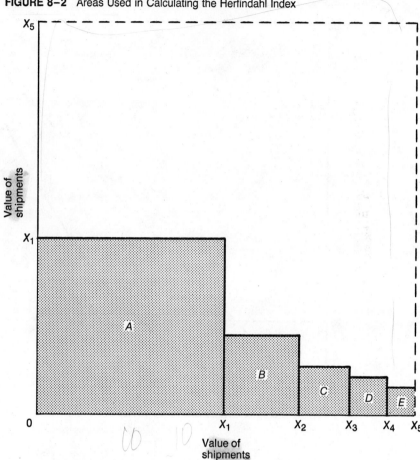

FIGURE 8–2 Areas Used in Calculating the Herfindahl Index

where S_i equals the percentage share or fraction of the market accounted for by the ith firm.

Figure 8–2 illustrates the principle behind the Herfindahl index. For interpretation of this diagram, the Herfindahl index may be rewritten as

$$H = \frac{\sum\limits_{i=1}^{n} X_i^2}{\left(\sum\limits_{i=1}^{n} X_i\right)^2}$$

where X_i equals the absolute value of shipments (or assets, employment, or value added) of the ith firm.

The value of shipments of the largest firm, OX_1, when squared, equals Area A. The square of the value of shipments of the second largest firm equals Area B. In this illustrative industry of five firms, the numerator of the Herfindahl index is the shaded area $A + B + C + D + E$. The denominator is the entire area of the large square, each side of which is equal in length to OX_5, the sum of the industry's shipments. The larger the number of firms, *ceteris paribus*, the smaller the value of the index; and the greater the degree of inequality, for a given number of firms, the larger the index. In a purely monopolistic market with only one seller, $H = 1$. If there are n firms of equal size in the market, $H = \frac{1}{n}$.

The Herfindahl index is often difficult to interpret because markets with quite different structures can have identical values for H. For example, in a market with five firms of equal size, $H = .20$. In a market that has one firm with 40 percent of value of shipments and nine others each with 6.67 percent, the value of H is also .20.

In June 1982, the Herfindahl index came into sudden prominence among antitrust lawyers as well as economists. The Antitrust Division of the Department of Justice announced that it would henceforth use this index to calculate the effects of horizontal mergers on market concentration. "Unlike the traditional four-firm concentration ratio," the division's "Merger Guidelines" explained, the Herfindahl index "reflects both the distribution of the market shares of the top four firms and the composition of the market outside the top four firms. It also gives proportionately greater weight to the market shares of the larger firms, which probably accords with their relative importance in any collusive interaction."[4]

Faith should not be placed in any single-number index of concentration. A market population consists of a number of firms of varying sizes. A single index number cannot encapsulate all relevant aspects of such a population.

TRENDS IN CONCENTRATION

Business concentration has been examined at two levels: the individual *industry* or *market* level (concentration in production and sales of specific goods and services) and the *aggregate, global,* or *overall* level (the extent to which the largest firms account for the nation's overall economic activity or some major sector such as manufacturing).

Industry or Market Concentration

Despite problems of measurement, current patterns of market concentration do indicate a number of basic structural features of the U.S. economy.

Structural Features of U.S. Economy. First, pure monopoly or even single-firm dominance of a market is virtually nonexistent at the national level. Market conquests such as Alcoa's 100 percent control of the domestic aluminum industry prior to World War II and the 80 to 95 percent market shares attained in the early 1900s by trusts such as Standard Oil and American Tobacco have been rolled back by a combination of time, flow of new capital, and public policy. General Motors' 46 percent share of the new car market (including imports) in 1980 and IBM's 65 to 73 percent share of the market for general-purpose computer systems in 1979[5] are exceptionally high and atypical.

Second, as illustrated in Table 8–1, the great majority of U.S. industrial markets range from oligopoly to imperfect or monopolistic competition. Several writers have treated CR4 of 50 percent and CR8 of 70 percent as the thresholds of "high" concentration.[6] In the United States, 134 of the nation's 452 four-digit industries were listed in the 1977 census as having a CR4 of 50 percent or over and 124 as having CR8 of 70 percent or over.

TABLE 8–1 Distribution of Four-Firm Concentration Ratios by Four-Digit Industries and Value of Shipments, 1977

CR4	Number of Industries*	Value of Shipments* ($ millions)
80–100%	22	$ 101,889.8
70–79	16	51,323.3
60–69	33	105,700.0
50–59	56	103,842.8
40–49	67	202,316.1
30–39	69	249,631.1
20–29	96	266,940.6
Less than 20	86	260,734.7
All industries	449	$1,358,526.4

*Less than total for all industries, as some have been excluded because of disclosure rules.
SOURCE: U.S. Department of Commerce, Bureau of the Census, *1977 Census of Manufactures: Concentration Ratios in Manufacturing*, subject series, May 1981 (Washington, D.C.: U.S. Government Printing Office, 1981), table 6, pp. 10–11.

Third, a common industrial pattern is a small core of very large firms surrounded by a fringe of much smaller ones. For example, the "big five" in industrial chemicals (Du Pont, Dow, Allied, Union Carbide, and Monsanto) dominate a total industry population of over 550 firms. Similarly, the giants of petroleum refining (Exxon, Shell, Mobil, Texaco, Chevron, Standard Oil of Indiana, and Atlantic Richfield) share their U.S. market with over 150 smaller, independent refineries.

Fourth, there is a statistically significant inverse correlation between concentration and size of market. Since, *ceteris paribus*, a large market can accommodate more firms than a small one, this is an intuitively plausible relationship. But it contradicts a common perception of giant corporations dominating the nation's major markets.

Fifth, manufacturing continues to decline in relative importance in the nation's overall economic activity. In 1950, manufacturing activity accounted for 29.2 percent of the gross national product. By 1970, the figure had fallen to 25.4 percent and, by 1981, to 21.9 percent.[7] Today, concentration in sectors such as wholesale and retail distribution, legal and medical services, and banking is attracting increased attention.

Historical Trends in Concentration. Beginning in the 1870s, industrialization resulted in a dramatic increase in the average size of firms and levels of concentration. But as Jesse W. Markham has noted, the effect on market power was offset by an equally dramatic expansion of average market size. By Markham's estimate, the average size of market served by a U.S. manufacturing establishment was about 3.24 times as large in 1900 as in 1882, as a result of rapid growth in the nation's transportation system, primarily railroad mileage, and a corresponding reduction in transportation costs.[8]

Data on industrial concentration were not collected on a systematic basis until 1935, and concentration ratios were not published until 1947.

One of the most interesting studies of changes in industrial concentration since World War II is that of Willard F. Mueller and Richard T. Rogers.[9] Their major findings are shown in Table 8–2. While average concentration for the 165 industries in Mueller and Rogers'

TABLE 8–2 Average Unweighted Four-Firm Concentration Ratios by Degree of Product Differentiation for 165 U.S. Manufacturing Industries, 1947–77

Year	Total Industries (165)*	Producer Goods (95)	Consumer Goods by Degree of Differentiation			
			All (70)	Low (21)	Moderate (33)	High (16)
1947	40.4%	43.8%	35.7%	26.0%	36.2%	47.7%
1954	39.8	42.5	36.0	23.8	35.9	52.3
1958	39.8	42.3	36.3	22.7	36.7	53.4
1963	41.0	42.3	39.3	24.8	39.6	57.8
1967	41.1	42.1	39.7	25.2	39.2	59.9
1972	41.8	42.0	41.4	27.0	41.4	60.6
1977	42.3	42.1	42.5	27.6	42.3	62.4
Change	+1.9%	−1.7%	+6.8%	+1.6%	+6.1%	+14.7%

*Numbers in parentheses indicate total number of industries in that category.
SOURCE: Willard F. Mueller and Richard T. Rogers, "Changes in Market Concentration of Manufacturing Industries, 1947–1977," *Review of Industrial Organization* 1, no. 1 (Spring 1984), pp. 1–14, at p. 3.

sample rose only slightly, this modest increase resulted from a decrease in concentration of producer goods industries offset by a substantial increase in concentration in consumer goods industries. By far the greatest increase occurred in those consumer goods industries with the highest ratios of advertising to sales.

To test more rigorously for the effect of advertising, Mueller and Rogers regressed the change in CR4 for each of their industries between 1947 and 1977 on the initial level of concentration, the industry's growth rate, industry size in 1977, and three variables measuring advertising intensity (total advertising, television and radio advertising, and newspaper, outdoor, and magazine advertising), each as a percentage of sales. Total advertising and advertising on television and radio, tested in separate regressions, had positive coefficients, statistically significant at the 5 and 1 percent levels, respectively. Newspaper, outdoor, and magazine advertising, included in the same regression as radio and television advertising, had negative but statistically insignificant effects. The rise of television advertising, Mueller and Rogers concluded, has played a particularly important role in increasing the levels of concentration in differentiated consumer goods industries. Television is an expensive medium that provides far greater advantages to national over local advertisers than the less costly media it replaced.

A major problem in ascertaining trends in market concentration is demonstrated in Mueller and Rogers' use of a sample of only 165 SIC four-digit industries. They had little choice—due to changes in census industry definitions, only these 165 (out of 452) were comparable over the entire period.

Aggregate, Global, or Overall Concentration

In describing the growth of aggregate concentration in 19th-century manufacturing, an early study (necessarily drawing on scattered and incomplete data) noted that from 1850 to 1910, average assets of manufacturing plants in the United States rose by a factor of 39, employment by a factor of 7, and value of output by 19. The authors were concerned that this increase in concentration was continuing, observing that in 1909, manufacturing plants with annual output over $1 million made up only 1.1 percent of the total number of such plants while accounting for 43.8 percent of the value of manufacturing output, up from 38 percent in 1904.[10]

In their 1932 book, Berle and Means estimated that at the beginning of 1930, the 200 largest nonfinancial corporations in the United States controlled 49.2 percent of the country's nonbanking corporate assets. The average annual rate of growth of these large corporations between 1909 and 1928 had been 5.4 percent, contrasted to only 2.0 percent for all other corporations. From projection of these figures, they calculated that if the growth trends continued, the 200 largest would control 70 percent of all nonfinancial corporate activity by 1950.[11]

But this trajectory did not continue. M. A. Adelman, in a study done 20 years later, found that the 139 largest manufacturing corporations in 1931 had owned 49.6 percent of the assets of all manufacturing corporations but that the share of the 139 largest in 1950 had fallen to 45.0 percent. Adelman concluded, "Concentration may be a problem, but for better or worse it is not threatening to engulf the economy. The moral, therefore, is simply that there is time to stop, look, and take thought."[12]

Following World War II, however, aggregate concentration of manufacturing again rose, as shown in Table 8–3. Between 1947 and 1954, there was a particularly sharp increase in the share of total value added accounted for by the 50 largest manufacturing companies; but since 1954, there has been little further change within this group. Aggregate concentration for the 200 largest, though, has continued to rise, especially within those ranking 101 to 200.

TABLE 8–3 Share of Total Value Added by Manufacture Accounted for by the 50, 100, 150 and 200 Largest U.S. Manufacturing Companies, 1947–77

Companies	1947	1954	1958	1962	1967	1972	1977
Largest 50	17%	23%	23%	24%	25%	25%	24%
Largest 100	23	30	30	32	33	33	33
Largest 150	27	34	35	36	38	39	39
Largest 200	30	37	38	40	42	43	44

SOURCE: U.S. Department of Commerce, Bureau of the Census, *1977 Census of Manufactures: Concentration Ratios in Manufacturing,* subject series, May 1981 (Washington, D.C.: U.S. Government Printing Office, 1981), p. 7.

Lawrence J. White[13] argued that figures such as those in Table 8–3 indicate that there was no increase in aggregate concentration between the early 1960s and 1977. He does not regard as significant the increased share of value added by manufacture among the firms in the bottom half of the top 200 over this period. To bolster his argument, he also presents census data measuring concentration by share of employment rather than by value added. By this measure, concentration among the top 200 in manufacturing declined from 1967 to 1976. Further, using data other than value added collected from various sources, White estimated changes in aggregate concentration, including sectors other than manufacturing, for various periods from the late 1950s through the late 1970s. Noting that the share of manufacturing in the nation's total value added had declined over this period, he concluded that "aggregate concentration in the private sector in the 1970s [measured for various periods and groupings of firms by employment, net income, and assets] apparently has not increased and probably has diminished slightly."[14]

Still, looking solely at the manufacturing sector (the only major sector for which we have value added data back to 1947), there does appear to be a continuing upward drift in aggregate concentration— slow and uncertain, but consistent with an overall trend since the last half of the 19th century. And heightened merger activity in the 1980s may be reinforcing that trend.

The conviction that aggregate concentration in manufacturing is rising over the long run (albeit by fitful leaps and starts) is supported by a study of asset concentration among the 500 largest industrial firms, as listed by *Fortune*, for 1967 to 1982. Edward Nissan and Regina Caveny reported that within the top 100, there had been virtually no change in concentration from the beginning of the period to the end, despite some year-to-year fluctuations, but for the bottom 400, there had been a steady increase.[15]

Aggregate Concentration and Diversification. One explanation of how aggregate concentration in manufacturing could rise from 1947 through the 1970s while average concentration in individual manufacturing markets remained nearly constant is that large firms were diversifying during the postwar years, both through internal expansion into new products and through conglomerate mergers. For diversification alone to lead to an increase in aggregate concentration, the largest firms must be growing overall at a more rapid pace than the average for all firms while, on the average, not expanding their shares of particular markets. A 1962 study by Michael Gort showed that growth and diversification are positively but only weakly related.[16] In examining the change in aggregate manufacturing concentration between 1947 and 1954, Ralph L. Nelson found that diversification had probably contributed to the increase but that its precise effect could not be identified.[17] He found that vertical integration among the top 50, leading to a more rapid growth in value added by manufacture than in value of shipments in any particular industry, had a larger and more perceptible effect than did horizontal diversification.

Aggregate Concentration: Aircraft and Automobiles. The principal causes of the 1947–54 increase in aggregate concentration, according to Nelson, were events in two industrial groups—aircraft and automobiles. Fifteen of the largest 50 firms in 1947 were replaced on the 1954 list. Seven of the 15 entrants were in SIC primary product group 372, Aircraft and Parts. As a result of the outbreak of the

Korean War in 1950, value of shipments of this group rose 571 percent between 1947 and 1954, while all manufacturing rose by only 51 percent. Even though CR4 fell in all of the four-digit SIC aircraft industries, the vastly increased value added by manufacture of these 7 newcomers raised the fraction accounted for by the top 50 by enough to account for almost half of the entire increase. Among the 35 firms that remained in the largest 50, the increased share in value added was accounted for almost entirely by firms in the Motor Vehicle and Parts industry (SIC 3717). In this instance, the increase in aggregate concentration was accompanied by a similar increase in market concentration, as CR4 in SIC 3717 rose from 56 percent in 1947 to 75 percent in 1954.

Nelson noted that a statistical problem arose in relating changes in aggregate concentration to changes in concentration in individual markets, since the former is reported as value added by manufacture (which cannot be broken down into the separate products of a firm) and the latter as value of shipments.

The relative roles played by diversification and other changes since 1954 remain problematic, as the Census Bureau has since denied outside researchers access to confidential data of the sort made available to Gort and Nelson.[18]

Turnover

In a 1954 study, A. D. H. Kaplan stressed the significance of turnover. "One way to test the competitiveness of big business," he argued, "is to find out the extent to which individual companies within the giant class have maintained their positions of leadership."[19] Kaplan found that these positions were "on the whole, unsure and maintained with great effort."[20] Of the 100 largest industrial corporations in 1909, only 36 remained in the 100 largest in 1948. Further evidence of the "precarious" nature of business leadership was found in analysis of the intervening years:

> Among the companies on the 1948 list there remained 31 which, disregarding changes of name, had maintained membership in the 100 largest in each of the selected years. Five more had appeared on the 1909 list but had fallen off in one or more of the three of the intervening years. Of the remaining 64 on the 1948 list, 25 appeared first in 1919, 14 in 1929, 5 in 1935, and 20 only in 1948.[21]

In a review of Kaplan's book, Markham noted that "it should come as a surprise to no one that between 1909 and 1948 steamship, express, sugar refining, locomotive, and ice companies gave way to producers of automobiles, aircraft, motion pictures, electrical appliances, and rubber tires."[22] A great deal of the turnover was the direct or indirect result of a single basic innovation—the internal-combustion engine. After regrouping Kaplan's firms within a revised market classification, Markham rejected Kaplan's conclusion that leading firms were in constant danger from dynamic competitive forces. Rather, he found that after allowance for mergers and the 1911 antitrust dissolutions, leading firms in particular industries (with few exceptions) had retained their positions. Kaplan's main point, however, is an important one—that is, turnover (as well as the level of concentration at any one time) is an indicator of the strength of competition.

A subsequent study by Norman R. Collins and Lee E. Preston noted that turnover *within* the ranks of the largest firms is as significant as entry to and exit *from* the group.[23] They proposed measuring stability over a period of time by calculating the correlation between the logarithms of assets (or some other measure of size) of each firm in the group at the beginning and end of the period. A perfect positive correlation would indicate that all of the firms in the group had grown at identical rates and thus preserved identical ranks and shares. The lower the correlation coefficient, the greater the instability, both within the group and in its turnover.

TABLE 8–4 Correlation Coefficients of Asset Sizes, by Pairs of Years, for the 100 Largest U.S. Manufacturing Firms, 1919–21 to 1962–64

Time Period	100 Largest Firms	200 Largest Firms
1919–21	.763	—
1921–23	.738	—
1923–25	.800	—
1925–27	.805	—
1927–29	.802	—
1929–31	.770	.790
1931–33	.871	.902
1933–35	.931	.924
1935–37	.886	.944
1937–39	.907	.920
1939–41	.840	.867
1948–50	.916	.915
1950–52	.879	.900
1952–54	.898	.913
1954–56	.831	.898
1956–58	.902	.934
1958–60	.859	.934
1960–62	.845	.937
1962–64	.841	.936

SOURCE: Stanley E. Boyle and Joseph P. McKenna, "Size Mobility of the 100 and 200 Largest U.S. Manufacturing Corporations: 1919–1964," *Antitrust Bulletin* 15 (Fall 1970), pp. 505–19, at p. 509.

Collins and Preston concluded that between 1909 and 1958, stability had increased, a finding corroborated by a number of more recent studies utilizing their measurement technique.[24] Results of one such study are shown in Table 8–4, where there appears to have been a sharp increase in stability after 1931. But a 1979 study, utilizing data through 1976, found no discernible trend toward either stability or instability among the 100 largest industrial firms since 1929.[25] Thus, there appears to be not so much a continuing increase in stability as a discrete shift reflecting somewhat greater turnover during the first three decades of the 20th century than since.

TABLE 8–5 Changes in Rank in Group Among 50 Largest Industrial Companies, 1947 and 1977

	1947	1954	1958	1962	1967	1972	1977
1977 group							
50 largest	23	30	32	36	39	43	50
51–100 largest	10	12	8	7	9	7	—
101–200 largest	10	1	6	4	1	—	—
Not in top 200	7	7	4	3	1	—	—
1947 group							
50 largest	50	35	34	29	24	25	24
51–100 largest	—	12	12	16	17	13	13
101–200 largest	—	3	4	5	5	6	5
Not in top 200	—	—	—	—	4	6	8

SOURCE: U.S. Department of Commerce, Bureau of the Census, *1977 Census of Manufactures: Concentration Ratios in Manufacturing*, subject series, May 1981 (Washington, D.C.: Government Printing Office, 1981), p. 8.

There is no unambiguous standard to determine if industrial turnover is high or low. Table 8–5 reproduces data from the *1977 Census of Manufactures*. Of the nation's 50 largest industrial corporations in 1949, only 24 remained in that group by 1977. Eight were no longer among the 200 largest. Similarly, only 23 of the 1977 top 50 had been among the 1947 group, and 7 had either risen from below the top 200 or did not exist in 1947.

DETERMINANTS OF CONCENTRATION

Several determinants of concentration widely recognized as among the most important in a modern industrial setting are enumerated and discussed below. However, an exhaustive study of an individual firm or industry is usually necessary to identify the sources of concentration in a specific case.

Economies of Scale and Scope Relative to Market Size

Perhaps the most obvious cause of concentration is that in many settings, the market can support only a limited number of firms. A number of sources of economies of scale exist at the levels of both the individual plant and the entire firm.

Operating Economies of Scale. Operating economies, determining optimal size of the plant, include the specialization of labor and machinery made possible both by the scale of production at any one time and by the length of production runs, technical economies of large machinery, the integration of processes of production, and massing of reserves.[26]

Specialization of Labor and Machinery. As workers specialize in one simple repetitive operation, they gain both speed and accuracy. Further, repetition of the same task eliminates time lost in turning from one operation to another. In his famous description of the division of labor in a small 18th century pin factory, Adam Smith noted that "One man draws out the wire, another straights it, a third cuts it, a fourth points it, a fifth grinds it at the top for receiving the head; to make the head requires two or three distinct operations; to put it on is a peculiar business."[27] The 10 employees in this factory turned out nearly 48,000 pins a day, whereas, according to Smith, one working alone could not have made 20. Dedication of a machine to a single function will yield similar economies of specialization and avoidance of downtime. (If a drill press can be used to drill holes of only one diameter, for example, and if work can flow smoothly past, the drill need be turned off and the bit changed only when a bit wears out.)

Technical Economies of Machine Size. Certain physical relationships determine optimal sizes for machinery. As E. A. G. Robinson described the matter, "If you take an ordinary container, such as a water tank, and double every dimension, so that it is twice as high, twice as wide, and twice as broad as it was before, the amount of water which the tank will hold has increased with the cube of the dimension; that is, in this case it has increased eight times."[28] The surface area of material needed to build the tank goes up by the square of the dimension, or only four times in this example. But Robinson might also have pointed out that the potential saving with increased size from this source is limited, as the pressure on the walls of the tank increases in the same proportion as the volume of water, while the bursting strength is a function of thickness of the wall alone. In other words, if the walls of the smaller tank had been just thick enough to contain the water, those of the larger one would have to be eight times as thick. For the same reason, there is a maximum length possible for a cable increased proportionally in length and diameter before its own weight tears it apart. (An ant the size of a human being, far from demonstrating the immense strength depicted in some science fiction, would crumble under the weight of its own exoskeleton.)[29]

Economies of Combination (Integration of Production). Because of economies of combination, the optimal scale of a plant is likely to be a multiple of the optimal scale of any of its production processes. Suppose, for example, that the minimum efficient scale (MES) of the first step in production, rough shaping of a block, is 300 units per hour. Suppose further that the MES of the second step, drilling holes in the blocks, is 500 units per hour and that of the third, finishing and smoothing, is 200. To carry out all three steps without any excess capacity at any stage would require a production of 3,000 units per hour (10 MES production lines shaping blocks, 6 drilling, and 15 finishing). Actual economies of combination or integration of production are, of course, usually much more complex.

Economies of Massed Reserves. There are economies of massed reserves in being prepared for unpredictable exigencies. If a transformer supplying power to a production line is prone to burnout, it might be prudent to have one on reserve. But even if the firm needs a separate transformer for each production line, the number of reserve transformers need not be equal to the number of production lines since the probability of two burning out at once is so much lower (the square of the probability of this happening to one) that one on reserve might be adequate. Economies of massed reserves, Robinson noted, may be multiplant economies—the excess capacity of one plant could be used to relieve overloads on others.

Multiplant Operations to Overcome Operating Diseconomies of Scale. At a certain rate of operation, all feasible economies of scale of plant may be fully exploited. But operating diseconomies need not set in at higher rates. Technical diseconomies such as bursting strength may limit the size of a particular machine or scale of a production operation; but once the optimum-sized production process has been designed and activated, it can be duplicated repeatedly, side by side with existing operations or, if necessary, in new locations.

To make a slightly subtle theoretical point: constraint of continued expansion, by the need to duplicate facilities in less suitable locations or by greater difficulties in obtaining scarce inputs, represents an upward shift of the entire average cost curve rather than an upturn in the curve. No diseconomy of scale has set in, since either an entrant building a single new facility or a firm building its 20th would face the identical higher location or material costs.

Operating Economies of Scope. In addition to operating economies of scale (lower unit costs of production and distribution of a single product at higher rates of output), a diversified firm may be able to obtain operating economies of scope, described by John C. Panzar and Robert D. Willig in a 1981 paper as a condition of production under which "it is less costly to combine two or more product lines in one firm than to produce them separately."[30] Several examples of such economies of scope given in a 1982 article by Elizabeth E. Bailey and Ann F. Friedlaender include joint production (mutton and wool), indivisible fixed assets (a stamping machine that can be used on both automobiles and trucks but with capacity in excess of the demand for either product), and combinations of robots and computer-controlled machine tools that can be switched from one job to another more flexibly than human assembly-line labor.[31]

Nonoperating Economies of Scale and Scope. Beyond operating economies at the plant level, there are economies of large transactions and volume of shipping in both purchasing and selling. Large firms have access to more varied and lower-cost sources of finance. There are advantages to a firm's having its own engineering, legal, R&D, and transportation departments rather than having to rely on outside services; but the amount of business needed to keep such departments occupied may be more than that generated by a single MES plant. The "span" of an outstanding manager may exceed the output of one MES plant: an executive who can save a firm 20 cents per unit is worth more to a firm producing 5 million units per year than to one producing 5,000.

Oliver E. Williamson discusses another important nonoperating economy of scope, internal allocation of capital among a firm's various divisions or products, in his multidivisional, or "M-form," firm.[32] Such firms, Williamson points out, can shift funds from less to more profitable lines more efficiently than can the capital market, both because the firm's internal flow of information is quicker, more accurate, and more complete than that available to an outside investor and because the internal transfer itself is quicker, simpler, and less costly than a transfer through payment of profits to investors and subsequent reinvestment by the recipients.

Illustrating Economies and Diseconomies of Scale. Economists working in the area of industrial organization conventionally treat the long-run average cost curve of the typical firm as J- rather than U-shaped, or as having a long flat bottom that may or may not turn up at very high rates of output. Such a curve is shown in Figure 8–3. The short-run average cost curves (*SATCs*) are U-shaped, since a firm will experience less efficient, higher-cost production as it deviates from the optimal mix of variable and fixed factors by producing either too much or too little with a particular combination of capital and land. At very high rates of output diseconomies of scale may cause the long-run average cost (*LATC*) to rise, as shown by the dotted portions of the curves on Figure 8–3. The most likely causes of diseconomies of scale, where they exist, are growing costs of communication and co-ordination within an organization as it grows in size and complexity, and less rapid and flexible responses to changing market or internal conditions. Employee alienation may be an integral part of these problems. But some argue that computerized data collection and communication coupled with decentralized management techniques may largely overcome these diseconomies of scale, at least to the extent that they pose virtually no constraints on expansion of the modern corporation.

FIGURE 8-3 J–Shaped Long-Run Average Cost Curve and Associated U–Shaped Short-Run Average Cost Curves

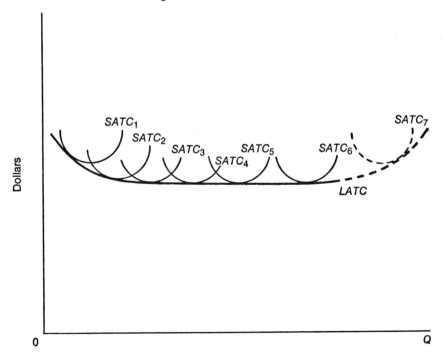

Economies of Scale and Scope: Multiplant Firms. Census Bureau data do not show ownership of individual plants, but the extent of multiplant operation is evident from several sources. In a special tabulation made for 1950, the Federal Trade Commission found the distribution of plant ownership shown in Table 8–6. Examples from *Moody's Industrial Manual* and the 1982 annual reports of some of the nation's largest firms include United Technologies with over 300 plants; Ford Motor Company with 87 domestic automobile plants, 149 overseas automobile plants, and 73 tractor plants; General Electric with 228 domestic and 135 foreign plants; and Exxon, which operated 70 domestic and 39 foreign refineries.

TABLE 8–6 Average Number of Establishments Operated by the 1,000 Largest U.S. Manufacturing Companies in 1950, by Size Class

Companies Ranked by Size	Number of Plants Operated
1–15	87
16–50	45
51–100	24
101–200	17
201–500	10
501–1,000	5

SOURCE: U.S. Federal Trade Commission, *Report of the Federal Trade Commission on Industrial Concentration and Product Diversification in the 1,000 Largest Manufacturing Companies: 1950* (Washington, D.C.: U.S. Government Printing Office, 1957), p. 37.

Virtually all large U.S. corporations are multiplant firms. Yet evidence analyzed throughout the 20th century repeatedly shows that economies of scale and scope in multiplant firms do not fully explain existing levels of concentration.

Investigations carried out before World War II included in-depth case studies of six of the largest trusts of the early 20th century,[33] analyses of the subsequent profit experiences of 35 combinations formed before 1904,[34] and several systematic examinations of the overall relationship between size of firm and profits throughout the entire economy.[35] Findings from these studies overwhelmingly rejected the hypothesis that the largest U.S. firms were by and large also the most efficient.

In a 1940 study carried out for the Temporary National Economic Committee, the Federal Trade Commission sampled both costs of production and rates of return on invested capital in 18 important industries from 1910 to 1938. The largest firm had the lowest costs in only 1 of 59 comparisons made. In 37 of these 59, a firm classed as small had the lowest costs. In the studies of rates of return, the largest company had the highest rate of return in 12 of 84 comparisons, while small firms were highest in 13. On the average, one third of the firms examined performed better than the largest in their comparison group in terms of both cost and profitability.[36]

A few years later, studies by the Department of Commerce concluded that firms in the middle size ranges, from $1 million to $50 million in assets, had higher average aftertax returns on owners' equity than did firms in either smaller or larger size classes.[37]

The most convincing postwar works on the issue of size and efficiency are those of Bain and of Scherer and his colleagues, based on questionnaires and in-depth interviews with business executives. In 17 of 20 industries studied, Bain found that the actual CR4s for 1947 were more than twice as high as could be justified by estimated optimal plant size. In 6 of his 20 industries, Bain's informants estimated that there were no economies of multiplant operation; in 8, it proved impossible to obtain definite estimates. In the remaining 6, estimated multiplant economies ranged from 0.5 percent of total unit cost to 5 percent, and the number of plants needed to obtain these economies ranged from 2 to 10.[38]

The results of the more recent study by Scherer et al. are shown for 12 U.S. industries in Table 8–7.

The authors interpreted the results shown in this table as confirming earlier studies.

TABLE 8–7 Extent of Multiplant Economies, Share of U.S. Market Required in 1967 to Obtain These Economies, and Actual Average 1970 Market Shares of Three Largest Firms, for 12 Manufacturing Industries

Industry	(1) Overall Disadvantage of Representative General-Line Single MES Plant Firms	(2) Number of MES Plants Needed to Have Not More than a Slight Overall Handicap	(3) Share of U.S. Market Required in 1967	(4) Average Market Share of U.S. Top-Three Members, 1970
Beer brewing	Slight to severe	3–4	10–14%	13%
Cigarettes	Slight to moderate (borderline)	1–2	6–12	23
Fabric weaving	Very slight to moderate	3–6	1	10
Paints	Slight	1	1.4	9
Petroleum refining	Very slight to moderate	2–3	4–6	8
Shoes	Slight to moderate	3–6	1	6
Glass bottles	Slight to moderate	3–4	4–6	22
Cement	Slight	1	2	7
Ordinary steel	Very slight	1	3	14
Bearings	Slight to moderate	3–5	4–7	14
Refrigerators	Moderate	4–8	14–20	21
Storage batteries	Slight	1	2	18

SOURCE: Frederic M. Scherer, Alan Beckenstein, Erich Kaufer, and R. Dennis Murphy, *The Economics of Multiplant Operation: An International Comparisons Study* (Cambridge, Mass.: Harvard University Press, 1975), p. 336.

In only three industries [in column (4)], brewing, refrigerators, and petroleum refining, are the observed leading firm market shares of about the same magnitude as the "required" estimates of column (3). In weaving and storage batteries, actual shares exceed "required" shares by roughly ten times; in paints, shoes, bottles, and steel, by four to six times; and in cigarettes, bearings, and cement, by two to three times. To the extent that our estimates are valid, national market seller concentration appears in most industries to be much higher than it needs to be for leading firms to take advantage of all but slight residual multi-plant scale economies.[39]

Thus, there is substantial evidence that we must look beyond economies of scale and scope, despite their importance, to fully explain current levels of concentration in U.S. industry.

Superior Product or Business Acumen

In a 1966 case alleging violation of Section 2 of the Sherman Act, the Supreme Court distinguished "growth or development as a consequence of a superior product, business acumen, or historic accident" as innocent and hence a legal source of monopoly power.[40] A firm may dominate a market by producing a better product than its competitors or by operating more efficiently. Yet only a minority of the nation's largest firms have grown to their present sizes and market positions through internal growth alone; most owe their rank and market share to growth through merger.[41]

There are, however, some very large firms whose success and growth are attributable primarily to outstanding competence and originality in leadership. Such firms pose an acute challenge to a public policy designed to restrain market power. "A single producer may be the survivor out of a group of active competitors, merely by virtue of his superior skill, foresight and industry," Judge Learned Hand wrote in 1945. "The successful competitor, having been urged to compete, must not be turned upon when he wins."[42]

Historic Accident or the Course of Events

As the Supreme Court noted, monopoly may arise from historic accident. Success in the race to develop a new product or process, discovery of a source of rare raw materials, and the perfectly timed introduction of a product in the face of a new consumer fad are likely to be the results of a combination of ability, diligence, and sheer good luck. Firms are both buffeted and blessed by external events—such as wars, major innovations and technical change, and the fortunes of customers and suppliers—that they can neither control nor often anticipate.

An intriguing illustration of the role of chance in determining market structure has been drawn from a stochastic, or random, process model. Suppose that a number of firms, all of equal size and managerial competence, enter a new market simultaneously. Suppose further that customers have no brand preferences and purchase from the firms at random. In the first year, some firms will make more than average sales and others will make less (at least, the probability is minuscule that customers choosing randomly will distribute themselves equally among the firms). Thus, by the beginning of the second year, some firms will have grown more than others, if growth occurs in response to demand. Some will have successive years of good luck; others will suffer a run of bad luck and perhaps leave the industry. The outcome compares to what one would expect if a number of gamblers, starting with equal stakes, played a night of roulette or some other game of pure chance, requiring no skill whatsoever. Some would leave the table penniless; while others would be many times richer by dawn than when they started.

If the assumptions of the stochastic model are made more restrictive, the end result can be described by use of a mathematical principle known as Gibrat's law. Assume that the percentage rates of growth in sales experienced in each year by the various firms are normally distributed and that each firm's chance of experiencing one of these growth rates in any given year is independent of its size or past rates of growth. According to Gibrat's law, if the mean growth rate and its standard distribution remain constant over time, the distribution of firm sizes will approach one that is normal in the *logarithms* of the sizes. Since each doubling of actual size represents an equal absolute increase in the logarithm of size, a log-normal distribution is one with a large number of small firms and only a few large ones. Simulations employing Gibrat's law have led to size distributions approximating those of actual markets.[43] While few, if any, industrial organization economists would ascribe current levels of concentration solely to chance, most believe that random processes do play an important role.

Product Life Cycle and Market Growth Rate

The product life cycle and market growth rate affect the level of concentration. A successful product typically goes through stages of introduction, rapid growth, slower growth in maturity, and decline. Investigators have also noted that, *ceteris paribus,* market growth tends to reduce concentration. The rapid growth stage, in the absence of effective patent protection or other barriers, promotes ease of entry; we might then expect that one or a few pioneers successfully introducing a product would find themselves faced with a number of new competitors and declining market shares. With market saturation at maturity, there may be product standardization, greater economies of scale in both production and distribution, and a subsequent industry "shakeout" involving both mergers and the departure of less efficient firms. Thus, barriers to entry and concentration should both increase.

Many of the nation's major industries, including automobiles, aircraft, semiconductors, and television sets, have evolved roughly as depicted in this model. But the model is not universally applicable: some products, such as aluminum and computers, did not experience significant market deconcentration in the growth stage; others, such as textiles, have remained at low levels of concentration into maturity and even decline.

Conscious Effort to Attain and Maintain Market Power

Since concentration enhances market power, which in turn provides the opportunity to earn monopolistic profits, concentration should be partly the result of purposive activities of profit-seeking businesses. Activities aimed primarily or exclusively at attaining market power seek to absorb rivals through merger, eliminate rivals through predatory and exclusionary practices, or restrict competition through collusion. The first two of these three strategies will, if successful, increase concentration.

Mergers. Analysts have identified two major merger waves before World War II. The first took place around the turn of the century, peaking between 1898 and 1902. The second, which served in part to restore levels of concentration that had eroded since the first, lasted from 1926 to 1930.[44]

Nelson identified 313 mergers resulting in the disappearance of 3,012 firms from 1895 to 1904. He noted that 48.6 percent of the disappearances and 70.4 percent of the capitalized values involved in the mergers led to combinations with leading or dominant market positions. He warned that it would be "extremely shaky reasoning" to attribute this pattern solely to an increased desire among American business leaders for market power, but he did detect "a fairly strong desire to avoid rigorous competition."[45] The development of an efficient capital market in the United States, Nelson contended, made the first merger movement possible. Promoters' profits, or the fees earned by investment bankers in managing a merger, provided an important motive not unrelated to the prospect of monopoly power, since promoters' fees were often paid in shares of the common stock of the new firm.

While growth of average firm size from the 1870s into the 20th century was clearly stimulated by such scale-enhancing factors as "the rate of industrial growth, the rise of technological innovation, and the growth of interregional transportation," Nelson concluded that these factors were not significant causes of the merger wave.[46] Companies formed by merger in this early period include such dominant firms as Standard Oil, American Tobacco, U.S. Steel, International Harvester, Du Pont, Anaconda Copper, General Electric, American Sugar Refining Company, and U.S. Rubber. In the aftermath of the merger wave, General Motors was put together in 1908, followed by IBM in 1911.

The mergers of the 1920s were, on the whole, of a different character. When measured by number of firms disappearing or dollar value of assets involved, this second merger movement was bigger than the first, but its impact on industrial structure was much slighter. Mergers of this decade added significantly to concentration in the distributive trades and in public utilities. Dissolutions required under the Public Utility Holding Company Act of 1935, however, reversed this last effect.

Markham, in a survey of the evidence on causes and effects of the merger movements, found that the prospect of promoters' profit, particularly during the stock market boom in the late 1920s, was a major cause of the merger wave. One result was to increase the extent of oligopoly, rather than single-firm dominance, in a number of industries; but Markham argued convincingly that attainment of oligopoly was an unlikely motive for, as distinguished from effect of, the mergers. Such a motive presumes a mutual recognition of the similar plans of others and of their subsequent behavior, requiring a greater awareness on the part of those considering merger than, in Markham's words, "logic can support."[47]

Since World War II, there have been a number of periods of high merger activity; but as a result of the 1950 Celler-Kefauver Act, which stiffened the Clayton Act's prohibition against anticompetitive mergers, most of these have been conglomerate or vertical mergers. They may have had a significant impact on aggregate concentration but have contributed little, if anything, to concentration in individual product markets.[48]

Predatory and Exclusionary Behavior. To identify the causes of market power in a particular industry, it is important to determine how the power was initially attained and subsequently maintained.[49] Concentration may result from economies of scale relative to market size, a patented invention, or some other "innocent" source yet be perpetuated by the deliberate erection of artificial barriers to entry after the market has expanded or the patent expired.

While predatory and exclusionary behavior may be ineffective in *attaining* monopoly power, such conduct is often crucial to *maintaining*

it. Pricing by an already dominant firm to deter entry is more feasible than predatory pricing to drive existing rivals out of a market, and foreclosure of markets through vertical integration is easier before competitors have entered.

Other Motives for Expansion

Growth of a firm, whether internal or through merger, may be motivated by other than economies of scale or scope or the prospect of market power. As noted previously, firms may integrate either upstream or downstream to reduce market uncertainty, and promoters' profit has provided a significant motive for merger. Several writers have suggested that management-controlled firms may expand beyond the optimal size, either because managerial compensation is more closely related to sales volume or number of individuals supervised than to profits or because managers are megalomanic and enjoy control of the largest possible organization.[50]

Government Policies

In 1955, Walter Adams and Horace M. Gray wrote *Monopoly in America: The Government as Promoter*.[51] The title describes the subject, one that has become of increasing importance and concern as government's role in the economy expands.

Barriers to entry (including patents, copyrights, tariffs, licenses, and franchises) are created by governmental action. H. O. Havemeyer of the American Sugar Refining Company remarked, in testimony before the U.S. Industrial Commission in 1899, that "the mother of all trusts is the customs tariff bill."[52] Havemeyer meant that a combination of U.S. sugar refiners would not have been worthwhile unless there had been some assurance that the trust would be able to exploit its market power without attracting foreign competition as soon as it raised the domestic price.

Tax laws have encouraged concentration. Through retained earnings, corporations may expand beyond otherwise preferable sizes, since stockholders pay personal income taxes only on that portion of earnings that they receive in dividends. Mergers have been encouraged by problems of uncertain valuation of family-owned firms for estate tax purposes and by tax code provisions allowing an acquiring firm to use past losses of an acquired firm to reduce its own future income tax liabilities.

Ironically, enforcement of the antitrust laws has promoted concentration. An early interpretation of the Sherman Act by the Supreme Court held that agreements (or "loose-knit" combinations) among firms to fix price, divide markets, or restrict output are per se illegal (see

Chapter Five). However, in the first case involving formation of a trust through merger (a "close-knit" combination), the Supreme Court held in 1895 that merely showing the manufacture of sugar was monopolized did not suffice to establish the requisite effect on commerce.[53] It was not until the 1904 *Northern Securities* decision that the Supreme Court asserted unambiguously that the Sherman Act could be used to attack close-knit combinations, regardless of organizational form.[54] Between 1895 and 1904, therefore, merger appeared to be a much safer device for limiting competition than collusion, and recognition of this situation by corporate lawyers and their clients stimulated the merger wave at the turn of the century.

Government procurement policies—particularly those of the Department of Defense (DoD) and the National Aeronautics and Space Agency (NASA)—may favor large and dominant firms. Since the end of the Korean War, the 100 largest defense contractors have received approximately two thirds of the total dollar value of DoD prime contract awards. Over the same period, small business firms have been receiving around 20 percent of DoD prime contracts, although small business accounts for roughly half of the nation's value added by manufacture.[55] In fiscal year 1981, 83 percent of the federal funds awarded to industry for R&D (the bulk of which came from DoD and NASA) went to firms with over 25,000 employees, while only 65 percent of all company-funded R&D was accounted for by firms in this size class.[56]

There may be "spillover" effects from government procurement to commercial civilian markets. As noted in a study of the U.S. commercial aircraft industry by Almarin Phillips,[57] firms obtaining contracts for both R&D and follow-on production of military aircraft gained knowledge and experience relevant to their subsequent development and introduction of new commercial aircraft. In this instance, the spillover effect heightened concentration in the commercial market; but spillovers from government to commercial markets may heighten competition in the latter, particularly if the firms benefiting from government contracts are not already among the larger and better established ones in the related commercial markets.

Finally, government regulation may promote concentration or retard the development of competition. Environmental and occupational safety rules may impose relatively greater cost burdens on small firms than on large ones. The major impetus for deregulation of airlines, trucking, and communications has stemmed from growing recognition that government regulation has removed competition from these industries, either by protecting the industry itself or preventing it from competing with another regulated industry. Regulation of trucking, for example, was imposed largely to prevent truckers from competing with the regulated railroads.

Alfred E. Kahn refers to the "oversimplified but illuminating generalization that regulatory commissions tend to go through a life cycle," beginning as "enthusiastic protagonists of the public interest" but "gradually becoming devitalized, limited in their perspective, routinized and bureaucratized in their policies and procedures, and increasingly solicitous and protective of the companies they are supposed to regulate."[58] He cites several reasons for this metamorphosis: the quality of personnel is higher and quantity of financial resources larger in the regulated industries; regulatory officials may suffer from the "subtle corruption" of prospects for later careers in the industries they regulate; producer interests are generally more effective in pressuring commissions and legislatures than consumer interests; and perhaps most important, since a regulatory commission is responsible for ensuring a service considered vital to the public interest, it understandably becomes solicitous of the industry's health.

ENDNOTES

[1]U.S. Department of Commerce, Bureau of the Census, *1977 Census of Manufactures*, vol. 1 (Washington, D.C.: U.S. Government Printing Office, 1981), pp. x–xi; U.S. Executive Office of the President, Office of Management and Budget, *Standard Industrial Classification Manual, 1972* (Washington, D.C.: U.S. Government Printing Office, 1972). For adaptations designed to yield industry definitions more in accord with the economist's concern for indicators of market power, see Carl Kaysen and Donald F. Turner, *Antitrust Policy: An Economic and Legal Analysis* (Cambridge, Mass.: Harvard University Press, 1959); Marshall Hall and Leonard W. Weiss, "Firm Size and Profitability," *Review of Economics and Statistics* 49, no. 3 (August 1967), pp. 319–31; William G. Shepherd, *Market Power and Economic Welfare* (New York: Random House, 1970).

[2]John E. Kwoka, Jr., "The Effect of Market Share Distribution on Industry Performance," *Review of Economics and Statistics* 61, no. 1 (February 1979), pp. 101–9; John E. Kwoka, Jr., "Does the Choice of Concentration Measure Really Matter?" *Journal of Industrial Economics* 29, no. 4 (June 1981), pp. 445–53.

[3]In the early 1970s, concentration measures based on the concept of entropy, or relative dispersion, were popular. For an excellent discussion, see Richard A. Miller, "Numbers Equivalents, Relative Entropy, and Concentration Ratios: A Comparison Using Market Performance," *Southern Economic Journal* 39, no. 1 (July 1972), pp. 107–12. For a systematic survey of a number of measures, see Christian Marfels, "A Bird's Eye View to Measures of Concentration," *Antitrust Bulletin* 20, no. 3 (Fall 1975), pp. 485–503.

[4]U.S. Department of Justice, "Merger Guidelines" (Washington, D.C.: June 14, 1982), p. 27. Reprinted in Commerce Clearing House, *Trade Regulation Reports*, no. 546 (June 16, 1982).

[5]Figures taken from Lawrence J. White, "The Automobile Industry," and Alan K. McAdams, "The Computer Industry," in *The Structure of American Industry*, 6th ed., ed. Walter Adams (New York: Macmillan, 1982), pp. 148, 288.

[6]See, for example, Joe S. Bain, "Relation of Profit Rate to Industry Concentration: American Manufacturing, 1936–40,"*Quarterly Journal of Economics* 65, no. 3 (August 1951), pp. 293–324; David Schwartzman, "Effect of Monopoly on Price," *Journal of Political Economy* 67, no. 4 (August 1959), pp. 352–62; H. Michael Mann, "Seller Concentration, Barriers to Entry, and Rates of Return in Thirty Industries, 1950–1960," *Review of Economics and Statistics* 48, no. 3 (August 1966), pp. 296–307.

[7]U.S. Council of Economic Advisers, *1983 Annual Report of the Council of Economic Advisers* (Washington, D.C.: U.S. Government Printing Office, 1983), p. 174.

[8]Jesse W. Markham, "Survey of the Evidence and Findings on Mergers," in *Business Concentration and Price Policy,* National Bureau for Economic Research (Princeton, N.J.: Princeton University Press, 1955), pp. 141–82, at pp. 155–6.

[9]Willard F. Mueller and Richard T. Rogers, "Changes in Market Concentration of Manufacturing Industries, 1947–1977," *Review of Industrial Organization* 1, no. 1 (Spring 1984), pp. 1–14. See also, by the same authors, "The Role of Advertising in Changing Concentration of Manufacturing Industries," *Review of Economics and Statistics* 62, no. 1 (February 1980), pp. 89–96.

[10]Jeremiah W. Jenks and Walter E. Clark, *The Trust Problem,* 4th ed. (Garden City, N.Y.: Doubleday Publishing, 1920), pp. 17–19.

[11]Adolf A. Berle, Jr., and Gardiner C. Means, *The Modern Corporation and Private Property* (New York: Macmillan, 1932), pp. 32–40.

[12]M. A. Adelman, "The Measurement of Industrial Concentration," *Review of Economics and Statistics* 33, no. 4 (November 1951), pp. 269–96, at p. 296.

[13]Lawrence J. White, "What Has Been Happening to Aggregate Concentration in the United States?" *Journal of Industrial Economics* 29, no. 3 (March 1981), pp. 223–30.

[14]Ibid., p. 229.

[15]Edward Nissan and Regina Caveny, "Relative Concentration of the Largest 500 Firms," *Southern Economic Journal* 51, no. 3 (January 1985), pp. 880–81.

[16]Michael Gort, *Diversification and Integration in American Industry* (Princeton, N.J.: Princeton University Press, 1962).

[17]Ralph L. Nelson, *Concentration in the Manufacturing Industries of the United States* (New Haven, Conn.: Yale University Press, 1963).

[18]Frederic M. Scherer, *Industrial Market Structure and Economic Performance,* 2d ed. (Skokie, Ill.: Rand McNally, 1980), p. 78.

[19]A. D. H. Kaplan, *Big Enterprise in a Competitive System* (Washington, D.C.: Brookings Institution, 1954), p. 132.

[20]Ibid., p. 141.

[21]Ibid.

[22]Jesse W. Markham, *American Economic Review* 45, no. 3 (June 1955), pp. 448–51, at pp. 449–50.

[23]Norman R. Collins and Lee E. Preston, "The Size Structure of the Largest Industrial Firms, 1909–1958," *American Economic Review* 51, no. 5 (December 1961), pp. 986–1011.

[24]For example, see David Mermelstein, "Large Industrial Corporations and Asset Shares," *American Economic Review* 59, no. 4 (September 1969), part 1, pp. 531–41; Stanley E. Boyle and Joseph P. McKenna, "Size Mobility of the 100 and 200 Largest U.S. Manufacturing Corporations: 1919–1964," *Antitrust Bulletin* 15 (Fall 1970), pp. 505–19; comments by David R. Kamerschen, Stanley E. Boyle, and David Mermelstein, *American Economic Review* 61, no. 1 (March 1971), pp. 160–74.

[25]Robert J. Stonebraker, "Turnover and Mobility among the 100 Largest Firms: An Update," *American Economic Review* 69, no. 5 (December 1979), pp. 968–73.

[26]The discussion here draws heavily on E. A. G. Robinson's classic contribution, *The Structure of Competitive Industry* (New York: Harcourt Brace Jovanovich, 1932).

[27]Adam Smith, *The Wealth of Nations,* ed. Edwin Cannan (New York: Modern Library, 1937), p. 4.

[28]Robinson, *Structure of Industry,* pp. 28–29.

[29]For a fascinating discussion of the relationships between size and dimensions of

animals and such features as cross-sectional bearing strength, surface tension of water, gravity, and oxygen absorption, see J. B. S. Haldane, "On Being the Right Size," *Possible Worlds and Other Papers* (New York: Harper & Brothers, 1928), pp. 20–28.

[30]John C. Panzar and Robert D. Willig, "Economies of Scope," *American Economic Review* 71, no. 2 (May 1981), pp. 268–72, at p. 268.

[31]Elizabeth E. Bailey and Ann F. Friedlaender, "Market Structure and Multiplant Industries," *Journal of Economic Literature* 20, no. 3 (September 1982), pp. 1024–48.

[32]Oliver E. Williamson, *Corporate Control and Business Behavior* (Englewood Cliffs, N.J.: Prentice Hall, 1970), pp. 138–41.

[33]Eliot Jones, *The Trust Problem in the United States* (New York: Macmillan, 1921).

[34]Arthur S. Dewing, "A Statistical Test of the Success of Consolidations," *Quarterly Journal of Economics* 36, no. 1 (November 1921), pp. 84–101. For somewhat different results more favorable to the hypothesis that concentration was a function of economies of scale and managerial ability, see Shaw Livermore, "The Success of Industrial Mergers," *Quarterly Journal of Economics* 50, no. 1 (November 1935), pp. 68–96.

[35]See, among others, William L. Crum, *Corporate Size and Earning Power* (Cambridge, Mass.: Harvard University Press, 1939); U.S. Temporary National Economic Committee, *Investigation of Concentration of Economic Power,* monograph no. 13: *Relative Efficiency of Large, Medium-Sized and Small Business* (Washington, D.C.: U.S. Government Printing Office, 1941); Joseph L. McConnell, "Corporate Earnings by Size of Firm," *Survey of Current Business* 25, no. 5 (May 1945), pp. 6–12; Joseph L. McConnell, "1942 Corporate Profits by Size of Firm," *Survey of Current Business* 26, no. 1 (January 1946), pp. 10–16, 20.

[36]U.S. Temporary National Economic Committee, *Investigation of Concentration,* Monograph no. 13.

[37]McConnell, "Corporate Earnings" and "1942 Corporate Profits."

[38]Joe S. Bain, *Barriers to New Competition* (Cambridge, Mass.: Harvard University Press, 1956), pp. 83–87.

[39]Frederic M. Scherer, Alan Beckenstein, Erich Kaufer, and R. Dennis Murphy, *The Economics of Multi-Plant Operation: An International Comparisons Study* (Cambridge, Mass: Harvard University Press, 1975), p. 93.

[40]United States v. Grinnell Corporation, 384 U.S. 563, 571.

[41]Ralph L. Nelson, *Merger Movements in American Industry: 1895–1956* (Princeton, N.J.: Princeton University Press, 1959), pp. 154–56, contains a table listing the 100 largest manufacturing corporations in the United States in 1955, with the dates of the most important mergers if mergers were important in the firm's history. Only 37 show no such mergers.

[42]United States v. Aluminum Company of America, 148 F. 2d 416, 430.

[43]Herbert A. Simon and C. P. Bonini, "The Size Distribution of Business Firms," *American Economic Review* 48, no. 4 (September 1958), pp. 607–17; Richard E. Quandt, "On the Size Distribution of Firms," *American Economic Review* 56, no. 3 (June 1966), pp. 416–32; Irwin H. Silberman, "On Lognormality as a Summary Measure of Concentration," *American Economic Review* 57, no. 4 (September 1967), pp. 807–31; Scherer, *Industrial Market Structure,* pp. 145–47.

[44]A definitive study is Nelson, *Merger Movements,* p. 135.

[45]Ibid., pp. 102–3.

[46]Ibid., p. 6.

[47]Markham, "Survey of the Evidence," p. 170.

[48]A study by members of the staff of the Bureau of Economics of the Federal Trade Commission concluded that rather than rising from 42.4 percent to 54.1 percent, aggregate concentration in the United States (as measured by the share of corporate manufacturing assets held by the 200 largest manufacturing corporations) would have

declined slightly between 1947 and 1968 in the absence of mergers. U.S. Federal Trade Commission, *Economic Report on Corporate Mergers* (Washington, D.C.): U.S. Government Printing Office, 1969), pp. 191–93.

[49]Such an approach was used effectively in Jones's 1921 study, *The Trust Problem in the United States.* This approach had become virtually the standard paradigm in industrial organization economics before Edward S. Mason introduced the structure-conduct-performance paradigm.

[50]For a survey of the extensive literature on the determinants of managerial compensation, see Mark J. Hirschey and Gregory J. Werden, "An Empirical Analysis of Managerial Incentives," *Industrial Organization Review* 8 (1980), pp. 66–78. For a model of organizational behavior based on managerial preferences for staff, emoluments, and the discretionary profits that both make these possible and provide self-fulfillment, see Oliver Williamson, *The Economics of Discretionary Behavior: Managerial Objectives in a Theory of the Firm* (Chicago: Markham, 1967). For evidence from seven countries on growth of firms through merger to sizes that cannot be explained by profitability, see Dennis C. Mueller, ed., *The Determinants and Effects of Mergers: An International Comparison* (Cambridge, Mass.: Oelgeschlager, Gunn & Hain, 1980).

[51]Walter Adams and Horace M. Gray, *Monopoly in America: The Government as Promoter,* (New York: Macmillan, 1955).

[52]U.S. Industrial Commission, "Hearings before the Industrial Commission," *Preliminary Report on Trusts and Industrial Combinations,* vol. 1 of the commission's reports (Washington, D.C.: U.S. Government Printing Office, 1900), p. 115.

[53]United States v. E. C. Knight Company, 156 U.S. 1, 12.

[54]United States v. Northern Securities Company, 193 U.S. 197.

[55]U.S. Department of Defense, Office of the Secretary of Defense, *100 Companies and their Affiliates, Listed according to Net Value of Military Prime Contract Awards* (various years) and *Military Prime Contract Awards* (various years).

[56]U.S. National Science Foundation, *Research and Development in Industry 1981* (Washington, D.C.: U.S. Government Printing Office, 1984), pp. 15, 20.

[57]Almarin Phillips, *Technology and Market Structure,* (Lexington, Mass.: D. C. Heath, 1971).

[58]Alfred E. Kahn, *The Economics of Regulation: Principles and Institutions,* vol. 2: *Institutional Issues* (New York: John Wiley & Sons, 1971), p. 11.

CHAPTER NINE

Underlying Models and Patterns of Business Conduct

An executive of E. I. du Pont de Nemours, one of the nation's most diversified and largest corporations, once commented that he found himself bemused by economists' preoccupation with pricing. There was, he explained, no companywide pricing policy. Pricing practices differed among and within divisions and were adapted to widely different conditions found in a great number of markets. Determination of specific product prices was viewed as a day-to-day, low-level, decentralized decision-making function, one that top management necessarily relegated to those more immediately concerned with sales.

From a managerial point of view, price determination undoubtedly is only one facet of the business decision-making process, often among the more routine and less challenging. Nevertheless, in the study of industrial organization, understanding how markets function is most crucial. And a market system is essentially one in which relative prices guide exchange of goods and services and, thus, the allocation of productive resources and distribution of final products. Economists have, therefore, traditionally regarded price determination as the most significant aspect of business conduct.

THE ELEMENTARY THEORY OF PRICE AND MARKET STRUCTURE: PURE COMPETITION AND PURE MONOPOLY

At the most basic level, firms are either price takers or price makers. Price takers sell in impersonal markets with so many sellers that no

individual firm can exert a perceptible influence on market supply—
and therefore affect price—by changing the amount it offers for sale.
(Similarly, no buyer in such an impersonal market can affect the price
by the quantities it demands.)   A price maker, on the other hand, sells
in a market with so few sellers that the price it quotes will determine
the quantity it can sell.   In other words, price takers, such as soybean
farmers or commercial fishermen, face horizontal or perfectly elastic
demand curves; price makers, such as automobile manufacturers and
portrait painters, face downward-sloping demand curves of less than
infinite elasticity.

Models of Pure Competition

Market models range between pure competition at one extreme and
pure monopoly at the other.   Under pure competition, all firms in an
industry are price takers.   The going price is determined by the intersection of market demand and supply.   Further, the model of pure
competition assumes that in the long run, there are no barriers to
entry or exit of firms or no impediments to the free flow of capital
investment.   In such a model, if the market-determined price rises
above the full opportunity costs of efficient production, the industry's
output will increase because of the expansion of existing firms and the
entry of new ones.   The added output causes price to fall, and raises
the cost of factors of production with less than perfectly elastic supply
to the industry.   Conversely, a fall in price below minimum long-run
average cost will lead to an outflow of capital, a drop in output, and a
subsequent rise in price.   Thus, in the long run, price will just cover
minimum average total costs.

In long-run equilibrium, a purely competitive firm operates under
the conditions depicted in Figure 9–1.   Since the demand curve (D) is
perfectly elastic, the price (P) or average revenue (AR) must be equal
to the marginal revenue (MR).   This merely illustrates that a price
taker need not reduce its price to increase its sales.   The free flow of
capital assures that economic profit (revenue in excess of full opportunity cost) is eliminated in long-run equilibrium, so that price equals
minimum long-run average cost, or P is just tangent to the minima of
both short-run average total cost ($SATC$), and long-run average cost
(LAC).   (Figure 9–1 is drawn on the conventional assumption that
LAC is U-shaped, with a unique rate of output, Q_e, at which long-run
average costs are minimized.   This assumption is often inappropriate
if economies of scale limit the number of firms; but in pure competition,
economies of scale relative to the size of the market are insignificant,
and the assumption adds precision without undue sacrifice of realism.)
Price equals both short- and long-run marginal costs (SMC and LMC).

FIGURE 9–1 Long-Run Equilibrium of the Firm in Pure Competition

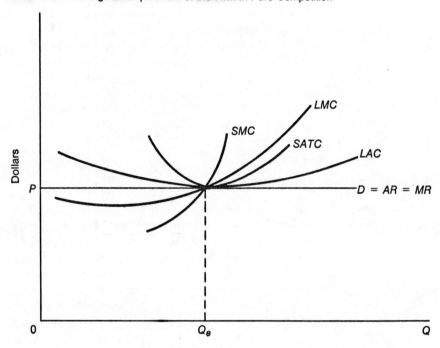

Thus, in the absence of externalities, the opportunity cost of the last unit produced by each firm in the industry is just equal to the value of that unit as determined by market demand. The Lerner index of monopoly power, $(P - MC)/P$, is zero.

Models of Pure Monopoly

In contrast, the pure-monopoly case assumes a single seller in a market with such severe barriers to capital mobility that the monopolist does not attract entrants by raising price to the profit-maximizing level, regardless of how far above full opportunity cost that price might be.

The long-run equilibrium position of the pure monopolist is shown in Figure 9–2. The demand curve (D) is, by definition, the downward-sloping market demand curve. Such a firm produces at the rate Q_e, equating marginal cost and marginal revenue—thereby setting price (P_e) higher than marginal cost, since MR lies everywhere below and to the left of the downward-sloping demand curve. Thus, the market value of the last unit produced at the monopolistically restricted rate of output is greater than the opportunity costs of the resources used in its production; the Lerner index rises from zero to some positive

FIGURE 9–2 Long-Run Equilibria of Firms in Pure Monopoly

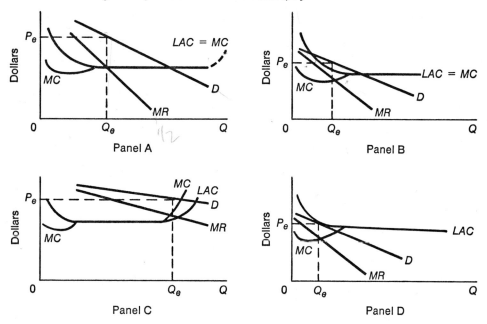

In long-run equilibrium, the monopolist may produce at the least-cost rate of output (Panel A), at a rate too low to obtain all available economies of scale (Panel B), or if diseconomies of scale set in, at an inefficiently high rate (Panel C). Monopoly power does not guarantee profit. Panel D depicts a situation in which the monopolist just covers all costs, at a point of tangency of D to LAC. If, in Panel D, demand were to fall or long-run average costs rise by a small amount, the monopolist would suffer loss and leave the industry. Panel D also illustrates the point that even without any economic profit, the monopolist's price exceeds its marginal cost, and the Lerner index is greater than zero.

number. (As discussed in Chapter Four, the degree to which price is raised above marginal cost is related to the elasticity of market demand by the expression $P/MC = \eta/(\eta - 1.)$

Models of Intermediate Cases

Pure competition and pure monopoly are extremes—more useful as benchmarks than as illustrations of real-world situations. Market models of intermediate cases—a small enough number of sellers so that each has some latitude in price setting, and neither absolute nor nonexistent barriers to entry—are more pertinent in studies of industrial organization.

OLIGOPOLY: THE COURNOT, BERTRAND, EDGEWORTH, AND VON STACKELBERG MODELS

In both pure competition and pure monopoly, the demand curve facing a firm is objectively determined. In the competitive case, the firm can sell all it wishes at the market-determined price: under pure monopoly, the market demand curve is identical with that facing the firm. But in intermediate cases, especially under oligopolistic conditions with a small number of competing sellers, each firm must predict rivals' reactions as well as customers' responses to its price changes. The demand curve facing an oligopolist thus becomes a subjective construct (subject to *conjectural variation*), and the theorist must model plausible conjectures that various firms might make about one another's behavior.

The Cournot Model

The earliest model of oligopoly pricing is that of Augustin Cournot. In an 1838 work,[1] he analyzed equilibrium shares in a market with various numbers of firms, each of which takes the output of its rivals as fixed, or at least as not influenced by its own output. Figure 9–3 illustrates the Cournot model under the simplest possible assumptions.

In Figure 9–3A, a single seller with constant unit cost of production (*AC*) and therefore an identical marginal cost curve (*MC*) faces the straight-line market demand curve (*D*). Since the firm's marginal revenue curve (*MR*) slopes down twice as steeply as the demand curve,[2]

FIGURE 9–3 Initial Price Adjustments in the Cournot Duopoly Model

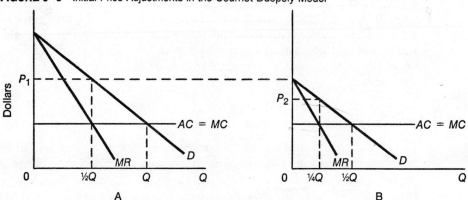

the monopolist produces an output of $\frac{1}{2}Q$, where Q represents the output that would be obtained with identical cost conditions under pure competition.

Suppose that a second firm, with unit cost identical to that of the first, enters the market. Under Cournot's assumption that the entrant, Firm 2, expects Firm 1 to maintain its existing level of production, Firm 2 faces a demand curve representing the potential buyers willing to pay less than the price (P_1) charged by Firm 1. This demand curve is shown in Figure 9–3B, which also indicates that Firm 2 will produce an output of $\frac{1}{2} \times \frac{1}{2}Q$, or $\frac{1}{4}Q$, lowering the price to P_2. The Cournot response of Firm 1 is to reduce its output to $\frac{1}{2}(Q - \frac{1}{4}Q)$, on the assumption that Firm 2's output is fixed at $\frac{1}{4}Q$. Firm 1 thus produces $\frac{3}{8}Q$. But Firm 2, in turn, sets its output at $\frac{1}{2}(Q - \frac{3}{8}Q)$, or $\frac{5}{16}Q$. In a number of such rounds, the output of both firms converges to $\frac{1}{3}Q$. Total market output has therefore risen from $\frac{1}{2}Q$ to $\frac{2}{3}Q$. with 2 firms

If a third Cournot-type firm enters the market, again with unit cost equal to those of the two existing firms, its initial rate of output would be $\frac{1}{2}(Q - \frac{2}{3}Q)$, or $\frac{1}{6}Q$. But after Firms 1 and 2 had adjusted fully to Firm 3's entry, and Firm 3 had adjusted to the new levels of output of the two older firms, each of the three would be producing $\frac{1}{4}Q$, so that the total output of the industry would have risen to $\frac{3}{4}Q$.

 In general, the output of each firm in a Cournot equilibrium will be $(\frac{1}{n+1})Q$, where Q equals the rate of output under pure competition, provided that there are no differences in unit costs of production among the firms, and constant costs for each regardless of rate of production. The industry's total output, therefore, is $(\frac{n}{n+1})Q$. As the number of firms increases, the total output gets continually closer to that of pure competition (Q), and further from that of pure monopoly ($\frac{1}{2}Q$). Thus, the Cournot model links price and output behavior directly to a single fundamental aspect of market structure—the number of firms.

The outcome of the Cournot model can be illustrated by use of curves known as *reaction functions*. In Figure 9–4, the more steeply sloping line represents Firm 1's reaction to any output of Firm 2, or Firm 1's output as a function of the output of Firm 2: $Q_1 = f_1(Q_2)$. Similarly, the less steeply sloping line shows Firm 2's output as a function of that of Firm 1.

Consider, first, Firm 1's reaction function. If Firm 2 were to produce at the competitive rate of output, indicated by Q on the vertical axis, Firm 1 would produce nothing. But if Firm 2 were to produce nothing, Firm 1 would produce at the monopolistic rate $\frac{1}{2}Q$. The line $Q_1 = f_1(Q_2)$ traces out the various intermediate combinations of outputs of Firms 1 and 2, treating Q_2 as the independent variable. Similarly, Firm 2's reaction function is a line connecting $\frac{1}{2}Q$ on the vertical axis with Q on the horizontal axis, showing Q_2 as a function of Q_1. At

FIGURE 9–4 Reaction Functions and Cournot Duopoly Equilibrium

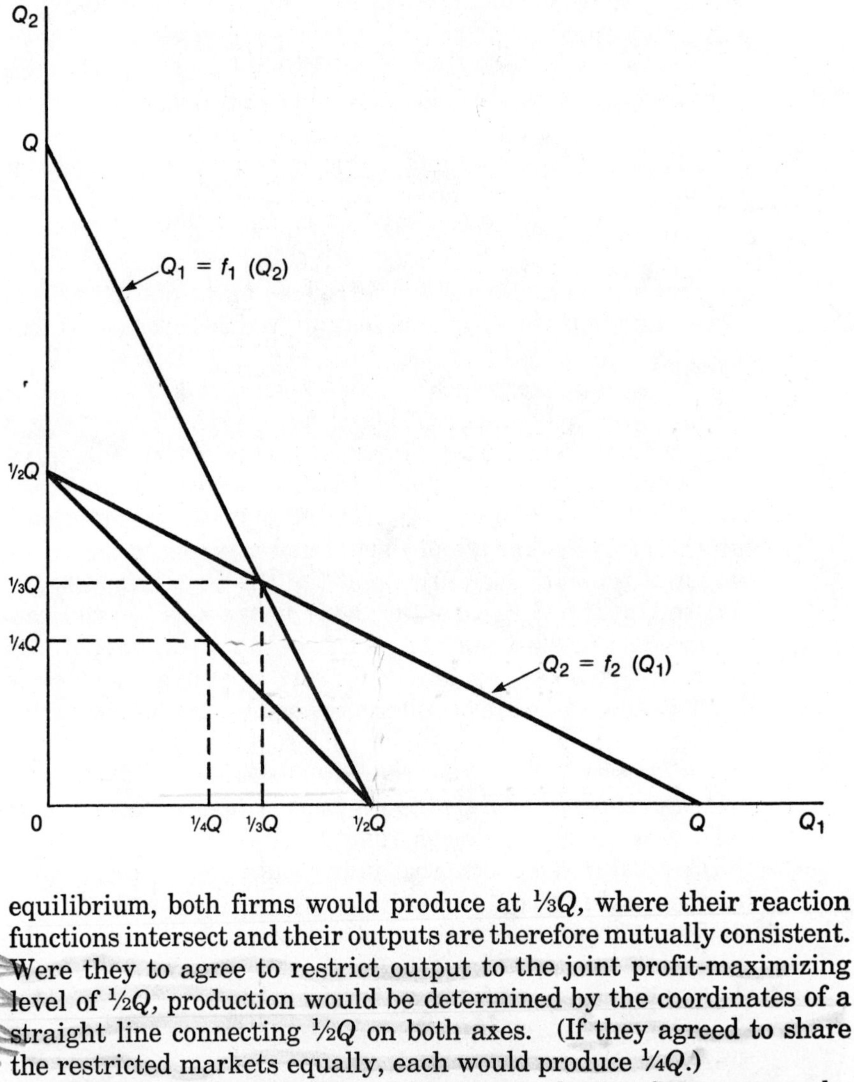

equilibrium, both firms would produce at $\frac{1}{3}Q$, where their reaction functions intersect and their outputs are therefore mutually consistent. Were they to agree to restrict output to the joint profit-maximizing level of $\frac{1}{2}Q$, production would be determined by the coordinates of a straight line connecting $\frac{1}{2}Q$ on both axes. (If they agreed to share the restricted markets equally, each would produce $\frac{1}{4}Q$.)

Stability of the Cournot equilibrium in the two-firm case can be shown by applying these reaction functions. In Figure 9–5, if Firm 2 produces Q_a, Firm 1 will respond with production of Q_b. But when Firm 1 produces Q_b, Firm 2 will cut back to a production rate of Q_c. Firm 1's reaction to this change in Firm 2's position will be to expand output to Q_d. The adjustments will proceed in a series of ever-diminishing stepwise changes until each of the two firms reaches equilibrium output of $\frac{1}{3}Q$.

Cournot recognized that in a market with a small number of sellers,

FIGURE 9-5 Adjustments to Cournot Duopoly Equilibrium along Reaction Functions

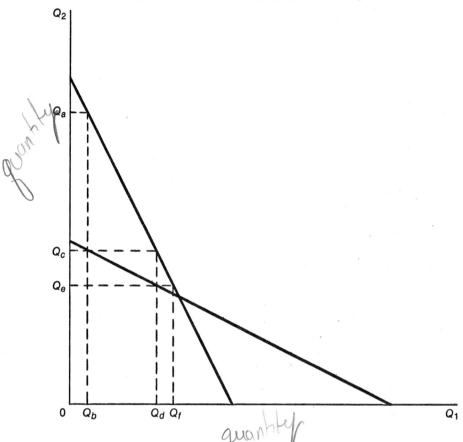

particularly in the duopoly situation, his firms were behaving in a short-sighted and even stupid way by persisting in taking their rivals' outputs as fixed even while adjusting their own to the changes made by others. "Why is it then," he asked rhetorically, "that, for want of an understanding, the producers do not stop, as in the case of a monopoly or of an association, at the value ... which would really give them the greatest income?" He continued, "The reason is that producer (1) having fixed his production ... the other will be able to fix his own production at a higher or lower rate with a *temporary benefit.* To be sure, he will soon be punished for his mistake, because he will force the first producer to adopt a new scale of production which will react unfavorably on producer (2) himself." The joint profit-maximizing or monopoly condition is not one of stable equilibrium, Cournot argued, "for in the moral sphere men cannot be supposed to be free of error and lack of forethought any more than in the physical world bodies can be considered perfectly rigid, or supports perfectly solid, etc."[3]

The Bertrand Model. Analysts in subsequent years developed models based on conjectural assumptions other than Cournot's. Joseph Bertrand noted that if each oligopolist assumes its rivals will hold their prices rather than their outputs constant, regardless of its own price reduction, each has an incentive to undercut the existing price just slightly; and even if there are only two rivals, equilibrium will be reached only when the price has dropped to the competitive level and all economic profit has been eliminated.[4]

The Edgeworth Model. F. Y. Edgeworth observed that if duopolists compete in the Bertrand manner but have limited production capacity such that both reach a limit to output before the price has fallen to the competitive level, each then has an incentive to raise price since its rival cannot accommodate any more customers. But if both raise their prices, their rates of production will decline below the capacity constraint, and both will then have an incentive to cut the price again. Thus, in the Edgeworth model, the equilibrium price is indeterminate and subject to continuing fluctuation as long as both firms keep behaving as Bertrand duopolists.[5]

The von Stackelberg Model. Heinrich von Stackelberg developed a duopoly model in which each firm must decide whether to be a "follower" (setting output to maximize profit on the assumption that the other firm's output is given, as in the Cournot model) or a "leader" (taking the other firm's reaction function into account and setting an output that maximizes profit, assuming the other firm will act as a follower).[6] If both become followers, the Cournot equilibrium results. If one becomes a leader and the other remains a follower, there is usually a definite equilibrium solution, but the follower will earn lower profits than the leader. If both firms attempt to be leaders, which von Stackelberg regarded as the most likely alternative, there is no stable equilibrium solution. Rather, the result is "a regular trial of strength,"[7] with both firms maintaining excessively high levels of output in the hope that the other will give up and become a follower. The combined output of the two may be so high that price is below unit cost, and the contest may then end in the ruin of at least one of the firms if one does not capitulate and accept the follower's role.

The reaction functions in Figure 9–6, illustrating the von Stackelberg model, are identical to those of Figure 9–4. At the Cournot equilibrium, Firm 1's output is Q_1 (identical to $\frac{1}{3}Q$ in Figure 9–4), and Firm 2's is Q'_1. Suppose that Firm 1 decides to adopt von Stackelberg's leadership strategy. Knowing Firm 2's reaction function and total market demand for the product and assuming that Firm 2 will remain a follower, Firm 1 can calculate the rate of its own output that maximizes its profits.[8] Such an output will be higher than Q_1, since Firm 2 (acting as a follower) will reduce its output in the face of Firm 1's expansion. Let Q_2 be Firm 1's calculated output. Firm 2 responds by reducing its output to Q'_2. The new equilibrium is stable only so long as Firm 2 is content with the lower output and lower profits of followership. Firm 2 might decide to become a leader itself, producing Q'_3, in the hope that such a rate of output and the concomitant fall in price would shock Firm 1 into becoming a follower and cutting pro-

FIGURE 9–6 Leadership and Followership in a von Stackelberg Duopoly Model

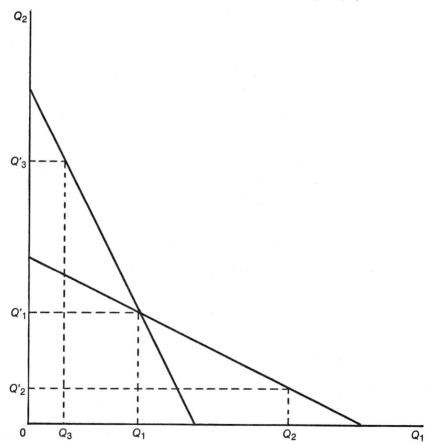

duction to Q_3. As drawn in Figure 9–6, the combined output Q_2 plus Q'_3 is greater than the competitive output; and in the constant-cost case, the price must therefore be below cost. If both firms persist in their efforts to assert leadership, the struggle will end only when one is driven from the market by its losses.

THE CHAMBERLINIAN SLIDE

In all of the oligopoly models discussed above, the conjectures made about rivals' behavior are simplistic and, in every case, are proven false as the market moves towards equilibrium. Yet the firms are assumed never to learn from their mistakes. Because no sensible business owner or manager would behave for long in such a short-sighted way, especially when confronted with only a few rivals of similar size, such models have proved unsatisfactory for analysis of real-world market situations. The most significant theoretical advance beyond this unsatisfactory state came from Edward H. Chamberlin in 1933.[9] The core of his insight and analysis is captured in a model illustrating the "Chamberlinian slide."

"Mutual Dependence Recognized"

Chamberlin introduced to economics jargon the somewhat cumbersome phrase "mutual dependence recognized." After discussing the Cournot, Bertrand, and Edgeworth models, he noted:

> When a move by one seller evidently forces the other to make a counter move, he is very stupidly refusing to look further than his nose if he proceeds on the assumption that it will not. . . . For one competitor to take into account the alternatives of policy which he forces upon the other is simply for him to consider the indirect consequences of his own acts. . . . He must consider not merely what his competitor is doing now, but also what he will be forced to do in the light of change which he himself is contemplating.[10]

In Figure 9–7, the demand curve facing an oligopolist in the case of mutual dependence fully recognized is the one labeled DD' (following Chamberlin's notation). DD' assumes that the oligopolist correctly takes into account all of the direct and indirect effects of its price on the quantities it can sell—that it can predict the adjustments and readjustments made by its rivals and itself, and the equilibrium that will result when all the repercussions have worked themselves out. The ability of individual firms to do this with approximate accuracy is enhanced by fewness of numbers, similarity of products, rough equality in size and costs of production, and barriers to entry. If rivals have

FIGURE 9–7 Chamberlinian Demand Curves with Mutual Dependence Fully Recognized and Ignored

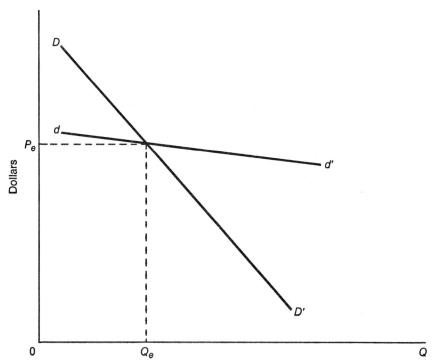

different enough rates of output, costs, or products, or if there are a large enough number of them, or if a firm's share becomes small enough (perhaps through entry of newcomers), such prediction is beyond human capacity. Firms must then make decisions based on existing circumstances and neglect changes that might result from their own actions. In this case, firms behave as posited in the Cournot model. The demand curve facing the firm becomes dd', defined by Chamberlin as showing the quantities a firm could sell at various prices provided the prices of all of its rivals remained constant. For any price and output combination shown on DD', there is an associated dd'. Necessarily, dd' is more elastic than DD', since a firm can obtain a greater increase in sales by reducing its price if rivals do not respond with their own price cuts.

Figure 9–8A shows the equilibrium profit-maximizing price (P_1) and output (Q_1) of an oligopolistic firm with full recognition of mutual dependence. If the firms in a market characterized by mutual de-

FIGURE 9–8 Chamberlinian Pricing under Mutual Dependence Recognized and Ignored

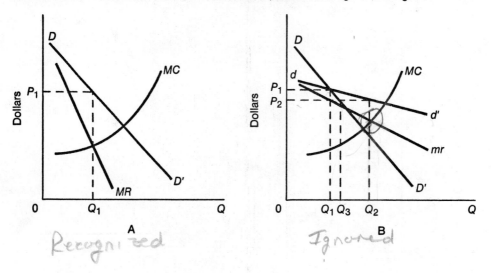

A

Recognized

B

Ignored

pendence recognized have constant shares at various prices and if their costs are identical—assumptions Chamberlin described as "heroic"— the market price and industry output will be the same as under pure monopoly and the joint profits of the firms maximized. In general, the closer to one another the firms are in size and cost conditions, the closer the equilibrium will be to joint profit maximization.

Figure 9–8B illustrates a possible set of consequences for the oligopolist that neglects its mutual interdependence. DD' and MC are identical with the curves in Figure 9–8A. If the firm, starting at P_1 and Q_1 (the equilibrium price and rate of output under recognition of mutual dependence), takes the prices of its rivals as independent of its own output, it will begin to think of dd' as the relevant demand curve it faces. It thus takes its profit-maximizing price to be P_2, expecting to sell an output of Q_2, at which rate mr (the marginal revenue curve associated with dd') is equal to MC. However, the industrywide reactions it neglected to consider in making this price cut will eventually lead to sales of only Q_3, after all of the moves and countermoves are completed.

Recognizing its mistake and realizing that the price of P_2 is below the optimal price for the industry as a whole, the firm that initiated the price cut might then take the lead in restoring a price of P_1. If recognition of mutual dependence has been fully reestablished, all other firms would follow in setting this price. An oligopolistic industry might, therefore, have a normal equilibrium characterized by recognition of mutual dependence, upset periodically by independent pricing but with the old equilibrium reestablished as firms learn their lesson from bitter experience.

The old equilibrium need not, however, always be restored. Over time, for example, a market may expand, so that each firm's share decreases. Firms, especially those differentiating their products, may develop different cost structures. Independent pricing, ignoring mutual dependence, may become more frequent. In many structural settings, such pricing is neither erroneous nor lacking in foresight but rather is part of a rational and effective policy of individual profit maximization—collusive agreements being ruled out by assumption. A firm with a small share of the market might believe, correctly, that its expansion of sales from Q_1 to Q_2 would have so small an impact as to be imperceptible to rivals or not warrant retaliation. For example, if 101 firms have initially equal market shares and one doubles its sales by winning customers from rivals, the other 100 will on the average lose only 1 percent of their sales. None of them may find it worthwhile to reduce the original price (at which the remaining 99 percent can still be sold) to restore its initial market position.

Second, retaliation may take substantial time. Rivals may initially assume that demand for the product has dipped and that all firms are experiencing similar declines in sales volume. After discovering the rival's price cut, retaliating firms must decide upon, announce, and implement their own price reductions. A firm may foresee an ultimate increase in sales from Q_1 to only Q_3 but also know that sales will first rise to Q_2 and then gradually decline to Q_3. The high profits made during the adjustment period may more than offset the later losses or reduced profits.

In a third possibility, several firms may realize that due to structural changes, at least one firm may start pricing on the basis of dd'. In this case, each realizes that it would be better to be the first to cut price and thereby increase market share for a time rather than be last and cut price merely to protect or regain its original share. When the probability of one or more rivals adopting an independent pricing strategy is high enough, a fully rational oligopolist may decide to be the first on the bandwagon.

The result of such a breakdown in recognition of mutual dependence is a "slide" of dd' down DD', as shown in Figure 9–9, where the initial neglect of mutual dependence, and pricing along $d_1d'_1$, leads to a price of P_2 and sales of Q_2 after industrywide reaction. But instead of awareness that DD' is the appropriate demand curve and a return to P_1 and Q_1 (as assumed in Figure 9–8), we now assume that a new subjective demand curve $(d_2d'_2)$ replaces $d_1d'_1$ in the pricing strategy of at least one firm. Another round of price cutting, output expansion,

FIGURE 9-9 The Chamberlinian Slide after a Breakdown of Mutual Dependence Recognized

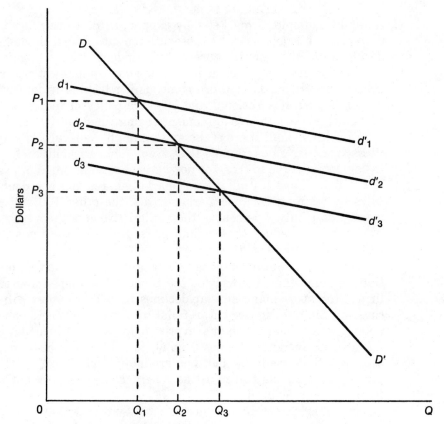

and retaliation leads to a price and output result of P_3 and Q_3, at which time $d_3d'_3$ springs into the minds of decision makers. Thus, dd' slides down DD'.

In the absence of entry or exit of firms, the slide will stop when each firm's expected sales at a particular price (on the assumption that the demand curve is dd') turns out to be the amount actually sold at that price after all industrywide adjustments. (See Figure 9-10.)

In Figure 9-10A, the intersection of DD' and dd' is labeled as Point A. The intersection of mr and MC is indicated as Point B. As dd' slides down DD', Point A moves down and to the right, along DD' and Point B moves down and to the left, along MC. When B is directly below A, as in Figure 9-10B, the slide will stop. The firm regarding dd' as the demand curve it faces, thereby ignoring indirect effects, expects to sell Q_n at the price of P_n, and this is indeed what happens,

FIGURE 9–10   Equilibrium of the Firm, without Entry, Following a Chamberlinian Slide

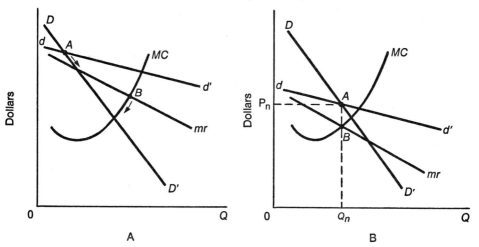

A   B

even after allowing for all of the unanticipated reactions of others that are incorporated in DD'.

Figure 9–10B does not, however, show the long-run equilibrium following a breakdown of recognition of mutual dependence. The slide may stop with a price above or below LAC. If we assume both an absence of barriers to entry and independent pricing, a price above LAC will attract entrants and one below it will lead to the exit of some firms. The entry of new firms causes the demand curves of the existing firms to shift to the left, as everyone's market share shrinks, and may cause average and marginal costs to rise in response to increased demand for factors of production. Exit results in a shift to the right in the demand curves facing those who remain, and a possible fall in their cost curves. Figure 9–11 illustrates the adjustment to long-run equilibrium when the slide overshoots, or ends in a price that does not cover LAC.

In the previous diagrams, average cost curves were omitted to avoid clutter and make the discussion easier to follow. In Figure 9–11, DD' is omitted for the same reason. Under the conditions assumed, the relevant demand curve facing the firm is dd'. In Figure 9–11A, firms are incurring losses because there is no output at which price covers long-run average cost. As a result of the exit of firms, dd' shifts to the right and LAC may fall. At the point where the two are tangent and full opportunity costs are just covered (as in Figure 9–11B), the exodus of firms ends and the curves no longer shift.

FIGURE 9–11 Long-Run Equilibrium of the Firm in Monopolistic Competition

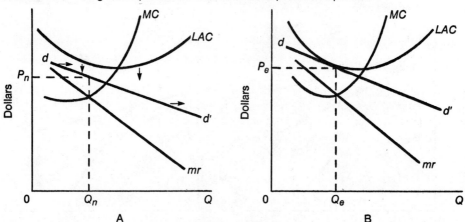

Monopolistic, or Imperfect, Competition

The Chamberlinian slide traces a transition from oligopoly to the market structure Chamberlin called *monopolistic competition* and Joan Robinson called *imperfect competition*.[11] Figure 9–11, depicting the result of a complete breakdown in recognition of mutual dependence, also shows the long-run equilibrium price and output of a firm in monopolistic or imperfect competition.

There are some differences between the original concepts of monopolistic and imperfect competition. Chamberlin emphasized product differentiation in explaining the less than perfectly elastic demand curve facing his monopolistically competitive firm and depicted substitution of similar but not identical products as the source of elimination of monopolistic profits, rather than entry to the specific product market. Robinson, however, stressed market imperfections (locational advantages of firms, customer attachment to a particular seller, differences in services and sales skills among firms, differences in reputation, and advertising by individual firms), along with a relatively small number of firms, as the reasons why even a firm without the ability to earn monopolistic profits might face a downward-sloping demand curve.

Most economists now regard these differences as unimportant, and many simply ignore them. For our purposes, the primary distinctions between oligopoly and either monopolistic or imperfect competition are (1) the crucial importance of conjectural variations, or assumptions about rivals' behavior, in oligopoly models, contrasted with the independent pricing assumed in monopolistic or imperfect competition, and (2) the absence of barriers to entry, either to the product market itself or to the manufacture of close substitutes, in monopolistically or imperfectly competitive markets.

At the "tangency solution," or the long-run equilibrium position in both Chamberlin's monopolistic competition and Robinson's imperfect competition, economic profit is eliminated, but monopolistic distortion of resource allocation remains since price is still above marginal cost (i.e., the Lerner index is still greater than zero). The price and output determined by the tangency point will not, however, differ too greatly from a purely competitive long-run equilibrium situation if *dd'* is elastic enough—and *dd'* is, by construction, more elastic than *DD'*.

Chamberlinian Theory: Comparisons

The Chamberlinian theory differs from other oligopoly models in three important aspects. First, it eliminates the basic flaw of assuming that oligopolists *always* make simplistic conjectures about rivals' behavior. In situations involving small numbers of similar firms, such an assumption is clearly inappropriate.

Second, in the Chamberlinian slide, the equilibrium price and output do not move steadily from those of pure monopoly toward those of pure competition as the number of firms increases, as happens in the Cournot model. Rather, there is a sudden and discrete shift in equilibrium conditions when independent pricing replaces recognition of mutual dependence. Thus, if mutual dependence breaks down only with the entry of the seventh firm, an increase from two firms to three would make little or no difference to the industry's price and output under Chamberlinian assumptions, though it would have a major effect on price and output in a Cournot type of market. More important, the determinants of recognition of mutual dependence include several structural factors in addition to number of firms.

Third, and perhaps most significant, Chamberlin identified circumstances under which oligopoly price and output would be the same as or close to those of pure monopoly, without any cartel agreement or explicit collusion. In the Cournot, Bertrand, Edgeworth, and von Stackelberg models, an industry of two or more firms could only earn monopoly profits through formal agreement or collusion. Indeed, in the Bertrand, Edgeworth, and von Stackelberg models, overt collusion was evoked to explain the very existence of equilibrium under assumed conditions of oligopoly.

THE THEORY OF GAMES

The most sophisticated and conceptually powerful technique for general theoretical analysis of oligopolistic market strategies and conjectural variation is the theory of games, initially formulated in 1944 by John von Neumann and Oskar Morgenstern.[12] While game theory has provided some important insights, its failure to meet early expectations attests to the difficulty—perhaps impossibility—of devising a single model capturing the essence of oligopolistic rivalry.

The elementary principles of game theory can be illustrated in a simple example of a two-person zero-sum game. The payoff matrix for such a game is presented in Figure 9–12. We assume two players, A and B. Player A has four strategies: a_1, a_2, a_3, and a_4. Player B has three: b_1, b_2, and b_3. Each number, or cell, in the matrix indicates the amount Player A will win or lose for the strategy pair indicated. Since the game is a zero-sum one, Player B wins whatever Player A loses, and loses whatever A wins. Thus, if Player A chooses Strategy a_3 and Player B chooses b_1, A loses 1 and B wins the same amount.[13]

FIGURE 9–12   Illustrative Payoff Matrix for a Two-Person Zero-Sum Game

	Player B's strategies		
Player A's strategies	b_1	b_2	b_3
a_1	12	−3	−6
a_2	5	2	−4
a_3	−1	−10	4
a_4	−6	8	2

Minimax and Maximin Strategies

Suppose both players know the entire matrix, but each must choose a strategy without first knowing the other's choice. Player A, choosing Strategy a_1, can win 12, the maximum gain possible—but only if Player

B chooses b_1. Player A will realize that Player B is not likely to choose b_1 and be exposed to a possible loss of 12. Similarly, the maximum gain possible for B is 10, but B is not likely to choose Strategy b_2 in the hope that A will choose a_3. Game theory posits a principle for strategy choice in such a situation: each player should choose the strategy that can lead to the least possible ex post regret. This implies either minimizing the maximum possible loss (called a "minimax" strategy) or maximizing the minimum possible gain (a "maximin" strategy). Player A chooses a_2, since the worst that can then occur will be a loss of 4, if Player B chooses b_3. Any other strategy choice exposes Player A to a still higher possible loss. Following the same principle, Player B does choose Strategy b_3. The result is a payoff of 4 to Player B and a corresponding loss of 4 suffered by Player A.

Why, if Player A knows that Player B will follow a minimax strategy and therefore choose b_3, does Player A not choose a_3 and thereby win 4? The problem is that the reasoning then becomes circular. Player B might well think, "If Player A expects me to be a minimaxer and choose b_3, he or she will choose a_3. But I'll outsmart Player A and pick b_2, so that I win 10." However, Player A might anticipate that Player B would think just this way and therefore reject a_3, with its possible loss of 10. In sum, this payoff matrix makes possible a conceivably unending chain of reasoning: "If my opponent thinks that I think that he or she thinks that I think . . ." Game theory posits that if the game is played only once, a minimax or maximin strategy is optimal. The game in the matrix of Figure 9–12 is, simply, loaded against Player A.

Mixed Strategy

If a game is to be played a number of times, a mixed strategy may be optimal, with certain strategies chosen in random order but according to a predetermined probability distribution. Even under a mixed strategy, however, the mean payoff should be selected according to the minimax or maximin principle.[14]

Although the minimax or maximin principle is optimal for a zero-sum game, it need not be if the game is nonzero-sum, or if one player's gain is not the other's loss. In particular, if various strategies lead to varying combinations of gain for both players, *cooperative solutions* become possible. Most economic games are of this type rather than zero-sum. Consider, for example, the payoff matrix in Figure 9–13, which depicts the payoffs available in a duopolistic market in which each firm can adopt a high-price strategy (H) or a low-price strategy (L). Market demand conditions are such that if both follow a high-price strategy their joint profits are greater than if both follow a low-price strategy. However, if one firm charges a high price, the other can adopt a low-price strategy and, by taking business away from its rival, earn even higher profits than its share under joint profit maximization. The first firm, as a consequence, experiences a loss.

FIGURE 9–13 Illustrative Payoff Matrix for a Two-Person Nonzero-Sum Game with a Possible Cooperative Solution

---

Firm 2's strategies

Firm 1's strategies	H_2	L_2
H_1	3, 3	−1, 4
L_1	4, −1	1,1

SOURCE: Adapted from Martin Shubik, *Strategy and Market Structure: Competition, Oligopoly, and the Theory of Games* (New York: John Wiley & Sons, 1959), p. 61.

The matrix in Figure 9–13 thus shows two payoffs in each cell—the first for Firm 1 and the second for Firm 2. In the absence of cooperation, the maximin solution calls for each firm to choose Strategy L. However, if cooperation is legal and feasible, both firms would benefit by agreeing to Strategy H, presumably to the detriment of their customers. The problem for the duopolists, however, is to prevent cheating. Either firm could gain still more by reverting back to Strategy L while its rival maintained Strategy H. The cooperative solution may be attainable only if agreements are *enforceable* as well as legal and feasible. But since the game in Figure 9–13 is played repeatedly, and both firms will learn the consequences of cheating and retaliation, the cooperative solution is quite likely to be an attainable and stable one.

This duopoly game is a variation of the well-known Prisoner's Dilemma game. Two suspected partners in crime, held in separate cells and not allowed to communicate with each other, are each offered a deal. The prisoner who confesses so that the other can be convicted will be given a two-year sentence. But, the prisoner who maintains innocence, does not confess, and is convicted through the testimony of the other will be given a 10-year sentence. Both prisoners know that if neither confesses, neither can be convicted. The noncooperative minimax solution is for both to confess, and game theoreticians regard this as a plausible solution if both are held in isolation. If, however, the two were able to communicate with each other, it is quite likely that they could reach the cooperative solution and that both could shortly thereafter walk out of prison as free persons.

The duopoly and Prisoner's Dilemma games may strike the reader as simplistic. They do, however, provide insights into two of the most fundamental features of oligopolistic markets—the problem of cheating and the role of communication or signaling of intent.

If games involve more than two players, some players may cooperate to form coalitions against others. A game with several players may resolve itself into a two-person game if two coalitions are formed. Game theorists have developed a number of principles for n-person games ($n > 2$). Most important, no coalition will survive if it contains a member whose payoff would be higher if it acted independently or joined another coalition. Thus, some coalitions will be maintained only by side payments to those who would otherwise defect. Solutions exist, but are typically complex, in games with several players, non-zero-sum payoffs, cooperative and noncooperative strategies, and side payments.

An n-person game is often impossible to solve without severely constraining conjectural assumptions. One of the most frequently used (incorporated into what is known as the Nash or Nash-Cournot equilibrium) is that each player maximizes its expected payoff on the assumption that the strategies of the others are fixed. Unfortunately, the Nash-Cournot equilibrium solution—closely analogous to the Chamberlinian solution under independent pricing or mutual dependence ignored—is often uninteresting in problems involving the interactions of small numbers of rivals.

In sum, game theory has contributed to a number of concepts useful in the analysis of oligopolistic market conditions. But it has not provided a general theory of oligopoly allowing us to move much beyond the Chamberlinian framework.

EXCLUSIONARY AND PREDATORY PRICING

Above-normal or monopolistic profits can persist only in the presence of barriers to entry or barriers to additional investment in existing rival firms—that is, barriers to expansion. Economic theorists have, therefore, observed that a firm that recognizes mutual interdependence with existing rivals in the short run may also take into account the long-run effects of its actions on inducing entry to or exit from its market. Further, such firms may devise pricing strategies to either deter entry or hasten the exit of existing rivals.

The Bain-Sylos Model

Joe S. Bain's *Barriers to New Competition*[15] and a study by Italian economist Paolo Sylos Labini[16] provided the path-breaking contribution to analysis of deliberate entry-deterring behavior by oligopolists. Both drew heavily on the "Sylos postulate"—the assumption that potential entrants make their entry decisions on the conjecture that the existing firms will maintain their present rate of output in the face of entry and allow the price to fall by whatever amount is necessary for the market to accommodate the newcomer's output. The Bain-Sylos analysis also assumes substantial economies of scale, such that the added output of a single entrant would have a noticeable effect on market output and price. Figure 9–14 illustrates the basic Bain-Sylos model of entry deterrence.

Figure 9–14A shows the market demand curve (labeled D_m). Under the Sylos postulate, the demand curve facing a potential entrant is that part of the market demand curve not satisfied by the existing firms. At price P, the demand curve facing an entrant is that part of D_m lying below and to the right of Point A, or beyond the output (Q), supplied by the existing firms. This demand curve can be shown as a separate curve by shifting it to the left until it intersects the vertical axis of the graph at P, indicating that an entrant would expect zero sales at that price and positive sales at lower prices, with the quantities sold at each price equal to the market demand minus the fixed output of the existing firms. Note that as the existing firms raise or lower price, moving Point A along D_m, the potential entrant's demand curve (D_e) shifts in or out.

The existing firms, or incumbents, are assumed to act as joint profit maximizers or, alternatively, there may be only one incumbent firm in the market. The incumbent(s) can manipulate the demand curve facing potential entrants by changing price. In Figure 9–14B, LAC is the long-run average cost curve of the entrant. It may be higher or lower than the incumbents' cost curves, or identical. The entry-deterring strategy calls for the existing firms to set a price (shown as P_{bar}) at which the potential entrant's demand curve has been shifted in and down until it is just below a point of tangency with LAC. P_{bar}, then, is the highest price existing firms can charge without making entry feasible and attractive.

Figure 9–14C illustrates one situation that incumbent firm(s) might face. Assume that LAC is the same for both existing firms and potential entrants. The joint profit-maximizing price, neglecting entry is P_{max}, and the corresponding output is Q_{max}. MR_m is drawn through the horizontal (constant-cost) range of LAC, where $MC = LAC$, for ease of exposition. If the incumbents set price at P_{max}, the demand

FIGURE 9-14 Pricing to Deter Entry

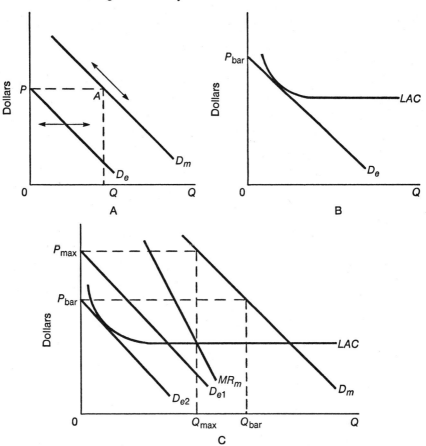

curve facing a potential entrant becomes D_{e1}, and entry is invited. To deter entry, D_e must be pushed down to D_{e2} by lowering the price to P_{bar} and thereby increasing output to Q_{bar}, with a resulting loss of profit. As drawn in Figure 9-14, P_{bar} does allow the existing firms to continue enjoying above-normal profits, since at Q_{bar} price is still above average cost. In such a situation, the incumbents must decide whether temporary monopoly profits eroded by entry are preferable to the lower but longer-lasting profits attainable while deterring entry. A profit-maximizing monopolist or collusive group would decide by comparing the net present discounted values of the two profit streams. Bain identified four basic entry conditions. Entry is *blockaded* when P_{max} is lower than P_{bar}. If P_{max} is greater than P_{bar}, but the two are close enough to each other so that the present value of the discounted profit stream associated with a price of P_{bar} is greater than that associated with P_{max}, entry is *effectively impeded*. Entry is *ineffectively impeded* if P_{max} is so far above P_{bar} that existing firms find it enhances profit to raise price above P_{bar} even if entry does result. And finally, if the price cannot exceed LAC of the established firms without attracting entrants, entry is *easy*.[17]

Criticisms and Modifications of the Bain-Sylos Model

Writers since Bain and Sylos have noted deficiencies in the model and have sought to improve it. The most important subsequent developments stemmed from dissatisfaction with the static nature of the formal model and skepticism as to the relevance of the Sylos postulate.

Dynamic Limit Pricing. Although Bain noted that conditions of entry would change over time (e.g., as some firms enter, it becomes progressively more difficult for others to follow), the formal analysis in the Bain-Sylos model is static, and the existing firms are presumed to choose one of only two alternatives. Either they set the profit-maximizing price and allow entry to occur, or they set the highest possible entry-barring price.

Darius W. Gaskins, Jr., applying an engineering concept known as optimal control theory to develop what is now known as limit-pricing strategy, made the initial contribution to dynamic analysis.[18] In dynamic limit-pricing models, entry and the subsequent erosion of profits are viewed as streams over time. The incumbent firm(s) will increase the rate of entry by raising price toward P_{max} and reduce the flow by lowering it toward P_{bar}. The incumbents need not choose either P_{max} or P_{bar}: they can choose any intermediate price, and they can raise or lower the price from time to time to alter the flow of entry. One highly significant result of the dynamic limit-pricing model is that an incumbent firm with no cost advantage should never maintain the entry-barring price indefinitely. Rather, there is always some rate of entry, allowing temporarily higher prices and profits, that yields a higher net present value for the profit stream. Clearly, the higher the firm's rate of discount, or preference for present over future income, the greater its preference for high profits in the near future and the more rapid the rate of entry it will find optimal.

A problem with simple control theory models is that market entry is not perfectly analogous to the flow of a liquid over time. Unless potential entrants differ markedly in their ability to enter and establish themselves, after a critical level of price and output restriction are reached, entry may be more like an avalanche. If economies of scale imply that entry will occur sporadically and involve only a few large firms, estimating the timing of such entry and the entrant's rates of output is an important consideration in incumbents' strategies. Models incorporating incumbents' subjective probability distributions have been developed to deal with such problems.[19]

Predatory Response to Entry. In a 1958 review article, Franco Modigliani described the Sylos postulate as the assumption that "potential entrants behave as though they expected existing firms to adopt the policy most unfavorable to them, namely, the policy of maintaining output while reducing price . . . to the extent required to enforce such an output policy."[20] Thus, the Sylos postulate prescribed a pattern of behavior for the potential entrant analogous to the minimax strategy in game theory. However, in some circumstances, maintenance of output in the face of entry may not be the worst possible outcome an entrant could expect; in other circumstances, it may not pose a credible threat.

Entry may lead to a breakdown of collusion or of Chamberlinian recognition of mutual dependence, leading to a price decline greater than that needed to absorb the entrants' output and to a concomitant increase in the outputs of the existing firms. Or, the incumbents might react in a predatory manner to repel the entrants. This latter possibility has led to debate on the appropriate definition of predatory pricing.

Phillip Areeda and Donald F. Turner have proposed that pricing be viewed as predatory when a firm drives out or excludes rivals by setting its price below average variable cost.[21] They contend that ideally, from the standpoint of consumer welfare, only a price below marginal cost should be considered predatory. But since marginal cost is hard to identify from accounting records, they propose use of average variable cost as an approximation. Oliver E. Williamson has objected to the Areeda-Turner rule because it permits strategic pricing by incumbent firms, who could hold price well above the entry-deterring level if potential entrants knew that existing firms could, in reaction to entry, expand output until price fell to average variable cost.[22] As an alternative, Williamson proposed an output limitation rule under which a firm could not expand its output in response to actual or threatened entry. In comparison with the Areeda-Turner rule, the Williamson rule (which would, by law, make the Sylos postulate the worst outcome a potential entrant could expect) would result in greater preentry output and hence a lower preentry price.

Although the Areeda-Turner rule has been adopted by the courts in several private-action antitrust cases,[23] both it and the Williamson rule have been criticized as allowing incumbents too much power to bar economically desirable entry.[24] The traditional Sherman Act approach, inferring intent to monopolize or restrain trade from the actions taken in specific cases, may be the best antitrust standard by which to identify predatory, entry-deterring behavior.[25]

Precommitment: A Credible Response to Entry. In many instances the prospect of existing firms maintaining output does not pose a credible threat to potential entrants. Unless incumbents expect to drive entrants out of the market in fairly short order, the strategy is likely to be self-defeating; certainly, if the entrants are expected to remain in the market, maintenance of preentry output levels by the existing firms is harmful to all. It would be in the mutual interest of old and new firms alike for the old ones to accommodate newcomers by reducing output, and to absorb the entrants into any overt or tacit restraint on competition that exists. Potential entrants may recognize that in such circumstances, the Sylos postulate prescribes irrational, indeed spiteful behavior. In John S. McGee's words, "The entrant should not expect that the monopoly would wreck itself to wreck others."[26]

One proposed set of solutions for the incumbents' problem of credibility is precommitment. Existing firms might lock themselves into the entry-deterring price and output levels, in advance of any actual entry, by long-term supply contracts or construction of plants designed so that it would be impossible or costly to retrench in a postentry period.[27] It may be perfectly rational for a firm to commit itself irrevocably to a course of action that will become harmful if a certain contingency occurs—if the commitment itself makes the contingency impossible or highly unlikely.

Judith R. Gelman and Steven C. Salop have noted that precommitment is a strategy also open to an entrant. What they call "judo economics" involves "a small firm using its rival's large size to its own advantage."[28] If a new firm enters a market with a small enough output plus a credible limitation on its capacity to produce, an incumbent may find it in its own interest to accommodate the entrant rather than incur the loss involved in maintaining output at the preentry level.

Predation against Existing Firms

Predation may occur against existing rather than entering firms and for the purpose of attaining rather than defending market power. It was alleged in the 1911 antitrust cases, and widely accepted among economists for many years thereafter, that both American Tobacco and Standard Oil engaged in widespread price warfare either to drive independent firms from their markets or to weaken them for acquisition on terms favorable to the trusts. Local price-cutting was regarded as the most vicious and effective form of such economic warfare available to a large and powerful trust, since discriminatory prices (even below costs of production) could be quoted in competitive areas and offset by monopolistic profits in other markets.

A Failure of Reason? Costs to the Predator and the Victim. In a 1958 article, McGee argued convincingly that this type of predatory pricing is rarely a rational tactic and, further, probably was not employed by the Standard Oil trust.[29] McGee and others have noted that such predation implies a failure of rational calculation. Predation imposes costs on both firms that could be avoided by a friendly merger; and the combined gain to both parties from the combination—however distributed—should be about the same whether the takeover results from early negotiations or after the financial ruin of the victim and an unnecessary drain on the predator's resources.

Predation for the purpose of driving a competitor from the market, without a subsequent merger, appears to be an even greater folly under most circumstances. Unless there are barriers to entry that did not exist when the attacked firm entered the market, the predator will be unable to enjoy the fruits of victory without attracting new competitors. Further, such entry is facilitated by the availability—perhaps at very low prices in bankruptcy or liquidation proceedings—of the physical plant of the firm or firms driven from the industry. Financial ruin does not imply the physical destruction of real capital such as buildings and machinery (although they may be subject to deterioration and deferred maintenance during a price war).[30]

If price discrimination is not possible, so that the predator must cut the price on all of its sales, its losses usually exceed those of an equally cost-efficient victim. If, as is usually the case, the predator has a larger share of the market, it must sell more than its rival at the predatory price. Also, to succeed in imposing the new price, the predator must increase sales to accommodate additional customers attracted by the bargain. The intended victim, on the other hand, can lower its output or perhaps close temporarily. And the larger the volume of sales, the greater the losses suffered in the struggle if the price is below cost. For this reason, a firm's vulnerability to predation depends greatly on the flexibility of its production scheduling or the magnitude of its fixed costs.

Rational Predatory Strategies. These arguments have not convinced all economists. Richard A. Posner noted that, under current antimerger law, acquisition to eliminate competitors is no longer a readily available option; therefore, predatory pricing to drive such firms from the market may be more attractive than it was in the heyday of the oil and tobacco trusts.[31]   In reply, McGee contended that Posner neglects the problem of disposition of the productive assets of the firms driven from the market.[32]

Kenneth G. Elzinga, in a study of alleged predatory pricing incidents in the Du Pont gunpowder trust case of 1911,[33] finds that predation can be ruled out in most, but not all, of these incidents.   He notes that business leaders can make mistakes, adding that if economists are still arguing over whether predation is ever rational, perhaps the business community at the turn of the century was also confused on the matter.

Further, predatory pricing aimed at existing competitors need not be intended to destroy them but merely to warn or discipline those whose pricing strategies undercut either an oligopolistic consensus or an outright conspiracy.   Even if these actions hurt the disciplinarians more than the errant competitors, they may still make sense as intimidating demonstrations, designed to warn all firms in the market against future transgressions.   At times, appearing to be indifferent to the harm one inflicts on oneself may be a perfectly rational business strategy.[34]

In sum, predation against existing competitors does occur.   But both a priori theoretical reasoning and empirical evidence strongly suggest that predation to acquire or eliminate a competitor is rare. Predation to discipline smaller rivals is a more plausible form of business conduct.

NONPRICE COMPETITION

Strategic Variables: Technological Improvement, Product Variation, and Advertising

While economists emphasize the effects of competitive behavior or its absence on price, they have not—and clearly could not have—ignored other aspects of market rivalry.   In a 1949 book, William Fellner contributed what is perhaps the most significant insight into nonprice competition in oligopolistic markets, building on the Chamberlinian concept of mutual dependence recognized.[35]   Fellner identified technological improvement, product variation, and advertising as the three most significant instruments, or strategic variables, of nonprice competition.

For two reasons, he argued, it is far more difficult for firms to come to an actual or implied understanding (a "quasi-agreement" in Fellner's terminology) regarding these variables than it is to reach a consensus on price.   First, firms cannot predict how market strength will change as a result of these forms of nonprice rivalry.   Therefore, it is extremely difficult for them to come to a mutually advantageous accommodation limiting such competition. Second, the unpredictability of the outcome of an R&D project, a new product introduction, or an advertising campaign makes the prospect of retaliation in these spheres less certain and less threatening than unrestrained price competition following a price cut by one group member. As Fellner put it, effective nonprice retaliation requires "inventiveness, which is in the nature of a scarce resource," while there is "no special skill (no unpredictable faculty) involved in undercutting a rival's price."[36]

From Fellner's analysis, a fairly common pattern in oligopolistic markets with mutual dependence recognized should be quasi agreement on price and market share coupled with independent and non-collusive behavior with respect to the nonprice competitive variables. As a result of the unpredictable outcomes of technical improvement, product variation, and advertising, relative market positions change. The continuing realignment of market share and power leads to periodic revision, and possible breakdown, of the understanding reached on price and output.

Market Power and Selling Effort: The Inverted-U Hypothesis

Subsequent work, both theoretical and empirical, suggests a relationship between a firm's market power and the intensity of its selling effort. Under market conditions approximating pure competition, firms have little or no incentive to promote their products. As a firm's market share and the impact of its output on price increase, it should find such activities a more effective way of competing. But if a firm enjoys market power close to pure monopoly, so that it is not greatly concerned with competition, it can relax its selling effort. This relationship—hypothesized to take an inverted-U shape—has most often been tested between concentration as an indicator of market power and the ratio of advertising expenditures to sales as a measure of selling effort.

Advertising in Pure Competition. For several reasons, advertising effort should increase as concentration rises from very low levels. Advertising affects demand and sales in two ways: (1) It attracts new customers and induces existing ones to buy more, thus expanding demand for the product—which benefits all firms in the market. (2) It diverts customers to the firm doing the advertising and away from its rivals. Under conditions near pure competition, with a homogeneous product and a large number of firms, no firm will advertise. If buyers make no distinction among products, any advertising by one firm will be diffused over the entire market. Under such circumstances, there is a powerful "free-rider" deterrent to advertising—each firm realizes that since it stands to gain just as much from others' advertising as from its own, it would be foolish to incur the cost, so no one advertises. In any event, if a firm's market share is so small that it considers itself a price taker, it will likely assume that it could not affect the market price through its own advertising any more than through varying the quantity it offers for sale.

Advertising under Monopolistic Competition and Oligopoly. Under monopolistic competition and oligopoly, advertising becomes an effective, perhaps necessary component of a firm's promotional and competitive strategies. If a product lends itself to differentiation, firms find it advantageous to publicize such things as unique brand characteristics and locational convenience. As numbers become small enough so that firms are no longer price takers but must quote price, and often compete in provision of services to customers as well, they must communicate these prices and services to potential customers.

With increasing concentration, the attractiveness of advertising is likely to grow. As Fellner noted, firms will recognize the inadvisability of competing in price, given the prospect of prompt and effective retaliation by rivals, and they may thus rely more on advertising as a competitive weapon.

A second effect of increasing concentration is reduction of the free-rider effect. As a firm's market share increases, so does its relative benefit from an increase in total market demand and, therefore, the positive relationship it perceives between its advertising effort and increased sales. Greater product differentiation has the same effect.

Advertising intensity throughout an industry feeds on itself. Firms facing loss of customers to rivals with more aggressive advertising will be forced to engage in higher levels of defensive advertising to stem the defections. As a result, advertising in oligopolistic markets may become excessive as one firm's efforts to attract customers and prevent defections merely counteract the similar efforts of rivals.

Advertising under Pure Monopoly. At high levels of market concentration, however, the incentives to advertise diminish. When rivals become few enough, their interdependence and vulnerability to retaliation extend to nonprice as well as price competition. Whether through overt collusion or recognition of mutual dependence, both aggressive and defensive advertising should decline. At the extreme of pure monopoly, the firm's only gain from advertising comes from expanding demand for the product. There are no competitors from whom to win customers and hence no need for defensive advertising—except, perhaps, as a barrier to entry.

Tests of the Inverted-U Hypothesis. A number of statistical and econometric studies provide statistically strong but qualified support for the inverted-U hypothesis.[37]

There are two main reasons for caution in interpreting the results of such regression analyses. First, a regression should control for a number of product characteristic variables, including numbers and skills of buyers (usually distinguishing between consumer and producer goods), elasticity of demand, rate of growth of the market, inherent differentiability of the product, importance of hidden product qualities that need to be called to buyers' attention, extent of impulse or otherwise emotional buying, and the importance of the product in purchasers' budgets.[38] Different researchers have controlled for some of these variables in different ways in their multiple regressions, while excluding others as neither measurable nor subject to inclusion through a reasonable proxy. As a result, correlation coefficients, or the percentages of variation accounted for by the included variables, tend to be low.

Second, as stressed by Douglas F. Greer, there is a reverse direction of causation in the underlying theory, implying simultaneity that makes ordinary least squares regressions inappropriate. Not only is concentration a determinant of advertising effort, but advertising may be a cause of concentration. Greer noted three sets of circumstances under which advertising efforts may promote concentration:

> First is the existence of internal economies of scale [to advertising]. . . .
> Second, assuming no economies of scale, one or more of the largest firms may consistently maintain greater advertising outlays relative to their sales . . . than those maintained by smaller firms because they possess larger financial resources, greater foresight, or predatory designs. Third, . . . some firms might be particularly successful in their advertising campaigns . . . [and] most of the remaining firms might respond in an attempt to emulate these successful companies by either eliminating the relative spending differential or establishing one in their own favor. Under certain conditions this competitive escalation may continue, resulting in a cost-price squeeze and, with failures and mergers, rising concentration.[39]

The inverted-U hypothesis has held up in multistage regression analyses of simultaneous-equation systems in which both advertising effort and concentration have been treated as endogenous variables.[40] The phenomenon, implying that advertising effort may frequently be excessive in moderately concentrated oligopolistic industries with products amenable to sales promotion, seems well established as a significant one linking market structure to business conduct and economic performance.

THE CENTRAL ROLE OF OLIGOPOLY THEORY IN INDUSTRIAL ORGANIZATION

Economists have long recognized that both pure monopoly and pure competition assume away the theoretical complexities raised by two essential structural features of most real-world markets: (1) product differentiation, which by definition is absent in both cases, and (2) barriers to entry, which must be effective enough to bar entry in pure monopoly but are assumed to be nonexistent in the model of pure competition. Thus, other models are necessary for the intermediate cases (where a certain level of monopoly power exists along with some degree of competition).

In light of the prevalence of these intermediate types of market structure, such theories are crucial to both the study of industrial organization and the evaluation of the nation's antitrust policy. The economists who have made the leading theoretical contributions—from Cournot through Chamberlin and Robinson to the game theorists, along with those who have considered the implications of entry-deterring, predatory, and nonprice strategies—have all had to come to terms with the basic and difficult problem of conjectural variation, or the extent to which mutual interdependence is recognized under oligopoly.

Next, we will consider more specific models of behavior, based on alternative conjectures a firm might make about its rivals' reactions in various oligopolistic market structures.

ENDNOTES

[1] Augustin Cournot, *Researches into the Mathematical Principles of the Theory of Wealth,* trans. Nathaniel T. Bacon (New York: Macmillan, 1897).

[2] The equation for a straight-line demand curve takes the form $P = a - bQ$. Multiplying both sides by Q yields $PQ = aQ - bQ^2$. Since PQ is total revenue, marginal revenue is equal to the first derivative of the latter expression with respect to Q, or $MR = a - 2bQ$.

[3] Cournot, *Researches,* p. 83.

[4] Joseph Bertrand, Review of Cournot, "Recherches," *Journal des Savants* (1883), pp. 499–508.

[5] Francis Y. Edgeworth, "The Pure Theory of Monopoly," *Papers Relating to Political Economy,* vol. 1 (London: Macmillan, 1925), pp. 111–42.

[6] Heinrich von Stackelberg, *The Theory of the Market Economy,* trans. Alan T. Peacock (New York: Oxford University Press, 1952).

[7] Ibid., p. 194.

[8] The calculation is complex. For an excellent graphical treatment, see Richard A. Bilas, *Microeconomic Theory: A Graphical Analysis* (New York: McGraw-Hill, 1967), pp. 219–24.

[9] Edward H. Chamberlin, *The Theory of Monopolistic Competition* (Cambridge, Mass.: Harvard University Press, 1933).

[10]Ibid., pp. 46–47.

[11]Joan Robinson, *The Economics of Imperfect Competition* (London: Macmillan, 1933).

[12]John von Neumann and Oskar Morgenstern, *Theory of Games and Economic Behavior* (Princeton, N.J.: Princeton University Press, 1944).

[13]Units of payoff may be expressed in terms of money, utility, or other quantitative measures. For example, one oft-cited game known as the Battle of the Bismark Sea has a payoff matrix expressed in the number of days a convoy will be exposed to aerial bombing. For a description of this game, see R. Duncan Luce and Howard Raiffa, *Games and Decisions* (New York: John Wiley & Sons, 1957), pp. 64–65.

[14]Ibid., chap. 4, "Two-Person Zero-Sum Games," pp. 56–87.

[15]Joe S. Bain, *Barriers to New Competition* (Cambridge, Mass.: Harvard University Press, 1956).

[16]Paolo Sylos Labini, *Oligopolio e Progresso Tecnico* (Milan: Guiffre, 1957).

[17]Bain, *Barriers,* pp. 21–22.

[18]Darius W. Gaskins, "Dynamic Limit Pricing: Optimal Pricing under Threat of Entry," *Journal of Economic Theory* 3, no. 3 (September 1971), pp. 306–22.

[19]Morton I. Kamien and Nancy L. Schwartz, "Limit Pricing and Uncertain Entry," *Econometrica* 39, no. 3 (May 1971), pp. 441–54; David P. Baron, "Limit Pricing, Potential Entry, and Barriers to Entry," *American Economic Review* 63, no. 4 (September 1973), pp. 666–74; Raymond R. De Bondt, "Limit Pricing, Uncertain Entry, and the Entry Lag," *Econometrica* 44, no. 5 (September 1976), pp. 939–46; Robert T. Masson and Joseph Shaanan, "Stochastic-Dynamic Limit Pricing: An Empirical Test," *Review of Economics and Statistics* 64, no. 3 (August 1982), pp. 413–22.

[20]Franco Modigliani, "New Developments on the Oligopoly Front," *Journal of Political Economy* 66, no. 3 (June 1958), pp. 215–32, at p. 217.

[21]Phillip Areeda and Donald F. Turner, "Predatory Pricing and Related Practices under Section 2 of the Sherman Act," *Harvard Law Review* 88, no. 4 (February 1975), pp. 697–733.

[22]Oliver E. Williamson, "Predatory Pricing: A Strategic and Welfare Analysis," *Yale Law Journal* 87, no. 2 (December 1977), pp. 284–340.

[23]See, for example, Hanson v. Shell Oil Co., 541 F. 2d 1352 (1976); Pacific Engineering and Production Co. v. Kerr-McGee Corp., 551 F. 2d 790 (1977); Outboard Marine Corp. v. Pezetel, 461 F. Supp. 384 (1978). For more recent decisions expressing skepticism toward judicial application of cost-based rules, see California Computer Products, Inc. v. International Business Machines Corp., 613 F. 2d 727 (1979); Chillicothe Sand & Gravel Co. v. Martin Marietta Corp., 615 F. 2d 427 (1980); William Inglis & Sons Baking Co., v. ITT Continental Baking Co., 668 F. 2d 1014 (1981).

[24]Frederic M. Scherer, "Predatory Pricing and the Sherman Act: A Comment," *Harvard Law Review* 89, no. 5 (March 1976), pp. 869–90; Joel B. Dirlam, "Marginal Cost Pricing Tests for Predation: Naive Welfare Economics and Public Policy,"*Antitrust Bulletin* 26, no. 4 (Winter 1981), pp. 769–814.

[25]For a convincing argument favoring the standard of intent in cases of predatory pricing aimed at existing rivals rather than to bar entry, see Douglas F. Greer, "A Critique of Areeda and Turner's Standard for Predatory Practices," *Antitrust Bulletin* 24, no. 2 (Summer 1979), pp. 233–61.

[26]John S. McGee, "Predatory Pricing Revisited," *Journal of Law and Economics* 23, no. 2 (October 1980), pp. 289–330, at p. 299.

[27]A. Michael Spence, "Entry, Capacity, Investment, and Oligopolistic Pricing," *Bell Journal of Economics* 8, no. 2 (August 1977), pp. 534–44; Steven C. Salop, "Strategic Entry Deterrence," *American Economic Review* 69, no. 2 (May 1979), pp. 335–38: Avinash Dixit, "The Role of Investment in Entry Deterrence," *Economic Journal* 90, no. 357 (March 1980), pp. 95–106; M. Therese Flaherty, "Dynamic Limit Pricing, Barriers to Entry, and Rational Firms," *Journal of Economic Theory* 23, no. 2 (October 1980),

pp. 160–82; Richard Schmalensee, "Economies of Scale and Barriers to Entry," *Journal of Political Economy* 98, no. 6 (December 1981), pp. 1228–38; Takashi Omori and George Yarrow, "Product Diversification, Entry Prevention, and Limit Pricing," *Bell Journal of Economics* 13, no. 1 (Spring 1982), pp. 242–48.

[28]Judith R. Gelman and Steven C. Salop, "Judo Economics: Capacity Limitation and Coupon Competition," *Bell Journal of Economics* 14, no. 2 (Autumn 1983), pp. 315–25, at p. 315.

[29]John S. McGee, "Predatory Price Cutting: The Standard Oil (N.J.) Case," *Journal of Law and Economics* 1 (October 1958), pp. 137–69.

[30]For an excellent summary of these arguments, see Robert H. Bork, *The Antitrust Paradox: A Policy at War with Itself* (New York: Basic Books, 1978), pp. 144–59. See also Lester G. Telser, "Cutthroat Competition and the Long Purse," *Journal of Law and Economics* 9 (October 1966), pp. 259–77.

[31]Richard A. Posner, *Antitrust Law: An Economic Perspective* (Chicago: University of Chicago Press, 1976), pp. 184–86.

[32]McGee, "Predatory Pricing Revisited," pp. 297–98.

[33]Kenneth G. Elzinga, "Predatory Pricing: The Case of the Gunpowder Trust," *Journal of Law and Economics* 13, no. 1 (April 1970), pp. 223–40.

[34]For example, for a firm launching a campaign of acquisitions, one or two purchases of firms ruined through price warfare and then bought out very cheaply might make negotiations easier and acquisitions cheaper in the future, even though the costs of predation could not be recouped by the direct results of the acquisitions of the original victims.

[35]William Fellner, *Competition Among the Few: Oligopoly and Similar Market Structures* (New York: Alfred A. Knopf, 1949).

[36]Ibid., p. 185.

[37]The earliest such study is Nicholas Kaldor and Rodney Silverman, *A Statistical Analysis of Advertising Expenditure and of the Revenue of the Press* (London: Cambridge University Press, 1948). More recent works include Douglas F. Greer, "Advertising and Market Concentration," *Southern Economic Journal* 38, no. 1 (July 1971), pp. 19–32; John Cable, "Market Structure, Advertising Policy and Intermarket Differences in Advertising Intensity," in *Market Structure and Corporate Behavior,* ed. Keith Cowling (London: Gray-Mills, 1972); C. J. Sutton, "Advertising, Concentration and Competition," *Economic Journal* 84, no. 333 (March 1974), pp. 56–69; Allyn D. Strickland and Leonard W. Weiss, "Advertising, Concentration, and Price-Cost Margins," *Journal of Political Economy* 84, no. 5 (October 1976), pp. 1109–21; John T. Scott, "Nonprice Competition in Banking Markets," *Southern Economic Journal* 44, no. 3 (January 1978), pp. 594–605; Stephen Martin, "Entry Barriers, Concentration, and Profits," *Southern Economic Journal* 46, no. 2 (October 1979), pp. 471–88; Richard E. Caves, Michael E. Porter, and A. Michael Spence with John T. Scott, *Competition in the Open Economy: The Model Applied to Canada* (Cambridge, Mass.: Harvard University Press, 1980).

[38]These characteristics are taken from Greer, "Advertising," pp. 19–20.

[39]Ibid., pp. 21–22.

[40]Greer, "Advertising"; Strickland and Weiss, "Advertising"; Martin, "Entry Barriers."

CHAPTER TEN

Types and Models of Oligopolistic Conduct

The crucial role of conjectural variation makes oligopoly theory the most intriguing and challenging branch of the theory of the business firm but at the same time the most difficult, controversial, and least complete. A number of specific models, mostly complementing one another, have been developed to analyze various observed types of oligopolistic business behavior.

OVERT COLLUSION

In a series of indictments in 1960, 29 electrical equipment manufacturers and 45 of their executives were charged with criminal violations of Section 1 of the Sherman Act, including agreements to fix and maintain prices, allocate sales to public agencies among themselves, and submit collusive and rigged bids to both government and private purchasers.[1] In imposing jail sentences on a number of these executives after the defendants had pled guilty, the trial judge stated, "This is a shocking indictment of a vast section of our economy, for what is really at stake here is the survival of the kind of economy under which America has grown to greatness, the free enterprise system."[2]

Although these cases provided a dramatic and highly visible example of overt collusion involving some of the nation's largest and best-known corporations, including General Electric Company and Westinghouse Corporation, the incident was not an isolated one. Roughly three quarters of all antitrust cases brought by the Department of Justice involve allegations of overt collusion. In fiscal year

1984, the Department of Justice filed 100 cases against 104 individuals and 131 corporations, charging criminal violations of the antitrust prohibitions against contracts, combinations, and conspiracies in restraint of trade. In the same year, fines of $22 million and jail sentences totaling 106 months of actual imprisonment were imposed.[3]

Since overt market collusion is illegal in the United States, it is impossible to accurately assess how widespread or effective the practice is in various sectors of the economy. Some commentators think it is endemic. According to one of the men who pled guilty in the electrical equipment conspiracy, "No one attending the gatherings was so stupid he didn't know [the meetings] were in violation of the law. But it is the only way a business can be run. It is free enterprise."[4]

The basic incentive to collude is self-evident. Firms hope that by coming to agreements on price levels or rates of output, they can end or limit competition among themselves and thus increase the group's overall profits or reduce its losses. The more inelastic the market demand curve, the greater the incentive to collude, *ceteris paribus*. If demand is highly inelastic, a uniform increase in price imposed at the same time by all of the firms in a particular market will lead to relatively small declines in sales volume and an increase in total revenue. (Conversely, competitive price-cutting is particularly harmful, as no seller will gain much in sales volume and all will lose revenue.)

Perfect Collusion

If collusion were *perfect*, in economic jargon, output would be restricted to the monopolistic rate and the joint profits of the conspirators would be maximized. Joint profit maximization would call for cooperative allocation of the monopolistic output in such a way that the marginal costs of all of the colluding firms were equal. Otherwise, once the optimal rate of output had been determined, the joint profit could be increased by expanding the output of the firms with lower marginal costs and imposing offsetting restrictions on those with higher costs. The opportunities to increase overall profitability by such shifts would not be exhausted until the marginal costs of all of the firms were equal and total costs thereby minimized. A strategy of equating marginal costs might require the closing of some high-cost plants and would, in any event, redistribute production and profits to favor the firms with the lower production costs at the restricted rate of industry output—even though some of the others might be equally or more efficient at other rates.

Where legal, cartels have often obtained the cooperation of the higher-cost firms through side payments, or payments made out of the enhanced profits of the low-cost producers to compensate the others for ceasing or drastically restricting production. But side payments may be only a short-run solution: in the long run, such payments have induced participants in profitable cartels to expand capacity—not to increase production but rather to claim higher side payments for not producing.

Imperfect Collusion

In most manufacturing industries, products are not identical. Product differentiation heightens the problem facing a group of colluders, since it is difficult if not impossible to determine the joint profit-maximizing prices—including optimal differentials among these prices—for related products. George Hay and Daniel Kelley have noted that product differentiation takes two forms.[5] *Intrafirm* differentiation involves one firm producing a line of products of varying sizes or grades, very likely with common costs attributable to the various products only by arbitrary accounting conventions. Would-be colluders may therefore disagree as to what the costs of a particular product are. *Interfirm* differentiation refers to real or perceived differences in the products of different firms, commonly leading to differences in the prices and outputs regarded as optimal by the various producers.

Thus, collusive agreements (even when successfully negotiated and implemented) are likely to result in price and output levels different from those of joint profit maximization or from those that would result from a full merger of the colluders. But though the profits from such imperfect collusion will necessarily be below the fully monopolistic level, the collusive price may conceivably be higher and the collective output lower than those that would maximize joint profits.

Motives for Collusion

Evidence—taken mostly from alleged conspiracies prosecuted by the antitrust agencies and thus drawn from atypical examples—suggests that the objective of collusive agreements may more often be to deal with adverse business conditions than to reap monopolistic profits. Almarin Phillips concluded that leading antitrust cases "raise the question of whether it is not more likely that overt conspiracies of this kind occur in markets in which rivalry is severe rather than in markets in which competition is stifled."[6] Phillips noted that the prominent Supreme Court cases out of which evolved the doctrine of per se illegality dealt with conspiracies in industries threatened with excessive competition stemming from high fixed costs relative to variable and inelastic and unstable demand—including steel, cement, cast-iron pipe, vitreous sanitary fixtures, and bituminous coal mining. Indeed, Phillips' study suggests that fear of such excessive competition may be a more powerful motive than greed in driving business firms to illegal conspiracy.[7]

Peter Asch and Joseph J. Seneca examined a sample of 101 large manufacturing firms. Fifty-one had been found guilty of or pled nolo contendere to charges of conspiracy under Section 1 of the Sherman Act; 50 had never been so charged and were included for comparison.[8] Asch and Seneca found a negative and statistically significant relationship between collusion and profitability. Rejecting the hypothesis that collusion leads to lower profits on grounds of elementary economic theory and common sense, they concluded that lower profits, or losses, provide the most powerful motives for collusion. But they were careful to warn readers that their sample might not be representative, because successful antitrust prosecutions tend to focus disproportionately on unsuccessful conspiracies.

Cheating and Its Detection

Once a collusive agreement is reached, the greatest short-run threat to its stability is cheating. The temptation to cheat is, ironically, heightened by others' resoluteness in adhering to the agreement. If a conspirator contemplating a possible price cut is confident that all the others will adhere to the higher agreed-upon price, it would assume that its potential gain in sales would include all of the new customers attracted by the lower price, plus a group of old customers from the other firms. In other words, its conjectured demand curve as a cheater is made a great deal more elastic by its faith that the others will not cheat.

Recognition that cheating poses such a great threat to collusion has led economists to analyze the problem of *detection*. George J. Stigler, in a 1964 article, noted that "it is a well-established proposition that if any member of the agreement can secretly violate it, he will gain larger profits than by conforming to it. . . . Enforcement consists basically of detecting significant deviations from the agreed-upon prices. Once detected, the deviations will tend to disappear because they are no longer secret and will be matched by fellow conspirators if they are not withdrawn."[9] Stigler envisaged three sources of evidence of cheating by others: the extent to which a noncheating firm lost old customers, the share of new customers it attracted, and the growth of sales of one or more rival firms.

The Number of Customers. As Stigler explained, if there is a certain probability that each sale in which the price is cut will be discovered, regardless of its size, a cheater may decide that only sales transactions above a certain value are worth the risk. Thus, only the larger buyers will be offered the lower price. Stigler also developed a model in which the sizes of all buyers were held constant. Under these circumstances, the larger the number of customers faced by each selling firm, the less the incentive to cheat. Each firm in the agreement is assumed to have a probability distribution of expected sales. If a firm's actual sales fall to a certain percentage below the expected level, that firm will suspect price-cutting. If, at the same time, a rival's sales have risen by more than a certain proportion, it will be identified as the probable cheater. The larger the number of transactions, or equal-sized buyers, the less the loss in sales revenue required to trigger a presumption of cheating.

For example, suppose a truck dealer averages three sales per week. If this dealer sells only two trucks per week for three weeks in a row, he or she might simply attribute the decline to a run of bad luck. But if a retail grocer expecting to make 1,000 sales per day dropped to around 667, he or she would suspect cheating much sooner.

The Number of Rival Firms. A second result of Stigler's model is that the larger the number of rival sellers, the greater the incentive for any one of them to cheat. The number of customers that a price-cutter can take from a given competitor without attracting its suspicion is not significantly affected by the number of competitors, while the gains from cheating are the sum of the gains extracted from each one. Alternatively, in a market with 101 initially identical firms, a firm can double its sales revenue by reducing that of each of the others by only one percent (neglecting new customers); if a firm in a market with four initially identical competitors doubled its sales at the others' expense, each of its rivals would lose one third of its sales. Detection of cheating is surely more likely in the latter case.

Price Visibility. Detection of secret price-cutting is also enhanced by the visibility of prices offered to prospective customers. Competitive sealed bidding procedures, for example, in which the buying agency opens each bid at a public meeting and announces both the identity of the bidder and the price bid, have been widely criticized as an invitation to the bidders to collude. Yet, state and federal laws often require public agencies to award procurement contracts through sealed bids, to avoid favoritism or bribery. In markets where prices are announced by public outcry—such as securities exchanges, cattle and tobacco auctions, and commodity marts—secret price-cutting is impossible. Prices published in catalogs may or may not be subject to unpublicized reductions when actual sales are made.

The easiest prices to conceal are those bid and offered in private face-to-face meetings between salespersons and purchasing agents. Indeed, collusive pricing may be disrupted by purchasing agents falsely claiming to be able to get better deals from one of the other colluders. Complex pricing schedules—involving such things as quality differentials, add-ons for extras (e.g., optional equipment on automobiles), custom orders, and discounts from list price for such things as large orders, prompt payment, or trade status (e.g., different prices to wholesalers and retailers)—facilitate secret price-cutting. Such "price shading" may be accomplished through false invoicing of customers for goods of lower quality than actually shipped, for example, or by allowing larger than normal discounts. Some large buyers routinely take the largest possible discounts for prompt payment, regardless of when payments are actually made.

Ability to Punish Violators. Still another determinant of a collusive agreement's viability is the ability to punish violators. In nations such as the United States, where price-fixing agreements are against the law and thus cannot be enforced through legal proceedings, retaliation must be implemented in the market. Such retaliation may not be as certain and automatic as Stigler suggested.

Large firms may decide not to punish much smaller rivals if they must match or exceed others' price cuts across the board. A firm selling 100,000 units per month, for example, might hesitate to match the price cut of a cheater selling 1,000 units, thereby sacrificing 100 times as much revenue. For this reason, the ability to discriminate in price (primarily the ability to prevent those receiving the lower price from reselling to those charged the higher price) enhances the ability to punish a cheater. If the large firm selling 100,000 units per month sold nationwide while the smaller price-cutter sold only in, say, the Los Angeles area, the large firm would be much more willing to retaliate if it could cut its prices only in the Los Angeles market while maintaining them elsewhere.

A second problem with retaliation is that it may require a number of firms to join in costly price-cutting, and it may be difficult to obtain the necessary cooperation.[10]

Timing of Retaliation. The timing as well as the probability of retaliation is an important consideration for the prospective cheater. Cheaters may expect a much greater sales volume at only a slightly lower price for some time before effective retaliation. In this case, temporary profit might more than offset the present discounted cost of any feasible punishment.

A related factor stems from size and frequency of sales. If sales are "lumpy," or infrequent and large, firms may be tempted to undercut the agreed-upon price to win one big order. A firm might find it impossible to resist a contract—for example, a major highway project or construction of an aircraft carrier—that would keep it operating at full capacity for several years.

As noted by Stigler, large and infrequent sales make detection more difficult. But even if detection is automatic—say the contract for highway or aircraft carrier construction is let by publicly opened and announced sealed bidding—retaliation may not be a credible deterrent. Such a problem surfaced in the electrical equipment conspiracy, as shown in the testimony of one of the participants, who stated:

> One company would be responsible one month for issuing these memorandums to the other companies . . . listing the pending propositions, what they calculated the book price to be, and the other companies were supposed to follow that price unless they caught an error in it. . . . That went on for quite a while, and seemed to work, because there wasn't much business. And then on the first real big job that came up, the memorandum scheme broke down.[11]

But despite bickering and breakdowns in the agreements, it appears that the electrical equipment conspiracy did succeed in raising the participants' profits and that the antitrust action was effective in reducing them.[12]

Barriers to Entry

In the long run, a collusive agreement will not be stable or workable unless there is some barrier to entry into the affected market—perhaps no more than the inability of new firms to earn more than a normal profit, even at the collusively determined price. If the collusion evolved in response to declining demand, cyclical overcapacity, or some other adverse development, the colluders themselves might not be making any excess profits.

Collusion that successfully raises conspirators' profits above normal, however, will be threatened by outsiders' attempts either to get in on the arrangement or to undercut the collusive price—unless barred by patents, economies of scale relative to market size, or some other constraint. The conspiracy may include some arrangement for absorbing newcomers and reallocating market shares to accommodate them, but only barriers to further entry at some point or erosion of profits to normal levels will end the long-run destabilizing effects of actual or anticipated inflow.

Donald Dewey has suggested a reason for collusive agreements, even where lack of barriers to entry assures that the conspirators will not be able to earn profits above the normal competitive level in the long run: in highly but less than perfectly competitive industries, price changes are initiated by individual firms rather than by some unspecified "impersonal market forces," even though no firm has the power to earn long-run monopolistic profits. Price changes made by competitors are a major source of uncertainty in such situations; and the rate of return required to attract or retain capital will be raised to reflect that uncertainty. A collusive agreement promotes price stability, both by reducing the number of price changes made and by providing information to each firm as to the others' current price. Such a reduction in uncertainty may lead to lower profits and higher rates of output in the industry. Dewey, like Phillips, concluded that collusive price-fixing may, in certain structural settings, promote economic welfare.[13]

Don E. Waldman, however, has taken issue with Dewey, arguing that successful collusion may lead to excess capacity, even in the absence of entry attracted by higher prices or profits, because the colluding firms will be reluctant to reduce their capacity for fear of being unable to maintain their market share if the conspiracy breaks down in the future.[14]

Waldman tested his hypothesis in a study of three well-known conspiracies in the cement, cardboard container, and electrical turbine industries. In all three, the expected increase in excess capacity did occur during the period of conspiracy—stemming from both entry and expansion of existing firms in cement, primarily from entry in cardboard containers, and from expansion of existing firms, coupled with greater penetration of the U.S. market by foreign suppliers, in the case of the electrical turbine industry. Further, according to Waldman, the excess capacity created by the conspiracies may have actually lowered prices in the cement and cardboard container industries.

In sum, price-fixing and other collusive activities are pervasive features of economic life even when subject to legal prohibitions, but their effectiveness is determined in large part by features of market structure, and their success is often problematic.

TWO OLIGOPOLY MODELS: THE KINKED DEMAND CURVE AND PRICE LEADERSHIP

Just as overt collusion is more often than not imperfect, so tacit collusion or recognition of mutual dependence is likely to be incomplete. Existing theories of oligopoly give little specific guidance as to how the individual business owner or manager is to think through the process of initial acts and marketwide reactions.

Economists' skepticism as to the seriousness and extent of effective tacit collusion was heightened by the revelations of the electrical equipment conspiracy trial. In markets populated by a small number of some of the nation's largest and most sophisticated sellers, not only had recognition of mutual dependence failed to evolve but even overt collusion proved erratic and only sporadically workable. Although 29 firms were indicted, the numbers alleged to be involved in specific product conspiracies were much smaller: 3 were indicted and 3 more named as coconspirators in a bid-rigging scheme for turbines and generators, 5 were named in a circuit-breaker conspiracy, and 3 were charged in the instance of meters. In each of these 3 indictments, the conspirators and coconspirators were alleged to control 100 percent of the market.[15]

A number of models have been developed employing conjectural variations less stringent than full recognition of mutual dependence and therefore leading to imperfect coordination among rivals. The more insightful of such models specify a set of structural conditions under which certain of these conjectural variations are plausible. Two of the most popular and enduring are the kinked demand curve and price leadership models.

The Kinked Demand Curve

The kinked demand curve model applies to an oligopolistic market structure with a small enough number of firms of roughly similar size for each one to know its rivals and to try to guess how each of them would respond to a price change. But no firm can be certain of the extent to which others will take account of their mutual interdependence. So a firm may behave as a minimaxer and act on the assumption that its worst expectations will be fulfilled: if it raised its price, none of the others would follow, resulting in a large loss of sales; but if it lowered its price, all of the others would make corresponding reductions, so that its sales volume would rise only by a fraction—roughly, its market share—of the overall increase.

Under these circumstances, the firm envisions itself as facing a demand curve such as D in Figure 10–1, with a kink at Point a, determined by the existing price and output. The more elastic upper segment is analogous to Chamberlin's dd' curve (i.e., others will maintain their prices), while the less elastic lower segment is based on a conjecture similar to that underlying DD' (i.e., the others will match the price reduction). The kinked demand curve model does not seek to explain how the initial equilibrium price and output (P_e and Q_e) were determined. A kink in the demand curve leads to a gap in the marginal revenue curve at Q_e. (The marginal revenue curve depicts the change in total revenue resulting from the sale of one more unit, and there is a discrete difference in the amount of that change depending on whether the last unit sold lies to the left or the right of Q.)

FIGURE 10–1 The Kinked Demand Curve

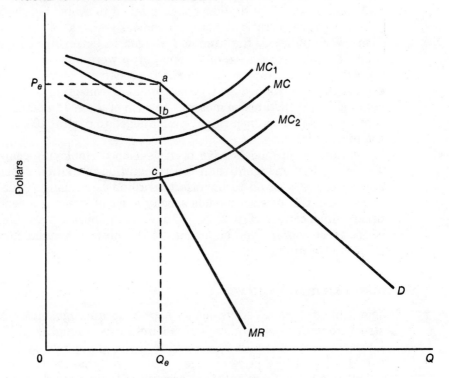

The result of the kinked demand curve model is that price and output will not change, despite fluctuations in cost, as long as the marginal cost curve (*MC*) passes through the gap between Points *b* and *c* in Figure 10–1. Thus, marginal cost could rise to MC_1 or fall to MC_2 without disturbing the equilibrium price and quantity.

The kinked demand curve model was developed originally as an explanation for price rigidity in oligopolistic sectors of the U.S. and British economies early in the 1930s Depression, when labor and raw material costs (including agricultural prices) fell much more sharply than the prices of manufactured goods. Paul M. Sweezy, one of the originators of the concept, noted that the shape, size, and direction of the kink would vary with conditions, since it resulted from an "imagined," or subjective, demand curve. In a period of declining demand, for example, in which each firm saw its demand curve shifting to the left, firms would be more likely to respond to a price cut with cuts of their own. If secret price-cutting was feasible, the kink would vanish; indeed, it could reverse itself, with the less elastic portion to the left of the existing price, if a firm thought others would follow its announced price increase but be unaware of an unannounced price cut.[16]

Despite such disclaimers, both Sweezy and the authors who independently introduced the kinked demand curve in a British journal[17]
probably made far too sweeping claims regarding its applicability and
capacity to explain the events of the Depression. Stigler, for example,
noted that the structural conditions under which the kink was plausible were quite restrictive.[18] Further, he pointed out, there were
other explanations for rigid prices in concentrated markets. These
include administrative lags in obtaining the necessary agreement to
change prices set by collusion, as well as the risk of precipitating
conflict over the appropriate change; the costs of advertising, revising
price lists, and issuing new catalogs to keep customers informed of
frequent small price changes; and the frequent use of long-term contracts providing that the buyer would receive any price cut given to
others over the life of the contract, which could make price cuts very
costly. Also, some buyers of intermediate-producers' goods are more
concerned with price stability than with level (particularly if the market demand for their own product is inelastic), since their primary
concern might be that competitors not obtain a cost advantage by
acquiring materials more cheaply. Comparing frequency and size of
price changes made in oligopolistic industries between 1929 and 1937
with the changes made over the same period in two monopolized industries, aluminum and nickel, Stigler found the monopolies to be far
more rigid even though they did not face a kink.[19]

The Price Leadership Model

The price leadership model presumes a quite different set of structural
conditions and conjectural variations. There is one firm substantially
larger than any of its rivals or a small group of large firms acting to
maximize their joint profits, along with a fringe group of smaller firms
that set output independently of the large firm(s). If we assume perfect
collusion or full recognition of mutual dependence among a small number of large firms, including restriction of output as well as price restraint, we can treat this group as one "leading" firm for analytical
convenience.

The leading firm determines its most profitable price and output
on the assumption that the smaller firms will adopt the same price.
The smaller firms may follow the leader's price by agreement or simply
because it is in their independent interests to do so. In the latter case,
the small firms are price takers, since no one of them has the power
to raise the price and there is no incentive for any of them to reduce
the price as long as there is no restraint on output. In this model,
none of the small firms believes that changes in its output, *ceteris
paribus,* will have a perceptible effect on the market price. A small

firm's profit-maximizing strategy, therefore, is to set output at the rate at which its marginal cost is equal to the price set by the leader. The optimal strategy for the leader in this situation is depicted in Figure 10–2. In both panels, the market demand curve is shown as D_m. At any price, the maximum quantity that the leader can put on the market without driving the price down is the total quantity that will be produced minus the quantity that the fringe firms will offer for sale. Each of the followers will produce a quantity equating its marginal cost with the price. Thus, the quantity that will be offered by the fringe as a whole is the horizontal sum of the marginal cost curves (above average variable cost) of all of the fringe firms. This is shown as ΣMC_f in Panel A.

FIGURE 10–2 Price Leadership

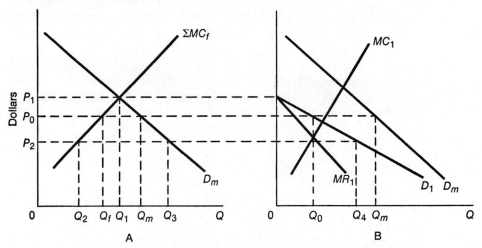

Assuming that the leader knows the costs of its small competitors, it then calculates the demand curve it faces by subtracting the output of the fringe firms from the total quantity demanded by the market at each price. For example, at a price of P_1, where $\Sigma MC_f = D_m$, the fringe firms would produce Q_1, and the leader could add nothing to market supply without lowering price. Thus, its demand is zero at P_1. At a price of P_2, the fringe would produce Q_2 and total market sales would be Q_3, so that the leader could sell Q_3 minus Q_2. This quantity is shown as Q_4 in Panel B (i.e., $Q_4 = Q_3 - Q_2$). The demand curve facing the leader, D_1 in Panel B, is constructed by calculating quantities such as Q_4 for all prices below $P_$ Given D_1, the leader maximizes profit by producing the output at which MR_1 (the marginal revenue curve associated with D_1) is equal to its marginal cost (MC_1).

The leader's optimal price is P_o, at which it sells Q_o, allowing the fringe of followers to sell Q_f. By construction as well as logic, $Q_o + Q_f = Q_m$, where the right-hand term is the total amount demanded by the market at the price P_o.

In both the short and long runs, the position of the price leader is frustrating and one that it would not tolerate could it control the followers' output. In the short run, an increase in price necessitating a reduction in the industry's output triggers an increase in the outputs of all of the firms except the price setter. The small fringe firms are acting against their own collective interest, as well as against that of the price leader, since their individual output strategies restrain the leader from raising the price to an effectively collusive level approaching that of joint profit maximization. Indeed, as can be shown from an unpublished set of formulations by Donald L. Basch, the equilibrium outcome of the price leadership model is typically closer to pure competition than to pure monopoly.

Table 10–1 contains some simple classroom types of illustrations, utilizing straight-line demand and cost functions with arbitrary price and output values ranging between zero and 10, employing Basch's formulations to compare the price and output results under pure competition (price = industry marginal cost), price leadership, and pure monopoly or joint profit maximization (industry marginal revenue = industry marginal cost). Results are presented for six cases in which the relationships between demand and marginal cost vary widely, the slopes of the demand curves are quite different, and both the leader and the competitive fringe have relative cost advantages. To limit the number of cases, the intercepts of the marginal cost curves are assumed to be the same for all firms in the industry. The values shown in Table 10–1 indicate that both the quantities and prices under price leadership are more similar to those of pure competition than to those of joint profit maximization.

Dean A. Worcester has shown that equilibrium in this price leadership model is unstable in the long run.[20] Unless the fringe firms' costs are substantially higher than those of the leader, they will earn economic profits; thus, the output of the fringe will expand, both through the growth of existing firms and the entry of new ones. Over time, these firms will take successively larger shares of the market away from a price leader that keeps passively adjusting its output to theirs. As the leader's share declines, it loses its dominant position and the dubious privilege of setting the market price.

Economists have distinguished three types of price leadership. First, there is the *dominant firm* case, in which one firm is so much larger than any of its competitors that it simply sets a price on the assumption that the others will follow in their own self-interest, perhaps bolstered

TABLE 10–1 Values Assumed and Equilibrium Results for Six Comparative Cases of Pure Competition, Dominant Firm Price Leadership, and Pure Monopoly

A. Values Assumed

	Case					
	I	*II*	*III*	*IV*	*V*	*VI*
Intercept of market demand curve	10.0	8.0	6.0	6.0	8.0	10.0
Slope of market demand curve	1.5	1.0	0.5	1.5	1.5	0.5
Intercept of marginal cost curve	1.0	3.0	5.0	5.0	3.0	1.0
Slope of dominant firm's marginal cost curve	1.0	1.0	1.0	1.0	1.0	1.0
Slope of followers' marginal cost curve	1.5	1.0	0.5	1.5	1.5	0.5

B. Equilibrium Results

Case		Competition	Dominant Firm	Joint Profit Maximization (Pure Monopoly)
I	Q	4.29	3.90	2.50
	P	3.57	4.15	6.25
II	Q	3.33	3.13	2.00
	P	4.67	4.88	6.00
III	Q	1.20	1.17	0.75
	P	5.40	5.42	5.63
IV	Q	0.48	0.43	0.28
	P	5.29	5.35	5.58
V	Q	2.38	2.17	1.38
	P	4.43	4.75	5.92
VI	Q	10.80	10.50	6.75
	P	4.60	4.75	6.63

by the leader's ability and willingness to discipline price cutters. Second, there is *collusive* price leadership, in which a group of firms—either the leading firms or all, including the fringe—agree to follow the price set by a designated leader. The lead may rotate among the firms, either because the conspirators do not wish to recognize a permanent leader, or to make the conspiracy less visible to antitrust authorities. Third, there is *barometric* price leadership, in which others usually follow the lead of one firm simply because and only so long as they respect its superior market knowledge or judgment. A barometric price leader need not possess substantial market power, and its announced price cuts may reflect nothing more than open recognition of industrywide secret price-cutting. In reality, the three cases blur into each other. The model encompasses the essential feature of all three cases—the pricing problem facing a firm that assumes the others will match its prices, but in which the collusion or recognition of interdependence does not extend to output.[21]

The kinked demand curve and price leadership models are both quite specific and are intended to apply only in particular oligopolistic structural settings. To be useful, such models must delineate clearly the relevant structural features assumed and the nature of the conjectures about rivals' behavior attributed to the firm being modeled. But when properly formulated and applied with skill, these and similar oligopoly models are effective and valuable tools for illuminating a broad spectrum of cases between mutual dependence fully recognized and completely ignored.

CORPORATE OBJECTIVES OTHER THAN PROFIT MAXIMIZATION

The profit motive plays a central role in microeconomic theory. But the large modern corporation often has both the ability and the organizational motivation to pursue other objectives. A firm capable of earning substantial monopolistic profits does not have to maximize such profits to stay in business or even to acquire additional productive resources for expansion. And the managers of a corporation in which ownership and control are separated may be free from unremitting pressure to run the firm for the sole purpose of earning the greatest possible profits for their stockholder-employers.

Some differences between the interests of owners and managers may reflect no more than division of the spoils, at least in the short run. A controlling group of executives may, for example, award themselves higher salaries, benefits, and emoluments than justified by the need to acquire, maintain, and motivate able management. Such outlays may be viewed as no more than a transfer of current profits from stockholders to managers and, indeed, as providing an incentive for managers to set price and production levels that maximize the profits available for distribution to both groups. But in the long run, excessive managerial "consumption" reduces the prospects for the firm's growth by reducing both retained earnings and the ability to raise additional funds from outside investors.

Other sources of conflict between managerial and ownership interests have more direct and immediate effects on business decisions and conduct. When a firm faces a declining market and, in the owners' best interests, should cut back or terminate operations, the very managers who make the decision may lose their jobs.

Managers may want to expand a financially healthy firm beyond its most profitable scale of operation, particularly if their compensation is related less to profits than to firm size. Further, since the sheer size of a firm may confer prestige on its managers, some may be driven by a desire to control the largest possible industrial empire. To achieve growth objectives, managers may try to maximize short-run profits but retain too great a portion of earnings for reinvestment, or they may expand through mergers and acquisitions on terms that are not in the stockholders' best interests.[22]

Managers may see stockholders as only one of many constituent groups to which the corporation is responsible. Such attitudes may lead to recognition of corporate obligations to its work force, its customers and suppliers (particularly those with long-term patron-client relationships such as franchised dealers and "customary" sources of supply),[23] and the communities in which it operates. Carl Kaysen has depicted—perhaps caricatured—this view in his comment that "The modern corporation is a soulful corporation."[24] Adolf A. Berle, Jr., attributes the recognition of corporate social responsibilities not to an organizational soul or conscience but rather to an institutional instinct for survival. In a pluralistic society such as the United States, Berle argues, positions of private power require social "legitimacy." He sees corporate recognition of such responsibilities as a response to the perceived—and real—need for justifying or giving legitimacy to managerial power.[25]

John Kenneth Galbraith argues that effective control of the modern large corporation is passing to the "technostructure," those who possess the "diverse technical knowledge, experience or other talent which modern industrial technology and planning require." The technostructure, he continues, "extends from the leadership of the modern industrial enterprise down to just short of the labor force."[26] The talents of the technostructure include skills in such areas as finance, procurement, labor relations, and merchandising, as well as more narrow technological fields. According to Galbraith, the technostructure's overriding goals are survival of the organization (which requires a minimum level of earnings) and the maximum possible rate of sales growth. Secondary goals include autonomy of the technostructure (particularly avoidance of subordination to either market forces or government regulation), technical virtuosity, and a rising dividend rate. The last two goals represent sources of prestige for the corporation that rub off on those identified with it. After these goals are met, tertiary goals of charitable giving, community service, and political participation may be indulged.

Sales Revenue Maximization

William J. Baumol identified several reasons why firms with market power might seek to maximize sales revenue (*not* physical volume) subject to a minimum-required-profit constraint.[27] In many ways, sales revenue maximization promotes long-run profits: Consumers may avoid a product if they believe its popularity is declining; credit may be harder to obtain with lower sales volumes; a firm's market power suffers if it loses either distributors or market share; and personnel relations are poorer in a firm that is firing than in one that is hiring.

Baumol's static model depicts a trade-off between maximization of sales revenue and profit, as shown in Figure 10–3. The situation shown is one of unconstrained sales revenue maximization. The total revenue and total cost functions (TR and TC) are drawn to correspond with a downward-sloping demand or average revenue schedule and a U-shaped average cost curve. The total profit function (TP) is merely the vertical distance between TR and TC. That is, the firm earns positive economic profits when it produces any output between Q_1 and Q_5. Profit is maximized at Q_2, the rate of output between Q_1 and Q_5 at which the vertical distance between TR and TC is at its greatest and at which TP is thus at its maximum height. Sales revenue is maximized at the output rate of Q_3, at which TR obtains its maximum value.

The rate of output that maximizes profit must be less than that which maximizes sales revenue, given the conventional shapes of TR and TC. The total revenue associated with a downward-sloping demand curve rises at a decreasing rate until it reaches the point of unit elasticity of demand, and then declines. Total cost must slope upward throughout, barring the extremely unlikely possibility of a range in

FIGURE 10–3 Static Sales Revenue Maximization

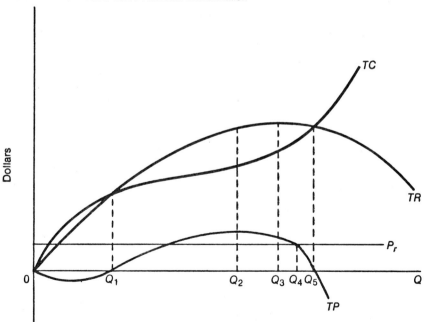

which marginal cost is negative. Profit, or the vertical distance between TR and TC, is maximized when their slopes, both necessarily positive, are equal (i.e., marginal revenue equals marginal cost, or the first derivative of $TR - TC = 0$). TR reaches its maximum only when output has further expanded to the point where its slope is zero (i.e., elasticity is unitary and marginal revenue is zero). Thus, the unconstrained sales revenue maximizer will always produce more and charge a lower price than a similarly situated profit maximizer.

Line P_r in Figure 10–3 represents the minimum profit required to keep the stockholders satisfied enough not to try to oust the management, to fend off takeover bids and corporate raiders, and perhaps to allow for the reinvestment needed to attain a desired growth rate. In Figure 10–3, the minimum-profit requirement allows the firm to produce as much as Q_4 and thus does not prevent the firm from maximizing sales revenue. If, however, P_r were to shift up, or an unfavorable shift in either TR or TC caused TP to fall, so that P_r intersected TP at an output of less than Q_3, we would have a case of *constrained* sales revenue maximization. A second source of constraint could arise if TC intersected TR to the left of the latter's maximum point, even if stockholders were content with a normal rate of return (i.e., $P_r = 0$).

Baumol noted that if we allow for advertising and other forms of nonprice competition, unconstrained sales revenue maximization is not a possible equilibrium outcome. If the firm is earning profits above the minimum required level and wishes to maximize sales revenue, it will devote the excess earnings to sales promotion, both increasing the sales that can be made at any price (i.e., shifting the demand curve out) and increasing its total costs. As long as added expenditures on sales promotion increase total revenue, they will be made, even though the increase in cost exceeds that in revenue and profit is thus reduced, until any further advertising outlay is checked by the minimum required level of profit.

The output under sales revenue maximization must be greater than that under profit maximization, and hence the price must be lower, except in the limiting case when the required level of profit is equal to the maximum attainable. Further, Baumol shows that for any given level of revenue, a sales revenue maximizer and a profit maximizer will use an identical set of inputs. Thus, faced with the same demand and cost curves, the sales revenue–maximizing oligopolist will in all likelihood come closer to a competitive allocation of resources than will a profit maximizer. But it is possible for the sales revenue maximizer to overdo a good thing, in a welfare sense, by producing even more and setting price even lower than would be the case under pure competition.[28]

Current Revenue and Growth

Robin Marris has shown that, if current profits are essential to finance asset expansion, and if the firm's objective is to maximize the present value of the expected stream of sales revenue, its current output will be higher than the static profit-maximizing rate.[29] The following equations and diagrams constitute a simplified version of this model.

Equation (10.1) shows the present value (PV) of the sales revenue stream for the next n periods.

$$PV = SR + \frac{SR(1 + g)}{(1 + r)} + \frac{SR(1 + g)^2}{(1 + r)^2} + \ldots + \frac{SR(1 + g)^n}{(1 + r)^n} \quad (10.1)$$

where

SR = Current period's sales revenue
g = Rate of growth of sales revenue, assumed to be constant
r = Discount rate reflecting the firm's preference for present over future income

As n approaches infinity, Equation (10.1) reduces to

$$PV = \frac{SR(1 + r)}{(r - g)} \quad (10.2)$$

provided that r is greater than g. (If r were less than g, PV would be infinitely large with each period's sales revenue having a greater present value than that of any of the preceding periods, into an infinite future.)[30]

Equation (10.2) shows that SR and g vary inversely for any given value of PV, provided the firm's discount rate (r) is held constant. Rearrangement of Equation (10–2) yields

$$g = r - \frac{(1 + r)}{PV} \cdot SR \quad (10.3)$$

Equation (10.3) allows us to draw a set of isovalue lines in Figure 10–4A, showing the varying combinations of SR and g that will yield a particular PV. In this figure, the higher subscripts indicate higher values, so that $PV_1 < PV_2 < PV_3$. The isovalue lines are downward sloping, with a constant slope of $-(1 + r)/PV$. In equation (10.3) the entire family of isovalue lines associated with a given value of r intersects the vertical axis at the point where $g = r$; but this merely gives us a guide to construction of Figure 10–4A, since the mathematical and economic interpretations of that point are not meaningful. When $g = r$, PV is infinite for any positive value of SR. But in the equation and on the graph, SR approaches zero as r approaches g.

The curved line (G) in Figure 10–4A plots the growth rates possible

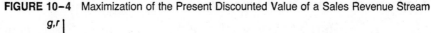

FIGURE 10-4 Maximization of the Present Discounted Value of a Sales Revenue Stream

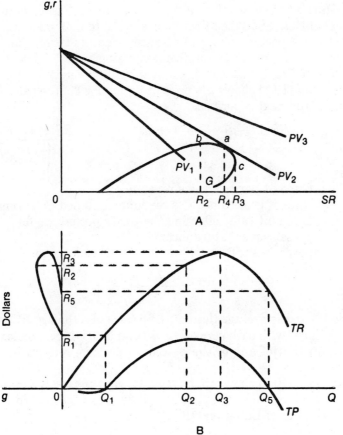

at various levels of *SR*. Assuming that the higher the level of profit, the higher the possible growth rate, and that some profit is required for growth, *G* can be derived from the *TP* and *TR* curves of Figure 10-3. Figure 10-4B reproduces the latter two curves and also indicates the maximum possible growth rate (*g*) on the left-side horizontal axis. Q_1, Q_2, Q_3, and Q_5 are rates of output identical to those of Figure 10-3. In particular, Q_2 is the profit-maximizing rate of output, and Q_3 is the sales revenue–maximizing rate.

At a rate of output of Q_1 and sales revenue of R_1, profit is zero, and thus the maximum possible growth rate is zero. At Q_2 and R_2, profit is maximized and so, therefore, is *g*. At sales revenue values above R_2, both profits and *g* decline. Q_3 yields the maximum value of *TR*, shown as R_3 on the vertical axis. As *Q* increases beyond Q_3,

TR falls towards R_5 at the rate of output Q_5, at which profit and thus *g* fall back to zero.

Referring again to Figure 10–4A, a firm seeking to maximize the present value of sales revenue (*PV*) will locate on the highest attainable isovalue line. This isovalue is PV_2, where the line is tangent to *G* at Point *a*. Thus, in the initial year, the firm will produce an output yielding sales revenue of R_4. The downward slope of the *PV* line assures that the point of tangency will lie between points *b* and *c*. Thus, R_4 must lie between R_2 (the sales revenue obtained by the profit maximizer) and R_3 (the revenue earned by the sales revenue maximizer in the static model). Similarly, the output associated with R_4 must lie between Q_2 and Q_3. The less steep the slope of the maximum *PV* attainable, or the lower *r* is, the closer the equilibrium positions of the present-value maximizer and the profit maximizer. Conversely, the higher *r* becomes, or the greater the subjective value to the firm of present earnings over future earnings, the closer the equilibrium of the present-value maximizer gets to that of the static revenue maximizer.[31]

Profitability and Form of Control

Later empirical work tended to cast doubt on one of the primary assumptions underlying managerial hypotheses such as sales revenue or growth maximization. Total management compensation—including bonuses, pension benefits, and stock option plans, in addition to salary—appears to be more closely related to profits than to sales revenue or size.[32]

Nevertheless, evidence from econometric studies seeking to determine the degree to which profitability is related to form of control suggests that, in the oligopolistic sector of the modern U.S. economy, owner-controlled firms are somewhat more profitable than comparable ones under managerial control.[33]

THE SHORT VIEW: AN ALLEGED FAILURE OF THE AMERICAN MANAGERIAL SYSTEM

Some are skeptical of the claim that separation of ownership and control allows managers to impose their own goals on the organization; they note that managers operate under severe restraints, including vulnerability to stockholder suits, takeover by dissident stockholders or outside "corporate raiders," unfriendly merger bids, and the growing influence of institutional investors holding large blocks of stock—the paraproprietal society. In every case, management's best protection is to maintain the highest possible market value of the outstanding common-stock equity. This, in turn, presumes profit maximization.

Until recently this external pressure for profit maximization was presumed to enhance business efficiency. But the conglomerate merger movement that peaked in the late 1960s and resurged in the early 1980s, and the rapid growth of institutional investors (particularly pension funds) through the 1960s and 1970s, have triggered new criticism of the modern large corporation. Critics now have at least one explanation for the apparent failure of American big business to meet the challenge of foreign competition—most notably from Japan. Managers, so the argument goes, are under unremitting pressure to generate the largest possible profits. The stock market and the institutional investors, however, put too much emphasis on short-term profits. A temporary drop in the market price of a firm's stock might attract the attention of an aggressive conglomerate or cause pension and mutual fund managers to unload large blocks of stock regardless of the downward impact on the stock's market price. Institutional investors are viewed as moving vast funds around the securities and money markets to take advantage of temporary swings, destabilizing both long-term capital and short-term credit positions of the affected corporations.

Managers, it is contended, have responded by an undue emphasis on short-term profitability at the expense of long-range strategies for sound and sustainable profits. Actions that could be taken to improve short-term profits to the detriment of long-term results include lowering quality standards to step up the immediate volume of production, cutting back on research and development and market research to improve current cash flow, deferring maintenance and repair expenditures, and running down year-end inventories to improve the reported rate of return. Further, reported short-term earnings may be no more than paper profits, involving "creative accounting" techniques by which the current bottom line can be inflated.[34]

Negative reactions to the literature concerned with the possible effects of such short-sighted corporate management have mostly taken two forms. First, it has been pointed out that the overall performance of the manufacturing and export sectors of the U.S. economy has actually been strong relative to that of the other industrialized nations. In a careful and thorough examination of the performance of U.S. and foreign manufacturing, Robert Z. Lawrence found that from 1973 to 1980, manufacturing production grew more rapidly in the United States than in any other industrialized nation except Japan. In 1980, per capita output in U.S. manufacturing was still the world's highest, although the gap was closing.[35]

Second, there has been a resurgence of the older view that the financial institutions and the market for corporate takeovers play an economically beneficial role in promoting managerial efficiency. The 1985 *Annual Report of the Council of Economic Advisers* gave national prominence to this view by devoting an entire chapter to the subject. According to the council, there is little evidence that the stock market undervalues companies with sound long-term programs and commitments—or, at least, programs and commitments that the investment community regards as sound. To the contrary, it is "well established that the stock market sees through accounting techniques and bases its evaluations on underlying market values." The evidence, the report notes, is "overwhelming" that target companies typically have been those suffering from mismanagement and that takeovers enhance efficiency, since "successful takeovers substantially increase the wealth of stockholders in the target companies . . . in the range of 16 to 34 percent of the value of the targets' shares."[36]

On the face of the matter, the concepts of the soulful corporation and what might be called the shortsighted one appear to pose a contradiction. The paraproprietal society envisioned by Berle and Harbrecht undoubtedly provides a more congenial environment for the shortsighted firm than for the soulful one. But it seems equally true that the two types of corporation can coexist—along with long-run profit maximizers—in an industrial economy as diverse as that of the United States. Perhaps the most that can be said at this time is that an investigator studying a particular firm or industry should be alert to the possibility that the form of control exerts a significant influence on the conduct and performance under examination, and should thus seek to identify the controlling groups, the pressures on them, and their motives. The corporate conscience appears to have had only a minor effect on the overall performance of U.S. business: it may be that the myopic view of profit will prove to be a temporary aberration, corrected by the harsh discipline of the financial markets and international competition.

ENDNOTES

[1]United States v. Westinghouse Electric Corporation et al., Criminal No. 20399, D. Ct. East. Pa., 1960. Reprinted in Clarence C. Walton and Frederick W. Cleveland, Jr., *Corporations on Trial: The Electric Cases* (Belmont, Calif.: Wadsworth, 1964), pp. **x**–xiv. See also John G. Fuller, *The Gentlemen Conspirators* (New York: Grove Press, 1962).

[2]Reproduced in Northwestern University School of Business, "General Electric and the Price Conspiracy Cases," Case Study MR 216RI, 1962, pp. 7–8.

[3]Statement of J. Paul McGrath, Assistant Attorney General, Antitrust Division, before the Subcommittee on Monopolies and Commercial Law of the Committee on the Judiciary, U.S. House of Representatives, concerning Department of Justice authori-

zation for fiscal year 1986, March 13, 1985 (Washington, D.C.: U.S. Department of Justice press release, March 13, 1985).

[4]*The Wall Street Journal,* January 10, 1962. Reprinted in Edwin Mansfield, ed., *Monopoly Power and Economic Performance,* 4th ed. (New York: W. W. Norton, 1978), pp. 163–64.

[5]George Hay and Daniel Kelley, "An Empirical Survey of Price Fixing Conspiracies," *Journal of Law and Economics* 17, no. 1 (April 1974), pp. 13–38.

[6]Almarin Phillips, *Market Structure, Organization and Performance* (Cambridge, Mass.: Harvard University Press, 1962), p. 195.

[7]For an earlier observation on the same point by a writer with experience managing government-sponsored cartels in Germany's Weimar Republic, see Herbert von Beckerath, *In Defense of the West* (Durham, N.C.: Duke University Press, 1942), especially p. 76.

[8]Peter Asch and Joseph J. Seneca, "Is Collusion Profitable?" *Review of Economics and Statistics* 58, no. 1 (February 1976), pp. 1–12.

[9]George J. Stigler, "A Theory of Oligopoly," *Journal of Political Economy* 72, no. 1 (February 1964), pp. 44–61, at p. 46.

[10]For an excellent discussion, see Oliver E. Williamson, *Markets and Hierarchies: Analysis and Antitrust Implications* (New York: Macmillan, 1975), pp. 238–44.

[11]Walton and Cleveland, *Corporations on Trial,* p. 46.

[12]David F. Lean, Jonathan D. Ogur, and Robert P. Rogers, "Does Collusion Pay . . . Does Antitrust Work?" *Southern Economic Journal* 51, no. 3 (January 1985), pp. 828–41.

[13]Donald Dewey, "Information, Entry, and Welfare: The Case for Collusion," *American Economic Review* 69, no. 4 (September 1979), pp. 587–94. See also critical comments by Kari Bullock and Sumner J. La Croix, Oliver Grawe and Thomas Overstreet, Roland I. Koller II, Don E. Waldman, and Philip L. Williams, along with a reply by Dewey, *American Economic Review* 72, no. 1 (March 1982), pp. 256–81.

[14]Don E. Waldman, "The Inefficiency of 'Unsuccessful' Price Fixing Agreements," paper presented at Eastern Economic Association Convention, Montreal, 1980.

[15]Walton and Cleveland, *Corporations on Trial,* p. 14.

[16]Paul M. Sweezy, "Demand Under Conditions of Oligopoly," *Journal of Political Economy* 47, no. 4 (August 1939), pp. 568–73.

[17]Robert L. Hall and Charles J. Hitch, "Price Theory and Business Behavior," *Oxford Economic Papers,* no. 2 (May 1939), pp. 12–45.

[18]George J. Stigler, "The Kinky Oligopoly Demand Curve and Rigid Prices," *Journal of Political Economy* 55, no. 5 (October 1947), pp. 432–49.

[19]Subsequent studies have confirmed Stigler's results but suffer from use of statistical samples of oligopoly that do not conform to the structural conditions on which the model is predicated. See Julian L. Simon, "A Further Test of the Kinky Oligopoly Demand Curve," *American Economic Review* 59, no. 5 (December 1969), pp. 971–75; Walter J. Primeaux, Jr., and Mark R. Bomball, "A Reexamination of the Kinky Oligopoly Demand Curve," *Journal of Political Economy* 82, no. 4 (July–August 1974), pp. 851–61.

[20]Dean A. Worcester, "Why 'Dominant Firms' Decline," *Journal of Political Economy* 65, no. 4 (August 1957), pp. 338–46.

[21]In addition to Worcester's, the leading studies of price leadership include Frederik Zeuthen, *Problems of Monopoly and Economic Warfare* (London: Routledge, 1930), pp. 15–23; George J. Stigler, "Notes on the Theory of Duopoly," *Journal of Political Economy* 48, no. 4 (August 1940), pp. 421–41; Jesse W. Markham, "The Nature and Significance of Price Leadership," *American Economic Review* 41, no. 5 (December 1951), pp. 891–905; Robert F. Lanzillotti, "Competitive Price Leadership—A Critique of Price Lead-

ership Models," *Review of Economics and Statistics* 39, no. 1 (February 1957), pp. 55–64; Joe S. Bain, "Price Leadership, Barometers, and Kinks," *Journal of Business* 33, no. 3 (July 1960), pp. 193–203.

[22]For extensive theoretical and empirical work on managerial motives and conglomerate mergers, see Dennis G. Mueller, ed., *The Determinants and Effects of Mergers* (Cambridge, Mass.: Oelgeschlager, Gunn & Hain, 1980), and Mueller's earlier article, "A Theory of Conglomerate Mergers," *Quarterly Journal of Economics* 83, no. 4 (November 1969), pp. 643–59.

[23]Carl Kaysen, "The Corporation: How Much Power? What Scope?" in *The Corporation in Modern Society*, ed. Edward S. Mason (Cambridge, Mass.: Harvard University Press, 1960), pp. 85–105.

[24]"The Social Significance of the Modern Corporation," *American Economic Review* 47, no. 2 (May 1957), pp. 311–19, at p. 314.

[25]Adolf A. Berle, Jr., *Power without Property: A New Development in American Political Economy* (New York: Harcourt Brace Jovanovich, 1959).

[26]John Kenneth Galbraith, *The New Industrial State* (Boston: Houghton Mifflin, 1967), p. 59.

[27]William J. Baumol, *Business Behavior, Value and Growth*, rev. ed. (New York: Harcourt Brace Jovanovich, 1967).

[28]William G. Shepherd, "On Sales-Maximising and Oligopoly Behavior," *Economica* 29, no. 116 (November 1962), pp. 420–24.

[29]Robin Marris, *The Economic Theory of "Managerial" Capitalism* (London: Macmillan, 1964).

[30]The derivation of this type of growth equation is described in a number of finance texts, usually in discussions of common-stock valuation. See, for example, James G. Van Horne, *Financial Management and Policy*, 6th ed. (Englewood Cliffs, N.J.: Prentice-Hall, 1983), pp. 27–29.

[31]Figure 10–4 and the associated discussion represent a modification of a similar presentation in Douglas Needham, *The Economics of Industrial Structure, Conduct and Performance* (New York: St. Martin's Press, 1978), pp. 9–13. I am grateful to one of my former students, Stephen M. Jennings, for substantial contributions to the modified version presented here.

[32]See, among others, Robert T. Masson, "Executive Motivations, Earnings, and Consequent Equity Performance," *Journal of Political Economy* 79, no. 6 (November–December 1971), pp. 1278–92; Wilbur G. Lewellen, *The Ownership Income of Management* (New York: Columbia University Press, 1971).

[33]John Palmer, for one, found that "among firms with a high degree of monopoly power, management-controlled firms report significantly lower profit rates than owner-controlled firms," in his study, "The Profit-Performance Effects of Separation of Ownership from Control in Large U.S. Corporations," *Bell Journal of Economics and Management Science* 4, no. 1 (Spring 1973), pp. 293–303, at p. 293. Others have found slight but statistically insignificant differences, or none. For a thoughtful survey and comparison of these studies, see William A. McEachern, *Managerial Control and Performance* (Lexington, Mass.: D. C. Heath, 1975).

[34]For discussions of the sources of this perceived overemphasis on short-term profits, its results, and policy recommendations, see Samuel M. Loescher, "Corporate Gigantism, Degradation of the Plane of Competition, and Countervailance," *Journal of Economic Issues* 8, no. 2 (June 1974), pp. 329–51; Robert H. Hayes and William J. Abernathy, "Managing Our Way to Economic Decline," *Harvard Business Review* 58, no. 4 (July–August 1980), pp. 67–77; Ira C. Magaziner and Robert B. Reich, *Minding America's Business: The Decline and Rise of the American Economy* (New York: Harcourt Brace Jovanovich, 1982); Robert B. Reich, *The Next American Frontier* (New York: New York Times Books, 1983); Samuel M. Loescher, "Bureaucratic Measurement, Shuttling Stock

Shares, and Shortened Time Horizons: Implications for Economic Growth," *Quarterly Review of Economics and Business* 24, no. 4 (Winter 1984), pp. 8–23; "Will Money Managers Wreck the Economy?" *Business Week*, August 13, 1984, pp. 86–93.

[35]Robert Z. Lawrence, *Can America Compete?* (Washington, D.C.: Brookings Institution, 1984).

[36]U.S. Council of Economic Advisers, *Annual Report of the Council of Economic Advisers, 1985* (Washington, D.C.: U.S. Government Printing Office, 1985), pp. 187–216, at p. 197.

CHAPTER ELEVEN

Economic Performance and the Competitive Norm: Resource Allocation

For most analysts, policymakers, and other outside observers of the business scene, interest in market structure and conduct stems from an even more basic concern with the economy's performance. Those involved with antitrust enforcement particularly need to understand how economic performance is affected by its structural and behavioral determinants, since the fundamental strategy underlying the antitrust laws is one of indirect influence on performance through restraints on certain types of business conduct and, to a lesser extent, through control of industrial structure. The antitrust authorities seek to establish and maintain a structural environment and code of conduct under which business activity motivated by private interest will lead to socially desirable performance. A consideration of performance, therefore, requires both formulation of standards or norms of ideal performance and identification of the significant structural and behavioral influences on actual performance.

THE COMPETITIVE MODEL AND THE WELFARE NORM

By far the most widely accepted criterion of an economy's overall performance is the material welfare of its members. If the technological knowledge, stock of productive resources, and income distribution are taken as given, consumer welfare is maximized when those resources are (1) fully utilized, (2) combined to produce goods in the most technically efficient ways, and (3) allocated to the production of various goods in such a way that no reallocation would result in a net increase in welfare. Under a set of restrictive assumptions, it can be shown that an economy characterized by pure competition attains such an optimal allocation of resources when it is in general equilibrium. It can also be shown that an economy in general equilibrium but with varying degrees of monopoly power in various markets is not allocating its resources optimally.

The Household Model

Suppose a household faces a set of consumer goods prices it has no power to change and it must decide how to allocate a limited budget among purchases of these goods. If the marginal utility, or the increase in satisfaction from consuming one more unit, of every good is declining, the household will maximize its total utility by distributing its expenditures to equate the utilities added by the last penny spent on every good. This implies that in equilibrium, the household has arranged its budget so that

$$mu_1/P_1 = mu_2/P_2 = \ldots = mu_n/P_n \qquad (11.1)$$

where mu_j equals the marginal utility to the household of the jth good, P_j equals the price of the jth good, and there are n consumer goods offered for sale in the economy ($j = 1$ to n).

The rationale for Equation (11.1) can be seen by assuming for the moment that utility can be measured in fixed units (utils). Suppose that our household can choose between only two goods, apples (a) and bananas (b) and that at an initial consumption combination, the last apple consumed yields 40 utils of satisfaction and the last banana yields 45. Suppose further that the price of an apple (P_a) is 20 cents and that of a banana (P_b) is 15 cents. From Equation (11.1),

$$mu_a/P_a = 40/20 = 2$$

and

$$mu_b/P_b = 45/15 = 3$$

or the last penny spent on an apple yields 2 utils while the last penny spent on a banana yields 3 utils. Now imagine that the household reduces its spending on apples by 60 cents, thus decreasing its purchases by three, and uses the same 60 cents to buy four additional bananas. The result is a net gain of somewhat under 60 utils, consisting of less than 180 utils of added satisfaction from consumption of bananas minus more than 120 utils of satisfaction lost from reduced apple consumption. The assumption of diminishing marginal utility lies behind the qualifying words *somewhat under, less*, and *more*. As more bananas are consumed, the utility added by the last one consumed decreases, while the marginal utility of apples rises as their consumption is curtailed. Thus, each additional 60 cents (or penny) transferred from the purchase of apples to bananas adds less to total utility. No further increase in satisfaction is possible when a penny's worth of apple and of banana yield equal marginal utility. This might occur when

$$mu_a/P_a = 50/20 = mu_b/P_b = 37.5/15 = 2.5$$

The result holds equally well for n goods as for two.

The reader who is unhappy with the concept of the util as a unit of measurement of happiness or satisfaction—as are many economists—should note that Equation (11.1) can be rearranged into a set of equations

$$mu_1/mu_2 = P_1/P_2$$
$$mu_1/mu_n = P_1/P_n \qquad (11.2)$$
$$mu_2/mu_n = P_2/P_n$$

and so on, including every possible pair of the n goods. In each of these equations, the utils in the numerator and denominator of the left side cancel out, leaving the ratios as pure numbers.[1]

A household will reach the utility-maximizing equilibrium of Equation (11.1) or Set (11.2) only if it knows all consumer goods prices and the utility-yielding characteristics of every available good. Further, those who make the decisions and control the spending must be equally concerned for the welfare requirements of all members of the household. The requisite knowledge of prices, product characteristics, and personal preferences and needs of oneself and others is embodied in the assumption of perfect information. The problem of equal concern for the welfare of all household members (e.g., elderly parents or small children) is assumed away by treating the household as a collective utility-maximizing unit.

If an economy is in general equilibrium, with all resources employed efficiently and every household maximizing its utility subject to a budget constraint and the existing set of prices, then the economy's total utility—simply, the sum of that of all households—is also maximized subject to the same income or budget and price constraints, provided there are no *externalities* of consumption. These externalities might be *negative,* such as one household reducing a neighboring one's utility by playing a radio at high volume at 2 A.M., or *positive,* such as installation of a smoke detector by an apartment dweller. But if we assume that all households' utilities are *independent* of others' consumption, then when all households are in equilibrium,

$$MU_1/P_1 = MU_2/P_2 = \ldots = MU_n/P_n \qquad (11.3)$$

where MU_j equals the marginal utility of consumption of good j for the entire economy, or its marginal social utility.

The General Equilibrium Model

Up to this point, prices have been taken as given. But under pure competition, each firm will receive a price for its product equal to its marginal cost (MC). Thus, $P_j = MC_j$, where all final-product markets in the economy are characterized by pure competition. By substitution into Equation (11.3),

$$MU_1/MC_1 = MU_2/MC_2 = \ldots = MU_n/MC_n \qquad (11.4)$$

Pareto Optimality. In the absence of any externalities of production and under conditions of pure competition in factor markets, the marginal cost of producing a final good reflects the value of the contribution the resources used in its production could have made in their next best alternative employments (i.e., their *opportunity* costs). Thus, Equation (11.4) depicts an allocation of society's resources that is *Pareto optimal*—there is no way to increase the welfare of one or more individuals or households without decreasing that of at least one other member of society. The concept of Pareto optimality rules out any transfer of income other than voluntary donations, or takes the existing income distribution as given, since an involuntary transfer of income from one person, no matter how wealthy, to another, no matter how impoverished, clearly reduces the welfare of the first.

The reasoning behind the assertion that Equation (11.4) depicts a situation of Pareto optimality is analogous to that just discussed for the household. Suppose that an all-wise, benevolent social planner with absolute economic power but no interest in redistribution of income directs the allocation of resources in an economy producing two goods: cookies (c) and doughnuts (d). Initially, let $MU_c = 10$ utils, $MU_d = 18$ utils, $MC_c = 5$ cents, and $MC_d = 12$ cents. Were the planner to transfer 60 cents worth of resources from the production of doughnuts to the production of cookies, social utility would rise by a little less than 30 utils. Subsequent transfers of similar quantities of the appropriate resources would yield successively lower increases in net utility, as MU_c fell, MC_c rose, MU_d rose, and MC_d fell. (Note that pure competition requires increasing marginal costs of production for all goods.) No further gain would be possible when $MU_c/MC_c = MU_d/MC_d$.

What the Model Means. The fundamental point of the model is that the equilibrium result under a regime of pure competition with no central direction is identical to the outcome that an absolute dictator would want to impose on the economy if interested only in the public welfare but unwilling to impose involuntary income transfers. Under varying degrees of competition and monopoly, where monopolistic prices exceed marginal costs, relative market prices will provide misleading guides to households, which will purchase too many competitively priced goods and too few of those sold at monopolistic prices. Aggregate welfare could be increased by reallocating society's given stock of resources so as to expand output in monopolized industries and reduce it in competitive ones.

The assumption of no externalities in production is a more severe one, especially for a modern industrialized country, than is the parallel assumption of no externalities in consumption. Essentially, the absence of externalities in production implies that private and social costs are equal, so that in pure competition the price of every product is equal to its marginal social cost. This rules out all external costs of pollution, congestion, and health hazards that firms impose on other firms and on individuals.

Factor Allocation. Finally, competition in factor as well as in product markets is needed to assure that individual factors of production are allocated to maximize their social productivity. A firm selling its product in pure competition has a *derived demand* for each of the factors of production it uses. This derived demand is calculated from the marginal physical product (*MPP*) schedule of a factor, which indicates the amount by which total output increases in response to application of an additional unit of the factor, *ceteris paribus,* for different levels of usage. A farmer, for example, would want to know how many more bushels of wheat the farm would yield if one more bag of fertilizer was added to the inputs. To convert the *MPP* of fertilizer into a derived demand schedule, the farmer would multiply its *MPP* at various levels of usage by the price of wheat, obtaining the marginal value product (*MVP*). As long as the *MVP* is above the price of fertilizer, the farmer will add more to total revenue than to total cost by applying another bag. Suppose the price of fertilizer is $15 per bag and the price of wheat is $3 per bushel. If the 200th bag of fertilizer is expected to increase the farm's yield by six bushels (i.e., *MPP* = 6 bushels), its use will add $18 to total revenue (i.e., *MVP* = $18). If the farmer applies that bag of fertilizer, making no other change in inputs, the farm's net surplus will rise by $3. An efficient farmer would use additional bags of fertilizer until its *MPP* fell to five bushels and its MVP therefore fell to the factor price of $15 per bag.

All other firms would, in similar fashion, use fertilizer—if they used it at all—up to the point at which its MVP was falling and equal to its market price. Thus, in general equilibrium,

$$MVP_{f1} = MVP_{f2} = \ldots = MVP_{fm} = P_f \qquad (11.5)$$

where *m* firms use a factor of production *f.* To continue our example, the *m* users of fertilizer would include other wheat farms, farms growing crops other than wheat, and landscape gardeners—that is, all producers using fertilizer in all of the industries for which it is a factor of production.

As long as the *MVP* of fertilizer, or any other factor of production, is higher in some uses than in others, its total value product can be increased by transferring some of it from lower to higher value uses. But since *MVP* is declining for every user, the opportunities for increasing a factor's total value product by such transfers will be exhausted when its *MVP*s in all uses are equal. Once again, the competitive market in equilibrium reaches the same result as the selfless and benevolent dictator.

Factor allocation will be optimal only under pure competition. Note that if our farmer had monopoly power in the market for the final product, wheat, he or she would not multiply the *MPP* of fertilizer by the *price* of wheat to determine a demand schedule for fertilizer but rather would multiply by a smaller number, the *marginal revenue* associated with the added output. Thus, a monopolized industry would use less of a factor of production, given its price, than would be the case if the industry were competitive. (This is, of course, consistent with the proposition that monopoly power results in a restriction of output.) Further, the equality of all *MVP*s for a specific factor requires that no user possess monopsonistic power—for example, our wheat farmer's purchases of fertilizer can not be large enough to have a perceptible and recognized effect on its price. In addition, there must be pure competition among the suppliers of each factor of production to assure that the factor price is equal for all users.

For Equation (11.5) to hold as a general-equilibrium condition, it must be assumed that all producers have complete information on the prices and productive qualities of all available factors of production and that these factors are mobile (can be transferred readily from one use to another). The model thus assumes away problems posed by such features of the real world as "sunk" capital—long-lived investments that are specialized in either location or purpose, such as coal mines and railroad tracks—and nontransferable labor skills.

The Competitive Model as a Norm for Economic Performance

The competitive model is not an accurate description of, or even a close approximation to, the way a real-world market economy works. But the model provides the economist with a norm or standard against which actual economic performance can be compared. Given the assumptions of the model, the norm becomes

$$P = MC \tag{11.6}$$

for all products, whether consumer or producer goods. As a corollary,

$$P_f = MVP_f \tag{11.7}$$

for all users of all factors of production.

If Equations (11.6) and (11.7) hold throughout an economy, the model demonstrates, no reallocation of resources can increase consumer welfare for a given income distribution. It is still possible, by a redistribution of income, to improve the lot of some while worsening that of others, but the general equilibrium is Pareto optimal.

CRITICAL ASSUMPTIONS UNDERLYING THE COMPETITIVE MODEL

The widespread conviction that a competitive system promotes economic welfare, despite the unrealistic assumptions of the underlying model, provides one of the strongest rationales for a procompetitive and antimonopolistic public policy. But some economists and policy analysts find the model's assumptions too restrictive. Indeed, it has been noted that under certain structural circumstances, some elements of competition are conducive to a worsening of economic performance. Two of the most critical assumptions are: (1) that there are no economies of scale inconsistent with a large number of efficient firms in every market and (2) that the economy's resources and technological knowledge are fixed.

Economies of Scale. In many industries, it is impossible for the market to contain enough firms of technically efficient size to even approximate pure competition. In a "natural monopoly," the level of demand is such that the market cannot accommodate more than one. In such instances, particularly where the product has no close substitutes and is viewed as a necessity (e.g., electric power, water, rail transportation), the natural monopolist has been subject to public regulation of price, output, and level of investment.

Three cases of natural monopoly are depicted in Figure 11–1. In all three panels, P_o and Q_o represent the socially optimal values of these variables, determined by the competitive norm $P = MC$, and are thus the prices and outputs that would be set under welfare-maximizing regulation (subject to the "second-best" qualification discussed later in this chapter). C_o is the long-run average cost (*LAC*) at the competitive rate of output. In Figure 11–1A, the demand curve (*D*) in-

FIGURE 11–1 Three Cases of Natural Monopoly

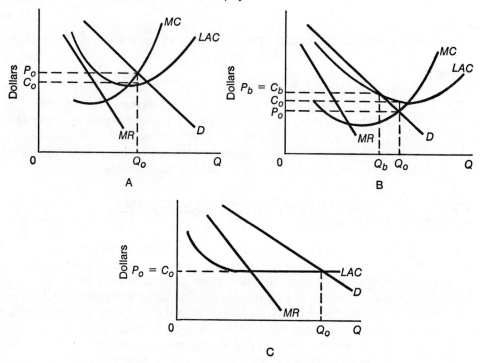

A

B

C

tersects the rising portion of LAC, so that long-run average cost must be increasing at the optimal rate of output (since MC must intersect LAC at the latter's minimum point). Thus, under optimal regulation, the monopolist can earn a profit equal to $(P_o - C_o)Q_o$. This profit is analogous to the inframarginal rent of a competitive industry and may or may not be recouped through taxation or franchise fees.

Figure 11–1B depicts a more problematic situation, in which D intersects LAC in the range in which it is still decreasing with output. The dilemma posed here for socially optimal pricing is that P_o is necessarily less than C_o in the decreasing-cost case. The regulator faces a choice of setting the optimal price of P_o and subsidizing the monopolist at the rate of $(C_o - P_o)Q_o$, or allowing it to break even at the suboptimal price of P_b and output of Q_b. Figure 11–1C, illustrating the case of constant cost in which there is no problem of either excess profit or enforced loss at the socially optimal price and output, is included for comparison.

In nonregulated markets, minimum-efficient-scale requirements are far more likely to impose an oligopolistic structure—with the important exception of local-market industries. Conventional economic wisdom holds that when economies of scale are such that there can be only a few firms of minimum efficient size in a market, there is an unavoidable trade-off in antitrust policy between technical and allocative efficiency. But the terms of the trade-off depend crucially on how much monopoly power actually exists in various concentrated markets.

Robert H. Bork argues that the sizes and market shares of large firms in the U.S. economy are almost always either justified by economies of scale or vulnerable to erosion by forces of competition. Any firm that had expanded to an inefficiently large size, Bork contends, would find itself unable to compete effectively against smaller, more efficient rivals. Such rivals, if not already in the market, would be attracted to it by the incumbent's weakness and the opportunity to wrest monopolistic gains from it. Further, Bork doubts that there are significant departures from competitive conduct and performance in markets with as few as three viable and noncollusive rivals.[2] He would, therefore, restrict antitrust laws to attacks on only three types of behavior: horizontal agreements to suppress competition, such as price-fixing and market-sharing; horizontal mergers leaving fewer than three viable rivals; and predation aimed at eliminating competitors, barring entry, or disciplining other firms.[3] "Antitrust," he avers, "should not interfere with any firm size created by internal growth, and this is true whether the result is monopoly or oligopoly."[4]

The conventional wisdom regarding the trade-off between allocative and productive efficiency is, however, bolstered by the empirical evidence reviewed in Chapter Eight, which strongly suggests that the sizes of the largest firms in most U.S. industries cannot be explained by either plant or multiplant economies of scale. Also, the typical long-run average cost curve for the modern large industrial firm probably has a long, flat bottom—a wide range in rates of output at which it has achieved full economies of scale but does not suffer from diseconomies. There may therefore be many oligopolistic industries whose largest firms could have their size and market power substantially reduced by divestiture or dissolution without any loss of productive efficiency. The contention that there would be little gain in allocative efficiency from restructuring oligopolistic markets, since even high concentration is conducive to competitive performance, is one that most economists would not make as unequivocally as Bork.

Resources and Technology. The most telling criticism leveled against the competitive model is that the twin assumptions of fixed resources and given technology render the model irrelevant to the most important feature of economic performance: technological advance and the resulting increase in welfare. Joseph A. Schumpeter's statement, quoted in Chapter Six, that "any system, economic or other—that at *every* given point of time fully utilizes its possibilities to the best advantage may yet in the long run be inferior to a system that does so at *no* given point in time, because the latter's failure to do so may be a condition for the level or speed of long-run performance."[5] Chapter Twelve is devoted to this crucial aspect of economic performance and to the questions it raises as to the compatibility of static and dynamic performance goals.

GENERAL EQUILIBRIUM AND THE THEORY OF SECOND BEST

The standard response to objections that the assumptions underlying the model of pure and perfect competition do not describe the real world is that these assumptions merely abstract from real-world imperfections and frictions to make a useful model feasible. But there is a logical flaw in this defense of the theory. J. M. Clark was perhaps the first to identify the problem in a partial-equilibrium context and to describe it clearly. In 1940, he wrote:

> If there are, for example, five conditions, all of which are essential to perfect competition, and the first is lacking in a given case, then it no longer follows that we are necessarily better off for the presence of any one of the other four. In the absence of the first, it is *a priori* quite possible that the second and third may become positive detriments; and a workably satisfactory result may depend on achieving some degree of "imperfection" in these other two factors.
>
> Suppose the first requisite is perfect two-way mobility of the factors of production, with no specialized and irrecoverable fixed capital. Granted this, an industry can stand the most rigorous competition in all other respects.... Take away the saving grace of perfect two-way mobility and leave the other conditions; let demand decline, and competition becomes too strong: you have a "sick industry" on your hands. Reduce the number of producers and let them sell on quoted prices and anticipate one another's reactions and you have a form of "oligopoly."[6]

It is neither intuitively obvious nor demonstrable from the competitive model whether the "sick industry" or the "oligopoly" is preferable from a welfare standpoint.

The theory of *second best* addresses this issue within a general-equilibrium framework. The fundamental proposition it demonstrates is a negative one: if anywhere in the economy one of the optimality conditions of the competitive model is missing, the next- or second-best situation probably is not one in which the rest of these conditions hold. Thus, the model yields an ambiguous norm if its assumptions are relaxed to incorporate such important real-world features and problems as economies of scale inconsistent with a competitive market structure, divergences between private and social marginal costs or utilities, or production and consumption decisions based on incomplete knowledge.[7]

Illustration of the Theory

To illustrate the theory of second best, consider an economy in which there is pure and perfect competition in the markets for all products except one monopolized final consumer good, k. Let the monopolist's profit-maximizing price exceed its marginal cost by a factor λ, so that $P_k = \lambda MC_k$, where $\lambda > 1$. In general equilibrium, then, as consumers seek to maximize household utility,

$$\frac{MU_1}{MC_1} = \frac{MU_2}{MC_2} = \ldots = \frac{MU_k}{\lambda MC_k} = \ldots = \frac{MU_n}{MC_n} \qquad (11.8)$$

In Equation (11.8), the increase in total utility yielded by the last dollar's worth of resources applied to the production of k is greater than that yielded by the last dollar's worth devoted to the production of any other consumer good available in the economy. Thus, welfare can be increased by transferring resources from the production of other goods into the production of k. Equation (11.8) depicts a clearly sub-..nal situation.

But suppose there is no way to eliminate the monopoly in k or to reduce k's price. Then the second-best solution is not to retain prices equal to marginal costs in all other markets. There is at least one better solution—as long as we make no judgments about the relative merits of different income distributions but are concerned only with the efficiency of resource allocation given the income distribution. All other prices can be raised by a factor of λ, so that

$$\frac{MU_1}{\lambda MC_1} = \frac{MU_2}{\lambda MC_2} = \ldots = \frac{MU_k}{\lambda MC_k} = \ldots = \frac{MU_n}{\lambda MC_n} \qquad (11.9)$$

If the equation is multiplied throughout by λ, we obtain the Pareto-optimal expression of Equation (11.4).

Demand Elasticity and Pareto-Optimal Equilibrium

In a chapter of *The Economics of Imperfect Competition* entitled "A World of Monopolies," Joan Robinson noted that profit maximization implied

$$P = \left(\frac{\eta}{\eta - 1}\right) MC$$

Therefore, if all producers in her world of monopolies faced demand curves that were of equal elasticity at the point of profit maximization (so that in terms of the present example, λ was equal for all firms), resource allocation would be identical with that of pure and perfect competition. Only the distribution of income would be changed—in favor of the monopolists.[8] The possibility of all firms in an economy facing demand curves of identical elasticity is infinitesimal.

But writers following Robinson did discuss the policy implications of a model world in which the benevolent dictator was able to set every price at λMC.[9] For example, in a real-world economy with unavoidably concentrated markets in the manufacturing sector, welfare could conceivably be raised by public actions restricting the outputs and raising the prices of agricultural products.

The world of monopolies will not, however, reach a Pareto-optimal equilibrium even if all demand elasticities are equal, unless all goods are sold on markets. Raising the prices of all traded goods above their marginal costs of production would lead to a household reallocation of labor, with more time devoted to such activities as housework, backyard vegetable gardens, do-it-yourself carpentry and crafts, and (probably most important) increased consumption of leisure time. The total amount of labor made available as a productive resource would decline, and a larger proportion would be allocated to the production of nontraded goods whose marginal utilities could be set equal to the marginal disutilities of the labor devoted to their production. Lionel McKenzie has noted another problem. Raising the prices both of producer goods used as inputs at different stages of production and consumer goods by a uniform percentage each time a sale is made will lead to suboptimal resource allocation, since the initial costs of the various inputs will be marked up different numbers of times before being reflected in final goods' prices.[10]

Second Best and the Competitive Norm

The theory of second best has dealt a damaging blow to the rigor of the logic underlying the welfare attributes of $P = MC$ in individual markets. Yet, its impact on acceptance of the competitive norm has been slight, in large part because it offers no solution to the problem it poses. Further, the problem is a serious one only in instances where the effects of one market on another are significant.

PARTIAL EQUILIBRIUM APPROACHES: CONSUMER SURPLUS, WORKABLE COMPETITION, AND CONTESTABLE MARKETS

Any logically rigorous and complete comparison of the welfare effects of competition and monopoly must be made in a general-equilibrium context. Nevertheless, most economists interested in antitrust policy have resorted to partial-equilibrium analysis to provide the theoretical underpinning for their assessments or proposals. Many economists retain a faith in the economic efficacy of the competitive process, holding that the restrictive assumptions and second-best limitations of the competitive general-equilibrium model are but minor qualifications in a basically sound demonstration of the superiority of a competitive market system. Others find the social and political case for competition and against monopoly compelling enough to overcome any doubts about the soundness of the economic case for competition. Finally, there is the operational problem of applying a general-equilibrium model to a specific market or form of business conduct. The ultimate repercussions that a change in one industry has on others may be both so small and so difficult to track that identification and estimation are simply not justified.

Consumer and Producer Surplus

In a partial-equilibrium context, the highest price a consumer would pay for a good minus the price actually paid represents the surplus enjoyed as the result of the purchase. If all of these surpluses are summed for all consumers, the total consumer surplus yielded by the sales made at a particular price equals the area under the demand curve but above the price, up to the quantity sold. Expressed mathematically, consumer surplus is the integral of $P_d - P_a$ over the interval from zero to Q_a, where P_d is the price consumers are willing to pay for a particular quantity, and P_a and Q_a represent the equilibrium price and quantity.

Similarly, the producer's surplus from the sale of a single item can be viewed as the difference between the price received and the lowest price at which the producer would have been willing to produce and sell the good. In a competitive industry, the supply curve is, by definition, a schedule of quantities firms would offer for sale at various prices. Therefore, under the assumption that the individual firms' costs are independent of the industry's output, producer surplus can be depicted as the area between the equilibrium price and the supply curve, up to the amount sold.[11] Figure 11–2 illustrates the proposition that the sum of consumer and producer surplus is maximized at the competitive market-clearing price.

In Figure 11–2A, the competitive equilibrium price is P_1, and the associated output is Q_1. At this equilibrium, consumer surplus is depicted by the area $A + B + C$, and producer surplus by $D + E$. If the price is raised to P_2 and output therefore falls to Q_2, consumer surplus falls to A while producer surplus becomes $B + D$. Area B, therefore, represents a transfer from consumers to producers. Under the Pareto welfare criterion, this transfer cannot be regarded as good

FIGURE 11-2 Consumer and Producer Surplus

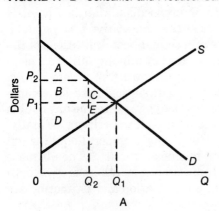
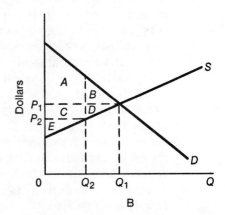

or bad. Such judgments are in the realm of normative economics. If B is greater than E, producers as a group gain from the price increase. But C and E represent "deadweight" losses of consumer and producer surplus, respectively, since they are simply eliminated at the higher price and lower output. This deadweight loss, C + E, is unambiguously bad.

Figure 11–2B illustrates a similar result when the price is reduced from that determined by a market equilibrium. In this panel, consumer surplus at the market equilibrium is A + B, and producer surplus is C + D + E. When the price is lowered from P_1 to P_2 and producers respond by cutting output from Q_1 to Q_2, Area C is transferred from producers to consumers, but B + D becomes a deadweight loss.

Workable Competition

Clark's 1940 article, in which he coined the term *workable competition,* was a pioneering effort to identify the factors that led to "the closest available working approximation to [the standard of pure and perfect competition] under actual conditions."[12] He was most concerned with short-run problems stemming from a high ratio of fixed to variable costs coupled with instability and unpredictable fluctuations in demand. Under such conditions, unregulated price competition can be destructive throughout an industry. Workable competition, Clark contended, would have to be "something intermediate between pure oligopoly and the ruinously low prices likely to result from unlimited market chaos."[13]

Fortunately, in Clark's view, many of the departures from purely competitive structure and conduct that make short-run competition workable are consistent with long-run performance approximating the efficient resource allocation of the competitive model. Potential competition and the competition of substitutes play important parts in monopolistic competition, and both of these factors tend to increase the elasticity of the demand curve facing the firm, particularly in the long run. Many large firms take a long-run viewpoint, recognizing the threats of potential competition and substitute products and, hence, refrain from restrictive practices that would increase short-run profits. And long-run cost curves tend to be flatter than the theory seemed to suggest.

Figure 11–3 illustrates the long-run equilibrium of a firm in monopolistic competition with demand and cost curves of the sorts Clark envisaged. The shallow long-run average and marginal cost curves (*LAC* and *LMC*) lead to only small divergences between the equilibrium price (P_e), where $LMC = MR$ (marginal revenue), and the optimal price (P_o), where $LMC = P$. Further, for any shapes of *LAC* and *LMC*, the flatter the demand curve, the smaller the Lerner index— $(P_e - P_o)/P_e$—and the less the divergence between the optimal output (Q_o) and the equilibrium output (Q_e).

In a 1958 article, Stephen H. Sosnick reviewed the works of 18 writers who had proposed "sophisticated criteria of workability."[14] Among the more prominent contributions are those of Corwin D. Edwards, Jesse W. Markham, and George W. Stocking.

FIGURE 11–3 Long-Run Equilibrium of the Firm in Monopolistic Competition, Illustrating the Case of Workable Competition

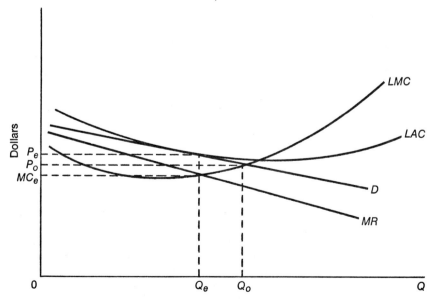

Edwards proposed that competition be viewed as workable when both buyers and sellers have access to a "substantial number" of alternatives and are able to reject those found to be "relatively unsatisfactory."[15]

Markham, adopting E. S. Mason's view that structure determines performance and pointing out that the practical prospect of remedy is essential to a delineation of workability, proposed the following standard:

> An industry may be judged to be workably competitive when, after the structural characteristics of its market and the dynamic forces that shaped them have been thoroughly examined, there is no clearly indicated change that can be effected through public policy measures that would result in greater social gains than social losses.[16]

Stocking stressed performance:

> If an industry is dynamic, if business firms are efficient, if prices respond quickly to changes in the conditions of demand and supply, if entrepreneurs pass on to consumers promptly the cost reductions that follow technological innovation, and if profits are reasonable, an industry is workably competitive regardless of the number and size of the firms that comprise it.[17]

There is, as Markham noted, an inevitable value judgment in formulating standards incorporating such phrases as "relatively unsatisfactory" alternatives, "clearly indicated" change, and "reasonable" profits. Perhaps the most that can be said is contained in the following comment made by a number of economists serving on the U.S. Attorney General's National Committee on the Antitrust Laws:

> [T]he "doctrine" of workable competition is only a rough and ready judgment by some economists, each for himself, that a particular industry is performing reasonably well—presumably relative to alternative industrial arrangements which are practically attainable. There are no objective criteria of workable competition, and such criteria as are proffered are at best intuitively reasonable modifications of the rigorous and abstract criteria of perfect competition.[18]

Contestable Markets

One of the most basic principles of microeconomic theory is that monopolistic profits cannot persist in the long run unless there is some barrier to entry. In the theory of contestable markets, the crucial structural precondition for socially optimal pricing is frictionless entry to and costless exit from markets, rather than the inability of any firm to influence price by changing its output. In a 1982 book, William J. Baumol, John C. Panzar, and Robert D. Willig show that in purely monopolistic and oligopolistic markets with certain cost and demand configurations, not only will economic profit be eliminated but price will equal marginal cost, provided entry and exit are unimpeded in the sense of being, respectively, frictionless and costless.[19] A market that fully meets their conditions qualifies as "perfectly contestable."

Illustration of a Contestable Market. Figure 11–4 depicts a market initially served by a single seller, with alternative demand and cost configurations. In Figure 11–4A, the demand curve (D) intersects the average cost curve (AC) at the right of the latter's minimum point. Conventional theory treats entry to such a market as barred by economies of scale if demand cannot sustain two or more firms of efficient scale. But under the assumption of frictionless entry and costless exit, the incumbent monopolist could not set a break-even price, much less equate price and marginal cost, without attracting entry. If the monopolist set the break-even price (P_b), an entrant with a similar average cost curve could enter the market, set a price of P_e, and sell at the rate of Q_e until the incumbent's price also fell. As soon as the incumbent's price fell below the entrant's average cost, the entrant would withdraw from the market. Given the assumption of absolutely unimpeded entry

FIGURE 11–4 Sustainable, Optimal, and Equilibrium Prices in Contestable Markets

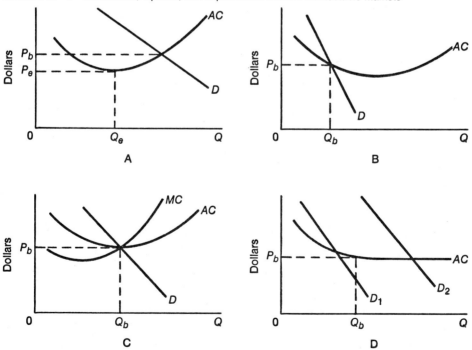

and exit, the period of time that the "hit-and-run" entrant remains in the market can be arbitrarily short. Hence, the situation illustrated in Figure 11–4A has no sustainable equilibrium.

Figure 11–4B illustrates the decreasing-cost case. In this case, it is impossible for the firm to set a first-best price where $P = MC$ and produce without incurring a loss. (The situation is analogous to that depicted in Figure 11–1B and discussed above.) But a price of P_b, so that $P = AC$, bars even free and instantaneous entry. An entrant offering less than Q_b for sale would have to set a price higher than P_b to cover its costs; if it offered more than Q_b, it would have to set a price below its average cost to sell the amount it had put on the market. Thus, the incumbent can set a second-best price at $P = AC$, and this second best will be sustainable. But P_b is the highest price the incumbent can set, even in the absence of regulation, since any higher price will attract hit-and-run entry.

In Figure 11–4C (where, by sheer chance, D intersects the lowest point on AC), the first-best price ($P = MC$) is also the sustainable natural-monopoly equilibrium price ($P = AC$). Hence, with U-shaped average cost curves, there is only an infinitesimal probability of the socially optimal price also being a sustainable one. This probability becomes the general case, however, if we drop the assumption that the average cost curve is U-shaped and assume instead that it is J-shaped, with a long, flat bottom, as in Figure 11–4D. (Note that with instantaneous entry assumed, the distinction between short- and long-run cost no longer holds.)

In Figure 11–4D, the monopolistic equilibrium is both sustainable and optimal if the demand curve intersects the average cost curve to the right of the lowest minimum-cost output (Q_b) as does D_2. If D intersects AC in the decreasing-cost range, as D_1 does, the second-best sustainable price is where $P = AC > MC$.

Thus, in a perfectly contestable market with a sustainable equilibrium price, entry to the market must be free and exit costless; incumbents and potential entrants must face identical cost functions; incumbents must be able to earn revenues equal to total costs of production at a market-clearing price; and there must be some lag between the response of demand to an entrant's lower price and the incumbent's response, so that potential entrants can use the incumbent's existing price to calculate the prospective profit from hit-and-run entry. Given these assumptions, a perfectly contestable market will yield the socially optimal price and output under a wide range of cost and demand configurations, even though occupied by only one firm.

Criticisms of the Theory. Critics have attacked the contestable market theory on the grounds that the necessary assumptions are so stringent as to rob the model of most of its empirical and theoretical relevance. Baumol et al. have two responses. First, and most important for our discussion of performance criteria, the principal value of the model is normative rather than descriptive:

> Perfect contestability is not likely to be satisfied exactly by any real market. Yet it does provide a standard against which actual markets can be compared, no matter if the relevant production techniques and market demands dictate production by a single giant firm or by a multitude of independent enterprises.

* * * * *

> [T]here are objective structural market conditions that can be examined to determine the relevance of contestability in practice. And where these conditions do not hold even approximately, actual industry configurations can, nevertheless, be usefully compared to those that would result if the markets were structurally contestable.[20]

Further, Baumol et al. argue, contestability as described in the model approximates actual conditions in some markets, such as airline service between city pairs. These markets, notes Elizabeth E. Bailey in a foreword to *Contestable Markets,* are "characterized both by easy entry and exit and significant economies of scale. Even if a route is flown by a single carrier, other carriers who have stations at both endpoint cities can readily enter if monopoly profits become evident."[21]

COMPETITION AND DEPLETABLE RESOURCES

Criteria for the socially optimal rate of exploitation of a depletable resource pose yet another issue involving the relevance of the competitive norm. These resources can be either nonrenewable, such as mineral ores and crude oil, or renewable, such as timber and fish.

Nonrenewable Resources: Economics of the Mine

The most straightforward model is that of the optimal rate of depletion of a nonrenewable resource—sometimes referred to as the economics of the mine.[22] The simplest case is that of a competitive mining industry extracting a fixed and known stock of ore. The individual mining firm faces two types of cost: (1) costs of extraction and (2) depletion costs (customarily referred to as user cost). User cost is the opportunity cost of selling the ore in the present period (the present value of the revenue, net of extraction costs, that could be obtained by waiting and selling the ore later). If a mine operator is considering extracting and selling ore now or waiting one period, marginal user cost may be expressed as

$$MUC_t = \frac{P^*_{t+1} - MEC^*_{t+1}}{1 + r} \qquad (11.10)$$

where MUC_t is marginal user cost in the current period, P^*_{t+1} and MEC^*_{t+1} are the expected price and marginal extraction cost in the next period, and r is the mine operator's discount rate for one period.

To maximize profit, a competitive mining firm will set price (which is not affected by its output) equal to total marginal cost, or $MEC + MUC$. Thus, the mine's rate of extraction will be that at which

$$P_t = MEC_t + \frac{P^*_{t+1} - MEC^*_{t+1}}{1 + r} \qquad (11.11)$$

Let $\pi = P - MEC$ (i.e., π = marginal user cost). Then, rearranging Equation (11.11) and substituting,

$$\pi^*_{t+1} = \pi_t(1 + r) \qquad (11.12)$$

Suppose $\pi^*_{t+1} > \pi_t(1 + r)$. The mine operator will respond to the relative increase in the future price by reducing present output and reserving more of its ore for sale in the next period. If all mining firms share the same expectations as to future prices and costs, all will cut back on extraction, and the current price of the ore will rise until Equation (11.12) is again satisfied. Similarly, if $\pi^*_{t+1} < \pi_t(1 + r)$, current output will expand, and the current price will fall until the equality is restored.

A mine operator's expected margin of price over MEC in Period $t + 1$ will be based on the margin expected in Period $t + 2$. Mathematically, $\pi^*_{t+2} = \pi^*_{t+1}(1 + r)$. The chain of reasoning extends into an indefinite future. Thus, if expectations are correct, π must rise through time by a factor of $1 + r$ per period. If demand and extraction cost schedules do not change, the price will continue to rise, and less of the ore will be used in each succeeding period.

Demand and Depletion. In the competitive model's treatment of nonrenewable resources, the price of a mineral ore may ultimately rise to a level where demand is zero. At and above such a price, consumers would resort to substitutes or simply forgo consumption of products containing the final metal. Such an eventuality implies that the resource is not essential for all time. A mineral ore may be completely used up if the highest price at which it will be consumed is greater than the marginal cost of extracting the last unit. Otherwise, it will never be entirely exhausted. If there is no upper limit to the price (demand remains positive at any price), reflecting the economy's inability to function without the resource, the ever-higher expected future prices would induce mine operators to limit the rate of extraction more and more severely, reserving dwindling supplies for the most pressing and costly uses. In theory, if there is no ceiling on the price, the resource will never be totally depleted.

The Competitive Welfare Norm. In this simple model, the competitive welfare norm holds for the mining industry in each period, since price equals total marginal cost. Further, intertemporal welfare is maximized (provided the miners' rate of discount and the social rate are equal), since the marginal value of the resource (measured as user cost, or the value in the ground net of extraction costs) is equalized over all periods. To appreciate this important result, consider the intertemporal allocation our benevolent dictator would impose. Such a dictator, at Time t, would be able to improve welfare if he or she could shift consumption of the resource among periods in such a way that the gain in net present value was greater in the periods in which consumption was increased than the discounted loss in the periods during which it was curtailed. Given downward-sloping market demand curves, reflecting diminishing marginal utility, the welfare maximum in each period would be reached when the discounted marginal values were equal in all periods—precisely the result yielded by the model for a purely competitive market.

Complications in the Theory. *Uncertainties Yield Indeterminate Effect.* The theory of the mine is complicated once the possibility of discovery of new ore deposits is introduced or when it is assumed that the mine operator is uncertain as to the quantity or grade of the deposit yet to be worked. The uncertainties associated with exploration and with working mine sites in which the extent and value of the unmined ore are unknown raise the discount rate applied by individual mine operators and thus encourage them to increase the rate at which they deplete existing mines. But risk aversion also discourages exploration and new investment and may therefore slow down the rate at which the resource is depleted. The net effect is indeterminate.

Monopoly and Intertemporal Allocation. Despite difficulties in modeling an extractive industry's performance over time, a recent survey of the literature concluded that "extractive resources are probably allocated by competitive markets about as well as other resources, subject to the usual variety of imperfections."[23] The most serious and widely held objection to this viewpoint is that a monopolistic mine operator, who will set a higher price and sell a smaller fraction of the mine's ore in the early years of operation, will in almost every conceivable case exhaust the mine at a later date than would be the case under competition. Conservationists have argued that the current private discount rate applied by mine operators will surely be higher than the appropriate social discount rate, both because private risk is higher than social risk and because individual members of the present generation do not put a high enough value on income streams accruing to future generations. According to this line of argument, monopoly's tendency to prolong extraction may provide a welfare-augmenting offset to the tendency of an unduly high private discount rate to accelerate depletion.[24]

The "Common Property" or "Oil Pool" Problem. Exploitation of some natural resources is subject to a phenomenon frequently referred to as the "common property" or "oil pool" externality. If a number of independently competitive oil companies have drilled successfully into the same underground pool, none can make a nice calculation of user cost and the optimal rate of depletion. Instead, following the logic of the Prisoner's Dilemma game, each will likely pump oil out as rapidly as possible, to obtain the largest possible share of the pool. Not only will the pool be exploited far too soon by intertemporal welfare standards, but extraction methods will probably be excessively costly and wasteful of the resource. Similar problems exist with such resources as natural gas, underground water, minerals and forests on public lands, and fish. The oil-pool problem constitutes a market failure that can be corrected either by single-firm control of each pool or by regulation—sometimes, as in ocean fishing, whaling, and seal hunting, by international agreement. Exploitation of a pool by one firm may involve monopoly power if the pool contains a large enough fraction of the resource, and most analysts would find regulation preferable.

Renewable Resources. The welfare theory of renewable-resource industries, such as forestries and fisheries, is more complex, especially if the renewal rate is determined more by natural forces of regeneration than by replenishment through business investment. But growth or decline in a timber stand or fish population is a problem in resource management; and whether or not a competitive structure or unregulated market is feasible, the competitive norm does provide an appropriate standard for both single-period and intertemporal resource allocation in such industries.[25]

MONOPOLY POWER AND THE COMPETITIVE NORM

The primary contribution of the theory of pure and perfect competition is a normative one. It is one thing to say that the effects of monopoly are to raise price above the competitive level and reduce output below that which would be produced under pure competition, given similar cost and market demand conditions. It is quite another to label the monopolistic price "too high" and the output "too low," while the competitive price and output are "just right." Analysis of general equilibrium in an economy with pure and perfect competition throughout gives us a logically rigorous basis for saying just that and for treating $P = MC$, with the Pareto-optimal resource allocation that results, as a norm, or standard, against which actual price-cost relationships can be judged.

The case for the competitive norm as a benchmark for evaluation of observed market performance and as a guide to antitrust policy is strengthened by acceptance of arguments for (1) its consistency with other standards for an economy's performance, such as full employment, equitable income distribution, and protection of the environment; (2) the infrequency, at least in the U.S. economy, of economies of scale relative to market size that would lead to severe trade-offs between allocative and productive efficiency; and (3) the broad though not universal applicability of $P = MC$ as an appropriate norm in partial-equilibrium analyses, despite second-best reservations. To a large extent, the economic case for competition has been made by those who accept these arguments. The competitive norm is equally essential to the theories of workable competition and contestable markets, since their purpose is to identify structural conditions other than those of pure competition that will lead to performance approximating this norm.

In Chapter Twelve, we turn to the issue that has posed the greatest challenge to the relevance of the competitive norm: the consistency or lack thereof between optimal allocation of existing resources under existing techniques of production, and the conditions most conducive to technological advance resulting in greater economic productivity over time.

ENDNOTES

[1]An alternative approach is through indifference curves, or schedules showing all combinations of two goods among which a household is indifferent. In this approach, the slope of the indifference curve at any point is equal to the marginal rate of substitution (MRS), or the amount of one good the household would be willing to give up in exchange for one additional unit of the other. Household utility is maximized when $MRS_{1,2} = P_1/P_2$ for all possible pairs of goods. A more general statement is that the util represents a hypothetical cardinal measure of utility, while all that is required to obtain the same result through indifference curve analysis is an ordinal ranking of household preferences.

[2]Robert H. Bork, *The Antitrust Paradox: A Policy at War with Itself* (New York: Basic Books, 1978), pp. 181–84.

[3]Ibid., pp. 405–6.

[4]Ibid., p. 178.

[5]Joseph A. Schumpeter, *Capitalism, Socialism, and Democracy* (New York: Harper & Bros., 1942), p. 83.

[6]J. M. Clark, "Toward a Concept of Workable Competition," *American Economic Review* 30, no. 2 (June 1940), Part 1, pp. 241–56, at p. 242.

[7]The leading work is Richard G. Lipsey and Kelvin Lancaster, "The General Theory of Second Best," *Review of Economic Studies* 24, no. 63 (1956), pp. 11–32.

[8]Joan Robinson, *The Economics of Imperfect Competition* (New York: Macmillan, 1933).

[9]For a discussion and critique, see Abba P. Lerner, *The Economics of Control* (New York: Macmillan, 1944), pp. 96–105.

[10]Lionel McKenzie, "Ideal Output and the Interdependence of Firms," *Economic Journal* 61, no. 244 (December 1951), pp. 785–803.

[11]In his leading treatment of consumer and producer surplus, Alfred Marshall noted that the supply curve used to depict producer surplus "is not a true supply curve adapted to the conditions of the world in which we live; but it has properties which are often erroneously attributed to such a curve." Marshall's concern was that a "normal" supply curve does not assume away the fact that individual firms' costs vary considerably with the industry's output. (Labor and material costs are particularly likely to rise as the industrywide demand for them increases.) Therefore, he warned, "This method of treating short-period normal value problems has attractions, and may perhaps ultimately be of service: but it requires careful handling, for the assumptions on which it rests are very slippery." See Alfred Marshall, *Principles of Economics,* 8th ed. (London: Macmillan, 1920), pp. 668, 669.

[12]Clark, "Toward a Concept," p. 241.

[13]Ibid., p. 253.

[14]Stephen H. Sosnick, "A Critique of Concepts of Workable Competition," *Quarterly Journal of Economics* 72, no. 3 (August 1958), pp. 380–423, at p. 380.

[15]Corwin D. Edwards, *Maintaining Competition* (New York: McGraw-Hill, 1949), p. 9.

[16]Jesse W. Markham, "An Alternative Approach to the Concept of Workable Competition," *American Economic Review* 40, no. 2 (June 1950), pp. 349–61, at p. 361.

[17]George W. Stocking, *Workable Competition and Antitrust Policy* (Nashville, Tenn.: Vanderbilt University Press, 1961), p. 190.

[18]*U.S. Attorney General's National Committee to Study the Antitrust Laws* (Washington, D.C.: U.S. Government Printing Office, 1955), p. 339.

[19]William J. Baumol, John C. Panzar, and Robert D. Willig, *Contestable Markets and the Theory of Industry Structure* (New York: Harcourt Brace Jovanovich, 1982). See also Baumol's presidential address at the 1981 meeting of the American Economic Association, "Contestable Markets: An Uprising in the Theory of Industrial Structure," *American Economic Review* 72, no. 1 (March 1982), pp. 1–15. For thoughtful critiques of the theory, see comments by Martin L Weitzman, and by Marius Schwartz and Robert J. Reynolds, *American Economic Review* 73, no. 3 (June 1983), pp. 486–90; Michael Spence, "Contestable Markets and the Theory of Industry Structure: A Review Article," *Journal of Economic Literature* 21, no. 3 (September 1983), pp. 981–90; and William A. Brock, "Contestable Markets and the Theory of Industry Structure: A Review Article," *Journal of Political Economy* 91, no. 6 (December 1983), pp. 1055–66.

[20]Baumol et al., *Contestable Markets,* pp. 35, 45.

[21]Ibid., p. xxi.

[22]The leading work is Harold Hotelling, "The Economics of Exhaustible Resources," *Journal of Political Economy* 39, no. 2 (April 1931), pp. 137–75. More recent treatments

include Orris C. Herfindahl and Allen V. Kneese, *Economic Theory of Natural Resources* (Columbus, Ohio: Merrill, 1974); Frederick M. Peterson and Anthony C. Fisher, "The Exploitation of Extractive Resources: A Survey," *Economic Journal* 87, no. 348 (December 1977), pp. 681–721; Richard Lecomber, *The Economics of Natural Resources* (New York: John Wiley & Sons, 1979).

[23]Peterson and Fisher, "Exploitation," p. 711.

[24]A monopolist, under certain exceptional conditions, may underconserve rather than overconserve a depleting resource. For analysis, see Milton G. Weinstein and Richard J. Zeckhauser, "Optimal Consumption of Depletable Resources," *Quarterly Journal of Economics* 89, no. 3 (August 1975), pp. 371–92.

[25]To pursue this assertion and its proof further, see Herfindahl and Kneese, *Economic Theory;* Peterson and Fisher, "Exploitation"; Lecomber, *Economics.*

CHAPTER TWELVE

Dynamic Aspects of Economic Performance: Technological Change and Progress[1]

THE SCHUMPETERIAN SYSTEM

In Chapter Eleven, economic performance was discussed from the point of view of *static allocative efficiency,* or standards of optimal allocation of existing resources, assuming a given level of technical knowledge and a fixed set of production techniques appropriate to the available technology. Joseph A. Schumpeter, more than any other social thinker, has illuminated the limitations of such an approach.

Innovation and Economic Development

Throughout his long career, Schumpeter stressed the importance of carefully distinguishing between economic development and economic growth, the latter recognized by classical economists as stemming from population growth and capital accumulation. Schumpeter was critical of leading economists, including such eminent figures as Adam Smith, John Stuart Mill, Leon Walras, and Alfred Marshall, for their failure to incorporate innovation in their formal analyses. "Obviously," he noted, "the face of the earth would look very different if people . . . had done nothing else except multiply and save." Rather, economic development had stemmed from new methods of production and commerce. "This historic and irreversible change in the way of doing things we call 'innovation' and we define: innovations are changes in production functions which cannot be decomposed into infinitesimal steps. Add as many mail coaches as you please, you will never get a railroad by so doing."[2]

Market Power and Innovation

For industrial organization economists, the most challenging aspect of Schumpeter's view of progress is his emphasis on the primacy of large firms with market power in the innovative process of a modern economy. He expressed this view most forcefully in his 1942 book, *Capitalism, Socialism, and Democracy*,[3] the most frequently cited source of the Schumpeterian "hypothesis" or "system."[4] Schumpeter threw down his challenge to the conventional wisdom regarding monopoly and competition in the following passage:

> As soon as we go into details and inquire into the individual items in which progress was most conspicuous, the trail leads not to the doors of those firms that work under conditions of comparatively free competition but precisely to the doors of the large concerns . . . and a shocking suspicion dawns upon us that big business may have had more to do with creating that standard of life than with keeping it down.[5]

There are two distinctly different elements in this Schumpeterian system—a causal relationship between size of firm and innovation and one between a firm's market power and its innovative activities. Schumpeter did not distinguish clearly between the two. Rather, he regarded size and market power as inextricably linked in modern capitalist reality as opposed to theory, at least to the extent that the primary sources of innovation are involved. "But 'monopoly' really means any large-scale business," he contended. "And since economic 'progress' in this country is largely the result of work done within a number of concerns at no time much greater than 300 or 400, any serious threat to the functioning of these will spread paralysis in the economic organism."[6]

Schumpeter did not spell out the significance of sheer size in the ability of the modern firm to innovate. He did, however, analyze the manner in which market power promotes innovation. Innovation is an activity fraught with uncertainty, and large-scale innovation may not be attractive unless some "insurance" is available to the potential entrepreneur. Noting that if "a war risk is insurable, nobody objects to a firm's collecting the cost of this insurance from the buyers of its products," Schumpeter argued that, by analogy, a firm unable to obtain insurance against the failure of an innovation should be able to engage in "a price strategy aiming at the same end."[7] Thus, monopolistic power in existing product markets may be a precondition for innovation.

Further, anticipated market power in new products may provide essential incentives to innovate, since "enterprise would in most cases be impossible if it were not known from the outset that exceptionally favorable situations are likely to arise," the exploitation of which "requires strategy that in the short run is often restrictive."[8]

"Creative Destruction"

One prominent feature of the Schumpeterian system is a short-term relationship in which aspects of industrial structure (size and market power) are viewed as determinants of the scope and rate of innovation; much of the subsequent study of the Schumpeterian hypothesis has dealt with this aspect of his system. But Schumpeter was equally concerned with a longer-term reverse relationship in which the impact of innovation on structure predominates. He referred to this impact as "creative destruction," or the competition from innovation that (unlike price competition) "strikes not at the margins of the profits and the outputs of the existing firms but at their foundations and their very lives."[9]

Thus, the full Schumpeterian system is one in which (1) size and market power are preconditions for the most efficient forms of innovative activity, and (2) successful innovation feeds back on market structure to produce or perpetuate an economy of large firms with market power—at least in the progressive sectors.

CONCEPTUAL AND THEORETICAL ISSUES

Schumpeter's distinction between invention and innovation is now widely accepted. He defined innovation as a change in a production function; in less rigorous terms, it is the economic implementation of knowledge and invention. Innovators, then, are those persons or firms who first make economic use of ideas or discoveries they may or may not have originated. The innovator brings together and organizes a set of factors of production either to produce a new product and introduce it to the market or to set up and put into operation a new process of production. In *Theory of Economic Development,* Schumpeter described an individual who borrowed all of the needed funds, purchased the rights to an invention made by another, set up a firm to exploit it, sold the firm as soon as it was established, and realized a profit from the proceeds of the sale after repayment of the loan, thus acting solely as an innovator and not as a capitalist, inventor, or manager.[10] Innovation, in the Schumpeterian system, is not confined to technological innovation. It includes, for example, the opening up of new markets and the establishment of new forms of organization. The evolution of the modern corporation, therefore, can be viewed as a succession of Schumpeterian innovations.

Technological innovation, of primary concern here, involves making use of discoveries stemming from both public and private research and development (R&D), including basic research, applied research, and development. The U.S. National Science Foundation (NSF) defines basic research as "original investigations for the advancement of scientific knowledge not having specific commercial objectives." Applied research consists of "investigations directed to the discovery of new scientific knowledge having specific commercial objectives with respect to products or processes." Development is defined as "technical activities of a nonroutine nature concerned with translating research findings or other scientific knowledge into products or processes."[11] In 1981, 3 percent of the nation's industrial R&D expenditures (both company- and government-financed) were for basic research, 21 percent were for applied research, and 76 percent were for development.[12]

Edwin Mansfield and his associates have identified a number of stages in the innovative process—applied research, formulation of specifications for materials and production processes, prototype or pilot plant construction, tooling and construction of manufacturing facilities, manufacturing start-up, and marketing start-up. R&D activities usually account for well under half of the total innovation costs identified by Mansfield et al.[13]

Economies of Scale in R&D

Several sources of economies of scale in R&D and innovation support the hypothesized relationship between size of firm and innovative activity. First, industrial R&D facilities may require sophisticated and expensive equipment or involve complex and costly experiments and tests. Teams of highly paid scientists and engineers may be necessary. Development may require pilot plants or full-scale experimental models.

Some of these economies in R&D performance, particularly those of equipment and personnel, could be obtained by using firms that specialize in doing R&D for others under contract. But contracted R&D has disadvantages relative to "in house" in cost and accuracy of communication between researcher and user, problems of confidentiality, and appropriation of valuable "spillover" findings.

Further, there are possible economies of scale in R&D relating to the size of the sponsoring firm, regardless of the optimal scale of the research facility itself. R&D can be risky, and only large firms may be able to absorb the losses associated with costly failures. A firm capable of engaging in a number of projects simultaneously reduces the overall risk by offsetting the losses from failures with the gains from successes. And to the extent that business enterprises are risk-averse, such a narrowing of the range of possible outcomes represents an economy of scale. Large firms may have the internal cash flow or favored access to credit needed to fund R&D programs.

Richard R. Nelson has hypothesized that diversification of a firm should promote R&D, particularly basic research, since unanticipated findings and spillovers are more likely to be exploitable in some product or process the greater the number of activities in which the sponsoring firm engages.[14]   As Frederic M. Scherer has observed, if a process innovation is more readily used by its innovator than licensed to others, the larger the firm's market for the product produced, the more valuable the cost-saving innovation.[15]   Similarly, a product innovation may be worth more to a firm with a large enough marketing organization to introduce it effectively.

Diseconomies of Scale

There are, on the other hand, conceivable diseconomies of scale in R&D—primarily managerial ones. Some of the ablest and most creative researchers, it has been argued, tend to be the least amenable to working in an organized hierarchy.[16]   Their originality and ingenuity may be frustrated by a chain of authority and responsibility, where they must justify and obtain approval for new projects or changes in existing ones and where their work is expected to complement and support that of others.

Large-scale organization of R&D may be inefficient. Supervision may be difficult (especially at levels more than one tier removed from the work) when only the technical person on the job is in a position to observe and interpret how well an investigation is proceeding. Flexibility may be essential to successful R&D, particularly in competitive situations where two or more firms are pursuing the same goal. The ability to shift to new lines of research, or to modify or terminate existing ones that appear to be going sour, may be impaired by the need for organizational approval.

The Relationship of Market Power to Innovation

Schumpeter also posited a positive relationship between at least a degree of market power and both the opportunity and the incentive to innovate—a causal link conceptually distinct from any advantages in R&D and innovation conferred by sheer size of firm. His argument that monopolistic profits in existing markets may enhance a firm's opportunities to engage in costly and risky R&D has been generally accepted as a theoretical proposition. However, theorists have identified both positive and negative incentives to R&D stemming from power in the markets in which the resulting innovations are to be exploited.

The fundamental theoretical point is that some economic reward must be expected from an innovation to induce firms to engage in R&D. Under pure and perfect competition, such profits could not be obtained, as imitators would immediately adopt the innovation and prices would promptly reflect only costs of production, with no possible recovery of the costs of innovation. Pure and perfect competition is, however, a theoretical construct: more realistic models of the competitive process allow for time in the adjustment process and for short-term frictional profits to be earned by innovators and early imitators.

Monopoly power in the post-innovative market does increase the profit to be gained and thus provides a positive incentive greater than that of frictional profit in a competitive setting. But competition with short-term disequilibrium profit attainable may provide a powerful negative incentive. The first firm (whether established or an entrant) to introduce an innovation may impose losses on the others. Fear of such preemption may spur competitors to R&D and innovations.

The problem may be particularly acute for firms faced with potential entry. The incumbent firms, with investment in plant and equipment designed for existing production techniques, would not want to introduce a process innovation unless the average total cost of the new process was lower than the average variable cost of the old one; an entrant would be attracted by the prospect if the average total cost of the new process was below the expected price of the product. Similarly, introduction of a new product might not appear profitable to an incumbent if the gain from the new product would be offset by loss of profit on the old product. A firm without existing profit to lose might find entry with the new product profitable. Thus, theory must allow for both the positive incentive of monopolistic profit and the negative incentive of potential losses to more highly innovative competitors in positing the effects of market structure on innovative activity, and it is not apparent which effect is likely to predominate.[17]

Time-Cost Trade-Offs and R&D. The essential features of these contrasting incentives are illustrated in Figure 12–1.[18] Line C shows the relationship between the length of time required for a firm to complete a project and total project cost, discounted to the current moment. This line reflects a commonly experienced trade-off between time and cost of innovation. The cost of a project is usually minimized by proceeding sequentially after an early exploratory stage, obtaining all information needed from one step before going on to the next.

Completion time can be accelerated by exploring several alternative research approaches simultaneously. Such a parallel strategy will almost always be more expensive than a cost-minimizing sequential one, as there will be duplication of effort, false starts, completed portions that do not mesh, and coordination costs. The decreasing slope of Line C indicates that it becomes more and more costly for the firm to make still further reductions as time to completion is shortened and

FIGURE 12–1 The Time-Cost Trade-Off and Levels of R&D under Monopoly and Competition

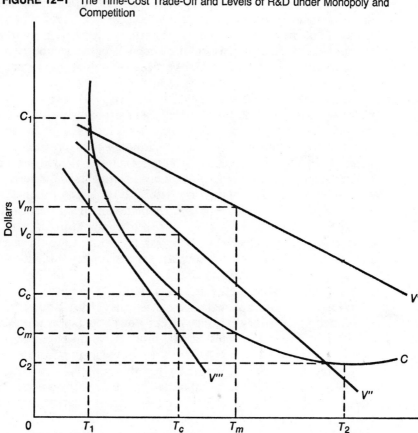

that at some expenditure, such as C_1, it becomes impossible. T_1, then, is the minimum time it will take to complete the project, regardless of the amount spent. Although the slower pace associated with a more sequential strategy lowers total project cost, some set of successive steps will minimize cost at the level shown as C_2, so that there is no gain to be had from delay beyond T_2.

The three lines labeled V represent the present discounted value of the net operating profit with the innovation introduced at various future dates. V' indicates this present value under pure monopoly. Even in the absence of competition, V declines with later introduction times, since the present discounted value of an income stream beginning in the near future is greater than that of an identical stream starting later. If the monopolist knows V' and C with certainty, it will choose the introduction time (T_m) that maximizes the positive difference between V' and C (at which the slopes of V' and C are equal). The return to the project will be V_m minus C_m.

The crux of the model lies in the effect of increasing intensity of competition on the position and slope of V. One effect will be to shift V in towards the origin of the graph, because rivals will imitate a successful innovation and, the greater the intensity of competition, the less the ultimate market share of the innovator. Further, the sum of the profits obtained by all firms, innovator and imitators, will be reduced if recognition of mutual dependence is lessened by heightened competition. This inward shift of V illustrates the decline in long-term profit as competition increases; but if the slope of the line does not change, the optimal amount of spending on R&D (C_m) remains the same—provided the profit incentive $(V_m - C_m)$ remains positive. If V_m falls below C_m, the firm will withdraw completely from R&D activity.

But greater competition will increase the steepness of the downward slope of V. Assuming that the other firms in the industry are engaged in similar R&D projects, the larger the number of competitors, the shorter the likely period before imitators enter and erode the innovator's income stream. Further and of greater significance in calculating V, the slower the pace of a project and the greater the number of competitors, the greater the probability of preemption. Preemption threatens not only a short-term loss until the firm can introduce its imitation but also a decline in long-term market share if customers tend to stay with the first firm to introduce a new product. The increasing steepness of V thus illustrates the negative incentive effect of competition. On a graph such as Figure 12–1, as the steepness of the slope of V increases, C remaining constant, the shorter the time period and the greater the cost at which the slopes of V and C are equal and V minus C is therefore maximized. (Compare $V_m - C_m$ with $V_c - C_c$ in the figure.)

Figure 12–1 thus depicts a situation in which some competition increases innovative effort over that of monopoly, as more is spent on R&D and projects are accelerated. if competition increases even more, however, and V shifts still further in until it lies entirely to the left of C, as does V''', the firm will not engage in any R&D or attempt to innovate, as all profit from innovation has been eliminated by competitive forces. R&D efforts are therefore maximized in market states lying somewhere between the extremes of pure monopoly and pure competition.

Refinements of the Model. Subsequent theoretical work has elaborated on and refined this basic and general model. Among the phenomena incorporated into more complex and highly specified models are:[19]

Uncertainty as to the time and cost of project completion and its success.

Winner-take-all situations in which imitation is impossible (perhaps because of fully effective patent protection) and the first firm to introduce the innovation reaps the entire reward.

Contrasting situations in which imitations can be made and introduced promptly and cheaply (perhaps because analysis of a competitor's new product, or "reverse engineering," is easy) and it may be more profitable to be an imitator than an innovator.

Strategic competitive interactions among rivals whose R&D programs can be adjusted as the programs of others change.

The results of these models differ considerably as to the relative effects of varying degrees of market power on innovative activity, not only because of differences in the market conditions and strategies posited but because the coefficients are allowed to vary for such parameters as the speed of market penetration, imitation lag, relative costs of innovation and imitation, and the decay rate at which old products or processes are replaced by new. The theoretical work taken as a whole strongly suggests that interrelations among market structure, technological opportunity, and innovation are complex and that the degree of competition most conducive to vigorous and effective R&D differs markedly from one industry to another.

Technological Change and Industry Structure

Schumpeterian evolution, or the long-run effect of technological change on industry structure, has been modeled by Richard R. Nelson and Sidney G. Winter.[20] In their basic simulation model, firms engage in R&D by paying to make "draws" from a technology pool according to a set of predetermined rules that are functions of firm size and profitability. Some firms make only innovative draws, while others make both innovative and imitative ones. Over a 200-period run, changes in firm size are determined by relative degrees of success and failure in the draws. Among other things, the number of firms initially in the industry, the ease of making major innovations, and the ease of imitating vary from run to run.

If technological advances are specified in the simulation runs as major and infrequent, so that each innovation has a marked effect on structure, concentration increases. But if there are numerous minor successful draws, all firms (innovators and imitators alike) tend to grow at roughly equal rates. In general, easy imitation leads to lower degrees of final concentration, since imitation contributes to a closer productivity race and thus greater similarity in growth rates.

In one set of runs, Nelson and Winter contrast the case in which the underlying technology is "science based" with a "cumulative technology" case. In the former, potential advances in the pool of technical opportunity are enhanced exogenously over time, so that the best productivity available is a function of external scientific advances. In the cumulative technology case, the gain in productivity made possible by a successful draw depends on the firm's present technology, so that the opportunities facing a firm come from its own past R&D successes rather than from outside science.

In simulations in which the pool consists of exogenous science-based technology, an occasional "hit" by an innovator, followed by widespread and aggressive imitation, is conducive to optimal perform-ance in a dynamic Schumpeterian sense, in that the average practice of the industry remains near the best available. This result obtains because in the science-based case, unlike the cumulative technology case, a decision to imitate rather than innovate has no adverse effect on the productivity advances subsequently available to a firm from the pool. This is a particularly interesting result, suggesting that the procompetitive effects of imitation might be most welcome and con-sistent with technical progress in those industries in which the basic technological advances are induced by external developments in sci-ence and engineering.

In almost all of Nelson and Winter's simulation runs, concentration tends to increase (although at varying rates) regardless of whether innovators or imitators fare the best, thus supporting the original Schumpeterian hypothesis. But their assumptions are quite stringent. In particular, their model does not allow for entry of new firms. In an econometric study of U.S. industries between 1963 and 1967, Arun K. Mukhopadhyay found that the effects of high and medium levels of R&D intensity were to reduce concentration and to increase profita-bility, since the net rate of entry was much higher than average in the technologically progressive industries.[21]

Another line of theoretical work has been the formulation of models consisting of an equation system in which both R&D and structural variables are endogenous: In one equation, R&D is treated as a function of industry structure; in another, the current structure is a function of past R&D.[22] These models tend to be highly abstract and solvable only for the equilibrium condition, lacking the rich descriptiveness of the dynamic processes contained in Nelson and Winter's less rigorous simulation models.

EMPIRICAL ANALYSES AND FINDINGS

The Role of Innovation in Economic Development

Schumpeter's stress on the importance of innovation in economic development and improvement in living standards has been amply supported by empirical study. Edward F. Denison has analyzed in detail the sources of economic growth in the United States from 1929 through 1978 (see Table 12–1).

TABLE 12–1 Indexes of Growth of National Income in the United States, 1929–78 (1972 = 100)

National Income	Year		Growth (Percent)
	1929	1978	
Total	26.86	116.69	434%
Per capita	45.83	111.51	243
Per person employed	47.68	101.90	214
Per hour worked	35.72	105.05	294

SOURCE: Edward F. Denison, *Accounting for Slower Economic Growth: The United States in the 1970s* (Washington, D.C.: Brookings Institution, 1979), pp. 8–9.

From 1929 to 1969, national income per employed person rose at an average annual rate of 1.89 percent. Denison estimated that 0.90 percent (just under half) was attributable to advances in knowledge (technological, managerial, and organizational) not reflected in any of the other sources identified. Economies of scale, made possible in part by advances in knowledge, accounted for another 0.35 percent. Better and more widespread education, stimulated by technological change among other things, accounted for 0.41 percent; and improved resource allocation accounted for 0.29 percent. The reallocation of resources was largely attributable to technological advances that made possible a shift of labor out of farming and low-productivity self-employment in retail trade and service industries. Capital accumulation, the primary source of per capita economic growth in the classical economics Schumpeter criticized, accounted for only 0.22 percent. Other sources were negligible. (The total exceeds 1.89 percent because increased productivity per hour worked was offset by lower hours of work, an alternative to increased consumption of goods and services in raising the quality of life.)[23]

The Schumpeterian hypotheses that size and market power promote innovative activity have not stood up to subsequent empirical examination in such an unqualified fashion as did his vision of the significance of the activity. We look first at size and then turn to market power.

The Effects of Size on Innovation

National Science Foundation Data and the "Schumpeterian Sector." At first glance, National Science Foundation (NSF) data such as shown in Table 12–2 appear to lend strong support to the hypothesis relating size of firm to innovation. In the table, the 141 firms with over 25,000 employees accounted for 71 percent of the total expenditures on R&D in U.S. industry in 1981, although they represented only about 1 percent of the firms estimated to be performing R&D in that year. At the other extreme, firms with fewer than 1,000 employees comprised 90 percent of those engaged in R&D but accounted for only 5 percent of the spending. Table 12–2 also indicates that federal funding of industrial R&D is much more highly concentrated within the larger performers than is the company-funded portion.

TABLE 12–2 Company, Federal, and Total Funds for R&D of U.S. Manufacturing Firms, by Size of Company, 1981

Number of Employees in Company	Number of R&D— Performing Firms	Funds for R&D ($ millions)		
		Company	Federal	Total
Less than 1,000	12,500*	$ 2,038	$ 484	$ 2,522
1,000 to 4,999	839	2,702	511	3,213
5,000 to 9,999	218	1,866	559	2,425
10,000 to 24,999	211	5,685	1,253	6,938
25,000 or more	141	23,071	13,661	36,732
Total	13,909	$35,362	$16,468	$51,830

*Estimated by the Bureau of the Census from 1981 survey of companies with fewer than 1,000 employees.
SOURCE: U.S. National Science Foundation, *Research and Development in Industry, 1981* (Washington, D.C.: U.S. Government Printing Office, 1984), pp. 12, 15, 20, 24.

However, when we focus on the "Schumpeterian sector," (the universe of large firms only) and on disaggregated data, support for the Schumpeterian hypothesis weakens. Table 12–3 indicates that overall, across various broad industry groups, the firms ranked in the 8 largest devoted a substantially lower percentage of sales revenue to R&D than did the 12 next largest (1.8 percent and 3.0 percent, respectively, weighted by sales). Although the 8 largest outperformed their 12 smaller rivals in most of the industry groups, the honors are split fairly evenly within the high-technology industries. The smaller firms were more active in industrial chemicals, drugs and medicines, and electronic components, while the larger ones predominated in office, computing, and accounting machines, communication equipment,

TABLE 12–3 Company R&D Funds as Percentages of Net Sales by R&D–Performing U.S. Manufacturing Companies, by Size Class, 1981

	Firm Size	
Industry Group	Eight Largest	Next 12
Food and kindred products	0.3%	0.3%
Textiles and apparel	0.3	0.5
Lumber, wood products, and furniture	1.0	0.9
Paper and allied products	1.2	1.0
Industrial chemicals	3.0	3.2
Drugs and medicines	5.5	7.7
Other chemicals	2.2	2.1
Petroleum refining and related industries	0.7	0.4
Rubber products	2.1	1.9
Stone, clay, and glass products	2.1	0.7
Ferrous metals and products	0.5	0.7
Nonferrous metals and products	0.6	1.0
Fabricated metal products	1.4	1.1
Office, computing, and accounting machines	10.4	10.1
Other machinery, except electrical	3.5	1.8
Radio and TV receiving equipment	2.6	2.3
Communication equipment	6.3	4.1
Electronic components	5.8	7.3
Other electrical equipment	3.0	2.6
Motor vehicles and motor vehicle equipment	4.2	1.0
Other transportation equipment	0.2	0.6
Aircraft and missiles	4.6	3.4
Professional and scientific instruments	7.7	5.4
Other manufacturing industries	0.4	0.9
Total	1.8%	3.0%

SOURCE: U.S. National Science Foundation, *Research and Development in Industry, 1981* (Washington, D.C.: U.S. Government Printing Office, 1984), p. 31.

aircraft and missiles, and professional and scientific instruments. In three of the four high-tech industries in which the eight largest firms were the more active R&D performers, the single largest firm seems to account for the superiority of the group, although NSF does not identify individual firms. Office, computing, and accounting machines includes IBM; communication equipment for the year 1981 includes AT&T prior to its 1982 breakup; and the broad category of professional and scientific instruments includes photographic instruments and, therefore, Eastman Kodak.

Richard R. Nelson, Merton J. Peck, and Edward D. Kalachek called attention to a misleading feature of the NSF data. "Certain industries, particularly aircraft, electronics and chemicals," they noted in a 1967 study, are "characterized by higher than average R&D intensity for all firms in the industry regardless of size, and also by high average firm size. Within an industry the tendency for R&D spending to rise more than proportionately with sales is far less marked than in the aggregate."[24]   In most industries, they continued, the ratios of R&D to sales did not increase from the 1,000–4,999-employee size class to that of 5,000 employees and over.

The problem identified by Nelson, Peck, and Kalachek stems primarily from high levels of aggregation in NSF's industry and size classifications.   Further, NSF's figures on R&D activity cover only expenditures and employment, both of which are indicia of R&D effort, or input.   If there are economies of scale in R&D, accruing to either the research establishment itself or the sponsoring firm, there should be some evidence that equal units of input (effort) yield greater results (innovative output) in larger organizations.   Until the early 1980s, therefore, authors of empirical studies had to either turn to data collected and published by private organizations or conduct their own field work to obtain information on individual firms and narrowly defined industries.

Nongovernmental Data, Case Studies, and Field Work.   Two early British studies were particularly significant in laying the groundwork for further studies.   C. F. Carter and B. R. Williams, on the basis of 152 case studies of individual firms in the early and mid-1950s, concluded that there were some advantages to size in conducting industrial R&D, especially in the incentives and ability to do basic research, but that an industry's scientific base (the relevance of some scientific discipline to its operations) and the resulting technological opportunities were the primary determinants of R&D activity.[25]

John Jewkes, David Sawers, and Richard Stillerman surveyed 61 important inventions made in Great Britain and the United States over the first half of the 20th century.   Their most widely cited finding was:

> More than one-half of the cases can be ranked as individual invention in the sense that much of the pioneering work was carried through . . . without the backing of research institutions and usually with limited resources and assistance or, where the inventors were employed in institutions, these institutions were, as in the case of universities, of such a kind that the individuals were autonomous, free to follow their own ideas without hindrance.[26]

Further, they wrote, "Even where inventions have arisen in the research laboratories of firms, the team responsible for it seems often to have been quite small."[27]   Jewkes et al. qualified their conclusions by noting that even though the industrial laboratories (including those of the largest firms) were small, development could be costly and require the resources of a large firm.   Inventions might at times be appropriated for development and commercial exploitation by large firms because of their superior resources and protected markets.

Pioneering statistical work of the 1960s confirmed skepticism as to the overall significance of economies of scale in R&D and innovation. James S. Worley[28] and Daniel Hamberg[29] both found slight but weak positive relationships between size and R&D *inputs* among the nation's largest firms; but when Scherer looked at patents as a measure of R&D *output* among 448 corporations listed in *Fortune*'s 500 largest U.S. industrials for 1955, he found no evidence that patenting increased more than proportionately with firm size. "If anything," he remarked, "the results show that firms below the half-billion dollar sales mark generate more innovations relative to their size than do giant firms."[30] Technological opportunity, indicated by dividing the firms into four groups (electrical, chemical, moderates, and unprogressives), accounted for a substantial portion of the differences in patenting activity.

William S. Comanor confirmed Scherer's general results, for a specific industry, in an examination of the pharmaceutical industry. Comanor measured innovative output as the sales revenue derived from new products for the first two years after introduction. He found substantial economies of scale to R&D input, measured in terms of employment of professional and research personnel, among the smaller of the 57 firms in his sample, but diseconomies among the larger ones. The most striking form in which Comanor reported his results is as elasticities of response of new-entity sales to size of R&D effort for various sizes of firms. He reported elasticities of 1.39 at annual sales of $1 million, .61 at $10 million, and .54 at $150 million.[31]

Mansfield and his colleagues have studied industrial R&D through case studies and surveys. Their studies of a number of industries (including iron and steel, petroleum refining, bituminous coal, chemicals, electronics, and machinery manufacture), and case studies of the nature and management of R&D activities within several firms, led Mansfield to conclude, in 1968:

> Contrary to the allegations of . . . Schumpeter . . . there is little evidence that industrial giants are needed in all or even most industries to insure rapid technological change and rapid utilization of new techniques. . . . There seem to be considerable advantages in a diversity of firm sizes, no single firm size being optimal in this respect. Moreover, the optimal average size is likely to be directly related to the costliness and scope of the inventions that arise.[32]

The Federal Trade Commission's Line of Business Data. In the early 1980s, a new data set became available through the Federal Trade Commission's Line of Business program.[33] A line of business (LB) was defined as an individual firm's activity in one of 261 manufacturing or 14 nonmanufacturing sectors—in contrast to the 25 in-

TABLE 12–4 Elasticities of R&D Spending with Respect to Size of Firm

	Number of Industries	Percentage
No significant departure from constant returns	140	71.4%
Increasing returns (elasticity greater than one)		
Throughout	29	
At higher sales levels	11	
Total	40	20.4
Diminishing returns (elasticity less than one throughout)	16	8.2

SOURCE: Frederic M. Scherer, *Innovation and Growth: Schumpeterian Perspectives* (Cambridge, Mass.: MIT Press, 1984), p. 233.

dustry groups included in the NSF reports. Under this program, several hundred of the largest U.S. manufacturing firms were required to report accounting data on sales, expenses, profits, and assets, as well as R&D data, for 1973 through 1977, all broken down by individual LBs.

Scherer combined LB data with an equally detailed and extensive set of patent data. For each of 196 industries, he calculated elasticities of R&D spending with respect to size of firm (measured in sales), using quadratic equations to ascertain whether the elasticity changed with size. In addition, he made similar calculations of elasticities of patenting with respect to size of firm for 124 industry categories in which five or more firms received patents. His results, shown in Tables 12–4 and 12–5, "tilt on the side of supporting the Schumpeterian

TABLE 12–5 Elasticities of Patenting with Respect to Size of Firm

	Number of Industries	Percentage
No significant departure from constant returns	91	73.4%
Increasing returns		
Throughout	9	
At higher sales levels	5	
Total	14	11.3
Diminishing returns		
Throughout	18	
At higher sales levels	1	
Total	19	15.3

SOURCE: Frederic M. Scherer, *Innovation and Growth: Schumpeterian Perspectives* (Cambridge, Mass.: MIT Press, 1984), p. 234.

hypothesis that size is conducive to the vigorous conduct of R&D," but "the evidence leans weakly against the Schumpeterian conjecture that the largest sellers are especially fecund sources of patented inventions."[34] These results were reconciled in a regression of patents on R&D spending, indicating that diminishing returns to R&D are frequent, as reflected in Table 12–6.

In all, the relationship between size of firm and innovation, at least within the ranks of the largest U.S. manufacturing firms, is tenuous; and empirical analysis has failed to reveal meaningful economies of scale in R&D at this level.

TABLE 12–6 Elasticities of Patenting with Respect to R&D Spending

	Number of Industries	Percentage
No significant departure from constant returns	74	59.7%
Increasing returns		
Throughout	16	
At higher R&D levels	3	
Total	19	15.3
Diminishing returns		
Throughout	30	
At higher R&D levels	1	
Total	31	25.0

SOURCE: Frederic M. Scherer, *Innovation and Growth: Schumpeterian Perspectives* (Cambridge, Mass.: MIT Press, 1984), p. 235.

The Effects of Market Power on Innovation

Much less empirical work has been done on the hypothesized effects of market power on innovative activity. Although the distinction between economies of scale and market power as incentives to innovate is clear enough conceptually, the two may be difficult to sort out empirically. Suppose, for example, the largest firm in a particular industry spends a higher percentage of its sales revenue on R&D than any other firm in the industry. Does it enjoy economies of scale because of its size, or does its market share allow it to exploit monopolistic power not possessed by smaller competitors? Most empirical studies have implicitly assumed the former. Market power is commonly assumed to be enjoyed by all of the firms (or at least by the large ones investigated) in an industry, either through overt or tacit collusion or because of the "umbrella effect"—all are able to set higher than competitive prices if the dominant firm does so. Thus, some measure of concentration is taken as an indicator of shared market power, and R&D activities throughout the industry are treated as a function of concentration.

Concentration and R&D Employment. Scherer analyzed the relationship between R&D employment as a percentage of total employment and concentration for a large and heterogeneous collection of firms, consisting of a 5 percent sample of companies classified into 56 industry groups from the 1960 *Census of Population.* The relationship was positive and significant, even when dummy variables for technological opportunity classes—electrical, chemical, and traditional— were incorporated; but the correlation was much higher in the traditional technology industries than in the other two classes. However, R&D effort appeared to increase only with lower levels of concentration. The correlation disappeared and perhaps even reversed its sign (although not at a statistically significant level) when the four-firm concentration ratio exceeded 50 or 55 percent, suggesting an inverted-U relationship similar to that found between ratios of advertising to sales and concentration.[35]

Concentration and Technological Change. In a 1977 book, Mansfield et al. observed that insufficient work had been done to support firm conclusions, but that evidence suggested "a slight amount" of concentration is conducive to technological change. "Very fragmented, splintered industries like construction do not seem able to promote a rapid rate of technological advance," they noted. "But beyond a moderate amount of concentration, further increases in concentration do not seem to be associated with more rapid rates of technological advance. In part, this may be due to less competitive pressure and fewer independent loci for decision making."[36] They also found, however, that another structural feature of market power, high barriers to entry, inhibited innovation within an industry. New firms and firms entering new markets, they reported, are disproportionately significant contributors to technological change.

Barriers to Entry and Innovation. The comments of Mansfield et al. on entry reinforced a previous study by Comanor, which verified the hypothesis that prompt and easy imitation tends to retard innovation, while moderate barriers to entry of imitators stimulate it. Foreclosure of imitators, however, was found to reduce the incentive to innovate. The overall effect was an inverted-U relationship between ease of entry by imitators and the propensity to innovate.[37]

An Inverted-U? Scott made use of the Federal Trade Commission's

LB data to test the inverted-U relationship between concentration and innovative activity. He first ran a quadratic regression of R&D intensity on concentration for 3,388 LBs (with no control variables) and found, in support of the hypothesis, that the coefficient on the unsquared term was positive while the coefficient on the squared term was negative, with both being highly significant. However, when control variables were added for each of the 437 firms in the sample and for 20 two-digit industries, the relationship vanished completely. Scott did not regard his econometric analysis as disproving the inverted-U hypothesis: rather he concluded that "the evidence from the ... model suggests caution when interpreting cross-sectional, multi-industry, inverted-U relations between seller concentration and nonprice competition." Indeed, until further work is done, "there is the presumption that all such previously adduced correlations may be artifacts of insufficient control for opportunity."[38]

Thresholds of Size and Power, and Innovation

A number of commentators have interpreted results of empirical work such as that reviewed here as refuting Schumpeter's hypotheses regarding both size and market power. Jesse W. Markham, however, has argued convincingly that such an interpretation reflects misunderstanding of Schumpeter's original argument. According to Markham, Schumpeter's theory must be viewed "as a 'threshold theory'; some departure from a state of perfect competition (or the presence of some monopoly) is a necessary concomitant of innovation, but it does not follow that twice this volume of departure, somehow measured, should lead to twice the volume of innovations."[39]

Nelson et al. followed Markham in noting that "in most industries there would appear to be a threshold on the size of an efficient program; if firms are not large enough to support a program of minimum efficient size, their efforts are ad hoc and informal or nonexistent." Moveover, "The optimum is a size distribution composed of small, medium, and large firms varying from industry to industry and from time to time. The optimum must further include a rate of turnover among firms sufficient to accommodate enough new firms to prevent excessive traditionalism."[40]

More recent work by Mansfield and his colleagues reinforced the finding (by then standard) of no significant relationship, beyond a certain threshold, between either size or market concentration as an explanatory variable and either R&D effort or relative innovative output. More specifically, small firms appeared to play a disproportionately large role at the stage of initial invention and in early, relatively inexpensive R&D. In the industries studied by Mansfield et al., development, even though expensive, rarely required the resources of the largest firms. Studies of the drug, petroleum, coal, and steel industries indicated that the firms responsible for the largest number of innovations relative to their size were not the largest ones. Further, the largest firms did not spend relatively more on R&D than did others of substantial size, although there were definite threshold effects.[41]

In a 1982 book, reviewing European data and studies, Christopher Freeman identified a somewhat different threshold in research-intensive industries:

> Each firm which wishes to stay in business must be capable, if not of making a major innovation itself, at least of imitating those made by its more advanced competitors within a short time. To do this it must have a certain R&D capacity, even if it also makes use of licensing and know-how agreements. This minimum level of "defensive" research and development may be termed the "threshold." It is an *absolute* level of resources, not a *ratio* of sales.[42]

Thus the existence of the threshold effect is well substantiated. It is equally clear that thresholds vary from industry to industry and, indeed, even from firm to firm within an industry if different types of R&D are done—such as smaller firms performing the original research and larger ones concentrating on development. But the evidence available to date suggests that only infrequently would there be a serious conflict between the minimum sizes and market power needed to promote optimal levels of innovative activity and industrial structures conducive to workable static competition.

The Feedback Effects of Innovation on Market Structure

Both a priori reasoning and a scattering of empirical evidence suggest that the long-term feedback effect of innovation on market structure may be profound and more important than the short-term effect of structure on innovation. But successful innovation may lead to lower rather than higher concentration and favor smaller rather than larger firms. Among the relevant circumstances appear to be the nature of the underlying technological opportunities, conditions of entry, and maturity of the industry.

The histories of firms such as Du Pont and IBM attest that in research-intensive industries, size and market power may owe much more to successful R&D than vice versa. This sort of casual empiricism is supported by more systematic, albeit scattered, evidence. Mansfield's studies in the 1960s of the steel and petroleum industries showed that "in every time interval and in both industries," successful innovators exceeded the growth rates of otherwise comparable firms by 4 to 13 percentage points over a 5- to 10-year period after the introduction of the innovation. "As one would expect," he reported, "a successful innovation had a much greater impact on the growth rate of a small firm than a large one."[43]

Ben S. Branch tested for a two-way causal relationship: successful R&D may lead to increased sales growth and profit, and both growth and profit may stimulate additional R&D. In a distributed lag analysis using patent counts as a measure of R&D success, he found strong support for the hypothesis that successful R&D does indeed lead to increased profits (though not necessarily increased rates of profit) and to more rapid sales growth. The results of his tests of the hypothesis that higher profit leads to greater R&D were mixed but yielded "some support."[44]

Perhaps the most influential work calling economists' attention to the effects of technological change on market structure is Almarin Phillips' 1971 study of the evolution of the U.S. commercial aircraft industry.[45] Phillips found that the impact of technological change on the structure of the industry has overwhelmed any reverse flow of causation from structure to technical activity. The primary cause of the growth of a few firms and the decline or demise of many more, resulting in high concentration, has been successful innovation. Two features of Phillips' study warrant emphasis here. First, in large part because of government-funded R&D on military aviation, the main sources of innovation in the commercial aircraft industry were exogenous science and technology, with great "spillover" advantages to those who had been awarded major military contracts. Second, successful entry into the industry involved "quantum leaps" in technology rather than imitation and minor improvements. Both of these features limit the relevance to other industries of Phillips' finding that successful innovation promotes high concentration but not of his more general conclusion that innovation can have a great impact on industry structure.

The effects of innovation on structure may vary with the maturity of a technologically based industry. James M. Utterback has argued that product innovations predominate in the initial stage of development of a new line of business. In this early period, technical virtuosity, product quality, and flexibility in adapting the new products to users' needs are the most important attributes of business success; and the advantage lies with small-scale, adaptable firms. New products are first introduced into small market niches where they face little or no competition and usually enjoy temporary monopoly. Through efforts of both innovators and imitators, the successful product spreads to new uses, coming more into competition with existing products as it does so. As the basic product penetrates the market, standardization and lower-cost processes of production become more important. Process innovation replaces product innovation, and production becomes more efficient—a change that Utterback equates with greater capital intensity and larger scale.[46]

In a 1983 article, Mansfield examined the question of whether technological change is typically scale-diminishing—as is the case with small, cheap printed circuits replacing complex wiring, capacitors, and resistors—or scale-augmenting—as when synthetic fibers produced in large factories replaced farm products such as cotton and wool.[47] He also investigated the follow-up issue of whether scale-augmenting innovation tends to promote concentration. His findings were drawn from a sample of major process innovations in the chemicals, petroleum, and steel industries, along with product innovations in these three plus the drug industry.

In summarizing his results, Mansfield noted that scale-increasing process innovations clearly predominated over scale-decreasing ones in the three industries for which he had data. But in chemicals and drugs, scale-decreasing product innovations occurred frequently, comprising a majority in the latter. To test the strength of the effect of innovation on concentration, Mansfield regressed change in the four-firm concentration ratio for each industry against the percentage of innovations that informants in 34 firms judged as concentration-increasing. The correlation coefficient was "moderate" and significant at only the 10 percent level, which Mansfield interpreted as indicating that the phenomenon was not an important determinant of concentration.

INDUSTRIAL INNOVATION AND ECONOMIC PERFORMANCE

If innovation and economic development are good, are more innovation and faster development better? Not necessarily. R&D, like any economic activity, requires resources that could be put to alternative uses. Too many as well as too few productive resources, including human talent, could be devoted to innovation. Further, resource allocation could be distorted by undue emphasis on certain types of innovation. For example, firms may have greater incentive to introduce a better-tasting candy coating on existing medicine than to improve the quality of the medicine. There is a socially optimal level and composition of innovative activity, and a crucial question for industrial organization is what sorts of market structures and public policies promote attainment of that optimum.

Divergences between Private and Social Benefits

The social benefits from R&D usually exceed the private benefits; at times the divergence is wide. In part, the difference reflects the increase in consumer welfare associated with any decline in cost or increase in demand, precisely as in static welfare theory. But the gap is widened in the case of successful innovation as the net result of two offsetting market failures.

Market Failures that Widen the Gap. First, public benefit tends to exceed private benefit because of the *appropriability* problem. Imitators will reap some of the gain, as the knowledge generated in the innovative activity spreads. Since the innovator cannot appropriate the full social value of the innovation, the incentive to innovate may be deficient.

The second source of market failure, generating excessive R&D, stems from the competitive process. Rivalrous R&D leads to duplication of effort and findings, results that are unusable because of preemption, and costs of imitation or "innovating around" an original discovery. Further, there is the cost of "cannibalization"—or the loss in value of investments in undepreciated, obsolete plant and equipment.

The "Wedge" of Competition. Mansfield and a group of his colleagues estimated the private and social returns to total technical innovation outlays—not just R&D costs—for 17 innovations. The analysis revealed the "key role of competition in driving a wedge between the private and social returns from innovation." The social rate of return averaged 56 percent for the 17 innovations; the private rate averaged 25 percent. In about 30 percent of the cases, the actual private rate of return was so low that the project would not have been undertaken had the return been forecast correctly. The social rates of return on "mundane" innovations were extremely high—300 percent on a thread and 200 percent on a household cleaner. "Without denying the importance of our 'high technology' industries," Mansfield et al. commented, "one is led to wonder whether there may not be a tendency in some quarters to underestimate the returns available from more R and D and related innovative activities in the relatively 'low technology' industries." In 4 of the 17 innovations studied, the private rate of return exceeded the social rate. The basic reason for this was that the innovator was able to divert a substantial amount of business from its competitors.[48]

Optimal Social and Private Returns. The fact that social returns are usually greater than private does not mean, however, that society necessarily would be better off if more resources were devoted to R&D. Figure 12–2 provides a simple diagrammatic illustration of this important point. In Panels (A) and (B), the lines labeled V_p represent the present discounted value of the stream of net private operating profits accruing to a firm, while those labeled V_s represent the net social benefit from an innovation. (The lines have a different shape from the V lines in Figure 12–1, because the values are now plotted as a function of cost (C) rather than of time.) All of the V functions in Figure 12–2 are drawn on the assumptions that both private profits and social benefits increase as project costs are increased from zero, but at a decreasing rate throughout, and that at some level of cost the profit or benefit is maximized with no further gain attainable from greater expenditure.

FIGURE 12–2 Optimal Social and Private Returns to R&D

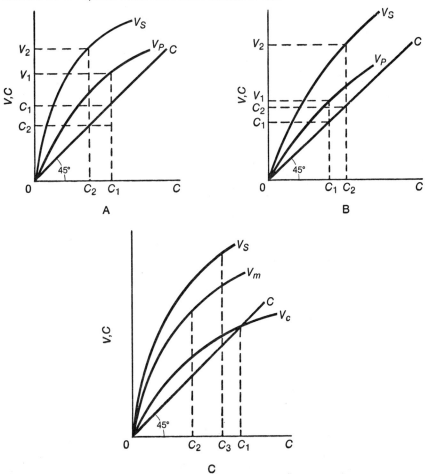

These assumptions reflect a time-cost trade-off, but the function need not be exactly as drawn. There may be a minimum level of expenditure necessary to obtain any results, so that V might intersect the horizontal axis to the right of the origin of the graph. There may be an initial stage of increasing returns to spending so that the function is S-shaped, or has a range of increasing slope. The precise shape and position of V do not matter as long as the value increases with cost but, beyond a certain level of expenditure, at a decreasing rate. C is merely a reference line, plotting coordinates on the vertical and horizontal axes where costs are equal.

Provided V_p in Panels (A) and (B) lies above C within some range of cost, it will be worthwhile for a firm to undertake the project. The net return, $V_p - C$, is maximized at the cost level where the slope of V_p is 45 degrees, or where $dV_p/dC = 1$, indicating that the marginal value of the project is equal to its marginal cost. In Panels (A) and (B), this level of cost is shown as C_1. Similarly, social benefit, $V_s - C$, is maximized at the level of expenditure (C_2) at which the slope of V_s is 45 degrees. V_s is drawn above V_p throughout, reflecting the assumption that social benefits exceed private; but a comparison of Panels (A) and (B) makes it evident that the socially optimal expenditure may or may not be greater than the private profit-maximizing one. Only by coincidence would the private level be exactly equal to the socially optimal level.

Panel (C) applies a similar technique to illustrate that even though the returns from innovation to a monopolist will inevitably be greater than those to a competitive industry because of greater appropriability, the monopolist will not necessarily do more R&D. There is one crucial difference in the private value function in Panel (C). In Panels (A) and (B), these functions represent the returns to the innovating *firm*. In Panel (C), V_m represents the private value of an innovation to a pure monopolist and, thus, to both the industry and a single firm. But V_c represents the net private value of an innovation to an entire competitive *industry*, summing the positive and negative values to the initial innovator and those preempted, whether or not the latter introduce imitations. In a winner-take-all race, competition may drive $V_c - C$ to zero, or C to C_1 in Panel (C).[49]

In Panel (C), the competitive industry's R&D spending (C_1) is somewhat greater than that of the monopolist (C_2). But the relative positions of V_m and V_c are arbitrary. An increase in appropriability by the monopolist, for example, could swing V_m up until the monopolist's optimal spending becomes greater. And to couple the results depicted in Panel (C) with those in Panels (A) and (B), under either competition or monopoly, an industry may devote more or less than the socially optimal amount of resources, C_3 in Panel (A), to innovation.

Dissemination, Imitation, and the Rate of Diffusion

The effect of technology on economic welfare is ultimately a result of the degree and rate at which innovations are diffused (made available to potential producers and users).

An innovation (such as the diesel engine) will diffuse among both users (railroads) and producers (manufacturers of railway equipment) and can originate at either level. From the innovator's viewpoint, diffusion among its suppliers or customers is generally beneficial, while diffusion among its competitors is unwelcomed. Diffusion may result, therefore, from deliberate efforts of the innovating firm or at least its acquiescence—or it may result from competitive imitation. The term *imitation* denotes diffusion by firms other than the innovator and without its permission or approval. Diffusion initiated or encouraged by the innovator is termed *dissemination*.[50]

The Diffusion of Disembodied Knowledge. Severe, even crippling sources of market failure have been identified when knowledge itself is viewed as a commodity to be transferred or diffused. Theorists have developed the concept of pure, disembodied knowledge that is not incorporated in any device and that can be transferred without cost or distortion. Discovering such knowledge (the original R&D) may be quite costly; but once a unit of knowledge exists, it can be reproduced (divulged to others) at no additional cost. Closely related to the idea of zero marginal cost of reproduction is that marginal *user* cost is also zero. The availability of a unit of knowledge to one person is in no way diminished by supplying it to another, although transfer may affect its private value. In this sense, knowledge is an inexhaustible common resource.

The implication of zero marginal reproduction and user cost of a unit of pure, disembodied knowledge is that its contribution to welfare is maximized when its price is zero. Thus, it should be made freely available. But free availability reduces or destroys the innovator's ability to appropriate gains from the innovation and hence lessens or eliminates the incentive to innovate. The result is a paradoxical situation noted by Kenneth J. Arrow: "In a free-enterprise economy, inventive activity is supported by using the innovation to create property rights; precisely to the extent that it is successful, there is an underutilization of the information."[51]

The concept of pure, disembodied knowledge with zero marginal costs of reproduction and use is highly abstract. The actual transfer of technology, whether by dissemination or imitation, is quite different.

Dissemination of Technology. Dissemination frequently takes the form of allowing another firm to produce a patented or proprietary product under license. If the innovator can protect the licensed technology from further unauthorized diffusion, it does not lose appropriability but merely chooses whether to reap its gains through profits on sales or royalty fees. The decision should reflect economies or diseconomies of scale in exploiting the technology, and perhaps short-run differences in available productive capacity or operating costs of various firms in the industry. Dissemination may also take the form of an inventor selling patent rights or an unpatented invention to another firm for development.

Influences on the Efficiency of Dissemination. According to Albert H. Rubenstein:

> Few transfers of technology beyond simple provisions of new parts or equipment embodying changes can be completed by "mail" or by "arms length" exchanges. They generally require "hands on" instruction and cooperation in installation, start-up, breaking in, adapting, improving training for use and maintenance, and going through the other activities that are required for effective and "full" transfer of technology.[52]

Dissemination, then, is made more or less efficient by characteristics of both the providing and receiving organizations. Providers may fail for lack of the capacity to write accurate specifications, provide repair and maintenance, give ongoing advice, or maintain an adequate inventory of replacement parts. Skills in contract and patent management may be required to protect the disseminated technology against subsequent competitive diffusion by customers or licensed suppliers. Backup skills in marketing, finance, and logistics may be required to exploit technological virtuosity effectively.

The buyer (user) of the technology may need skills similar to those of the disseminator. Use of a new technology may require retraining the work force or recruiting people with specific skills. The using firm may need sophisticated technical expertise to absorb and manage the technology, particularly in areas such as proper operation of complex machinery, shop layout, use of appropriate materials, and quality control. Originators may refuse to provide new technology to users who have inadequate safeguards against leakage of proprietary information; alternatively, users that fail to provide the required protection may incur costly legal liabilities.

David J. Teece has studied dissemination by multinational firms, incuding transfers of technology to wholly owned subsidiaries, joint ventures, independent private enterprises, and government enterprises. He found that transfer costs tend to be high, averaging 19 percent of total project costs across his sample but ranging widely from 2 percent to 59 percent.[53]

Problems of communication, marketing, servicing, and absorption of new technologies affect diffusion in two different ways. First, they may limit the process of dissemination to innovators large enough to transmit information efficiently and to recipients with adequate absorptive capacity. Second, and perhaps more important, such problems raise barriers to unauthorized dissemination or imitation, particularly by smaller firms, and therefore make dissemination by the innovators more profitable.

Diffusion is also affected by *first start* advantages. A decline in costs associated with production experience may put later adopters at a serious enough disadvantage to retard both dissemination and imitation.

Unauthorized Diffusion: Imitation. Imitation provides a major mechanism of diffusion. A common quip in industry is that a patent is often little more than a "license to sue"; and reverse engineering (analysis of how a competitor's product was made) has become a routine feature of industrial R&D work. Imitation may, in some circumstances, augment the welfare benefits of innovation by speeding the diffusion process and extending the spread of the innovation closer to the theoretical optimum where the marginal social cost of adoption equals the marginal social benefit. Alternatively, by reducing the anticipated earnings from innovation, imitation may retard the incentive to innovate.[54]

Mansfield and his colleagues have found that firms that are relatively large spenders on innovative R&D also tend to be prompt to adopt others' technologies, confirming the hypothesis that innovative R&D and imitative R&D are likely to be complementary rather than substitute strategies. Imitation is often costly and time consuming: the ratio of imitation to innovation costs in firms that Mansfield and his colleagues have studied averaged around 65 percent, and the similar ratio for total project development time was approximately 70 percent. In one seventh of the cases, imitation costs were equal to or greater than those of innovation. The higher the ratio of research expense to development expense, the lower are imitation costs relative to development, indicating that the diffusion of research findings is easier than the transmission of production know-how.[55]

Original R&D did not appear to be dampened by the prospect of imitation. Among the firms Mansfield et al. studied, this willingness to innovate was based on the belief that innovation would be profitable even though imitations appeared within a few years. The average ratio of imitation cost to innovation cost was found to be positively and significantly correlated with the industry's concentration level. Mansfield et al. hypothesized that a feedback phemonenon might explain this finding: ease and cheapness of imitation of competitors' processes and products should lower concentration.

Anthony A. Romeo, one of Mansfield's collaborators, found diffusion of numerically controlled (NC) machine tools in a number of using industries positively and significantly related to the number of firms in the industry but negatively and significantly related to differences in firm sizes, supporting the hypothesis that competition stimulates diffusion among users.[56]

Diffusion of a Major Innovation. The process of diffusion has been studied in the context of an industry life cycle. Dennis C. Mueller and John E. Tilton identified four general, stylized stages in the development of an industry created by a major innovation. At the first, or "innovation," stage (in which the new product or process is invented, developed, and introduced to the market), its spread is limited and perhaps inadequate; the innate conservatism and "not invented here" bias of large corporations impedes the introduction of innovations made by smaller units without the capacity to develop and market them. In Mueller and Tilton's second stage, labeled the "imitation stage," uncertainty about technical obstacles and market potential fades. New firms rush to enter, often with different or superior variants. Typically, in this second stage, the underlying science and technology are poorly understood, and their pragmatic application does not require large-scale institutionalized industrial research facilities. Thus, small firms may be as successful as large in entry through imitation at this stage.

In the third stage, that of "technological competition," transformations tend to favor large industrial laboratories. The scientific and technological base becomes firmer, R&D becomes more specialized and sophisticated, and technical advance more commonly takes the form of improvement in specific aspects of the underlying technology. Concentration increases in this stage. Economies of scale favor large industrial laboratories. Knowledge becomes embodied in production experience, and small-scale imitation becomes more difficult.

In the fourth and final stage, "standardization," patents expire, technological advance slows, the knowledge appears in textbooks, and production becomes standardized. Technological barriers to entry and imitation fall, perhaps to be replaced by barriers to entry such as economies of scale in production and marketing.[57]

Modifications of the Model. Mueller and Tilton's highly stylized model will not fit all industries. In an analysis of the life-cycle of 46 new products, Michael Gort and Stephen Klepper found that changes in economies of scale did not adequately explain concentration in the later stages of the cycles. Of greater importance, they concluded, is a distinction between information as organizational capital and as human capital. The former adheres to a firm either through patent ownership or because it is embedded in the collective knowledge or experience of the organization; the latter can be taken from one organization to another by an individual who possesses the information. Organization capital, according to Gort and Klepper, is associated more with minor modifications than with major innovations, and it grows over time relative to human capital, thus raising a barrier to entry by imitators.[58] Other empirical studies indicate that standardization of technology and production need not increase in the mature stages of an innovation's life cycle. To the contrary, product diversification may grow with maturity of a technologically based industry.[59]

Summary. In sum, invention, innovation, and diffusion are the three sequential and equally essential steps in the overall process of technological change. Although the concept of pure, disembodied knowledge abstracts from transfer costs and thus exaggerates the extent of market failure in diffusion, the paradoxical conclusion remains that adequate rewards to stimulate optimal private efforts at innovation are generally incompatible with the optimal degree of diffusion of existing innovations. Although the life-cycle phenomenon is not yet thoroughly understood and varies considerably from industry to industry, it is clear that diffusion both is influenced by industry structure and, concurrently, shapes changes in that structure.

The Quality of Innovation and Technological Advance: Socially Undesirable R&D

Commercial R&D may have deleterious as well as beneficial effects. Competitive duplication and reverse engineering are sources of excessive and wasteful R&D. Efforts to differentiate products and segment markets may lead to excessive R&D on minor improvements or on distinctive but trivial characteristics.

Product Debasement. Market power, either existing or attainable, may promote socially undesirable R&D. At a time when General Electric held the basic patents on the incandescent light bulb, for example, the following memo was sent by a GE engineer to his superior:

> Two or three years ago we proposed a reduction in the life of flashlight lamps . . . to a point where the life of the lamp and the life of the battery

under service conditions would be approximately equal. Sometime ago, the battery manufacturers went part way with us on this and accepted lamps of two battery lives instead of three.... We have been continuing our studies and efforts to bring about the use of one battery life lamps.... We estimate that it would result in increasing our flashlight business approximately 60 per cent.[60]

Shortly thereafter, however, after expiration of the patents, another memorandum was written by a GE officer:

We are being pushed very hard by non-Mazda competition. Most of these lamps are at somewhat lower efficiency than ours and inherently have a longer life.... We realize that the constant reduction of lamp life that we have been in the process of carrying on has kept the volume of business up, but cannot refrain from giving a word of warning and a suggestion that it is about time to call a halt on this in view of the competitive situation.[61]

Although GE maintained that lower-life bulbs used less electricity and thus in net saved money for the user, the company did not make any effort to promote its products on that basis. To the contrary, yet another company officer wrote, "Decision has just been made to change the life of the 200-watt 110–120 volt P530 bulb lamp from 1000 hours design and published to 750 hours design and published.... We do not know just when this change will go into effect, and we are giving no publicity whatever to the fact that the change is contemplated."[62]

Another example is found in the proposal of a Du Pont research director, following development of a pigment that could be used in either paints or dyes. "Further work may be necessary," the researcher wrote, "on adding contaminants to 'Monastral' colors to make them unsatisfactory on textiles but satisfactory for paints."[63] The recommendation was not adopted.

In both instances, the incentives to engage in R&D aimed at debasing products rather than improving them stemmed from monopoly power in the product markets. Once GE's patents expired, it could no longer increase sales by producing shorter-lived bulbs in the face of quality as well as price competition. Similarly, Du Pont would have had no apparent motive for inhibiting new textile dyes while promoting new coloring agents for paints unless the company believed there was a market to capture in paint, while the new dyes would simply render obsolete existing Du Pont products in which the company had a domestic monopoly.

Blocking Patents. Product debasement is not the only harmful or socially wasteful form of R&D that firms might undertake in the interest of exploiting or attaining monopoly power. Firms have engaged in R&D to obtain "fencing" or "blocking" patents that covered substitutes for their own products or processes, thus raising barriers to entry. U.S. automobile manufacturers were charged with agreeing to exchange R&D information on emission-control devices, including proposals made by independent inventors, to restrain their development so that regulations requiring their use would be delayed. The case was settled by a consent decree in which the firms agreed to end the practice but did not admit guilt.[64]

Physical Tie-Ins. Another restrictive type of R&D involves what are known as "physical tie-ins." Products compatible only with complementary products produced by the same firm have been developed and introduced to raise barriers to entry and extend market power from one product to another. For example, in 1972, Eastman Kodak Company simultaneously introduced its 110 Pocket Instamatic camera and a new, faster Kodacolor II film, which fit only the 110 camera. Thus, buyers attracted by the new camera had to buy the film, and those attracted by the new film had to buy the camera. Further, Kodacolor II required a new development process, and independent photofinishers were not advised in advance of either the film's introduction or the formula for the chemicals used to develop it. In a private antitrust suit, the jury found that independent photofinishers were required to buy chemicals and equipment from Kodak at "excessive" prices and that "almost certainly" the kits sold were "vastly inferior" to those Kodak used itself.[65]

SOME IMPLICATIONS FOR PUBLIC POLICY

In the early and mid-1950s, a number of economists influenced by the Schumpeterian vision expressed concern that traditional antitrust goals of preserving and promoting price competition were incompatible with the degrees of size and market power needed for optimal levels of technological development. Subsequent work, both theoretical and empirical, indicates that this dilemma is illusory. In most U.S. industries, the threshold levels of size and concentration required for effective R&D appear to be consistent with those conducive to workably competitive conduct and performance.

Findings on the important role in innovation played by new firms and entrants from other industries suggest strongly that barriers to entry through innovation are particularly pernicious and that policies designed to remove such barriers can make a significant contribution to technical progress.

The long-term feedback effect of successful innovation may, from time to time, increase concentration. The decision in a well-known antitrust case posed the issue: "The successful competitor, having been urged to compete, must not be turned upon when he wins."[66] The opinion in a later case, elaborated on this point, stating:

> The defendant may escape statutory liability if it bears the burden of proving that it owes its monopoly solely to superior skill, superior products, natural advantages, (including accessability to raw materials or markets), economic or technological efficiency, (including scientific research), low margins of profit maintained permanently and without discrimination, or licenses conferred by, and used within, the limits of law, (including patents on one's own inventions, or franchises granted directly to the enterprise by a public authority).[67]

Under current interpretation of the Sherman Act, market power resulting from innovation is not illegal as long as it is not deliberately maintained through subsequent exclusionary conduct.[68] This interpretation of the law seems appropriate to the underlying economic phenomena.

The most difficult problems for public policy designed to promote optimal levels of innovation involve appropriability. A certain level of protection from prompt imitation—whether through time lags resulting from friction, secrecy, market power, or issuance of a patent—is required in order to provide adequate incentive to private innovative activity; but excessive protection from the threat of competitive innovation may lessen a firm's incentive to do R&D. The problem is a subtle one—the proper degree of protection involves not only providing appropriability to the innovator but limiting wasteful competitive R&D in reverse engineering and imitation.[69] The threshold and life-cycle concepts suggest that the appropriate level of protection and the forms it might take vary from industry to industry and within an industry over time. But empirical work indicates that the degree of concentration called for is usually modest; and private restrictive practices, outside of legitimate use of patents, are generally unwarranted and harmful.

ENDNOTES

[1]This chapter draws heavily on William L. Baldwin and John T. Scott, "Market Structure and Technological Change," in *Pure and Applied Economics* (forthcoming). Scott's major contributions, both in substance and expression, to this chapter are gratefully acknowledged.

[2]Joseph A. Schumpeter, "The Creative Response in Economic History," *Journal of Economic History*, November 1947, pp. 149–59, at p. 152. Reprinted in *Essays of J. A. Schumpeter*, ed. Richard V. Clemence (Reading, Mass.: Addison-Wesley Publishing, 1951).

[3]Joseph A. Schumpeter, *Capitalism, Socialism, and Democracy* (New York: Harper & Row, 1942).

[4]For a thoughtful, integrative exposition of this system, see Richard V. Clemence

and Francis S. Doody, *The Schumpeterian System* (Reading, Mass.: Addison-Wesley Publishing, 1951).

[5]Schumpeter, *Capitalism,* p. 82.

[6]Joseph A. Schumpeter, *Business Cycles,* 2 vols.   (New York: McGraw-Hill, 1939), p. 1044.

[7]Schumpeter, *Capitalism,* p. 88.

[8]Ibid., pp. 89–90.

[9]Ibid., p. 84.

[10]Joseph A. Schumpeter, *Theory of Economic Development,* trans. Redvers Opie (Cambridge, Mass.: Harvard University Press, 1934), chap. 4.

[11]U.S. National Science Foundation, *Research and Development in Industry, 1981* (Washington, D.C.: U.S. Government Printing Office, 1984), p. 2.

[12]Ibid., p. 33.

[13]Edwin Mansfield, John Rapoport, Jerome Schnee, Samuel Wagner, and Michael Hamburger, *Research and Innovation in the Modern Corporation* (New York: W. W. Norton, 1971), p. 221.

[14]Richard R. Nelson, "The Simple Economics of Basic Scientific Research," *Journal of Political Economy* 67, no. 3 (June 1959), pp. 297–306.

[15]Frederic M. Scherer, "Concentration, R&D, and Productivity Change," *Southern Economic Journal* 50, no. 1 (July 1983), pp. 221–25.

[16]The point is developed at some length and argued forcefully in John Jewkes, David Sawers, and Richard Stillerman, *The Sources of Invention* (London: Macmillan, 1958).

[17]Joe S. Bain, *Pricing, Distribution and Employment,* rev. ed. (New York: Holt, Rinehart & Winston, 1953), pp. 225–31, has an excellent discussion of these incentives.

[18]The model was originally presented in Frederic M. Scherer, "Research and Development Resource Allocation under Rivalry," *Quarterly Journal of Economics* 81, no. 3 (August 1967), pp. 359–94.   For the diagrammatic version, see Frederic M. Scherer, *Industrial Market Structure and Economic Performance,* 2d ed. (Skokie, Ill.: Rand McNally, 1980), pp. 426–30.   A similar diagram and discussion appears in Mansfield et al., *Research and Innovation,* pp. 152–55.

[19]A number of these models are reviewed in Morton I. Kamien and Nancy L. Schwartz, *Market Structure and Innovation* (London: Cambridge University Press, 1982); and in Baldwin and Scott, "Market Structure."

[20]Richard R. Nelson and Sidney G. Winter, *An Evolutionary Theory of Economic Change* (Cambridge, Mass.: Harvard University Press, 1982).

[21]Arun K. Mukhopadhyay, "Technological Progress and Change in Market Concentration in the U.S., 1963–77," *Southern Economic Journal* 52, no. 1 (July 1985), pp. 141–49.

[22]See especially Glenn C. Loury, "Market Structure and Innovation," *Quarterly Journal of Economics* 93, no. 3 (August 1979), pp. 395–410; Partha Dasgupta and Joseph E. Stiglitz, "Uncertainty, Industrial Structure, and the Speed of R&D," *Bell Journal of Economics* 11, no. 1 (Spring 1980), pp. 1–28; Partha Dasgupta and Joseph E. Stiglitz, "Industrial Structure and the Nature of Innovative Activity," *Economic Journal* 90, no. 358 (June 1980), pp. 266–93; Carl A. Futia, "Schumpeterian Competition," *Quarterly Journal of Economics* 94, no. 4 (June 1980), pp. 675–95.   For a pioneering attempt at formulating and testing an empirical model based on Dasgupta and Stiglitz' theoretical one, see Richard C. Levin and Peter C. Reiss, "Tests of a Schumpeterian Model of R&D and Market Structure," in *R&D, Patents, and Productivity,* ed. Zvi Griliches (Chicago: University of Chicago Press, 1984), pp. 175–204.

[23]Edward F. Denison, *Accounting for United States Economic Growth, 1929–1969* (Washington, D.C.: Brookings Institution, 1974).

[24]Richard R. Nelson, Merton J. Peck, and Edward D. Kalachek, *Technology, Economic Growth, and Public Policy* (Washington, D.C.: Brookings Institution, 1967), p. 67.

[25]C. F. Carter and B. R. Williams, *Industry and Technical Progress* (London: Oxford University Press, 1957).

[26]Jewkes et al., *Sources*, p. 82.

[27]Ibid., p. 88.

[28]James S. Worley, "Industrial Research and the New Competition," *Journal of Political Economy* 69, no. 2 (April 1961), pp. 183–86.

[29]Daniel Hamberg, "Size of Firm, Oligopoly, and Research," *Canadian Journal of Economics and Political Science* 30, no. 1 (February 1964), pp. 62–75.

[30]Frederic M. Scherer, "Firm Size, Market Structure, Opportunity, and the Output of Patented Inventions," *American Economic Review* 55, no. 5 (December 1965), pp. 1097–125 at p. 1114.

[31]William S. Comanor, "Research and Technical Change in the Pharmaceutical Industry," *Review of Economics and Statistics* 47, no. 2 (May 1965), pp. 182–90.

[32]Edwin Mansfield, *The Economics of Technological Change* (New York: W. W. Norton, 1968), p. 217.

[33]U.S. Federal Trade Commission, Bureau of Economics, *Statistical Report: Annual Line of Business Report* (Washington, D.C.: U.S. Government Printing Office, 1974, 1975, and 1976).

[34]Frederic M. Scherer, *Innovation and Growth: Schumpeterian Perspectives* (Cambridge, Mass.: MIT Press, 1984), pp. 234–35.

[35]Frederic M. Scherer, "Market Structure and the Employment of Scientists and Engineers," *American Economic Review* 57, no. 3 (June 1967), pp. 524–31.

[36]Edwin Mansfield, John Rapoport, Anthony Romeo, Edmond Villani, Samuel Wagner, and Frank Husic, *The Production and Application of New Technologies* (New York: W. W. Norton, 1977), p. 16.

[37]William S. Comanor, "Market Structure, Product Differentiation, and Industrial Research," *Quarterly Journal of Economics* 81, no. 4 (November 1967), pp. 639–57.

[38]John T. Scott, "Firm versus Industry Variability in R&D Intensity," in *R&D, Patents and Productivity*, ed. Zvi Griliches (Chicago: University of Chicago Press for the National Bureau of Economic Research, 1984) pp. 236–37.

[39]Jesse W. Markham, "Market Structure, Business Conduct, and Innovation," *American Economic Review* 55, no. 2 (May 1965), pp. 323–32, at p. 325.

[40]Nelson et al., *Technology*, pp. 67, 71.

[41]Mansfield et al., *Production and Application*.

[42]Christopher Freeman, *The Economics of Industrial Innovation*, 2d ed. (Cambridge, Mass.: MIT Press, 1982), p. 146 (italics original).

[43]Mansfield, *Economics*, pp. 106–7.

[44]Ben S. Branch, "Research and Development Activity and Profitability: A Distributed Lag Analysis," *Journal of Political Economy* 82, no. 5 (September–October 1974), pp. 999–1011.

[45]Almarin Phillips, *Technology and Market Structure* (Lexington, Mass.: D. C. Heath, 1971).

[46]James M. Utterback, "The Dynamics of Product and Process Innovation," in *Technological Innovation for a Dynamic Economy*, ed. Christopher T. Hill and James M. Utterback (Elmsford, N.Y.: Pergamon Press, 1979).

[47]Edwin Mansfield, "Technological Change and Market Structure: An Empirical Study," *American Economic Review* 73, no. 2 (May 1983), pp. 205–9.

[48]Mansfield et al., *Production and Application*, pp. 188, 189. See also Edwin Mansfield, John Rapoport, Anthony Romeo, Samuel Wagner, and George Beardsley, "Social

and Private Rates of Return from Industrial Innovations," *Quarterly Journal of Economics* 91, no. 2 (May 1977), pp. 221–40.

[49]This discussion is drawn from a related but somewhat different model in Yoram Barzel, "Optimal Timing of Innovations," *Review of Economics and Statistics* 50, no. 3 (August 1968), pp. 348–55.

[50]Jack Hirschleifer, "The Private and Social Value of Information and the Reward for Innovative Activity," *American Economic Review* 61, no. 4 (September 1971), pp. 561–74.

[51]Kenneth J. Arrow, "Economic Welfare and the Allocation of Resources for Invention," in *The Rate and Direction of Inventive Activity,* Universities-National Bureau Committee for Economic Research (Princeton, N.J.: Princeton University Press, 1962), p. 617.

[52]Albert H. Rubenstein, "The Role of Embedded Technology in the Industrial Innovation Process," in *Special Study on Economic Change,* vol. 3: *Research and Innovation: Developing a Dynamic Nation,* U.S. Congress, Joint Economic Committee (Washington, D.C.: U.S. Government Printing Office, 1980), p. 395.

[53]David J. Teece, *The Multinational Corporation and the Resource Cost of International Technology Transfer* (Cambridge, Mass.: Ballinger, 1978).

[54]The effects of imitation on the incentive to innovate have been discussed in Scherer, "Research and Development"; William L. Baldwin and Gerald L. Childs, "The Fast Second and Rivalry in Research and Development," *Southern Economic Journal* 36, no. 1 (July 1969), pp. 18–24; Morton I. Kamien and Nancy L. Schwartz, "Potential Rivalry, Monopoly Profits, and the Pace of Innovative Activity," *Review of Economic Studies* 45, no. 141 (October 1978), pp. 547–57.

[55]Edwin Mansfield, Anthony Romeo, Mark Schwartz, David Teece, Samuel Wagner, and Peter Brach, *Technology Transfer, Productivity, and Economic Policy* (New York: W. W. Norton, 1982); Edwin Mansfield, Mark Schwartz, and Samuel Wagner, "Imitation Costs and Patents: An Empirical Study," *Economic Journal* 91, no. 364 (December 1981), pp. 907–18.

[56]Anthony Romeo, "Interindustry and Interfirm Differences in the Rate of Diffusion of an Innovation," *Review of Economics and Statistics* 57, no. 3 (August 1975), pp. 311–19; Anthony Romeo, "The Rate of Imitation of a Capital-Embodied Process Innovation," *Economica* 44, no. 173 (1977), pp. 63–69.

[57]Dennis C. Mueller and John E. Tilton, "Research and Development Costs as a Barrier to Entry," *Canadian Journal of Economics* 2, no. 4 (November 1969), pp. 570–79.

[58]Michael Gort and Stephen Klepper, "Time Paths in the Diffusion of Product Innovations," *Economic Journal* 92, no. 367 (September 1982), pp. 630–53.

[59]Morris Teubal, "On User Needs and Need Determination: Aspects of the Theory of Technological Invention," in *Industrial Innovation: Technology, Policy, Diffusion,* ed. Michael J. Baker (London: Macmillan, 1979); Mariluz Cortez, "The Transfer of Petrochemical Technology to Less Developed Countries," in *The Transfer and Utilization of Technical Knowledge,* ed. Devendra Sahal (Lexington, Mass.: D. C. Heath, 1982); and Edwin Mansfield, "Technology Transfer, Innovation, and Public Policy," in *Transfer and Utilization,* ed. Sahal.

[60]Quoted in George W. Stocking and Myron W. Watkins, *Cartels in Action* (New York: Twentieth Century Fund, 1946), p. 354.

[61]Ibid., p. 356.

[62]Ibid., p. 359.

[63]Quoted in Walter Adams, "Technological Progress and Economic Institutions—Discussion," *American Economic Review* 44, no. 2 (May 1954), pp. 190–93, at p. 191.

[64]United States v. Automobile Manufacturers Association, General Motors Corporation, Ford Motor Company, Chrysler Corporation, and American Motors Corporation, CCH Trade Cases, ¶72,907 (1969).

[65]Berkey Photo Incorporated v. Eastman Kodak Company, 603 F.2d 263, 290 (1979).

[66]United States v. Aluminum Company of America, 148 F.2d 416, 430 (1945).

[67]United States v. United Shoe Machinery Corporation, 110 F.Supp. 295, 342 (1953).

[68]The Supreme Court has held that the requirement for violation of Section 2 of the Sherman Act is "the willful acquisition or maintenance of that power as distinguished from growth or development as a consequence of a superior product, business acumen, or historic accident." United States v. Grinnell Corporation, 384 U.S. 563, 570–71 (1966).

[69]A detailed theoretical examination of this problem is found in Carl Christian von Weizsäcker, *Barriers to Entry: A Theoretical Treatment* (Berlin: Springer-Verlag, 1980).

CHAPTER THIRTEEN

The Concentration Doctrine and the Chicago School

The structure-conduct-performance paradigm is central to the study of industrial organization and is emphasized throughout this book. This chapter and the next treat more recent approaches as supplementing and enriching this paradigm. But, as will become evident, the various approaches to industrial organization and appropriate antitrust policy cannot be neatly synthesized. Acceptance of a common paradigm does not eliminate controversy and even contradiction.

A number of economists have emphasized industrial concentration as the primary determinant of economic performance. Their broadly shared conclusions, especially those pertaining to the relationship between concentration and profits, have been called the "concentration doctrine."

The major attack on the concentration doctrine came from a cluster of economists and lawyers (the Chicago school) who hailed their own collective approach as the "new learning" of industrial organization. These economists and lawyers share a tradition associated with the University of Chicago's Department of Economics and its Law School, stressing a commitment to the economic, political, and social values of a free-market system and a corresponding antipathy toward most government interference with its workings. Prominent among this group, and concerned with concentration and antitrust policy, are Robert H. Bork, Ward S. Bowman, Jr., Harold Demsetz, John S. McGee, Stanley I. Ornstein, Sam Peltzman, Richard A. Posner, George J. Stigler, and Lester G. Telser.[1]

These labels are a convenient expository device, applied to distinguish various strands of the leading paradigms of industrial organization economics. However, there are important differences among those espousing the concentration doctrine and among those within the Chicago school.

THE CONCENTRATION DOCTRINE

Industry structure is a multifaceted concept, consisting of a set of overlapping and often unquantifiable characteristics. When structure is thought of as the set of external considerations business owners and managers take into account in making their decisions, it is a subjective concept (although objective reality can inject itself painfully into business affairs if important elements of actual structure are ignored or misunderstood). Aspects of structure such as the "degree" of product differentiation or the "height" of barriers to entry cannot be measured in precise numerical units. Other aspects of structure such as elasticity of market demand, the ratios of fixed to variable costs at different rates of output, or economies of scale in production, while measurable in principle, are often extremely difficult or impossible to quantify in empirical study of actual industrial situations.

Concentration Indices

There is, however, one feature of structure, "the numbers and relative sizes of buyers and sellers" in Edward S. Mason's words,[2] or concentration of the industry, that is amenable to numerical measurement and for which substantial data are available. The use of concentration indices as explanatory variables in studies comparing the performance of various industries was encouraged and given greatly enhanced statistical legitimacy by a 1955 study in which Gideon Rosenbluth reported that the most widely used concentration indices and bases were highly consistent with one another.[3]

Concentration, however measured, is only one aspect of structure. But in the theory of oligopoly, it is crucial, since control of a large share of an industry's market by a small number of firms is necessary though not sufficient to sustain prices above costs and restrict output. Other important attributes of structure (such as barriers to entry, degree of product differentiation, and economies of scale) are commonly associated with concentration, so that a concentration index can often serve as a proxy for a set of structural conditions conducive to or limiting exercise of market power. (Indeed, one criticism of the concentration doctrine is that its adherents link concentration too directly to market power, sometimes even indiscriminantly equating the two.)

Thus, because of data availability, the feasibility of constructing simple numerical indices, and the inherent attractiveness of such an index as a reasonable and available surrogate for market power, many economists concerned with problems of industrial organization have focused primarily on the concept of concentration.[4]

In a 1974 review of 46 previous studies, Leonard W. Weiss noted that "the concentration-profits relationship has been one of the most thoroughly tested hypotheses in economics" and that "the bulk of the studies show a significant positive effect of concentration on profits or margins."[5] Weiss concluded that, in spite of problems of data and measurement, the relationship was well established for "normal" years, although it became less apparent during or immediately after periods of accelerating inflation, when differences between accounting and actual valuations became most acute and when the tendency for price adjustments in concentrated markets to lag behind changes in other prices had the most pronounced effect.

The Neal Report

The high point of the concentration doctrine's influence was reached in the late 1960s. In 1968, a special task force set up by President Lyndon B. Johnson submitted the Neal Report (after task force chairman Phil C. Neal, dean of the University of Chicago Law School, but far from a Chicagoan). One of the Neal Report's principal findings was:

> Highly concentrated industries represent a significant segment of the American economy. . . . An impressive body of economic opinion and analysis supports the judgment that this degree of concentration precludes effective market competition and interferes with the optimum use of economic resources. Past experience strongly suggests that, in the absence of direct action, concentration is not likely to decline significantly.[6]

On the relationship between concentration and profits, the report made the following observations:

> The adverse effects of persistent concentration on output and price find some confirmation in various studies that have been made of return on capital in major industries. These studies have found a close association between high levels of concentration and persistently high rates of return on capital, particularly in those industries in which the largest four firms account for more than 60% of sales. High profit rates in individual firms or even in particular industries are of course consistent with competition. . . . It is the persistence of high profits over extended time periods and over whole industries rather than in individual firms that suggests artificial restraints on output and the absence of fully effective competition. The correlation of evidence of this kind with the existence of very high levels of concentration appears to be significant.[7]

The Neal Report recommended passage of a statute to be known as the "Concentrated Industries Act," under which a special antitrust court would be set up to restructure highly concentrated industries.

Summary

The concentration doctrine is a variant of the structuralist position. Concentration is regarded as clear and convincing evidence of the existence of market power; and adherents contend that economic performance will be improved (those espousing various versions of the doctrine emphasize different aspects of performance) by reducing concentration in most industries in which it exceeds some predetermined standard. The doctrine, as stated here in its simplest and most general form, is predicated on the assumption that in a majority of industries, or at least in enough to justify sweeping public action, existing levels of concentration are not the result of real economies of scale or the technological preeminence of large firms achieved through their own innovative efforts.

CHALLENGES TO THE CONCENTRATION DOCTRINE AND THE EMERGENCE OF THE CHICAGO SCHOOL'S NEW LEARNING

The Stigler Report

In an immediate response to the Neal Report, incoming President Richard M. Nixon established a new antitrust task force, chaired by George J. Stigler. The ensuing Stigler Report noted three determinants of the degree to which an oligopolistic industry would behave in a competitive manner. First, the "easier (quicker and cheaper) new firms can enter the industry, the smaller and more short lived will be the monopolistic restrictions." Second, the "more elastic the demand for the product . . . the less the reward from restrictions of output below the competitive level, and hence the less the inducements to act collusively." Third, as the number of firms increases, the probability of collusion grows smaller; but the more production is concentrated within a few, the more likely a given number of firms will collude.[8] Since they had concluded that other factors also play important roles in determining an industry's performance, the Stigler task force members reported that "on the basis of existing knowledge," they could not endorse proposals "to deconcentrate highly oligopolistic industries by dissolving their leading firms."[9]

In a 1970 lecture commenting on the Neal and Stigler reports, Jesse W. Markham observed that "industries having similar structural characteristics may have widely different behavioral and conduct patterns. . . . This fact alone makes it extremely difficult if not impossible to erect structural standards separating tolerable from intolerable levels of concentration in the hope that the standards will be applicable to industry generally."[10] In other words, even if concentration has a statistically clear and demonstrable effect on price, competition, and profit in various industries, it does not follow that one particular numerical value for a given concentration index will be associated with equally deleterious effects in otherwise different industries.

This point could be based, as Markham chose to do, on an argument in the tradition of Joel Dirlam and Alfred Kahn that identical structures (and thus, necessarily, identical levels of concentration) are consistent with very different types of conduct (see Chapter 6). Alternatively, the Stigler task force posed the argument in structuralist terms: There are many more aspects to structure than concentration alone; thus, the market power of individual firms in a particular industry will depend on such structural factors as barriers to entry, heterogeneity of the product, demand and supply elasticities, cost flexibility, and the state of technology, as well as on the level of concentration. Under either formulation then, antitrust policy should be based on a great deal more than the broad proposition that, other things being equal, high concentration is associated with poor performance.

Even granting the truth of the proposition, other things are not equal. Frederic M. Scherer made the point in the following way: "I know of no economist who holds that this relationship [high concentration leads to high prices] is applicable for every industry at every moment in time. Rather, it is believed to be a statistical tendency— prevailing on the average over a large sample of cases, like (but perhaps stronger than) the tendency for lung cancer to be contracted more frequently by heavy smokers."[11]

The Chicago View of Concentration and Oligopoly Theory

In 1973, Harold Demsetz described the "market concentration doctrine" simply as the widespread belief "that a reliable index of monopoly power can be obtained by measuring the degree to which the output of an industry is produced by a few firms."[12] Demsetz and others of the Chicago school go far beyond Markham, Scherer, and the Stigler task force members, denying that there is acceptable theoretical support for the contention that higher levels of concentration are associated with lower degrees of competition. In addition, they contend that concentration is more often a consequence of economic efficiency than a cause of allocative inefficiency.

The Chicago critics of the concentration doctrine have no quarrel with the elementary theoretical proposition that the effect of monopoly is to raise price and restrict output, *ceteris paribus*. But they maintain that there is no theoretical basis for assuming that as some concentration index increases, price will fall and output rise in some systematic proportion to the increase in the index number.

Chamberlinian Theory and Concentration. The Chamberlinian concept of mutual dependence recognized is most commonly cited to support the view that concentration short of pure monopoly is a source of market power. In *The Theory of Monopolistic Competition*, Edward H. Chamberlin observed that if a monopolistic industry became a duopoly, producing a homogeneous product, and if each firm took full account of its rival's reactions to any attempt to change price or output, both would realize that their long-run advantage lay in setting the monopoly price and sharing in the necessary restriction of output— "the equilibrium result is the same as though there were a monopolistic agreement between them." Overt collusion would not be necessary, and Chamberlin assumed that it did not occur. Full recognition of mutual dependence, however, was considered to be a form of implicit or tacit collusion. "If the sellers are three or more," Chamberlin noted, "the results are the same, so long as each of them looks to his ultimate interest." But, he continued, "There is no gradual descent to a purely competitive price with increase of numbers, as in Cournot's solution. The break comes when the individual's influence on price becomes so small that he neglects it."[13]

This last observation of Chamberlin's has been highlighted by the Chicagoans. The recognition of mutual dependence may vanish when the number of competitors rises from three to four or from eight to nine. The theory gives us no guidance on this matter. Further, if the break occurs between, say, 6 and 7, Chamberlinian theory does not suggest that there will be any significant change in industrywide price and output if the number of firms is increased from 4 to 5, or from 9 to 10. Chamberlin warned his readers that the theory gave no indication as to where this break would occur, or if it would be a clean one: "At what point exactly do the effects of a price cut upon others become 'negligible'? It is undeniable that they are not so when numbers are small and that they become so when numbers are very large. Between these limits the result is unpredictable."[14]

The Debate Continues. Theoretical work done on oligopoly markets since the appearance of Chamberlin's and Joan Robinson's works has not resolved the debate on the concentration doctrine. A survey by John S. McGee concluded that some of these more recent models, particularly those focusing on costs of acquiring information about competitors' behavior and of imposing sanctions on cheaters, support the position that competitiveness increases with the number of firms; others, notably those incorporating conditions of entry and potential competition, show no such relationship. "Thus," McGee concludes, "there are many conflicting theories of oligopoly, and predicted behavior depends crucially on the types of assumptions made."[15]

In a similar vein, Stanley I. Ornstein focused on theories of both overt and tacit collusion, emphasizing the costs of colluding. Collusion presumably will occur when the benefits to the colluders exceed costs, including costs of negotiation, coordination, and enforcement. These costs decrease as the number of colluders becomes smaller. On the other hand, collusive agreements become less stable with increases in product heterogeneity, nonprice competition, cost differences among firms, differences in size and market share, potential for entry, and returns to cheating. "Without a complete theory of oligopoly relating the cost of collusion, concentration, and the cost of competing," he concluded, "it is a heroic assumption to simply relate concentration and collusion."[16]

The Chicago View of Concentration and Economic Efficiency

The Counterproposition. The concentration doctrine, which states that industrial concentration leads to excessively high or rigid prices or to persistent excess profits, is thereby asserting that, in general, concentration is a cause of economic inefficiency. In addition to denying that this proposition has ever been demonstrated, the Chicago school has also made the far more devastating criticism that, to the contrary, economic efficiency is the principal cause of concentration. Robert H. Bork stated this counterproposition in a dissenting comment in the Neal Report:

> When firms grow to sizes that create concentration or when such a structure is created by merger and persists for many years, there is a very strong *prima facie* case that the firms' sizes are related to efficiency. By efficiency I mean "competitive effectiveness" within the bounds of the law, and competitive effectiveness means service to consumers. If the leading firms in a concentrated industry are restricting their output in order to obtain prices above the competitive level, their efficiencies must be sufficiently superior to that of all actual and potential rivals to offset that behavior. Were this not so, rivals would be enabled to expand their market shares because of the abnormally high prices and would thus deconcentrate the industry. Market rivalry thus automatically weighs the respective influences of efficiency and output restriction and arrives at the firm sizes and industry structures that serve consumers best.[17]

In *The Antitrust Paradox,* Bork added, "Today, I would add only two thoughts. First, I doubt that there is any significant output restriction problem arising from the concentration of any industry. Second, there is no coherent theory based on consumer welfare that supports a policy of industrial deconcentration when concentration has been created either by the internal growth of the firms or by merger more than ten or fifteen years old."[18]

Research Pro and Con. Research by Demsetz supports the contention that large firms attain their size and win dominant market shares because they are more efficient than either actual or potential competitors. Demsetz pointed out that a correlation between concentration and profitability is a priori consistent either with market power derived from the level of concentration or with greater efficiency of the larger firms. If the market power hypothesis is correct, all of the firms (large and small alike) in a concentrated industry should enjoy the monopolistic profits. There is, presumably, no way that the large firms could prevent equally efficient small rivals with an identical product from sharing in the profits obtainable from restriction of output and enhancement of price. If, on the other hand, an industry had become concentrated through the superior efficiency of one or a few firms, those dominant firms should be earning higher profits than their less efficient smaller rivals.

To test these two alternative hypotheses, Demsetz classified firms into size groups and calculated correlation coefficients between four-firm concentration ratios and rates of return for each size class. In a sample of 95 industries in 1963 and 69 comparable industries in 1969, he obtained negative correlation coefficients for his smaller size classes and positive correlations for the larger ones. His results are shown in Table 13–1. Demsetz concluded:

> The data strongly suggest that the relatively large firms in concentrated industries produce at lower cost than their smaller rivals. It is difficult to explain how large firms in concentrated industries earn rates of return significantly higher than smaller firms in the same industries without attributing superior performance to the larger firms (whether or not collusion becomes easier in more concentrated markets).[19]

Demsetz's findings have been questioned by non-Chicago critics. He used the broad census three-digit "industry group" classification consisting of 144 such groups for the manufacturing sector. The logic of his test rests on the assumption that the large and small firms in an industry are providing identical products or such close substitutes that the small firms benefit from any price "umbrella" established by the large ones. But in many three-digit groups, the small firms are

TABLE 13-1 Correlations between Rate of Return and Concentration by Asset Size of Firms

1963		1969	
Asset Size ($000)	Correlation Coefficient	Asset Size ($000)	Correlation Coefficient
$50 or less	−.12	Under $10	−.09
50–100	−.24	$10–25	−.10
100–500	−.05	25–50	−.40
500–1,000	+.20	50–100	.00
1,000–2,500	−.03	100–250	−.14
2,500–5,000	−.10	250–500	−.23
5,000–10,000	+.06	500–1,000	−.09
10,000–25,000	+.11	1,000–2,500	−.07
25,000–50,000	+.09	2,500–5,000	−.27
50,000–100,000	+.03	5,000–10,000	.00
100,000–250,000	+.21	10,000–25,000	−.06
250,000 and up	+.21	25,000–35,000	−.05
		35,000–50,000	+.20
		50,000 · 100,000	+.05
		Over 100,000	+.24

SOURCE: Harold Demsetz, *The Market Concentration Doctrine* (Washington, D.C.: American Enterprise Institute for Public Policy Research, 1973), pp. 23, 25.

actually producing quite different products from those of the large ones. For example, SIC 371, motor vehicles and motor vehicle equipment, includes both automobile manufacturers and the many small producers of automotive parts and accessories. Further, since concentration ratios are published only for four-digit industries, a finer classification with 451 manufacturing industries, Demsetz had to calculate weighted-average concentration ratios for his three-digit industries although it has been shown that such weighted-average ratios distort the actual degree of concentration.[20] Finally, the explanatory power of Demsetz's correlation coefficients is quite low.

In 1974 I attempted to verify Demsetz's results for a sample consisting only of firms listed by *Fortune* magazine as among the 500 largest manufacturing firms in the United States and also among the 4 largest in their respective three-digit industry groups, on the ground that these were the firms of interest in testing the policy implications of the concentration doctrine. In other words, I argued that the advocates of deconcentration programs similar to those of the Neal Report might contemplate breaking up the one or two largest firms in an industry but would be most unlikely to impose divestiture on the fourth or to break the giants up into sizes smaller than that of the fourth. (Three-digit industries were used, since the sample would have been much smaller with the finer four-digit classification. Further, the objection involving comparisons of dissimilar firms seemed less serious for a sample confined to *Fortune*'s 500 and the four largest firms.)

Statistically significant results confirming Demsetz's findings occurred only for consumer goods industries, suggesting that the superior efficiency of the larger firms might lie in advertising and product differentiation rather than in production and distribution. In 1966, the largest firm was the most profitable of the big four in 16 out of the 48 industry groups, or in one third of the cases studied. In 1972, the number was 19 out of 49, or 39 percent. Thus, the proportion of instances in which the largest firm was the most profitable far exceeded the chance figure of 25 percent in both years examined; but the frequency with which smaller firms were more profitable suggests that efficiency considerations alone could not account for the general level of concentration.[21]

A subsequent study by John R. Carter, however, lent added support to the efficiency argument. To avoid the criticisms leveled at Demsetz, Carter used four-digit industries and compared average profit rates of the four largest firms with the averages of the next four largest, or those ranking five through eight, in each industry. He found that differences in the average profit rates between his two groups were positively and significantly correlated with concentration, supporting Demsetz's conclusion to the extent that the comparison relevant for deconcentration as a part of antitrust policy is between the largest four firms taken as a group and the next four, rather than within the top four themselves.[22]

Sam Peltzman found that increases in concentration between 1947 and 1967 were positively associated with greater than average declines in both labor and material costs in those industries with rapid sales growth. In industries with little or no growth, on the other hand, he found no significant relationship between changes in concentration and cost reductions. Increases in concentration also led to increases in price-cost margins, corroborating the hypothesis that concentration was positively related to market power. But the cost reduction overwhelmed the increase in the price-cost margin, leading Peltzman to conclude that the efficiency effect identified by Demsetz was far more important than the offsetting market power effect. Peltzman hypothesized that in some industries, one firm or a small number were able to make substantial cost reductions, leading to expansion of both their market shares and sales of the industry's product.[23] Scherer, however, noted that the industries with the highest rates of increase in concentration during the period Peltzman studied were predominantly consumer goods industries and that, by and large, they had not made the sort of cost-reducing innovations posited by Peltzman.[24]

In general, subsequent empirical research bearing on the Chicago school's position has yielded mixed and inconclusive results.

The Third Firm Effect. Bork's assertion that virtually all of the gains in allocative efficiency attributable to competition are likely to be achieved when an industry moves from single-firm monopoly to rivalry between two independent firms, each large enough to compete effectively with the other, recalls John E. Kwoka's finding that CR2 is more closely correlated with profit rates than is any other measure of concentration. Kwoka suggested that the crucial role in injecting competitive behavior might be played by the third rather than second firm. In industries with high CR2, he found, profit margins were reduced sharply when the third firm was large relative to the first two. The problem was that only a few industries have this characteristic. The larger CR2, the less room there is for the third firm to have a relatively high share of the market. Nevertheless, on the basis of a limited number of observations, Kwoka concluded that "industry margins when all three firms are large are much the same as when all are small. Equality of size among three large firms appears to breed a rivalry capable of simulating competitive performance levels."[25]

Disentangling Market Share and Concentration. Several econometric studies have sought to disentangle the effects of market share from those of industry concentration as determinants of a firm's profitability. If one but not the other is included as an explanatory variable in a regression analysis, it may falsely show an effect actually due to the absent variable. In regressions including both as explanatory variables, William G. Shepherd,[26] Bradley T. Gale and Ben S. Branch,[27] and David J. Ravenscraft[28] have all found that market share takes on virtually all of the significance attributed to industry concentration in previous studies that did not include a market share variable. Branch and Gale, along with Ravenscraft, interpreted their results as supporting Demsetz's position that superior efficiency rather than market power is the source of the observed higher profits. Shepherd, however, rejected this interpretation, contending that the market share of an individual firm is a better measure of its monopolistic power than is the level of concentration of the industry as a whole. He thus considered his findings consistent with the older view that market power is the primary source of above-normal long-run earnings.[29]

The logic behind interpreting a large market share as an indication of market power not enjoyed by all of the firms in an industry requires rejecting the umbrella hypothesis—that smaller firms are usually able to bask under a price umbrella erected by their larger rivals. Product differentiation, market segmentation, and perhaps bargaining power in setting collusive agreements may all give larger firms a higher degree of market power than that available to smaller firms classified as being in the same industry.[30] Richard E. Caves and Michael E. Porter's distinction between barriers to entry into an industry and barriers to mobility of firms within an industry (see Chapter 7) suggests that the latter may be an important phenomenon protecting larger firms from the competition of their smaller rivals.[31]

Ravenscraft's analysis was based on the Federal Trade Commission's line of business data. Two subsequent studies using that same data base came to different conclusions. Employing dummy variables for both firms and industries, Richard Schmalensee found that unspecified effects attributable to phenomena at both the firm and the industry levels were significant determinants of industry rates of return; but his analysis was incapable of determining whether concentration was one of these industry effects.[32] John T. Scott and George Pascoe noted that rate of return on assets should decline as the ratio of assets to sales increases, for any given degree of power to raise price over marginal cost. Market power is the power to control price, yet the objective of a profit-maximizing firm is to maximize the rate of return on owners' investment, or on its assets in the absence of debt, for any given asset base. In regression analysis in which the asset-to-sales ratio and the debt-to-equity ratio were both included as control variables, Scott and Pascoe found that the rate of return on assets rose significantly with industry concentration.[33]

Ravenscraft, Schmalensee, and Scott and Pascoe all recognize that one serious limitation of the line of business data is its short time span. The program collected data only for the years 1973 through 1977 before being terminated under President Reagan's administration. Yet the underlying theory recognizes that short-run profits will result from all sorts of disequilibrium shifts in demand and supply and that only persistent, long-run profits are necessarily attributable to the exercise of market power. To make matters worse, 1973–77 was a turbulent period of recession and recovery.

Replacing Profit with Price. A 1983 article by Franklin M. Fisher and John J. McGowan argued that accounting conventions—especially depreciation methods—lead to such serious differences between accounting rates of return (net income divided by undepreciated cost of assets) and the economic rate of return (the discount rate that sets the present value of the expected income stream equal to the original investment) that "examination of absolute or relative accounting rates of return to draw conclusions about monopoly profits is a totally misleading enterprise."[34] While subsequent articles maintain that Fisher and McGowan have exaggerated the seriousness of the shortcomings of accounting profits,[35] no one denies that the divergence from economic profits is real and often large.

A promising alternative to comparison of reported profits is comparison of the prices charged in highly concentrated markets and others.

Such comparisons cannot be made among different products. But in a few cases, investigators have been able to identify separate markets in which identical or very similar products are sold, sometimes by the same firms.

Reuben Kessel studied the tax-exempt bond market, taking the number of underwriters who bid on various issues as an index of concentration.[36] He found that the underwriter's spread, or gross fee, declined smoothly with the number of bidders, supporting the general notion that concentration reflects market power but contradicting Chamberlin's view that recognition of mutual dependence should keep prices at the joint profit-maximizing level until some critical number of competitors is reached. Howard P. Marvel compared gasoline retail prices in 22 cities and found that the prices rose with the Herfindahl index for a particular city.[37] The effects were more marked and statistically significant for regular gasoline than for premium.

Peter J. Meyer and a group of researchers compared grocery prices in neighborhood markets in the Santa Cruz and Berkeley areas of California.[38] They found that prices in monopolized markets and those with only two supermarkets were substantially higher than prices in neighborhoods with three or more stores. But there were no significant differences in the single-store and two-store markets. In several instances, stores owned by the same chain had higher prices in monopolized markets than in competitive ones. Further, the stores in competitive neighborhood markets had a better selection and, in the field researchers' judgment, cleaner premises and better services.

Summary

Overall, the empirical work gives limited support to the Chicago view. The traditional view that market power matters seems unshaken. Whether this power can be exercised by only one pure monopolist or can be effectively shared among two, three, or some other number of the larger firms in an industry is uncertain. Probably, the critical number or market share varies from industry to industry, depending on elasticity of demand for the product, ease of entry and intraindustry mobility, economies of scale, homogeneity of product, and other structural features. Thus, the Chicagoans' contention that differences in profitability among U.S. firms are almost inevitably the result of differences in efficiency and not in market power has not been sustained. But the view that individual market share matters as much if not more than industry concentration has held up well; and, in some markets at least, large shares have been won by superior efficiency. The statistical difficulties in ascertaining how frequently this occurs are formidable. Finally, the relation between concentration and economic performance is more complex than presumed in the simpler versions of the concentration doctrine.

THE EFFICIENCY DOCTRINE

The Chicago school's attack on the concentration doctrine centers on the contention that economic efficiency is the primary cause of concentration, coupled with a denial that any systematic relationship has been shown to exist between concentration short of pure single-firm monopoly and poor economic performance. This attack has led to a public policy position labeled the "efficiency doctrine."

The gist of the efficiency doctrine is that the sole purpose of antitrust laws should be to promote economic efficiency. For most members of the Chicago school, economic efficiency is clearly equated with maximization of economic benefits to consumers. Bork, for example, asserts that the responsibility of the courts "requires that they take consumer welfare as the sole value that guides antitrust decisions."[39] Consumer welfare, in turn, is determined by two types of economic efficiency: allocative and productive. Bork concludes, therefore, that "the whole task of antitrust can be summed up as the effort to improve allocative efficiency without impairing productive efficiency so greatly as to produce either no gain or a net loss in consumer welfare."[40]

McGee similarly argues that current antitrust policy would be much more "sensible" if the only legal criterion was "efficiency, broadly considered." But he does not define efficiency any more narrowly than to note that the objective is to "maximize economic benefit."[41] Posner states that " 'efficiency' means exploiting economic resources in such a way that 'value'—human satisfaction *as measured by aggregate consumer willingness to pay for goods and services*—is maximized."[42]

The Welfare Triangle

These views of economic efficiency are illustrated in Figure 13–1 by a graphical construct known as the welfare triangle. The figure depicts long-run equilibrium, in which case it is not unreasonable to assume perfect mobility of capital and constant returns to scale, or a horizontal long-run marginal cost schedule for the industry as a whole. (This assumption is unnecessary for any of the analytical conclusions reached here, but is commonly made for expositional convenience. Similarly, the demand curve is drawn as a straight line merely for simplicity.)

The competitive equilibrium in Figure 13–1, with price equal to marginal cost, is shown by the output Q_c and the price P_c, where P_c is equal to long-run average as well as marginal cost. Marshallian con-

FIGURE 13–1 The Welfare Triangle

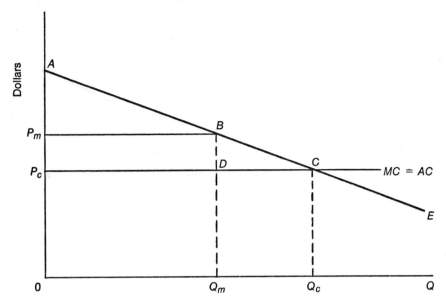

sumer surplus—defined as the excess of the price that consumers would be willing to pay over actual price, summed for all consumers at the quantity actually purchased—is represented by the large triangle ACP_c, where AC represents a segment of the market demand curve AE. The social efficiency of competition is illustrated by noting that if the rate of production increased beyond Q_c, the costs of producing extra units of the product (MC) would exceed the added value to consumers (the demand segment CE).

If there was enough monopoly power in the industry to raise the price to P_m, restricting output to Q_m, consumer surplus would fall by the area P_mBCP_c. Assuming no changes in costs or demand resulting from concentration, producer surplus (monopolistic profit) would rise by the rectangle P_mBDP_c. The so-called deadweight social loss, then, is shown by the small triangle BCD, equal to the decline in consumer surplus minus the offsetting gain in producer surplus.

As implied in measuring the net social loss only by the area of the "welfare" triangle BCD, this brand of welfare analysis is absolutely value free. Rectangle P_mBDP_c, representing the wealth transferred from consumers to producers as a result of the latter's market power, does not reflect any social loss, since there are no objective grounds for preferring the welfare of consumers to that of producers. Some readers may regard this neutrality as offensive, but it reinforces the point that the goal of economic efficiency can be distinguished from

other economic or social goals such as equity in income distribution—
a distinction the Chicagoans contend is essential to proper antitrust
policy.

The wealth transfer, rectangle $P_m BDP_c$ in Figure 13–1, is likely
to be many times larger than the welfare triangle BCD. The area of
BCD, designated as DW for deadweight loss, can be approximated by
the expression

$$DW = 1/2 \cdot \left(\frac{P_m - P_c}{P}\right)^2 \cdot P \cdot Q \cdot \eta$$

where η equals the absolute value of the market elasticity of demand.
The expression $(P_m - P_c)/P$ represents the percentage change in price
brought about by the increase in monopolistic market power; and
$P \cdot Q$ approximates total sales revenue of the industry.[43]

The wealth transfer, designated by WT, is equal to $(P_m - P_c) \cdot Q_m$.

Assuming small changes, so that Q_m is approximately equal to Q,
we obtain

$$\frac{DW}{WT} = 1/2 \cdot \frac{P_m - P_c}{P} \cdot \eta$$

Suppose that the market power in a particular industry is great
enough to raise price by 25 percent above the competitive level. If
$\eta = 1$, $DW/WT = .125$, or the wealth transfer will be eight times as
large as the deadweight loss. If the price is raised by only 10 percent,
still assuming unit elasticity of demand, the wealth transfer will exceed
the deadweight loss by a factor of 20. Virtually all plausible values
for the elasticity of market demand and the percentage increases in
price associated with increases in market power short of pure monopoly
will yield results in which WT is much larger than DW.

The Social Costs of Monopoly

Posner has argued that the case for a vigorous antitrust policy based
solely on considerations of efficiency is considerably strengthened by
recognizing that a rectangle such as $P_m BDP_c$ represents the potential
or actual gains from monopolization rather than a transfer from consumers to the owners of the firms in the monopolized industry. Such
monopoly gains, Posner notes, have a tendency to be converted into
social costs. These gains are not costless to obtain and will be sought
by knowledgeable profit maximizers until the marginal cost of monopolizing is equal to the marginal gain available from obtaining further market power. Costs of monopolizing include those of cartel for-

mation and maintenance, erection of barriers to entry and efforts to overcome these barriers, and the forms of nonprice competition used to maintain or expand the various firms' shares of a lucrative market. Posner concludes that an area such as P_mBDP_c is "at best a rough approximation of the actual costs resulting from the competition to become a monopolist,"[44] which may turn out to be somewhat smaller or larger. In any event, these costs are safely assumed to be substantially in excess of the deadweight loss. Other Chicagoans, including Bork, accept Posner's point and agree, although with varying degrees of enthusiasm, that it does strengthen the case for antitrust. Bork has pointed out that taking these costs into account makes very little difference to the actual application of the efficiency doctrine, since there is invariably a deadweight loss associated with any successful effort to obtain monopoly power, regardless of the cost of this effort.[45]

The costs of acquiring and maintaining monopoly power may not represent complete social waste. Posner has also noted that firms may seek to deter entry as well as increase their market shares through product improvement and better service. To the extent that this enhances the product's value to consumers, resources expended on market control provide a real benefit to society. Posner concludes, however, that expenditures for establishing and perpetuating positions of market dominance are largely wasteful from society's point of view. He cites, as an extreme example, the experience of airlines operating under regulations that required prices far above competitive levels. The potential monopoly gains were competed away entirely by nonprice competition, particularly by providing an excessive number of flights. Passengers benefited from the added convenience, but empty seats reflected the waste involved.[46]

One of the efficiency doctrine's basic tenets is that market power often results from the greater efficiency of large firms. Society's trade-off, in such an instance, can be illustrated by a welfare triangle such as Figure 13–2, where $P_c = C_c$ represents both price and long-run marginal cost under competition. Partial monopolization raises the price to P_m; but at the same time, real economies of scale associated with the reduction in the number of firms in the industry reduce marginal cost to C_m. Neglecting the extent to which resources are wastefully expended to achieve market power, or treating P_mACP_c as a transfer of wealth, a pure welfare trade-off remains between the deadweight loss ABC and a real resource saving of C_cCDC_m. Oliver E. Williamson has shown that under reasonable assumptions as to elasticity of demand, the favorable welfare effects of small percentage reductions in cost can offset the unfavorable effects of much larger increases in price.[47]

FIGURE 13–2 The Welfare Triangle and Social Gain from Decreased Cost

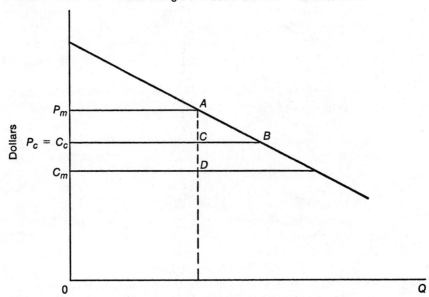

Summary

While the efficiency doctrine sets very different criteria for appropriate antitrust activities from those of the concentration doctrine, an emphasis on economic efficiency in and of itself in no way weakens the underlying case against tolerating monopolistic restraints on output and enhancement of price. But when coupled with the Chicago school's assumptions that competition among a few firms may be just as effective as competition among many and that efficiency is the primary cause of concentration, the efficiency doctrine does suggest that structural remedies are usually inappropriate in instances short of pure monopoly and that the major job of the antitrust authorities should be to control or eliminate overtly collusive conduct.

THE CHICAGO CONTRIBUTION IN RETROSPECT

The new learning is not necessarily the last word. But a fresh and invigorating challenge has been laid down to the relevance of oligopoly theories, to interpretation of statistical relationships between industrial concentration and economic performance, to identification of sources of efficiency related to economies of scale, and to determination of the scope of competitive or collusive behavior among the large firms in concentrated industries. An indisputable contribution of the Chicago school's new learning is its contribution to the research agenda of industrial organization.

ENDNOTES

[1]For an insider's review and evaluation of the Chicago school's contribution to antitrust economics and policy, see Richard A. Posner, "The Chicago School of Antitrust Analysis," and Richard R. Nelson, "Comments on a Paper by Posner," *University of Pennsylvania Law Review* 27, no. 4 (April 1979), pp. 925–52. For a broader perspective on the Chicago school's development and overall approach to economics, see Melvin W. Reder, "Chicago Economics: Permanence and Change," *Journal of Economic Literature* 20, no. 1 (March 1982), pp. 1–38.

[2]Edward S. Mason, "Price and Production Policies of Large-Scale Enterprise," *American Economic Review* 29, no. 1 (March 1939), part 2, pp. 61–74, at p. 69.

[3]Gideon Rosenbluth, "Measures of Concentration," in *Business Concentration and Price Policy,* National Bureau of Economic Research (Princeton, N.J.: Princeton University Press, 1955), pp. 57–95.

[4]For leading examples of research relating structure to performance that were not limited to concentration as the single explanatory structural variable, see Joe S. Bain, *Barriers to New Competition* (Cambridge, Mass.: Harvard University Press, 1956); H. Michael Mann, "Seller Concentration, Barriers to Entry, and Rates of Return in Thirty Industries," *Review of Economics and Statistics* 48, no. 3 (August 1966), pp. 296–307; William S. Comanor and Thomas A. Wilson, "Advertising, Market Power, and Performance," *Review of Economics and Statistics* 49, no. 4 (November 1967), pp. 423–40. Multiple regression techniques, allowing for use of several independent variables, are now commonplace.

[5]Leonard W. Weiss, "The Concentration-Profits Relationship and Antitrust," in *Industrial Concentration: The New Learning,* ed. Henry J. Goldschmid, H. Michael Mann, and J. Fred Weston (Boston: Little, Brown, 1974), pp. 184–233, at pp. 201–22.

[8]*Report of the Task Force on Productivity and Competition,* February 1969, reprinted in *Antitrust Law and Economics Review* 2, no. 3 (Spring 1969), pp. 13–52, at pp. 25–6.

[7]Ibid., p. 29.

[8]*Report of the Task Force on Productivity and Competition,* February 1969, reprinted in *Antitrust Law and Economic Review* 2, no. 3 (Spring 1969), pp. 13–52, at pp. 25–6.

[9]Ibid., p. 26.

[10]Jesse W. Markham, "Structure versus Conduct Criteria in Antitrust," in *Antitrust Policy and Economic Welfare,* ed. Werner Sichel (Ann Arbor, Mich.: Bureau of Business Research, Graduate School of Business Administration, University of Michigan, 1970), pp. 102–18, at pp. 106–7.

[11]Frederic M. Scherer, "Structure-Performance Relationships and Antitrust Policy," *Industrial Concentration and the Market System,* ed. Eleanor M. Fox and James T. Halverson (Chicago: American Bar Association Press, 1979), pp. 128–36, at p. 128.

[12]Harold Demsetz, *The Market Concentration Doctrine* (Washington, D.C.: American Enterprise Institute for Public Policy Research, 1973), p. 2.

[13]Edward H. Chamberlin, *The Theory of Monopolistic Competition* (Cambridge, Mass.: Harvard University Press, 1933), p. 48.

[14]Ibid., pp. 53.

[15]John S. McGee, *In Defense of Industrial Concentration* (New York: Praeger Publishers, 1971), p. 74.

[16]Stanley I. Ornstein, "Concentration and Profits," in *The Impact of Large Firms*

on the U.S. Economy, ed. J. Fred Weston and Stanley I. Ornstein (Lexington, Mass.: D. C. Heath, 1977), pp. 87–102, at p. 88.

[17]*Report of the White House Task Force,* p. 54.

[18]Robert H. Bork, *The Antitrust Paradox: A Policy at War with Itself* (New York: Basic Books, 1978), p. 178.

[19]Demsetz, *The Market Concentration Doctrine,* p. 22.

[20]Eugene M. Singer, *Antitrust Economics* (Englewood Cliffs, N.J.: Prentice-Hall, 1968), pp. 167–74; Stanley E. Boyle, "The Average Concentration Ratio: An Inappropriate Measure of Industry Structure," *Journal of Political Economy* 81, no. 2 (March–April 1973), part 1 pp. 414–26.

[21]William L. Baldwin, "Industrial Structure, Size and Rates of Return among *Fortune*'s 500: Some Implications for Antitrust," *Industrial Organization Review* 2, no. 3 (1974), pp. 169–85.

[22]John R. Carter, "Collusion, Efficiency, and Antitrust," *Journal of Law and Economics* 21, no. 2 (October 1978), pp. 435–44.

[23]Sam Peltzman, "The Gains and Losses from Industrial Concentration," *Journal of Law and Economics* 20, no. 2 (October 1977), pp. 229–63. See also Steven Lustgarten, "Gains and Losses from Concentration: A Comment," *Journal of Law and Economics* 22, no. 1 (April 1979), pp. 183–90.

[24]Frederic M. Scherer, "The Causes and Consequences of Rising Industrial Concentration," *Journal of Law and Economics* 22, no. 1 (April 1979), pp. 191–211.

[25]John E. Kwoka, "The Effect of Market Share Distribution on Industry Performance," *Review of Economics and Statistics* 61, no. 1 (February 1979), pp. 101–9, at p. 107. For a critical rejoinder, see Willard F. Mueller and Douglas F. Greer, "The Effect of Market Share Distribution on Industry Performance Reexamined," *Review of Economics and Statistics* 66, no. 2 (May 1984), pp. 353–58. Mueller and Greer find that the share of the fourth firm, when added to CR2, has virtually the same statistical effect as the share of the third and that most of the statistical significance of Kwoka's findings vanish when separate regressions are run for consumer goods and producer goods industries. Further, they argue that Kwoka may not have identified the largest firms in regional and local market industries, since he used national concentration figures.

[26]William G. Shepherd, "The Elements of Market Structure," *Review of Economics and Statistics* 54, no. 1 (February 1972), pp. 25–37.

[27]Bradley T. Gale and Ben S. Branch, "Concentration versus Market Share: Which Determines Performance and Does It Matter?" *Antitrust Bulletin* 27, no. 1 (Spring 1982), pp. 83–105.

[28]David J. Ravenscraft, "Structure-Profit Relationships at the Line of Business and Industry Level," *Review of Economics and Statistics* 65, no. 1 (February 1983), pp. 22–31.

[29]For a more recent statement on this matter than his 1972 article, see William G. Shepherd, *The Economics of Industrial Organization* (Englewood Cliffs, N.J.: Prentice-Hall, 1985), pp. 129–30.

[30]For a leading discussion, see Bradley T. Gale, "Market Share and Rate of Return," *Review of Economics and Statistics* 54, no. 4 (November 1972), pp. 412–23.

[31]Richard E. Caves and Michael E. Porter, "From Entry Barriers to Mobility Barriers," *Quarterly Journal of Economics* 91, no. 2 (May 1977), pp. 241–61.

[32]Richard Schmalensee, "Do Markets Differ Much?" *American Economic Review* 75, no. 3 (June 1985), pp. 341–51.

[33]John T. Scott and George Pascoe, "Beyond Firm and Industry Effects on Profitability in Imperfect Markets," *Review of Economics and Statistics* 68, no. 2 (May 1986), pp. 284–92.

[34]Franklin M. Fisher and John J. McGowan, "On the Misuse of Accounting Rates of Return to Infer Monopoly Profits," *American Economic Review* 73, no. 1 (March 1983), pp. 82–97, at p. 91.

[35]See comments by Ira Horowitz, William F. Long and David J. Ravenscraft, Stephen Martin, and Michael F. van Breda, and rejoinder by Fisher, in *American Economic Review* 74, no. 3 (June 1984), pp. 492–517; Gerald L. Salamon, "Accounting Rates of Return," *American Economic Review* 75, no. 3 (June 1985), pp. 495–504.

[36]Reuben Kessel, "A Study of the Effects of Competition in the Tax-Exempt Bond Market," *Journal of Political Economy* 79, no. 4 (July–August 1971), pp. 706–38.

[37]Howard P. Marvel, "Competition and Price Levels in the Retail Gasoline Market," *Review of Economics and Statistics* 60, no. 2 (May 1978), pp. 252–58. For a discussion of Kessel's, Marvel's, and another study, see also Frederick E. Geithman, Howard P. Marvel, and Leonard W. Weiss, "Concentration, Price, and Critical Concentration Ratios," *Review of Economics and Statistics* 63, no. 3 (August 1981), pp. 346–53.

[38]Peter J. Meyer, "Concentration and Performance in Local Retail Markets," in *Industrial Organization, Antitrust, and Public Policy*, ed. John V. Craven (Boston: Kluwer-Nijhoff, 1983), pp. 145–61.

[39]Bork, *The Antitrust Paradox*, p. 51.

[40]Ibid., p. 91.

[41]McGee, *In Defense*, pp. 136–37.

[42]Richard A. Posner, *Economic Analysis of Law*, 2d ed. (Boston: Little, Brown, 1977), p. 10.

[43]By construction,

$$DW = 1/2 \cdot (P_m - P_c) \cdot (Q_c - Q_m) \tag{13.1F}$$

By definition,

$$\eta = \frac{dQ}{dP} \cdot \frac{P}{Q}$$

Let $P_m - P_c \approx dP$, and $Q_c - Q_m \approx dQ$. Dividing both sides of Equation 13.1F by $\eta \cdot P$, we obtain

$$\frac{DW}{\eta \cdot P} = 1/2 \cdot \left(\frac{P_m - P_c}{P}\right)^2 \cdot Q \tag{13.2F}$$

[44]Richard A. Posner, *Antitrust Law: An Economic Perspective* (Chicago: University of Chicago Press, 1976), p. 13.

[45]Bork, *The Antitrust Paradox*, p. 113.

[46]Posner, *Economic Analysis*, 2d ed., pp. 202–4.

[47]Oliver E. Williamson, "Economics as an Antitrust Defense: The Welfare Trade-offs," *American Economic Review* 58, no. 1 (March 1968), pp. 18–36.

CHAPTER FOURTEEN

Organization and Strategy of the Firm

Both the concentration doctrine and the Chicago school's new learning follow the structure-conduct-performance paradigm in focusing on the organization of an entire industry; that is, how business firms interact with suppliers, customers, and competitors within various markets. The internal organization of the firm is taken as given in both approaches. But ever since 1932 when Adolf A. Berle, Jr. and Gardiner C. Means first examined the shift from owner to management control in the modern corporation, industrial organization economists have been concerned with corporate control, mainly because control is assumed to affect the degree to which firms are profit maximizers. In recent years, there has been greater interest in the processes by which firms' internal organizations respond to changes in the economic environment (structure) and how changes in organization in turn influence firms' strategies and performance.[1]

TRANSACTIONS, MARKETS, AND FIRMS

One of the most fundamental economic activities is the exchange transaction. Presumably, completion of any voluntary exchange leaves both parties better off. Exchanges can be categorized in various ways: for example, monetary exchanges and barter exchanges; ephemeral exchanges, such as the sale and purchase of a bag of groceries, and exchanges that continue until expressly terminated by one party, such as employment.

Transactions and the Nature of the Business Firm

Ronald H. Coase, seeking to apply the concept of the transaction to an understanding of the business firm, noted in a 1937 article that price was thought of as the coordinating mechanism in a market economy, in that resource use depended on relative market prices. Yet, he continued, resource flows within the firm were determined quite differently. A worker moves from one department to another because ordered to do so rather than in response to a change in relative prices. Outside of the firm, economic activity is coordinated by market exchange transactions; within the firm, direction is substituted for voluntary exchange. These considerations led Coase to define the business firm as "a system of relationships which comes into existence when the direction of resources is dependent on an entrepreneur."[2]

That definition was merely a prelude to the central question of Coase's article. If market exchange and entrepreneurial authority are alternative ways of setting resources to work, why do firms come into being? (Or, to turn the question around, why is all production not centralized in one huge firm?) Coase concluded that the main reason for establishment of firms is to avoid the costs to individual economic agents of ascertaining relevant prices. Further, the costs of negotiating each transaction separately are eliminated. Workers, for example, are employed not to do specific jobs with specific remuneration set for each task but rather are offered periodic wages in exchange for agreeing to obey the entrepreneur's orders within predetermined limits. Also, if supplies are purchased on short-term (say, day-to-day) contracts, renegotiation costs may be high and supply uncertain. Alternatively, as conditions change, long-term supply contracts may lock the purchaser into unsuitable contractual provisions. Internal production of material may reduce costs of both acquisition and risk while preserving flexibility. In all, Coase doubted that the business firm would even have been devised in the absence of uncertainty.

Given these advantages of internal coordination, why do markets continue to exist? There are, Coase pointed out, diseconomies of management. The larger the number of transactions being organized internally, the greater the cost of organizing still another. Growing complexity within the firm leads to increased inefficiencies. Further, the costs of hiring some factors of production might rise with size of the firm. People with managerial skills, for example, may prefer to run their own firms.

Ideally, firms should expand up to the point at which the internal organization of one more transaction would cost the firm just as much as obtaining the same commodity or service through an exchange transaction on the market.

The traditional theory of the firm, Coase observed, held that, in a perfectly competitive market, firm size would be limited by rising costs of production, since profit would be maximized by expanding output up to the point where the product's marginal cost equaled its price. In other markets, firm size would be limited by declining marginal revenue, which would fall below marginal cost at some level of sales and production even if marginal cost did not rise. The flaw in this view, however, is that the firm can produce more than one product. The limit on size, therefore, is instead determined by the relative costs of internal and external coordination of resource flows.

Transactional Analysis and Internal Organization

Until Oliver E. Williamson's 1975 work, *Markets and Hierarchies: Analysis and Antitrust Implications,* there was virtually no follow-up on Coase's provocative article. As the title indicates, Williamson concentrates on distinguishing between transactions carried out in markets and those occurring in hierarchical (intrafirm) settings. Like Coase, he views the transaction as fundamental to any economic analysis; and he notes the need for development of a "transactional paradigm."[3]

Organizational Failure. Williamson centers his analysis on the concept of organizational failure—either market failure or internal organization failure. Market failure simply means a situation in which a transaction can be consummated more efficiently within a firm; an internal organization failure depicts the opposite situation.

Williamson cites two basic causes of organizational failure: bounded rationality and opportunism. The concept of bounded rationality recognizes that even human behavior intended to be rational is limited or bounded by (1) the ability to acquire, recall, assimilate, and use information correctly and (2) the ability to communicate accurately. Opportunism recognizes that individuals acting in their own self-interest may withhold, misrepresent, or distort information. Bounded rationality coupled with opportunism gives rise to the pervasive problem of information impactedness—when one of two parties to a prospective transaction has more information than the other and cannot be relied on to reveal it.

The human factors of bounded rationality and opportunism lead to market failure only in the presence of certain environmental conditions—uncertainty, complexity, and small numbers involved in the exchange nexus. Uncertainty as to the future and complexity of the transaction mean that contractual agreements negotiated in open market settings may involve contingent provisions and claims that, because of bounded rationality, are difficult to frame, interpret, and enforce, even presuming good faith on both sides. Such problems are compounded by opportunism. In the absence of the small-numbers condition, opportunism is not a serious source of market inefficiency; when new transactions are negotiated, opportunists will simply be bypassed in favor of competitors who deal candidly and in good faith. For similar reasons, information impactedness is alleviated as the number of market participants grows and competition in the sale of information therefore increases.

Intrafirm Transactions. The substitution of intrafirm hierarchical transactions for market transactions may overcome problems of bounded rationality in several ways. Internal organization permits adaptive and sequential decisions to be made more easily and flexibly than would be the case with either frequently negotiated spot transactions or complex contingent long-term contracts. This advantage holds for both labor and materials. In comparison with long-term contracts, internal control economizes on decision-making capacity because managers need be concerned only with actual events, not with all possible outcomes. Further, internal organization may routinize repetitive transactions, ensuring understanding of all involved with minimal communication; language within an organization may be reduced to a code. Finally, people in the same organization are more likely to share expectations of a transaction's effect.

Williamson notes that internal organization has three advantages in coping with opportunism. First, employees have less incentive to behave opportunistically than those engaging in market transactions since they are not normally in positions to make immediate financial gain by doing so. Second, internal organizations can more effectively monitor how well various parties are living up to their agreements, particularly since an internal auditor is allowed more freedom of action and access than an external auditor. Third, disputes between members of the same organization usually can be mediated easily and informally—or settled by arbitrary decision of those in authority. Such decisions by fiat, impossible in resolving market disputes, are far more efficient (even if less equitable) than formal and legalistic mediation between two independent parties.

Causes of Internal Organizational Failure. To complete his analysis, Williamson (as Coase before him) had to address the question of why firms reached limits of efficient size. In his terminology, he had to identify causes of internal organizational failure. He cited several such causes, including inefficiencies of internal procurement, biases toward program persistence and unwarranted expansion, limits on managers' span of control, and bureaucratic insularity. All are affected by problems of distorted communications and by conflicts between rational pursuit of subgroup goals and those of the overall organization.

Internal Procurement and Program Persistence. If a firm owns and operates its own supply sources, it eventually becomes biased against market procurement. Even if managers know that outside procurement would be less costly or would provide a superior product, they may hesitate to advise abolishing their own subgroup. Intrafirm reciprocity ("I'll help your subgroup if you'll do the same for mine") favors internal procurement. And similar considerations allow other programs and projects to persist in the face of preferable market alternatives.

Unwarranted Expansion. Mediation favors inefficient expansion when compromises give both subgroups at least some of what they want. Since internal disputes frequently involve control of resources and allocation of organizational functions, such compromises typically are expansionary and inefficient. (In *Markets and Hierarchies*, Williamson did not discuss the problem of unwarranted expansion initiated by top management out of self-interest in the perquisites and personal satisfactions gained from control of a large enterprise or large subgroup, but he has dealt at length with this phenomenon elsewhere.[4])

Span of Control and Bureaucratic Insularity. One aspect of bounded rationality is that an individual manager can supervise only a limited number of individuals and activities. Consequently, expansion requires a larger and more complex hierarchical superstructure, thus increasing the chance that ultimate decision makers will get distorted, incomplete, inaccurate, or out-of-date information. Further, growth of the hierarchy reduces top management's ability to control and coordinate subgroups, fostering bureaucratic insularity and thereby exacerbating such problems as excessive emphasis on subgroup goals and impersonality in intrafirm exchanges that lessen the advantages of internal over open market transactions. In such a setting, opportunism may lead subgroup managers to transmit deliberately misleading information to protect themselves from the unfavorable attention of top management or to bias their information in favor of their subgroups.

For Williamson as for Coase, technical considerations do not determine optimum firm size. Rather, the optimum size is determined by a balance between stimuli to growth (including vertical integration and product diversification) stemming from market failures and the offsetting constraints and incentives to rely on markets stemming from internal organization failures.

BUSINESS STRATEGY AND FIRM STRUCTURE

In two books widely acclaimed for their insightful analyses, Alfred D. Chandler examined the internal organization of the business firm from the viewpoint of U.S. economic history.[5] Through the 1840s, Chandler notes, business forms, practices, and institutions changed little from those "which had evolved to meet the growth of trade and the coming of market economies in the Mediterranean basin in the twelfth and thirteenth centuries,"[6] largely because merchandise trade remained the predominant form of large-scale business.

The Organizational Revolution: Development of the Managerial Hierarchy

The need for a managerial hierarchy—formally organized and assigned specific duties, including the coordination and supervision of the work of lower managers—first arose in the 1850s with the emergence of large railroad lines. The earlier railroads, normally between 30 and 50 miles long, sometimes with only a single train and thus only one-way traffic, employed about 50 workers and could be administered by one superintendent and a few functional managers. When railroads grew to some 500 miles in length, with a number of trains going in both directions each day, often on a single track and without telegraphic signals, problems of scheduling and freight handling became complex.

By the outbreak of the Civil War, modern forms of hierarchical management had spread through the nation's long-haul railroads. "Middle and top managers supervised, coordinated, and evaluated the work of lower level managers who were directly responsible for the day-to-day operations," Chandler noted. "No private business enterprise with as many managers or with as complex an internal organization existed in the United States—nor, except for railroads in Britain and western Europe, in any other part of the world."[7]

Hierarchical, structured, and specialized management spread first to other forms of transportation (initially to steamship lines and then to urban public transportation systems) and to the communication industries (the postal service, telegraph, and telephone). In these sectors, as in railroading, new managerial forms had to be developed to coordinate flows through large complex networks. Improved transportation and communication services linked the nation and facilitated the burgeoning mass distribution and marketing of goods from raw farm commodities through manufactured consumer products. As a result, the new forms of management were adopted by commodity trading houses, wholesale jobbing firms, and mass retailing department stores. Last, the organizational revolution spread to manufacturing, as the new technologies of transportation and communication inexorably made mass production more economically and technically feasible.

Strategy and Structure. Chandler analyzes this process through a paradigm involving his concepts of strategy and structure. Strategy is defined as "the determination of the basic long-term goals and objectives of an enterprise, and the adoption of courses of action and the allocation of resources necessary for carrying out these goals."[8] Strategy evolves to meet new opportunities and challenges posed by changes in a firm's economic environment—developments in technology, markets, other institutions, population, and national income. In sharp distinction to its meaning in the structure-conduct-performance paradigm, structure is defined as "the design of the organization through which the enterprise is administered," including "first, the lines of authority and communication between the different administrative offices and officers and, second, the information and data that flow through these lines of communication and authority."[9] Thus, business strategy is formulated to meet new external conditions, and the firm's organizational structure evolves in response to changing strategies. (From here on, a modifier such as *organizational* or *firm* will be attached to the word *structure* whenever it is being used in the Chandlerian sense, to distinguish it from market or industrial structure.)

The Influence of the Organization on the Economic Environment

In his 1977 book, Chandler adds another extremely significant step to the process: structural changes in organizations feed back on the economic environment, altering industrial structures throughout the economy. Two stages in this feedback process are relevant to industrial organization: (1) the initial impact of the widespread adoption of hierarchical organization by large manufacturing firms and (2) more recent changes made possible by the 20th century's major innovation in organizational structure—the multidivisional firm.

Integration and the Merger Movement. "In modern mass production," Chandler notes, contrary to the conventional wisdom, "economies resulted more from speed than from size."[10] To obtain these economies of speed, manufacturers not only had to coordinate activities and material flows within the plant but had to assure reliable and prompt provision of raw materials. Further, to avoid inventory pileups, manufacturers needed reliable channels of wholesale and retail distribution. Thus, the mass-production manufacturers came into close and sustained contact with the mass traders of commodities and the merchandisers of finished goods. The result was integration. Such integration, as it turned out, led to more efficient management of high-speed flows from raw materials through sale of finished products; but Chandler notes that the first industrial firms to integrate vertically, both upstream into supply of raw materials and downstream into mass distribution of their products, did not do so in pursuit of these economies but rather because existing merchandisers could not expand to meet their growing needs.

Integration, and the resulting growth in firm size, took place through both internal expansion and merger. "Some small single-unit firms," Chandler observed, "moved directly into building their own national and global marketing networks and extensive purchasing organizations and obtaining their own sources of raw materials and transportation facilities."[11] Others, however, first expanded to nationwide scope by merger with similar firms, centralized the management of the combined enterprise, and then integrated backward and forward.

But simple horizontal merger, whether in pursuit of economies of scale or monopoly power, rarely succeeded. Rather, successful mergers "consolidated production, centralized its administration, and built their own marketing and purchasing organizations. And they operated in industries where technology and markets permitted such integration to increase the speed and lower the cost of materials through the processes of production and distribution."[12] In the process, the U.S. economy was transformed into one with modern levels of industrial concentration.

The Multidivisional Organizational Structure. The second major historical development in modern U.S. business organization—the creation and spread of the multidivisional form—began in the years immediately following World War I. Chandler details the administrative reorganizations of the four pioneers: Du Pont, General Motors, Sears Roebuck, and Standard Oil of New Jersey.

The hierarchical organizational structure that had evolved in the 19th century in railroading, communications, marketing, and manufacturing was one that Chandler characterizes as centralized and functionally departmentalized (Williamson labeled it the unitary or U-form enterprise). The U-form can be illustrated by the organizational chart in Figure 14–1.

In the design of their hierarchical management structures, indus-

FIGURE 14–1 An Example of the Unitary Form of Business Organization

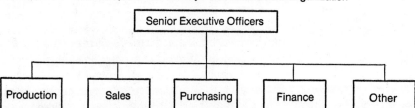

trial firms tended to imitate the railroads. But those that had complex manufacturing processes and had integrated into new activities found the centralized, functionally departmentalized structure inadequate. Senior executives were too involved in the day-to-day chain of command and tended to neglect strategic, long-run planning and overall organizational problems. With continuing growth, the difficulties of efficient management increased.

Chandler notes two significant phenomena. First, in all four companies, the introduction of the multidivisional form was preceded by managerial crises. Second, the organizational innovation spread most rapidly and pervasively in industries characterized by technical complexity, a diverse mix of products, and integration into either or both raw material manufacture and end-product distribution. Thus, by 1962, virtually all large firms in electrical and electronic machinery, power machinery (including automobiles), and chemicals had adopted the multidivisional structure, while very few firms in steel and nonferrous metals had done so.

The multidivisional firm—or the M-form enterprise, as Williamson calls it—has an organizational chart similar to Figure 14–2. Decentralization is inherent in multidivisional structure. Division managers are responsible for day-to-day supervision of both line and staff operations, leaving top management free for strategic planning.

Coincident with the emergence of the multidivisional firm in the 1920s, large manufacturing firms moved toward strategic product diversification. Chandler points out that before that decade, many successful integrated industrial firms had adopted a so-called full-line approach; but only in the 1920s did diversification become a deliberate strategy as the integrated industrial firms sought to make better use of their purchasing and marketing capabilities and take advantage of by-products associated with complex production operations. The multidivisional form easily accommodated such horizontal or conglomerate expansion and indeed may have stimulated it—a new semiautonomous division could be added without disturbing existing divisions.

Williamson, using his concepts of bounded rationality and oppor-

FIGURE 14–2 An Example of the Multidivisional Form of Business Organization

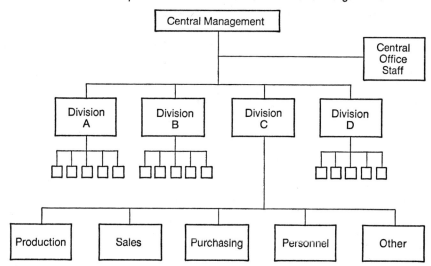

tunism, noted that the M-form ameliorates or overcomes a number of the internal organization failures limiting the sizes of firms. He states:

> Operating decisions were ... resolved at the divisional level, which relieved the communication load. Strategic decisions were reserved for the general office, which reduced partisan political input into the resource allocation process. And the internal auditing and control techniques ... served to overcome information impactedness conditions and permit fine tuning controls to be exercised over the operating parts.[13]

By far the most important advantage of the M-form, in Williamson's opinion, is that it allows the diversified firm to substitute internal allocation of capital for that of the market. Cash flows generated by operating divisions are subject to control and diversion by the central management, which can usually reallocate funds among divisions more efficiently than if the divisions were independent firms competing for funds on the capital market. As a result of centralized control of investment funds (usually coupled with an insistence that divisions support their competing investment proposals to top management in terms of estimated rates of return), Williamson concludes that the M-form of organization is more conducive to profit maximization than the U-form.

Both Williamson and Chandler note dramatic feedback effects on the overall structure and performance of the U.S. economy as the M-form spread from the 1940s through the 1970s. In Williamson's view, the M-form has facilitated diversification rather than specialized growth in a single product or market. The result, he concludes, has been to increase economywide concentration without affecting concentration in individual product markets.

Chandler points out that the multidivisional form, with an institutional commitment to strategic planning and a structure facilitating diversification, is highly conducive to industrial R&D. Not only can research establishments be financed and managed efficiently in such a firm but the results can be easily assimilated by the organization. This strength has led, in turn, to advantages in meeting the government's sophisticated military needs. The ease with which new operations can be integrated and the ability to create and market new products have made the M-form an excellent organizational structure for movement into foreign markets, thus facilitating the transformation of multidivisional firms into multinational ones.

The single most important feedback effect, in Chandler's view, is that the managements of large enterprises have supplanted the market in "the coordination and integration of the flow of goods and services from the production of raw materials through the several processes of production to the sale to the ultimate consumer."[14] He states:

> In many sectors of the economy the visible hand of management replaced what Adam Smith referred to as the invisible hand of market forces. The market remained the generator of demand for goods and services, but modern business enterprise took over the functions of coordinating flows of goods through existing processes of production and distribution, and of allocating funds and personnel for future production and distribution. As modern business enterprise acquired functions hitherto carried out by the market, it became the most powerful institution in the American economy and its managers the most influential group of economic decision makers. The rise of modern business enterprise in the United States, therefore, brought with it managerial capitalism.[15]

THE PRODUCT LIFE CYCLE AND THE EXPERIENCE CURVE[16]

Two managerial planning concepts—the market life cycle of a product from introduction through obsolescence, and the reduction in unit costs gained through cumulative experience—are prominent elements in the business strategies proposed for large diversified firms. To the extent that they are adopted, these strategies pose major issues for industrial structure and antitrust policy.

The Product Life Cycle

According to this concept, a product goes through four stages of growth and decline, as illustrated in Figure 14–3.

FIGURE 14–3 The Product Life Cycle

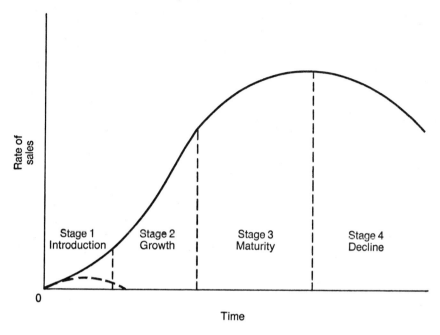

When a product is first marketed, the seller must inform potential buyers, overcome customer resistance, and develop channels of distribution. Thus, early market penetration is likely to be slight and growth sluggish. But if the product satisfies a substantial customer need, growth will accelerate. (Many new products, of course, never get beyond this first stage. Such an unhappy experience is illustrated by the small dashed line in Figure 14–3.)

A product that survives its birth pangs and wins market acceptance should enjoy a stage of rapid growth as interest spreads, and the number of first-time users increases. This second stage ends with market saturation—all potential buyers know of the product and those who are favorably disposed have already made their initial purchases.

With market saturation, the product enters its third stage, maturity. Sales of a mature product may grow slowly or level off, and sellers will find themselves relying more on replacement sales and less on initial sales. The maturity stage may continue for a long time, but sooner or later customer tastes or needs will change or the product will be replaced by a new one. Then the product will enter its fourth and final stage—decline.

The product life cycle is a marketing rather than statistical concept and is more useful in strategic planning than in forecasting actual sales volume. Firms may try to stretch the life cycle by successive penetrations of new markets. For example, Theodore Levitt has described how Du Pont introduced nylon into the military market and then, when that market matured, turned to nylon stockings, followed by knits, tire cord, textured yarn, and carpet material.[17] Raymond Vernon has pointed out how the product life cycle may be prolonged by moving into foreign markets as domestic markets become saturated.[18]

The Experience Curve

The idea that a new product's production costs will fall as workers and managers gain experience—the learning curve phenomenon—has long been recognized. In the 1960s, the Boston Consulting Group (BCG) introduced a new and broader variation on the learning curve. The experience curve embraces all costs, such as capital, marketing, purchasing, administrative, and research, as well as the direct labor and production supervision costs on which the older learning curve concentrated. Costs, according to the current experience curve concept, can be expected to fall by a constant percentage with each doubling of accumulated production experience.[19]

The experience curve is as depicted in Figure 14–4. Note that in Panel A, using a linear scale on both axes, the rate of cost reduction declines throughout the product's lifetime, both because the cost reduction is a constant percentage of a declining cost base and because an equal percentage reduction occurs only in a geometric progression with each successive doubling of cumulated production. In Panel B, using a log-log scale, the cost decline becomes a straight line.

The Experience Curve versus Traditional Cost Curves. The experience curve is distinct from the traditional cost curves of economic

FIGURE 14–4 The Experience Curve

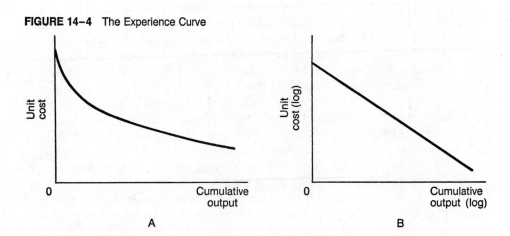

theory. Cost reductions due to accumulated experience are quite different from those due to economies of scale. In both panels of Figure 14–4, total output to date (cumulated from the inception of production) is shown on the horizontal axis. Standard average and marginal cost curves, in contrast, are static, showing costs as a function of the current rate of production. The cost reduction depicted by the experience curve is a function of total output over the product's lifetime and not of the rate of production at any one time.

According to experience curve advocates, a number of sources of cost reduction are related to experience and unattainable without it. First, the experience curve does incorporate the cost reductions depicted in the learning curve. Production costs should fall as both workers and supervisors learn new techniques and acquire new skills. Further, as production proceeds, work routines will be simplified and standardized and managers will discover better floor layouts, material flows, and coordination techniques. New materials, machines, tools, and variations on the product itself will be discovered. Contacts with suppliers will improve; and the best, cheapest, and most reliable sources of materials will become known. New suppliers can be developed and old ones encouraged to improve their production techniques and products. Similarly, access to and use of creditors will improve.

Exploiting the Life Cycle and the Experience Curve

The experience curve concept suggests that the firm that promptly wins the largest market share for a new product will gain a major competitive advantage. In the first and early second stages of the product life cycle, when sales volume is small but growing rapidly, the most crucial strategic objective is to accumulate experience faster than competitors, since costs are posited to fall by some constant percentage with every doubling of cumulative production and a large cost advantage can be gained quickly at relatively low rates of output. Later, when the market approaches saturation, it will be far more difficult to achieve comparable cost reductions, and competitive cost advantages and disadvantages will be harder to realign.

For this reason, "riding down the experience curve" implies a highly aggressive early pricing strategy. A firm that has just introduced a new product should press vigorously for the largest possible market share, a drive that will often mean pricing the product below cost. The essential goal is to obtain and maintain market share dominance to enjoy the greatest cumulative experience and hence the lowest costs.

As the product matures and the rate of growth slows, cost should be allowed to fall below price. One way to achieve this is to hold price steady until cost has fallen to a level at which the margin is adequate

FIGURE 14–5 A Pricing Strategy to Exploit the Experience Curve

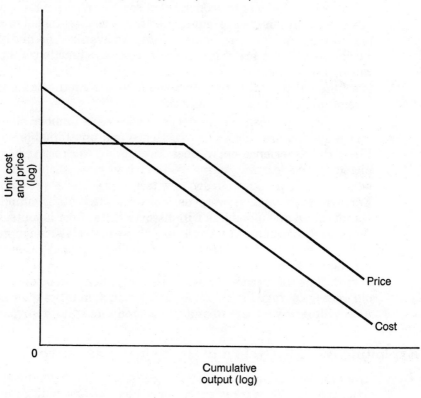

and then reduce price to maintain that margin as cost continues to fall. The cost-price relationship inherent in this strategy is shown in Figure 14–5.

In addition to early pricing below cost, the firm must be prepared to supply the market with sufficient product. It must therefore make a prompt capital investment in production facilities in anticipation of rapidly expanding output. Both of these cash drains—below-cost pricing and investment outlay—must be incurred while the product is still in its introductory stage—a time when its success is most problematic. Such a high-risk strategy is thus most suitable for a multiproduct firm that can spread the risks and smooth out the cash drain over a number of new products.

Implications for Competition and Antitrust Policy

A product strategy predicated on attaining the lowest cost by obtaining and maintaining the largest market share implies that the successful competitor will obtain a near monopoly. Such a monopoly may be in the public interest, since many of the hypothesized cost savings are real rather than pecuniary, and thus enhance productive efficiency. Further, the degree of contradiction between the competitive model and the business strategy model based on the product life cycle and experience curve concepts ought not be exaggerated. One of the crucial features of the strategy is market segmentation. The experience curve presumably applies to specific products and not to the firm as a whole. Accordingly, the strategy involves some narrowly defined market segment that the firm thinks it has a reasonable chance of dominating— for example, mentholated cigarettes, portable electric typewriters, and steel ply radial tires. Monopoly power in such narrow markets should be severely limited by the existence of close substitutes.

Questions about the Experience Curve. Perhaps the best critique of the product strategy model for economic analysis and antitrust policy is Richard B. Craswell's.[20] Craswell notes that little is yet known about how the experience curve operates in various industries, warning that "the strength of the experience curve in the industry actually being studied is thus one question that must always be asked." Granting that some form of the experience curve is a widespread economic phenomenon, it is not evident that its benefits accrue solely to the firm that has accumulated the experience. "How much of the cost reductions are due entirely to economies of scale, which can be obtained by any firm (regardless of past experience) whose current operations are large enough?" Craswell asks. "How much of the reductions are due to unpatented improvements which can be copied by less-experienced firms, or to trained employees who can be hired away?"[21] Still another question might be added: If part of the cost reduction comes from developing capable suppliers, why won't these suppliers sell to competitors?

Craswell asks how changes in industrial structure would affect the experience curve. If firms merge, are their respective experiences combined in some way? Or what would happen to the experience curve effect if an operating division was spun off? These are not frivolous questions, Craswell notes, in light of the emphasis put on market share as the principal indicator of cumulative experience.

The Experience Curve and Antitrust Laws. Turning to antitrust, Craswell points out that the strategy model does not have any particular implications for change in antitrust laws' current opposition to price-fixing and other forms of collusion. The emphasis put on market segmentation suggests that antitrust authorities might want to concentrate on more narrowly defined markets. Much more must be known about how experience is transmitted before the implications can be assessed for public policy toward horizontal and conglomerate mergers.

Similarly, it is not clear whether the benefits of past experience would be lost if an industry was deconcentrated by dissolution of its largest firms or divestiture of some of their divisions.

The strategy model does have direct relevance to two aspects of antitrust policy, Craswell continues. The first is predation. The model suggests that firms should occasionally cut price below cost, expand capacity to preempt future demand, and promote their products aggressively, particularly in the early stages of growth. Such behavior is presumed to be socially beneficial, pushing down costs. Antitrust, on the other hand, proscribes such behavior where the firm's purpose is to eliminate or harm specific competitors. Craswell notes that current legal rules for identifying predation are already confused and that introduction of the experience curve "complicates matters greatly."[22]

Second, the strategy model raises issues of antitrust policy toward monopolization. The law, Craswell points out, does not forbid monopoly itself but only monopoly coupled with some form of restrictive or exclusionary conduct. And strenuous efforts to increase output can hardly be regarded as restrictive or exclusionary if carried out independently.

He concludes that the business strategy model, in its present state, contributes little to general reform of antitrust policy, although it does identify some new factors to be considered in individual cases.

THE PARADIGMS IN RETROSPECT

One inescapable conclusion follows from a survey of the current paradigms of industrial organization: the basic structure-conduct-performance approach, the structuralist and conduct-oriented variants of that framework, the concentration doctrine, the new learning of the Chicago school, the efficiency doctrine that grew out of the Chicagoans' line of thought, the transactional paradigm, the strategy and structure approach, and the business strategy models just discussed. Any attempt to integrate or synthesize these paradigms into a single coherent and internally consistent analytical framework would be futile.

Industrial organization, therefore, remains in what Thomas S. Kuhn, a leading philosopher of science, regards as an immature or preparadigmatic state. (For Kuhn, a body of knowledge becomes a mature science only when a single paradigm is accepted throughout the discipline.) Kuhn's description of pre-Newtonian studies of the nature of light is analogous to the current state of industrial organization. He writes,

> One group took light to be particles emanating from material bodies; for another it was a modification of the medium that intervened between the body and the eye; still another explained light in terms of an interaction of the medium with an emanation from the eye; and there were

other combinations and modifications besides. Each . . . emphasized, as paradigmatic observations, the particular cluster of optical phenomena that its own theory could do most to explain.[23]

Kuhn then adds, "At various times all these schools made significant contributions . . . from which Newton drew the first nearly uniformly accepted paradigm for optical physics."[24] Similarly, all of the industrial organization paradigms are making positive contributions. Each one is useful in helping to solve specific problems, yet none is clearly superior to the others as a general framework.

The industrial sector of a large, modern economy is highly diverse. In some industries, concentration is the result of superior efficiencies of large firms; in others, smaller firms are the more efficient. In some markets, only one type of performance will be consistent with the underlying structure of the industry, and in others, various kinds of behavior are feasible. Some types of industrial activity seem more amenable to the M-form enterprise than others. Some products and some markets lend themselves more readily to the product life-cycle, experience curve strategy than others.

The attitude expressed by Oliver Williamson is commended to all industrial organization students. Emphasizing the contribution a transactional paradigm could make, Williamson writes:

> For those who, like myself, are inclined to be eclectic, no comprehensive commitment to one approach rather than another needs to be made. What is involved, rather, is the selection of the approach best suited to deal with the problems at hand. Although the matching of models to problems is not always easy, I find the alternative of forcing one model to handle all the issues to be even less satisfactory.[25]

The original structure-conduct-performance paradigm does have one distinct and important characteristic not found in the others. As initially formulated by Edward S. Mason, it simply provides an approach: first examine industrial structure, then analyze conduct after identifying its structural determinants, and finally ascertain and evaluate economic performance resulting from conduct within a structural context. Such a general framework can encompass the other paradigms and, in the process, accommodate widely diverse modes of analysis, viewpoints, and ideological predilections.

ENDNOTES

[1] The literature is surveyed in Oliver E. Williamson, "The Modern Corporation: Origins, Evolution, Attributes," *Journal of Economic Literature* 19, no. 1 (December 1981), pp. 1537–68.

[2] Ronald H. Coase, "The Nature of the Firm," *Economica* 4, no. 16 (November 1937), pp. 386–405, at p. 393.

[3]Oliver E. Williamson, *Markets and Hierarchies: Analysis and Antitrust Implications* (New York: Free Press, 1975).

[4]Oliver E. Williamson, "Managerial Discretion and Business Behavior," *American Economic Review* 53, no. 5 (December 1963), pp. 1040–57; Oliver E. Williamson, *Managerial Objectives in a Theory of the Firm* (Chicago: Markham, 1967).

[5]Alfred D. Chandler, *Strategy and Structure: Chapters in the History of the Industrial Enterprise* (Cambridge, Mass.: MIT Press, 1962); Alfred D. Chandler, *The Visible Hand: The Managerial Revolution in American Business* (Cambridge, Mass.: Harvard University Press, 1977). For a thoughtful assessment of Chandler's work and a survey of its contribution to subsequent business literature, see Richard E. Caves, "Industrial Organization, Corporate Strategy and Structure," *Journal of Economic Literature* 18, no. 1 (March 1980), pp. 64–92.

[6]Chandler, *The Visible Hand,* p. 16.

[7]Ibid., pp. 107, 109.

[8]Chandler, *Strategy and Structure,* p. 13.

[9]Ibid., p. 14.

[10]Chandler, *The Visible Hand,* p. 244.

[11]Ibid., p. 286.

[12]Ibid., p. 336.

[13]Williamson, *Markets and Hierarchies,* pp. 137–38.

[14]Chandler, *The Visible Hand,* p. 11.

[15]Ibid., p. 1.

[16]This section draws heavily on Edward E. Morrison, "An Introduction to Four Business Strategy Models," in *Papers on Business Strategy and Antitrust,* Office of Policy Planning, U.S. Federal Trade Commission (Washington, D.C.: September 1980).

[17]Theodore Levitt, "Exploit the Product Life Cycle," *Harvard Business Review* 43, no. 6 (November–December 1965), pp. 81–94, at pp. 87–91.

[18]Raymond Vernon, *Storm over the Multinationals* (Cambridge, Mass.: Harvard University Press, 1977), pp. 89–98.

[19]Boston Consulting Group, *Perspectives on Experience* (Boston: Boston Consulting Group, 1968); Bruce Henderson, *Henderson on Corporate Strategy* (Cambridge, Mass.: Abt Books, 1979); Bruce Henderson, *The Logic of Business Strategy* (Cambridge, Mass.: Ballinger, 1984).

[20]Richard B. Craswell, "Antitrust Issues Raised by Some Business Strategy Models," in *Papers on Business.*

[21]Ibid., pp. 17–18.

[22]Ibid., p. 30.

[23]Thomas S. Kuhn, *The Structure of Scientific Revolutions* (Chicago: University of Chicago Press, 1962), pp. 12–13.

[24]Ibid., p. 13.

[25]Williamson, *Markets and Hierarchies,* p. 249.

PART THREE

Antitrust Policy

CHAPTER FIFTEEN

Monopolization and the Rule of Reason: Section 2 of the Sherman Act

The basic antitrust laws of the United States, enacted in 1890 and 1914, long antedate the formulation and development of the structure-conduct-performance paradigm. Yet the special, indirect character that sets antitrust apart from other types of government regulation of business can best be understood within that paradigm's framework. Most forms of public regulation identify desired characteristics of business *performance* and seek to compel that performance directly through legislation or edict. A public utility commission, for example, sets the rates that a firm under its jurisdiction (presumably a natural monopoly) can charge, as well as prescribing the types of service the firm must provide. Other government regulatory bodies specify standards for product quality, labeling, product safety, workplace safety, pollution, and fair employment practices; and firms' premises and products are subject to inspection to see that these standards are met.

In contrast, no official of the Antitrust Division or the FTC can order a business firm to lower its price or increase its output. Rather, the antitrust agencies can and do try to lower prices and raise output by attacking market *structures* that give firms the power to raise prices and restrict output, and by enforcing prohibitions against collusive agreements and other forms of *conduct* designed to attain, maintain, or exploit such power. The antitrust authorities, in sum, seek to influence performance indirectly, by policies aimed at market structure and business conduct.

In Chapters Fifteen and Sixteen, we examine structural antitrust: the remedial or "trust-busting" approach under Section 2 of the Sherman Act and the preventive, antimerger approach under Section 7 of

345

the Clayton Act. Chapters Seventeen–Nineteen are devoted to conduct-oriented provisions of antitrust law.

ROUND ONE OF THE RULE OF REASON

Judicial development of the rule of reason has proceeded episodically. At least two and perhaps three distinct "rounds" can be distinguished in application of the rule to monopolization.[1] Round One was dominated by the *Standard Oil* and *American Tobacco* decisions of 1911, discussed at some length in Chapter Five.[2]

John Bates Clark, a leading economist and until that time one of the Sherman Act's harshest critics, noted in a 1912 book coauthored with his son John M. Clark, "We know to-day that we *can* dissolve the trusts—that we can break up the big corporations into smaller ones—and this is distinctly more than we once knew."[3] But they still questioned the wisdom of a vigorous dissolution policy. The problem, they argued, was to see that the trusts continued to be agents of progress, for stagnation would be a far worse failing than a tendency to higher prices and restricted output. The trusts that proved to be true monopolies—that could stand still because they feared no competition, actual or potential—should be dissolved. Such an attitude toward antitrust, cautious but basically accepting and even welcoming, spread among economists over the decade following the *Standard Oil* and *American Tobacco* cases.

The first round continued with successful dissolutions in the explosives, farm machinery, photographic equipment, and glucose and cornstarch industries.[4] But the government lost monopolization cases against the American Can Company in 1916, United Shoe Machinery Company in 1918, and United States Steel Corporation in 1920.[5] The Supreme Court's decision in the last of these signals the end of Round One.

The *U.S. Steel* case was decided by a bare majority of four to three, with two justices disqualifying themselves because of previous public advocacy of the company's breakup. The Court interpreted the case strictly as one of monopolization and not as merely an attempt to monopolize, in light of the language of the government's complaint and the remedy of dissolution that was sought. At the time of the case, U.S. Steel's market share was somewhat under 50 percent and declining. "Monopoly, therefore, was not achieved, and competitors had to be persuaded by pools, associations, trade meetings, and through the social form of dinners, all of them, it may be, violations of the law, but transient in their purpose and effect."[6] Further, these practices had been abandoned before the suit was brought in 1911, not in fear of litigation but because they were not working in the face of vigorous competition.

The Court was impressed that U.S. Steel had engaged in "no act of aggression upon its competitors," in contrast to the "brutal" behavior of the Standard Oil Company and the similar conduct of the American Tobacco Company. Finally, the majority noted that U.S. Steel was regarded as an efficient firm and an important factor in the nation's foreign trade. U.S. Steel was "of impressive size," the Court observed. "But we must adhere to the law, and the law does not make mere size an offense, or the existence of unexerted power an offense. It, we repeat, requires overt acts, and trusts to its prohibition of them and its power to repress or punish them."[7]

In sum, U.S. Steel did not have the market share or power of Standard Oil and American Tobacco nor had it engaged in any of the same predatory tactics. The Supreme Court clearly regarded these two distinguishing factors as related: Private monopoly could not arise and persist without conduct designed to eliminate rivals. Round One thus ended with the proposition that monopoly power evidenced by overwhelming market share (80 to 90 percent), coupled with aggressive tactics demonstrating a clear intent to attain or maintain that power, fell afoul of Section 2; but the Sherman Act was not designed to break up large firms in the absence of one or both of these elements.

ROUND TWO OF THE RULE OF REASON

The opening bell of Round Two sounded with the *Alcoa* decision of 1945.[8] John J. Flynn, writing in 1981, noted that this round (or wave, in his terminology) "evolved after the shattering experience of the depression and national flirtation with cartelization early in the New Deal." The view of the rule of reason emerging from this second round "has dominated the training and thinking of today's generation of judges, lawyers, and economists" and "reflected a growing use of economic theory as a tool for analysis."[9]

Alcoa: The Intent to Monopolize

Judge Learned Hand, who wrote the final opinion for a circuit court of appeals since a majority of the Supreme Court disqualified themselves, followed White's outline of the rule of reason, addressing the question of monopoly and then that of intent. The market controlled by Alcoa, he concluded, included all virgin aluminum ingot but excluded secondary or scrap aluminum. By this calculation, Alcoa accounted for over 90 percent of the market. Had secondary aluminum been included in the definition of the relevant market, Alcoa's share would have been about 64 percent; and had secondary aluminum been included while Alcoa's production for internal use was excluded, its share would have been only around 33 percent. Hand concluded, "That percentage [over 90] is enough to constitute a monopoly; it is doubtful whether sixty or sixty-four percent would be enough; and certainly thirty-three percent is not."[10]   Hand's uncritical and unqualified reliance on market share has been harshly criticized by economists. But virtually all critics have failed to note that Hand was scrupulously respecting precedent in contrasting the market shares of the 1911 and 1920 defendants and in placing Alcoa squarely in the category of those the Supreme Court had held to possess monopoly power.

Turning to intent, Hand observed that "It does not follow that because 'Alcoa' had such a monopoly, that it 'monopolized' the ingot market: it may not have achieved monopoly; monopoly may have been thrust upon it." As examples, Hand cited a market so limited that it would be impossible to produce at feasible cost in more than one plant, changes in cost or taste that drive out all but one producer, or a single firm surviving out of a group "merely by virtue of superior skill, foresight and industry." Such a "successful competitor, having been urged to compete, must not be turned upon when he wins."[11]

Alcoa, as the holder of the original patents on the electrolytic reduction process, had a legitimate monopoly on the commercial production of aluminum until 1909. Thereafter, however,

> Nothing compelled it to keep doubling and redoubling its capacity before others entered the field. It insists that it never excluded competitors; but we can think of no more effective exclusion than progressively to embrace each new opportunity as it opened, and to face every newcomer with new capacity already geared into a great organization. . . . Only in case we interpret "exclusion" as limited to manoeuvres not honestly industrial, but actuated solely by a desire to prevent competition, can such a course, indefatigably pursued, be deemed not "exclusionary". . . . In order to fall within §2, the monopolist must have both the power to monopolize, and the intent to monopolize. To read the passage as demanding any "specific" intent, makes nonsense of it, for no monopolist monopolizes unconscious of what he is doing. So here, "Alcoa" meant to keep, and did keep, that complete and exclusive hold on the ingot market with which it started. That was to "monopolize" that market, however innocently it otherwise proceeded.[12]

The problem of remedy that had so troubled the Supreme Court in the *U.S. Steel* case did not loom large in *Alcoa*. Expansion of aluminum production during World War II had been financed by the government; and in 1945, about two thirds of the industry's capacity was owned by the government although operated under lease by Alcoa. Hand ruled that the district court should retain jurisdiction and determine if any further dissolution was required after disposal of the government-owned plant and equipment. In 1950, the court ruled that the disposal program that established Kaiser Aluminum and Reynolds

Metals as large, integrated aluminum firms had been adequate to restore competition.[13]

In the 1911 *Standard Oil* and *American Tobacco* cases, intent had been inferred from specific acts aimed at eliminating, weakening, or absorbing specific competitors. No such specific intent could be shown in *Alcoa*. Rather, Hand reverted to a concept developed by the Supreme Court in 1905, in an opinion holding that a "general" intent to monopolize could be inferred from a series of acts, each legal in itself but which taken as a whole constituted a pattern evidencing a plan to attain or maintain a monopoly position.[14] Hand considered this requisite general intent established by Alcoa's actions.

Despite his caveat that a firm might have monopoly "thrust upon it" and thus escape liability, his standard of general intent seemed so strict and encompassing that it was difficult to see how any monopolist could engage in general business operations without violating the law. Indeed, Eugene V. Rostow commented that the decision "finally interred and reversed the old dictum that size is not an offense under the Sherman Act."[15]

United Shoe Machinery: Highlight of Round Two

The meaning of intent to monopolize was further analyzed and refined in the *United Shoe Machinery Corporation* case of 1953,[16] generally regarded as the highlight of Round Two.[17] Before turning to intent, Judge Charles Wyzanski had to ascertain whether United Shoe held monopoly power. He defined the market as including all types of shoe-making machinery and observed that United held between 75 and 85 percent of that market. But Wyzanski went beyond Hand in taking note of other factors. In particular, United's business practices resulted in substantial barriers to entry. United leased its machines on staggered long-term contracts with penalties for early cancellation and discounts for renewal. Since United refused to sell its machines, there was no secondhand market available to those who wanted to buy from another source nor could potential competitors acquire a United machine for reverse engineering and imitation. The leases contained a "full-capacity" clause requiring that the leased machine be fully utilized before any other machine could be acquired or utilized. Sales of materials such as tacks and threads were tied to leasing of machinery. Repair and maintenance services were similarly incorporated in the leases and not otherwise available. The results, according to Wyzanski, were barriers affecting both actual and potential competition.

In 1918, the government had lost a case alleging that the original formation of United—by merger of three firms, each of which was the product of earlier consolidations—violated the Sherman Act. Accordingly, Wyzanski accepted the initial market power of the corporation as legitimate. He also took note of the "high quality of United's products, its understanding of the techniques of shoemaking and the needs of shoe manufacturers, its efficient design and improvement of machines, and its prompt and knowledgeable service." These, he observed, are beyond reproach. Further, "United's power does not rest on predatory practices. Probably few monopolies could produce a record so free from any taint of that kind of wrong doing."[18] But, he concluded:

> United's control does not rest solely on its original constitution, its ability, its research, or its economies of scale. There are other barriers to competition, and these barriers were erected by United's own business policies. Much of United's market power is traceable to the magnetic ties inherent in its system of leasing, and not selling, its more important machines. . . . In addition . . . brief reference may be made to the fact that United has been somewhat aided in retaining control of the shoe machinery industry by its purchases in the secondhand market, by its acquisitions of patents, and, to a lesser extent, by its activities in selling to shoe factories supplies which United and others manufacture. . . . In one sense, the leasing system and the miscellaneous activities . . . were natural and normal, for they were, in Judge Hand's words, "honestly industrial." They are the sort of activities which would be engaged in by other honorable firms. And, to a large extent, the leasing practices conform to long-standing traditions in the shoe machinery business. Yet, they are not practices which can be properly described as the inevitable consequences of ability, natural forces, or law. They represent something more than the use of accessible resources, the process of invention and innovation, and the employment of those techniques of employment, financing, production, and distribution, which a competitive society must foster. They are contracts, arrangements, and policies which, instead of encouraging competition based on pure merit, further the dominance of a particular firm.[19]

As to intent, "Defendant intended to engage in the leasing practices and pricing policies which maintained its market power. That is all the intent which the law requires when both the complaint and the judgment rest on a charge of 'monopolizing,' not merely 'attempting to monopolize.' Defendant having willed the means, has willed the end."[20] Thus, as evidence of general intent to monopolize, Wyzanski sought to identify conduct representing an "intermediate case where the causes of an enterprise's success were neither common law restraints of trade, nor the skill with which the business was conducted, but rather some practice which without being predatory, abusive, or coercive was in economic effect exclusionary."[21]

The government had asked that United be dissolved into three separate firms, although all manufacture of machinery was conducted in one plant. Given his diagnosis of the barriers to entry, Wyzanski identified a remedy short of dissolution. The restrictive lease terms were eliminated, United was required to offer repair and maintenance services separately from its leases, and the company was also required to offer for sale any machine that it leased. The last provision, Wyzanski noted, would have a long-term impact on United's market power because the machines would ultimately reach a second-hand market.

The major contribution of the *United Shoe Machinery* opinion, affirmed by the Supreme Court in 1954,[22] was to impose a standard of intent to monopolize that preserved the concept of general intent, yet mitigated the apparent harshness of Hand's formulation.

Du Pont: Defining Monopoly Power

The next advance, completing Round Two, emerged from the Supreme Court's 1956 decision in the *Du Pont* cellophane case,[23] in which the primary issue involved determining the existence of monopoly power. The Court noted, almost in passing, that Du Pont accounted for nearly 77 percent of U.S. cellophane sales during the relevant period, but it took no further notice of market share. The defense contended that Du Pont did not "have the power to control the price of cellophane or to exclude competitors from the market in which cellophane is sold."[24] Such carefully chosen language followed a definition of monopoly given in 1908 by the trial court in the *American Tobacco* case.[25]

The 1956 *Du Pont* Court repeated the definition, stating that "monopoly power is the power to control prices or exclude competition."[26] In terms of economic analysis, this concept of monopoly power is vastly superior to mere market share. The power to control price can be related directly to price elasticity of the demand facing the firm, while the power to exclude competition translates readily into the barriers to entry needed for monopolistic profit to persist in the long run.

The *Du Pont* cellophane decision was unfortunately marred by a crucial error in economic analysis, as the Court observed that the cross-elasticity of demand between cellophane and other flexible packaging materials determined whether cellophane comprised a separate market. Accepting the trial court's finding that this cross-elasticity was high, the Supreme Court ruled that the relevant market was flexible packaging materials and that Du Pont did not have monopoly power therein.

The fallacy of this reasoning, pointed out in an article by George W. Stocking and Willard F. Mueller, is that a profit-maximizing monopolist would exercise its power over price by raising the price until customers were almost (but not quite) driven to the use of substitutes, or where cross-elasticity was quite high. The relevant measure for market definition would be cross-elasticity at a price equaling marginal cost rather than, as observed, at the monopolistic price.[27] The Court formulated an alternative test for demarcation of the relevant market, the so-called reasonable interchangeability test, that has been the basic guideline for subsequent Section 2 cases. "That market is composed of products that have reasonable interchangeability for the purposes for which they are produced—price, use and qualities considered."[28]

Round Two ended with the *Du Pont* cellophane case. A Supreme Court decision written 10 years later, in 1966, encapsulated the results. In the *Grinnell* case, the Court noted that there are two elements to the offense of monopolizing under Section 2 of the Sherman Act. First, there is "the possession of monopoly power in the relevant market," with monopoly defined as "the power to control prices or exclude competition." Second, there is "the willful acquisition of or maintenance of that power as distinguished from growth or development as a consequence of a superior product, business acumen, or historic accident."[29]

THE AFTERMATH OF ROUND TWO: IS IT ROUND THREE?

In January 1969, the Department of Justice filed a complaint against IBM under Section 2 of the Sherman Act, alleging monopolization of the market for general-purpose computer systems. And in 1974, the department brought suit against AT&T, seeking a major restructuring. Over the same period, the FTC initiated structural actions against the four largest breakfast cereal manufacturers, eight major oil companies, and Du Pont, all on the legal theory that monopolization prohibited by Section 2 of the Sherman Act was inherently an unfair method of competition and hence subject to attack under Section 5 of the Federal Trade Commission Act.[30] Concurrently, the number of private treble-damage suits alleging monopolization or attempts to monopolize rose sharply, stimulated by court decisions easing the plaintiff's burden in showing damages suffered.[31] In 1960, 228 private antitrust suits were filed. By 1980, the number had risen to 1,457, after peaking at 1,611 in 1977.[32] It appeared that a lively third round was under way.

But, whether gauged by developments in interpretation of the law or by the economic impact of antitrust action, Round Three has been little more than shadowboxing compared to Rounds One and Two— with one dramatic exception, the breakup of AT&T by consent decree.

The AT&T Breakup

In its initial complaint, the government alleged that AT&T had monopolized the U.S. telecommunications market through its ownership of 22 regional operating telephone companies; the parent corporation's Long Lines Division; the Western Electric Company, which manufactures telephones, switchboards, and other communications equipment; and Bell Telephone Laboratories, one of the nation's leading research institutions. According to the complaint, AT&T had used this corporate structure to monopolize by restricting communication services through the Long Lines Division and by foreclosing competition in communications equipment through encouraging the operating companies to acquire nearly all of their equipment from Western Electric.

In January 1982, lawyers for the Antitrust Division and AT&T filed pleadings to end the case with a consent decree; and after a period of public comment and further negotiations with the presiding judge, the decree was entered the following August.[33] In one sense, that of advancing interpretation of the law, the *AT&T* case made no contribution, since a consent decree terminates a case with neither a determination of guilt or innocence nor any opinion by the court on the legal issues. But the settlement represents by far the largest restructuring of an industry accomplished under the antitrust laws, rivaling if not exceeding the 1911 dissolutions of Standard Oil, American Tobacco, and Du Pont in impact on the U.S. economy.

The decree called for AT&T to divest itself of its operating subsidiaries, thus removing itself from provision of local telephone service. These 22 subsidiaries, since recombined into seven regional operating companies, are completely independent of AT&T and of one another. AT&T kept the Long Lines Division, Western Electric, and Bell Laboratories. But the new operating companies are prohibited from discriminating against AT&T's competitors, so Long Lines now faces competition in providing long-distance interconnection services as does Western Electric in supplying equipment to users and operating companies.

Perhaps the most important long-run provision of the 1982 decree is that it supersedes a 1956 consent decree that prohibited the Bell System from engaging in any line of business other than common-carrier public communications.[34] While the seven operating companies remain subject to regulation of their rates and services, the new AT&T is no longer prohibited from entering and competing in any aspect of electronic data processing and transmission.

The IBM Antitrust Suit

The 1969 complaint against IBM alleged that during the 1960s, the company had monopolized the market for "general purpose electronic digital computer systems," a charge that led to dispute over the appropriate definition of the market. The defense contended that the relevant market was a much broader one, the "computer systems" or "electronic data processing (EDP)" market. Under the broader definition, IBM's share of the market fell from roughly 70 to 80 percent, as alleged by the government, to around 30 percent.[35]

The indictment further charged IBM with several instances of aggressive and predatory conduct, cited as evidence of the company's intent to monopolize. These included "preannouncement" of a forthcoming new computer line one to two years before any such systems could be put on the market to limit sales of a competitor's new product, use of "fighting machines" (computers sold at below-cost prices in the face of competition), and "bundling" (quoting a single price for hardware, software, and maintenance services) to limit entry of firms offering only software or services.

The same day the AT&T agreement was announced, the Antitrust Division withdrew its case against IBM. The case had dragged on for 13 years, during which the practices that had formed the basis for the government's complaint had purportedly ended and, in the opinion of the assistant attorney general in charge of the Antitrust Division, the structure of the industry had changed considerably.[36]

The Implications for Round Three

The Department of Justice Suits. Even if actions taken to end the *AT&T* and *IBM* cases were decided independently, the effects must be considered jointly. Technological developments in computers and communications have blurred the distinction between these two industries, and a new "information industry" is rapidly becoming one of the nation's largest and most extensive. Voice communication now represents only a minor portion of the information transmitted over a vast and complex network linking input and output terminals with central processing, storage, and switching units.[37] The restructuring of the telephone industry reflects this fundamental change, and surely the competition in both R&D and manufacturing that IBM would soon face from the new AT&T must have been one consideration in withdrawing the case against IBM. (Undoubtedly, a second factor was the increasingly effective competition from abroad, particularly from Japan.)

Failure of the FTC's Shared-Monopoly Concept. The FTC's initiatives ended in failure across the board. In its cases against the petroleum refiners[38] and the breakfast cereal manufacturers,[39] the commission had sought to gain legal acceptance for the concept of "shared monopoly." According to this concept, embraced by both the Antitrust Division and the FTC during the 1970s, the leading firms in highly concentrated industries with behavior evidencing full recognition of mutual dependence should be viewed as jointly holding and sharing monopoly power; therefore, they should be subject to structural remedy under Section 2 of the Sherman Act or Section 5 of the Federal Trade Commission Act.

In 1981, the commission dismissed the complaint against the oil companies. William S. Comanor, former director of the FTC's Bureau of Economics, observed:

> In the spring of [1981], attorneys for both the Commission and the oil companies agreed that trial was still three years off. Little political support remained for an action so far from resolution. The political spotlight had changed from the oil companies to the regulatory agencies themselves, and it was time to dispose of old baggage. Partially in self-defense, the Commission concluded, "that further proceedings . . . are not in the public interest," and dismissed the case.[40]

The breakfast cereal case was heard by an administrative law judge who handed down a ruling in favor of the companies in the fall of 1981. Early in 1982 the full commission approved this ruling and dismissed the case.[41] In part, this outcome can be attributed to a new administration and commission (as was true in the oil case), but it also reflected the administrative law judge's doubts about the legal standing of the theory of shared monopoly. Under the law, he concluded, it is still necessary to prove conspiracy in such a case, and the FTC staff had failed to do so.

The three respondent firms, Kellogg, General Mills, and General Foods (Quaker Oats had been charged but was later dropped from the case), controlled 80 to 90 percent of the market for ready-to-eat cereals and enjoyed sustained high profits. These supracompetitive profits, according to the complaint, resulted from the dominant firms' brand proliferation, or aggressive expansion into every product niche with highly advertised brands, thus raising artificial barriers to entry by smaller, single-brand firms. The evidence further indicated parallel behavior in such matters as price leadership, avoidance of competition for retail shelf space, common refusal to produce cereals for private-label marketers, coordinated restrictions on the timing and extent to which cereals were fortified with vitamins, and highly similar limitations on in-pack promotions such as cents-off coupons and premiums.

Since shared monopoly failed to meet Section 2 criteria for monopoly under these circumstances of highly oligopolistic structure and conduct, at least in the opinions of the administrative law judge and the FTC commissioners, it is doubtful that the concept would hold up in application elsewhere. (John Shenefield, assistant attorney general in charge of the Antitrust Division during the Carter administration, who had initially been enthusiastic about shared-monopoly cases, came to a similar conclusion after failing to find a single industry suitable for prosecution.)[42]

The *Du Pont* case alleged attempted monopolization of titanium dioxide pigments through such tactics as announcements of intended expansion to discourage competitors, premature expansion for preemptive purposes, refusal to raise price in the face of favorable market conditions so as to deny smaller competitors funds for investment, and refusal to license its production technology. Both the administrative law judge and the commissioners, however, found that Du Pont's conduct resulted from its lower costs, sophisticated forecasts of demand, and economies of scale, and was therefore legitimate under the test of "superior skill, foresight and industry" enunciated in the *Alcoa* case.[43]

Treble-Damage Suits: The Main Arena. The main arena for Round Three—or what there was of it—turned out to be private treble-damage cases. Plaintiffs won suits in the district courts against IBM in 1973 and Eastman Kodak in 1978 and, in both cases, were awarded heavy damages. But on appeal, both decisions were reversed.[44] IBM defended itself successfully at the district court level in a number of other private suits.

In a suit brought by MCI Communications Corporation, AT&T was found to have injured MCI by refusing to provide telephone interconnections for intercity messages transmitted by MCI's microwave relay system, and by predation in the form of charges below fully distributed costs for competing long-distance services. The jury awarded MCI $600 million in damages out of $900 million claimed ($1.8 billion trebled). The appeals court reversed on the allegations of predation, ruling that only prices below long-run incremental costs (or the cost of adding the new service) rather than fully distributed costs should be regarded as predation, but it upheld the jury verdict that refusal to interconnect was an act of monopolization that damaged MCI. The case was remanded for redetermination of damages.[45] In 1985 a trial court jury reduced damages to $37.8 million, trebled to $113.3 million.

Flynn expressed concern over interpretations of the rule of reason growing out of private monopolization suits because private litigation requires proof of standing, causation, and damages as well as substantive violation. Also, "Private damage actions, unlike most government litigation, usually entail a jury trial, further complicating the evolution of substantive standards by the need to separate judge and jury functions. Doubts about these added factors or confusing them with a proof of violation in a private suit may influence or significantly alter assessments of the substantive offense."[46] The *Telex* and *Berkey* cases illustrate some of the fundamental problems.

In *Telex,* the plaintiff alleged predatory actions by IBM in response to independent firms selling peripheral equipment that was plug-compatible with IBM's central processing units. The trial judge agreed and awarded damages of $86.5 million, $259.5 million trebled.

The appeals court focused on two issues. First, although the trial court had defined the market as peripherals that were plug-compatible with IBM's central processing units (a market in which, by definition, IBM held a monopoly prior to the entry of the independent producers), the appeals court held the market to be peripherals compatible with *any* central processing unit. Second, and more relevant to development of the rule of reason, the appeals court did not agree that the cited conduct represented monopolization under the rule. Rather, after noting that the "thrust upon" exception formulated in *Alcoa* and elaborated on in *United Shoe Machinery* had never been clearly defined, the opinion continued:

> There must be some room to move for a defendant who sees his market share acquired by research and technical innovations being eroded by those who market copies of its products. It would seem that technical attainments were not intended to be inhibited or penalized by a construction of section 2 of the Sherman Act to prohibit the adoption of legal and ordinary marketing methods already used by others in the market, or to prohibit price changes which are within the "reasonable" range, up or down.[47]

Despite the court of appeals' invitation—indeed plea—to the Supreme Court to define the exception, that Court declined to hear the case on appeal.

Berkey Photo's claim against Kodak grew out of the latter's simultaneous introduction of a new camera and a new film. The 110 Instamatic camera could use only Kodacolor II film, yet the company had made no prior announcement of the "system" to competing manufacturers of film or cameras. This marketing strategy gave Kodak an 18-month lead before competitors could introduce cameras that could use Kodacolor II. Further, Kodak did not disclose the process for developing Kodacolor II to competing film producers. The core issue in the case was the correctness of the trial judge's instructions to the jury:

> Standing alone, the fact that Kodak did not give advance warning of its new products to competitors would not entitle you to find that this conduct was exclusionary. Ordinarily a manufacturer has no duty to predisclose its new products in this fashion. It is an ordinary and acceptable business practice to keep one's new developments a secret. However, if you find that Kodak had monopoly power in cameras or in film, and if you find that this power was so great as to make it impossible for a competitor to compete with Kodak in the camera market unless it could

offer products similar to Kodak's, you may decide whether in the light of other conduct you determine to be anticompetitive, Kodak's failure to disclose was on balance an exclusionary course of conduct.[48]

The appeals court held these instructions to be in error. The opinion noted:

> While proclaiming vigorously that monopoly power is the evil at which §2 is aimed, courts have declined to take what would have appeared to be the next logical step—declaring monopolies unlawful *per se* unless specifically authorized by law. To understand the reason for this, one must comprehend the fundamental tension—one might almost say the paradox—that is near the heart of §2. This tension creates much of the confusion surrounding §2. . . . [In the *Alcoa* decision,] Hand . . . told us that it would be inherently unfair to condemn success when the Sherman Act itself mandates competition. Such a wooden rule, it was feared, might also deprive the leading firm in an industry of the incentive to exert its best efforts. Further success would yield not rewards but legal castigation. The antitrust laws would therefore compel the very sloth they were intended to prevent. We must always be mindful lest the Sherman Act be invoked perversely in favor of those who would seek protection against the rigors of competition.[49]

Applying this line of reasoning to the facts of the case at hand, the appeals court concluded, "Because . . . a monopolist is permitted, and indeed encouraged, by §2 to compete aggressively on the merits, any success that it may achieve through 'the process of invention and innovation' is clearly tolerated by the antitrust laws."[50]

Finally, the court of appeals held that the introduction of the new film and camera in a format where one could not be used without the other did not violate the antitrust laws. The conclusion that a monopolist could not use its power in one market to gain an advantage in another was "an inexorable interpretation of the antitrust laws."[51] However, the 110 Instamatic and Kodacolor II did not constitute separate products, according to the opinion, but rather were a "system," since a new film yielding sharp and clear reproductions from a small negative was necessary to introduce the new pocket camera.

Conclusion

The cases reviewed suggest that the primary contribution of Round Three has been a negative one. The simple elements of the rule of reason—monopolization under Section 2 of the Sherman Act requires monopoly power plus general intent to acquire or maintain that power—are complex in application and subject to differing interpretations. In the borderline cases where the established doctrines prove inadequate or unclear, lower courts have admitted to uncertainty and confusion.

From 1967, the year Round Two closed with the Supreme Court's *Grinnell* decision, through 1984, that Court made no interpretation of the rule of reason. But in 1985 the Supreme Court did rule on a case similar to *Telex* and *Berkey* in that the conduct of a dominant firm injuring a smaller competitor was alleged to be monopolization violating Section 2.[52] At issue was the unilateral termination by Aspen Skiing Company of an arrangement whereby it and the only other operator of downhill skiing facilities in the Aspen, Colorado, area, Aspen Highlands Skiing Corporation, sold six-day tickets good for use on either's slopes. Entry was barred by environmental and resort development regulations of the U.S. Forest Service and county government. Following the termination, the smaller firm's share of revenue fell from 20.5 percent to 11 percent. The Court noted that no firm, even a monopolist, had a general obligation to cooperate with a competitor, but that the dominant firm's conduct in terminating the agreement was, in this case, evidence from which the jury could properly conclude that there was an intent to monopolize. The opinion was, however, a narrow one, confined to the jury issue. The lower courts' Round Three monopolization opinions were not discussed or even cited. The *Aspen Ski* case, therefore, did nothing to resolve the questions troubling the lower courts.

THE AFTERMATH OF ROUND THREE: MAJOR UNRESOLVED ISSUES

Flynn, in his comprehensive review of Round Two and Three cases ("waves II and III," in his terminology), describes the rule-of-reason formulation developed in Round Two as a "gumball machine" approach: "The facts are plugged into the model and out pops the 'right answer' neatly packaged for consumption." Round Three courts, he continues, have been "faced with a legacy from *ALCOA* and *Grinnell* requiring categorization of the facts into a market definition, power, and conduct sequence without regard to whether the thrust of the evidence is a behavioral theory of unlawful monopolization or a structural theory of illegality." As a result, courts wrestling with the structural issue of monopoly power have been unnecessarily plunged into the "black hole of conduct issues."[53]

The Conduct Issue

Flynn and others, including a commission appointed by President Jimmy Carter to review the antitrust laws,[54] have therefore advocated a "no conduct" standard of monopolization in which persistent monopoly power would establish a violation, and efficiency defenses could be introduced only when remedy is being considered. A. D. Neale and D. G. Goyder, however, note that "monopoly as such is not and cannot be illegal *per se*. The reason for this is obvious. The first firm to bring a new product on to the market is inevitably a monopolist for a time, but it would be ludicrous to charge it with a criminal offense against the system of free competition." Similarly, an established firm may temporarily capture an entire market through superior efficiency, which "surely must be counted a success of the competitive system, not an assault upon it." Thus, they conclude, the primary responsibility of the courts "in seeking to isolate the element of positive drive which constitutes *monopolizing* is to identify the *intent* of the firm."[55]

The basic difference between those advocating a no-conduct standard and those who support the current approach appears to be a disagreement as to how long monopoly power is likely to persist without some kind of conduct designed to preserve it. Hence, Flynn would apply the no-conduct standard only to "persistent" monopolies, while Neale and Goyder are careful to note that monopolies should last only "for a time."

The nature and height of barriers to entry, therefore, are crucial to the issue, since profitable monopoly is difficult or impossible to retain in the absence of such barriers. Artificial barriers (except governmental ones such as patents and franchises), usually result from conduct from which intent can be inferred. It therefore seems unnecessary to sacrifice the fairness to those charged with monopolizing that is inherent in requiring proof of intent under a rule of reason.

Alternatively, we might argue that since monopoly will not persist without some purposive conduct, it is not necessary to identify the actual conduct to infer intent. But this line of reasoning makes it difficult to prescribe effective remedies other than dissolution: If we do not discover the current cause of monopoly (such as United Shoe Machinery's leasing practices), we cannot formulate an effective remedy (such as requiring that machines be offered for sale as well as lease).

The principal economic defect of the rule of reason's inclusion of intent is its inability to get at monopolies based on natural barriers to entry, such as innocently acquired sole ownership of a scarce resource or an absolute-cost advantage. Fortunately, barriers of this type appear to be rare. Similarly, natural monopoly based on economies of scale relative to size of market (restructuring of which would pose a real social cost) is uncommon in the United States outside of regulated public utilities.

Although commentators may disagree as to the role that conduct *should* play in determining illegal monopolization, there is no argument as to its crucial importance in the rule of reason as currently applied. Monopolization is the possession of monopoly power plus some additional element from which intent can be inferred. That element is some form of conduct. A judge or jury is not expected to ascertain criminal intent, whether in an antitrust case or any other, from direct evidence of what passed in a person's mind. Rather, it is a long-established principle of common law that an individual's intent is indicated by the natural, inevitable, or expected consequences of his or her acts, unless that individual pleads insanity or some other form of legal incompetence. In Judge Wyzanski's words, "Defendant having willed the means, has willed the end."

This injection of conduct led to a core problem in Rounds Two and Three. A firm with little or no market power would unquestionably be free to lease rather than sell its product or to terminate an agreement with a competitor. But according to the courts, neither United Shoe Machinery nor the Aspen Skiing Company enjoyed such freedom. In other cases, the challenged conduct was allowed. Eastman Kodak was ruled to have the same right as others not to predisclose its plans for introduction of a new camera/film system, and Du Pont's aggressive investment in expansion of its titanium dioxide facilities was treated as legitimate business conduct. Probably the single most important unanswered question pertaining to monopolization is how one distinguishes behavior that should be permissible for most firms but not for a monopolist. The analogy has been drawn to an elephant in a chicken coop. There is no problem if the chickens want to dance, but the elephant should be denied such recreation. Similarly, a monopolist may have to accept constraints not imposed on others if its actions have untoward effects on competition. The analogy can be pushed further. Suppose the elephant knows that it cannot dance without crushing chickens, but it is indifferent to the chickens' fate. If it dances, it has evidenced *intent* to kill chickens since it knew the likely result of its action, even though such mayhem was not its motive. It is not clear how solicitous a monopolist should be of others, assuming its conduct is not deliberately predatory.

Defining the Market

Identifying monopoly power involves defining the monopolized market. In theory, markets are delineated by Joan Robinson's "gaps in the chain of substitutes," resulting from either differences in the nature of products or separation of the geographical areas in which firms can sell.[56] In specific cases, these gaps have been identified by expert witnesses with knowledge of the business, or by examination of the trade press. But courts struggling with this question in Round Three have not been guided by any generally applicable and accepted framework. The *Telex* decision, for example, hinged on a ruling that there was no separate market for peripheral devices that were plug-compatible with IBM's central processing units, as distinct from compatibility with any other computer manufacturer's units. The 110 Instamatic camera and Kodacolor II film were held to comprise a photographic system rather than separate products. The absence of a standard approach to market definition is reflected in the appeals courts' reversals of the district courts' findings on this matter in both of these cases.

The Problem of Appropriate Remedies

Successful prosecution of a monopolization case (other than a private treble-damage suit) ends with the imposition of an appropriate remedy. The obvious remedy for an illegal monopoly may appear to be dissolution. Yet courts have been reluctant to impose such a remedy, viewing it as a drastic solution to be resorted to only if less severe alternatives (such as were found in *Alcoa* and *United Shoe Machinery*) are not available.[57] Wyzanski, in rejecting the government's proposal for dissolution of the United Shoe Machinery Corporation, stated:

> Judges in prescribing remedies have known their own limitations. They do not *ex officio* have economic or political training. Their prophesies as to the economic future are not guided by unusually subtle judgment. . . . In the anti-trust field the courts have been accorded, by common consent, an authority they have in no other branch of enacted law. . . . They would not have been given, or allowed to keep, such authority in the anti-trust field, and they would not so freely have altered from time to time the interpretation of its substantive provisions, if courts were in the habit of proceeding with the surgical ruthlessness that might commend itself to those seeking absolute assurances that there will be workable competition, and to those aiming at immediate realization of the social, political, and economic advantages of dispersal of power.[58]

Dissolution of a going concern destroys an organization, but it does not destroy productive capital: Factory buildings, machines, and other real assets are merely transferred to new ownership. Further, there need be no loss of employment: Indeed, if output was restricted, successful dissolution should lead to increased production and employment. Thus, dissolution is not the corporate analogue to capital punishment. Dissolution, however, may be a complicated and lengthy process, involving protracted participation by the court in formulating and implementing the transfer of millions or even billions of dollars of assets. Some judges are concerned that dissolution imposes losses on shareholders and destroys economies of scale or scope, although such concerns may be exaggerated.

If a monopolist had exploited its market power and the dissolution had successfully eliminated or reduced that power, the profits of the successor companies should be lower, in total, than those of their predecessor, *ceteris paribus*. Thus, the stockholders would bear the brunt of the remedy. Concern about equity arises because the stockholders at dissolution are often not those who reaped the gain from monopoly power.

Yet, curiously, stockholders do not usually suffer financially from dissolution.[59] The absence of such loss might indicate that the original monopoly power was less than thought or was not exercised. It also suggests that restructuring monopolies into oligopolies, without restraining the conduct of successor companies, may merely transform single-firm monopoly into the shared variety. A third possibility is that competition may energize firms.

Further, it is not obvious why dissolution should have a more serious impact on earnings and stock prices than an effective conduct remedy. (Following the 1953 decree, for example, the United Shoe Machinery Corporation's market share fell to under one half, it suffered several years of poor earnings and losses, and in 1975 was acquired by the Emhart Corporation, a smaller but more profitable concern.) There is, however, one important distinction: A conduct-oriented remedy can be modified later if its provisions turn out to be unduly harsh or inappropriate, while it would most likely be impossible to reassemble a dissolved company.

Economies of scale or scope in production, distribution, or R&D should be important factors in framing a remedy. As Wyzanski noted, in harsh criticism of the proposed dissolution of the United Shoe Machinery Corporation:

> The Government's proposal that the Court dissolve United into three separate manufacturing companies is unrealistic. United conducts all machinery manufacture in one plant. . . . A petition for dissolution should reflect greater attention to practical problems and should involve supporting economic data and prophesies such as are presented in corporate reorganization and public utility dissolution cases.[60]

But very few large U.S. corporations operate only one plant, and existing levels of concentration are typically greater than can be explained by economies of scale.

The Protracted "Big Case"

A final problem, recognized throughout the history of the Sherman Act but grown to what some commentators fear may be unmanageable proportions during Round Three, is that of adjudicating the "big case." The *IBM* case—settled 13 years after filing and involving 700 trial days, 104,000 pages of transcript, and 17,000 exhibits—exemplifies the problem.[61] Pretrial discovery proceedings took six years, and presentation of the government's case took another three. Costs were well over $100 million. In settling the case, the Justice Department noted that many of the issues originally involved were no longer pertinent.

The *IBM* case is not unique in this respect. Both the breakfast cereals and petroleum cases took eight years before being dismissed by the FTC. The latter cost the commission nearly $12 million and the defendants an estimated $75 million.[62]

The President's National Commission for the Review of Antitrust Laws and Procedures, writing in 1979, apportioned the blame among judges, the judicial system, parties to the suit, and attorneys. Judges were cited for failure to exercise stronger judicial management and control of complex, lengthy cases. Parties to the suit were seen as protracting cases to extend the life of profitable but challenged business practices. And lawyer excesses and inefficiencies were criticized, in particular the abuse of discovery and unnecessary motions.[63] The flow of documentary evidence, particularly in the pretrial discovery period, may be immense. A former FTC official sardonically cited IBM's tactics as a model and "advised corporate attorneys to make certain that the Government gets enough documents and data so that personnel on the Government team will turn over several times during the law suit."[64]

The problem is not, however, insoluble. The antitrust commission found that when the parties to the case lack incentives to move forward, judges can and should set time limits for various phases of the litigation, actively control the discovery process, and require parties to define and focus on central issues through pretrial conferences and increased willingness to hand down summary judgments on disputed legal questions.

The antitrust commission reserved its harshest criticisms and most draconian recommendations for the lawyers.

> Dilatory and abusive conduct occurs far too frequently in complex litigation. . . . Lawyers, particularly in "high-stakes" antitrust litigation, too often file meritless claims, defenses, or counterclaims, make excessive or abusive discovery demands, unreasonably resist legitimate discovery requests, provide unresponsive, "stonewalling" answers, and unreasonably produce masses of insignificant, unresponsive information. Other dilatory behavior may take the form of unjustified refusals to stipulate or admit facts, unwarranted motion practice, mishandling of documents, bad faith claims of privilege or confidentiality, and disruption of depositions.[65]

Judges, the commission recommended, should be more willing to impose personal sanctions on lawyers, including assessments for the costs of delay, disallowance of reimbursement for unnecessary time spent, contempt-of-court rulings, fines, and disciplinary proceedings before bar association panels. Sanctions can also be imposed on litigants to reduce or eliminate the financial incentives to delay, including assessments of costs, dismissal, default judgments, and prejudgment interest added to damage awards.

Unnecessary delay and obfuscation can and certainly should be eliminated from Section 2 proceedings. Nevertheless, cases of monopolization tried under the rule of reason are inherently complex. At the end of Round Two, it appeared that legal and economic approaches to the problem of monopoly were coalescing and that the reformulated rule of reason would provide a powerful and discriminating guide to the enforcement agencies and the courts. Round Three, while in no way discrediting the new rule of reason or the advances made in Round Two, brought to light a number of problems. Sophisticated legal and economic thinking needs to be directed to these problems if antitrust policy is to move forward in some future Round Four.

ENDNOTES

[1] An excellent discussion and clear demarcation of these rounds, or waves, is found in John J. Flynn, "Monopolization under the Sherman Act: The Third Wave and Beyond,"*Antitrust Bulletin* 26, no. 1 (Spring 1981), pp. 1–131.

[2] Standard Oil Company of New Jersey v. United States, 221 U.S. 1 (1911); United States v. American Tobacco Company, 221 U.S. 106 (1911).

[3] John Bates Clark and John M. Clark, *The Control of Trusts,* rewritten and enlarged (New York: Macmillan, 1912), p. 3 (italics original).

[4] United States v. E. I. du Pont de Nemours & Company, 188 Fed. 127 (1911); United States v. International Harvester Company, 214 Fed. 987 (1914); United States v. Eastman Kodak Company, 230 Fed. 522 (1916); United States v. Corn Products Refining Company, 234 Fed. 964 (1916).

[5] United States v. American Can Company, 230 Fed. 859 (1916); United States v. United Shoe Machinery Company of New Jersey, 247 U.S. 32 (1918); United States v. United Steel Corporation, 251 U.S. 417 (1920).

[6] 251 U.S. 417, 444–45.

[7] 451.

[8] United States v. Aluminum Company of America, 148 F. 2d 416 (1945).

[9] Flynn, "Monopolization under the Sherman Act," pp. 8–9.

[10] 148 F. 2d 416, 424.

[11] 429, 430.

[12] 431, 432.

[13] United States v. Aluminum Company of America et al., 91 F. Supp. 333 (1950).

[14] Swift and Company v. United States, 196 U.S. 375 (1905).

[15] Eugene V. Rostow, "The New Sherman Act: A Positive Instrument of Progress," *University of Chicago Law Review* 14, no. 4 (June 1947), pp. 567–600, at p. 577.

[16] United States v. United Shoe Machinery Corporation, 110 F. Supp. 295 (1953).

[17] For an authoritative discussion of this case, see Carl Kaysen, United States *v.*

United Shoe Machinery Corporation: *An Economic Analysis of an Antitrust Case* (Cambridge, Mass.: Harvard University Press, 1956); also see A. D. Neale and D. G. Goyder, *The Antitrust Laws of the U.S.A.*, 3d ed. (London: Cambridge University Press, 1980), p. 113.

[18]110 F. Supp. 295, 345.

[19]344–45.

[20]346.

[21]341.

[22]United States v. United Shoe Machinery Corporation, 347 U.S. 521 (1954).

[23]United States v. E. I. du Pont de Nemours & Company, 351 U.S. 377 (1956).

[24]380.

[25]United States v. American Tobacco Company et al., 164 Fed. 700, 721 (1908).

[26]351 U.S. 377, 391.

[27]George W. Stocking and Willard F. Mueller, "The Cellophane Case and the New Competition," *American Economic Review* 45, no. 1 (March 1955), pp. 29–63.

[28]351 U.S. 377, 404.

[29]United States v. Grinnell Corporation, 384 U.S. 563 (1966) at 570–71.

[30]See Federal Trade Commission v. Cement Institute, 333 U.S. 683 (1948); Atlantic Refining Company v. Federal Trade Commission, 381 U.S. 357 (1965); Federal Trade Commission v. Brown Shoe Company, 384 U.S. 316 (1966); Sperry and Hutchinson Company v. Federal Trade Commission, 432 F. 2d 146 (1970), affirmed 405 U.S. 233 (1972).

[31]The leading case is Bigelow v. RKO Radio Pictures Incorporated, 327 U.S. 251 (1946). See also Atlantic City Electric Company v. General Electric Company, 226 F. Supp. 59 (1964); Hanover Shoe Incorporated v. United Shoe Machinery Corporation, 392 U.S. 481 (1968); Zenith Radio Corporation v. Hazeltine Research Incorporated, 395 U.S. 100 (1969).

[32]Louis B. Schwartz, John J. Flynn, and Harry First, *Free Enterprise and Economic Organization: Antitrust,* 6th ed. (Mineola, N.Y.: Foundation Press, 1983, p. 22.

[33]United States v. Western Electric Incorporated, and American Telephone & Telegraph Company, CCH Trade Cases, ¶64,900 (1982).

[34]United States v. Western Electric Company, Incorporated, and American Telephone & Telegraph Company, CCH Trade Cases, ¶68,246 (1956).

[35]On this issue, see Alan K. McAdams, "The Computer Industry," in *The Structure of American Industry,* 6th ed., ed. Walter Adams (New York: Macmillan, 1982), pp. 249–97; Franklin M. Fisher, John J. McGowan, and Joen E. Greenwood, *Folded, Spindled, and Mutilated: Economic Analysis and U.S. v. IBM* (Cambridge, Mass.: MIT Press, 1983); Hendrik S. Houthakker's review of *Folded, Spindled, and Mutilated* in *Journal of Political Economy* 93, no. 3 (June 1985), pp. 618–22.

[36]U.S. Department of Justice, *Annual Report of the Attorney General of the United States, 1982* (Washington, D.C.: U.S. Government Printing Office, 1983), p. 135. For a study of the emergence of IBM as the world's leading computer manufacturer and of the issues leading to the 1969 indictment, see Gerald W. Brock, *The U.S. Computer Industry* (Cambridge, Mass.: Ballinger, 1975). For a spirited defense of IBM's economic performance and a biting critique of the government's case, written by three consultants to IBM in formulating and presenting the company's defense, see Fisher et al., *Folded, Spindled, and Mutilated.*

[37]See, for example, Manley R. Irwin and Steven C. Johnson, "The Information Economy and Public Policy," in *Electronics: The Continuing Revolution,* ed. Philip A. Abelson and Allen L. Hammond (Washington, D.C.: American Academy for the Advancement of Science, 1977).

[38]In the Matter of Exxon Corporation et al., docket no. 8934.

[39]In the Matter of Kellogg Company et al., docket no. 8883.

[40]William S. Comanor, "Antitrust in a Political Environment," *Antitrust Bulletin* 27, no. 4 (Winter 1982), pp. 733–52, at p. 749.

[41]In the Matter of Kellogg Company et al., docket no. 8883, 99 FTC 8 (1982).

[42]"Touted Search by Justice Department Fails to Find a Solid Case of Shared Monopoly," *The Wall Street Journal*, January 16, 1981, p. 21.

[43]In the Matter of E. I. du Pont de Nemours & Company, docket no. 9108, 96 FTC 653 (1980).

[44]Telex Corporation v. IBM Corporation, 367 F. Supp. 258, reversed 510 F. 2d 894 (1975); Berkey Photo Incorporated v. Eastman Kodak Company, 457 F. Supp. 404, reversed 603 F. 2d 263 (1979).

[45]MCI Communications Company v. American Telephone & Telegraph Company, 708 F. 2d 1081 (1983).

[46]Flynn, "Monopolization under the Sherman Act," p. 41.

[47]510 F. 2d 894, 927.

[48]603 F. 2d 263, 281.

[49]273.

[50]281.

[51]275.

[52]Aspen Skiing Company v. Aspen Highlands Skiing Corporation, 86 L. Ed. 2d 467 (1985).

[53]Flynn, "Monopolization under the Sherman Act," pp. 30, 95.

[54]U.S. National Commission for the Review of Antitrust Laws and Procedures, *Report to the President and the Attorney General*, 2 vols. (Washington, D.C.: U.S. Government Printing Office, 1979).

[55]Neale and Goyder, *Antitrust Laws*, pp. 90, 92 (italics added for emphasis).

[56]Joan Robinson, *The Economics of Imperfect Competition* (London: Macmillan, 1933), p. 17.

[57]Richard A. Posner noted that the courts resorted to dissolution as a remedy in monopolization cases brought under Section 2 of the Sherman Act in only 32 cases between passage of the act in 1890 and 1969, in "A Statistical Study of Antitrust Enforcement," *Journal of Law and Economics* 13, no. 2 (October 1970), pp. 365–419, at p. 406.

[58]110 F. Supp. 295, 347–48.

[59]For an influential and pioneering study, see Donald Dewey, "Romance and Realism in Antitrust Policy," *Journal of Political Economy* 63, no. 2 (April 1955), pp. 93–102. For a survey of the literature and a finding of financial hurt due to the American Tobacco Company dissolution ordered in 1911, see Malcolm R. Burns, "An Empirical Analysis of Stockholder Injury under §2 of the Sherman Act," *Journal of Industrial Economics* 31, no. 4 (June 1983), pp. 333–62.

[60]110 F. Supp. 295, 348.

[61]Schwartz et al., *Free Enterprise*, p. 66.

[62]Comanor, "Antitrust in a Political Environment," p. 747.

[63]National Commission, *Report to the President*, vol. 1, pp. 12–13.

[64]Quoted in Schwartz et al., *Free Enterprise*, p. 50.

[65]National Commission, *Report to the President*, vol. 1, p. 82.

CHAPTER SIXTEEN

Mergers and Section 7 of the Clayton Act

ORIGINAL SECTION 7 AND THE CELLER–KEFAUVER AMENDMENT

Until 1950, no section of the U.S. antitrust laws dealt specifically and unambiguously with merger.   Indeed, until that year, many felt that the nation had no meaningful policy on anticompetitive mergers.

As enacted in 1914, Section 7 of the Clayton Act forbade a corporation from acquiring, "directly or indirectly, the whole or any part of the stock or other share capital of another corporation . . . where the effect . . . may be to substantially lessen competition between the corporation whose stock is so acquired and the corporation making the acquisition or . . . tend to create a monopoly of any line of commerce."[1] The law was silent on merger through acquisition of assets, leading to subsequent concern about an "asset loophole."

To understand original Section 7 and the failure of Congress to address merger through outright purchase of assets, recall that the Clayton Act was passed in the aftermath of the *Standard Oil* and *American Tobacco* cases of 1911 and that Congress was strongly influenced by revelations of predatory and unethical behavior.

Acquisition of competing companies' shares was thought to be prominent among the unsavory tactics used in forming the trusts. Control of a corporation could be obtained through ownership of a majority or "working minority" of its voting common stock at far less cost than outright purchase of assets, particularly if debt was a significant portion of the target firm's capitalization.   The investment required to control an operating company could be further reduced by using holding companies to own the shares of one or more corporations.

Shares of stock could be bought without the permission or even knowledge of the target firm's owners and managers; sometimes a controlling interest could be kept secret from competitors and customers, leading to the "bogus independents" complained of in the *Standard Oil* decision. Through holding companies and other corporate devices, varied and complex business organizations could be assembled. The corporate structure of the old American Tobacco Company, for example, was so tangled that the court needed help from company creator James B. Duke to frame a dissolution decree.[2]

In an early set of cases, the Federal Trade Commission (FTC) sought to use Section 7 to undo or forbid merging of the assets of firms already under common stockholder control. In 1926, the Supreme Court held that the commission had no authority to do so under the Clayton Act and indicated that if stockholdings were used to bring about a merger of assets, the combination could only be dissolved by action brought under the Sherman Act by the Department of Justice and adjudicated under the rule of reason.[3] In 1934, the Supreme Court went further, holding that if illegally acquired stock was used to bring about a combination of assets, even after the FTC had initiated an action to compel divestiture of the stock, the commission had no authority to order that the newly acquired assets be divested.[4] In both 1926 and 1934, the Supreme Court decisions were made by 5-to-4 votes, with strongly worded dissenting opinions.

In a 1950 opinion, Judge Irving R. Kaufman summarized the situation by noting that "the Section was designed primarily to deal with the evil of the secret acquisition by one corporation of the stock of another, principally those acquisitions by 'holding companies.' Congress intended that the public should not be deceived into believing that their companies were competing when their stock was actually commonly owned either by one of the 'competing' corporations or by a third corporation."[5]

The situation was not satisfactory to those who saw merger as a primary source of undue concentration in the U.S. economy and who believed the Clayton Act was designed to prevent such concentration from rising to levels that met Sherman Act standards of monopolization. Every big monopolization case in the Sherman Act's early years, successful and unsuccessful, involved firms formed by mergers of previously independent and competing firms—American Tobacco, Standard Oil, Du Pont, American Sugar Refining, Corn Products Refining, Eastman Kodak, American Can, International Harvester, United Shoe Machinery, and U.S. Steel.

This concern reached a crescendo in the early years following World War II, a time when a third merger wave was widely perceived. In 1947, a report of the House Judiciary Committee noted "the great increase in recent years of competition-destroying mergers" and called for "the enactment of legislation to stop the rising tide of monopoly."[6] The following year, an FTC report noted that at least 2,450 firms in manufacturing and mining had been absorbed in mergers from 1940 to 1947.[7] Congress responded in 1950 by enacting the Celler-Kefauver amendment to Section 7. The key passage reads:

> No corporation engaged in commerce shall acquire, directly or indirectly, the whole or any part of the stock or other share capital and no corporation subject to the jurisdiction of the Federal Trade Commission shall acquire the whole or any part of the assets of another corporation engaged also in commerce, where, in any line of commerce in any section of the country, the effect of such acquisition may be substantially to lessen competition or to tend to create a monopoly.[8]

The substance and the intent of the amendment were precisely summarized in Judge Edward Weinfeld's 1958 opinion in the *Bethlehem-Youngstown* case, the first to reach the courts under the amended Section 7:

> The 1950 amendment to section 7 expanded its sweep so as: (1) to prohibit the acquisition of assets as well as stock; (2) to broaden the area in which competition may be adversely affected by eliminating the test of whether the effect may be to substantially lessen competition *between the acquiring and the acquired corporation;* (3) to eliminate the prior test of whether the acquisition might restrain commerce "in any * * * community" and instead, to make the test whether "in any line of commerce in any section of the country" the acquisition may substantially lessen competition, or tend to create a monopoly; and (4) to cover vertical as well as horizontal mergers. . . . Its major objectives . . . [were] (1) to limit future increases in the level of economic concentration resulting from corporate mergers and acquisitions; (2) to meet the threat posed by the merger movement to small business fields and thereby aid in preserving small business as an important competitive factor in the American economy; (3) to cope with monopolistic tendencies in their incipiency and before they attain Sherman Act proportions; and (4) to avoid a Sherman Act test in deciding the effects of a merger.[9]

LEGAL INTERPRETATION OF SECTION 7 AS AMENDED BY THE CELLER–KEFAUVER ACT

Although the 1958 *Bethlehem-Youngstown* case was the first under amended Section 7 in which a lower court rendered an opinion, the impact of the Celler-Kefauver Act was portended one year earlier in the Supreme Court's *Du Pont–General Motors* opinion. In a 1949 indictment, the government alleged that Du Pont's ownership of 23 percent of the outstanding common stock of General Motors, acquired from 1917 to 1919, violated Sections 1 and 2 of the Sherman Act as well as the original Section 7 of the Clayton Act. On appeal, the Supreme Court concentrated on the Clayton Act aspect of the case, explicitly omitting the Sherman Act charges. The Court, mindful of passage of the Celler-Kefauver amendment, made two basic points, equally applicable to either version of Section 7. First, the congressionally declared objective of the Clayton Act was "by making these practices illegal, to arrest the creation of trusts, conspiracies, and monopolies *in their incipiency and before consummation.*" Thus, the government could proceed not only at "the time the stock was acquired, but at any time when the acquisition threatens to ripen into a prohibited effect." Second, while "proof of a *mere possibility* of a prohibited restraint or tendency to monopoly" would not suffice, the burden on the government under the Section 7 phrase "where the effect may be" was to show a reasonable probability of the proscribed effects and not necessarily a high likelihood.[10]

In his *Bethlehem-Youngstown* decision, Judge Weinfeld also addressed a central economic issue in merger policy—the possible denial of real economies of scale or scope. Economies of scale and scope, he argued, afford no defense to an otherwise objectionable merger because the intent of Congress was to prevent undue concentration even at the sacrifice of productive efficiency. But an important economic consideration justified the trade-off Congress had been prepared to make: the sacrifice would be small, since internal expansion is usually a feasible and less anticompetitive alternative to expansion through merger if the economies are real and significant. (Within a few years after Judge Weinfeld's decision, both Bethlehem and Youngstown did engage in major expansion and modernization.)

In the 1960s, the Supreme Court moved further toward rigorous interpretation of amended Section 7 as a strict preventive antimerger statute, at least in cases that involved *horizontal* mergers—ones in which the acquiring and acquired firms are competitors and the merger eliminates competition between them. Thus, the issue under Section 7 is whether such lessening of competition is "substantial" or whether the merger may "tend to create a monopoly."

Vertical mergers involve firms formerly in an actual or potential buyer-seller relationship. In a vertical merger, other firms at the buying (downstream) level may be *foreclosed,* or denied access to goods or services formerly provided by the selling (upstream) firm. Also, firms that formerly competed with the upstream firm in selling to the downstream partner to the merger may be foreclosed from such sales. Since the *Du Pont–General Motors* decision, the courts have held that such foreclosure constitutes an elimination of competition. The issue, as in horizontal merger, is whether such elimination is "substantial."

In a *conglomerate* merger, the situation is more complex. By definition, a merger of this type takes place between firms that neither compete nor are significant supply or sales sources for each other.

Horizontal and Vertical Mergers

The first Celler-Kefauver Act case heard by the Supreme Court involved a merger with both horizontal and vertical aspects—the acquisition of G. R. Kinney Company by Brown Shoe Company.[11] Both firms manufactured shoes, and both were vertically integrated into retailing. Brown, however, produced more shoes than it sold through its retail outlets, while Kinney sold more at retail than it produced and thus purchased shoes from other manufacturers. The issues before the Supreme Court were whether the merger had the proscribed effects, horizontally in the retail market for shoes and vertically through foreclosure of sales to Kinney by manufacturers other than Brown.

Market Definition. The horizontal feature of the case concentrated on proper definition of the market—both "line of commerce" and "section of the country" in legal language, or "product" market and "geographic" market in economic terminology. Brown was the third largest seller of shoes; it owned or franchised 1,230 retail outlets. Kinney, the eighth largest retailer, had over 350 retail outlets. The government contended that the affected line of commerce was "footwear," or, alternatively, men's, women's, and children's shoes, each as a separate line, and that the section of the country within which an anticompetitive effect might be found was the whole nation or, alternatively, "each city or city and its immediate surrounding area in which the parties sell shoes at retail." The defendants, however, maintained that "not only were the age and sex of the intended customers to be considered in determining the relevant line of commerce, but that differences in grade of material, quality of workmanship, price and customer use of shoes resulted in establishing different lines of commerce." The distinction was important because Brown produced a higher grade of shoes than Kinney. The geographic market, the defendants argued, "must vary with economic reality from the central business district of a large city to the 'standard metropolitan area' for a smaller community."[12]

The Supreme Court disposed of the issue in a sweeping statement.

> The outer boundaries of a product market are determined by the reasonable interchangeability of use or the cross-elasticity of demand between the product itself and substitutes for it. However, within this broad market, well-defined submarkets may exist which, in themselves, constitute product markets for antitrust purposes. The boundaries of such a submarket may be determined by examining such practical indicia as industry

or public recognition of the submarket as a separate economic entity, the product's peculiar characteristics and uses, unique production facilities, distinct customers, distinct prices, sensitivity to price changes, and specialized vendors.[13]

If there was a reasonable probability that competition would be lessened in *any* submarket, the opinion continued, the merger would be illegal. Applying this reasoning, the Supreme Court held that men's, women's, and children's shoes did constitute separate lines of commerce but that there were no separate markets for different "price/quality" lines. The geographic markets were held to be "cities with a population exceeding 10,000 and their environs in which both Brown and Kinney retailed shoes through their own outlets."[14] The lower bound of 10,000 was set because Kinney had no retail stores in smaller communities.

Incipiency and Foreclosure. In assessing the vertical aspect of the merger, the Supreme Court upheld the district court's opinion that the relevant market comprised the entire nation. Since the Clayton Act's objective was to check concentration in its incipiency, the merger had to be evaluated in the context of industrywide trends. Further, although intent itself was not relevant under the Clayton Act test of illegality, evidence of intent could be used to help infer probable effect. Thus, the Court concluded: "The trend toward vertical integration in the shoe industry, when combined with Brown's avowed policy of forcing its own shoes upon its retail subsidiaries, seems likely to foreclose competition from a substantial share of the markets for men's, women's, and children's shoes, without producing any countervailing competitive, economic, or social advantages."[15]

The "Deep Pocket." Foreclosure was not the only anticompetitive effect seen to be associated with vertical merger. In the same year the Supreme Court ruled against the Brown-Kinney merger, an appeals court upheld an FTC order requiring an aluminum manufacturer, Reynolds Metals Company, to divest itself of the stock and assets of Arrow Brands, a small firm that processed raw aluminum foil into decorative florist's foil. The court noted, with approval, that the commission's decision did not rest on the "minor anticompetitive effect" of foreclosure. Rather:

> Arrow's assimilation into Reynolds' enormous capital structure and resources gave Arrow an immediate advantage over its competitors who were contending for a share of the market for florist foil. The power of the "deep pocket" or "rich parent" for one of the florist foil suppliers in a competitive group where previously no company was very large and all were relatively small opened the possibility and power to sell at prices

approximating cost or below and thus to undercut and ravage the less affluent competition.[16]

Does Foreclosure Really Lessen Competition? Despite the courts' concern, foreclosure will result in a substantial lessening of competition only in special circumstances. First, either the upstream or downstream market share of the merged firm must be large enough to result in a significant reduction in overall market size. Second, no matter how great the market share involved, foreclosure will be effective only if there are barriers to entry into the foreclosed market. Suppose, for example, that a firm acquires the sole producer of a necessary raw material and refuses to supply its competitors with that material. Unless there is some barrier preventing new firms from entering the raw material industry or deprived firms from integrating backwards, foreclosure will not eliminate or disadvantage rivals. Or, if a manufacturer were to purchase all of the existing retail outlets for its industry's product, it would be able to squeeze out its competitors only if new outlets did not appear. In any event, even if entry were barred, the basic structural problem from the point of view of economic performance would be the monopolization of the raw material or of retailing, rather than the vertical integration.

In 1972, the Supreme Court did uphold a district court finding that Ford Motor Company's acquisition of the Electric Autolite Company's spark plug manufacturing facilities violated Section 7 by foreclosing Ford as a purchaser of spark plugs.[17] But since then, there have been few vertical integration cases brought by the Justice Department or the FTC, and the Supreme Court has not issued another opinion. The 1969 Stigler Report to President Nixon (discussed in Chapter Thirteen) argued that vertical integration rarely added to a firm's market power and was usually motivated by the prospect of more efficient methods of distribution or production. The report therefore recommended that the law against vertical mergers not be vigorously enforced.[18] The antitrust agencies have followed this advice.

Presumptive Illegality. In 1963, the Supreme Court considered and ruled against the merger of two Philadelphia banks. Two aspects of this ruling strengthened Section 7's application to horizontal merger. First, the Court applied the doctrine of *presumptive illegality* to mergers that lead to substantial increases in concentration. Citing congressional fears, the Court held:

> This intense congressional concern with the trend toward concentration warrants dispensing, in certain cases, with elaborate proof of market structure, market behavior, or probable anticompetitive effects. Specifically, we think that a merger which produces a firm controlling an undue per-

centage share of the relevant market, and results in a significant increase in the concentration of firms in that market is so inherently likely to lessen competition substantially that it must be enjoined in the absence of evidence clearly showing that the merger is not likely to have such anticompetitive effects.[19]

Procompetitive Effects Provide No Defense.   The defendants in the bank case had argued that the merger's effect on concentration in the Philadelphia area would be offset by the combined banks' ability to compete against New York and California banks in the national market for large business loans and that the larger bank could attract business to the Philadelphia area and thereby contribute to local economic development.   In rejecting these arguments, the Court held:

> If anticompetitive effects in one market could be justified by procompetitive consequences in another, the logical upshot would be that every firm in an industry could, without violating §7, embark on a series of mergers that would make it in the end as large as the industry leader. . . .
>
> We are clear, however, that a merger the effect of which "may be substantially to lessen competition" is not saved because, on some ultimate reckoning of social or economic debits and credits, it may be deemed beneficial. . . .   Congress . . . proscribed anticompetitive mergers, the benign and malignant alike, fully aware, we must assume, that some price might have to be paid.[20]

Further Strengthening of Section 7.   Throughout the 1960s, other horizontal merger decisions of the Supreme Court further strengthened Section 7.

Relaxing the Definition of Relevant Market.   Market definition arose in two cases.   In a 1964 case involving a merger between a metal can and a glass bottle manufacturer, the Court held the relevant market to be the two types of containers, since "where the area of effective competition cuts across industry lines, so must the relevant line of commerce."[21]   Justice John M. Harlan dissented however, noting that the requisite effect on competition could not have been shown either if glass bottles and tin cans had been considered as separate lines of commerce or if all containers had been included in a broad definition. "In any event," he wrote, "the Court does not take this tack.   It chooses instead to invent a line of commerce the existence of which no one, not even the Government, has imagined; for which businessmen and economists will look in vain; a line of commerce which sprang into existence only when the merger took place and will cease to exist when the merger is undone.   I have no idea where §7 goes from here, nor will businessmen or the antitrust bar."[22]

In a 1966 case involving the merger of two beer brewers, the defense challenged the government's definition of the relevant market as too vague and unproven. The Supreme Court brusquely rejected this defense and the district court's acceptance of it:

> Apparently the District Court thought that in order to show a violation of §7 it was essential for the Government to show a "relevant geographic market" in the same way the corpus delicti must be proved to establish a crime. But when the Government brings an action under §7 it must, according to the language of the statute, prove no more than that there has been a merger between two corporations engaged in commerce and that the effect of the merger may be substantially to lessen competition or tend to create a monopoly in any line of commerce *"in any section of the country."*... This phrase does not call for the delineation of a "section of the country" by metes and bounds as a surveyor would lay off a plot of ground.[23]

Per Se Illegality of Acquisition by a Dominant Firm. In 1964, Alcoa, the largest producer of aluminum conductor cable with 27.8 percent of the market, was barred from acquiring Rome Cable Corporation, a small firm that accounted for 1.3 percent of sales. The Supreme Court noted that Rome was "an aggressive competitor" and that "preservation of Rome, rather than its absorption by one of the giants, will keep it as 'an important competitive factor.' ... Rome seems to us the prototype of the small independent that Congress aimed to preserve by §7."[24] Commentators interpreted this decision to mean that the acquisition of any competitor, no matter how small, would be per se illegal for an industry leader.

"The Government Always Wins." The high-water mark of Section 7 is generally recognized as the 1966 *Von's–Shopping Bag* case.[25] In this case a merger of the third and sixth largest retail grocery chains in the Los Angeles area led to a combined firm with a 7.5 percent market share. In ruling the merger illegal, the Supreme Court relied heavily on the incipiency argument and on the point that a merger must be evaluated in the context of marketwide trends. In a biting dissent, Justice Potter Stewart lashed out at the Court's overall interpretation of Section 7. "The sole consistency that I can find is that in litigation under §7, the Government always wins."[26]

Conglomerate Mergers

Amended Section 7 has had only limited success in checking conglomerate mergers. The problem, for both enforcement agencies and those concerned with the sociopolitical and economic consequences of conglomerates, has been to identify any effect on competition from a merger of noncompeting firms. Firms' market-related interests, however, extend beyond competitors, suppliers, and customers, and most mergers presumably yield some particular advantages to the parties.

Recognizing this, the FTC has distinguished three types of conglomerate merger. In *market extension* mergers, a firm enters a new market by acquiring a firm already in that market (e.g., a commercial bank in Seattle acquires another in Spokane). A *product extension* merger involves firms that produce different but related products—that is, the products are sold to common customers, use similar manufacturing techniques, or are otherwise linked in production, distribution, or management (e.g., an international airline merges with an international hotel chain). Finally, in a *pure* conglomerate merger, the firms have no apparent relationship (e.g., a steel company merges with a bakery).

Market Extension Mergers. The anticompetitive effect most often alleged in market extension mergers is a lessening of *potential* competition: If merger with an established firm enjoying a substantial market share is disallowed, the would-be acquiring firm might enter the market *de novo* (by establishing a new facility or by a "toehold" merger with a small firm followed by later internal growth). Even if the anticipated entry does not occur, the argument goes, fear that it might, or of potential competition, limits the ability of existing firms to exercise market power and earn monopolistic profits.

Prosecutions based on this argument have been somewhat successful in Section 7 cases. El Paso Natural Gas Company, which supplied California, was required to divest itself of Pacific Northwest Pipeline Corporation. Prior to the merger, Pacific Northwest did not supply California, but it had made two unsuccessful attempts to do so.[27] A joint venture of Pennsalt Chemicals and Olin Mathieson to establish a jointly-owned subsidiary to produce a bleaching agent in a fast-growing market area was successfully challenged on the theory that, in the absence of the joint venture, one of the two might enter the market alone and the other "might have remained at the edge of the market, continually threatening to enter."[28] In an attempt to enter the New England beer market, Falstaff Brewing Corporation acquired Narragansett Brewing Company. In ruling that Falstaff was not a potential competitor, the district court relied heavily on testimony by Falstaff executives who stated that Falstaff had no intention of entering the New England market by any route other than merger with an established firm. The Supreme Court reversed, noting: "The specific question with respect to this phase of the case is not what Falstaff's internal company decisions were but whether, given its financial capabilities and conditions in the New England market, it would be reasonable to consider it a potential entrant into that market."[29]

Limits to the potential competition doctrine were spelled out in the 1974 *Marine Bancorporation* decision approving the acquisition of a Spokane bank by one in Seattle. Justice Lewis F. Powell summarized the development of precedent through the *Falstaff* case and concluded:

> The principal focus of the doctrine is on the likely effects of the premerger position of the acquiring firm on the fringe of the target market. In developing and applying the doctrine, the Court has recognized that a market extension merger may be unlawful if the target market is substantially concentrated, if the acquiring firm has the characteristics, capabilities, and economic incentive to render it a perceived potential *de novo* entrant, and if the acquiring firm's premerger presence on the fringe of the target market in fact tempered oligopolistic behavior on the part of existing participants in that market. In other words, the Court has interpreted §7 as encompassing what is commonly known as the "wings effect"—the probability that the acquiring firm prompted premerger procompetitive effects within the target market by being perceived by the existing firms in that market as likely to enter *de novo*.[30]

The government, Powell asserted, had tried to push the potential competition doctrine too far in contending that a market extension merger could be held illegal solely on the ground that it eliminated the prospective competition the acquiring firm's entry would provide. To succeed, the prosecution would have to show, first, "that feasible alternative means of entry in fact existed" and, second, "that the alternative means offer a reasonable prospect of long-term structural improvement or other benefits in the target market."[31]

Product Extension Mergers. Product extension mergers can be challenged on various grounds. One early and successful basis was that such a merger could lead to *reciprocity*—i.e., favored vendors would be expected to reciprocate by placing orders with another division of the buying firm. In the leading case, Consolidated Foods Corporation (a food processor, wholesaler, and retailer) acquired Gentry, Inc. (a manufacturer of dehydrated onion and garlic seasonings). Evidence showed that food-processing firms selling their products to Consolidated tended to favor Gentry as a supplier of seasonings. The Supreme Court, in proscribing the merger, stated that reciprocity "is one of the congeries of anticompetitive practices at which the antitrust laws are aimed."[32]

The FTC cited a number of anticompetitive results stemming from the acquisition of Clorox Chemical Corporation, a leading manufacturer of household liquid bleach, by Procter & Gamble Company, the nation's leading producer of soaps, detergents, and cleansers. As summarized in the Supreme Court's opinion:

> The Commission found that the substitution of Procter with its huge assets and advertising advantages for the already dominant Clorox would dissuade new entrants and discourage active competition from the firms already in the industry due to fear of retaliation by Procter. . . . Retailers might be induced to give Clorox preferred shelf space since it would be manufactured by Procter, which also produced a number of other products marketed by the retailers. There was also the danger that Procter might underprice Clorox in order to drive out competition, and subsidize the underpricing with revenue from other products. The Commission . . . not[ed] that "[t]he practical tendency of the . . . merger . . . is to transform the liquid bleach industry into an arena of big business only, with the few small firms that have not disappeared through merger falling by the wayside, unable to compete with their giant rivals." Further, the merger would seriously diminish potential competition by eliminating Procter as a potential entrant into the industry. Prior to the merger, the Commission found, Procter was the most likely prospective entrant, and absent the merger would have remained on the periphery, restraining Clorox from exercising its market power. If Procter had actually entered, Clorox's dominant position would have been eroded and the concentration of the industry reduced.[33]

Note the cross-subsidization, "deep pocket," predation, potential competition, and protection of small business arguments, as well as two theories of anticompetitive effects not yet discussed: *leverage*, the idea that monopoly power in one area can be used to enhance power in others, and *triggering*, the concern that one merger might have a secondary effect on concentration by stimulating other mergers or driving small independent firms from the market.

Markham has investigated the prevalence of cross-subsidization and reciprocity among large diversified firms.[34] His survey indicated that the greater the degree of diversity, the more autonomy each division was given in pricing its products and the more likely it was to be identified as a separate "profit center." Under these circumstances, divisional managers had no incentives to give up their own profits to help other divisions through either reciprocity or cross-subsidization. The statistical result of this managerial phenomenon was that the greater the diversification of a firm, the less likely it was to engage in either practice.

Pure Conglomerate Mergers. The enforcement agencies have not succeeded in cases involving pure—or nearly pure—conglomerate mergers. The courts have not yet accepted the concept of *mutual forbearance*, the argument made by some economists that firms that share a number of markets may be more reluctant to compete in any one of them, since they are vulnerable to retaliation in others.[35]

In 1969, the Antitrust Division filed five pure conglomerate merger cases, but all were settled by negotiation and consent decree before reaching the Supreme Court.[36] Three involving International Telephone & Telegraph were dropped as part of a 1971 consent decree in which IT&T was permitted to keep its largest acquisition, the Hartford Fire Insurance Company, but agreed to divest itself of a number of other subsidiaries. IT&T further agreed not to acquire any firm with assets of over $100 million without prior approval from the Justice Department or the district court administering the decree for 10 years after the date of filing.[37] In settlement of another of the 1969 conglomerate cases, Ling-Temco-Vought was permitted to keep Jones & Laughlin Steel Corporation provided it divested itself of Braniff Airways and the Okonite Corporation and agreed to refrain from acquiring any other firm with assets of over $100 million for the next 10 years.[38]

By the time of the IT&T settlement, the government had lost cases in the district courts challenging IT&T's acquisitions of Hartford and Grinnell. The decision in the *Grinnell* case is significant for its rejection of the government's argument that an increase in aggregate concentration would lead to a violation of Section 7. In rejecting this contention, Judge William H. Timbers wrote:

> Whatever may be the merits of the arguments as a matter of social and economic policy in favor of, or opposed to, a standard for measuring the legality of a merger under the antitrust laws by the degree to which it may increase economic concentration rather than by the degree to which it may lessen competition, that is beyond the competence of the Court to adjudicate. . . . [I]f that standard is to be changed, it is fundamental under our system of government that any decision to change the standard be made by the Congress and not by the courts.[39]

AGENCY ENFORCEMENT UNDER MERGER GUIDELINES AND THE HART–SCOTT–RODINO ACT

The Supreme Court's 1974 decision in the *Marine Bancorporation* case, allowing the merger of the two Washington banks, was one of two major cases that year in which the Supreme Court ruled against the government. The second was a horizontal merger case involving the combination of two coal mining companies in which the acquiring firm subsequently became a subsidiary of General Dynamics Corporation. The Court noted that the government's case rested mainly on statistics "showing that within certain geographic markets the coal industry was concentrated among a small number of large producers; that this concentration was increasing; and that the acquisition of United Electric would materially enlarge the market share of the acquiring company." Further, "In prior decisions involving horizontal mergers between competitors, this Court has found prima facie violations . . . from aggregate statistics of the sort relied on."[40] However, the Court pointed out that United's uncommitted reserves were nearly depleted and it was not in a position to replace them. Regardless of United's current market share, the Court held, it was not likely to remain an effective competitor for any substantial length of time, and therefore, its acquisition would not pose a reasonable probability of substantially lessening competition.

So ended Justice Stewart's sole source of consistency in interpreting Section 7—"the Government always wins" in horizontal and vertical merger cases. Some interpreted the Court's language in *General Dynamics* as indirectly criticizing the "statistical approach" of earlier decisions and as presaging a new, more permissive approach to mergers. Such a change never had a chance to materialize. By the late 1970s and early 80s, the main scene of action shifted to the enforcement agencies.

Merger Guidelines

In 1968, the Antitrust Division spelled out the criteria it intended to use in deciding whether to challenge a merger. In published guidelines, the division indicated the market shares of both acquiring and acquired firms that it would find objectionable in horizontal mergers, with smaller shares allowed in more highly concentrated industries. Maximum market shares supplied and purchased by the merging firms were established as standards for evaluating vertical mergers. In 1982 and again in 1984, the guidelines were revised, with the Herfindahl index substituted for market share and the concentration ratio as the measure of concentration. The 1984 guideline standards for horizontal mergers are:

> 3.11 *General Standards*
>   In evaluating horizontal mergers, the Department will consider both the post-merger market concentration and the increase in concentration resulting from the merger. . . . *However, market share and concentration data provide only the starting point for analyzing the competitive impact of a merger. Before determining whether to challenge a merger, the Department will consider all other relevant factors that pertain to its competitive impact.*
>   The general standards for horizontal mergers are as follows:
>   a) *Post-Merger HHI Below 1000.* Markets in this region generally would be considered to be unconcentrated. Because implicit coordination among firms is likely to be difficult and because the prohibitions of section

1 of the Sherman Act are usually an adequate response to any explicit collusion that might occur, the Department *will not* challenge mergers falling in this region, *except in extraordinary circumstances.*

b) *Post-Merger HHI Between 1000 and 1800.* Because this region extends from the point at which the competitive concerns associated with concentration are raised to the point at which they become quite serious, generalization is particularly difficult. The Department, however, is unlikely to challenge a merger producing an increase in the HHI of less than 100 points. The Department is *likely* to challenge mergers in this region that produce an increase in the HHI of more than 100 points. . . .

c) *Post-Merger HHI Above 1800.* Markets in this region generally are considered to be highly concentrated. Additional concentration resulting from mergers is a matter of significant competitive concern. The Department is unlikely, however, to challenge mergers producing an increase in the HHI of less than 50 points. *The Department is likely to challenge mergers in this region that produce an increase in the HHI of more than 50 points, unless the Department concludes . . . that the merger is not likely substantially to lessen competition. However, if the increase in the HHI exceeds 100 and the post-merger HHI substantially exceeds 1800, only in extraordinary cases will [other] factors establish that the merger is not likely substantially to lessen competition.*

3.12 *Leading Firm Proviso*

In some cases, typically where one of the merging firms is small, mergers that may create or enhance the market power of a single dominant firm could pass scrutiny under the standards stated in Section 3.11. Notwithstanding those standards, the Department is likely to challenge the merger of any firm with a market share of at least one percent with the leading firm in the market, provided the leading firm has a market share that is at least 35 percent. Because the ease and profitability of collusion are of little relevance to the ability of a single dominant firm to exercise market power, the Department will not consider the presence or absence of the factors [relating to the likelihood of collusion].[41]

The 1984 guidelines cite a number of factors other than concentration to be considered in assessing the competitive effects of a horizontal merger, including the impact of new technology on market conditions and on the firms' likely future shares, firms' financial strengths and weaknesses in the market, the significance of foreign competition, ease of entry, nature of the product and terms of sale, ease of detection of changes made by others in prices and terms of sale, the ease and speed with which small firms might expand their output in response to a price increase, and the past and current conduct of firms in the market. Further:

Some mergers that the Department might otherwise challenge may be reasonably necessary to achieve significant net efficiencies. If the parties to the merger establish by clear and convincing evidence that a merger will achieve such efficiencies, the Department will consider those efficiencies in deciding whether to challenge the merger. . . . In addition, the Department will reject claims of efficiencies if equivalent or comparable savings can reasonably be achieved by the parties through other means.[42]

The 1984 guidelines distinguish between horizontal and nonhorizontal mergers rather than among horizontal, vertical, and conglomerate. They do note that a vertical merger may pose problems of heightened barriers to entry, but it is unlikely to be challenged in the absence of exacerbating circumstances unless the Herfindahl index for the market most affected is above 1800 (.18). The rationale is that markets with lower levels of concentration are likely to be so highly competitive that barriers to entry will not have a deleterious effect on performance and collusion cannot be effective. The guidelines' only ground for challenging conglomerate mergers is lessening of potential competition. Such a lessening is considered likely to be serious only if the Herfindahl index in the acquired firm's market exceeds 1800.

Although the FTC did not explicitly endorse and adopt any of the guidelines, it has announced and applied similar ones.

The Hart-Scott-Rodino Act: Premerger Notification

The 1968 guidelines succeeded to some extent in deterring mergers that the enforcement agencies were likely to challenge, thus curtailing the courts' role. The courts' participation was further reduced by the premerger notification requirement in the Hart-Scott-Rodino Act. Under this 1976 amendment to Section 7, all firms involved in a prospective merger must notify both the Antitrust Division and the FTC if sales or assets of the acquiring firm exceed $100 million and if sales or assets of the acquired firm exceed $10 million. The notification is followed by a 30-day waiting period (15 days in the case of a cash tender offer) before the merger can be consummated; and this waiting period can be extended by 20 days if one of the enforcement agencies asks for additional information.

The Premerger Process. Since passage of Hart-Scott-Rodino, the standard practice has been for either agency that questions a proposed merger to notify the other. The agency agreed on to handle the matter negotiates with the parties during the waiting period. The enforcement agencies can also file in a district court for a preliminary injunction forbidding consummation until the merger's legality is determined or for a "hold separate" order under which neither the assets nor the records of the acquired company can be mingled with those of the acquiring one until the case is settled. The courts have almost routinely granted such requests, despite pleas that equity demands greater consideration for the interests of the companies' stockholders in allowing the merger to proceed before the terms become obsolete.[43]

Under these circumstances, companies have been extremely reluctant to contest the antitrust agencies in the courts and suffer both the economic and the legal uncertainties associated with protracted litigation. Thus, the fate of large mergers has come to be settled by negotiation between an enforcement agency and the firms involved, rather than by the courts.

In the face of opposition by the Antitrust Division or the FTC, some proposed mergers have simply been dropped. In 1981, for example, the Justice Department successfully blocked Mobil Oil's intended acquisition of Marathon Oil, and Heileman Brewing Company withdrew an offer to purchase Schlitz Brewing Company. In early 1984, the Antitrust Division's objections ended U.S. Steel's effort to acquire National Steel. In 1982, Gulf Oil's proposal to acquire Cities Service was challenged by the FTC, which refused to approve the merger unless Gulf divested itself of a major refinery and terminal facilities in 19 localities. Gulf was amenable to selling the terminals but unwilling to give up the refinery; when the FTC would not modify its position, the company withdrew its merger offer.

The Shift from Court to Enforcement Agencies. The enforcement agencies may play a crucial role in determining the final composition of a contested merger. In 1981, for example, Joseph E. Seagram & Sons, Du Pont, and Mobil Oil were all actively seeking to acquire Continental Oil Company (Conoco). The Antitrust Division held up Mobil's exercise of a tender bid opposed by Conoco management and made an agreement with Du Pont that it would not challenge that company's acquisition of Conoco provided Du Pont purchased Monsanto Chemical Company's share in a joint petrochemical venture between Conoco and Monsanto. The anticompetitive effect seen was that both Du Pont and Monsanto produced synthetic fibers from petrochemicals. After being cleared to proceed, Du Pont outbid Seagram.

Typically, the enforcement agencies have not just blocked mergers but rather tried to eliminate their anticompetitive aspects. This approach is workable because firms rarely file merger proposals that clearly violate the guidelines. In 1982, Stroh Brewing Company was permitted to acquire Schlitz provided it divested itself of one of Schlitz's two plants in the southeastern United States. Later that year, Heileman was permitted to acquire Pabst Brewing Company, including Pabst's 49 percent ownership of the Olympia beer brewery in which Heileman already had a 2 percent interest, but only if Heileman divested itself of approximately 83 percent of Pabst's tangible assets. Heileman was permitted to keep two Pabst breweries and the Olympia brewery, but its most important acquisition was the rights to a number of Pabst's brand names. In 1983, the purchase of Wheelabrator-Frye Inc. by the Signal Companies was approved subject to the proviso that Wheelabrator-Frye sell its patents on two petroleum-refining processes. In early 1984, the Federal Trade Commission approved the largest merger then on record, a $13.4 billion acquisition of Gulf Corporation by Standard Oil Company of California (SoCal). However, the merger was subject to extensive divestiture requirements including one refinery, an interest in a pipeline company, and Gulf's southeastern distribution system consisting of 30 wholesale terminals and 4,000 service stations throughout six states—about one third of Gulf's entire wholesale and retail operations. Further and for the first time in a merger case, SoCal agreed, but only under strenuous protest, to "hold separate" all of Gulf's assets until the divestitures were completed.

One obvious result of this shift from the courts to the enforcement agencies is an increase in discretionary enforcement of antimerger policy and less concern with consistency and precedent. The guidelines are subject to administrative change and reflect the views of current Justice Department officials. And unlike the courts, the antitrust agencies are subject to direct political pressure.

SOME ECONOMIC CONSIDERATIONS IN MERGER POLICY

Productive versus Allocative Efficiency

The economic rationale behind the courts' refusal to accept economies of scale as a defense for an otherwise unjustified merger is that the sacrifice of productive efficiency is likely to be small relative to the gain in allocative efficiency. Oliver E. Williamson has pointed out, however, that the welfare losses from large increases in price can be offset by small gains in productive efficiency.[44]

Figure 16–1 illustrates the point. In what Williamson refers to as the "naive trade off model," P_c and Q_c show the premerger equilibrium price and output assuming constant costs and no market power. If one or more mergers both reduce cost and create market power allowing the merged firms to raise price, cost falls from AC_c to AC_m, and the price rises from P_c to P_m. The pure welfare loss from monopoly power is thus shown by Triangle ABC. The resource saving from the lower cost is shown by Rectangle P_cFEB. The net social gain is therefore $P_cFEB - ABC$. Williamson has shown that a percentage decrease in cost will offset a much larger percentage increase in price under reasonable assumptions as to elasticity of demand.[45]

FIGURE 16–1 The "Naive" Welfare Trade-Off between Allocative and Productive
Efficiency

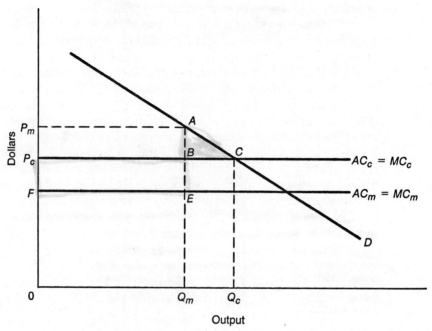

The model is considered "naive" because it assumes the economies
are attainable by merger rather than through internal expansion.
Further, it compares the price and output of certain firms before and
after merger without taking into account that other firms in the industry may be able to raise prices when the merged firms exploit their
newly gained market power. Also, the model is a pure welfare one,
neglecting any questions of distributive equity.

In any event, cost saving does not appear to have been a significant
motive for merger. Economies of scale or scope not matched by rivals
through internal growth should enhance postmerger profits. But evidence indicates that on the whole, large mergers since World War II
have not increased participants' rates of return. Indeed, some studies
suggest that the financial performance of merged firms has been slightly
poorer than that of initially comparable firms.[46] An interesting dis-
tributional issue has emerged from some of these studies. In general,
merger terms have favored the stockholders of acquired companies,
who tend to gain at the expense of acquiring companies' stockholders,
suggesting to some that managerial goals of growth, size, and the
pecuniary rewards for managing large enterprises may have been more
important motives than profitability and efficiency.[47] The relatively

poorer profit showing of large merged firms also suggests that monopoly has not been a significant motive since World War II, perhaps because antitrust enforcement has been effective in checking merger for market power.

The growing threat of hostile takeover has pressured some conglomerates to undo mergers that, in retrospect, have reduced rather than increased the overall value of the combined firms. In a 1985 article, *Business Week* noted that "a growing number of companies that once thought diversification and expansion were vital are abruptly changing course. They are slimming down and narrowing their focus, lopping off divisions and selling assets and product lines." Describing the phenomenon as a "riot of voluntary restructuring," *Business Week* continued, "Many conglomerates jettisoned bad acquisitions in the early 1970s, but the current, far more pervasive sell-off spree is different. Rather than simply dumping dogs, companies are making moves to spin off and scale down healthy businesses to concentrate on what they do best."[48]

Motives for Merger

Risk Reduction. There are motives for merger other than economies of scale, market power, and managerial gratification.[49] Vertical mergers, in particular, may be motivated by the desire to reduce risk by assuring sources of supply or outlets for production. Similarly, conglomerate mergers may be designed to reduce the risks of dependence on one market. But in most cases, the reductions in risk are private rather than social and therefore afford little justification for otherwise objectionable mergers. A firm that integrates upstream to assure supply of a critical raw material, for example, exposes its unintegrated rivals to even greater risks of unavailability in time of shortage. And firms need not diversify to reduce the risk exposure of their stockholders, since stockholders can diversify for themselves by balancing their portfolios.

Short-Term Investment Gains. Mergers may lead to short-term gain in the market values of firms' stocks, unrelated to actual profitability. Firms with high price-earnings ratios—that for some reason, look attractive to investors—may be able to acquire firms with much lower ratios and find that the stock market subsequently capitalizes the combined earnings at the rate originally applied to the acquiring company alone. At the height of 1960s merger boom, a conglomerate craze developed in which stock values of "go-go" firms could be and were inflated by such acquisitions. But as investors grew more familiar with these firms and the market value of several glamorous conglomerates collapsed, opportunities dwindled for exploiting differences in price-earnings ratios.

Profits for Promoters and Advisors. Promoters could earn large profits from engineering go-go mergers—as long as they sold their shares before reality caught up with the market. (Many, however, believed in the magic themselves and thus went down with their creations.) But promoter profits remain a source of merger activity.[50] Law firms, brokerage houses, and consultants can earn high fees for their services as intermediaries and advisors in merger negotiations. Both individuals and firms have acted as "marriage brokers," seeking out prospective partners for clients, as well as identifying and initiating promising merger opportunities—customarily for a large finder's fee.

The Opportunity to Sell a Firm. Probably most important among the motives for merger are those of the acquired firms' owners and managers. A 1951 study, for example, found that a majority of the postwar mergers investigated stemmed from the initiatives of the acquired firms.[51] Owners facing retirement might find that selling the business is the most profitable way to disengage. Sale of a firm before the owner's death establishes a value and can avoid protracted and costly problems with estate taxes. It has been argued that the opportunity to sell a successful business to a larger firm is an important incentive to small-business entrepreneurship.

Tax Considerations. Incentives to merge are heightened by other tax considerations. In calculating corporate income tax, firms can carry losses forward (deduct them from future years' earnings). These carryovers can be transferred to an acquiring company. A corporation with accumulated losses thus has a marketable asset.

While a corporation's entire income is subject to the corporate income tax, its aftertax earnings are further taxable to stockholders only when paid out in dividends. There is, thus, an incentive to retain earnings. But as earnings accumulate, how do owners realize their gains? In publicly held corporations, individuals may be able to withdraw their share of retained earnings by selling stock and paying only the capital gains tax. But the shares of small companies may be hard to sell, especially in large blocks, without depressing the price. Merger sometimes provides a solution to this problem. For example, if a merger is accomplished through an exchange of stock, the owners of the acquired company receive shares of the acquiring company tax-free. Such shares may be more widely traded and thus easier to liquidate without disturbing the market.

The Failing Company. A going concern is often worth far more to society and its owners than its assets would be if sold separately. For a failing company, merger may be the only feasible alternative to liquidating assets. Congress and the courts have recognized this by providing a "failing-company" defense in Section 7 cases. If a firm can show that it is in grave danger of failing and that no less anticompetitive alternative exists, it will be allowed to merge with a competitor. Economic justifications include the arguments that a failing firm is unlikely to be a significant competitor and that allowing others to bid for the failing firm should raise the price and lessen the probability of collapse, giving some protection to employees, creditors, and owners.[52]

The Market for Control

Henry G. Manne has distinguished a "market for control" within the broader market for mergers.[53] He sees "a high positive correlation between corporate managerial efficiency and the market price of the shares of that company."[54] Inefficient firms are, therefore, attractive takeover targets, primarily because more effective management may raise the market value of their shares. Those who carry out the takeover will benefit if they hold shares in the acquired company or can assign themselves high-paying managerial positions. But, Manne continued:

> The greatest benefits of the take-over scheme probably inure to those least conscious of it. . . . Only the take-over scheme provides some assurance of competitive efficiency among corporate managers and thereby affords strong protection to the interests of vast numbers of small, noncontrolling stockholders.[55]

Manne argued that if monopoly or economies of scale were the objective of a merger, both parties would gain and the terms of the merger would appear equitable to an outside observer. But if the objective is to purchase control, the acquiring firm would have to pay more than the asset value of the acquired firm, and the terms would appear unfavorable to the acquiring firm's owners. He considered his argument significantly verified by researchers' findings that financial benefits of mergers accrued disproportionately to stockholders of acquired firms.

Officials of the Reagan administration have accepted and endorsed Manne's views. James C. Miller III, then chairman of the FTC, commented in the spring of 1985, "It may be best to leave decisions concerning takeover tactics to the market." Contrasting antitrust and securities regulation, he observed that "the emphasis on economic efficiency that has come to dominate antitrust policy has not yet had the same impact on regulatory policy toward takeover tactics. A policy that enhances economic efficiency will be in the interest of the economy as a whole. This is the direction in which antitrust policy has moved, and we should attempt to do so here [regulation of securities markets] as well."[56] And a chapter devoted to the same issue in the 1985 *Report of the Council of Economic Advisers* concluded, "The public has a legitimate interest in the continued strength and vitality of the market for control. Publicly traded corporations account for a substantial portion of the Nation's wealth and productive capacity, and it is important that the management of these firms not be insulated from competition in the market for corporate control. The available evidence is that the operation of this market has generated net benefits for the economy."[57]

The market for control, if it functions effectively, should promote efficiency in allocation and utilization of resources. Yet in assessing the adequacy of information and degree of rational investor behavior required for the beneficial working of this market, we must keep in mind the misinformation and excesses of the conglomerate merger movement.

ENDNOTES

[1]Public Law No. 212, approved October 15, 1914 (2d sess. 63d Cong., U.S. Stat. L., vol. 38, p. 730).

[2]United States v. American Tobacco Company et al., 191 Fed. 371 (1911).

[3]Federal Trade Commission v. Western Meat Company; Thatcher Manufacturing Company v. Federal Trade Commission; Swift & Company v. Federal Trade Commission, 272 U.S. 554 (1926).

[4]Arrow-Hart & Hegeman Electric Company v. Federal Trade Commission, 291 U.S. 584 (1934).

[5]United States v. Celanese Corporation of America, 91 F. Supp. 14, 17 (1950).

[6]Quoted in Jesse W. Markham, "Survey of the Evidence and Findings on Merger," in *Business Concentration and Price Policy,* Universities–National Bureau Committee for Economic Research (Princeton, N.J.: Princeton University Press, 1955), pp. 141–82 at p. 142.

[7]U.S. Federal Trade Commission, *The Merger Movement: A Summary Report* (Washington, D.C.: U.S. Government Printing Office, 1948).

[8]Public Law 899, approved December 29, 1950 (2d sess. 81st Cong., U.S. Stat. L., vol. 64, p. 1125).

[9]United States v. Bethlehem Steel Corporation, 168 F. Supp. 576, 582–83 (1958). (Italics and asterisks original.)

[10]United States v. E. I. du Pont de Nemours & Company, 353 U.S. 586, 597–98 (1957). (Italics original.)

[11]Brown Shoe Company v. United States, 370 U.S. 294 (1962).

[12]297–98.

[13]325.

[14]339.

[15]334.

[16]Reynolds Metals Company v. Federal Trade Commission, 309 F. 2d 223, 229–30 (1962).

[17]Ford Motor Company v. United States, 405 U.S. 562 (1972).

[18]*Report of the Task Force on Productivity and Competition,* February 1969, reprinted in *Antitrust Law and Economics Review* 2, no 3 (Spring 1969), pp. 13–52.

[19]United States v. Philadelphia National Bank, 374 U.S. 321, 363 (1963).

[20]370–71.

[21]United States v. Continental Can Company, 378 U.S. 441, 457 (1964).

[22]476–77.

[23]United States v. Pabst Brewing Company, 384 U.S. 546, 549 (1966). (Italics original.)

[24]United States v. Aluminum Company of America, 377 U.S. 271, 281 (1964).

[25]United States v. Von's Grocery Company, 384 U.S. 270 (1966).

[26]301.

[27]United States v. El Paso Natural Gas Company, 376 U.S. 651 (1964).

[28]United States v. Penn-Olin Chemical Company, 378 U.S. 158, 173 (1964).

[29]United States v. Falstaff Brewing Corporation, 410 U.S. 526, 532–33 (1973).

[30]United States v. Marine Bancorporation, Inc. 418 U.S. 602, 624–25 (1974).

[31]638–39.

[32]Federal Trade Commission v. Consolidated Foods Corporation, 380 U.S. 592, 594 (1965).

[33]Federal Trade Commission v. Procter & Gamble Company, 386 U.S. 568, 575 (1967).

[34]Jesse W. Markham, *Conglomerate Enterprise and Public Policy* (Boston: Graduate School of Business Administration, Harvard University, 1973).

[35]See, for example, Corwin D. Edwards, "Conglomerate Bigness as a Source of Power," in *Business Concentration and Price Policy,* pp. 331–59; U.S. Federal Trade Commission, Bureau of Economics, *Economic Report on Corporate Mergers* (Washington, D.C.: U.S. Government Printing Office, 1969); John T. Scott, "Multimarket Contact and Economic Performance," *Review of Economics and Statistics* 64, no. 3 (August 1982), pp. 368–75.

[36]United States v. Northwest Industries, Inc., 301 F. Supp. 1066 (1969); United States v. Ling-Temco-Vought, Inc., 315 F. Supp. 1301 (1970); United States v. International Telephone & Telegraph Corporation, 324 F. Supp. 19 (1970); United States v. International Telephone & Telegraph Corporation, CCH Trade Cases, ¶73,619 (1971); United States v. International Telephone & Telegraph Corporation, CCH Trade Cases, ¶73,666 (1971).

[37]CCH Trade Cases, ¶73,665, ¶73,666, and ¶73,667 (1971).

[38]CCH Trade Cases, ¶73,105 (1970).

[39]324 F. Supp. 19, 52, 54 (1970).

[40]United States v. General Dynamics Corporation, 415 U.S. 486, 494, 496 (1974).

[41]U.S. Department of Justice, "Merger Guidelines," June 14, 1984 (mimeographed). Reprinted as *CCH Trade Regulation Reports,* no. 665, (June 18, 1984), part II, pp. 21–24. The traditional expression for the Herfindahl index, as discussed in Chapter Ten, yields a figure ranging from 0 to 1. The 1984 "Merger Guidelines" calculate the index

to four significant decimals and multiply the expression by 10,000, thus eliminating the decimal point. The guidelines also refer to the index as the "Herfindahl-Hirschman Index" (HHI), recognizing the contribution of Albert O. Hirschman to its development.

[42]Ibid., pp. 35–36.

[43]Rudolf W. Buettenmuller, "The Goal of the New Premerger Notification Requirements: Preliminary Relief against Anticompetitive Mergers," *Duke Law Journal* 1979, no. 1 (February 1979), pp. 249–85.

[44]Oliver E. Williamson, "Economies as an Antitrust Defense: The Welfare Trade-offs," *American Economic Review* 58, no. 1 (March 1968), pp. 18–36; Oliver E. Williamson, "Economies as an Antitrust Defense Revisited," *University of Pennsylvania Law Review* 125, no. 4 (April 1977), pp. 699–736.

[45]Using the notation of Figure 16–1, the area of Triangle ABC equals $\frac{1}{2}(P_m - P_c)$ $(Q_c - Q_m)$. The area of rectangle P_cFEB equals $(AC_c - AC_m)Q_m$. Therefore, the gain exceeds the loss if

$$(\Delta AC)Q_m > \frac{1}{2}(\Delta P)(\Delta Q)$$

Dividing both sides by P_cQ_c and substituting $\eta(\Delta P/P_c)$ for $(\Delta Q/Q_c)$ yields

$$\left(\frac{\Delta AC}{AC_c}\right) > \frac{1}{2}\,\eta\left(\frac{Q_c}{Q_m}\right)\left(\frac{\Delta P}{P_c}\right)^2$$

If, for example, $\eta = 2$, the welfare gain from a 1.05 percent decrease in cost will offset the welfare loss from a 10 percent increase in price.

This expression is discussed and developed in "Economies as an Antitrust Defense: Correction and Reply," *American Economic Review* 58, no. 5 (December 1968), part 1, pp. 1372–76.

[46]A leading study is Samuel R. Reid, *Mergers, Managers and the Economy* (New York: McGraw-Hill, 1968). See also H. Igor Ansoff, Richard G. Brandenburg, Fred E. Portner, and Raymond Radosevich, *Acquisition Behavior of U.S. Manufacturing Firms, 1946–1965* (Nashville, Tenn.: Vanderbilt University Press, 1971); U.S. Federal Trade Commission, *Conglomerate Merger Performance: An Empirical Analysis of Nine Corporations* (Washington, D.C.: U.S. Government Printing Office, 1972); Robert L. Conn, "Acquired Firm Performance after Conglomerate Merger," *Southern Economic Journal* 43, no. 2 (October 1976), pp. 1170–73. A number of case studies of unprofitable mergers in the late 1970s and early 1980s are included in "Do Mergers Really Work?" *Business Week*, June 3, 1985, pp. 88–100. The phenomenon is not a new one. See Shaw Livermore, "The Success of Industrial Mergers," *Quarterly Journal of Economics* 50, no. 1 (November 1935), pp. 68–96.

[47]Dennis C. Mueller, "A Theory of Conglomerate Mergers," *Quarterly Journal of Economics* 83, no. 4 (November 1969), pp. 643–59; Michael Gort and Thomas F. Hogarty, "New Evidence on Mergers," *Journal of Law and Economics* 13, no. 1 (April 1970), pp. 173–76; Paul J. Halpern, "Empirical Estimates of the Amount and Distribution of Gains to Companies in Mergers," *Journal of Business* 46, no. 4 (October 1973), pp. 554–73.

[48]"Splitting Up: The Other Side of Merger Mania," *Business Week*, July 1, 1985, pp. 50–55, at p. 55.

[49]A perceptive and comprehensive discussion of motives for merger, especially conglomerate, is found in Peter O. Steiner, *Mergers: Motives, Effects, Policies* (Ann Arbor: University of Michigan Press, 1975).

[50]A pioneering and excellent discussion of the role of promoters' profits in earlier merger waves is found in Markham, "Survey of the Evidence."

[51]J. Keith Butters, John M. Lintner, and William L. Cary, *Effects of Taxation on Corporate Mergers* (Boston: Harvard Business School, 1951).

[52]Derek C. Bok, "Section 7 of the Clayton Act and the Merging of Law and Economics," *Harvard Law Review* 74, no. 2 (December 1960), pp. 226–355.

[53]Henry G. Manne, "Mergers and the Market for Corporation Control," *Journal of Political Economy* 73, no. 2 (April 1965), pp. 110–20, at p. 112.

[54]Ibid.

[55]Ibid., p. 113.

[56]James C. Miller III, quoted in *CCH Trade Regulation Reports,* no. 703 (May 13, 1985), p. 7.

[57]U.S. Council of Economic Advisers, *Economic Report of the President and Annual Report of the Council of Economic Advisers, 1985* (Washington, D.C.: U.S. Government Printing Office, 1985), p. 216.

Joint Actions in Restraint of Trade: Sections 1 and 2 of the Sherman Act

Nearly all "big" antitrust cases—the complex, lengthy, and costly ones—involve structural issues of monopolization or merger and pose hard problems of effective and equitable remedy in response to civil complaints. But the great majority of antitrust actions, the "bread and butter" conspiracy cases, deal with anticompetitive conduct that is proscribed regardless of market structure. If the defendant loses such cases, the outcome is usually straightforward: fines, jail sentences, treble-damage awards, and judicial decrees ordering the illegal conduct ended. In fiscal year 1984, for example, the Antitrust Division filed 100 criminal cases alleging "price fixing and kindred activities," but brought only 14 civil actions.[1] These enforcement agency activities are not only central to the goal of preserving a competitive economy but also raise important economic and legal questions regarding appropriate antitrust policy and enforcement.

AGREEMENTS AMONG COMPETITORS AND THE PER SE RULE

With only one major but temporary lapse,[2] the Supreme Court has consistently adhered to and strengthened the per se doctrine first formulated in 1898 by Circuit Court Judge William Howard Taft.[3] As interpreted by Taft in the *Addyston Pipe & Steel* case, Section 1 of the Sherman Act followed the common law in banning every "naked" restraint of trade—i.e., every restraint not ancillary to a legitimate business purpose.

Price-Fixing Agreements

All agreements to fix prices, Taft concluded, whether directly or through division of markets as in *Addyston,* were illegal per se (in and of themselves) without regard to intent or economic circumstances. Two landmark Supreme Court decisions reaffirmed and reinforced the per se rule.

In the 1920 *Trenton Potteries* case, the trial court judge refused to instruct the jury that "only an undue and unreasonable restraint" leading to "injury to the public" was illegal under the 1911 interpretation of the Sherman Act.[4] On appeal, the Supreme Court reaffirmed Peckham's and Taft's earlier refusals to consider the reasonableness of prices fixed by collusion.

> The aim and result of every price-fixing agreement, if effective, is the elimination of one form of competition. The power to fix prices, whether reasonably exercised or not, involves power to control the market and to fix arbitrary and unreasonable prices. The reasonable price fixed today may through economic and business changes become the unreasonable price of tomorrow. . . . Agreements which create such potential power may well be held to be in themselves unreasonable or unlawful restraints. . . . Moreover, in the absence of express legislation requiring it, we should hesitate to adopt a construction making the difference between legal and illegal conduct in the field of business relations depend upon so uncertain a test as whether prices are reasonable—a determination which can be satisfactorily made only after a complete survey of our economic organization and a choice between rival philosophies.[5]

In 1940, the Court dealt similarly with the defense's contention that a jury should have been allowed to decide whether agreements among several major oil companies were unreasonable restraints of trade. The agreements were designed to check sales below cost in a period of severe depression by purchase of so-called distress gasoline from independent refiners. Justice William O. Douglas wrote:

> Ruinous competition, financial disaster, evils of price cutting and the like appear throughout our history as ostensible justifications for price-fixing. If the so-called competitive abuses were to be appraised here, the reasonableness of prices would necessarily become an issue in every price-fixing case. In that event the Sherman Act would soon be emasculated; its philosophy would be supplanted by one which is wholly alien to a system of free competition; it would not be the charter of freedom which its framers intended. . . .
>
> Congress has not left with us the determination of whether or not particular price-fixing schemes are wise or unwise, healthy or destructive. It has not permitted the age-old cry of ruinous competition and competitive evils to be a defense to price-fixing conspiracies. . . . Under the Sherman Act, a combination formed for the purpose and with the effect of raising,

depressing, fixing, pegging, or stabilizing the price of a commodity in interstate or foreign commerce is illegal per se.[6]

Subsequent decisions have confirmed Justice Douglas's sweeping assertion that the per se rule applies both to collusion aimed at lowering or stabilizing prices and to collusion aimed at raising them.[7]

Territorial and Output Restrictions

Price-fixing may be accomplished indirectly through agreements to divide markets or restrict output. If the clear objective is to raise, depress, fix, peg, or stabilize prices, such agreements are per se illegal. Territorial market division was the central feature of the agreement in *Addyston Pipe;* and *Socony-Vacuum* involved restriction on output through joint purchase and removal of independent refiners' gasoline.

A 1972 case established the precedent that horizontal agreements to divide markets are per se illegal even without evidence that the intent or effect was to influence price. In *Topco,* an association of small and medium-sized retail grocery chains formed a joint purchasing agency "to obtain high quality merchandise under private labels in order to compete more effectively with larger national and regional chains."[8] Most member firms were licensed to sell Topco brand products in exclusive territories. The defense alleged that such exclusivity was necessary for effective promotion and marketing of private-label products and that Topco's assignment of exclusive territories should therefore be judged under the rule of reason. In rejecting this argument, the Supreme Court pointed out that the courts' inability to weigh procompetitive and anticompetitive effects of naked restraints of trade was an important reason for introducing the per se rule. Further:

> Without the *per se* rules, businessmen would be left with little to aid them in predicting in any particular case what courts will find to be legal and illegal under the Sherman Act. Should Congress ultimately determine that predictability is unimportant in this area of the law, it can, of course, make *per se* rules inapplicable in some or all cases and leave courts free to ramble through the wilds of economic theory in order to maintain a flexible approach.[9]

The courts have not dealt with a case in which a joint restriction on output with no clear effect on price was at issue, presumably because the relationship between quantity offered for sale and price is so close and obvious. A. D. Neale and D. G. Goyder conclude, "There can, however, be little doubt that collusive arrangements to limit the amount of a product reaching the market are illegal *per se* under section 1 of the Sherman Act and would be so found even if no evidence of concomitant effects on prices could be produced, which is unlikely."[10]

In sum, application of the per se rule has been justified on at least four grounds. First, an intent to restrain trade is inherent in any direct agreement to fix prices, and because of the necessary and obvious consequences for price such intent is presumed in any agreement to restrict output or share markets. Wrongful intent can therefore be inferred from the act and need not be proved. Second, the anticompetitive consequences of price-fixing, output restrictions, and market-sharing are so preponderant that occasional procompetitive results are properly sacrificed in the interests of efficient and prompt enforcement. If every Section 1 case were tried under the rule of reason, the courts could face an unacceptably heavy burden. Third, even if possible beneficial results ought to be considered in every case, as Almarin Phillips[11] and a few other economists have argued, the courts are not capable of the "ramble through the wilds of economic theory" that such consideration would require. Fourth, business people are better off knowing what sorts of conduct are proscribed than they would be by operating in a more permissive but less certain environment.

Limits of the Per Se Doctrine

Exchange of Price Information. Limits of the per se doctrine in agreements affecting price were probed, but not clearly defined, in two cases. In both, competitors exchanged information on current prices and terms of sale but had no agreement as to how individual companies would use the information to determine their prices. In the 1969 *Container Corporation* case, 18 manufacturers of corrugated containers, accounting for approximately 90 percent of industry sales, exchanged information on specific sales made to identified buyers. Justice Douglas, writing for the majority of the Court, concluded that the practice was unlawful under the particular circumstances.

> The result of this reciprocal exchange of prices was to stabilize prices though at a downward level. . . . The corrugated container industry is dominated by relatively few sellers. The product is fungible and competition for sales is price. The demand is inelastic, as buyers place orders only for immediate, short-run needs. The exchange of price data tends toward price uniformity. . . . The inferences are irresistible that the exchange of price information has had an anticompetitive effect in the industry, chilling the vigor of price competition.[12]

Justice Abe Fortas wrote a concurring opinion, noting, "I do not understand the Court's opinion to hold that the exchange of specific information among sellers as to prices charged to individual customers, pursuant to mutual arrangement, is a *per se* violation of the Sherman Act." Rather, the "evidence, although not overwhelming, is sufficient in the special circumstances of this case to show an actual effect on pricing and to compel us to hold that the court below erred in dismissing the Government's complaint."[13]

The *Container* case was a civil action; it sought to establish the legality of the behavior and end it in the corrugated container industry, not to punish the individuals involved. In 1973, a criminal indictment was brought against six manufacturers of gypsum board and several of their officials for engaging in a similar exchange. In a 1978 opinion, Chief Justice Warren E. Burger held that the case should have been tried under the rule-of-reason standard, stating that "we hold that a defendant's state of mind or intent is an element of a criminal antitrust offense which must be established by evidence and inferences drawn therefrom and cannot be taken from the trier of fact [in this case, the jury] through reliance on a legal presumption of wrongful intent from proof of an effect on prices." A few pages later, he developed his line of argument further. "With certain exceptions for conduct regarded as *per se* illegal because of its unquestionably anticompetitive effects, the behavior proscribed in the Act is often difficult to distinguish from the gray zone of socially acceptable and economically justifiable business conduct. Indeed, the type of conduct charged in the indictment in this case—the exchange of price information among competitors—is illustrative in this regard."[14]

Justice Burger disposed of the question of whether the mere exchange of price information could be held illegal per se in a civil case by noting the Court had already decided to the contrary in the *Container* case. He did not, however, discuss what role, if any, proof of intent should play in a civil case.

Commercial Boycott. In the 1959 *Klor's* case, the Supreme Court held yet another collective restraint of trade—concerted refusal to deal (commercial boycott)—to be per se illegal.[15] The defendant, Broadway-Hale, had organized a collective boycott of the plaintiff by inducing manufacturers (including General Electric, RCA, Admiral, Zenith, and Emerson) to either raise the prices they charged Klor's or refuse to sell to it. Klor's, a small retail store located next to Broadway-Hale, was an aggressive discounter of brand-name goods also carried by Broadway-Hale.

The per se prohibition of collective boycotts, however, appears to apply only under a narrow concept of the practice. Robert H. Bork has argued that the courts have applied the per se rule only to what he calls naked boycotts, not to ancillary collective refusals to deal that serve a legitimate purpose. For example, Bork pointed out, "All league sports from the Ivy League to the National Football League ... rest entirely on the right to boycott.... No court is likely to hold that every sandlot team in America is given the right by the Sherman Act to play baseball in the American League. The league would be destroyed."[16] Noncommercial boycotts, organized for social or political objectives, have been held to be "a form of speech or conduct" constitutionally protected under the 1st and 14th amendments.[17] A court of appeals held that the National Football League's player draft system, while an unreasonable restraint of trade under the rule of reason, was not a per se illegal boycott. The opinion described the sort of boycott that the court held would be per se illegal as follows.

> The classic "group boycott" is a concerted attempt by a group of competitors at one level to protect themselves from competition from non-group members who seek to compete at that level. . . . The group may accomplish its exclusionary purpose by inducing suppliers not to sell to potential competitors, by inducing customers not to buy from them, or, in some cases, by refusing to deal with would-be competitors themselves. In each instance, however, the hallmark of the "group boycott" is the effort of competitors to "barricade themselves from competition *at their own level*."[18]

EXEMPT ACTIVITIES

Collective activities by certain groups, even with an obvious effect on price and an undisguised intent to restrain trade, are partially or totally exempt from liability under the antitrust laws.

Federal Legislative Exemptions

Federal legislation exempts export associations, agricultural marketing organizations with membership limited to farmers and primary processors, and groups formed by insurance companies to exchange information on risk exposure and discuss appropriate rates.[19] These exemptions, however, are subject to limitation and public control. Export agreements must be registered with the Federal Trade Commission or filed with the Departments of Commerce and Justice, and can be challenged if they have a direct and substantial effect on domestic prices and competition. Agricultural marketing cooperatives are regulated by the Department of Agriculture. And insurance is subject to the federal antitrust laws in areas not regulated by state law.

Regulated Industries

Federal regulatory agencies (e.g., the Interstate Commerce Commission, Federal Communications Commission, and Securities and Exchange Commission), bank regulatory bodies, and state and local public utility commissions have authority over pricing, service, entry to and exit from the industries they regulate, and sometimes over structure, including merger. There are, thus, many points of overlap and possible conflict between regulatory and antitrust enforcement agencies. In the *AT&T* case, the trial judge noted two types of such exemptions: statutory, through act of Congress, and implied, through the courts' interpretations of congressional intent. Exemption, he noted, should not be implied lightly in the absence of specific statutory provisions:

> Regulated industries are not per se exempt from the Sherman Act, and they are not necessarily exempt even if the conduct complained of in an antitrust context has been expressly approved by the agency charged with regulating the particular industry. . . .
>
> Regulated conduct is, however, deemed to be immune by implication from the antitrust laws in two relatively narrow instances: (1) when a regulatory agency has, with congressional approval, exercised explicit authority over the challenged practice itself (as distinguished from the general subject matter) in such a way that antitrust enforcement would interfere with regulation, and (2) when regulation by an agency over an industry or some of its components or practices is so pervasive that Congress is assumed to have determined competition to be an inadequate means of vindicating the public interest.[20]

State and Local Government Actions

State regulatory bodies may allow or even encourage private firms or local governmental agencies to engage in activities that ordinarily would violate antitrust laws. Such activities have included provision of "free" light bulbs to customers of an investor-owned electric utility company in Detroit, Michigan (a tying arrangement under which the cost of the bulbs was included in the rates); price-fixing and resale price maintenance by private wine producers in California; monopolization of cable television service in Boulder, Colorado; collective setting of freight rates by interstate trucking companies; provision of gas and water by the city of Plaquemines, Louisiana, only to those who also purchased their electricity from the city; and refusal by Eau Claire, Wisconsin, to provide sewage services to adjacent townships unless they agreed to annexation. Under the *state action* doctrine, such activities are exempt from antitrust only if authorized by a clearly articulated state policy.[21]

On the ground that local governments, unlike state, are not sovereign, the courts have refused to extend the exemption to acts engaged in or authorized by local government agencies unless pursuant to explicit state policies.[22] But local governments, their officials, and private firms operating under local grants of special privilege are sheltered from exposure to treble damages by the Local Government Antitrust

Act of 1984, which prohibits antitrust suits for damages against any of these parties if the action was authorized and directed by the local government. The act does not prevent either private or public antitrust suits seeking injunctive remedy against a local government or its agents.

Industry-Specific Exemptions

Occasionally Congress or the courts have been persuaded that a specific industry warrants special antitrust treatment. In 1970, for example, Congress passed the Newspaper Preservation Act to preserve independence and competition in a newspaper's reporting and editorial policies, even when its financial independence was no longer feasible. This act provided more lenient standards for newspaper mergers in which business operations were combined but the reporting and editorial staffs remained separate. In 1980, over the strong opposition of the antitrust agencies, Congress enacted the Soft Drink Interbrand Competition Act, legitimizing territorial agreements between soft-drink syrup manufacturers and bottlers that had been held to be unreasonable restraints of trade by the FTC in 1978.[23]

A longstanding exemption, later recognized by the Supreme Court as an anachronism but not overruled, stems from the Court's 1922 decision that professional baseball is not subject to the Sherman Act.[24] Indeed, the entire field of sports (professional and amateur alike) has posed troublesome problems for antitrust. In 1984, for example, the Supreme Court held that the National Collegiate Athletic Association's plan to limit members' televised football games, and to allocate televised games among member colleges, eliminated price competition and restricted output. But the Court refused to apply the per se doctrine on the ground that "[W]hat is critical is that this case involves an industry in which horizontal restraints on competition are essential if the product is to be available·at all." The opinion went on to note that the NCAA played a "vital role" in preserving the "character and quality" of collegiate football by enforcing mutual agreement that "athletes must not be paid, must be required to attend class, and the like." In general, sports required agreements among competitors as to rules of the game and restraints on "the manner in which institutions compete."[25]

The National Cooperative Research Act of 1984 was designed to encourage firms to participate in joint research and development projects. The act provides, first, that any suit brought against an R&D joint venture be tried under the rule of reason rather than by a per se standard and, second, that if the Federal Trade Commission and the Antitrust Division are given advance notice of a proposed R&D joint venture, participants will be liable only for actual damages and costs.

RESTRAINTS OF TRADE BY LABOR UNIONS IN COLLABORATION WITH EMPLOYERS

Section 6 of the Clayton Act declares that:

> The labor of a human being is not a commodity or article of commerce. Nothing contained in the antitrust laws shall be construed to forbid the existence and operation of labor, agricultural, or horticultural organizations, instituted for the purposes of mutual help, and not having capital stock or conducted for profit, . . . nor shall such organizations, or the members thereof, be held or construed to be illegal combinations or conspiracies in restraint of trade, under the antitrust laws.[26]

Bolstered by the Norris–LaGuardia Act of 1932, Section 6 of the Clayton Act has been interpreted to exempt from antitrust prosecution all labor union activities in restraint of trade if the actions are taken independently, in the interests of the union's members, and not in collusion with employers.[27] For example, rules of the American Federation of Musicians requiring a band to charge a 10 percent premium when accepting an engagement outside the territory of its members' local union, and to accept engagements only from booking agents licensed by the union, were held to be valid exercises of the union's independent bargaining rights.[28] On the other hand, collaboration among an electrical workers' local union, manufacturers of electrical equipment, and contractors in the New York City area, allowing the contractors to install only electrical equipment manufactured by New York firms whose employees were represented by the union local, was regarded as a conspiracy in violation of Sections 1 and 2 of the Sherman Act.[29]

Industrywide collective bargaining, including negotiation of uniform wage scales, is unquestionably legal; but an understanding between the United Mine Workers and certain large coal mine operators that the union would impose identical wage scales on large and small mines, with both parties aware that many small mines would have to close as a result, was condemned under Sections 1 and 2.[30] The union allegedly agreed with the large operators that increased wages and benefits could be obtained only by eliminating overproduction.

ACTIVITIES OF TRADE ASSOCIATIONS AND PROFESSIONAL SOCIETIES

According to the 1983 directory *National Trade and Professional Associations of the United States*,[31] there were more than 3,400 active trade associations in the United States, up from about 1,900 in 1943.

Trade Association Activities and Restraint of Trade

These associations, which vary widely in size and scope, provide a major vehicle for communication and cooperation among competing firms. Much of this mutual self-help enhances the efficiency of an industry and improves its economic performance. But joint activities of competitors inevitably give rise to a danger of blunting competition and thereby enhancing prices.

Virtually every trade association holds an annual convention and sends publications to its members. Other important activities include compilation of statistical data; market research; sponsorship of research on new products, materials, and more effective production methods; quality certification and standardization; cooperative advertising and other forms of public relations; political lobbying; and advice on accounting, tax, and legal matters.

Some of these activities are clearly procompetitive. Information from trade associations may allow firms to compete more effectively and intelligently. Other activities may make economies of scale available to small firms and thus strengthen competition. On the other hand, trade association meetings can be natural settings for conspiracy. Articles, editorial comments, and letters in trade association publications may call attention to "soft" prices or "overhanging" inventories. Dissemination of information on prices, production, and inventory may lessen rather than invigorate competition. In an early case, for example, a trade association described the objective of its plan for collecting and reporting price information:

> The Open Competition Plan is a central clearing house for information on prices, trade statistics and practices. By keeping all members fully and quickly informed of what others have done, the work of the Plan results in *a certain uniformity of trade practice.* There is no agreement to follow the practice of others, *although members do follow their most intelligent competitors,* if they know what these competitors have been actually doing.[32]

Guidelines for Trade Associations

A number of general rules or guidelines for trade associations have emerged from a series of antitrust cases.[33] The courts have held that trade associations must report only past and current prices and production rates. In particular, advance notice of a price change cannot be disseminated to competitors through the trade association. There can be no agreement to adhere to prices filed with an association. Associations cannot publish blacklists or otherwise encourage or engage in boycotts. Information sent to members must also be made available to the public. Member firms may be required to report off-list sales and special credit terms, but individual buyers cannot be identified. Trade association officials must be careful not to advocate or suggest specific prices, sales terms, or production volumes.

Professional Societies

Until the mid-1970s it was widely believed that the "learned" professions were exempt from antitrust scrutiny. The Supreme Court decided to the contrary in the 1975 *Goldfarb* case. The Fairfax County Bar Association had set a schedule of minimum fees for routine legal services, and adherence was enforced by the Virginia State Bar. The Court held that the schedule and its enforcement constituted price-fixing and, more important, that the defense argument that Congress "never intended to include the learned professions within the terms 'trade' or 'commerce' in §1 of the Sherman Act" was not supported by any "explicit exception or legislative history."[34] In the *Goldfarb* case, however, the Court was not prepared to declare that the per se rule applied to the professions, noting in a footnote, "The public service aspect, and other features of the profession, may require that a particular practice, which could properly be viewed as a violation of the Sherman Act in another context, be treated differently. We intimate no view on any other situation than the one with which we are confronted today."[35]

In 1976 and 1977 the Court struck down bans on advertising of prescription drugs and legal services and fees, but on grounds of First Amendment protection of the rights of free speech rather than as violations of the antitrust laws.[36] The following year, the Court did find a provision in the National Society of Professional Engineers' "Code of Ethics" to be in violation of Section 1.[37] The challenged provision barred members of the society from negotiating or even discussing fees until a prospective client had selected an engineer. The society relied heavily on the cautionary footnote in *Goldfarb* as its defense, averring that price competition among professional engineers would adversely affect engineering quality and be dangerous to public health, welfare, and safety.

The Court responded by noting, "[While] an agreement among competitors to refuse to discuss prices with potential customers until after . . . selection of an engineer . . . is not price-fixing as such, no elaborate industry analysis is required to demonstrate the anticompetitive character of such an agreement." The agreement was, therefore, per se illegal. As to the defense contention that the agreement restrained a type of competition that was "dangerous to the public health, safety, and welfare," the Court replied:

The Sherman Act reflects a legislative judgment that ultimately competition will not only produce lower prices, but also better goods and services. . . . The assumption that competition is the best method of allocating resources in a free market recognizes that all elements of a bargain—quality, service, safety, and durability—and not just the immediate cost, are favorably affected by the free opportunity to select among alternative offers.[38]

EXPLOITATION OF PATENTS

A patent is an award of temporary monopoly, giving the grantee the exclusive right for 17 years to make, use, and sell the patented article and to transfer these rights to others by license. Exploitation of such a monopoly does not violate the antitrust laws. However, uses of the patent privilege can conflict with antitrust proscriptions, particularly when firms suppress inventions, enhance market power through agglomerations of patents, restrict licensees, and require that nonpatented articles be used with patented ones.

The Test for Antitrust Liability: Magnification of Monopoly Power

The general test for antitrust liability of patent-based restraints of trade is whether the monopoly power inherent in the original grant is in any way increased by the challenged practice.[39]

Since 1896 the courts have held that a patent holder can refrain from using a patent and refuse to license it to others—that is, suppress its use completely.[40] In a 1945 case, the Supreme Court refused to overturn this precedent. In a dissenting opinion, Justice Douglas discussed the problem of "fencing," or obtaining patents solely to block competitors' access to a technology: "It is difficult to see how that use of patents can be reconciled with the purpose of the Constitution 'to promote the progress of science and the useful arts.' Can the suppression of patents which arrests the progress of technology be said to promote that progress?"[41]

Two or more patents under the same ownership may reinforce each other and magnify the monopoly power conferred in the original grants. Such patent agglomerations are tested under a straightforward application of the rule of reason—did the acquirer intend to augment market power? It is illegal for a group of firms to pool patents or for one firm to purchase patent rights for this purpose.[42] But there is no judicial limit on the number of patents a firm may amass through its own research and discovery.[43]

Although the test of intent is easy enough to frame, it may be difficult to apply in specific cases involving patent pooling and acquisition. There are valid reasons for combining patent rights. The most efficient manufacturing method may require the rights to complementary patents covering various steps in the process. If patents overlap, the best way to avoid questions of infringement may be to acquire the rights to all, even if only one is used.

Licensing Agreements

A patent holder may limit the quantities a licensee can produce. Similarly, licenses may restrict the licensee to sales in a particular territory or to specified classes of customers. And in a 1926 case involving General Electric's licensing of Westinghouse to produce patented incandescent light bulbs, the Supreme Court held that a patentee can set the price that a licensee is allowed to charge, reasoning as follows:

> We think he may do so, provided the conditions of sale are normally and reasonably adapted to secure pecuniary reward for the patentee's monopoly. . . . When the patentee licenses another to make and vend, and retains the right to continue to make and vend on his own account, the price at which his licensee will sell will necessarily affect the price at which he can sell his own patented goods. It would seem entirely reasonable that he should say to the licensee, "Yes, you may make and sell articles under my patent, but not so as to destroy the profit that I wish to obtain by making them and selling them myself."[44]

In 1948, the Supreme Court held that the organizers of a pool of complementary patents had violated Section 1 by issuing licenses that prescribed prices. Four justices urged that the case be used to overrule *General Electric,* but the majority distinguished between the right of a single patentee to restrict price, which presumably does not enhance the patent's power, and the denial of that right to a group, in which pooling may augment the value of the individual patents.[45]

Cross-licensing agreements sometimes call for exchanges of future patents and for "grant-backs," in which the licensee agrees that if it obtains any patents covering improvements on or extensions of the original patent, it will license them to its current licensor. The pooling agreement may call for *exclusive* cross-licensing, preventing any present or future patent covered by the agreement from being licensed to nonmembers. Such agreements may be constructive, allowing industrywide access to the best technology, more rapid technological advance, less duplicated research, and fewer infringement suits. But they may also retard the research of firms obligated to share the results, restrict entry, and perpetuate the dominance of certain firms.

In the 1963 *Singer* case, for example, the Supreme Court dealt with a cross-licensing agreement involving three sewing machine companies. Singer in the United States and two European firms, Vigorelli in Italy and Gegauf in Switzerland, negotiated a cross-licensing agreement covering a multicam zigzag mechanism. One consideration was that Singer would use the U.S. patent to bring infringement suits against Japanese firms manufacturing zigzag sewing machines. The Court found a Sherman Act violation, since "the facts as found by the trial court indicate a common purpose to suppress the Japanese machine competition in the United States through the use of the patent, which was secured by Singer, on the assurances to Gegauf and its co-licensee, Vigorelli, that such certainly would be the result."[46]

OLIGOPOLY AND TACIT COLLUSION

Competitors may, through conspiracy or overt collusion, devise a scheme to fix price, restrict output, or divide markets. Such explicit agreements, as we have seen, are per se illegal in most instances. But as Edward H. Chamberlin reasoned in his concept of mutual dependence recognized,[47] it may not be necessary for oligopolists to communicate or negotiate joint behavior to arrive at prices and output similar to levels that would be set by conspirators or a monopolist. If the number of firms is small and their costs, products, and market situations are similar, the Chamberlinian argument goes, each firm may weigh the consequences of its own actions on the behavior of its rivals; and the result may be independently determined restraints on production and pricing that approximate joint profit-maximizing levels.

Conspiracy Inferred from a Course of Action

In 1946, the Supreme Court upheld the conviction of three major cigarette manufacturers, American Tobacco, Liggett & Myers, and R. J. Reynolds, on charges that they violated both Sections 1 and 2 of the Sherman Act. These three companies, formed in the dissolution of the old American Tobacco Company after its 1911 Sherman Act conviction, accounted for approximately two-thirds to nine-tenths of the nation's cigarette production in the late 1920s and early 1930s. Conspiracy charges, both in restraint of trade and to monopolize, were supported almost entirely by evidence of parallel behavior.

The record showed that prices charged by the three were almost always identical, that Reynolds took the lead in announcing price changes, and that each of the three refused to participate in tobacco auctions unless buyers from the other two were also present for the bidding. The conduct of the big three during the worst of the Depression was considered particularly blatant. In late 1929 and again in 1931, Reynolds announced and the other two promptly adopted substantial increases in wholesale cigarette prices. Then, faced with inroads from the so-called "10-cent" brands of small producers, the big three made simultaneous 20 percent price cuts in early 1933, followed by a series of lockstep increases after the market share of the 10-cent brands had fallen. During this period, the three also purchased large quantities of low-priced tobacco used in the 10-cent brands but not in their own cigarettes.

The trial judge instructed the jury that it could infer a conspiracy from the circumstantial evidence provided by such conduct. The Supreme Court upheld this instruction, stating, "No formal agreement is necessary to constitute an unlawful conspiracy. Often crimes are a matter of inference deduced from the acts of the person accused and done in pursuance of a criminal purpose.... The essential combination or conspiracy in violation of the Sherman Act may be found in a course of dealings or other circumstances as well as in an exchange of words."[48]

Conscious Parallelism

In a series of subsequent cases, the term *conscious parallelism* entered the literature. The antitrust enforcement agencies sought to establish that the *American Tobacco* opinion outlawed tacit as well as overt collusion. For a brief period, it appeared that the effort might succeed. But the courts soon made it clear that they would not equate independent decisions with conspiracy merely on evidence of uniform behavior. A circuit court of appeals judge, in a 1951 private treble-damage case, commented on evidence that eight motion-picture distributors had refused to provide films to the plaintiff for first-run showings: "This uniformity in policy forms the basis of an inference of joint action. This does not mean, however, that in every case mere consciously parallel business practices are sufficient evidence, in themselves, from which a court may infer concerted action."[49] And in a 1954 case, the Supreme Court's opinion noted:

> This Court has never held that proof of parallel business behavior conclusively establishes agreement or, phrased differently, that such behavior itself constitutes a Sherman Act offense. Circumstantial evidence of consciously parallel behavior may have made heavy inroads into the traditional judicial attitude toward conspiracy; but "conscious parallelism" has not yet read conspiracy out of the Sherman Act entirely.[50]

The current state of the law on parallel behavior was described by Judge Marvin E. Frankel in 1968 jury instructions: "It is not sufficient to show that the parties acted uniformly or similarly or in ways that may seem to have been mutually beneficial. If such actions were taken independently as a matter of individual business judgment, without any agreement or arrangement or understanding among the parties, then there would be no conspiracy."[51] Or, as Peter Asch interprets what he describes as the "somewhat ambiguous status" of conscious parallelism: "The pertinent question in conspiracy cases is apparently whether parallel business behavior could have been the product of independent decisions. If an independence hypothesis does not tax the credulity of the court, a conclusion of innocence may be reached."[52]

Imperfect Collusion

Some practices reflect only partial recognition of mutual dependence, or *imperfect collusion*. The three most significant are price leadership, basing-point pricing, and price signaling.

Price Leadership. Price leadership, without evidence of collusion, is entirely legal. As the Supreme Court noted in the 1927 *International Harvester* case, "The fact that competitors may see proper, in the exercise of their own judgment, to follow the prices of another manufacturer, does not establish any suppression of competition or show any sinister dominance."[53]

Basing-Point Pricing. Basing-point pricing is a system in which one or more sellers quote customers only a delivered price, consisting of a mill net price plus freight from a location designated as a basing point, whether or not the product is actually shipped from that point. Under the multiple basing-point system, freight is charged from the nearest basing point. When coupled with price leadership, a pricing system in which all firms in an industry use the same set of basing points confronts buyers with identical delivered prices regardless of the seller's location and actual freight costs.

Basing-point pricing allows firms to sell to more distant customers without cutting prices to those closer to the plant and makes price leadership more feasible in industries with scattered production facilities and high shipping costs. But it involves additional costs to the sellers, as well as social waste, since buyers have no incentive to keep transportation costs down by ordering from nearby producers. Further, buyers have no incentive to locate their facilities near sources of supply.[54] Basing-point systems that have been adopted by an entire industry, with all firms using the same basing points and following a leader's price, have been held indicative of more than conscious parallelism and have been declared illegal under the antitrust laws.[55]

Price Signaling. Economists have long realized that recognition of mutual dependence can be facilitated by actions short of collusion.

Barometric price leadership, for example, is a form of signaling. The leader indirectly communicates its opinion of market conditions by raising or lowering price and other firms indicate their agreement or disagreement by following the leader or refusing to go along with its change. Advance notification of intended price changes, with opportunity for retraction if others do not follow, is often even more effective. Firms can also signal one another through speeches, press releases, or advertising.

The problem of signaling was highlighted when General Electric and Westinghouse adopted parallel policies for determining bid prices on heavy electrical equipment almost immediately after their conviction in the electrical equipment conspiracy. In 1976, the Antitrust Division negotiated modifications in the 1962 consent decrees, based on the following allegation:

> In 1963 both General Electric and Westinghouse published similar and unusually extensive price books enabling each to predict not only the exact price that the other would bid in a particular situation, but also the precise type and size of the machine. Both companies also adopted a price protection plan which provided that if the price was lowered by a manufacturer for a particular customer, any buyer within the previous six month period would be given an identical discount retroactively. Thus, each manufacturer was assured that the other would not engage in discounting because of the substantial self-imposed penalty involved.[56]

The modified decrees enjoined the two companies "from publishing or distributing any 'price-signalling' information, offering a price protection policy, using any price book, price list or compilation of prices other than its own, and from using or retaining those prepared by another manufacturer." Each was also forbidden to reveal information to others regarding its prices and bidding policies.[57]

In 1979, the FTC pressed the attack on signaling further. It alleged that three manufacturers of gasoline antiknock additives attained uniform pricing by making all sales at delivered prices, promising customers that they would receive any lower prices or more favorable credit terms offered to another customer ("most favored nation" clauses), giving 30-day advance notice of price increases, and making public announcements of intended price changes. In 1983, the commission upheld an administrative law judge's cease and desist order. A court of appeals, however, reversed in 1984, noting the commission was asking that "non-collusive, non-predatory and independent conduct of a non-artificial nature" be declared illegal, "at least when it results in a substantial lessening of competition." The court found the signaling theory to be little more than conscious parallelism in new dress and stated that even within an oligopolistic setting, "at least some indicia of oppressiveness must exist such as (1) evidence of anticompetitive intent or purpose on the part of the producer charged, or (2) the absence of an independent legitimate business reason for the conduct."[58]

How Serious Is the Problem?

Economists do not agree on the pervasiveness of mutual dependence recognized or on the structural conditions necessary for it to be effective. For those who perceive oligopolistic behavior as a serious problem, the courts' treatment of mere conscious parallelism as legal represents the greatest failure of antitrust law—a gaping loophole between strict interpretation of the rule of reason in monopolization cases and the per se illegality of most overt collusion. Those who doubt the widespread applicability of the Chamberlinian model—such as the Chicago school—are less troubled.

PUNISHMENT AND REMEDY

Indictments or complaints charging conspiracy in restraint of trade under Section 1 of the Sherman Act, or conspiracy to monopolize under Section 2, necessarily allege illegal conduct. Resolution of these cases may be frustrating. Under the Sherman Act, the Antitrust Division can file a criminal indictment, seeking punishment of the alleged perpetrators, or it can bring a civil complaint, seeking relief "effective to redress the antitrust violation proved."[59] Frequently, companion (concurrent) criminal and civil suits are brought against the same defendants seeking fines or imprisonment, or both, and an end to the conduct.

Penalties for Criminal Antitrust Violations

In 1974, criminal violation of the Sherman Act was elevated from a misdemeanor to a felony. Since that time, convicted corporations can be fined up to $1 million for each violation, and individuals can be fined up to $100,000 and sentenced to up to three years in prison. Fines against individuals can be severe sanctions if the court forbids company reimbursement.

Since the publicity surrounding the electrical equipment conspiracy, the Justice Department has pressed for jail sentences in flagrant cases; but only rarely are business executives imprisoned for more than 30 days for an antitrust violation. The department considers criminal prosecution appropriate and asks for jail sentences in cases of price-fixing, predatory practices, other restraints of trade where specific intent can be shown, or where the defendant has a record of previous antitrust violation. Criminal charges are not usually made when the alleged offense involves an unsettled legal issue or a type of conduct not previously challenged. Thus, only a civil complaint was filed in the *Container Corporation* case, the first to allege that a mere exchange of price information violated Section 1. But in *U.S. Gypsum*, the second case involving the practice and following the conviction of the *Container* defendants, criminal charges were brought.

Problems of Structure

Inadequacy of Criminal Punishment. Criminal punishment alone may be virtually irrelevant when the root of the problem is structural—that is, in highly concentrated, oligopolistic industries where full or partial recognition of mutual dependence is inevitable. Such a difficulty surfaced in the 1946 *American Tobacco* case. Throughout the proceedings, defense lawyers maintained that the companies were acting independently in a setting in which each had to consider the actual and prospective behavior of the other two.

In argument before the appeals court, counsel for the American Tobacco Company asked:

> Whether in an industry such as this, the antitrust laws are violated by uniformity of conduct, where normal business factors cause each company, acting individually, to adopt practices and policies that are, in many instances, similar to those of its competitors. If there be a violation of the law under such circumstances, every businessman who meets the competition of a rival by similar action or who responds to external economic stimuli in the same way as his competitors operates his business under serious peril. For that matter, the competitor whose methods are imitated is brought under the same peril by the very act of imitation.[60]

Liggett & Myers' counsel, arguing that the government's case hinged on the consequences of price uniformity, contended that cigarette prices "are based to a considerable extent on consideration by the management of a company of what its chief competitors are doing and what they are likely to do in respect of price changes.... Believing that, in general, imitation minimizes risk, Liggett & Myers ... has followed its principal rivals in pursuance of its own independent judgment as to the company's best interest."[61]

In effect, these lawyers were asking what sorts of conduct the cigarette manufacturers could engage in to avoid further prosecutions, given the structure of the industry. They received no answer from the courts—only convictions and fines for their clients.

Civil Antitrust Actions. The filing of civil complaints, alone or concurrently with criminal indictments, does not necessarily solve such problems. The law requires that the remedy in a civil case be reasonably related to the complaint; thus, structural remedies are legally inappropriate in cases attacking conduct, however much economic sense such a remedy might make.

A successful civil case typically terminates with a consent decree or judicial order barring the firm from behaving in specified ways in the future. If the Antitrust Division or the court has singled out and attacked behavior that creates or perpetuates market power, a conduct-oriented decree can be highly effective. Terminating United Shoe Machinery's leasing practices and refusal to sell its machinery, for example, almost surely led to the subsequent decline of the company's market power. Indeed, the consequences of the decree in that case may have been greater than foreseen. Don E. Waldman has argued that barring similar practices by American Can and Continental Can resulted in structural changes and improved performance in the can manufacturing industry, and that eliminating basing-point pricing in the cement industry led to more efficient resource use even though concentration was not reduced.[62]

But the conduct commonly complained of in Section 1 cases—collusion in restraint of trade—may result from structural conditions that are not likely to change by ending the practices. Further, as long as the underlying structure remains unchanged, other practices may lead to the same or similar results. The shift of the two largest electrical equipment companies from overt collusion to price signaling is a case in point.

The aftermath of the *Container Corporation* case offers an even more dramatic example. The 1969 decree ending the practice of exchanging price information did not change the conditions of high concentration, inelastic demand, and a homogeneous product. In 1976, the Department of Justice filed a criminal case alleging that 23 folding-box manufacturers (including the Container Corporation and other principal defendants in the 1969 case) and 50 of their executives conspired to fix price, rig bids, and allocate customers. All but one of the corporations and two of the individuals pleaded nolo contendere.[63]

Assessing the Structural Context. Business behavior takes place within a structural context, and that context is important in assessing how a conduct-changing decree will affect performance. Examination of structure may suggest appropriate ways to modify conduct or lead to the conclusion that such changes will have little or no effect on performance.

In the latter instance, the economic question is whether the potential improvement in performance is great enough to warrant an attack on the industry's structure or whether the illegal conduct is harmless enough to be ignored. The third alternative, repeated criminal prosecution, is not a promising way to improve an industry's performance. Thus, there is cause for concern that the antitrust laws and their current interpretation do not allow adequate consideration of structural features in cases involving collusive restraints of trade.

ENDNOTES

[1]Statement of J. Paul McGrath, Assistant Attorney General, Antitrust Division, before the Subcommittee on Monopolies and Commercial Law, Committee on the Judiciary, House of Representatives, concerning the Antitrust Division's authorization for fiscal year 1986, March 13, 1985 (Washington, D.C.: U.S. Department of Justice press release, March 13, 1985.)

[2]Appalachian Coals v. United States, 288 U.S. 344 (1933).

[3]United States v. Addyston Pipe & Steel Company et al., 85 Fed. 271 (1898).

[4]United States v. Trenton Potteries Company et al., 273 U.S. 392, 395 (1927).

[5]397–98.

[6]United States v. Socony-Vacuum Oil Company, Inc. et al., 310 U.S. 150, 221–23 (1940).

[7]Kiefer-Stewart Company v. Seagram & Sons, Inc., 340 U.S. 211 (1951); Albrecht v. Herald Company, 390 U.S. 145 (1968); Arizona v. Maricopa County Medical Society et al., 457 U.S. 332 (1982).

[8]United States v. Topco Associates, Inc., 405 U.S. 596, 599 (1972).

[9]609–10.

[10]A. D. Neale and D. G. Goyder, *The Antitrust Laws of the U.S.A.*, 3d ed. (London: Cambridge University Press, 1980), p. 59.

[11]Almarin Phillips, *Market Structure, Organization and Performance* (Cambridge, Mass.: Harvard University Press, 1962).

[12]United States v. Container Corporation of American et al., 393 U.S. 333, 337 (1969).

[13]338–39.

[14]United States v. United States Gypsum Company, 438 U.S. 422, 435, 440–41 (1978).

[15]Klor's, Inc. v. Broadway-Hale Stores, Inc., 359 U.S. 207, 211 (1959).

[16]Robert H. Bork, *The Antitrust Paradox: A Policy at War with Itself* (New York: Basic Books, 1978), p. 332.

[17]NAACP v. Claiborne Hardware Company, 458 U.S. 886, 907 (1982).

[18]Smith v. Pro Football, Inc. 593 F. 2d. 1173, 1178 (1978). (Italics added.)

[19]The exception for export associations is provided in the Webb-Pomerene Act of 1918; for agricultural marketing groups, the Capper-Volstead Act of 1922 and the Cooperative Marketing Act of 1926; for insurance, the McCarran-Ferguson Act of 1945. For discussion of the Export Trading Company Act of 1982, which provides limited antitrust immunity to individual exporters as well as associations, see Chapter Twenty.

[20]United States v. American Telephone & Telegraph Company, 461 F. Supp. 1314, 1322–23 (1978).

[21]For development of the state action doctrine, see Parker v. Brown, 317 U.S. 341 (1943); Cantor v. Detroit Edison Company, 428 U.S. 579 (1976); California Retail Liquor Dealers Association v. Midcal Aluminum, Inc., 445 U.S. 97 (1980); Southern Motor

Carriers Rate Conference, Inc., et al. v. United States, 85 L. Ed. 2d 36 (1985); and cases involving state-sanctioned activities of professional associations discussed in this chapter.

[22]See City of Lafayette v. Louisiana Power & Light Company, 435 U.S. 389 (1978); Community Communications Company, Inc. v. City of Boulder, 455 U.S. 40 (1982); Town of Hallie v. City of Eau Claire, 85 L. Ed. 2d 24 (1985).

[23]In the Matter of Coca-Cola Company, docket no. 8855, 91 FTC 517 (1978); In the Matter of Pepsico, Inc., docket no. 8856, 91 FTC 680 (1978).

[24]Federal Base Ball Club of Baltimore v. National League, 259 U.S. 200 (1922); Toolson v. New York Yankees, Inc., 346 U.S. 356 (1953).

[25]National Collegiate Athletic Association v. Board of Regents of the University of Oklahoma and University of Georgia Athletic Association, 82 L. Ed. 2d 70, 84 (1984).

[26]Public Law No. 212, approved October 15, 1914 (2d sess. 63d Cong., U.S. Stat. L., vol. 38, p. 730).

[27]Unfair labor practices by unions and abuses of their economic power are dealt with in other laws, particularly the National Labor Relations (Wagner) Act of 1935, the Labor-Management Relations (Taft-Hartley) Act of 1947, and the Labor-Management Reporting and Disclosure (Landrum-Griffin) Act of 1959.

[28]American Federation of Musicians v. Carroll, 391 U.S. 99 (1968).

[29]Allen Bradley Company v. Local Union No. 3, International Brotherhood of Electrical Workers, 325 U.S. 797 (1945).

[30]United Mine Workers of America v. Pennington, 381 U.S. 657 (1965).

[31]*National Trade and Professional Associations of the United States* (Washington, D.C.: Columbia Books, 1983).

[32]American Column & Lumber Company v. United States, 257 U.S. 377, 393 (1921). (Italics in original.)

[33]The leading cases include Eastern States Retail Lumber Dealers Association v. United States, 234 U.S. 600 (1914); American Column and Lumber Company, cited above; Maple Flooring Manufacturers Association v. United States, 268 U.S. 563 (1925); Sugar Institute v. United States, 297 U.S. 553 (1936); Federal Trade Commission v. Cement Institute, 333 U.S. 683 (1948); Tag Manufacturers Institute et al. v. Federal Trade Commission, 174 F. 2d 452 (1949).

[34]Goldfarb et ux. v. Virginia State Bar et al., 421 U.S. 773, 786 (1975).

[35]788–89.

[36]Virginia State Board of Pharmacy v. Virginia Citizens Consumer Council, Inc., 425 U.S. 748 (1976); Bates v. State Bar of Arizona, 433 U.S. 350 (1977).

[37]National Society of Professional Engineers v. United States, 435 U.S. 679 (1978).

[38]692, 695.

[39]For a thoughtful discussion, coupled with the argument that conflict between the patent law and the economic objectives of the antitrust laws is more apparent than real, see Ward S. Bowman, Jr., *Patent and Antitrust Law: A Legal and Economic Appraisal* (Chicago: University of Chicago Press, 1973).

[40]Heaton-Peninsular Button-Fastener Company v. Eureka Specialty Company, 77 Fed. 288 (1896).

[41]Special Equipment Company v. Coe, 324 U.S. 370, 383 (1945).

[42]Hartford-Empire Company v. United States, 323 U.S. 386 (1945); Kobe, Inc. v. Dempsey Pump Company, 198 F. 2d 416 (1952).

[43]Transparent-Wrap Machine Corporation v. Stokes & Smith Company, 329 U.S. 637 (1947); Automatic Radio Manufacturing Company v. Hazeltine Research, Inc., 339 U.S. 827 (1950); Zenith Radio Corporation v. Hazeltine Research, Inc., 395 U.S. 100 (1969).

[44]United States v. General Electric Company, 272 U.S. 476, 490 (1926).

[45]United States v. Line Material Company, 333 U.S. 287 (1947).

[46]United States v. Singer Manufacturing Company, 374 U.S. 174, 194–95 (1963).

[47]Edward S. Chamberlin, *The Theory of Monopolistic Competition* (Cambridge, Mass.: Harvard University Press, 1932).

[48]American Tobacco Company v. United States, 328 U.S. 781, 809–10 (1946).

[49]Milgram v. Loew's, Inc., 192 F. 2d 579, 583 (1951).

[50]Theatre Enterprises, Inc. v. Paramount Film Distributing Corporation, 346 U.S. 537, 541 (1954).

[51]United States v. Charles Pfizer and Company, 281 F. Sup. 837 (1968). Passage from trial record as quoted in Frederic M. Scherer, *Industrial Market Structure and Economic Performance,* 2d ed. (Skokie, Ill.: Rand McNally, 1980), p. 518.

[52]Peter Asch, *Industrial Organization and Antitrust Policy,* rev. ed. (New York: John Wiley & Sons, 1983), p. 225.

[53]United States v. International Harvester Company, 274 U.S. 693, 708 (1927).

[54]For an excellent treatment of the economics of basing-point pricing, see Fritz Machlup, *The Basing Point System* (Philadelphia: Blakiston, 1949). See also Samuel M. Loescher, *Imperfect Collusion in the Cement Industry* (Cambridge, Mass.: Harvard University Press, 1959). Systematic "freight absorption"—or charging a customer lower than actual freight costs in order to match the delivered price of a rival located nearer to the customer—may be a form of competition of benefit to customers under certain circumstances and assuming otherwise independent and noncollusive behavior. See Stephen J. DeCanio, "Delivered Pricing and Multiple Basing Point Equilibria: A Reevaluation," *Quarterly Journal of Economics* 99, no. 2 (May 1984), pp. 329–49.

[55]Corn Products Refining Company v. Federal Trade Commission, 324 U.S. 726 (1945); Federal Trade Commission v. A. E. Staley Manufacturing Company, 324 U.S. 746 (1945); Triangle Conduit and Cable Company v. Federal Trade Commission, 168 F. 2d 175 (1948); Cement Institute, cited above. But, see also Boise Cascade Corporation v. Federal Trade Commission, 637 F. 2d 573 (1980), where an appeals court held that in the absence of any evidence of collusion or an actual effect on competition, the adoption of the same West Coast basing point by the major plywood producers in the Southeast did not constitute a violation.

[56]United States v. General Electric Company and Westinghouse Electric Corporation, CCH Trade Cases, ¶61,659 (1977–2), at p. 72,716.

[57]United States v. General Electric Company, CCH Trade Cases, ¶61,660 (1977–2); United States v. Westinghouse Electric Corporation, CCH Trade Cases, ¶61,661 (1977–2). For an interesting commentary on these decrees, see Barbara Epstein, " 'Theory of Second Best' in Operation: A Comment on the 1976 Modification of the Electrical Equipment Consent Decrees," *Antitrust Bulletin* 22, no. 3 (Fall 1977), pp. 503–16.

[58]E. I. du Pont de Nemours & Company v. Federal Trade Commission, and Ethyl Corporation v. Federal Trade Commission, 729 F. 2d 128, 137, 139 (1984).

[59]United States v. E. I. du Pont de Nemours & Company et al., 366 U.S. 316, 323 (1961).

[60]Quoted in William H. Nicholls, *Price Policies in the Cigarette Industry* (Nashville, Tenn.: Vanderbilt University Press, 1951), p. 363.

[61]Ibid., p. 364.

[62]Don E. Waldman, *Antitrust Action and Market Structure* (Lexington, Mass.: D.C. Heath, 1978). See also William L. Baldwin, "Feedback Effect of Business Conduct on Industry Structure," *Journal of Law and Economics* 12, no. 1 (April 1969), pp. 123–53.

[63]BNA Antitrust and Trade Regulation Report, no. 921 (July 5, 1979), p. A–13 (Washington, D.C.: Bureau of National Affairs).

CHAPTER EIGHTEEN

Price Discrimination: Section 2 of the Clayton Act

Because economic and legal approaches to antitrust issues differ, economists may find some interpretations and applications of the law anomalous. For instance, in economic models of monopoly power that assume profit-maximizing behavior, evidence of intent to monopolize is irrelevant. Also, the criteria for successful antitrust actions are different in each approach: Law enforcement agencies seek to end illegal practices and bring lawbreakers to justice; economists are interested in how an outcome will improve market performance and consumer welfare.

Still, in the areas reviewed in the last three chapters—monopolization, merger, and horizontal restraints of trade—the objectives of the antitrust laws are fundamentally consistent with the implications of various market structures and forms of business behavior for economic welfare. Unfortunately, the same cannot be said of the areas considered in this and the following chapter, price discrimination and vertical restraints of trade. Rather, many economists regard current antitrust enforcement in these two areas as illogical, perverse, and even bizarre.

ECONOMIC ANALYSIS OF PRICE DISCRIMINATION

In its simplest and clearest form, price discrimination is the sale, at the same time and place, of different units of an identical commodity at different prices. For example, a motion picture theater may set lower prices for children, tomato soup may sell for 40 cents a can and two for 75 cents, or a bus line may offer special fares for senior citizens. Virtually all economists prefer a broader definition—that price discrimination is the sale of identical or similar goods at price differences that do not reflect differences in manufacturing or sales costs. Indeed, the economic view is that sales at identical prices are discriminatory if costs are different. In this chapter, we follow the broader definition.

Systematic Price Discrimination

Economists have developed models distinguishing three general forms of *systematic* price discrimination, or pricing designed to exploit differences in demand among various buyers of the same commodity. These are referred to as first-degree (or perfect), second-degree, and third-degree price discrimination. First- and second-degree price discrimination are similar in nature, while third-degree is a distinctly different pricing strategy.

First-Degree Discrimination. In the model of perfect, or first-degree, discrimination a firm charges the highest price anyone will pay for each unit it sells. Although such discrimination is rare, this model is important in highlighting the economic effects of more realistic cases.

Perfect price discrimination is illustrated in Figure 18–1. Suppose a discriminating monopolist can quote a separate price for each unit sold and knows the highest, or *reservation,* price anyone would be willing to pay for each of these units. P_1, at the intersection of the demand curve (D) and the vertical axis of Figure 18–1A, is the highest price at which any of the commodity can be sold. The monopolist identifies the buyer willing to pay P_1 and sells that buyer one unit at that price. (Strictly, at the price shown at the intersection of the demand curve with the vertical axis, sales are zero. But, we are assuming that the scale on the horizontal axis yields a continuous demand curve so that the drop in price from P_1 needed to sell one unit is infinitesimal.) The monopolist also ascertains the highest price anyone would be willing to pay for the second unit—either a different buyer or the same buyer who bought the first unit and regards the second as worth only slightly less. The monopolist "moves down" the demand curve, charging P_i for the Q_ith unit without having to reduce the price of any other unit. Under perfect price discrimination, the demand curve facing the firm becomes its marginal revenue curve (i.e., D is a schedule showing the amount added to total revenue by selling one more unit) and the firm maximizes its profit by producing Q_e, the rate of output at which $MC = MR = P_e$, where P_e is the price charged for the final unit sold.

FIGURE 18–1 First- and Second-Degree Price Discrimination

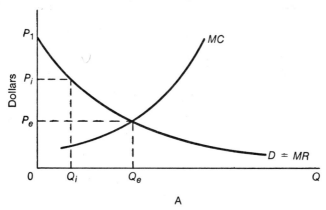

A

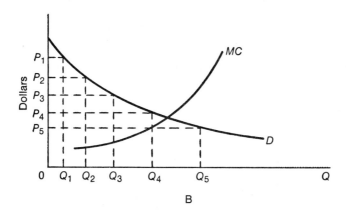

B

Second-Degree Discrimination. Second-degree price discrimination, sometimes described as "block pricing," is a variant of perfect
discrimination. In this more realistic case, the firm is not able to sell
each unit in a separate and independently priced transaction but is
able to sell blocks of product at different prices. Electricity and gas
are often priced at block rates, such as charging each customer the
highest rate for the first 50 kilowatt hours used per month and progressively lower rates for blocks of 51 to 100, 101 to 300, and over 300
per month. A restaurant may charge 50 cents for the first cup of coffee
and 10 cents for each refill (representing true discrimination only if
the cost of refilling a cup differs from the cost of filling and serving it
the first time by less than 40 cents). Bargaining over the price of each
transaction is a form of second-degree price discrimination common in

bazaar markets in many parts of the world, although the ability of each seller to discriminate is usually limited by the proximity of other sellers of similar products.

Second-degree price discrimination is illustrated by Figure 18–1B, in which a price of P_1 is charged for the first Q_1 units, P_2 is charged for each unit between Q_1 and Q_2, and so on. In this figure, Q_4 units will be produced and sold, since at that rate of output, marginal revenue drops from above to below marginal cost.

Perfect price discrimination poses, in a stark and simple fashion, the fundamental welfare issues surrounding price discrimination, as illustrated in Figure 18–2. The demand curve (D) represents the average revenue (AR_s) of a nondiscriminating monopolist who charges a single price (P_s) and who produces the output Q_s. (For the moment, ignore the dashed line ATC.) Consumer surplus is shown by the area ABP_s, and the deadweight loss of monopoly is shown by the area BCE. If the monopolist becomes a perfect price discriminator, D becomes its marginal revenue (MR_d), and its output rises to Q_d. Since P_d (the price charged to the marginal buyer) is equal to the price that all buyers

FIGURE 18–2 Output under Nondiscriminating Monopoly and Perfect Price Discrimination

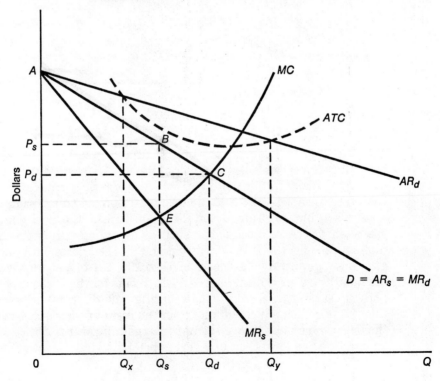

would pay under pure competition, Q_d is equal to the competitive output. Thus, the resource misallocation of single-price monopoly is eliminated by perfect price discrimination. The deadweight loss, the area BCE, disappears. But the entire consumer surplus that would exist under pure competition, the area ACP_d, is now appropriated by the discriminating monopolist, who has squeezed this surplus out of its customers by charging the full reservation price for each unit sold.

It is possible that a particular product will be produced and sold only under price discrimination. If average total cost (the dashed line ATC in Figure 18–2) lies as shown—everywhere above D but at some rates of output below AR_d—there will be no rate of output at which a nondiscriminating firm can cover costs; thus, the product will not be produced in the long run in the absence of price discrimination. Under perfect price discrimination, the average revenue curve (AR_d) lies above the demand curve, as any downward-sloping average revenue curve lies above its associated marginal revenue curve; and production by a private firm becomes possible without subsidy at any rate of output between Q_x and Q_y. Joan Robinson noted that price discrimination of this sort might be necessary to cover the costs of a doctor practicing in a rural area or to justify provision of railroad service to a small and isolated community.[1]

Third-Degree Discrimination. The other major type of systematic price discrimination, third-degree, has a different nature: The seller is assumed to sell in two or more separated markets, each with its own demand curve.

For systematic, profit-maximizing third-degree price discrimination to be feasible, three conditions must be met: (1) The firm must be a monopolist, or have some degree of market power, so that it faces

FIGURE 18–3 Third-Degree Price Discrimination

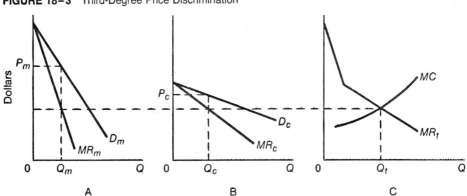

downward-sloping demand curves and has the ability to set prices. (2) It must face demand curves of differing elasticities in each of the markets in which it wishes to set a separate price. The need for this condition can be understood by recalling that the profit-maximizing price is equal to $[\eta/(\eta-1)]MC$, where η is the absolute value of the elasticity of demand and MC is the firm's marginal cost. Given the product's marginal cost, the profit-maximizing prices in the firm's various markets will be different only if the demand elasticities at these prices are different. (3) There must be some barrier to prevent customers from transferring the product among themselves. Such barriers may result from transportation or other transfer costs, customer ignorance of price differences, or the inherent nature of the commodity. (A surgeon could base appendectomy fees on patients' incomes, for example, without worrying about poor patients reselling the operation to rich ones.)

Suppose a patented and therefore monopolized chemical compound can be used by firms other than its producer for making both medicine and candy. Only poor substitutes are available to pharmaceutical companies, but a number of good substitutes are available to candy manufacturers. If the patent holder can prevent pharmaceutical firms from acquiring batches intended for sale to candy manufacturers, demand in the medicinal and candy markets might be as depicted in Panels A and B of Figure 18–3, with the demand in the medicinal market (D_m) assumed to be less elastic throughout and more limited than that in the candy market (D_c). The discriminating monopolist would maximize its profit by calculating its total marginal revenue, which is the horizontal sum of the marginal revenues in the two markets ($MR_m + MR_c$). This total marginal revenue is shown as MR_t in Figure 18–3C. The rate of total output (Q_t) would be determined by the equality of MR_t and the marginal cost MC. The total revenue obtainable from any rate of output is maximized by distributing that output among markets until the marginal revenue is equal in all markets. Thus, in the two markets shown in Panels A and B, Q_m would be sold in the medicinal market at a price of P_m, and Q_c would be sold in the candy market at a price of P_c.

Figure 18–4 assumes price discrimination between the two markets is no longer possible. Since the maximum prices at which the compound can be sold in the two markets differ, there will be a kink in the total demand curve (D_t) at the price at which candy manufacturers enter the market. Such a kink in the demand curve leads to a discontinuity in the associated marginal revenue curve. The manufacturer of the compound now faces the choice of selling only to the medicinal market (supplying that market with Q_1 and obtaining a price of P_1) or cutting the price to P_2 for all customers to attract candy

FIGURE 18–4   Price and Output Alternatives for a Nondiscriminating Monopolist Selling in One or in Two Separated Markets

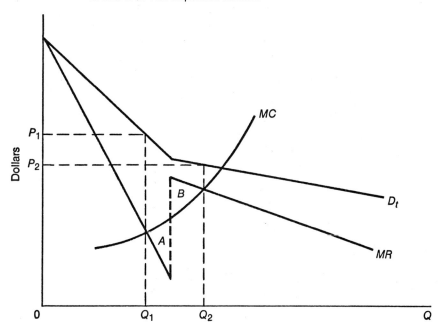

manufacturers and sell the larger quantity (Q_2). Note that the profit-maximizing conditions of $MR = MC$ is met at both Q_1 and Q_2, or that both are *local* maximizing equilibria. If Area A, in which marginal cost exceeds marginal revenue, is larger than Area B, in which marginal revenue exceeds marginal cost, the compound manufacturer will earn greater profits by confining itself to the higher-priced medicinal market. But if B is larger than A, the profit-maximizing monopolist will expand its sales to Q_2 and sell the compound to pharmaceutical and candy producers alike at the lower price of P_2.

The effect of third-degree price discrimination on output is inde-terminate. It has been shown that with straight-line demand curves the output under price discrimination is identical to that under non-discriminating monopolistic pricing, provided the firm sells in both markets. Q_t in Figure 18–3C is therefore equal to Q_2 in Figure 18–4. If the demand curves are not straight lines, the theoretical problem becomes complex, and the solution depends on the relative convexities or concavities of the two (or more) demand curves.[2]

Robinson concluded that more often than not, output would be higher under third-degree price discrimination; and some of the sub-sequent literature supports that conclusion. The underlying theory, however, is still indefinite. But if third-degree discrimination leads a firm to sell in a market in which it would otherwise not participate, output must increase.

Predatory and Sporadic Price Discrimination

Not all price discrimination results from monopolistic power designed to exploit differences in customer demand. Two other types, *predatory* and *sporadic,* are engaged in for other purposes and with other effects.

Predatory Price Discrimination. Empirical and theoretical studies discussed in Chapter Nine, notably those of John S. McGee[3] and Kenneth G. Elzinga,[4] cast serious doubt on the prevalence of predatory pricing by demonstrating that it is rarely the most efficient way for a dominant firm to eliminate or reduce competition. The ability to discriminate in price, however, makes predatory pricing somewhat more attractive for a large firm seeking to injure or destroy a smaller rival; the predator may be able to cut price only to actual or potential customers of the small firm. Still, McGee's basic arguments hold: In almost every instance, it would be less costly for the larger firm to buy out its smaller competitors than to eliminate them through mutually harmful price-cutting, and predation will not effectively eliminate competitors in the long run unless there are barriers to entry by new firms.

Predatory price discrimination has been used to discipline competitors rather than destroy them. The FTC and the courts have recognized multiple basing-point pricing as a particularly effective device for enforcing price leadership. If one firm cuts its price, others can retaliate by soliciting customers located near the price-cutter, matching or even undercutting its mill-gate price and charging freight only from the errant firm's place of production, even though the goods are actually shipped from much farther away. If the price-cutting firm is located at a basing point, the process of retaliation involves only aggressive solicitation of orders from customers near its mill and the willingness to collect less than actual freight charges, or to "absorb" freight, to a greater extent than usual. If a firm is not located at an existing basing point, its mill can be declared a "punitive" basing point by the others. The tactic will not be too costly to any one of the predators, since delivered prices to customers close to the disciplining firms need not be cut when a rival's territory is penetrated in this way. When the victim sees the error of its ways, the others simply stop soliciting its nearby customers, eliminating the cost of absorbing freight on such sales.

Predatory price discrimination is not an effective tactic against firms with low fixed costs of production. Although, in the 1911 *American Tobacco* case, James B. Duke was charged with using such discrimination to put together the tobacco trust, it was not a workable device for bringing in cigar manufacturers. Until 1920, cigar manufacture was carried out on a small scale, mainly by hand labor. Because cigar tobacco needed only three months of curing time, cigar manufacturers could cut operations whenever prices fell and expand when prices rose.

That response to the trust was not so readily available to other firms in the tobacco industry with higher fixed costs (from more mechanized production) and greater inventory requirements (up to three years of curing time for cigarette tobacco).[5] Thus, by 1910, when Duke's American Tobacco Company controlled 86 percent of the domestic market for cigarettes and almost the same percentages for smoking, chewing, and snuff tobacco products, it accounted for only 14.4 percent of the domestic market for cigars.[6]

Sporadic Price Discrimination. Sporadic price discrimination may reflect competitive responses to disequilibrium situations and, indeed, may be a part of the process of moving to a new market equilibrium position. The model of pure and perfect competition notwithstanding, shifts in supply and demand need not lead to immediate adoption of the new equilibrium price by all firms in an industry. Rather, a firm may respond initially to competitive pressures by lowering price in the areas or to the customers immediately affected. Its actions may, in turn, trigger partial and tentative responses by others. A price reduction may thus spread through a market over time, perhaps through a series of smaller and uneven price cuts to particular customers.

If firms had to respond to a situation affecting only part of their sales by changing prices across the board, many might ignore the situation as long as possible and maintain the current price to all customers. The result might be periods of price rigidity punctuated by periods of turmoil and overreaction as pent-up pressures on price suddenly took marketwide effect. In general, the fewer the number of transactions and the more costly the product, the more likely it is that discrimination will facilitate the adjustment process. Price changes are likely to take place smoothly enough in markets with large numbers of small transactions, and in such markets, the ability to discriminate may retard or distort the processes of adjustment.

Another type of procompetitive sporadic price discrimination is associated with secret price-cutting by cheating members of a cartel, or by firms in concentrated markets who fear retaliation if detected. Such price shading is the main reason for the unsustainability of collusive prices or those reflecting recognition of mutual dependence and is more likely to occur if price offers can be made surreptitiously to individual customers.

Ruinous Competition. In 1923, John M. Clark identified a form of sporadic price discrimination that can lead to excessive or, as he termed it, "ruinous" competition in industries with high fixed costs.[7] In such an industry, short-run average and marginal costs decline over a wide range of output, as the fixed or overhead costs are spread over larger volumes of production. Marginal cost through this range is below average cost; hence, a price that is below average cost may yet exceed marginal cost. But a unit of the product sold at a price above its marginal cost is always profitable (even if below average cost), yielding a surplus that helps cover fixed costs, so long as it is not necessary to lower the price charged for other units.

In periods of low sales, the pressures to get the volume up and spread the overhead by cutting prices to new customers may become intense. And as the firms seek to attract customers from one another, defensive discounts must be given to retain existing customers. The competition may become ruinous as greater proportions of total industry sales are made at prices below average cost. Richard A. Posner suggested that this phenomenon was behind the railroad rebates that figured so prominently in the 1911 *Standard Oil* case and might explain why the railroad industry supported passage of the Interstate Commerce Act of 1887, under which such rebates were forbidden.[8]

THE WELFARE EFFECTS OF PRICE DISCRIMINATION

Systematic price discrimination is one way to exploit market power. Thus, to isolate welfare effects, we must compare the results of price discrimination to the results of nondiscriminatory pricing by firms with the same market power.

Output and Equity

Transfer of Consumer Surplus to Producers. In most cases, systematic noncollusive price discrimination results in a greater rate of output than does uniform nondiscriminatory monopolistic pricing. But this increased output is obtained through a transfer of consumer surplus to producers—a transfer that reaches its extreme in the model of perfect price discrimination. Thus, this model highlights the essential welfare trade-off involved in many forms of price discrimination: more efficient resource allocation versus redistributive effects of questionable equity.

Distributive equity, a normative rather than a positive issue, involves value judgments that are not amenable to purely objective economic analysis. For this reason, some antitrust scholars regard the issue as irrelevant. Robert H. Bork, for example writes:

> The evil of monopoly is restriction of output and consequent misallo-
> cation of resources. . . . If discrimination increases output, it tends to
> move resource allocation and value of the marginal product toward that
> which would obtain in a competitive industry. A decrease in output has
> the opposite effect. The impact of discrimination on output, therefore,
> may be taken as a proxy for its effect on consumer welfare.[9]

However, as Bork himself notes in another context, "Value trade-offs
must be made, and to refuse to deal with them is to make the choice
of letting the status quo decide the trade-off."[10] For some, the redistributive effects of price discrimination are quite important—at times,
the crux of the issue—and redistribution from consumers to producers
through a device that permits more effective exploitation of monopoly
power is regarded as inherently unfair.

Transfers from Unfavored to Favored Customers. A second issue
of redistribution involves the effects on different groups of customers—
for example, the doctor who sets rich patients' fees high enough to earn
an acceptable income and still treat poor patients at cost or less. In
most instances, under third-degree price discrimination, customers in
the low-elasticity group pay a higher price than what would be charged
under uniform pricing by the monopolist, while those in the high-
elasticity group pay a lower price. Indeed, as illustrated in Figure
18–4, price discrimination may be necessary to induce the monopolist
to make any sales at all in the market with the lower price. Thus,
price discrimination is sometimes necessary to make a product available to low-income consumers. The cut-rate pricing of generic and
private-label products exemplifies this phenomenon.

Low demand elasticity may, however, reflect a need for a product
rather than the ability to afford it comfortably. For example, consumers at all income levels may have highly inelastic demands for
some medical products and thus be vulnerable to exploitation by a
price-discriminating manufacturer. In a situation like that illustrated
in Figures 18–3 and 18–4, the question of increased output might be
less important than whether the manufacturer would cut the price in
the medicinal market to be able to make sales in the candy market if
discrimination became impossible.

Resource Misallocation

Even if systematic price discrimination does enhance output, its effects
on resource allocation may not be entirely benign. Posner noted two
such effects. First, the prospect of engaging in profitable price discrimination will encourage firms to devote resources to socially un-
productive activities such as attaining market power and erecting barriers against transfer of goods from low- to high-priced markets. Second,

price discrimination may perpetuate inefficient resource use and monopolistic positions among business customers since the favored ones will enjoy a competitive advantage unrelated to any real differences in economic efficiency.[11]

Identifying Predation

Virtually by definition, little if anything can be said in favor of predatory price discrimination. Conversely, most forms of sporadic price discrimination are procompetitive and thus make a positive contribution to economic performance. Yet, in practice, it may be difficult to distinguish between the two.

Suppose, for example, that the Boston Company (a hypothetical firm making sales in the northeastern United States) finds that its sales in Delaware are slipping because the Richmond Company, a rival it faces only in that state, has cut its price. Boston responds by lowering its price in Delaware but nowhere else. Is the response predatory if Richmond is a large firm selling throughout the southeastern United States? What if Richmond is a small firm operating only in Delaware? Should Boston's intent be a consideration? (Suppose Boston's president states, "We've got to protect our Delaware market" or "We're really going to teach Richmond a lesson this time.") What if Boston undercuts rather than meets Richmond's price in Delaware? Under what circumstances would Richmond's initial price cut in Delaware be regarded as predatory? What if Richmond had never before sold in Delaware and was trying to penetrate a new market by selling at prices lower than elsewhere? Should market shares, past pricing policies, and past competitive behavior of the two companies be considered? This barrage of questions indicates that whether a discriminatory price cut is predatory may depend largely on its context.

Phillip Areeda and Donald F. Turner proposed one possible solution to this problem, arguing that theoretically any price below marginal cost can be deemed predatory because no firm would make such a sale other than to harm a competitor.[12] (Since marginal cost is often difficult or impossible to identify in practice, they proposed use of average variable cost in applying antitrust law to cases of alleged predation.) Further, they contended that no price above marginal or average variable cost ought to be regarded as predatory, although admittedly such a standard would exclude a few cases in which the intent behind a price cut is to harm a competitor. Virtually all economists who have commented on the question accept the point that in the absence of a "race down the experience curve," a price below marginal cost is necessarily a predatory one; but some criticize Areeda and Turner's criterion as too restrictive in that it excludes pricing policies that should be condemned as predatory.[13]

In sum, price discrimination is a complex phenomenon with varied results. Economic analysis does not justify banning the practice in the absence of predation; to the contrary, economists have identified several reasons for not doing so. But the theory does indicate that price discrimination can be harmful and that economic performance might be improved by appropriate controls and limits. However, such controls and limits have not even been identified, much less put into place.

THE ROBINSON–PATMAN ACT

When the original Clayton Act was passed in 1914, shortly after the 1911 *Standard Oil* and *American Tobacco* cases, nearly all members of Congress, leading economists, lawyers, and journalists believed that selective, local, and temporary price-cutting, sometimes below cost, had been a major device used to put together the large industrial combinations. Thus, eliminating predatory price discrimination was one of the Clayton Act's most important preventive objectives. Section 2 of that act made it illegal in interstate commerce "to discriminate in price between different purchasers of commodities . . . where the effect of such discrimination may be to substantially lessen competition or tend to create a monopoly in any line of commerce." However, Section 2 also provided that "nothing herein contained shall prevent discrimination in price between purchasers of commodities on account of differences in the grade, quality, or quantity of the commodity sold, or that makes only due allowance for differences in the cost of selling or transportation, or discrimination in price in the same or different communities made in good faith to meet competition."

The Failure of Original Section 2

The original Section 2 turned out to be an insignificant addition to antitrust law probably because its proponents exaggerated the role of predatory price discrimination. And whatever potential this section may have had was further diminished by court interpretation. In 1923, an appeals court held that since congressional intent was to curb predatory price discrimination, the law was violated only on a showing of a substantial lessening of competition at the level of the discriminating seller. Effects on competition among favored and disfavored buyers were not to be considered.[14] In 1929, this decision was overruled by the Supreme Court, which interpreted the phrase "in any line of commerce" to modify "substantial lessening of competition" and "tend to create a monopoly," so that an effect on competition at any level was covered.[15] But by that time, most antitrust lawyers thought that the proviso that "nothing herein contained shall prevent discrimination in price ... on account of differences in ... quantity of the commodity sold" rendered Section 2 virtually unenforceable.[16]

Passage of Robinson–Patman

The impetus to passage of the Robinson-Patman Act came from the rise of the chain store—principally in food, drug, and department store retailing—and from the distress of small businesses during the Depression of the 1930s. Members of Congress (some sincerely and others demagogically) linked the two phenomena, arguing that chain stores were able to obtain supplier discounts not available to smaller retailers and that this economic power, rather than superior efficiency, allowed the chains to sell at lower prices. Chain store buying practices threatened brokers and wholesalers as well as retailers, since many of the chains were vertically integrated and performed their own brokerage and distribution functions.

The version of the Robinson-Patman bill first submitted to Congress was drafted by a private attorney serving as counsel for the United States Wholesale Grocers Association.[17] The atmosphere in which the bill was debated and passed was heated. In reviewing the legislative history of the act, the Department of Justice noted that "anti-chain sentiment became virulent. Emotions were so strong that many Congressmen would have supported a bill legislating the absolute prohibition of chain stores."[18]

Provisions of the Amendment

Section 2(a) of the Clayton Act as amended by the Robinson-Patman Act made it unlawful "to discriminate in price between purchasers of commodities of like grade and quality ... where the effect of such discrimination may be substantially to lessen competition or tend to create a monopoly in any line of commerce, or to injure, destroy, or prevent competition with any person who either grants or knowingly receives the benefit of such discrimination, or with customers of either of them."

Closing the "Loopholes" in Original Section 2. The basic objectives of Congress are evident. The reference to commodities of like grade and quality eliminated the debilitating quantity exception in original Section 2. The amendment also removed any ambiguity involving the lines of commerce; it covers price discrimination whenever competition is injured, destroyed, or prevented at the level of the seller (now known as primary-line injury), or of the buyer (secondary-line), or of customers of either (tertiary-line).

Injury to a Competitor Rather than to Competition. Perhaps the single most important feature of Robinson-Patman is its modification of the Clayton Act's basic test of illegality, which it expanded to include injuring, destroying, or preventing competition "with any person." Under this phrasing, it is only necessary to show that one firm competing with the seller, the buyer, or a customer of either of them has been harmed by the discriminatory price, rather than a lessening of competition or a tendency toward monopoly.

Defense Provisions. Section 2(a) provides a cost-justification defense for otherwise illegal discrimination, stating that "nothing herein contained shall prevent differentials which make only due allowance for differences in the cost of manufacture, sale, or delivery resulting from the differing methods or quantities in which such commodities are to such purchasers sold or delivered." This defense is qualified, however, by giving the FTC authority to investigate the effects of particular quantity discounts and to fix maximum limits if it "finds that available purchasers in greater quantities are so few as to render differentials on account thereof unjustly discriminatory or promotive of monopoly."

Section 2(b) states, "Upon proof . . . that there has been discrimination . . . the burden of rebutting the prima facie case thus made by showing justification shall be upon the person charged." One rationale for imposing the burden in this fashion is that the alleged offender should have access to internal information needed to establish a cost justification, while it would be extremely difficult or impossible for a prosecutor or plaintiff to show that a price differential was not justified by differences in cost.

Section 2(b) goes on to establish a second defense, providing that "nothing herein contained shall prevent a seller rebutting the prima facie case thus made by showing that his lower price or the furnishing of services or facilities to any purchaser or purchasers was made in good faith to meet the equally low price of a competitor, or the services or facilities furnished by a competitor."

Brokerage Fees and Promotional Allowances. Section 2(c) makes it unlawful to pay a brokerage fee or grant a brokerage allowance to anyone other than an independent broker. The prohibition is per se and not subject to any justification on grounds of brokerage services performed by an integrated customer. Section 2(d) forbids any payment to a customer for services performed, such as local media advertising, window displays, or other point-of-sale promotion, "unless such payment is available on proportionately equal terms to all other customers competing in the distribution of such products or commodities."

Section 2(e) contains a similar ban against promotional and other services or facilities provided by the seller, unless offered to "all purchasers on proportionately equal terms." The prohibitions of Sections 2(d) and 2(e), like that of Section 2(c), are per se.

Inducing Discrimination. Section 2(f) states, "It shall be unlawful for any person engaged in commerce, in the course of such commerce, knowingly to induce or receive a discrimination in price which is prohibited by this section."

Violations of Sections 2(a) through 2(f) of the Robinson-Patman Act are civil offenses. A final section of the act, rarely enforced, makes it a criminal offense to be a party to or knowingly assist in discriminatory practices for the purpose of destroying competition or eliminating a seller, or to sell goods at "unreasonably low prices" for such a purpose.

INTERPRETATION AND ENFORCEMENT OF THE ROBINSON–PATMAN ACT

Given the mixed character of price discrimination, widely held misperceptions of its motivations and effects, and the circumstances under which the Robinson-Patman Act was passed, it is not surprising that the courts and the FTC have had trouble interpreting and enforcing it. (By mutual understanding, the Antitrust Division has left enforcement almost entirely to the FTC.)

Posner noted that into the 1960s, the FTC used a two-pronged strategy to try to reduce the evidentiary requirements for successful prosecution of a Robinson-Patman case. First, the commission concentrated its efforts on bringing cases under Sections 2(c), 2(d), and 2(e), where the prohibitions are per se. (From 1936 through 1971, 964 of the 1,305 Robinson-Patman complaints filed by the FTC were brought under these sections.) Second, the commission argued for interpretations both of Section 2(a) and of the good-faith defense in Section 2(b) that would have made price discrimination, as defined in the act, virtually per se illegal.[19]

Primary-Line Injury

The courts have recognized that the primary intent of Congress in passage of Robinson-Patman was to deal with perceived problems of secondary-line injury. Nevertheless, the Supreme Court has held that "it is certain at least that §2(a) is violated where there is a price discrimination which deals the requisite injury to primary-line competition even though secondary-line and tertiary-line competition are unaffected. The statute could hardly be read any other way."[20]

The Supreme Court's 1967 *Utah Pie*[21] decision, dealing with standards for ascertaining primary-line injury, remains a landmark case and leading precedent despite harsh and widespread criticism of the criteria adopted.[22] The Utah Pie Company, a Salt Lake City firm engaged in baking pies that were sold in Utah and surrounding states, began selling frozen pies in Salt Lake City in 1957. Three large firms, Continental Baking Company, Carnation Company, and Pet Milk Company, had for several years been selling frozen pies, shipped from outside the state, in Salt Lake City. With its locational advantage, Utah Pie entered the market with lower prices than the incumbents. Continental, Carnation, and Pet all responded, at one time or another, with prices "lower than they sold pies of like grade and quality in other markets considerably closer to their plants."[23]

In 1958, its first full year of participation in the frozen-pie market, Utah Pie accounted for 66.5 percent of sales in the Salt Lake City market; by 1961, its share had fallen to 45.3 percent. Over the same period, Utah Pie's price fell from $4.15 per dozen to $2.75. Its total sales revenue rose, however, because the market was growing rapidly. And throughout the period, Utah Pie remained profitable, with its net worth rising from $31,652 to $68,802.

In 1961, Utah Pie brought a private suit, seeking both treble damages and injunctive relief. In an opinion reversing a court of appeals decision for the respondents, Supreme Court Justice Byron White wrote:

> We believe that the Act reaches price discrimination that erodes competition as much as it does price discrimination that is intended to have immediate destructive impact. In this case, the evidence shows a drastically declining price structure which the jury could rationally attribute to continued or sporadic price discrimination. The jury was entitled to conclude that "the effect of such discrimination," by each of these respondents, "may be substantially to lessen competition . . . or to injure, destroy, or prevent competition with any person who either grants or knowingly receives the benefit of such discrimination."[24]

In dissent, Justices Potter Stewart and John M. Harlan noted, "Unless we disregard the lessons so laboriously learned in scores of Sherman and Clayton Act cases, the 1961 situation has to be considered more competitive than that of 1958. Thus, if we assume that the price discrimination proven against the respondents had any effect on competition, that effect must have been beneficient." The Court, they asserted, "has fallen into the error of reading the Robinson-Patman Act as protecting competitors, instead of competition."[25]

In an article published shortly after the Supreme Court's decision, Ward S. Bowman observed, "Mr. Justice White, as clearly and unambiguously as anyone could, used the very evidence of competition which convinced the court of appeals that no violation existed to decide that there was an antitrust violation."[26]

Presumably unwittingly, White illuminated the conflict between the implications of economic analysis and of his decision by noting that the jury could infer injury from sporadic price discrimination—the type of discrimination economists view as most procompetitive.

Secondary-Line Injury

The leading secondary-line injury case is *Morton Salt,* decided by the Supreme Court in 1948.[27]   At issue was a schedule of quantity discounts offered by Morton.   Less-than-carload shipments were priced at $1.60 per case, delivered.   Carload purchases were priced at $1.50. Extra discounts of 10 cents and an additional 5 cents were given for purchases of 5,000 cases and 50,000 cases, respectively, if purchased within any 12-month period.   By the time the complaint was brought, only five large chain stores had purchased large enough quantities of salt to obtain the lowest price of $1.35 per case.   In its defense, Morton argued that the discounts, being available to all customers, were not discriminatory under the concept of price discrimination incorporated in the Robinson-Patman Act.   The Court noted that, in reality, the larger discounts were unavailable to many independent wholesalers and retail grocers with smaller salt purchases.   Further, the opinion continued:

> Congress considered it to be an evil that a large buyer could secure a competitive advantage over a small buyer solely because of the large buyer's quantity purchasing ability.   The Robinson-Patman Act was passed to deprive a large buyer of such advantages except to the extent that a lower price could be justified by reason of a seller's diminished costs due to quantity manufacture, delivery or sale, or by reason of a seller's good faith effort to meet a competitor's equally low price.[28]

The Court noted that the burden of showing that price differentials were justified by cost differences was on the respondent rather than the commission.   To establish a prima facie showing of illegality in a case alleging secondary-line injury, "the Commission need only prove that a seller had charged one customer a higher price for like goods than he had charged one or more of the purchaser's competitors."[29]   To support this view, the Court cited an earlier case in which it had held that "the statute does not require that the discriminations must in fact have harmed competition, but only that there is a reasonable possibility that they 'may' have such an effect."[30]   Note that the standard of "reasonable possibility" applied here is more rigorous than that of "reasonable probability" adopted by the Court in interpreting the test of legality for mergers evaluated under Section 7 of the Clayton Act.

"Trade" or "functional" discounts, such as separate price schedules for sales to wholesalers and retailers, are not regarded as violations of the law in markets where sets of distributors are clearly distinct and do not compete with one another. But functional discounts have been found to cause secondary-line injury in instances where some firms make both wholesale and retail sales. The Supreme Court has held that if buyers compete at any level, they must be offered the same discounts unless differences can be justified by differences in cost.[31]

Since it is usually difficult to make a successful cost-justification defense, suppliers have been driven to quoting identical prices and terms to all customers, regardless of differences in sales costs, or refusing to sell to any retailers. Quoting identical prices to all customers, no matter how different sales circumstances may be, is perfectly legal under the Robinson-Patman Act, although in an economic sense, such actions constitute price discrimination. This interpretation of Section 2(a) has also frustrated retailers' efforts to form joint buying organizations. The FTC has held it illegal to grant wholesalers' discounts to such organizations on the ground that competition with retailers who buy from independent wholesalers may be injured.[32]

Problems in Using Defense Provisions

The cost-justification and good-faith defenses against a prima facie showing of illegal discrimination are of limited usefulness and, according to many critics, based on dubious logic.

Cost Justification. A fundamental theorem of economics is that if there are common or joint costs of production or distribution, there is no one correct way to allocate these costs. For example, how should fuel costs and pilots' salaries be allocated between first-class and coach passengers? As Morris A. Adelman noted:

> The burden of proof of a cost differential is on the seller; any cost differential is presumed to be "unjustified" unless and until the Commission finds to the contrary. The procedural requirements are such that a cost differential must be disregarded unless it is certain and precise. But, since cost differentials are inherently uncertain and imprecise, most of them cannot exist in the contemplation of the law.[33]

Some costs can be separated and allocated precisely enough to satisfy the FTC and the courts (although an economic theorist might regard the results as nonsense) by keeping elaborate accounting records (number of salespersons' calls per unit sold, differences in time and labor required to make small and large deliveries, etc.). But such record-keeping is expensive and can be challenged by the FTC.

Good-Faith Defense. Several pitfalls hinder successful use of the

Section 2(b) defense based on meeting competition in good faith. First, the seller must show that it has tried to ascertain that a competing seller is offering a lower price. A seller cannot rely on a customer's statement to that effect.[34] In the 1978 *Gypsum* case[35] (discussed in Chapter Seventeen), the Supreme Court rejected the defendants' contention that they should have been allowed to exchange price information with competitors in order to avail themselves of the good-faith defense. But the Court could not say what efforts a seller should be expected to make. The Court admitted:

> Given the fact-specific nature of the inquiry, it is difficult to predict all the factors the FTC or a court would consider in appraising a seller's good faith in matching a competing offer in these circumstances. ... In a limited number of situations a seller may have substantial reasons to doubt the accuracy of reports of a competing offer and may be unable to corroborate such reports in any of the generally accepted ways. Thus the defense may be rendered unavailable.[36]

Further, courts of appeal have held that if the good-faith defense is to prevail, discriminatory price cuts cannot be offered too broadly but only to meet those made by competitors, thereby indiscriminately limiting the economic role of price discrimination in transmitting price cuts throughout a market.[37] In a 1951 case, the Supreme Court held that the Section 2(b) defense applied to the meeting of only a "lawful" price;[38] but an appeals court subsequently interpreted that opinion as requiring merely that the seller not know that the price it was meeting was unlawful.[39] A seller may "meet but not beat" a competitor's price;[40] and two courts of appeal have ruled differently on whether a seller can seek only to retain old customers rather than win new ones and still claim the good-faith defense.[41] Finally, in a case involving a discount given by a refiner to a gasoline service station to help it meet competition in a local price war, the Supreme Court ruled that the good-faith defense held only in meeting the price offers of competing sellers and did not apply to helping a customer meet the competition it faced.[42]

Per Se Prohibitions

The per se prohibitions of Sections 2(c), 2(d), and 2(e) were designed primarily to avoid subterfuge—to prevent firms from evading the intent of the Robinson-Patman Act through use of substitutes for price discrimination.

Brokerage Payments. Thus, to eliminate bogus brokerage payments made to large chain stores in lieu of price discounts, Section 2(c) prohibits a seller from making brokerage payments to anyone but an independent broker. The principal effect, however, has been to protect independent brokers from the competition of buyers that otherwise could integrate backwards, setting up their own purchasing departments to provide internal brokerage services. Ironically, the chains at which Section 2(c) was aimed have largely escaped the law's impact by entering into contracts under which suppliers sell their entire output of a product to the chain, often under a private label or special brand name.

Promotional Allowances. Sections 2(d) and 2(e) have confronted the FTC and the courts with the virtually impossible task of applying the test of "proportionately equal terms" to varied forms of sales promotion. In *Exquisite Form*,[43] for example, a court had to rule whether customers were treated on proportionately equal terms under a particular promotion program: Exquisite Form offered allowances on future purchases to reimburse customers for advertising that prominently displayed Exquisite's products, and also offered premiums based on purchases to customers that chose not to engage in such advertising. Economies of scale in promotional services were denied in *Elizabeth Arden*,[44] in which demonstrator services were provided to large department stores with adequate facilities for such demonstrations but not, on grounds of infeasibility, to smaller retail outlets.

However unsuited the legal process may be to make such determinations, in *Simplicity Pattern* the Supreme Court not only accepted the burden but sought to rationalize its acceptance in replying to a defense claim that Sections 2(d) and 2(f) were "bad law and bad economics."

> Entirely aside from the fact that this Court is not in a position to review the economic wisdom of Congress, we cannot say that the legislative decision to treat price and other discriminations differently is without a rational basis. In allowing a "cost justification" for price discriminations and not for others, Congress could very well have felt that sellers would be forced to confine their discriminatory practices to price differentials, where they could be more readily detected and where it would be much easier to make accurate comparisons with any alleged cost savings.[45]

Induced Discriminatory Discounts

Section 2(f) is the only section of the Robinson-Patman Act that deals directly with the primary evil at which the act was aimed: the ability of the chains and other powerful buyers to demand and obtain discriminatory discounts from their suppliers. Yet only a few cases have been brought under this section, and the FTC lost the significant ones it did bring.

In *Automatic Canteen,* the leading decision, the Supreme Court ruled against the FTC and an appeals court, holding that the phrase "knowingly to induce or receive a discrimination in price which is prohibited by this section" must be construed to mean "that a buyer is not liable under §2(f) if the lower prices he induces are either within one of the seller's defenses such as the cost justification or not known by him not to be within one of these defenses."[46]   Further, the part of Section 2(b) that put the burden of rebutting a prima facie case on the person charged was held not to apply to Section 2(f).   Rather, the burden of showing that the buyer knew that the price it received was an illegal one rests on the complainant.   The principal effect intended by Congress, the Court stated, was to make it possible for suppliers to resist pressure from powerful buyers by informing them that the preferential treatment sought would be illegal under the Robinson-Patman Act.

In marked contrast to its decisions in cases involving other sections of the Robinson-Patman Act, the Supreme Court in *Automatic Canteen* was solicitous of competition and concerned over conflicts between the objectives of the Robinson-Patman Act and those of the other antitrust statutes.   After commenting on the lack of precision of expression in the Robinson-Patman Act, Justice Felix Frankfurter noted in the opinion that "we are unable, in the light of congressional policy as expressed in other antitrust legislation, to read this ambiguous language as putting the buyer at his peril whenever he engages in price bargaining. Such a reading must be rejected in view of the effect it might have on that sturdy bargaining between buyer and seller for which scope was presumably left in the areas of our economy not otherwise regulated."[47]

In a 1979 opinion, the Supreme Court reaffirmed its views, holding that The Great Atlantic & Pacific Tea Company did not violate the law in accepting a price offer from the Borden Company to supply a private-label milk after A&P's buyer had advised Borden that "I have a bid in my pocket.   You are so far out of line it is not even funny," even though Borden did not know that the bid it subsequently made was far below the competitor's.   Recognizing a basic economic principle, the Court explained that "in a competitive market, uncertainty among sellers will cause them to compete for business by offering buyers lower prices."[48]

VIEWS ON ROBINSON–PATMAN

Criticisms

Criticisms of the Robinson-Patman Act, by both lawyers and economists, are not only widespread but border on the vituperative.   Bork, for example, has referred to "the Robinson-Patman Act, that misshapen progeny of intolerable draftsmanship coupled to wholly mistaken economic theory."[49] Fredric M. Scherer, whose views on antitrust policy are distinctly different from those of Chicagoans such as Bork, has noted:

> The Robinson-Patman Act is an extremely imperfect instrument. It is questionable whether the circle of its beneficiaries extends much wider than the attorneys who earn sizeable fees interpreting its complex provisions. In many ways it conflicts with both the spirit and the letter of other antitrust laws. It certainly has the potential of encouraging competitors to pull their punches. . . . The brunt of the Commission's enforcement effort fell upon the small businesses Congress sought to protect.[50]

Perhaps the gist of the criticisms is best captured in a comment of A. D. Neale and D. G. Goyder, nominally addressed to a European reading audience:

> There is a real danger that an account of the case-law under the Robinson-Patman Act—particularly an account intended primarily for readers outside the United States—will be met with frank unbelief. The idea that a manufacturer may break the law by granting a wholesaler's discount to a wholesaler who also runs retail shops, or by selling goods directly to retailers at a price higher than one of his wholesalers may be charging, or by beating an offer made to an important customer by a rival manufacturer, or even by matching that offer unless he is satisfied that his rival can justify his low price by cost savings—all this may seem impossible to square with the purpose of the antitrust policy to preserve a system of free competition.[51]

Defending the Act

The Robinson-Patman Act does, of course, have its defenders. Efforts to repeal or amend it have been defeated repeatedly. In a 1976 report of an ad hoc subcommittee of the House Committee on Small Business, the Robinson-Patman Act was hailed in several passages as the "Magna Carta of small business."[52] In a letter requesting information from the Antitrust Division, the subcommittee chairman described the act as "a vital factor in aiding, counseling, and assisting small business in order through that means to aid in the preservation of our free competitive enterprise."[53] Jerrold G. Van Cise, testifying before the subcommittee, described himself as a devout advocate of the Robinson-Patman Act,[54] although in a book published in the same year this distinguished antitrust lawyer described it thus:

> [The act is] the most awkwardly drafted of all antitrust legislation. The statute was a roughly hewn unfinished block of legislative phraseology when it left Congress, and has required much interpretive refinement by

the Commission and the courts to reveal the contours of its meaning and application. Indeed, so confusing is certain of this language that experience in applying its provisions is the only reliable prophecy of the wise practitioner.[55]

Van Cise reconciled these views by contending that the courts' interpretations of the Robinson-Patman Act have removed much of its original ambiguity and that the protection the act affords small business is essential to the political and ethical objectives of antitrust, whatever the criticisms of economists may be.

Earl W. Kintner, former chairman of the FTC, reflected his more general views of the Robinson-Patman Act in commenting on the *Elizabeth Arden* case:

> The whole thing is that large stores would be able to induce suppliers of cosmetics to give them live demonstrators, and that is a great service. It encourages people to come in and to patronize the large department store. But what about the little store down on the corner that has the same cosmetics and no demonstrator? They fall farther and farther behind in the competitive race, simply because they are not receiving equal treatment.[56]

The dominant theme of the act's defenders is that the preservation of small business is worth the costs of supporting higher prices, denying real economies of scale in distribution and sales promotion, and supporting inefficient resource use (i.e., a particular set of social and political values is placed above the economic norm of consumer welfare). And they seem untroubled by persuasive arguments that the Robinson-Patman Act is an inefficient instrument for this purpose and cannot be applied in a just and equitable manner.

The FTC's Response

In the mid-1960s, the FTC initiated a drastic turnaround in its enforcement of the Robinson-Patman Act, as a succession of chairmen and other commissioners became progressively more disenchanted with the act and more receptive to the unremitting barrage of economic and legal criticism.[57] (From a high point of 530 Robinson-Patman complaints filed by the FTC between 1960 and 1964, the number dwindled to less than 10 per year by the early 1970s, and to zero from 1982 through 1984.)[58] Economists and legal scholars have welcomed this change. But administrative action, even if supported by Republican and Democratic administrations alike, is not a satisfactory solution. Future commissions may reverse course again. And in the meantime, private treble-damage suits are still being brought and tried.

ENDNOTES

[1] Joan Robinson, *The Economics of Imperfect Competition* (London: Macmillan, 1933), p. 203.

[2] The straight-line case was first analyzed in Arthur C. Pigou, *The Economics of Welfare* (London: Macmillan, 1920). For analyses of the more general case see Robinson, *Economics;* Edgar O. Edwards, "The Analysis of Output under Discrimination," *Econometrica* 18, no. 2 (April 1950) pp. 163–72; Thomas J. Finn, "The Quantity of Output in Simple Monopoly and Discriminating Monopoly," *Southern Economic Journal* 41, no. 2 (October 1974), pp. 239–43; Richard Schmalensee, "Output and Welfare Implications of Monopolistic Third-Degree Price Discrimination," *American Economic Review* 71, no. 1 (March 1981), pp. 242–47; John P. Formby, Stephen K. Layson, and W. James Smith, "Price Discrimination, 'Adjusted Concavity,' and Output Changes under Conditions of Constant Elasticity," *Economic Journal* 93, no. 372 (December 1983), pp. 892–99.

[3] John S. McGee, "Predatory Price Cutting: The Standard Oil Case," *Journal of Law and Economics* 1 (October 1958), pp. 137–69.

[4] Kenneth G. Elzinga, "Predatory Pricing: The Case of the Gunpowder Trust," *Journal of Law and Economics* 13, no. 1 (April 1970), pp. 223–40.

[5] Richard B. Tennant, *The American Cigarette Industry* (New Haven, Conn.: Yale University Press, 1950); Richard B. Tennant, "The Cigarette Industry," in *The Structure of American Industry*, ed. Walter Adams (New York: Macmillan, 1950).

[6] Tennant, "The Cigarette Industry," p. 239.

[7] John M. Clark, *Studies in the Economics of Overhead Costs* (Chicago: University of Chicago Press, 1923).

[8] Richard A. Posner, *The Robinson-Patman Act: Federal Regulation of Price Differences* (Washington, D.C.: American Enterprise Institute, 1976), p. 22.

[9] Robert H. Bork, *The Antitrust Paradox: A Policy at War with Itself* (New York: Basic Books, 1978), p. 395.

[10] Ibid., p. 79.

[11] Posner, *The Robinson-Patman Act*, p. 127.

[12] Phillip Areeda and Donald F. Turner, "Predatory Pricing and Related Practices under Section 2 of the Sherman Act," *Harvard Law Review* 88, no. 4 (February 1975), pp. 697–733.

[13] See especially Frederic M. Scherer, "Predatory Pricing and the Sherman Act: A Comment," *Harvard Law Review* 89, no. 5 (March 1976), pp. 869–90; Oliver E. Williamson, "Predatory Pricing: A Strategic and Welfare Analysis," *Yale Law Journal* 87, no. 2 (December 1977), pp. 284–340; Douglas F. Greer, "A Critique of Areeda and Turner's Standard for Predatory Practices," *Antitrust Bulletin* 24, no. 2 (Summer 1979), pp 233–61; Joel B. Dirlam, "Marginal Cost Pricing Tests for Predation: Naive Welfare Economics and Public Policy," *Antitrust Bulletin* 26 no. 4 (Winter 1981), pp. 769–814.

[14] Mennen Company v. Federal Trade Commission, 288 Fed. 774 (1923). See also National Biscuit Company v. Federal Trade Commission, 299 Fed. 733 (1924).

[15] Van Camp and Sons v. American Can Company, 278 U.S. 245 (1929).

[16] An appeals court, in a case decided after Section 2 had been amended by the Robinson-Patman Act, held that the exemption of quantity discounts was, as critics feared, absolute. Goodyear Tire and Rubber Company v. Federal Trade Commission, 101 F. 2d 620 (1939).

[17] U.S. Department of Justice, *Report on the Robinson-Patman Act* (Washington, D.C.: U.S. Government Printing Office, 1977), p. 114.

[18] Ibid., p. 104.

[19] Posner, *The Robinson-Patman Act*, p. 30.

[20]Federal Trade Commission v. Anheuser-Busch, Inc., 363 U.S. 536, 542–43 (1960).

[21]Utah Pie Company v. Continental Baking Company et al., 386 U.S. 685 (1967).

[22]See, among others, Ward S. Bowman, "Restraint of Trade by the Supreme Court: The Utah Pie Case," *Yale Law Journal* 77, no. 1 (November 1967), pp. 70–85.

[23]386 U.S. 685, 690.

[24]703.

[25]705.

[26]Bowman, "Restraint of Trade," p. 73.

[27]Federal Trade Commission v. Morton Salt Company, 334 U.S. 37 (1948).

[28]43.

[29]45.

[30]Corn Products Refining Company v. Federal Trade Commission, 324 U.S. 726, 742 (1945).

[31]Standard Oil Company (Indiana) v. Federal Trade Commission, 340 U.S. 231 (1951); Federal Trade Commission v. Ruberoid Company, 343 U.S. 470 (1952).

[32]In the Matter of Alhambra Motor Parts, 68 FTC 1039 (1965).

[33]Morris A. Adelman, *A&P: A Study in Price-Cost Behavior and Public Policy* (Cambridge, Mass.: Harvard University Press, 1959), pp. 164–65.

[34]Viviano Macaroni Company v. Federal Trade Commission, 411 F. 2d 255 (1969).

[35]United States v. United States Gypsum Company, 438 U.S. 422 (1978).

[36]454–55.

[37]Standard Motor Products, Inc. v. Federal Trade Commission, 265 F. 2d 674 (1959); Surprise Brassiere Company v. Federal Trade Commission, 406 F. 2d 711 (1969).

[38]Standard Oil Company (Indiana) v. Federal Trade Commission, 340 U.S. 231 (1951).

[39]Standard Oil Company v. Brown, 238 F. 2d 54 (1956).

[40]National Dairy Products Corporation v. Federal Trade Commission, 395 F. 2d 517 (1968).

[41]Sunshine Biscuits, Inc. v. Federal Trade Commission, 306 F. 2d 48 (1962); Standard Motor Products, Inc. v. Federal Trade Commission, 265 F. 2d 674 (1959).

[42]Federal Trade Commission v. Sun Oil Company, 371 U.S. 505 (1963).

[43]Exquisite Form Brassiere, Inc. v. Federal Trade Commission, 301 F. 2d 499 (1961).

[44]Elizabeth Arden v. Federal Trade Commission, 156 F. 2d 132 (1946).

[45]Federal Trade Commission v. Simplicity Pattern Company, Inc., 360 U.S. 55, 67–68 (1959).

[46]Automatic Canteen Company of America v. Federal Trade Commission, 346 U.S. 61 (1953).

[47]73–74.

[48]Great Atlantic & Pacific Tea Company, Inc. v. Federal Trade Commission, 440 U.S. 69, 73, 80 (1979).

[49]Bork, *The Antitrust Paradox*, p. 382.

[50]Frederic M. Scherer, *Industrial Market Structure and Economic Performance,* 2d ed. (Skokie, Ill.: Rand McNally, 1980), pp. 580–81.

[51]A. D. Neale and D. G. Goyder, *The Antitrust Laws of the U.S.A.,* 3d ed. (London: Cambridge University Press, 1980), p. 245. © Cambridge University Press. Reprinted by permission of Cambridge University Press.

[52]U.S. Congress, House Committee on Small Business, Ad Hoc Subcommittee on Antitrust, the Robinson-Patman Act, and Related Matters, *Report: Recent Efforts to*

Amend or Repeal the Robinson-Patman Act (Washington, D.C.: U.S. Government Printing Office, 1976), p. 49, for example.

[53]Ibid., p. 64.

[54]Ibid., p. 42.

[55]Jerrold G. Van Cise, *Understanding the Antitrust Laws*, 7th ed. (New York: Practising Law Institute, 1976), p. 67.

[56]Ad Hoc Subcommittee, *Report*, p. 118.   Kintner's views on the Robinson-Patman Act and proposed amendments, including portions of his testimony before the subcommittee, are set forth in some detail in Earl W. Kintner, Lawrence F. Henneberger, and Marc L. Fleischaker, "Reform of the Robinson-Patman Act: A Second Look," *Antitrust Bulletin* 21, no. 2 (Summer 1976), pp. 203–36.

[57]This redirection of policy is discussed in Posner, *The Robinson-Patman Act,* and in Kenneth W. Clarkson and Timothy J. Muris, eds., *The Federal Trade Commission since 1970: Economic Regulation and Bureaucratic Behavior* (London: Cambridge University Press, 1981).

[58]Richard A. Posner, *The Robinson-Patman Act: Federal Regulation of Price Differences* (Washington, D.C.: American Enterprise Institute, 1976), pp. 32–33; Commerce Clearing House, CCH Trade Regulation Reporter, Transfer Binder, *Federal Trade Commission Complaints and Orders, 1973–1976, 1976–1979; and 1979–1983;* CCH Trade Regulation Reporter, *Law Reports,* vol. 3; *FTC Procedure, Rulings, Docket of Complaints* (loose-leaf).

CHAPTER NINETEEN

Vertical Restraints of Trade: Section 3 of the Clayton Act and Section 1 of the Sherman Act

THE PRINCIPAL FORMS OF VERTICAL RESTRAINT

Vertical restraints of trade are those imposed by a firm either downstream on its customers or upstream on its suppliers. The most common restraints—dealt with in various and inconsistent ways by the antitrust laws—are downstream, including tying arrangements, exclusive-dealing agreements, resale price maintenance, and territorial or customer restrictions on resale.

In a *tying arrangement,* the sales or rentals of two or more goods are tied—that is, the seller or lessor offers one (the tying product) only on the condition that the buyer or lessee also purchase or rent one or more other goods (the tied product or products). For example, in an early case, A. B. Dick Company attached a notice to its patented mimeograph machines informing buyers that use of any ink other than Dick's would constitute patent infringement.[1] Sinclair Refining Company required that only Sinclair gasoline be stored in and sold from a tank and pump combination leased from Sinclair.[2]

Tying arrangements may take the form of *full-line forcing,* in which a seller or lessor requires a buyer or lessee to purchase or rent an entire line of products in order to acquire any. An automobile manufacturer, for example, might require its dealers to carry all models of a particular line of car rather than just compacts or just luxury models. Until 1922, shoe manufacturers were required to lease all of their shoemaking machinery from the United Shoe Machinery Corporation in order to obtain any, and were also required to use only United-supplied materials, such as thread and tacks, in the machines.[3]

In *exclusive-dealing agreements,* a wholesale or retail distributor agrees not to handle the products of a supplier's competitors but to confine itself to a single manufacturer's product line. James B. Duke's American Tobacco Company was accused of refusing to sell to jobbers who handled other brands and granting special discounts to those who agreed to handle the trust's products exclusively.[4]

 A variant on exclusive dealing is the *requirements contract,* in which a buyer agrees to take all of its product requirements from one particular supplier. Requirements contracts are often long-term (Tampa Electric Company agreed to purchase from Nashville Coal Company all the coal needed for an electrical generating plant for a 20-year period[5]). Requirements contracts are often desired by buyers who want an assured source of supply and sellers who want assured outlets for their products.

In *resale price maintenance,* a manufacturer sets the price at which its product is to be resold by wholesalers or retailers and makes resale at that price a condition of sale. Other restrictions on resale may limit the territories in which distributors can sell, or confine them to particular classes of customers. The White Motor Company, for example, included territorial and customer clauses in its contracts with dealers. A typical territorial clause specified a geographical area in which the dealer was granted an exclusive right to sell White trucks and added, "Distributor agrees . . . not to sell such trucks except to individuals, firms, or corporations having a place of business and/or purchasing headquarters in said territory." A typical customer clause read, "Distributor further agrees not to sell nor to authorize his dealers to sell such trucks to any Federal or State government or any department or political subdivision thereof, unless the right to do so is specifically granted by Company in writing."[6]

Section 3 of the Clayton Act, which addressed tying arrangements and exclusive-dealing agreements, reflects congressional concern with the use of exclusive dealing alleged in the 1911 *American Tobacco* case and also with the acquittals of A. B. Dick in 1912 and United Shoe Machinery in 1913, in which the Supreme Court held that the tying arrangements used by these two companies were legal under the Sherman Act. In the cases decided since, the courts have ruled that tying arrangements "serve hardly any purpose beyond the suppression of competition"[7] and have thus dealt with them strictly, while recognizing that exclusive-dealing agreements may serve legitimate business purposes and therefore ought to be evaluated on a case-by-case basis.

Resale price maintenance has repeatedly been held to constitute a per se violation of Section 1 of the Sherman Act. But territorial and customer restraints, although also coming within the scope of Section 1, are now evaluated under the rule of reason, with emphasis on the intended effects of the restraint on intrabrand and interbrand competition.

The distinctly different judicial treatments given to the various types of vertical restraints result from a widespread perception among legislators, antitrust enforcement officials, and judges that the motives for and effects of these trade practices differ in basic aspects. But economic analysis has identified underlying similarities and indicates that the current legal views are based on some fundamental misperceptions.

TYING ARRANGEMENTS

Judicial hostility towards tying arrangements stems from two widely perceived anticompetitive effects. First, tying arrangements are said to facilitate *leverage*—the transfer of monopoly power from one market to another, perhaps somehow increasing the overall degree of market power exercised. A. B. Dick, for example, presumably attained increased power to raise the price of its ink by requiring exclusive use of said ink in its mimeograph machines—a product line in which the company enjoyed a monopoly by virtue of patent protection. Second, courts have held that tying arrangements may raise *barriers to entry* for the tied product, particularly if its sales in conjunction with the tying product are substantial. Eastman Kodak's practice of selling its color film only with processing charges included, a tie-in ended by a 1954 consent decree, allegedly made it difficult for independent film developers to enter the market for color film processing.[8]

Per Se Illegality

In a 1947 case striking down a requirement that only salt supplied by the International Salt Company could be used in patented machines leased from that firm, the Supreme Court emphasized the exclusion of competitors as an evil to be condemned per se. "Not only is price-fixing unreasonable, *per se*," the opinion noted, "but it is also unreasonable, *per se*, to foreclose competitors from any substantial market. The volume of business affected by these contracts cannot be said to be insignificant or insubstantial and the tendency of the arrangement to accomplishment of monopoly seems obvious."[9] The *International Salt* case had alleged violation of both Section 1 of the Sherman Act and Section 3 of the Clayton Act.

Section 3 of the Clayton Act covers only commodities. In a 1953 case, *Times-Picayune,* the Department of Justice attacked an arrange-ment whereby those who wished to purchase advertising space in that company's morning *or* evening newspaper had to pay for and run the identical advertisement in both papers. The case was brought under Section 1 of the Sherman Act to avoid the issue of whether advertising space was a commodity as understood in the Clayton Act. Justice Tom C. Clark's opinion elaborated on the application of the per se rule under both statutes.

> When the seller enjoys a monopolistic position in the market for the "tying" product, *or* if a substantial volume of commerce in the "tied" prod-uct is restrained, a tying arrangement violates the narrower standards expressed in §3 of the Clayton Act because from either factor the requisite potential lessening of competition is inferred. And because for even a lawful monopolist it is "unreasonable, *per se,* to foreclose competitors from any substantial market," a tying arrangement is banned by §1 of the Sherman Act whenever *both* conditions are met.[10]

In its 1958 *Northern Pacific* opinion, the Supreme Court held that the cumulative effect of the previous decisions was to make tying arrange-ments illegal per se, stating,

> However, there are certain agreements or practices which because of their pernicious effect on competition and lack of any redeeming virtue are conclusively presumed to be unreasonable and therefore illegal without elaborate inquiry as to the precise harm they have caused or the business excuse for their use. .... Among the practices which the courts have here-tofore deemed to be unlawful in and of themselves are price-fixing, division of markets, group boycotts, and *tying arrangements.*[11]

Justice Clark's 1953 *Times-Picayune* opinion was interpreted as consistent with this view of per se illegality: "We do not construe this general language as requiring anything more than sufficient economic power to impose an appreciable restraint on free competition in the tied product (assuming all the time, of course, that a 'not insubstantial' amount of interstate commerce is affected)."[12] *Northern Pacific's* con-cept of the per se illegality of tying arrangements is certainly very different from the concept used in condemning horizontal restraints of trade. As noted in a leading antitrust law case book: "When is there 'sufficient economic power with respect to the tying product to appre-ciably restrain free competition in the market for the tied product'? How much is a 'not insubstantial' amount of interstate commerce af-fected by the tie? Litigation since *Northern Pacific* has repeatedly encountered each of these questions and has regularly failed to resolve finally most of them."[13]

The issue was squarely put to the Supreme Court in *Jefferson Parish,* a 1984 case in which the Department of Justice filed a friend-of-the-court brief asking the Court to overrule its earlier decisions and abandon its per se treatment of tying arrangements. In a five-to-four decision, the Supreme Court declined to do so. Justice Sandra Day O'Connor wrote, in the concurring opinion of the four justices who supported the Department of Justice's brief:

> The "per se" doctrine in tying cases has always required an elaborate inquiry into the economic effects of the tying arrangement. As a result, tying doctrine incurs the costs of a rule of reason approach without achieving its benefits: the doctrine calls for the extensive and time-consuming economic analysis characteristic of the rule of reason, but then may be interpreted to prohibit arrangements that economic analysis would show to be beneficial. Moreover, the per se label in the tying context has generated more confusion than coherent law because it appears to invite lower courts to omit the analysis of economic circumstances of the tie that has always been an [sic] necessary element of tying analysis.
>
> The time has therefore come to abandon the "per se" label and refocus the inquiry on the adverse economic effects, and the potential economic benefits, that the tie may have.[14]

Justice O'Connor went on to cite some of the economic literature discussing the benefits as well as harm that can result from tying arrangements.[15]

Leverage and Monopoly Power

Economic analysis of leverage demonstrates that it rarely increases monopoly power, suggesting that tying arrangements must usually be used for other purposes. If an unwanted tie-in is imposed on a monopolized product, it makes that product less attractive at any price and thus shifts its demand curve down and to the left. For example, A. B. Dick was undoubtedly in a position to raise the price of its ink and perhaps to increase the quantity of ink sold. But any increase in its ink price would make its mimeograph machines less attractive and hence would lower the demand for these machines.

Model of Leverage in a Tying Arrangement. The point is illustrated in Figure 19–1. Panel A depicts the situation facing a firm selling, say, soap powder. Initially, in the absence of a tie-in, the firm is assumed to have no monopoly power in that market. The market-determined price is P_a; and with a marginal cost curve of MC, the firm sells soap powder at a rate of Q_a. Panel B depicts the situation if the firm also sells a second product (washing machines in this example) in which it has monopoly power. If the initial demand curve facing the firm for its washing machines is D_1, it will set a profit-maximizing price and output of P_1 and Q_1.

Now suppose the firm ties the two products—it requires that a

FIGURE 19–1 Leverage in a Tying Arrangement

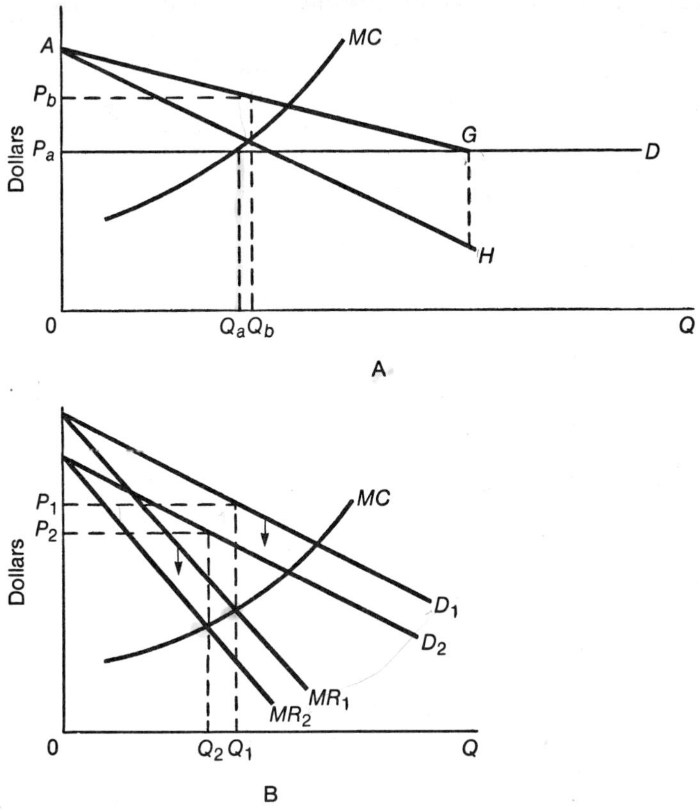

customer who purchases its washing machine use only its own soap powder in the machine. (How this requirement could be enforced is left to the reader's imagination.) As a result, the firm obtains monopoly power over the portion of soap powder sales made to owners of its washing machines. The demand curve facing the firm becomes the line AGD in Panel A, where the segment AG represents demand for soap powder by the owners of the firm's washing machines. The marginal curve associated with AGD is the kinked line $AHGD$. The firm will maximize the profits now available to it in the soap powder market by raising its price to P_b and increasing its sales to Q_b. (The quantity sold may rise or fall, depending on the slopes and positions of the marginal cost and marginal revenue curves.)

The firm faces a problem, however, in its washing machine market. The demand curve D_1 in Figure 19–1B shows the quantities of these machines that the firm can sell at various prices, *ceteris paribus*. However, every increase in the price of the firm's soap powder from the original level of P_a causes the demand curve for the firm's washing machines to shift down. The demand curve D_2 and its marginal revenue curve MR_2 are shown as the curves facing the firm when it has raised the price of its soap powder to P_b. Thus, the monopolistic profits made in the formerly competitive soap powder market as a result of the tie-in are offset by reduced profits in the monopolized washing machine market. The leverage exerted by the tying arrangement may or may not increase net profits.

Enhancing Monopoly Profit through Leverage. In certain cases, it is impossible to enhance monopoly profit through leverage. For example, when the goods are perfect complements and used in fixed proportions, such as nuts and bolts or left and right shoes, leverage cannot raise profit above the level available from simply charging the profit-maximizing price for the tying (monopolized) product. If each product is useless without the other, the customer considers only the total price of the two. Any increase in the price of the tied product would reduce sales of both in precisely the same way as an equal increase in the price of the tying product.

If the goods are complementary, however, and used in variable proportions, profit-enhancing leverage is possible, depending on the elasticity of demand for the tied product and the cross-elasticity of demand between the tying and tied products. If the demand curve for the tied product is highly inelastic at and near the price at which it was formerly sold (so that total revenue rises substantially with a price increase) and if the demand curve for the tying product is not very responsive to changes in the price of the tied product, the tying arrangement may, through leverage, result in increased profits.

Two-Product Monopoly Power. Most analyses of leverage in tying arrangements have considered a case in which a firm possesses monopoly power in the tying product but faces competitive conditions in the other product market in the absence of a tie-in. Another opportunity for leverage arises when a firm enjoys monopoly power in two complementary products. A firm in this position may use a joint profit-maximizing pricing strategy that takes into account the effects of each product's price on the demand for the other. But this type of leverage, in its pure form, involves adjusting the prices of the two goods rather than tying the sales of one to the other.[16]

Barriers to Entry

Virtually all economists agree that the courts have erred in treating leverage as a major motive for tying arrangements. But they disagree over how extensively tying arrangements have been used to foreclose portions of the markets for tied goods or to erect barriers to entry. If the tying product is not patented and can be imitated, the barrier involves either capital requirements or economies of scale relative to size of the market for the tying product, since potential competitors must acquire capacity of their own in the tying product to make sales of the tied product to those using it in conjunction with the tying product. As noted in Chapter Seven, higher capital requirements constitute a barrier to entry only to the extent that capital markets are imperfect and favor established larger firms, or if the entry of a new firm raises capital costs for all. But if, at worst, the tying product is protected by a strong patent and the only use for the tied product is with the tying product, the tying arrangement will result in an absolute barrier to entry until the patent expires.

Thus, judicial concern over the erection of barriers to entry through tying arrangements is warranted. Such concern does not, however, appear to justify application of a per se rule to tying arrangements. In most cases with a patented tying product and no alternative use for the tied product, the latter would not have been produced before introduction of the former. Therefore, there would be no existing competitors foreclosed. Any quarrel with such a tying arrangement, provided there was no increase in monopoly power through leverage, would be a criticism of the powers granted by the patent.

If the tying product is not patented, a tying arrangement may put on competitors the burden of acquiring enough capital to produce a similar or substitute product. In some cases, this may be unreasonable: the predatory purpose of the tying arrangement may be evident. In others, the burden may be fairly light or justified by the objectives of the firm imposing the tying arrangement. If competitors are spurred to improve on the tying product, competition may be promoted. Where there are alternative uses for the tied product, even if the tying product is thoroughly protected by a patent, the question of whether the foreclosure is substantial involves the proportion of the market affected and the alternatives open to competitors. Such cases should be tried on their merits rather than subjected to a per se prohibition.

Discriminatory Prices

Despite their criticism of the judicial approach, economists have recognized that tying arrangements may be used to increase the profits available from market power in the tying product. The most common mechanism is not leverage, however, but using the tied product to facilitate discriminatory pricing of the tying product. A firm producing a mimeograph or salt-processing machine may wish to charge prices based on how intensely customers use the machine but be unable to do so because of ease of resale, legal constraints, or inability to determine intensity. It can, however, achieve the same result by selling the machine at cost or a minimal markup, and then charging a substantial premium for the ink or salt used. The tied product thus becomes the counting device to measure rate of usage, and the premium becomes a royalty fee based on that usage. The tying product is made available to many who would not buy it at the nondiscriminatory monopoly price.

George J. Stigler offered a similar explanation for film producers' practice of block booking—offering two or more films for rent as a package while refusing to make them available separately—a practice that was found to be an illegal tie-in in the 1962 *Loew's* case.[17] Consider, he suggested, two potential renters of two films. Theater A is willing to pay $8,000 for Film X and $2,500 for Film Y, while Theater B is willing to pay $7,000 for Film X and $3,000 for Film Y. If the producer rented each film separately but charged each theater the same rental, it could obtain a maximum of $19,000—two copies of Film X at $7,000, yielding $14,000, and two copies of Film Y at $2,500, yielding an additional $5,000. However, the package could be rented to each buyer for $10,000, for a total revenue of $20,000. (If perfect discrimination were possible, so that each theater was charged its reservation prices for both films, total revenue would rise to $20,500.)[18]

To the extent that tying arrangements substitute for and have similar effects as straightforward price discrimination in the tying product, the implications for economic performance and public policy are similar. Neither tying arrangements nor price discrimination are harmful enough to be banned per se, but both have enough potential for misuse to call for antitrust control.

Exceptions to Per Se

Lack of Monopoly Power. Although the Supreme Court has persisted in applying its per se rule to most tying cases, it has recognized a number of exceptions. In the *Sinclair* case cited above (one of a number of "tank and pump" cases brought concurrently by the FTC against the major gasoline refiners), the Supreme Court upheld the tying arrangement. It noted that a gasoline refiner had a legitimate interest in proper handling of a dangerous product and in assuring customers that they would get the brand named on the pump. The legal basis for the decision, though, was that Sinclair had no monopoly power in either gasoline or tank-and-pump combinations. In 1984, however, 13 major oil companies agreed in an out-of-court settlement to allow their franchised service stations to sell other brands of gasoline, provided the service stations used their own tanks and pumps for such sales or indicated on the pumps that other gasoline brands were being dispensed.[19]

Establishing a New Technology. In a 1936 case, IBM contended that its practice of leasing tabulating machines on the condition that lessees use only IBM-manufactured punch cards ought to be allowed because it was intended "only to preserve to appellant the good will of its patrons by preventing the use of unsuitable cards which would interfere with the successful performance of its machines."[20] The Supreme Court rejected this contention on the grounds that IBM could specify the size, thickness, and quality of cards needed and hold lessees responsible for damage to machines resulting from failure to use proper cards, but it could not forbid lessees to use other firms' cards meeting those requirements.

In a 1960 case, however, Jerrold Electronics Corporation was partially successful in arguing before a district court that its package of complete community television antenna systems, including maintenance service and repair parts, ought to be allowed since the firm's technology was new and the purpose was to establish the quality and reliability of the full Jerrold system. The court upheld this method of selling, but only for a limited time, ruling that since Jerrold had become well established, its full system and replacement contracts had become per se illegal tying arrangements. The Supreme Court affirmed without comment.[21]

In 1961, the holder of patents on a glass-lined silo and a special unloading device successfully defended itself, without any time limitation, against a private treble-damage suit by arguing that it had tied sales of the two products because neither functioned properly when used with other unloaders or containers.[22]

Franchise Agreements. The growth of franchising has led to a number of tying cases. In 1964, an appeals court upheld Carvel Corporation's requirement that its franchisees purchase not only the basic Carvel ice cream mix but also Carvel cones, toppings, and extracts. The opinion noted that "the true tying item was rather the Carvel trademark, whose growing repute was intended to help the little band of Carvel dealers swim a bit faster than their numerous rivals up the highly competitive stream."[23] But, as in *Sinclair,* Carvel was not exonerated on grounds of legitimate intent or purpose but on a finding that the Carvel trademark did not give the firm sufficient economic power to restrain competition.

Seven years later, another appeals court ruled against Chicken Delight, Inc.'s contractual requirements that franchisees purchase certain cooking equipment, batter and seasoning mixes, and packaging items bearing the Chicken Delight trademark exclusively from Chicken Delight. The court rejected the argument that Chicken Delight's "trademark and franchise licenses are not items separate and distinct from the packaging, mixes, and equipment," but rather that "all are essential components of the franchise system."[24] The franchise and license permitting use of the Chicken Delight trademark constituted the tying product, the court ruled, and the remaining items were those tied. Contrary to the *Carvel* court, the appeals court in *Chicken Delight* upheld the trial judge's ruling that Chicken Delight's ability to impose the tie-ins established, as a matter of law, the requisite market power.

Since the *Chicken Delight* decision, the lower courts have become more receptive to allowing tying arrangements in franchise agreements. In the 1980 *McDonald's* case, an appeals court noted that "franchising has come a long way since the decision in *Chicken Delight*" and observed:

> Far from merely licensing franchisees to sell products under its trade name, a modern franchisor such McDonald's offers its franchisees a compete method of doing business. . . . Its regime pervades all facets of the business, from the design of the menu board to the amount of catsup on the hamburgers, nothing is left to chance. This pervasive franchisor supervision and control benefits the franchise in turn. His business is identified with a network of stores whose very uniformity and predictability attracts customers. In short, the modern franchisee pays not only for the right to use a trademark but for the right to become part of a system whose business methods virtually guarantee his success. It is often unrealistic to view a franchise agreement as little more than a trademark license.
>
> Given the realities of modern franchising, we think the proper inquiry is not whether the allegedly tied products are associated in the public mind with the franchisor's trademark, but whether they are integral components of the business methods being franchised. Where the challenged aggregation is an essential ingredient of the franchised system's formula for success, there is but a single product and no tie exists as a matter of law.[25]

In 1982, an appeals court met head-on the issue evaded in the *Carvel* decision, holding that the Baskin-Robbins trademark and Baskin-Robbins ice cream comprise one product.[26]

As of this writing, the Supreme Court has not yet ruled on tying arrangements involved in a franchise system.[27]

EXCLUSIVE DEALING

In marked contrast to their treatment of tying arrangements, the courts consistently have recognized that exclusive-dealing agreements may have legitimate business purposes and may serve procompetitive as well as anticompetitive ends. Thus, in its initial interpretation of Section 3 of the Clayton Act, the Supreme Court observed:

> Section 3 . . . deals with consequences to follow the making of the restrictive covenant limiting the right of the purchaser to deal in the goods of the seller only. But we do not think that the purpose in using the word "may" was to prohibit the mere possibility of the consequences described. It was intended to prevent such agreements as would under the circumstances disclosed probably lessen competition, or create an actual tendency to monopoly. That it was not intended to reach every remote lessening of competition is shown in the requirement that such lessening be substantial.[28]

Curiously, the distinction between the applications of Section 3 to tying arrangements and to exclusive-dealing agreements was made most explicitly in a merger case. In *Brown-Kinney,* the Supreme Court turned to established Section 3 standards for guidance as to how the phrase "substantially lessen competition or tend to create a monopoly" should be interpreted in evaluating mergers under the Celler-Kefauver Act.

> A most important such factor to examine is the very nature and purpose of the arrangement. . . . The usual tying contract forces the customer to take a product or brand he does not necessarily want in order to secure one which he does desire. Because such an arrangement is inherently anticompetitive, we have held that its use by an established company is likely "substantially to lessen competition" although only a relatively small amount of commerce is affected. . . . On the other hand, requirement contracts are frequently negotiated at the behest of the customer who has chosen the particular supplier and his product on the basis of competitive merit. . . . [A] requirement contract may escape censure if only a small share of the market is involved, if the purpose of the agreement is to insure to the customer a sufficient supply of a commodity vital to the customer's trade or to insure to the supplier a market for his output and if there is no trend toward concentration in the industry.[29]

In recognition of the irrelevance of intent to the Clayton Act's standards, the Court explained in a footnote its emphasis on purpose as "an aid in predicting the probable future conduct of the parties and thus the probable effects."[30]

Quantitative Substantiality

Thus, most exclusive-dealing cases have focused on the question of whether there has been a substantial lessening of competition. In these Section 3 cases, as in the vertical-merger cases brought under Section 7, the courts have put more emphasis on the mere volume of business foreclosed than most economists find warranted. In the 1949 *Standard Stations* case, the Supreme Court agreed with the district court's decision and the trial judge's ruling

> that the requirement of showing an actual or potential lessening of competition or a tendency to establish monopoly was adequately met by proof that the contracts covered "a substantial number of outlets and a substantial amount of products, whether considered comparatively or not." Given such quantitative substantiality, the substantial lessening of competition—so the [district] court reasoned—is an automatic result, for the very existence of such contracts denies dealers opportunity to deal in the products of competing suppliers and excludes suppliers from access to the outlets controlled by those dealers.[31]

This doctrine of quantitative substantiality evoked a storm of criticism from economists and lawyers alike.[32] The Court, critics contended, was imposing a virtual per se rule and evading its responsibility under the statute. Richard A. Miller, for example, noted, "It is not difficult to sympathize with the Supreme Court's reluctance to undertake complete analysis of each exclusive dealing case. Easily applied rules benefit the courts as well as businessmen in their interpretations of socially acceptable behavior. On the other hand, the qualifying clause of Section Three does imply questions of economic analysis."[33]

In 1961, in the *Tampa Electric* case, the Supreme Court in effect dropped the standard of quantitative substantiality, although not explicitly overruling *Standard Stations,* and formulated a set of alternative criteria comprising a standard of qualitative substantiality.

> To determine substantiality in a given case, it is necessary to weigh the probable effect of the contract on the relevant area of effective competition, taking into account the relative strength of the parties, the proportionate volume of commerce involved in relation to the total volume of commerce in the relevant market area, and the probable immediate and future effects which pre-emption of that share of the market might have on effective competition therein. It follows that a mere showing that the contract itself involves a substantial number of dollars is ordinarily of little consequence.[34]

Economic Objectives and Analysis

The economic objectives of an exclusive-dealing agreement that have been most discussed by the courts are those related to requirements contracts. But an exclusive-dealing agreement may merely specify that the distributor will not carry any competing goods. Such garden-variety exclusive dealing is economically akin to a tying arrangement. It imposes a condition of sale on potential buyers that, *ceteris paribus,* reduces dealers' freedom thereby making the product less attractive to them. The demand curve facing the manufacturer will, therefore, shift inwards.

There must be some offsetting consideration that motivates a manufacturer to use such a device. A manufacturer with so dominant a share of the market that virtually all distributors would prefer selling only its products to being denied any might, in the short run, be able to exclude smaller competitors by foreclosing sales outlets, as in the instance of the tobacco trust. But in the long run, the entry barrier thereby raised is usually only that of capital requirements preventing foreclosed firms from integrating forward to establish their own distributive outlets. The advantage to the manufacturer most commonly cited, in the absence of market dominance, is the establishment of a group of "loyal" wholesalers or retailers who will concentrate their selling efforts on promoting that manufacturer's products. Such increased dealer loyalty may promote interbrand competition and may be particularly important for an entrant seeking to introduce and establish a new brand.

In a 1982 article, however, Howard P. Marvel questioned this traditional explanation.[35] In most instances, he argued, dealers' promotional efforts could be stimulated more efficiently by resale price maintenance or by grants of exclusive territorial or customer markets, since exclusive dealing must be imposed on reluctant dealers. A more likely explanation, according to Marvel, is that manufacturers who promote their own products vigorously rather than relying on their dealers to do so can protect themselves from a form of "free-riding" through exclusive dealing. Such a manufacturer's advertising, if successful, will encourage potential customers to shop at outlets carrying the advertised products. The manufacturer may resort to exclusive dealing to prevent these customers from having their interest diverted to competing products at the point of purchase through either the "disloyalty" of sales personnel who push other manufacturers' products or mere exposure to others' wares.

Marvel's observation does not deny the value to a supplier of having dealers handling and, thus, promoting its products exclusively. As he himself noted, one quid pro quo is that exclusive dealing is often used in combination with resale price maintenance, or with nonprice restrictions on resale giving exclusive markets to dealers. The risk of losing outlets by imposing exclusive dealing varies with the alternatives available to dissatisfied dealers; but those who remain undoubtedly have a greater incentive to push the manufacturer's products. Further, the other forms of vertical restraint are not always as feasible as exclusive dealing. In particular, it may be harder for manufacturers to detect cheaters who sporadically undercut an announced resale price, or make "hit-and-run" sales outside of their assigned territories, than it is to enforce an exclusive dealing agreement—perhaps through occasional unannounced inspections of dealers' warehouses, showrooms, and invoices.

RESALE PRICE MAINTENANCE

Tying arrangements and exclusive-dealing agreements impose downstream restraints that make a manufacturer's products less attractive to distributors. In contrast, resale price maintenance and nonprice restraints on trade that divide and insulate markets are designed to limit or eliminate competition in the resale of a particular manufacturer's product line (that is, *intrabrand* competition) and are generally welcomed by dealers. Indeed, as noted by Chief Justice Charles Evans Hughes in the 1911 *Dr. Miles* case, when a manufacturer sets the prices at which dealers can resell its products, it is engaged in an act that would be per se illegal if performed by the dealers themselves.[36] The same may be said for allocations of either territories or customers.

Manufacturers' Motivations

It is not in a manufacturer's interest, *ceteris paribus,* to raise dealers' margins above the competitive level. As noted in a leading article by Lester G. Telser, "If manufacturers set a floor to the resale price then they also set a ceiling to their sales and thus apparently support a policy that runs counter to their own self-interest. . . . Would not the manufacturers' sales and profits be greater the lower is the price at which distributors resell their products to consumers?"[37]

The point is illustrated in a simple diagram drawn from Telser's article and a later analysis by Lawrence J. White.[38] There are two sets of firms involved in the situation depicted in Figure 19–2, a single manufacturer selling to a group of retailers. D_c represents the ultimate demand curve of consumers for the product. The demand curve facing the manufacturer (D_m) is derived by subtracting the retailer's margin from the prices along D_c. The manufacturer determines the price it will charge retailers (P_m) and the associated output (Q_m) by equating its marginal revenue (MR_m) with its marginal cost (MC_m). The product is sold to consumers at the price P_c, and the retailers' margin is $P_c - P_m$. The lower the margin, the higher the demand curve facing the manufacturer, *ceteris paribus*. "Competition," White noted, "will normally insure that this margin is at a minimum, for any given wholesale price. Consequently, it would normally appear to be in the manufacturer's interest to encourage the maximum amount of competition among his retailers."[39]

Thus, the crucial economic question is why manufacturers impose such restraints.

Avoiding Use as Loss Leaders. One of the earliest and most durable explanations is that manufacturers with reputations for high

FIGURE 19–2   Price Received by Manufacturer, Price Paid by Consumers, and Retailers' Margin, with a Single Manufacturer Selling Directly to a Group of Retailers

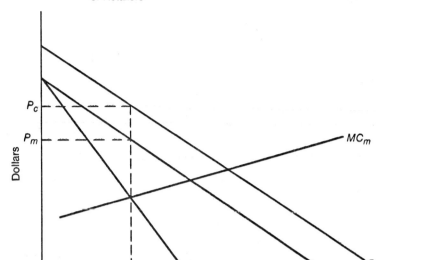

quality and value want to prevent retailers from using their products as *loss leaders*.[40]   A loss leader is an item a retailer advertises at an extremely low price to attract customers in the hope of then selling them other items with higher markups.   To minimize the cost of using this tactic, it is alleged, the retailer stocks only a few of the loss-leader items and tries to steer disappointed customers to alternatives.

Manufacturers claim to be hurt in two ways: First, use of an item as a loss leader detracts from the manufacturer's high-quality image (only products with such an image make good loss leaders).   Second, more scrupulous retailers are less interested in carrying the same item since they must explain to customers why they are charging a higher price.   But there is a question as to how extensive loss-leader selling is and how serious a problem it poses for manufacturers.   One study, surveying six countries and the European Economic Community, concluded that "the prominent place it frequently has assumed in public discussion and political debate . . . [is] wholly disproportionate to the intrinsic importance and quantitative extent of loss-leader selling (unless it is meaninglessly equated with all retail price competition)."[41]

Covering Promotional and Service Costs. Telser, White, and other economists who analyzed resale price maintenance stressed different considerations.[42] One manufacturers' desire is to assure dealers an adequate margin to cover local promotion and point-of-sale customer services. These dealer services include provision of attractive show-rooms; demonstrator models; knowledgeable salespeople; delivery, setup, and repair services; adequate stock of product and spare parts; dealer warranties; advertising in local media; and so on. In most instances, such services and promotional activities are provided more efficiently by an on-the-spot dealer than by the manufacturer.

We could argue that, if customers regard dealer services as worth the cost, resale price maintenance ought not be necessary. Dealers would offer them in their own self-interest, and customers would be willing to pay more to cover the cost. Further, those who do not want such services could buy the product at discount stores.

The flaw in this argument is that it overlooks a free-rider problem similar to that in the *Klor's* case discussed in Chapter Seventeen. Customers are free to visit full-service dealers, confer with informed sales-people, inspect and try out various models, and then make their purchases at discount stores or through mail-order catalogs. Sales clerks in the low-overhead, low-service outlets may encourage this behavior, suggesting that customers look over the product elsewhere and then return to buy it at a discount. Such free-riding may lead to the elimination of dealers' services even if nearly all customers consider them worth their costs. Resale price maintenance, by requiring all dealers to sell a product at an identical price, eliminates this free riding. Also, dealers who are forbidden to compete in price may be forced by nonprice competition to provide the point-of-sale services manufacturers desire.

Fully effective nonprice competition should absorb all of the dealers' margin over and above a normal rate of return. Thus, by increasing or decreasing the difference between the price it charges dealers and the resale price, the manufacturer can exert a great deal of control over the total level of dealer services provided.

Competition for Dealers. Resale price maintenance may also play a role in the competition for dealers. For some manufacturers, the market for dealerships is imperfect, and it may be difficult to attract and keep qualified dealers. Rivalry for dealers may become intense; and dealers' margins guaranteed by resale price maintenance may become an important competitive weapon, especially in market situations where experienced and qualified dealers with established reputations can move easily from one manufacturer to another. Dealers' market power may even enable a colluding group to fix the resale price and put the responsibility of enforcing that price on the manufacturer through resale price maintenance.

Building a Reputation for Quality. A series of case studies commissioned by the Federal Trade Commission indicated that, at least in some industries, resale price maintenance played a constructive role as a signal of quality early in a product's life cycle, although a more ambiguous and perhaps socially detrimental one later.[43] In studies of the marketing of designer jeans, audio components, and shoes, researchers concluded that the manufacturers had adopted resale price maintenance to induce prestigious retail outlets with reputations for stocking only high-quality merchandise to carry their brand name products. The shoe manufacturer also wanted its products to retail only at prices indicative of high quality. Audio components manufacturers were concerned with retailers' demonstration and repair services; but Japanese manufacturers, in particular, also used resale price maintenance to attract U.S. dealers that had "developed some good will and respectability in their market and could thereby cloak the foreign product in this mantle of respectability and, to some extent, certify product quality."[44]

In the jeans and shoe cases, the manufacturers coupled resale price maintenance with selective choice of retailers. By the time the FTC brought cases against the jeans and audio component manufacturers, brand reputations for quality had been established and the original need for resale price maintenance had disappeared. Continuation of the practice appeared to be limiting competition unnecessarily among jeans retailers and to be retarding the spread of more efficient mass-merchandizing methods of less expensive, low-end audio products.

Price-Fixing. Finally, resale price maintenance may be a part of collusive or tacit price-fixing arrangements among manufacturers of similar products, particularly in industries in which a manufacturer's price to a dealer is not easily detectable by other manufacturers. As Telser pointed out, a group of colluding manufacturers might agree to impose resale price maintenance on their dealers, so that the dealers could not pass on to customers a manufacturer's secret price concession. The price-cutting manufacturer would not, therefore, gain any increased sales, but merely transfer profit to its dealers. A cheating manufacturer might, nevertheless, offer secret concessions to woo dealers away from the other conspirators. This tactic, Telser observed, could be countered by having the conspirators impose exclusive dealing on all retailers, along with a requirement that retailers not shift from one manufacturer to another without the approval of the first.[45]

Apart from overt collusion, resale price maintenance may facilitate recognition of mutual dependence among oligopolistic manufacturers. It eliminates outbreaks of sporadic or predatory price-cutting at the dealer level that might pressure manufacturers to lower their prices to help their dealers cope with the unexpectedly intense competition.

The Legal View of Resale Price Maintenance

The law has been untroubled by any of these economic subtleties. In the 1911 *Dr. Miles* case, Justice Hughes applied the analogy to a dealers' conspiracy in holding the resale price maintenance contracts at issue to be per se illegal. He commented:

> If there be an advantage to the manufacturer in the maintenance of fixed retail prices, the question remains whether it is one which he is entitled to secure by agreements restricting the freedom of trade on the part of dealers who own what they sell. As to this, the complainant can fare no better with its plan of identical contracts than could the dealers themselves if they formed a combination and endeavored to establish the same restrictions, and thus to achieve the same result, by agreement with each other.[46]

The Colgate Doctrine. In 1919, the Supreme Court enunciated what came to be known as the *Colgate* doctrine, ruling that the Colgate Company had the right to specify resale prices for its products and to refuse to sell to anyone who resold at a lower price, provided it did not enter into any contract (express or implied) with its wholesale and retail dealers respecting the resale price. The indictment failed to allege any such contract.[47] Since that time, however, the Colgate doctrine has been severely eroded by a number of decisions holding that if the firm imposing resale price maintenance requests and obtains any cooperation from any of its dealers in implementing and enforcing its pricing policy, a combination in a restraint of trade results, violating Section 1 of the Sherman Act.[48]

The Issue of Per Se Illegality. A 1980 Supreme Court decision cited the *Dr. Miles* case as current authority for the assertion that "this Court has ruled consistently that resale price maintenance illegally restrains trade."[49] In 1983, at the same time that it filed its friend-of-the-court brief in *Jefferson Parish,* the Antitrust Division filed a second such brief in a private action in which a terminated dealer, Spray-Rite Service Corporation, alleged that Monsanto Company had refused to renew its franchise as part of a conspiracy to maintain resale prices.[50] The brief asked that *Dr. Miles* be overruled and that the Supreme Court hold resale price maintenance subject to the rule of reason. In its 1984 opinion, the Court declined the opportunity to reverse the per se rule of *Dr. Miles,* not on the merits of the issue, but on the grounds that neither party had argued for the application of the rule of reason before the district court or had raised the point on appeal. In this way, the Court left the issue open to argument in future pleas.

The Miller-Tydings Act. For nearly 40 years federal legislation permitted and even encouraged resale price maintenance. The Miller-Tydings Resale Price Maintenance Act of 1937 exempted resale price maintenance contracts made lawful by state legislation from prosecution under the Sherman and Federal Trade Commission Acts. This law was passed over the opposition of both the FTC and President Franklin D. Roosevelt.

Shortly before the Miller-Tydings Act passed, 10 states had so-called fair-trade laws making resale price maintenance contracts within the state legal. By 1941, there were 45.[51] The Miller-Tydings Act and the state fair-trade laws were enacted in circumstances similar to those surrounding the passage of the Robinson-Patman Act—the primary concern was to protect small independent retailers from price-cutting by large chain, department, and mail-order stores. The anticompetitive potential of resale price maintenance was recognized, however, in a proviso in the Miller-Tydings Act that the exemption was to apply only to products sold in "free and open competition with commodities of the same class sold by others."

By the mid-1950s and throughout the 1960s, pressure was growing to repeal the Miller-Tydings Act and the associated McGuire Act. (The latter was enacted in 1952 to legitimize "non-signer" clauses under which a resale price maintenance contract entered into with one dealer could be made binding on all.) Many manufacturers, finding that large retailers enjoying economies of scale were becoming more important outlets for their products than traditional small retailers, were losing interest in resale price maintenance. Private and governmental studies indicated that prices in states permitting resale price maintenance were higher than those charged for identical goods in states where the practice was still subject to the antitrust laws. Some discount stores and mail-order houses openly defied non-signer clauses, challenging the constitutionality of both federal and state laws allowing resale price maintenance to be imposed on unwilling retailers.

A number of states repealed their fair-trade laws or had them declared invalid by state courts. A 1966 study reported that most manufacturers in the electrical appliance, typewriter, fountain pen, camera, watch, and phonograph record industries had abandoned resale price maintenance but that the practice was still prevalent in the drug, cosmetic, and toiletries industry and in the book trade.[52] In 1975, Congress passed the Consumer Goods Pricing Act, repealing both the Miller-Tydings and McGuire Acts.

The Central Issue: Balancing Operating and Allocative Efficiency

The central economic issue in the debate over resale price maintenance is one of ascertaining the proper trade-off between operating efficiency in distribution and allocative efficiency. The practice clearly restrains intrabrand competition among dealers handling the same product and is particularly pernicious if it facilitates collusion among dealers or manufacturers. Yet, it may promote both interbrand competition and efficient methods of distribution, particularly if a free-rider problem would lead to an inadequate level of nonprice competition.

However, resale price maintenance may not be the best way to eliminate this free-rider market failure. We must ask whether less anticompetitive alternatives would achieve the same end. Manufacturers might provide some services now offered by dealers and alleviate consumer demand for others by expanding warranties. Private firms can inspect and rate products and publish the results.

The extent to which such services are valued by consumers, provided more efficiently by dealers, and depend on resale price maintenance varies from product to product. Further, the anticompetitive effects of resale price maintenance may be severe in some markets and negligible in others. These considerations do not justify a moratorium on enforcement of the law against resale price maintenance, but they do present a strong case for substituting a rule-of-reason approach for the present per se prohibition.

TERRITORIAL AND CUSTOMER RESTRICTIONS ON RESALE

The courts have dealt with nonprice restraints on resale far more circumspectly than they have with resale price maintenance. The issue did not reach the Supreme Court until the *White Motor* case in 1963. White assigned exclusive territories to its dealers and reserved government sales for itself. White contended that the territorial clauses were necessary to stimulate dealers and distributors to make "vigorous and intensive efforts in a restricted territory," therefore allowing White to compete effectively with larger truck manufacturers, and that the clauses reserving government sales were designed to meet a market in which White faced "especially severe competition with other makes of trucks" and wanted to assure itself that "appropriate discounts" and repair and maintenance services were given.[53] The district court held against White on a motion for summary judgment. The Supreme Court, taking note of White's contentions, reversed and remanded the case for trial on its merits, explaining, "We need to know more than we do about the actual impact of these arrangements on competition to decide whether they have such a 'pernicious effect on competition and lack . . . any redeeming virtue' and therefore should be classified as *per se* violations of the Sherman Act."[54]

Invoking Per Se

But in 1967 the Supreme Court decided it did know enough to resolve the issue. In the *Schwinn* case, the Court upheld territorial restrictions on wholesalers who took bicycles owned by Arnold, Schwinn & Company on consignment and shipped them to retailers but condemned similar restrictions on bicycles sold by Schwinn to either wholesalers or retailers. "Once the manufacturer has parted with title and risk," the opinion asserted, "he has parted with dominion over the product, and his effort thereafter to restrict territory or persons to whom the product may be transferred—whether by explicit agreement or by silent combination or understanding with his vendee—is a *per se* violation of §1 of the Sherman Act."[55] Rather than an evaluation of economic effects, the primary basis for the ruling was that to allow a manufacturer control over goods it has sold "would violate the ancient rule against restraints on alienation," or the freedom of owners to dispose of their property as they saw fit.[56]

Returning to the Rule of Reason

Schwinn did not stand for long, however. In the majority opinion in the 1977 *Sylvania* case, Justice Lewis F. Powell, Jr., commented that "*per se* rules of illegality are appropriate only when they relate to conduct that is manifestly anticompetitive" and that such a rule ought not be applied to territorial restraints. "The market impact of vertical restrictions is complex," he explained, "because of their potential for a simultaneous reduction of intrabrand competition and stimulation of interbrand competition." A divided Court overruled *Schwinn*, and Powell wrote for the majority: "The appropriate decision is to return to the rule of reason that governed vertical restrictions prior to *Schwinn*. When competitive effects are shown to result from particular vertical restrictions they can be adequately policed under the rule of reason, the standard traditionally applied for the majority of anticompetitive practices challenged under §1 of the Act."[57]

Since *Sylvania*, territorial and customer restrictions on resale have been tested, as Powell suggested, by weighing the countervailing effects on intrabrand and interbrand competition. The decision epitomizes the merits and drawbacks of a per se rule. Introducing the rule of reason opened a floodgate of private treble-damage litigation and scholarly commentary. Standards for weighing relative effects on the two types of competition are necessarily imprecise, thus leading to complicated and costly cases. Although the certainty of guidance given by the per se rule has been lost, refined and more clear-cut standards should ultimately emerge from the welter of cases and articles; and

Justice Powell's approach seems consistent with—indeed, called for—
by economic analysis of the practice.

Uses of Territorial and Customer Restrictions

Eliminating the Free Rides. Territorial or customer exclusivity ob-
viates a type of free-rider problem that cannot be dealt with through
resale price maintenance. Certain promotional activities, particularly
local media advertising, can be performed more efficiently by local
dealers than by national manufacturers, even though they do not involve point-of-sale services. A dealer is more likely to promote a brand
if it has been granted an exclusive market. In the absence of such
exclusivity, each dealer may opt to free-ride on the advertising expenditures of others, resulting in a less than optimal level of local
brand name advertising.

Competitive Efficiency. In parceling out exclusive territories or
customers to dealers, a manufacturer may limit the number of dealers.
This barrier to entry may promote efficiency if dealers would otherwise
face conditions of Chamberlinian monopolistic competition. White has
analyzed such a case with the aid of a diagram similar to Figure
19–3.

D_1 in Figure 19–3 is the demand curve facing a representative
dealer where the manufacturer allows unrestricted entry—that is, will

FIGURE 19–3 Dealer's Price and Output under Monopolistic Competition, with Unrestricted and Restricted Entry

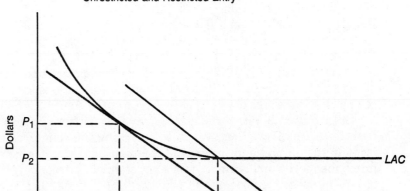

sell its product to any wholesaler or retailer. (Note that D_1 is *not,* as are the demand curves in Figure 19–2, a market demand curve.) Under conditions of monopolistic competition, entry will shift D_1 to a point of tangency with the long-run average cost curve (*LAC*), resulting in a price of P_1 at which the dealer will sell at the rate of Q_1. By limiting dealerships, the manufacturer can shift out the demand curve facing the dealer until, as shown by D_2, it intersects *LAC* at the minimum efficient scale of operation. White suggests that in return for the grant of exclusivity the manufacturer can force the dealer to take the larger quantity Q_2 per unit of time, thus lowering the retail price to P_2.[58] Alternatively, this line of analysis suggests a rationale for a manufacturer imposing a maximum resale price on its dealers.[59]

Attracting Dealers. Like resale price maintenance, territorial or customer exclusivity may be a competitive device for attracting and maintaining dealers. Such exclusivity might be particularly important to induce a dealer to introduce and promote a new product or to assure a new dealer that free-riding competitors will not enter after it has incurred developmental expenses.

Influencing Price. In the *White Motor* case, customer restrictions were explained—indeed, defended—as a form of price discrimination. Territorial exclusivity can clearly serve the same purpose if dealers are assigned markets with different elasticities of demand.

Grants of exclusive territories or customers may reduce dealers' incentives to cut prices or prevent price-cutting from spreading, thus serving the same function as resale price maintenance in reducing the concern of oligopolistic manufacturers that dealers may pressure one of them to cut price. But unlike resale price maintenance, territorial or customer exclusivity cannot be used by colluding manufacturers to detect cheating. Finally, nonprice restrictions on resale, as well as resale price maintenance, may be imposed on a reluctant manufacturer by a powerful collusive group of retailers.

As White notes, the current legal standard, which weighs the effects of territorial and customer restrictions on intrabrand competition against those of interbrand competition, must be used with caution. Such restrictions may reduce competition among manufacturers by facilitating tacit or overt collusion or by raising barriers to entry at the manufacturing level. But a manufacturer has no other interest in reducing intrabrand competition and artificially enhancing the monopoly power of its distributors in their selling market: rather, its own interests are promoted, *ceteris paribus,* by minimizing the dealers' margin. In the absence of collusion or foreclosure, downstream monopoly is an unwanted side effect of improved efficiency in the distributive process. Thus White argued, "there needs to be some kind of weighing of the *decrease in competition at the upstream level* against the increase in efficiency at the downstream level. This heightened upstream collusion is the only legitimate reason for forbidding vertical restraints."[60]

VERTICAL RESTRAINTS AND THE VIRTUE OF CONSISTENCY

The Inconsistencies

The current inconsistent treatment of vertical restraints is troubling. To recapitulate: Tying arrangements are held to be per se illegal, but under definitions of per se that are applied to no other form of restraint and that vary depending on whether a violation of Section 3 of the Clayton Act or Section 1 of the Sherman Act is alleged. Exclusive-dealing agreements are tested by a rule-of-reason standard of purpose and probable effect, whether challenged as a "qualitatively substantial" lessening of competition under Section 3 of the Clayton Act or as a contract in restraint of trade under Section 1 of the Sherman Act. Resale price maintenance constitutes a per se violation of Section 1 of the Sherman Act and is treated as analogous to a horizontal combination in restraint of trade. And territorial or customer restrictions on resale are evaluated for violation of Section 1 under a particular formulation of the rule of reason requiring that the effects on intrabrand and interbrand competition be compared.

Yet analysis indicates that the basic economic characteristics of these practices are similar—indeed, close to identical in the instances of resale price maintenance and nonprice restrictions on resale. All of these vertical restraints can be used to enhance economic efficiency or to restrain trade. All differ from horizontal restraints in that the potential for efficiency is considerably greater and the capacity to restrain trade is considerably less. Thus, whether the justification for treating a restraint as per se illegal is that "the restrictive intent is clear and unmistakable," as posited by A. G. Neale and D. G. Goyder,[61] or that "the gains from forbidding the specified conduct far outweigh the losses," as asserted by Carl Kaysen and Donald F. Turner,[62] the application of a per se rule appears inappropriate to any of the vertical restraints discussed here.

New Guidelines for Vertical Restraints

In January 1985, in the aftermath of the *Jefferson Parrish* and *Monsanto* decisions of the previous spring, the Department of Justice issued a set of guidelines for vertical restraints.[63]

Nonprice Restraints. The guidelines primarily addressed themselves to exclusive dealing agreements and to territorial and customer restraints, which the guidelines distinguished from resale price maintenance as "nonprice" restraints. According to the guidelines, the courts now determine the legality of these two types of nonprice restraint, unlike tying arrangements, by a rule-of-reason standard. Under the guidelines, a two-part screen is applied. The first part is structural:

> Firms with very small market shares, firms operating in unconcentrated markets, and firms operating in markets where a significant share of sales or capacity is not under restraints, are unlikely to be able to collude effectively or foreclose competitors from the market. Accordingly, under the market structure screen, the use of vertical restraints by very small firms (having market shares of under 10 percent), by firms operating in unconcentrated markets, or by firms operating in markets that are not "covered extensively" by restraints (i.e., a significant share of capacity or sales is not subject to restraint) will be presumed legal without further analysis by the Department.[64]

If a restraint is not eliminated from further consideration by this first "market structure" screen, the Antitrust Division will apply a second "structured rule of reason" screen, examining such matters as conditions of entry to both supplier and dealer markets, the extent to which the markets appear amenable to effective collusion, evidence of intent to exclude or collude, use of the restraint by small firms and new entrants, and whether the firms using the restraint can present credible evidence that they gained efficiencies. The department was candid in announcing that it expected almost all nonprice vertical restraints to pass muster under these guidelines.

Tying Arrangements and Resale Price Maintenance. The guidelines deal only briefly with tying arrangements and resale price maintenance. Noting that tying arrangements are illegal per se only if the seller has monopolistic power in the tying-product market, the guidelines state that a tying arrangement will not be challenged if the seller's market share is 30 percent or less, except in cases in which it can be shown that the tie-in "unreasonably restrained competition" in the tied product. If the firm's market share in the tying-product market is 30 percent or over, the Antitrust Division will seek to ascertain whether it possesses "dominant market power." A tying arrangement will be challenged only if both the "unreasonable restraint" and "dominant power" criteria are met.[65]

The guidelines recognize that resale price maintenance is per se illegal, despite the Justice Department's efforts to have the Supreme Court reverse its earlier rulings, but state that the Antitrust Division will prosecute under the per se rule only in instances where there is evidence of "an explicit agreement as to the specific prices at which goods or services would be resold" and where the price restraints are not merely ancillary to nonprice restraints "plausibly designed to create efficiencies."[66]

CONCLUSION

Per se rules do not seem appropriate in dealing with vertical restraints. The traditional rule of reason that has been applied to monopolization cases seems workable in vertical-restraint cases brought under Section 1 of the Sherman Act. The plaintiff should bear the burden of showing (1) that the challenged restriction materially restrained trade and (2) that the defendant intended to do so. As in monopolization cases, probable effect should be one source of evidence from which intent can be inferred. The defendant could rebut a charge of intent to restrain trade by demonstrating efficiencies substantial enough to convince the judge or jury that the restraint was ancillary to a legitimate business purpose. The only additional burden that ought to be imposed on a defendant is that of rebutting a claim by the plaintiff that there were less restrictive ways of obtaining the same efficiencies.

Tying and exclusive-dealing cases, however, are brought under the Clayton as well as the Sherman Act. Section 3 of the Clayton Act proscribes these practices "where the effect may be . . . to substantially lessen competition or tend to create a monopoly in any line of commerce." Similar language in Section 7 has been interpreted to mean that neither economic efficiencies nor procompetitive effects in other lines of commerce provide a defense. In exclusive-dealing cases, the courts have reconciled the language of the statute with the fundamental economic issue of evaluating trade-offs between productive and allocative efficiency by taking intent and probable effect into account. A welcome result is to inject an element of the Sherman Act's rule of reason into Section 3 of the Clayton Act. Full consistency in treatment of vertical restraints, as well as a great deal of economic sense, would be incorporated into the antitrust laws should the courts apply the same approach to tying arrangements.

ENDNOTES

[1]Henry v. A. B. Dick Company, 224 U.S. 1 (1912).

[2]Federal Trade Commission v. Sinclair Refining Company, 261 U.S. 463 (1923).

[3]United States v. Winslow, 227 U.S. 202 (1913); United Shoe Machinery Corporation v. United States, 258 U.S. 451 (1922).

[4]U.S. Industrial Commission, *Report of the Industrial Commission on Trusts and Industrial Corporations,* vol. 13 (Washington, D.C.: U.S. Government Printing Office, 1901), pp. 333–37. See also Harry L. Purdy, Martin L. Lindahl, and William A. Carter, *Corporate Concentration and Public Policy* (New York: Prentice-Hall, 1945) pp. 184–85. For an assessment of the extent and effectiveness of the practice, see Richard B. Tennant, *The American Cigarette Industry* (New Haven, Conn.: Yale University Press, 1950), pp. 304–6.

[5]Tampa Electric Company v. Nashville Coal Company, 365 U.S. 320 (1961).

[6]White Motor Company v. United States, 372 U.S. 253, 255–56 (1963).

[7]Standard Oil Company of California v. United States, 337 U.S. 293, 305–6 (1949).

[8]United States v. Eastman Kodak Company, CCH Trade Cases, ¶67,920 (1954).

[9]International Salt Company v. United States, 332 U.S. 392, 396 (1947).

[10]Times-Picayune Publishing Company v. United States, 345 U.S. 594, 608–9 (1953). (Italics original.)

[11]Northern Pacific Railway Company v. United States, 356 U.S. 1, 5 (1958). (Italics original.)

[12]11.

[13]Louis B. Schwartz, John J. Flynn, and Harry First, *Free Enterprise and Economic Organization: Antitrust,* 6th ed. (Mineola, N.Y.: Foundation Press, 1983), p. 699.

[14]Jefferson Parish Hospital District No. 2 et al. v. Hyde, 80 L. Ed. 2d, 27 (1984).

[15]Justice O'Connor cited Robert H. Bork, *The Antitrust Paradox: A Policy at War with Itself* (New York: Basic Books, 1978); Phillip Areeda, *Antitrust Analysis: Problems, Text, Cases,* 3d ed. (New York: Little, Brown, 1981). Among the more significant contributions to this literature are Ward S. Bowman, Jr., "Tying Arrangements and the Leverage Problem," *Yale Law Journal* 67, no. 1 (November 1957), pp. 19–36; Meyer L. Burstein, "The Economics of Tie-In Sales," *Review of Economics and Statistics* 42, no. 1 (February 1960), pp. 68–73; Eugene M. Singer, "Market Power and Tying Arrangements," *Antitrust Bulletin* 8, no. 4 (July–August 1963), pp. 653–67; James M. Ferguson, "Tying Arrangements and Reciprocity: An Economic Analysis," *Law and Contemporary Problems* 30, no. 3 (Summer 1965), pp. 552–80; William J. Adams and Janet L. Yellen, "Commodity Bundling and the Burden of Monopoly," *Quarterly Journal of Economics* 90, no. 3 (August 1976), pp. 475–98; Roger D. Blair and David L. Kaserman, "Vertical Integration, Tying, and Antitrust Policy," *American Economic Review* 68, no. 3 (June 1978), pp. 397–402. The discussion of tying arrangements in this chapter draws heavily on William L. Baldwin and David McFarland, "Tying Arrangements in Law and Economics," *Antitrust Bulletin* 8, nos. 5–6 (September–December 1963), pp. 743–80.

[16]Martin J. Bailey, "Price and Output Determination by a Firm Selling Related Products," *American Economic Review* 44, no. 1 (March 1954), pp. 82–93.

[17]United States v. Loew's, Inc., 371 U.S. 38 (1962).

[18]George J. Stigler, "United States v. Loew's, Inc.: A Note on Block Booking," in *The Supreme Court Review,* ed. Philip B. Kurland (Chicago: University of Chicago Press, 1963).

[19]*New York Times,* September 25, 1984, pp. A1, D8.

[20]International Business Machines Corporation v. United States, 298 U.S. 131, 134 (1936).

[21]United States v. Jerrold Electronics Corporation, 187 F. Supp. 545 (1960); 365 U.S. 567 (1961).

[22]Dehydrating Process Company v. A. O. Smith Corporation, 292 F. 2d 653 (1961).

[23]Susser v. Carvel Corporation, 332 F. 2d 505, 519 (1964).

[24]Siegel v. Chicken Delight, Inc., 448 F. 2d 43, 47–48 (1971).

[25]Principe v. McDonald's Corporation, 631 F. 2d 303, 309 (1980).

[26]Krehl v. Baskin-Robbins Ice Cream Company, 664 F. 2d 1348 (1982).

[27]For an excellent discussion of the relative merits of franchising and vertical integration, with emphasis on the pervasiveness of tying arrangements in the relationship between franchisors and franchisees, see Richard E. Caves and William F. Murphy II, "Franchising: Firms, Markets, and Intangible Assets," *Southern Economic Journal* 42, no. 4 (April 1976), pp. 572–86.

[28]Standard Fashion Company v. Magrane-Houston Company, 258 U.S. 346, 356–57 (1922).

[29]Brown Shoe Company v. United States, 370 U.S. 294, 330–31 (1962).

[30]329.

[31]Standard Oil Company of California v. United States, 337 U.S. 293, 298 (1949).

[32]See, for example, the dissenting opinion of Justices Robert H. Jackson, Fred M. Vinson, and Harold H. Burton; *U.S. Attorney General's National Committee to Study the Antitrust Laws* (Washington, D.C.: U.S. Government Printing Office, 1955), pp. 137–49; Richard A. Miller, "Exclusive Dealing in the Petroleum Industry: The Refiner-Lessee Dealer Relationship," *Yale Economic Essays* 3, no. 1 (Spring 1963), pp. 223–47.

[33]Miller, "Exclusive Dealings," p. 225.

[34]365 U.S. 320, 329.

[35]Howard P. Marvel, "Exclusive Dealing," *Journal of Law and Economics* 25, no. 1 (April 1982), pp. 1–25.

[36]Dr. Miles Medical Company v. John D. Park & Sons Company, 220 U.S. 373 (1911).

[37]Lester G. Telser, "Why Should Manufacturers Want Fair Trade?" *Journal of Law and Economics* 3 (October 1960), pp. 86–105, at p. 86.

[38]Lawrence J. White, "Vertical Restraints in Antitrust Law: A Coherent Model," *Antitrust Bulletin* 26, no. 2 (Summer 1981), pp. 327–45.

[39]Ibid., pp. 330–31.

[40]L. A. Skeoch notes that the loss-leader problem was emphasized by the Dominion Grocers' Guild in hearings before a committee of the Canadian House of Commons in 1888. See L. A. Skeoch, "Canada," in *Resale Price Maintenance,* ed. Basil S. Yamey (Hawthorne, N.Y.: Aldine Publishing, 1966).

[41]Yamey, *Resale Price Maintenance,* p. 18.

[42]For a survey and review of the issues see the several articles in "Resale Price Maintenance: Theory and Policy in Turmoil," *Contemporary Policy Issues* 3, no. 3 (Spring 1985), part 1, pp. 1–58.

[43]Ronald N. Lafferty, Robert H. Lande, and John B. Kirkwood, eds, *Impact Evaluations of Federal Trade Commission Vertical Restraints Cases* (Washington, D.C.: Federal Trade Commission, 1984). See especially, Sharon Oster, "Levi Strauss," pp. 47–90; Timothy Greening, "Interco-Florsheim Shoes," pp. 92–178; William A. McEachern and Anthony A. Romeo, "Vertical Restraints in the Audio Components Industry: An Analysis of FTC Intervention," pp. 201–57.

[44]McEachern and Romeo, "Vertical Restraints," p. 225.

[45]Telser, "Why Should Manufacturers Want Fair Trade?" pp. 96–99.

[46]220 U.S. 373, 407–8.

[47]United States v. Colgate & Company, 250 U.S. 300 (1919).

[48]United States v. Schrader's Son, Inc., 252 U.S. 85 (1920); Federal Trade Commission v. Beech-Nut Packing Company, 257 U.S. 441 (1922); United States v. Bausch & Lomb Optical Company, 321 U.S. 707 (1944); United States v. Parke, Davis & Company, 362 U.S. 29 (1960); California Retail Liquor Dealers Association v. Midcal Aluminum, Inc., 445 U.S. 97 (1980).

[49]California Retail Liquor Dealers, cited above, 102.

[50]Monsanto Company v. Spray-Rite Service Corporation, 79 L. Ed. 2d 775 (1984).

[51]A. D. Neale and D. G. Goyder, *The Antitrust Laws of the United States of America,* 3d ed. (London: Cambridge University Press, 1980), p. 262.

[52]S. C. Hollander, "United States of America," in *Resale Price Maintenance,* ed. Yamey, pp. 83–91.

[53]372 U.S. 253, 256–57.

[54]263.

[55]United States v. Arnold, Schwinn & Company et al., 388 U.S. 365, 382 (1967).

[56]380.

[57]Continental T.V., Inc. v. GTE Sylvania, Inc., 433 U.S. 36, 50, 51–52, 59 (1977).

[58]White, "Vertical Restraints," pp. 334–36.

[59]Such a practice was ruled illegal in Albrecht v. Herald Company, 390 U.S. 145 (1968).

[60]White, "Vertical Restraints," p. 328 (italics original).

[61]Neale and Goyder, *The Antitrust Laws,* p. 447.

[62]Carl Kaysen and Donald F. Turner, *Antitrust Policy: An Economic and Legal Analysis* (Cambridge, Mass.: Harvard University Press, 1959), p. 43.

[63]U.S. Department of Justice, "Guidelines for Vertical Restraints," January 23, 1985, mimeographed. Reprinted as *CCH Trade Regulation Reports,* no. 687 (January 30, 1985).

[64]Ibid., p. xii.

[65]Ibid., p. 41–42.

[66]Ibid., p. 10–11.

CHAPTER TWENTY

Unfair Methods of Competition and Deceptive Practices in Commerce, Antitrust in International Trade, and Interlocking Directorates

This final antitrust chapter covers miscellaneous areas, each important in a comprehensive and balanced exploration of antitrust law and economics. The prohibition against interlocking directorates in Section 8 of the Clayton Act is seldom enforced and easily evaded. But unfair and deceptive practices and restraints on international trade are aspects of antitrust policy with wide-ranging effects on fundamental sectors of economic activity.

UNFAIR METHODS OF COMPETITION AND DECEPTIVE PRACTICES IN COMMERCE

The Intent of Section 5 of the Federal Trade Commission Act

As initially enacted in 1914, Section 5 of the Federal Trade Commission Act stated simply and tersely that "unfair methods of competition in commerce are hereby declared unlawful." Congress clearly intended to give the FTC authority to investigate and issue cease and desist orders against competitive practices already condemned as unfair in the common law. Such practices included misrepresenting a product's nature or quality, false disparagement of competitors' products, misrepresenting a product's origin by copying the trademark or approximating the brand name of another, imitating another product's appearance, industrial espionage, industrial sabotage, and commercial bribery. But it seems clear that Congress also intended to grant the

FTC authority to expand and modify the concept of unfair competition to meet changing business conditions and practices. The report of the Senate Committee on the Trade Commission Bill stated, "It is believed that the term 'unfair competition' has a legal significance which can be enforced by the commission and the courts, and that it is no more difficult to determine what is unfair competition than it is to determine what is a reasonable rate or what is an unjust discrimination."[1] And the conference report on the bill noted:

> It is impossible to frame definitions which embrace all unfair practices. There is no limit to human inventiveness in this field. Even if all known unfair practices were specifically defined and prohibited, it would be at once necessary to begin over again. . . . Whether competition is unfair or not generally depends upon the surrounding circumstances of the particular case. What is harmful under certain circumstances may be beneficial under different circumstances.[2]

The FTC has, from its inception, identified two facets to enforcement of Section 5. The commission's annual report for 1916 made a clear distinction:

> Thus far the Commission has been of the opinion that at least those cases in which the method of competition restrains trade, substantially lessens competition, or tends to create a monopoly are subject to a proceeding under section 5 of the Federal Trade Commission Act. The Commission has gone further than this, however, and in some instances where these elements did not appear, as in certain cases of misbranding and falsely advertising the character of goods where the public was particularly liable to be misled, the Commission has taken jurisdiction.[3]

Restraint of Trade or Competition. In holding that practices which restrain trade, substantially lessen competition, or tend to create a monopoly are unfair methods of competition subject to Section 5, the commission was asserting that violations of the Sherman and Clayton Acts are also violations of the Federal Trade Commission Act. Initially, the FTC faced resistance from the courts in pressing this interpretation of the law. In a 1920 case involving a tying arrangement, the Supreme Court held that "it is for the courts, not the commission, ultimately to determine as a matter of law" what forms of conduct constitute unfair methods of competition.[4] However, in 1940, the Supreme Court upheld an FTC finding that a collective boycott was an unfair method of competition, noting that "if the purpose and practice of the combination . . . runs counter to the public policy declared in the Sherman and Clayton Acts, the Federal Trade Commission has the power to suppress it as an unfair method of competition."[5]

In the years that followed, the courts moved toward complete acceptance of the FTC's view. In the 1948 *Cement Institute* case, the

Supreme Court ruled that any practice prohibited by the Sherman Act was also illegal under Section 5.[6] In 1953, the Supreme Court held that Section 5 covered not only violations of the other antitrust statutes, but even incipient violations, observing, "it is also clear that the Federal Trade Commission Act was designed to supplement and bolster the Sherman Act and the Clayton Act—to stop in their incipiency acts and practices which, full blown, would violate those Acts."[7] And in 1962, an appeals court upheld the commission's ruling that conduct that violated the spirit but not the letter of the Robinson-Patman Act was in violation of Section 5.[8]

Advertising Abuses. The commission's second line of early activity under Section 5, actions against misbranding and false advertising, burgeoned into an active campaign against false and misleading advertising. However, in the 1931 *Raladam* case, the Supreme Court accepted the company's contention that the FTC had no authority to proceed against any claims made by advertisers, even admittedly false or misleading ones, unless the commission could show that there was an actual or threatened injury to competition.[9] This decision led Congress, in 1938, to pass the Wheeler-Lea Act, amending Section 5 to read, "Unfair methods of competition in commerce, *and unfair or deceptive acts or practices in commerce,* are hereby declared unlawful" (the phrase added by the amendment is in italics). The Wheeler-Lea Act further strengthened the FTC by providing that a cease and desist order issued by the commission under either the Federal Trade Commission Act or the Clayton Act became final unless appealed to the courts within 60 days.

The Economic Cost of Consumer Ignorance. Economic analysis shows the important role played by truthful and nondeceptive advertising in providing information and reducing search costs. The cost of consumer ignorance is illustrated in Figure 20–1.[10] In both panels, D_t represents the "true" demand curve of a consumer for a particular good, or the quantities that a fully informed, utility-maximizing buyer would purchase at various prices. D_u represents the "uninformed" demand curve of the same consumer. In Panel A, the consumer faced with a price of P_1 purchases the good at the rate of Q_u per unit of time in the absence of full information. In this case, the consumer is not aware of certain qualities that make the good more useful or attractive than he or she realizes. The product might, for example, disinfect as well as clean or repel insects as well as smell pleasant. If fully and accurately informed, by advertising or otherwise, this consumer's demand curve would shift out to D_t, and at the prevailing price, his or

FIGURE 20–1   The Welfare Loss from Consumer Ignorance

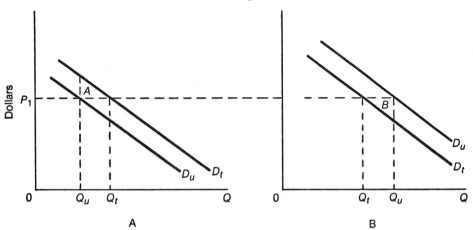

her purchases would rise to Q_t.   As a result of the information, the consumer's surplus is increased by the area of Triangle A.   Panel B illustrates a case in which consumer ignorance of certain undesirable features of the product or an exaggerated belief as to its merits (perhaps resulting from false advertising) leads to an uninformed demand higher than the true demand.   Since the consumer would, at price P_1, reduce purchases from Q_u to Q_t if aware of the truth, the loss of consumer surplus due to ignorance equals the area of Triangle B.

Consumers do not necessarily bear the costs of advertising.   Successful advertising will shift out the demand curve facing the firm, but it will also raise its costs.   The firm achieves its optimal level of advertising when the marginal dollar of selling expenditure yields one dollar in added operating profit (marginal revenue minus marginal operating cost) from the increased sales it generates.[11]   In most but not all cases, the shift up and out of both cost and demand curves will raise the price paid by the consumer.

Figure 20–2 depicts long-run equilibrium in monopolistic competition and illustrates situations in which an increase in advertising expenditures may either increase or decrease price.   In both panels, LAC_1 and D_1 represent long-run average cost and demand curves at relatively low levels of advertising, yielding an equilibrium price of P_1 and a rate of output of Q_1. LAC_2 represents long-run average cost at a higher level of advertising, with demand shifted to D_2.   In both panels, output rises from Q_1 to Q_2 with the increase in advertising; but while price rises to P_2 in Panel A, it falls to P_2 in Panel B, with a different cost and demand configuration.

FIGURE 20–2 Price and Output at Low and High Levels of Advertising

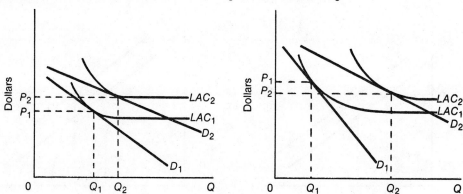

A

B

Search, Experience, and Credence Qualities. Advertised goods can be categorized as having *search* and *experience* qualities. A product characterized by search qualities is one whose essential attributes can be determined by inspection. Clothing, for example, can be examined for fabric, construction, color, style, and fit. One can listen to audio equipment, look at a painting, or push and even bounce on a mattress. Produce can be examined for ripeness, wilted leaves, and soft spots. These goods need not be purchased until they have been inspected. Advertising of these kinds of goods is mostly *informative,* advising buyers where products with certain characteristics are available, and at what price.

Experience qualities, in contrast, cannot be evaluated by prepurchase inspection but must be discovered through use or consumption. Canned or prepackaged food, headache remedies, and grass seed are examples of goods that are high in experience qualities. Effective advertising of such goods usually must be *persuasive* as well as informative (i.e., "Try it, you'll like it"), since first-time buyers must be induced to purchase a product whose qualities are not evident.

These two categories are abstractions; virtually no products are pure search or pure experience goods. An automobile, for example, has many search qualities. A prospective buyer can examine color, design, and seating and trunk capacity in a dealer's showroom and can test drive the vehicle to ascertain acceleration, braking, smoothness of ride, and cornering. But only through experience will the buyer discover the vehicle's reliability and durability. Similarly, most advertising messages have both informative and persuasive content. The abstractions are useful, however, to analyze the market incentives for informative and truthful advertising.

Phillip Nelson found that the 1957 average ratio of advertising expenditure to sales revenue for a group of consumer goods classified as "experience durables" was 2.177 percent, while the ratio for those classified as "experience nondurables" was 4.085 percent. In contrast, a group of "search" goods had an average advertising-to-sales ratio of only 1.395 percent. This finding supported Nelson's initial hypothesis that "producers of experience goods advertise more than producers of search goods" because "advertising of experience qualities increases sales through increasing the reputability of the seller, while advertising of search qualities increases sales by providing the consumer with 'hard' information about the seller's products."[12]

As Nelson noted, the incentive to mislead is small although not entirely absent in advertising of search goods. Exaggerated claims will lead to greater sales only if the disutility of going to an alternative seller is greater than the difference between the expected utility of purchasing elsewhere and the utility revealed by inspection of the falsely advertised good. Further, misleading advertising will lower a seller's credibility, reducing the effectiveness of future advertising in inducing prospective buyers to inspect its products. As a result, Nelson concluded, "consumers can have some confidence that the advertising of search qualities bears a close relation to the truth."[13]

In advertising an experience good, the seller attempts to induce buyers to incur the time and cost of making a purchase, and, in the case of an initial purchase, to try a good of unknown qualities. Thus, *ceteris paribus,* the advertising of experience goods should be more intensive than the advertising of search goods. Further, the incentive to mislead is greater, but only to the extent that first purchases are an important source of revenue. "The major control consumers have over the market for experience qualities," Nelson observed, "is whether they repeat the purchase of a brand or not."[14]

A more important yet less obvious explanation for the greater intensity of experience goods advertising, Nelson added, is that heavy advertising typically reflects high quality relative to price. Sellers who believe their products are a good buy—that many who try the brand will become regular purchasers and recommend it to others— have a greater incentive to advertise than those primarily interested in making initial sales. Further, brand name advertising keeps the advertiser's name in the minds of customers. This effect reinforces both favorable and unfavorable impressions, so the better the image of a firm and its products, the more effective advertising becomes as a selling tool. The mere volume of advertising, therefore, regardless of whether the content is primarily informative or persuasive (or whether actual attributes and price are even mentioned), conveys information to potential buyers as to the value obtainable for the price.[15]

Michael R. Darby and Edi Karni, however, noted a major qualification to Nelson's argument. A number of products, they observed, embody what they refer to as *credence* qualities, which they defined as "those which, although worthwhile, cannot be evaluated in normal use."[16] As examples, they cite an appendectomy, replacement of a television tube, and certain automobile repairs. In all of these, experience cannot tell a buyer whether the good or service was worth its cost, since there is no way of knowing what would have been experienced had the purchase not been made. (I.e., would the appendix really have ruptured, or did the doctor misdiagnose an attack of indigestion and remove a healthy appendix? How much trust can be put in the diagnosis of a television repairman or garage mechanic who assures a customer that a part is about to wear out?) The value of credence goods, if determinable at all, can be assessed only through acquisition of costly information. Credence qualities, therefore, leave consumers more vulnerable to fraud than either search or experience qualities.

Consumers can protect themselves from such fraud by acquiring technical expertise themselves or by incurring the costs of obtaining information—a second medical opinion, for example, or repair estimates from two or more garages. Another possible form of protection is "internalizing" the cost of fraudulent misrepresentation by putting the burden of fulfilling the claims on the seller. Examples include long-term service contracts, warranties, and health maintenance plans. Business firms may integrate upstream into performing services for themselves if they fear their exposure to fraud is too great. Franchising can be used to put the reputation of a national or regional firm behind locally provided goods. Darby and Karni concluded that the fraud associated with credence goods could not be eliminated, and that government regulation is unlikely to be any more cost effective than private efforts in curbing such fraud.

Robert Pitofsky, a former director of the FTC's Bureau of Consumer Protection (later a commissioner), took issue with the market orientation of Nelson and of Darby and Karni. Although conceding that in most situations market forces ensured adequate information to consumers, he noted that "most government charges of deceptive advertising have to do with product claims that are extremely difficult or impossible to measure by observation or use" and asked rhetorically, "How can a consumer determine the accuracy of a claim that a product has 'twice as much vitamin C' as a competing brand? How can a consumer reliably evaluate a claim that a particular disinfectant 'helps prevent colds and flu'?" And rather than accept Darby and Karni's assessment that the government could not control fraudulent advertising any more effectively than the private sector, he asserted, "Government regulation is essential to prevent the market distortion that such claims would otherwise produce."[17]

In another paper, Pitofsky noted that "there may be no repeat purchase opportunities with certain kinds of products—encyclopedias, houses, swimming pools, hearing aids, and so forth—so that consumer dissatisfaction can rarely be expressed by refusal to make a second purchase. Indeed, some of the most blatantly false claims occur precisely in those markets where repeat purchases are unlikely."[18]

As noted in Chapter Seven, consumers are far more vulnerable to deceptive advertising than business purchasers, mainly because they buy a greater variety of goods in smaller quantities. There is little incentive—or indeed, possibility—for consumers to take the time and bear the cost of acquiring expertise, engage in thorough search, or even accurately recall past experiences with many goods when faced with a wide variety and constantly changing mix of brands, most of which take up only a tiny fraction of a household's income.[19]

FTC Enforcement Powers and Procedures

Until 1962, the FTC used only two approaches to enforce Section 5 against false and misleading advertising and other deceptive and unfair selling tactics (such as shipping unordered goods). First, the commission could file a complaint that, if successful, would end in a consent order in which the respondent agreed to terminate the challenged practice or, after litigation, in a cease and desist order. Such action could end the deception, but not punish the offender.

The second early approach, initiated in 1919, was the *trade practice conference,* in which representatives of the firms in an industry met by invitation with members of the FTC staff to formulate *trade practice rules,* covering both practices the FTC regarded as violations of the law and those that members of the industry considered unfair or unethical. These trade practice rules did not have the force of law. If a rule was violated, the commission had to challenge it under the language of the statute rather than under the rule.

In 1962, the commission began issuing *trade regulation rules.* Such rules are initially published in the *Federal Register* as proposed trade regulation rules, and public comment is invited. Formal hearings before the commissioners cover matters of both law and fact; and after these hearings and consideration of written submissions, the trade regulation rule is promulgated as a finding of the commission. Unlike a trade practice rule, a trade regulation rule now has the legal force of a commission decision. Like any commission decision, however, the application of a trade regulation rule can be challenged by appeal to the courts.

The legal basis for the commission's authority to issue trade regulation rules was questioned both within and outside of the FTC until 1975. The Magnuson-Moss Federal Trade Commission Improvement

Act of that year explicitly authorized the FTC to issue such rules, under which particular practices could be designated as unfair or deceptive acts. The commission promptly issued a trade regulation rule against restraints on the advertising of eyeglass prices; and shortly thereafter, it proposed a rule dealing with advertising directed to young children. The commission also proposed rules covering sales practices of funeral parlors and used car dealers. The commission's investigations had led to findings that funeral directors frequently took advantage of a customer's emotional state by refusing to quote prices or show inexpensive coffins, misrepresenting that embalming was legally required or that cremation was regulated in various costly ways by health authorities, and disparaging low-cost funeral arrangements. The commission had also found that in the sales of used cars, deception was endemic as to both the car's mechanical condition and the services the dealer would provide to correct problems.

Procedures for Controlling Advertising. In 1971, the FTC initiated an *advertising substantiation* program requiring advertisers in selected industries to demonstrate the basis (laboratory tests, surveys, etc.) for the claimed merits of their products. The information provided by the advertisers is made public by the commission. In several cases, the FTC issued formal complaints when claims were not adequately substantiated.

The FTC has also used the complaint procedure to obtain remedies other than cease and desist orders. In 1977, the Supreme Court left standing an appeals court decision that upheld the main thrust of an FTC *corrective advertising* order. The order required Warner-Lambert Company, maker of Listerine, to include the statement "Contrary to prior advertising, Listerine will not help to prevent colds or sore throats or lessen their severity" in its advertising of that product until it had spent $10 million on such ads.[20] (The figure was determined as approximately the average annual spending on Listerine advertising between 1962 and 1972.) The court did rule, however, that the phrase "contrary to prior advertising" be deleted from the required statement. The court held that corrective advertising orders were within the implied remedial authority of the FTC, though not mentioned in the Federal Trade Commission Act, and were proper in cases where misleading impressions would remain after the advertising was halted. A similar remedy is the *affirmative disclosure* order, such as the requirement that cigarette advertising warn of the dangers of cigarette smoking.

Published Guides and Opinions. The FTC publishes and distributes guides that grow out of trade practice conferences or reflect the commission's concern with certain practices, such as *Guides Against Deceptive Pricing, Guides Against Bait Advertising, Guides Against Deceptive Advertising of Guarantees,* and *Guides Concerning Use of Endorsements and Testimonials in Advertising.*

Finally, FTC staff members may give *advisory opinions* to officers of firms and their counsel seeking information on the legality of proposed actions. If these advisory opinions are considered to be of general interest, they are published by the FTC, though they do not identify the firms that initiated the inquiries.

What Makes Advertising Deceptive?

Equally as important as the FTC's enforcement powers and procedures are the standards it uses to ascertain deceptive trade practices. In a 1971 book, Earl W. Kintner, who was chairman of the FTC from 1959 to 1961, identified six basic rules that had come to guide the FTC.[21]

1. Advertising need have only a tendency to deceive; the FTC does not necessarily have to prove actual deception. To establish a tendency to deceive, however, the FTC must show that the representations made in the advertisement would be a "material factor" in a decision to buy. Some instances of so-called puffing (unsupported statements that others would consider clear exaggerations) have been held not to be material in this sense and therefore permissible. Words like *perfect* and *best* have been allowed as "mere puffing."

2. It is immaterial whether the seller knew that the claims made in its advertisements were false.

3. Intent is likewise immaterial.

4. The commission can insist on literal truthfulness. Obvious fantasy might be permitted, recognizing that falsity is not always misleading (e.g., one television advertisement for a scouring powder depicted hundreds of tiny scrub brushes rubbing a grimy pan). But according to an appeals court, Section 5 was not framed "for the protection of experts, but for the public—that vast multitude which includes the ignorant, the unthinking and the credulous." Therefore, "the fact that a false statement may be obviously false to those who are trained and experienced does not change its character, nor take away its power to deceive others less experienced."[22]

5. The literal truth may sometimes be deceptive and thus unlawful. Perhaps the clearest example of this principle is the FTC's ban, upheld on appeal, against advertisements for Old Gold cigarettes. The ads claimed that research described in a *Reader's Digest* article had found Old Gold lowest in nicotine and tar. However, the article had stressed that the differences in the tested brands were so small that they provided no basis for choosing one particular brand.[23]

6. Regardless of its overt message, an advertisement can be held false because of a message conveyed by ambiguity and innuendo. In banning an advertisement that indirectly and falsely promoted a medicinal preparation as inducing abortion, the commission's opinion observed that "this advertisement seems to invite a reading between the lines. It is reminiscent of the situation existing in bootlegging days when a knowing wink might convey to the prospective purchaser the thought that the liquid being sold as 'cold tea' was in fact intoxicating liquor."[24] More common are ads that imply medical or scientific endorsement by depicting scientific instruments, symbols such as a red cross or a caduceus, laboratory surroundings, or models in doctors' or nurses' garb.

In the 1980s, both the commission's expanded rulemaking power and the standards it applied to advertising came under attack. The FTC's proposed "kidvid" rule on children's advertising was assailed as discriminatory and unduly paternalistic by advertisers, television producers, and press commentators. Criticisms of the rules proposed for funeral parlors and used car dealers were also widespread.

Congress responded to the outcry from representatives of these two typically independent and locally owned small businesses and enacted legislation to constrain the FTC. The Federal Trade Commission Improvements Act of 1980 limited the extent to which the FTC could regulate the practices of funeral parlors. Far more significant, it imposed a legislative veto on future trade regulation rules by requiring that any proposed rule be submitted to Congress, where it could be vetoed by both the House and Senate within 90 days of initial submission. In response, the FTC dropped its proposed "kidvid" rule and relaxed the rule for funeral parlors, requiring only that funeral directors make price lists available and not misrepresent laws or public health regulations. In May 1982, Congress vetoed a used car rule that would have required dealers to disclose all known defects to customers.

However, the Supreme Court ruled the legislative veto unconstitutional in June 1983.[25] The FTC reconsidered its used car rule and issued a proposal in July 1984 that would require dealers to place a sticker in the window of any used car describing the terms of any warranty or whether the car was being sold "as is," advising the prospective purchaser to get promises in writing and to obtain an independent inspection of the car, listing the major defects most often found in used cars, and explaining the terms and coverage of any service contract available.

The revised and relaxed funeral parlor and used car rules were issued by the FTC during the Reagan administration. But by 1984, President Reagan's appointees to the commission were deemphasizing the use of industrywide rulemaking. A new policy concentrated instead on case-by-case prosecution of individual instances of consumer fraud and deception, beginning with some specific actions taken against firms offering diamond investment schemes and lotteries on land that might possibly be oil-bearing. At the same time, the commission was considering repeal of a number of existing trade regulation rules.[26]

In October 1983, by a three-to-two vote, FTC commissioners adopted a new policy toward deceptive practices, utilizing definitions Chairman James C. Miller had earlier urged Congress to incorporate in legislation. There are three elements to this policy:

> *First,* there must be a misrepresentation, omission, or practice that is likely to mislead the consumer. Practices that have been found misleading or deceptive in specific cases include false oral or written representations, misleading price claims, sales of hazardous or systematically defective products or services without adequate disclosures, failure to disclose information regarding pyramid sales, use of bait and switch techniques, failure to perform promised services, and failure to meet warranty obligations.
>
> *Second,* we examine the practice from the perspective of a consumer acting reasonably in the circumstances. If the representation or practice affects or is directed primarily at a particular group, the Commission examines reasonableness from the perspective of that group.
>
> *Third,* the representation, omission, or practice must be a "material" one. The basic question is whether the act or practice is likely to affect the consumer's conduct or decision with regard to a product or service. If so, the practice is material, and consumer injury is likely, because consumers are likely to have chosen differently but for the deception. In many instances, materiality, and hence injury, can be presumed from the nature of the practice. In other instances, evidence of materiality may be necessary.
>
> Thus, the Commission will find deception if there is a representation, omission or practice that is likely to mislead the consumer acting reasonably, to the consumer's detriment.[27]

The vote on this policy reflected a fundamental split within the commission—the commissioners appointed by President Reagan supported it and the holdovers from the previous administration opposed it. The newer commissioners, including Chairman Miller, were adherents of the Chicago school of industrial organization and thus inclined toward the free-market arguments stemming from Nelson's analysis.

In a dissenting statement, Commissioner Patricia P. Bailey (a Republican appointee of President Carter's) objected to (1) the substitution of "likelihood" of deception for the earlier standard of "tendency" to deceive in the first element of the new policy, (2) the substitution of "reasonable action" by consumers for the courts' standard which included protection of "the ignorant, the unthinking and the credulous" in the second element, and (3) the equating of materiality with injury in the third element. She wrote:

> Rather than clarifying . . . the law of deception, the statement writes new law that is destined to confuse and confound its readers. The three part definition of deception, if applied literally, could substantially narrow the Commission's authority to prosecute a wide range of dishonest and deceptive conduct, while creating enormous complications and uncertainty about the legitimacy of the cases we do bring.[28]

Subsequently, in March 1984, Chairman Miller replied that the new policy is intended to "define for the public the parameters of [the FTC's] jurisdiction" rather than modify the commission's practice as guided by judicial precedents and that "the October statement still stands and is the policy of this Commission."[29] Whether the new standards prove similar to or more permissive than those laid out by former Chairman Kintner must await the test of time.

ANTITRUST IN INTERNATIONAL TRADE[30]

The basic antitrust laws of the United States were intended to apply to foreign as well as domestic trade. Section 1 of the Sherman Act states that every contract, combination, or conspiracy "in restraint of trade or commerce among the several States, *or with foreign nations,* is hereby declared to be illegal," and Section 2 similarly forbids monopolization or attempts to monopolize "any part of the trade or commerce among the several States, *or with foreign nations*" (italics added for emphasis). The Wilson Tariff Act, enacted in 1894, supplemented the Sherman Act by providing:

> Every combination, conspiracy, trust, agreement, or contract is hereby declared to be contrary to public policy, illegal, and void, when the same is made by or between two or more persons or corporations either of whom is engaged in importing any article from any foreign country into the United States, and when such combination, conspiracy, trust, agreement, or contract is intended to operate in restraint of lawful trade, or free competition in lawful trade or commerce, or to increase the market price in any part of the United States of any article or articles imported or intended to be imported into the United States, or of any manufacture into which such imported article enters or is intended to enter.

Both Section 1 of the Clayton Act and Section 4 of the Federal Trade Commission Act define commerce, for purposes of the statutes, to include trade or commerce among the various jurisdictions of the United States and "with foreign nations." Finally, the Webb-Pomerene Act, passed in 1918, provides that the prohibition against unfair methods of competition in Section 5 of the Federal Trade Commission Act "shall be construed as extending to unfair methods of competition used in export trade against competitors engaged in export trade, even though the acts constituting such unfair methods are done without the territorial jurisdiction of the United States."

Areas of Enforcement

This comprehensive authority to enforce the U.S. antitrust laws in international trade has led to nearly as wide a variety of foreign commerce actions as domestic ones. The following cases capture the international aspects of antitrust rather than provide a detailed account of the scope and development of the law.[31]

Monopolization. The United Fruit Company was charged in 1954 with monopolizing both interstate and foreign trade in bananas through acquisition of virtually all of the banana-growing land in Central America; control of needed wharf, communications, and shipping facilities in that area; and predatory pricing. The case was settled by a consent decree. United Fruit agreed to divest itself of International Railways of Central America and, either through sale of other assets in the area or spin-off, to create a new company with the capacity to import 9 million stems of bananas per year into the United States.[32] Alleging monopolization of U.S. import markets, cases have been brought against foreign firms as well, notably against the International Nickel Company of Canada and the South African diamond producer De Beers Mines.[33]

Collusive Restraint of Trade. There have been a number of cartel cases. Two, involving dyestuffs and tungsten, stemmed from revelations during World War II of German firms' prewar cartelization that had restricted U.S. production and investment as well as exports.[34] In *National Lead,* two U.S. and several foreign firms were found to have violated the law by dividing the world market for titanium pigments among themselves through exclusive licensing agreements and joint ownership of production facilities.[35] A similar arrangement between Du Pont and Imperial Chemical Industries of Great Britain, primarily affecting chemicals and processes used in synthetic fibers, was held per se illegal.[36] In the *Quinine* case, a foreign cartel without participation by U.S. firms but limiting imports into this country, was attacked successfully under the Sherman Act.[37] But in 1979, in a private suit brought against OPEC by the machinists' union, the court held that activities of the oil cartel were exempt from legal attack in the United States as within the sovereign rights of the OPEC nations to control the exploitation of their natural resources.[38]

Merger. Mergers involving firms in two or more nations have been challenged successfully on several grounds. The merger of Schlitz Brewing Company and John LaBatt, Limited, a Canadian beer manufacturer, was held illegal in part because of the potential import competition from LaBatt.[39] Similarly, in the *Gillette* case, a merger between the largest U.S. manufacturer of safety razors and Braun, A. G., the third largest European manufacturer of electric razors, was modified by a consent decree to meet the Antitrust Division's concern that Braun was a potential entrant into the domestic shaving-instrument market.[40] In the *British Petroleum–Sohio* case, a foreign firm's acquisition of a domestic firm was allowed only subject to divestiture of part of the foreign firm's U.S. holdings.[41] Even a merger, consummated abroad, of two foreign firms, Ciba, Ltd. and J. R. Geigy, was challenged and subject to settlement by consent decree because each of the two firms had a U.S. subsidiary and the Justice Department contended that the combination of these two subsidiaries constituted a horizontal merger between two domestic companies that lessened competition in the U.S.[42]

Predatory Practices. In the 1927 *Sisal Sales* case, the Justice Department successfully alleged that U.S. defendants had obtained a monopolistic position in the export of sisal fiber (used in cordage and binder twine) through predatory acts done abroad—in particular, by inducing the governments of Mexico and Yucatan to enact legislation that barred other firms from buying sisal for export to the U.S. market.[43] Similar predation was found nearly 50 years later in the *Timberlane* case, upholding a private plaintiff's allegation that the defendants, Bank of America and a Honduran lumber firm, had prevented it from entering the lumbering and lumber export business in Honduras through, among other things, causing a Honduran court to issue an order preventing Timberlane from engaging in operations in Honduras, having its local manager arrested, and promoting publication of articles hostile to Timberlane in the Honduran press.[44] However, Occidental Petroleum Company was unsuccessful in pressing its allegation that a predatory competitor had induced the ruler of Sharjar (one of the Persian Gulf Trucial States), and later Iran, to claim ownership of an area in which Occidental had previously obtained a drilling concession from Umm al Qayayn, another of the Trucial States. The court denied Occidental's complaint as an unwarranted and unenforceable challenge to the sovereign rights of Sharjar and Iran.[45]

Vertical Restraints. Vertical restraints in import and export trading have also been barred. Foreign automobile manufacturers, including Volkswagen, Renault, and Nissan, have been prohibited from imposing resale price maintenance and exclusive territories on their U.S. dealers.[46] A restriction by Anheuser-Busch, under which its U.S. wholesalers were forbidden to sell Budweiser beer to competitors of a designated Anheuser-Busch retail outlet in the Bahamas, was held illegal.[47] And an exclusive territorial arrangement under which Sony dealers in the United States had to compensate other dealers for sales made in their territories was condemned as evidencing anticompetitive intent and effect.[48]

Scope of Enforcement

Many of the cases just reviewed were settled by consent decree and, therefore, without an opinion; others were private suits in which neither side had any concern for the development of antitrust law or for national policy. Further, the number of antitrust cases involving international trade is relatively small. Thus, the case law where issues of foreign commerce are involved is not well formulated. One of the most crucial issues is the extent to which the United States has a legitimate concern with such commerce. In 1976, the Department of Justice published an *Antitrust Guide for International Operations,* in which it held that antitrust enforcement with respect to international trade had two major purposes: "The first is to protect the American consuming public by assuring it the benefit of competitive products and ideas produced by foreign competitors as well as domestic competitors," the *Guide* noted. "Competition by foreign producers is particularly important when imports are or could be a major source of a particular product, or where the domestic industry is dominated by a single firm or a few firms." The second purpose "is to protect American export and investment opportunities against privately imposed restrictions."[49]

Protection Limited to U.S. Consumers and Businesses: Pros and Cons. The Department of Justice argued for limiting protection to U.S. consumers and businesses on grounds of both congressional intent and respect for the sovereignty of other nations, noting that U.S. antitrust actions against "foreign activities which have no direct or intended effect on United States consumers or export opportunities would, we believe, extend the Act beyond the point Congress must have intended. This could encroach upon the sovereignty of a foreign state without any overriding justification based on legitimate United States interests."[50]

This view has been criticized as narrow and selfish, allowing U.S. firms to exploit consumers in foreign markets in ways that would be prohibited if the victims were residents of this country. Such an apparently cynical lack of concern for the economic damage done abroad, it has been argued, could result in "ill will and possible retaliation by our trading partners."[51] Third-world countries have contended that the industrialized nations ought to exercise more control over the worldwide operations of multinational firms whose trade practices outside of the host country may retard as well as promote economic development.

James R. Atwood and Kingman Brewster, on the other hand, strongly support the Justice Department's position "if coupled with an unequivocal willingness by the United States government to lend assistance to foreign antitrust authorities."[52] They argue that the limitation of U.S. enforcement gives clarity to the law and thus promotes international trade, and encourages foreign governments to develop and strengthen their own antitrust laws. Enhancement of foreign antitrust laws, they conclude, should be encouraged and supported by the United States both by participation in international organizations and through bilateral channels.[53]

However limited the reach of U.S. antitrust laws may be, the courts are open to anyone alleging injury from an antitrust violation. By a four-to-four tie vote in a 1978 case, the Supreme Court upheld a lower court ruling that foreign governments as well as foreign nationals can sue for treble damages under the U.S. antitrust laws. In the *Pfizer* case, the government of India was one of a number of institutional buyers to sue U.S. pharmaceutical manufacturers following an FTC complaint of anticompetitive practices in both domestic and foreign markets. But in its opinion, the Court avoided facing the issue of precisely who the U.S. antitrust laws are designed to protect. It noted that even if the intent of Congress was to protect U.S. and not foreign consumers, the deterrent effect of potential treble-damage suits by foreigners alleging injury from restraints in domestic markets adds to the protection of U.S. consumers.[54]

Export Activities. The intended thrust of U.S. antitrust law toward domestic interests is evidenced by legislation exempting exporters and by enforcement policies of the Department of Justice. The 1918 Webb-Pomerene Act declared that an association "entered into for the sole purpose of engaging in export trade," and actually so engaged, would not be subject to Section 1 of the Sherman Act "provided such an association, agreement, or act is not in restraint of trade within the United States and is not in restraint of the export trade of any domestic competitor of such an association." The Webb-Pomerene Act further provided that an export association must not do anything that "artificially or intentionally enhances or depresses prices within the United States . . . substantially lessens competition . . . or otherwise restrains trade therein." All such export associations are required to file statements of organization and periodic reports of their activities with the FTC, which is charged with responsibility for oversight and for taking remedial actions against export associations whose practices turn out to have the prohibited effects on domestic commerce or competing exporters.

The Export Trading Company Act of 1982 further amended the Sherman and Federal Trade Commission Acts to make them inapplicable to conduct in trade with foreign nations, other than import, unless such conduct has "a direct, substantial, and reasonably foreseeable effect" on domestic or import commerce of the United States or on another person in the United States engaged in exporting. Title III of the act further provides that any firm or group of firms can apply for a *certificate of review*, to be issued by the Department of Commerce after both that department and the Antitrust Division have determined that the export activities described in the application will "(1) result in neither a substantial lessening of competition or restraint of trade within the United States nor a substantial restraint of the export trade of any competitor of the applicant," and "(2) not unreasonably enhance, stabilize, or depress prices within the United States." Further, it must be determined that the proposed export activities do not constitute unfair methods of competition against competing exporters and cannot reasonably be expected to result in resale of the exported products in the United States. A firm or association holding such a certificate cannot be held liable in either a criminal or a civil suit for conduct specified in and complying with the terms of the certificate. And if a certificate holder is successfully sued by a private plaintiff on the grounds that the challenged conduct does not meet the standards of the certificate, it is liable only for actual damages.

The Webb-Pomerene and Export Trading Acts notwithstanding, it may be impossible to cordon off export activities so completely as to prevent spillovers into domestic trade. In a 1950 case in which "a combination of dominant American manufacturers" had established joint subsidiaries abroad "for the sole purpose of serving the internal commerce" of the nations in which they were located, Judge Charles Wyzanski expressed such a concern, noting that "the intimate association of the principal American producers in day-to-day manufacturing operations, their exchange of patent licenses and industrial know-how, and their common experience in marketing and fixing prices may inevitably reduce their zeal for competition *inter sese* in the American market."[55]

Atwood and Brewster note that agreements made in the export trade may promote covert or tacit understandings affecting U.S. markets or competitors.[56] An exporter, for example, who agrees to sell to only one distributor in a foreign country or to stay out of certain foreign markets might expect some reciprocal consideration in its domestic markets. U.S. firms that meet, share information, and take cooperative action through an export association or export agent may, either deliberately or inadvertently, exchange information or behave in a way that restrains domestic trade. Mere interaction on matters affecting foreign commerce may give firms insights into rivals' ways of doing business that strengthen the recognition of mutual dependence. Atwood and Brewster are probably correct in concluding that the dangers of anticompetitive spillovers into domestic markets vary considerably depending on the structural situation (for example, the number of competitors involved) and the degree to which cooperation in the export market is related to the firms' domestic marketing and competitive strategies.

Jurisdictional Issues. Another major issue in international antitrust is when it is appropriate for U.S. enforcement agencies and courts to exercise jurisdiction once they establish that U.S. consumers or exporters are affected. The disputed acts may affect those in other nations as well, or remedial actions may involve U.S. courts handing down orders to or imposing penalties on foreign firms and individuals.

Foreign governments, sometimes acrimoniously, have resisted attempts by U.S. courts to require their firms to produce documents or other evidence located abroad, to appear before U.S. courts, and to obey remedial orders. On several occasions, firms have been ordered by their governments not to produce the documents or comply with U.S. court orders.[57]

Perhaps the most heated controversy grew out of a private treble-damage suit brought by Westinghouse Electric against U.S. and foreign firms in an international uranium cartel. The cartel was formed in the 1960s in response to a U.S. ban on the import of uranium. The governments of Great Britain, Canada, Australia, and South Africa all took steps to block their national firms from disclosing information or appearing in a U.S. court. An appeals court judge lashed out with a statement that "shockingly to us," these governments had "subserviently" presented the defendants' case against U.S. jurisdiction.[58] The U.S. State Department, in turn, protested that the court was embarrassing the nation and ignoring accepted principles of international comity. According to Atwood and Brewster, controversy over the Westinghouse case reached the point where "political relations with at least some of these countries in other areas had been damaged."[59]

Another case that escalated to the highest levels of government grew out of a grand jury investigation of a complaint filed by the Department of Justice in 1983. The complaint alleged an international conspiracy to drive the no-frills, low-fare British firm of Laker Airways out of the transatlantic airline business. Those charged included a U.S. aircraft manufacturer and a number of airline carriers, both U.S. and foreign, including one government-owned firm, British Airways. Shortly before the Antitrust Division's investigation began, Laker's liquidators had filed a private suit against the same firms, so the U.S. government's action appeared to support the private complaint. The British government objected that the allegedly predatory fares had been approved by that nation's Civil Aviation Authority and therefore represented an "instrument of national policy," as well as being exempt from U.S. antitrust attack under international aviation treaties.

More important, Great Britain's Prime Minister Margaret Thatcher was interested in "privatizing" British Airways by selling its stock to the public. This could not be done as long as the litigation was pending. In June 1983 the British Transport Department issued an order forbidding British Airways and British Caledonian Airways from providing any information requested by either the grand jury or the court hearing the private suit.[60] Then, in November 1984, the U.S. Justice Department issued a press release announcing that it was closing the grand jury hearing, stating that "it was the President's decision based on foreign policy reasons that this should be done." The private suit was later settled, with the defendants paying $40 million to Laker's creditors, $8 million to Laker's founder Sir Freddie Laker, and $12 million toward creditors' attorneys' fees.[61]

In some instances, acts attacked by the U.S. antitrust enforcement agencies or private plaintiffs may involve acts of state by foreign governments, or feasible remedies may impinge on the sovereignty of other nations, as in the *Sisal, Occidental Petroleum, Timberlane,* and *OPEC* cases reviewed above. The question of acts of state was partially resolved by the Sovereign Immunities Act of 1976. The act provides that antitrust suits challenging foreign states for sovereign acts of government will be dismissed, but it distinguishes between commercial activities and governmental functions. The commercial activities of governments, according to the act, are not acts of state and are therefore subject to the antitrust laws. Thus, a Polish government enterprise producing and importing golf carts was subject to a private suit charging predatory pricing subsidized by the Polish government and anticompetitive exclusive-dealing agreements with its U.S. distributors. (On the merits, the trial court dismissed the case.)[62]

In the absence of clear guidance from the Supreme Court, the enforcement agencies, most legal commentators, and several other courts have endorsed Judge Herbert Y. C. Choy's 1977 opinion in the *Timberlane* case, described by the then assistant attorney general in charge of the Antitrust Division as "a masterful combination of substantive antitrust law and the analysis [of foreign relations law]."[63] Judge Choy, writing for an appeals court, held that a court must balance the interests of the United States and those of other nations in determining whether to exercise jurisdiction. He added:

> The elements to be weighed include the degree of conflict with foreign law or policy, the nationality or allegiance of the parties and the locations or principal places of business of corporations, the extent to which enforcement by either state can be expected to achieve compliance, the relative significance of the effects on the United States as compared with those elsewhere, the extent to which there is explicit purpose to harm or affect American commerce, the foreseeability of such effect, and the relative importance to the violations charged of conduct within the United States as compared with conduct abroad.[64]

In the 1979 *Mannington Mills* case, another appeals court endorsed Judge Choy's balancing approach and formulated its own list of elements to be weighed:

1. Degree of conflict with foreign law or policy;
2. Nationality of the parties;
3. Relative importance of the alleged violation of conduct here compared to that abroad;
4. Availability of a remedy abroad and the pendency of litigation there;
5. Existence of intent to harm or affect American commerce and its foreseeability;
6. Possible effect upon foreign relations if the court exercises jurisdiction and grants relief;
7. If relief is granted, whether a party will be placed in the position of being forced to perform an act illegal in either country or be under conflicting requirements by both countries;
8. Whether the court can make its order effective;
9. Whether an order for relief would be acceptable in this country if made by the foreign nation under similar circumstances;
10. Whether a treaty with the affected nations has addressed the issue.[65]

Ultimately, any workable solution must include continuing consultation with foreign governments, sensitivity to their concerns, notification of pending actions that might impinge on other nations' interests and of negotiations on remedies, and commitments to mutual assistance in enforcement of the antitrust laws of various nations. In 1977, 1982, and 1984, the U.S. government made such cooperative agreements with West Germany, Australia, and Canada. The Department of Justice endorses and has actively sought such agreements, but this form of international cooperation can have little effect on controlling or restraining private treble-damage suits.

Antitrust Laws of Other Nations

Since the end of World War II, international organizations and nations around the world have enacted antitrust laws, codes, and resolutions. Virtually all of the nations of Western Europe and Scandinavia, Canada, Japan, and Australia have antitrust laws. So do some developing nations, including Argentina, Brazil, India, and Pakistan. The Treaty of Rome, establishing the European Economic Community (now the European Communities, or EC), contains articles dealing with restrictive practices and abuse of dominant market positions. The EC antitrust law is binding on all 13 member nations, and is enforceable in their courts. The Organization for Economic Cooperation and Development (OECD) has developed a code of conduct for multinational firms. A United Nations code on antitrust was framed under the auspices of the United Nations Conference on Trade and Development (UNCTAD). Both the OECD and UNCTAD codes call for voluntary adherence and have no legal force.[66]

Typically, foreign antitrust laws put much more emphasis on administrative enforcement through informal discussions, negotiations, and directives handed down by bureaucratic agencies and much less reliance on enforcement through the courts than does the U.S. system. As a result, national policies and interests—such as full employment, national defense, balance of payments, and the development of particular firms and industries—are taken into account in evaluating specific restrictive practices. Such discretion and flexibility do, however, carry a price. Neale and Goyder, for example, note that "the fact that American courts are at pains to avoid making their decisions depend on economic analysis and prediction" is a key factor that "enables the main lines of the policy to operate through a body of compliable and reasonably predictable law enforced by the courts and the legal advisers of industry rather than through decisions of administrators and economic advisers."[67]

Japan's antitrust experience, beginning with the 1947 Act Concerning Prohibition of Private Monopoly and Maintenance of Fair Trade enacted under guidance of the U.S. occupation authorities, is particularly interesting. The substantive law, including post-occupation amendments in 1953 and 1977, bears many similarities to that of the United States. There is a single enforcement agency, the Fair Trade Commission, attached to the Prime Minister's Office. Only one court, the Tokyo High Court, hears appeals in cases initiated by the Fair Trade Commission. Fugate, writing in 1982, observed a current "disposition to make competition a strong national policy" in Japan. "The Fair Trade Commission," he wrote, "has acted vigorously in the face of considerable odds. Concepts of competition and antitrust were distinctly foreign to the Japanese economy, and Japan has made great strides in the last two decades in changing over from an economy dominated by large government-supported enterprises with practically monopoly power to an essentially competitive economy."[68]

Fugate's account is borne out in a 1981 *Wall Street Journal* article.[69] The author, Ken Ohmae, managing partner of McKinsey and Company's Tokyo office, noted the utter falsity of the perception that Japanese firms compete so effectively in export markets partly because of strength derived from cartelized domestic markets. Rather, he wrote, "in almost every industry where Japanese industries have done well in export markets, they have honed their teeth in fierce domestic competition." For example, Nikon, Canon, Olympus, Minolta, Pentax, and Konica compete in the camera industry, as do Matsushita, Sony, Toshiba, Hitachi, Mitsubishi, Sanyo, Sharp, and Nippon Electric in color television. He noted similar intensely competitive situations in the domestic markets of other export-oriented industries, including plain-paper copiers, hi-fi audio equipment, automobiles, steel, and computers. More concentrated and less competitive industries, including cosmetics, breweries, construction machinery, and pianos, have been less successful in export markets, with most foreign sales made in developing countries. Ohmae concluded that "to understand why Japanese companies do well on world markets, it's important to recognize that they have built up their competitive strengths in perhaps the world's most competitive domestic marketplace." The lesson from Japan seems stunningly clear for U.S. policymakers faced with pleas that antitrust enforcement at home be relaxed or exceptions be made so that some American industry can regain its competitive edge in world trade.

INTERLOCKING DIRECTORATES

Section 8 of the Clayton Act forbids any one person from serving on the boards of directors of two or more large corporations if "the elimination of competition by agreement between them would constitute a violation of any of the provisions of any of the antitrust laws." Yet, a study of the 250 largest U.S. corporations in 1935, 21 years after passage of the Clayton Act, found that 225 had at least one director on the board of at least one of the others. Further, analysis of these interlocking directorates indicated eight financial and family "interest groups" (such as Rockefeller, du Pont, Mellon, and Morgan Stanley) involving 106 of these corporations.[70]

A later study of the 250 largest U.S. corporations in 1965 found that 233 were interlocked through common directors and that of a total of 2,480 such interlocks, 297 were among firms within the same SIC five-digit industry classification and, therefore, presumably among competitors in most of the cases.[71] (There were 1,720 interlocks among 200 nonfinancial firms in the study, of which 160 were among presumed competitors.) In 1965, this study found, the 4,007 directorships in the 250 largest corporations were filled by 3,165 individuals. Of these men and women, 2,603 served on only one board, while 562 held two or more directorships. Five were each members of six boards.[72]

And in a study by the staff of the Senate Committee on Governmental Affairs, 600 instances of common directors were found among 100 leading companies in the United States in 1980.[73] The introduction to the committee's study contains the following observation:

> Interlocking directorates provide a special opportunity for intercompany communication and consensus. The linkages at the boardroom table are personal connections by which key information can be passed, arrangements can be made and policies formed. Board meetings are corporate proceedings where management policies are specifically reviewed and approved or corrected. Thus, to the extent that a board contains members who are also directors of actual or potential competitors, suppliers, customers or financial organizations, there is a potential for anticompetitive abuse.[74]

Clearly, Section 8 has not succeeded in eliminating interlocking directorates.

For several reasons, the FTC and the Antitrust Division have chosen not to devote any substantial portion of their limited resources to detecting and attacking violations of the section. The scope of the law is limited, proscribing only *direct* interlocks, in which one individual sits on the boards of two or more competing firms. The law does not reach a situation in which an officer of one firm is a director of a competitor; nor does it prohibit *indirect* interlocks, in which a firm (typically a financial institution or a law firm) has representatives on the boards of two or more industrial or commercial firms that are in competition with one another. Alternatively, the directors or executives of competing firms may serve together on the boards of other firms. The presidents of two automobile companies, for example, might both be directors of the same bank.

Indirect interlocks such as these are far more common than direct ones: The 1980 Senate study that found 600 direct interlocks among the 100 leading firms it examined also found 16,959 indirect interlocks within the same group. Further, Section 8 does not cover even direct *vertical* interlocks between suppliers and customers, since they do not compete with each other, even though agreement between them could injure third parties and conceivably violate the exclusive-dealing provision of Section 3 of the Clayton Act. Finally, the prohibition of Section 8 is easy to evade if a person legally ineligible to serve on two boards controls enough voting stock to place a family member or other representative on one of them.

Sporadic efforts to enforce Section 8 in the courts have resulted in further weakening of the law. Such cases have been rare; in virtually every instance of challenge to an apparently illegal interlock, the individual involved has resigned from one of the boards rather than litigate the issue, with no assurance that the offense will not be repeated. In a 1953 case, the Supreme Court agreed with a district court's refusal to uphold an FTC order forbidding an individual to engage in future activity violating Section 8, even though evidence showed he had been involved in three previous violations, had contested their illegality, and had refused to agree with the FTC not to repeat the violation.[75] Another district court held that to constitute a violation under the test of illegality of Section 8, there must be actual and not merely potential competition between the two firms with common directors.[76] In 1978, an appeals court ruled that Section 8 did not forbid an interlock between two firms whose subsidiaries were in competition, absent a showing that both parents exercised a high degree of control over their subsidiaries.[77] Confusion within the enforcement agencies on the reach of the statute was shown when, in 1981, the FTC and the Antitrust Division gave conflicting advisory opinions on whether Section 8 would be violated if representatives of the United Auto Workers sat on the boards of competing automobile manufacturers.[78]

Despite these frustrations, the weakness of Section 8 does not seem to be a serious flaw in antitrust policy. Typically, outside directors do not dominate the boards on which they sit. Although the enforcement agencies have taken little initiative in enforcing the law, flagrant cases or those coming to their attention through outside complaints are generally handled easily if not always permanently: A notification of alleged violation usually leads to a resignation, solving the problem. Further, if directors do abuse their positions and put the firms they represent in legal jeopardy in the way Section 8 seeks to prevent, they and the corporations on which they sit are vulnerable to attack under the other provisions of the antitrust laws.

ENDNOTES

[1]U.S. Senate *Report* no. 597, 63d Congress, 2d Session (1914). Quoted in Section of Antitrust Law of the American Bar Association, *Antitrust Developments, 1955–1968: A Supplement to the Attorney General's National Committee to Study the Antitrust Laws* (Chicago: American Bar Association, 1968), p. 252.

[2]U.S. House of Representatives *Report* no. 1142, 63d Congress, 2d Session (1914). Quoted in ABA, *Antitrust Developments*, pp. 252–53.

[3]Quoted in Earl W. Kintner, *A Primer on the Law of Deceptive Practices* (New York: Macmillan, 1971), pp. 16–17.

[4]Federal Trade Commission v. Gratz, 253 U.S. 421, 427 (1920).

[5]Fashion Originators' Guild v. Federal Trade Commission, 312 U.S. 457, 463 (1940).

[6]Federal Trade Commission v. Cement Institute, 333 U.S. 683 (1948).

[7]Federal Trade Commission v. Motion Picture Advertising Service Company, 344 U.S. 392, 394–95 (1953). See also Federal Trade Commission v. Brown Shoe Company, 384 U.S. 316 (1966).

[8]Grand Union Company v. Federal Trade Commission, 300 F. 2d 92, 95 (1962).

[9]Federal Trade Commission v. Raladam Company, 258 U.S. 643 (1931).

[10]The presentation is derived from Sam Peltzman, "An Evaluation of Consumer Protection Legislation: The 1962 Drug Amendments," *Journal of Political Economy* 81, no. 5 (September–October 1973), pp. 1049–91; Thomas McGuire, Richard Nelson, and Thomas Spavins, "An Evaluation of Consumer Protection Legislation: The 1962 Drug Amendments: A Comment,"*Journal of Political Economy* 83, no. 3 (June 1975), pp. 655–61; Michael R. Darby and Edi Karni, "Free Competition and the Optimal Amount of Fraud," *Journal of Law and Economics* 16, no. 1 (April 1973), pp. 67–88.

[11]For a full graphical and theoretical exposition of this point, see Norman S. Buchanan, "Advertising Expenditures: A Suggested Treatment," *Journal of Political Economy* 50, no. 4 (August 1942), pp. 537–57.

[12]Phillip Nelson, "Advertising as Information,"*Journal of Political Economy* 82, no. 4 (July–August 1974), pp. 729–54, at p. 740.

[13]Ibid., p. 730.

[14]Ibid.

[15]For further discussion of this point, see Richard E. Kihlstrom and Michael H. Riordan, "Advertising as a Signal," *Journal of Political Economy* 92, no. 3 (June 1984), pp. 427–50.

[16]Darby and Karni, "Free Competition," pp. 68–69.

[17]Robert Pitofsky, "Advertising Regulation and the Consumer Movement," in *Issues in Advertising,* ed. David G. Tuerck (Washington, D.C.: American Enterprise Institute, 1978), p. 34.

[18]Robert Pitofsky, "Changing Focus in the Regulation of Advertising," in *Advertising and Society,* ed. Yale Brozen (Washington, D.C.: American Enterprise Institute, 1974), p. 136.

[19]For a perceptive discussion of the influence of income level on consumers' search efforts, see Richard H. Holton, "Consumer Behavior, Market Imperfections, and Public Policy," in *Industrial Organization and Economic Development,* ed. Jesse W. Markham and Gustav F. Papanek (Boston: Houghton Mifflin, 1970), p. 107. Holton has noted that both high and low incomes dampen consumers' search efforts.

[20]Warner-Lambert Company v. Federal Trade Commission, 562 F. 2d 749 (1977).

[21]Kintner, *A Primer,* pp. 30–40.

[22]Charles of the Ritz Distributors v. Federal Trade Commission, 143 F. 2d 676, 679 (1944); drawing on Federal Trade Commission v. Standard Education Society, 302 U.S. 112, 116 (1937).

[23]P. Lorillard Company v. Federal Trade Commission, 186 F. 2d 52 (1950).

[24]In the Matter of Doris Savitch Trading as Personal Drug Company, and Leo Savitch, 50 FTC 828, 834 (1954).

[25]Immigration and Naturalization Service v. Chadha, 77 L. Ed. 2d 317 (1983).

[26]*The Wall Street Journal,* July 3, 1985, p. 17.

[27]*CCH Trade Regulation Reports,* ¶50,455, pp. 56,071–72.

[28]Ibid., pp. 56,080–82.

[29]"Analysis of the FTC Law of Deception: FTC Members Bailey and Pertschuk," *CCH Trade Regulation Reports,* no. 641 (March 27, 1984), p. 73.

[30]This section relies heavily on the major contributions of James R. Atwood and Kingman Brewster, *Antitrust and American Business Abroad,* 2 vols., 2d ed. (Colorado Springs, Colo.: Shepard's/McGraw-Hill, 1981); Wilbur L. Fugate, *Foreign Commerce and the Antitrust Laws,* 2 vols., 3d ed. (Boston: Little, Brown, 1982).

[31]Readers interested in such accounts are referred to Atwood and Brewster, *Antitrust;* Fugate, *Foreign Commerce.*

[32]United States v. United Fruit Company, CCH Trade Cases, ¶68,941 (1958).

[33]United States v. International Nickel Company of Canada, CCH Trade Cases, ¶62,280 (1948–9); United States v. De Beers Consolidated Mines, Ltd., 325 U.S. 312 (1945); United States v. De Beers Industrial Diamond Division, Ltd., CCH Trade Cases, ¶60,825 (1976–1); United States v. De Beers Industrial Diamond Division (Ireland) Ltd., CCH Trade Cases, ¶62,056 (1978–1). The government lost the first of the cases against De Beers for lack of jurisdiction.

[34]United States v. General Dyestuff Corporation, 57 F. Supp. 642 (1944); United States v. General Electric Company, 80 F. Supp. 989 (1948).

[35]United States v. National Lead Company, 63 F. Supp. 513 (1945).

[36]United States v. Imperial Chemical Industries, Ltd., 100 F. Supp. 504 (1951); and supplemental opinion on remedy, 105 F. Supp. 215 (1952).

[37]United States v. NV Nederlandsche Combinatie Voor Chemische Industrie, CCH Trade Cases, ¶75,434 (1974–2).

[38]International Association of Machinists v. Organization of Petroleum Exporting Countries, 477 F. Supp. 553 (1979).

[39]United States v. Schlitz Brewing Company, 253 F. Supp. 129 (1966).

[40]United States v. Gillette Company, CCH Trade Cases, ¶60,691 (1976–1).

[41]United States v. Standard Oil Company, CCH Trade Cases, ¶72,988 (1970).

[42]United States v. CIBA Corporation, CCH Trade Cases, ¶73,269 (1970).

[43]United States v. Sisal Sales Corporation, 274 U.S. 268 (1927).

[44]Timberlane Lumber Company v. Bank of America, 549 F. 2d 597 (1976).

[45]Occidental Petroleum Corporation v. Buttes Gas & Oil Company, 331 F. Supp. 92 (1971).

[46]United States v. Volkswagen of America Corporation, CCH Trade Cases, ¶70,256 (1962); United States v. Renault, Inc., CCH Trade Cases, ¶70,386 (1962); United States v. Nissan USA, CCH Trade Cases, ¶74,333 (1973).

[47]Todhunter-Mitchell and Company, Ltd., v. Anheuser-Busch, Inc., 383 F. Supp. 586 (1974).

[48]Eiberger v. Sony Corporation of America, 622 F. 2d 1086 (1980).

[49]U.S. Department of Justice, *Antitrust Guide for International Operations* (Washington, D.C.: U.S. Government Printing Office, 1977), p. 5.

[50]Ibid., p. 7.

[51]Atwood and Brewster, *Antitrust,* vol. 1, p. 188.

[52]Ibid., vol. 2, p. 315.

[53]Ibid., pp. 324–25.

[54]Pfizer, Inc. v. Government of India, 434 U.S. 308 (1978).

[55]United States v. Minnesota Mining and Manufacturing Company, 92 F. Supp. 947, 963 (1950).

[56]Atwood and Brewster, *Antitrust,* vol. 2, pp. 320–21.

[57]Many of these incidents are discussed at length in Atwood and Brewster, *Antitrust;* Fugate, *Foreign Commerce.*

[58]In re Uranium Antitrust Litigation, 617 F. 2d 1248, 1256 (1980).

[59]Atwood and Brewster, *Antitrust,* vol. 1, p. 170.

[60]The Wall Street Journal, June 27, 1983, p. 32; July 11, 1983, p. 23.

[61]The Wall Street Journal, July 15, 1985, p. 4; August 22, 1985, p. 27.

[62]Outboard Marine Corporation v. Pezetel, 461 F. Supp. 384 (1978).

[63]Quoted in Fugate, *Foreign Commerce,* vol. 1, p. 84.

[64]549 F. 2d. 597, 614.

[65]Mannington Mills, Inc. v. Congoleum Corporation, 595 F. 2d 1287, 1297–98 (1979).

[66]Readers with a more detailed interest in the contents of these foreign antitrust laws and codes are referred to excellent discussions in the studies of Fugate, *Foreign Commerce;* Atwood and Brewster, *Antitrust;* A. D. Neale and D. G. Goyder, *The Antitrust Laws of the U.S.A.,* 3d ed. (London: Cambridge University Press, 1980).

[67]Neale and Goyder, *The Antitrust Laws,* pp. 493–94.

[68]Fugate, *Foreign Commerce,* vol. 2, pp. 398–99.

[69]Ken Ohmae, "Japan vs. Japan: Only the Strong Survive," *The Wall Street Journal,* January 26, 1981, p. 20.

[70]U.S. National Resources Committee, *The Structure of the American Economy* (Washington, D.C.: U.S. Government Printing Office, 1939).

[71]Peter C. Dooley, "The Interlocking Directorate,"*American Economic Review* 59, no. 3 (June 1969), pp. 314–23.

[72]Ibid., p. 315.

[73]U.S. Senate, Committee on Governmental Affairs, *Structure of Corporate Concentration,* vol. 1 (Washington, D.C.: U.S. Government Printing Office, 1980).

[74]Ibid., pp. 5–6.

[75]United States v. W. T. Grant Company, 345 U.S. 629 (1953).

[76]Paramount Pictures Corporation v. Baldwin-Montrose Chemical Company, CCH Trade Cases, ¶71,678 (1966).

[77]Kennecott Copper Corporation v. Curtiss-Wright Corporation, 584 F. 2d 1195 (1978).

[78]Noted in Louis B. Schwartz, John J. Flynn, and Harry First, *Free Enterprise and Economic Organization: Antitrust,* 6th ed. (Mineola, N.Y.: Foundation Press, 1983), p. 214.

PART FOUR

Epilogue

CHAPTER TWENTY-ONE

In Retrospect

QUESTIONS (MANY) AND ANSWERS (FEW)

The most common complaint of students who have taken my courses in industrial organization and public policy toward business is that they have been confronted with more questions than answers. While I cannot deny the truth of the assertion, neither can I accept it as a valid criticism. There are many unanswered questions in industrial organization, and it would be a disservice to students to gloss over these questions or to give glib and superficial answers. A certain degree of informed confusion may be a necessary precondition for insight and understanding.

Unresolved Issues of History, Theory, and Statistics

Controversy and unresolved questions pervade Joseph Schumpeter's triad of basic economic techniques: history, theory, and statistics. Compare, for example, Hans B. Thorelli's conclusion that "the Sherman Act embodies what is to be characterized as an eminently 'social' purpose"[1] with Robert H. Bork's finding that "there would be little point in reviewing here all of the positions that have been advanced concerning the broad social, political and ethical mandates entrusted to the courts through the Sherman Act . . . as there is not a scintilla of support for such views anywhere in the legislative history."[2] Both of these interpretations were based on painstaking study of the historical record. Such differences are of far more than pedantic interest. In the 1980s, public policy is still being influenced by this debate.

Similarly, neither theory nor quantitative analysis is free from controversy. In a 1979 paper, Richard A. Posner noted the major contributions made by Chicago school theorists to evaluation of forms of conduct such as tie-in sales, resale price maintenance, and predatory pricing. He concluded that "partly as a result of the growing sophistication of economic analysis, the traditional industrial organization is being discredited in academic circles. The Chicago school," he continued, "has largely prevailed with respect to its basic point: that the proper lens for viewing antitrust problems is price theory."[3] But in a comment on Posner's paper, Richard R. Nelson responded that "the price theory to which Posner refers is the old-fashioned price theory of the textbooks of twenty years ago. What Posner does not see is that over the last decade or so a newer price theory is replacing the old. I suggest that the new price theory probably provides better support for the old industrial organization than it does for what Posner calls the new."[4]

To cite a final example from statistical analysis, there is continuing dispute between adherents to the concentration doctrine and members of the Chicago school as to whether the observed correlation between concentration and profitability reflects the exercise of monopolistic power in concentrated markets, or whether it results from greater profitability and hence expansion of the most efficient firms. That is, correlation does not demonstrate causality, and it remains an open question whether the primary direction of causation runs from concentration to profits or from profits to concentration.

Conflict-Generating Characteristics of Industrial Organization

At least three basic characteristics of industrial organization give rise to unresolved issues and controversy—and make the subject challenging and stimulating. First, ideology is rarely far from the surface. The major contributions to industrial organization have been greatly influenced by the social, ethical, and political values of individual researchers and writers. Leading scholars may—indeed, almost always do—carry out analyses with a rigor and discipline that precludes ideological bias; but the questions asked, the abstractions employed in theoretical models, the phenomena examined, and the interpretations of the results emerging from such analyses are all shaped by the investigator's values.

Second, the real-world phenomena that make up the subject matter of industrial organization—private business activities in relatively free markets—are diverse and constantly changing. Policy prescriptions for improving the economic and perhaps social performance of business must be reexamined, debated, and modified as the impact of structure and conduct on performance changes over time and among industries.

Third, industrial organization can be viewed in large part as applied microeconomic theory. The industrial organization economist, as a user of theory, puts that theory to the harshest of tests: How well do the theoretical constructs and abstractions stand up in application to actual market structures and forms of business behavior, and does the theory shed light on the issues of greatest significance in real-world settings? Inevitably, when preconceptions are challenged and deficiencies alleged, controversy will be high.

THE STRUCTURE–CONDUCT–PERFORMANCE PARADIGM REVISITED

Unanswered questions at the basic level of a discipline may, paradoxically, be a sign of strength rather than weakness. A sound and useful paradigm helps pose the right questions, and the right questions are often the hard ones.

Getting the Questions Right

The structure-conduct-performance approach, as developed and refined over some 50 years, remains of the utmost value to industrial organization economists in framing the questions that have advanced both the techniques of the field and the knowledge gained.

While the basic paradigm is broad enough to encompass such diverse views as structuralism, behavioralism, the concentration doctrine, and the efficiency doctrine, it focuses the analyst's attention on a common set of crucial issues. A broad theoretical question such as "Does resale price maintenance enhance or detract from economic efficiency?" would be reformulated under the structure-conduct-performance approach into the more precise and meaningful query, "Under what sets of structural conditions will resale price maintenance be likely to enhance or detract from economic efficiency?" While the answer to the latter is not a simple yes or no, it is more likely to pinpoint areas of agreement and dispute, as well as to provide guidance in assessing the sources of good or bad performance in specific markets.

In this book's discussion of various forms of business conduct I emphasize that the underlying structure is a crucial factor in the analysis. For example, the likelihood that collusive price-fixing will exist and will succeed was examined as a function of such structural features as the number of firms in the market, their relative sizes, the degree to which costs and products are similar, barriers to entry of new firms, elasticity of demand for the product, and the vulnerability of cheaters to effective retaliation. An alternative hypothesis, that some lines of business are populated by less ethical individuals, was rejected not so much for being erroneous as for being uninformative. Further, it was observed that the effects of successful price-fixing on the economic performance of an industry may be quite different—perhaps socially preferable—in a market characterized by the structural attributes of unstable demand and high fixed costs than they would be in an industry with steady growth and flexible rates of production in the short run.

Fitting the Paradigm to the Subject

More generally, the structure-conduct-performance paradigm is uniquely suited to industrial organization's primary subject matter: how such *organization* of industries and markets affects the performance of an economy. Central to this approach are the precepts that (1) we must look at the business environment, or structure, within which business decisions are made to understand the conduct of firms that results from these decisions and (2) that the effects of that conduct on performance, as well as its feedback effects on structure, will be influenced by the surrounding structural context. Not only do these two precepts provide a general framework for assimilating the contributions and proffered answers of the various schools of economists, they are particularly appropriate for analysis and evaluation of U.S. antitrust policies, since these policies seek to improve performance indirectly through alterations in structure and conduct rather than directly through proscribing or requiring certain kinds of performance.

The Pitfall of Mechanistic Application

The structure-conduct-performance approach is, however, not a simple and mechanistic prescription—a "gumball machine," to borrow John J. Flynn's analogy. That is, we cannot simply plug a set of predetermined characteristics of structure and types of conduct found in an industry into such a hypothetical machine, turn a crank, and grind out a solution describing and evaluating the performance of that industry. In an apt but caustic comment on the 1955 report of the Attorney General's National Committee to Study the Antitrust Laws, George J. Stigler noted, "To determine whether any industry is workably competitive, therefore, simply have a good graduate student write his dissertation on the industry and render a verdict. It is crucial to this test, of course, that no second graduate student be allowed to study the industry."[5]

Stigler's 1956 observation has lost none of its pertinence with time. Yet, he himself, in his major 1964 analytical study of collusion, stressed the centrality of the basic proposition underlying the structure-conduct-performance paradigm, albeit in more general phraseology:

> If we adhere to the traditional theory of profit-maximizing enterprise, then behavior is no longer something to be assumed but rather something

to be deduced. The firms in an industry will behave in such a way, given the demand-and-supply functions (including those of rivals), that their profits will be maximized. . . . Our modification of this theory consists simply in presenting a systematic account of the factors governing the feasibility of collusion, which like most things in this world is not free.[6]

From Analysis to Value Judgments

Further, the sharpest disagreements among experts in industrial organization involve value judgments rather than analysis. Steven R. Cox examined 42 responses to a questionnaire sent to academic economists specializing in industrial organization, professors of marketing, business specialists, and editors and writers associated with leading business magazines and newspapers. The respondents were asked to evaluate various aspects of the performance of 14 industries as well as to choose which industry in each of all possible pairings had the better overall performance. In his conclusion, Cox cited Stigler's 1956 quip and commented:

> The experimental results reported here are more promising. If one chooses a sizeable panel of economics graduate students, and lets them study a diverse sample of industries, the experiment's results suggest that it is likely they will agree strongly on at least those industries which display widely contrasting performance, even if not on those which lie close together on the performance spectrum. The real problem, however, would seem to lie in the formation of a panel of graduate students from diverse fields—economics, business administration, engineering, etc. Then substantial disagreements are likely, the experiment suggests, because panelists of varying occupational backgrounds attach widely divergent weights to different sub-dimensions of performance.[7]

Business panelists, for example, regarded high profit margins and aggressive advertising as positive aspects of an industry's performance, while academic panelists viewed these as indicia of poor performance. More to the point, differences in the performance rankings assigned by the 25 academic economists in the sample were significantly influenced by how "Schumpeterian" their views were, or how important they considered current resource allocation to be relative to technological progress.

COMPETITION, ANTITRUST, AND THE PERFORMANCE OF THE U.S. ECONOMY

By both the standard of static allocative efficiency and the dynamic criteria of technological progress and productivity growth, and given the common objective of maximizing consumer welfare, the overall performance of the U.S. economy has been impressive. From the point of view of a student of industrial organization, the two most pertinent questions are (1) the extent to which this performance is attributable to effective competition and (2) the degree to which the antitrust laws have contributed to the preservation of such competition.

Static Allocative Efficiency

Several researchers have estimated the deadweight welfare loss to the U.S. economy from monopolistic power, applying the welfare triangle approach discussed in Chapter Thirteen.[8] Such estimates of the economy-wide losses associated with the sum of these triangles have consistently yielded very small numbers relative to the scale of the nation's total economic activity; most researchers and their critics conclude that the loss is probably somewhat under 1 percent of the gross national product.

But a number of these same researchers have noted that the losses are distributed unequally among industries and the bulk is concentrated in a few. In some cases, the welfare costs of market power may be quite high relative to the size of the specific industry. One study of 734 large U.S. firms, mostly manufacturing, found a deadweight loss between 4 and 13 percent of the firms' contributions to the nation's gross corporate product, with the range resulting from alternative treatments of advertising expenditures and corporate profit taxes.[9] A small number of firms accounted for most of the loss.

The Impact of Competition. Robert T. Masson and Joseph Shaanan's 1984 study dealt with the question of competition's role in holding down deadweight loss. They estimated the actual deadweight losses for 37 U.S. industries and compared these losses with those they calculated would have obtained had the firms in the industry maximized their joint profit in the absence of any threat to entry. They concluded that, had the firms acted as pure monopolists, the welfare loss would have been 11.6 percent of their value of shipments, while the actual welfare loss was 2.9 percent. The difference, 8.7 percent of value of shipments, was attributed to the effects of actual and potential competition. Since the average level of CR4 in the 37 industries was 68 percent, the deadweight welfare loss of 2.9 percent of value of shipments in this oligopolistic group is consistent with a substantially lower economy-wide figure expressed as a percentage of the gross national product. Masson and Shaanan felt that their most significant finding was the large divergence between the actual welfare losses and the potential losses from pure monopoly. They noted that this difference could be due to either "natural market forces" or "strict antitrust enforcement" and refused to speculate on the matter, with its "weighty and differing policy conclusions."[10]

The Impact of Antitrust.   Others have not been so hesitant to speculate on the roles of market forces and antitrust. Stigler, for example, took issue with the pioneering estimate of Arnold C. Harberger but concluded that "whatever it [the deadweight welfare loss] may be, we may still properly devote much attention to monopoly. The loss would be much larger if we were less diligent in combating monopoly, and the cumulative effects of widespread cartelization would eventually move the losses into a new order of magnitude."[11]

William G. Shepherd examined changes in the degree of competition in the U.S. economy between 1939 and 1980 and concluded that from 1939 to 1958, the economy became more competitive "but at no more than the pace of a glacial drift," while from 1958 to 1980, the pace stepped up substantially. "A trend formerly measured in inches," he reported, "has jumped to a much higher level. The U.S. economy now appears to be far more competitive than at any time during the modern industrial period."[12]   More significantly, according to Shepherd, this growing competitiveness primarily resulted from public policies (particularly antitrust), international trade policies leading to increased import competition, and deregulation.

Using both structural criteria (market share stability, concentration, and entry barriers) and behavioral evidence on pricing, supplemented by information on profitability and innovation as dimensions of performance, Shepherd categorized industries as pure monopoly, dominant firm, tight oligopoly, and effectively competitive. His results are shown here.[13]

Industry Category	Share of Total National Income		
	1939	1958	1980
Pure monopoly	6.2%	3.1%	2.5%
Dominant firm	5.0	5.0	2.8
Tight oligopoly	36.4	35.6	18.0
Effectively competitive	52.4	56.3	76.7

Import competition, Shepherd found, had increased competition in 13 major industries and had accounted for about one sixth of the increase in competitiveness from 1958 to 1980. Deregulation was hard to disentangle from antitrust action during the 1970s, particularly in industries such as banking, security trading, and telephone communication that were subject to both; but Shepherd estimated that deregulation coupled with antitrust actions in the deregulated industries was responsible for about 20 percent of the rise in competition from

1958 to 1980. By far the greatest impact, Shepherd noted, came from antitrust, with the overall effectiveness of enforcement bolstered from three sources: the dramatic rise in private antitrust cases through the 1960s and 70s; the 1975 repeal of the Miller-Tydings and McGuire Acts; and the stiffening of penalties, both fines and jail sentences, for criminal antitrust violations.

Shepherd's procedure was "to assemble the main cases and informal actions that have affected industries, and then to estimate whether those actions have significantly raised competition."[14] Antitrust, he concluded, led to an increase in competition in 20 industries other than deregulated ones and accounted for 40 percent of the 1958–80 rise in effective competition (57 percent if the deregulated industries also affected by antitrust were included). Further, "Antitrust performs an additional continuing function because it maintains competition throughout the economy much higher than it would otherwise exist. If antitrust were suddenly to cease, then a large wave of new mergers and collusion would soon raise the degree of market power in a wide range of sectors. By continuing to prevent that rise, antitrust has made possible the overall trend toward a rise in competition."[15]

As noted in Chapter Thirteen, the wealth transfer from buyers to monopolistic sellers amounts in most instances to many times the welfare triangle loss. Such transfers must be added to the deadweight costs of monopoly, and thus strengthen the case for antitrust, unless one is willing to take the distribution of income as given in assessing the efficiency with which an economy allocates its resources to alternative uses. Further, some of the potential transfer may reflect wasteful use of resources to attain or maintain monopoly power, or sheer dissipation of resources through X-inefficiency.

Marx's Vision and Antitrust. Yet another argument for antitrust policy is provided by Karl Marx's apocalyptic vision that a capitalist economy, left to itself, will inevitably evolve into monopoly capitalism ("one capitalist always kills many") and that monopoly capitalism must, in turn, collapse from its internal contradictions. The vision is shared by such modern antitrust scholars of distinctly non-Marxist persuasions as Jerrold G. Van Cise, who wrote, "The dogma of Karl Marx that the competition of capitalism will necessarily lead to jungle warfare, in which competitor will eat competitor until only monopoly remains, has been refuted by our antitrust laws."[16]

Dynamic Criteria: Technological and Productivity Growth

Although the static allocative inefficiencies of private market power in the United States have been held to a low level overall, with effective competition evidently being primarily responsible, some are concerned that the nation cannot take similar pride in the growth and development of the economy, or in the dynamic aspects of performance.

The Challenge of World Competition. Ira C. Magaziner and Robert B. Reich, for example, noted the decline in U.S. world competitiveness throughout the 1960s and 70s, observing that growth in per capita productivity was substantially slower in this country than in the Western European nations and Japan. As a result, U.S. gross domestic product (GDP) fell from first in the world to a tie with France, behind Switzerland, Denmark, Sweden, West Germany, Iceland, Norway, Belgium, Luxemburg, and the Netherlands. In Japan, where per capita GDP was 16 percent of that in the United States in 1960, the figure rose to 82 percent by 1979.[17] Magaziner and Reich further cited other indices of quality of life, including unemployment rates, average lengths of paid vacations, life expectancies, infant mortality rates, pollution levels, and deaths by homicide, in which by 1980 the United States compared poorly with other nonsocialist industrialized nations.

U.S. Response to the Challenge. The United States appears to be responding well to the challenge of world competition. We must recognize that the overwhelming superiority of the U.S. economy in the early years after World War II was a historical aberration and that the indicia of good and even excellent economic performance should not include outstripping every other nation in every significant respect. In an October 1984 article, *The Wall Street Journal* observed that "the U.S. economy, recently trailing the growth rate of Japan and West Germany, now is running ahead of its major industrial rivals. America's industries, particularly in new technologies, are gaining ground against foreign competitors." The article cited data from the Organization for Economic Cooperation and Development (OECD) indicating that the U.S. GDP rose from 38 percent of the total GDP of all OECD members in 1975 to 40 percent in 1982 and 42 percent in 1983. "That means," the article continued, "the U.S., with 5% of the world's population, produces and consumes a third of its wealth, up from just a quarter nine years ago. What's more, rapid economic growth and a 30% gain in the dollar's value have probably made the U.S. standard of living, as measured by per capita income, the highest in the industrialized world again."[18]

From the point of view of global economic development, it is neither likely nor desirable that 5 percent of the world's population should continue to produce and consume one third of its output. Ideally, the gap will be narrowed through expansion of world output rather than struggles over shares. In any event, experience since World War II suggests that world competition will play an increasing, crucial, and generally beneficial role in this process of development and growth, providing increasing opportunities for developing nations both to draw on and penetrate world markets, while at the same time posing a stimulating challenge to the developed nations already established in these markets.

Experience further suggests that vigorous competition at home enhances the ability of a nation to compete effectively on world markets. The United States is particularly fortunate among the nations of the world. Due to the sizes of our markets, incompatibilities between workably competitive industry structures and minimum efficient scales of operation are the exception rather than the rule, as are serious trade-offs between structures conducive to efficient static resource allocation and those conducive to vigorous R&D and innovation.

The Vital Roles of Antitrust and Competition in the Modern Economy

A national public policy aimed at promoting competitive market structures and business behavior is certainly no panacea for all the ills of a modern industrialized economy. Vigorous competition in free markets is not the solution for problems of environmental degradation, congestion, occupational safety, public health and welfare, macroeconomic stability, or a number of other significant indicia of overall economic performance and quality of life. Economies of scale or externalities leading to market failures may, in certain instances, require public regulation or even toleration of an otherwise unacceptable degree of private market power rather than free competition. Further, the antitrust laws of the United States and their interpretations in the nation's courts suffer from some serious flaws and inconsistencies. But competition has provided an essential stimulus to the high overall level of the nation's economic performance; and antitrust, in turn, has been necessary to preserve effective competition—to say nothing of the free-enterprise system itself.

ENDNOTES

[1]Hans B. Thorelli, *The Federal Antitrust Policy: Organization of an American Tradition* (London: George Allen & Unwin, 1954), p. 227.

[2]Robert H. Bork, "Legislative Intent and the Policy of the Sherman Act," *Journal of Law and Economics* 9 (October 1966), pp. 7–48, at p. 10.

[3]Richard A. Posner, "The Chicago School of Antitrust Analysis," *University of Pennsylvania Law Review* 127, no. 4 (April 1979), pp. 925–48, at pp. 932–33.

[4]Richard R. Nelson, "Comments on Paper by Posner,"*University of Pennsylvania Law Review* 127, no. 4 (April 1979), pp. 949–52, at p. 949.

[5]George J. Stigler, "Report of the Attorney General's Committee on Antitrust Policy—Discussion," *American Economic Review* 46, no. 2 (May 1956), pp. 504–7, at p. 505.

[6]George J. Stigler, "A Theory of Oligopoly," *Journal of Political Economy* 72, no. 1 (February 1964), pp. 44–61, at p. 44.

[7]Steven R. Cox, "An Industrial Performance Evaluation Experiment," *Journal of Industrial Economics* 22, no. 3 (March 1974), pp. 199–214, at p. 213.

[8]See especially Arnold C. Harberger, "Monopoly and Resource Allocation," *American Economic Review* 44, no. 2 (May 1954), pp. 77–87; David Schwartzman, "The Burden of Monopoly,"*Journal of Political Economy* 58, no. 6 (December 1960), pp. 627–30; Dean A. Worcester, Jr., "New Estimates of the Welfare Loss to Monopoly, United States: 1965–1969," *Southern Economic Journal* 40, no. 2 (October 1973), pp. 234–45; Abram Bergson, "On Monopoly Welfare Losses,"*American Economic Review* 63, no. 5 (December 1973), pp. 853–70; John J. Siegfried and Thomas K. Tiemann, "The Welfare Cost of Monopoly: An Interindustry Analysis," *Economic Inquiry* 12, no. 2 (June 1974), pp. 190–202; Richard L. Carson, Dean A. Worcester, Jr., and Abram Bergson, "On Monopoly Welfare Losses: Comment" and "On Monopoly Welfare Losses: Reply," *American Economic Review* 65, no. 5 (December 1975), pp. 1008–31; Keith Cowling and Dennis C. Mueller, "The Social Costs of Monopoly Power," *Economic Journal* 88, no. 352 (December 1978), pp. 727–48; Frederic M. Scherer, *Industrial Market Structure and Economic Performance,* 2d ed. (Skokie, Ill.: Rand McNally, 1980), pp. 459–71; Robert T. Masson and Joseph Shaanan, "Social Costs of Oligopoly and the Value of Competition," *Economic Journal* 94, no. 375 (September 1984), pp. 520–35.

[9]Cowling and Mueller, "The Social Costs."

[10]Masson and Shaanan, "Social Costs of Oligopoly," p. 354.

[11]George J. Stigler, "The Statistics of Merger and Monopoly," *Journal of Political Economy* 64, no. 1 (February 1956), pp. 33–40, at p. 35.

[12]William G. Shepherd, "Causes of Increased Competition in the U.S. Economy, 1939–1980," *Review of Economics and Statistics* 64, no. 4 (November 1982), pp. 613–26, at p. 613.

[13]Ibid., pp. 618–19.

[14]Ibid., p. 623.

[15]Ibid.

[16]Jerrold G. Van Cise, *The Federal Antitrust Laws,* 4th ed. (Washington, D.C.: American Enterprise Institute, 1982), p. 68.

[17]Ira C. Magaziner and Robert B. Reich, *Minding America's Business: The Decline and Rise of the American Economy* (New York: Random House, 1982), p. 13.

[18]"U.S. Economic Surge, A Source of Pride Here, Causes Envy Overseas," *The Wall Street Journal,* October 8, 1984, pp. 1, 27, at p. 1.

CASE INDEX

517

SUBJECT INDEX

*This book has been set in Linotron 202N in 10 and
9 point Century Schoolbook, leaded 2 points. Part and
chapter numbers are 12 point Century Schoolbook;
part and chapter titles are 24 and 18 point Century
Schoolbook. The size of the type page is 30 by 47 picas.*